THE MEMOIRS OF HECTOR BERLIOZ

THE MEMOIRS OF HECTOR BERLIOZ has long been considered to be among the best of musical autobiographies. Like his massive compositions, Berlioz (1803–1869) was colorful, eloquent, larger than life. His book is both an account of his important place in the rise of the Romantic movement and a personal testament. He tells the story of his liaison with Harriet Smithson, and his even more passionate affairs of the mind with Shakespeare, Scott, and Byron. Familiar with all the great figures of the age, Berlioz paints brilliant portraits of Liszt, Wagner, Balzac, Weber, and Rossini, among others. And through Berlioz's intimate and detailed self-revelation, there emerges a profoundly sympathetic and attractive man, driven, finally, by his overwhelming creative urges to a position of lonely eminence.

The Memoirs of Hector Berlioz

Translated and edited by David Cairns

E V E R Y M A N ' S   L I B R A R Y

Alfred A. Knopf New York Toronto

231

THIS IS A BORZOI BOOK

PUBLISHED BY ALFRED A. KNOPF

This title first included in Everyman's Library, 1912
This translation published in Everyman's Library, 2002

Typography by Peter B. Willberg

 Published in the United States by Alfred A. Knopf, a division of Random House, Inc., New York, and simultaneously in Canada by Random House of Canada Limited, Toronto. Distributed by Random House, Inc., New York

www.randomhouse.com/everymans

Originally published in somewhat different form in the United Kingdom by Victor Gollancz, London, in 1969, and in the United States by Alfred A. Knopf, New York, in 1969

ISBN 0-375-41391-X

Book Design by Barbara de Wilde and Carol Devine Carson

Printed and bound in Germany
by GGP Media, Pössneck

THE MEMOIRS OF HECTOR BERLIOZ

Hector Berlioz (1803–69).
Photograph by Nadar, January 1857

CONTENTS

EDITOR'S INTRODUCTION

THE LAST HALF-CENTURY has seen a striking change in the general attitude to Berlioz and his work. For the modern generation of musicians and music-lovers, beneficiaries of the revival and reappraisal of his music which followed the first complete production of *The Trojans*, at Covent Garden in 1957, the old myth of the freakish outsider, master only of the grotesque, has faded. The revelation—it was nothing less—of the opera's purposeful beauty and grandeur made us listen to all his music afresh and see his achievement in a new light. A historically-minded age, and one that has outgrown the long reaction against Romanticism, is now better placed to assess the nature and the value of that achievement and also to recognize that so far from springing out of nowhere Berlioz had many roots—in eighteenth-century *tragédie-lyrique*, in the opera and sacred music of the French Revolution and First Empire, and in a local and popular folk-art of great antiquity; indeed it was precisely because of this ancestry that his music in many ways ran counter to the dominant ideals and practices of its time. Today on the contrary the characteristics which once made it bizarrely unconventional—emphasis on extended melody, linear approach to orchestration, irregularity of phrase-length, the use of timbre and even of space as elements of composition, and a quality of objectivity at the core of his art (which is romantic without living up to all the expectations aroused by Romanticism)—are once again quite natural; his originality, without having lost its vividness, no longer seems eccentric. We can enjoy him, greatness and limitations, for what he is, a remarkable composer but one among many.

The man likewise: we have accepted him. Sacheverell Sitwell's 'being set apart, physically and mentally', 'like no one else who has ever existed' is not valid any more. He was an extraordinary being—exceptionally imaginative and highly strung, an unusual and intricate mixture of passion and detachment, at once masterful and incurably naïve, with an impressionability and capacity for intense feeling that seem never to have been overlaid by worldly accommodations, and a faculty for reliving childhood experiences, combined with a tenacious clinging to ideals, that cost him dear, though it made him the artist he was; a being born for suffering, if you like. But the personality which emerges from his account of himself strikes chords of fellow-feeling. We recognize it, and instead of shaking our heads over it are stirred to sympathy. The 'inexorable need of affection' to which he confesses, the terrifying sense of isolation that could sweep over him, are not peculiar to Berlioz nor confined to the nineteenth century. It is a strange tale but it carries conviction, and in the light of the music it acquires an even greater interest, poignancy and truth.

The veracity of the *Memoirs* has been much contested. In the age of the debunking biographer the book was a byword for exaggeration and distortion and the unconscious or wilful garbling of facts. It is this view that now seems distorted. In any case we look for other things in an artist's autobiography than a catalogue of daily events—though simply as a factual record it is more accurate than overhasty commentators would have had us believe.

Even so, we may still feel inclined to see hyperbole in what Berlioz writes. To take one example, could he really have been so overwhelmed by Shakespeare, and in a foreign tongue at that? To answer, we must think ourselves back to that time and try to conceive what Shakespeare's advent meant to young artists brought up on the rigid rules of the great classical dramatists and their feeble contemporary imitators. There is plenty of testimony to support Berlioz. Dumas', for instance: 'Imagine a man, blind from birth, receiving the gift of sight and discovering a world of which he had no inkling. Imagine Adam waking after his creation to find the flower-strewn earth before him, the glorious sky overhead, round him trees laden with golden fruit, in the distance a great shining river, at his side a naked, pure young woman—and you will have some idea of the enchanted Eden which that performance [of *Hamlet*] disclosed to me.'

What of the violent antipathies expressed in the *Memoirs*, the persistent complaints of intrigue and opposition? Berlioz's picture of his struggle to establish himself in Paris has often been thought overdone. Certain French scholars, for the honour of France, make a half-hearted show of discrediting it. One understands the desire. Great artists are generally said to exaggerate the obstacles they had to overcome; in this way we seek to appease our guilt or anger at the spectacle of outraged genius. It is more comfortable not to believe it. English people are particularly prone to this mistake, because for the English art is largely a world apart, neither a preoccupation of society nor a function of bureaucracy, as it is in France. We find it hard to credit that things can have been quite so bad, and the conspiracy and double-dealing quite so dirty, as Berlioz says they were. In fact he could have been louder in his complaints without straining the truth. Read Stendhal's *Lucien Leuwen* if you find the description of his relations with the Ministry of the Interior over the Requiem implausible.

As Ernest Newman remarks, Berlioz 'had the imprudence to be born into a not very musical nation in one of its least truly musical periods'. Mediocrity will naturally fight to protect itself against talent and 'the painful impact of new ideas'. No doubt, too, Berlioz's caustic pen helped to stimulate opposition. But such opposition was already inherent in the situation, as he himself recognized. 'What the devil was the Good Lord thinking of when he had me born in "this pleasant land of France"?' His opinions on so many questions were so deeply at variance with those of his time. How thoroughly and eternally un-Parisian he was, for instance, in preaching the inviolability of the work of art and the sanctity of the composer's intentions. Castil-Blaze, the arranger of *Der Freischütz*, is singled out for attack in the *Memoirs*; but his activities, if unusually flamboyant, were far from uncommon in that age of rudimentary copyright laws, and the attitude behind them was widely shared; he was voicing a conventional view when he claimed that there 'is nothing wrong in transposing movements from one Beethoven symphony to another—on the contrary, everything is to be gained, for the audience will have more chance of enjoying the work if a livelier minuet, an andante of greater charm and melodic originality, are substituted for the original movement'.

At the second performance of the Ninth Symphony in Paris, in 1832, the work was divided in two, the first part consisting of the opening movement and the scherzo, the second of the adagio and the finale, with excerpts from Weber and Cherubini in between—this from the hallowed Société des Concerts, no less. The same plan was adopted next time the work was given, two years later, with the difference that the adagio preceded the scherzo. Ernest Reyer, writing in 1864 apropos of *The Trojans*, confirms that operas were habitually cut and altered in Paris: 'I am not saying that composers are infallible. [. . .] I am merely protesting at the systematic and senseless cutting which destroys a work's shape and even its character. And look how we treat the dead, who have no way of protesting or defending themselves. There is not a work of the old German school—not one—and scarcely any of the French that is not hacked about and changed at the whim of the director or the irrepressible creative urge of some artist or other.' Berlioz did not invent the fundamental antagonism between himself and Parisian musical custom.

Again, the violence of his reaction against Rossini (which did not however preclude admiration of particular works) is explained not only by Rossini's dominance of operatic life in Paris in the middle and late 1820s but by his almost universal deification by the French intelligentsia of the day, who freely compared the composer of *Semiramide* and *Moïse* with Raphael or Titian. To Berlioz, with his quite different ideas of dramatic music based on Gluck, Spontini, Weber and Beethoven, this was the very ecstasy of wrong-headedness.

Between such divergent views a head-on confrontation was inevitable; and it was inevitable that Berlioz should lose. When we consider how France treated him the outbursts in the *Memoirs* seem almost modest. His greatest error was that despite every encouragement to do so he could never bring himself to leave Paris, 'that unique, electrifying city' (though he came near to settling in London). Having failed in his first attempt on the Opéra—the centre of Paris musical life, where reputations and fortunes were made—he never really had another chance. Concerts paid very little; and after 1843 the risks were increased by his no longer being allowed to use the Conservatoire hall, where he had had a small but regular public. Tiersot calculates that between 1832 and 1840, the period of his greatest activity as composer and concert-promoter, Berlioz earned about ten thousand francs from his music. A rough modern equivalent would be two thousand pounds. He never obtained a position as conductor, though he was the best of his time; the jobs always went elsewhere. Academic recognition, for most of his career, was likewise not vouchsafed him. His main income came from music criticism. The journeys he went on in the 1840s and 1850s provided artistic stimulus in all sorts of ways, and they played an important part in the development of the orchestra and of modern techniques of orchestral playing and conducting. But in the last resort they were a diversion from the course he ought to have followed.

Granted the fact of his genius and his not unreasonable belief in it, Berlioz's predicament was an appalling one. Before *The Trojans* became well known it was possible, and consoling, to postulate a decline in creative vitality due to exhaustion, disappointment and disease. We can see that this was not so. Berlioz in the 1850s was at the height of his powers. He knew it himself. 'I feel that my faculties have never been so great; but material obstacles prevent me from using them. This frustration of my creative impulses makes me literally ill.' The financial catastrophe of *The Damnation of Faust* was the watershed of his career; incalculable consequences flowed from it. It is heartbreaking to think of all that he might have written with a little more encouragement from the authorities of the day; the known list includes an opera on *Antony and Cleopatra*, one on *Romeo and Juliet*, and a symphony, all of which projects belong to the 1850s and the last-named of which he deliberately suppressed, knowing it would commit him to an expense he could not possibly afford. This grim episode comes in the three-year gap which separates the inception and completion of *The Childhood of Christ*, a period filled by foreign tours and journalism. During this time he composed nothing of importance and reviewed the following thirty-two operas: Halévy's *La dame de pique*, Grisar's *Bonsoir, Monsieur Pantalon*, Rosenhain's *Le démon de la nuit*,

Gounod's *Sapho*, Thalberg's *Florinda*, Saint-Jullien's *Serafina*, Boisselot's *Mosquita la sorcière*, Gautier's *Murdock le bandit*, David's *La perle de Brésil*, Limnander's *Le château de Barbe-Bleue*, Louis Boïeldieu's *La butte des moulins*, Déjazet's *Le mariage en l'air*, Grisar's *Le carillonneur de Bruges*, Villeblanche's *Les fiançailles des roses*, Adam's *La poupée de Nuremberg*, Maillard's *La croix de Marie*, Cadaux's *Les deux Jakel*, Reber's *Le père Gaillard*, Gautier's *Flore et Zéphire*, Auber's *Marco Spada*, Clapisson's *Les mystères d'Udolphe*, Verdi's *Luisa Miller*, Gastinel's *Le miroir*, Grisar's *Les amours du diable*, Thomas' *La torelli*, Niedermeyer's *La fronde*, Adam's *Le roi de Hall*, Duprez's *La lettre au bon dieu*, Halévy's *Nabab*, Vogel's *La moissonneuse*, Poise's *Le voisin*, Adam's *Le bijou perdu*, and Prudent's *La danse des fées*.

No wonder the *Memoirs* is a passionate cry of protest. The remarkable thing is that it is not more bitter, that the protest is largely untouched by self-pity and the passion can still be tempered with irony. When he began compiling the book, in London in 1848, he was still without a settled position in Paris and seemed about to lose even what he had. Six years later, when the first draft was completed, nothing had changed. The struggle—what he called his 'Thirty Years War against the routineers, the academics and the deaf'—concentrated his energies and narrowed his sympathies. The former Saint-Simonian, who had dreamed of a society renewed by art in the interests of the people, came to hate republicanism, unfairly identifying it with the philistine forces which denied his talents full expression; he preferred despotism to constitutional monarchy: it actually paid you as much for your work as the other obliged you to spend on it. But this artistic egoism did not dehumanize him. It was only the fate of *The Trojans* that broke his spirit. 'I cannot conceal from you', he writes to Princess Wittgenstein after a private performance of a few excerpts with piano, 'that the thought of the quarantine imposed on the work [. . .] has tormented me day and night. I had not heard any of it before, and those great phrases, brought to life by Madame Charton's splendid voice, intoxicated me. I now imagine its effect in the theatre; and, against my will, the crass opposition of those idiots at the Opéra breaks my heart.' For Berlioz, the rejection of the work he knew to be the culmination of his existence was a total and unmitigated defeat which he bore only with a kind of bitter dignity. As Gounod remarks, it 'finished him; one may say of him, as of his namesake Hector, that he died beneath the walls of Troy'. He was an old man at sixty.

Yet the *Memoirs*, profoundly sad as it is, is not a gloomy book to read. This is partly because of the humour and saving irony that run through so much of it, and the vitality and virile simplicity of mind; partly because we can see that his career as a composer was not unfulfilled, that he did write a crowning masterpiece in which all aspects of his art meet; above all because it shows someone broken by his fate yet refusing to give up his ideals, still vulnerable to experience, still prepared to feel. He remained open to life. 'Listen,' he writes to a friend who had forwarded a letter from a young Russian woman with whom Berlioz had been in love, 'I suffer keenly; yet I'm grateful to her for reviving in me the pain I was trying to forget. There are so many kinds of love. The kind I feel is the true full-blown poetic love. I have known it since the first time of all, and nothing is more beautiful. It alone, and love of art, can raise our souls to the divine. With it, the world grows radiant, horizons expand, the whole of nature glows and pulsates with infinite harmonies—one loves, that's all, one loves!' It was the text of his life, and it is the theme of the account he has left us of it.

*

When Berlioz began the *Memoirs*, in his Harley Street lodgings in March 1848, he made his intentions perfectly clear. He would not be writing 'confessions': he would tell only what he wished to tell about his private life; at the same time he would attempt to give an idea of 'the difficulties confronting those who try to be composers at the present time, and to offer them a few useful hints'.

The result was a book with no pretensions to be the full story of his life; and the commentators who made it their business to demonstrate its inaccuracy—chief among them Hippeau, Boschot and Newman—could have spared themselves a lot of trouble if they had taken note of this, instead of approaching it with minds primed to detect the muddled recollection or 'the plain protective lie'. They might then have been less disconcerted to find not the meticulous day-to-day record they seem mistakenly to have expected but a composed work of literature, partly didactic and objective, wholly personal, organized by sequence of ideas as much as of time. Newman, for instance, would have had less reason to object that 'Berlioz's chronology' is frequently 'confused', or that a sequence like that of Chapters 26 (second half), 27, 28 and 29, which describes events in 1830 belonging respectively to May, autumn, spring and July, is 'very confused', when it is patently logical, given that it is dictated not by chronology but by subject-matter.

Cross-questioning an autobiography demands a care that Boschot, in particular, often neglected: with all the documents in front of him he sometimes contrived to get things more muddled than Berlioz writing in the midst of an active and embattled career, and to obscure the very record he set out so eagerly to put right. The commentator who would test the truth of an author's account against contemporary newspapers, official documents and the writer's own letters must observe certain salutary cautions. No one with any idea how journalists work and in what conditions newspapers are produced will be disposed to accept their testimony as incontrovertible fact; the case of the music critic who reviews an item omitted from the programme after he or she left the hall is only an extreme example. Official documents can blur the truth or even lie (a decision can be recorded and then not be carried out, a payment can be entered before it has been made). As Barzun says, 'if we believed the papers signed by the kindly Horace Vernet as director of the Academy in Rome, we would suppose Berlioz had never left it'; his account of the tragi-comic escapade to Nice would have to be set down as pure fabrication.

Neither are letters necessarily to be treated at face value. Being written to a particular person they take on to a greater or lesser degree the colour of that person; or they may tell only what the writer wishes that person to hear (or what at the time he or she wrongly believes to be true). When Berlioz, writing to his family, omits to mention or makes light of some disaster which in the *Memoirs* he describes at length, we should be wary of using the letter to refute the autobiography. Equally, we should not hasten to convict the autobiographer of falsehood when what he says appears to be unsupported by independent evidence. Hippeau assumed that the episode of the mathematician at the Opéra (Chapter 15) was sheer fantasy—only for a letter to turn up that corroborated it.

Nor is it enough to pit an earlier recension of some passage against the more vivid or elaborate final version to prove the writer an embellisher of the truth. In the *Memoirs* the Institute usher, Pingard, is made to refer to the ceremonial vessel in which the academicians cast their votes as the 'hurn'. This detail is absent from the *Voyage musical* of 1844 (and from the original newspaper article). But we cannot therefore conclude that we have caught Berlioz in the act of touching up his picture: it is just as possible that, after the book came out, some former fellow-student reminded him of how Pingard 'always used to say hurn'. Similarly *Voyage musical*, in its account of the Rákóczy March and the inarticulate Hungarian enthusiast, does not include the words 'Germans—dogs!' which appear in the later version. The phrase may be an embroidery, but is at least as likely to have been omitted from the original—which was first and foremost an account of a tour of Germany—on grounds of diplomacy and tact.

All autobiographies contain errors, of fact and of emphasis. The *Memoirs* is no exception. Neither is it exceptionally inaccurate. On some matters the writer's memory is not to be trusted. But this should not surprise us. The human memory is naturally selective. Though Berlioz reserved the right to keep silent, sometimes silence can amount to falsification. He tends to play down the part taken in his mature works by music written in his student days. He apparently fails to recognize the importance, for his whole career, of the year spent in Italy. Remembering the frustrations he experienced there—'used to an extremely active mental life, I am trapped in a country where there are no books, no theatres, no music'—he cannot see the fruitful influence of this period of inaction but intense receptivity.

Sometimes, especially in the tales of his dealings with officialdom, though the emphasis is wrong—a sum of money or a period of time exaggerated—the substance is correct. It took the Ministry of the Interior five months, not eight, to pay him for the rehearsals of the Requiem; but the point is made. His fondness for tall stories can get the better of him (one of them, he admits in a footnote, is 'an example of the proneness of artists to write for effect'), though the dramatized dialogues which punctuate the narrative are surely not meant to be taken absolutely literally. Sometimes he deliberately heightens some quirk of his nature or makes himself out to be a wilder or more uncultivated fellow than he really was. When recalling Paganini's princely gift, his memory transmutes the relief he felt at no longer having to depend for a living on writing articles into an actual interruption of his journalistic career during the composition of the *Romeo and Juliet* symphony which the gift made possible. He can certainly be casual about dates. Out of hurt pride and the deep wound it dealt him, he minimizes the seriousness of his relationship with Camille Moke. Such things are normal. To an impartial critic the *Memoirs* must none the less appear a largely and essentially true account of an artist's life and of the feelings and thoughts that inspired it.

*

In this edition my principle has been that Berlioz's text should be left where possible uncorrected; discussion of errors is in most cases confined to the back of the book. The reader will find them—those that I have spotted—listed, with chapter, page and line reference and identifying phrase, in Appendix III. The same appendix also gives my opinion on various controversial questions and enlarges on other matters of possible interest. With a few exceptions, the notes at the foot of the page are concerned with matters of immediate relevance. Under this heading come dates of journeys and concerts and other significant events, sources of literary allusions, and so on. Editor's footnotes are distinguished from author's by square brackets.

I have included among the appendices a glossary of characters and institutions, a short anthology (chronologically arranged) of descriptions of Berlioz, a list of newspaper articles which served as sources for certain chapters in the book, and a bibliography. A chronology of the main events of Berlioz's life follows this introduction.

For my translation I have felt free to borrow ideas or phrases from the two previously published English versions, the one by Rachel and Eleanor Holmes (1884), which was used with minor revisions by Newman in his edition of the *Memoirs* (1932), and the Everyman edition (1912) by Katharine F. Boult (mother of Sir Adrian). This last, though heavily abridged, is full of character. As my introduction to Berlioz's autobiography it first aroused my interest in the man, and I gratefully acknowledge the debt.

I realize that in my rendering of French titles and quotations I may have laid myself open to criticism on the score of inconsistency. I have no defence, except to say that if consistency were one's aim one would not attempt a translation. Berlioz did not quote Molière or Auguste Barbier in English, nor did he say London or the July Revolution; but such logic, once admitted, would strangle the act of translation at birth. I have tried to make my version as English as possible while stopping short of the pretence that the *Memoirs* is an English book. In general I follow English usage, which speaks of *Harold in Italy*, the Conservatoire library, and the Institute, but also of the Champs-Elysées, *Les nuits d'été* and the Prix de Rome (*The Count of Monte-Cristo* but *Les misérables*). Passages from poems or vocal works are given in English, where the meaning of the words is the point of the quotation. The result is not consistent; but I hope it justifies itself pragmatically.

CHRONOLOGY

DATE	AUTHOR'S LIFE	ARTISTIC CONTEXT
1802		de Staël: *Delphine*. Chateaubriand: *Génie du Christianisme*.
1803	Born at La Côte Saint-André Isère, 11 December.	Beethoven: *Eroica* Symphony.
1804		Schiller: *William Tell*.
1805		Chateaubriand: *René*.
1806	Nanci (sister) born (February).	
1807		de Staël: *Corinne*. Spontini: *La Vestale*. David: 'The Coronation of Napoleon'.
1808		Beethoven: Fifth and Sixth Symphonies completed. Goethe: *Faust* (1).
1809		
1810		de Staël: *De l'Allemagne*.
1811	Uncle Félix Marmion with Grande Armée in Spain.	
1812		Byron: *Childe Harold* (1 & 2).
1813		
1814	Educated at local school, then at home by his father. Adèle (sister) born (May).	Beethoven: *Fidelio* (revised version).
1815	First communion. Falls in love with Estelle Dubeuf.	Scott: *Guy Mannering*.
1816	Learns to play the flageolet.	Rossini: *The Barber of Seville*. Scott: *Old Mortality*. Constant: *Adolphe*.
1817	Learns the flute under Imbert. First compositions.	
1818	Imbert replaced by Dorant. Learns the guitar.	
1819	Begins medical studies with father. Attempts to get compositions published.	de Maistre: *Du Pape*. Géricault: 'The Raft of the Medusa'. Ingres: 'La grande Odalisque'.
1820		Lamartine: *Méditations poétiques*.

Peace of Amiens between France and Britain (at war since 1793). Concordat between France and Roman Catholic Church. Napoleon made Consul for life.

Renewal of war with Britain. Sale of Louisiana to United States.

Civil Code promulgated. Napoleon crowned emperor.

Third Coalition against France. Nelson victorious at battle of Trafalgar. French army defeats Austrians at Ulm and Austerlitz and occupies Vienna. Peace of Pressburg.

Prussian army defeated at Jena and Auerstadt. French occupation of Berlin and Warsaw. Blockade of Britain declared.

Russians sign treaty of Tilsit with France, following defeat at Eylau and Friedland.

Joseph Bonaparte made King of Spain. Peninsular War begins.

War between France and Austria resumed; French victory at Wagram.

Napoleon divorces Joséphine and marries Archduchess Marie Louise of Austria.

Birth of Napoleon's son, the Duc de Reichstadt.

Napoleon invades Russia. Battle of Borodino. Retreat from Moscow. Wellington takes Madrid.

Napoleon defeated by Allied forces at battle of Leipzig.

Allies invade France. Fall of Paris. Abdication of Napoleon and exile to Elba.

First Bourbon Restoration. First Treaty of Paris. Louis XVIII signs Constitutional Charter. Congress of Vienna (to 1815).

Napoleon's Hundred Days and defeat at Waterloo. Second Bourbon Restoration. White Terror in Midi. *Chambre introuvable* elected. Government of Talleyrand and Fouché (July–September). Ministry of Richelieu (to 1818). Second Treaty of Paris. Execution of Marshal Ney.

Dissolution of *Chambre introuvable*. Election of new Chamber.

Congress of Aix-la-Chapelle: end of occupation of France. Richelieu replaced by Decazes.

Peterloo Massacre in England. Metternich's repressive Carlsbad Decrees (German Confederation).

Assassination of Duc de Berry, heir presumptive to French throne. Second Richelieu ministry. Revolutions in Spain and Naples.

DATE	AUTHOR'S LIFE	ARTISTIC CONTEXT
1821	Passes baccalaureate at Grenoble. Goes to Paris to study medicine (October). Frequents Opéra and hears Salieri's *Les Danaïdes*, Méhul's *Stratonice* and Gluck's *Iphigénie en Tauride*.	Weber: *Der Freischütz*.
1822	Studies Gluck and Spontini scores in Conservatoire library. Beginning of conflict with family over career. Composes *Le cheval arabe*. Becomes pupil of Lesueur. Medical School closed for five months (November). Publishes songs.	Géricault: 'The Madwoman'.
1823	Composes *Estelle et Némorin* and *The Crossing of the Red Sea*. Defends Gluck in the *Corsaire*.	Rossini: *Semiramide*. Lamartine: *Nouvelles Méditations poétiques*.
1824	Composes *Beverley* and *Messe solennelle* (Mass). *Robin des bois* (*Der Freischütz*) at Odéon. Abortive rehearsal of Mass (December).	Beethoven: Ninth Symphony completed. Delacroix: 'The Massacre of Scio'.
1825	Successful performance of Mass at St Roch (July). Composes *Scène héroique*.	Saint-Simon: *Nouveau Christianisme*.
1826	Weber in Paris. Failure in preliminaries of Prix de Rome. Completes *Les francs-juges*. Joins chorus at the Nouveautés.	Weber: *Oberon*. Mendelssohn: *A Midsummer Night's Dream* Overture. Hugo: *Odes et ballades*. Vigny: *Cinq-mars*.
1827	Prix de Rome cantata (*Orphée*). Sees *Hamlet* and *Romeo and Juliet* at Odéon, with Harriet Smithson as Ophelia and Juliet (September). Second performance of Mass.	Nerval: *Faust* Part I (translation of Goethe). Hugo: Preface to *Cromwell*. Delacroix: 'Death of Sardanapalus'.
1828	Hears Beethoven symphonies at Conservatoire concerts. Puts on concert of his own music at Conservatoire (May). Second prize in Prix de Rome (*Herminie*). Reconciliation with family. Composes *Eight Scenes from Faust*.	Auber: *La muette de Portici*. Delacroix: *Faust* lithographs.
1829	Publishes *Eight Scenes*. Prix de Rome (*Cléopâtre*). Puts on second concert (November). Composes *Neuf mélodies* to Thomas Moore poems.	Rossini: *William Tell*. Hugo: *Les orientales*; *Le dernier Jour d'un condamné*. Dumas: *Henri III*.

HISTORICAL BACKGROUND

Death of Napoleon on St Helena. Revolutionary movement of the Charbonnerie. Fall of Richelieu: Ultras take over government. Laibach Conference: Austria authorized to suppress Neapolitan revolution. Greek War of Independence begins.

Villèle President of the Council. Congress of Verona.

French invasion of Spain. Guizot publishes *Essais sur l'histoire de France*, and Thiers his *Histoire de la révolution française* (to 1827).

Death of Louis XVIII; accession of Charles X. Death of Byron at Missolonghi.

Law against sacrilege. Indemnity to *émigrés* voted.

Niepce photographs from nature.

Combined French, British and Russian fleets defeat Turks in the battle of Navarino.

Resignation of Villèle.

Polignac forms government.

DATE	AUTHOR'S LIFE	ARTISTIC CONTEXT
1830	Affair with Camille Moke, leading to engagement. Composes Fantastic Symphony. Wins Prix de Rome (*Sardanapale*). Meets Liszt. Première of symphony (December).	Stendhal: *Le rouge et le noir.* Hugo: *Hernani.* Delacroix: 'Liberty leading the People'.
1831	Travels to Rome. Meets Mendelssohn. Receiving no word from Camille, returns to Florence and, learning of her marriage to Pleyel, continues to Nice. Composes *King Lear* overture and begins *Rob Roy.* Return to Rome. Completes *Le retour à la vie* (*Lélio*). Visits Naples and Pompeii.	Bellini: *Norma.* Meyerbeer: *Robert le Diable.* Hugo: *Notre-Dame de Paris.* Dumas: *Antony*; *Les feuilles d'automne.* Balzac: *Le peau de chagrin.*
1832	Composes *La captive.* Revises Fantastic Symphony. On return to France stays five months at La Côte. Puts on performances of symphony and *Lélio* (December) and is introduced to Harriet Smithson.	Mendelssohn: *Hebrides* overture (revised version). Donizetti: *L'elisir d'amore.* Goethe: *Faust* (2). Sand: *Indiana.* Ingres: 'Portrait of Louis Bertin'.
1833	Marries Harriet (October). Writes articles for *L'Europe littéraire.* Music critic of *Rénovateur.* Liszt makes piano arrangement of Fantastic Symphony, which he publishes (1834) at his own expense.	Mendelssohn: 'Italian' Symphony. Heine: *De la France.*
1834	Composes *Harold* for Paganini, and *Sara la baigneuse.* Move to Montmartre. Louis Berlioz born (August). Libretto of *Benvenuto Cellini* rejected by Opéra-Comique. Four concerts of recent works in Conservatoire Hall (November–December). Writing regularly for newly founded *Gazette musicale.*	Balzac: *Le père Goriot.* Lemaître: *Robert Macaire.* Sand: *Lettres d'un voyageur.* Lamennais: *Paroles d'un croyant.* Daumier: 'Massacre in the rue Transnonain'.
1835	Music critic of *Journal des débats.* Works on seven-movement *Fête musicale funèbre à la mémoire des hommes illustres de la France,* but completes only *Le cinq mai.* Takes over conducting of his own concerts.	Donizetti: *Lucia di Lammermoor.* Bellini: *I puritani.* Halévy: *La Juive.* Vigny: *Servitude et grandeur militaires, Chatterton.* Gautier: *Mademoiselle de Maupin.*
1836	Composes *Benvenuto Cellini.* Supervises rehearsals of Louise Bertin's *Esmeralda* at Opéra.	Meyerbeer: *Les Huguenots.* Liszt: *Album d'un voyageur.*

HISTORICAL BACKGROUND

Conquest of Algiers. The Four Ordinances: King dissolves newly elected Chamber, restricts the franchise and suppresses freedom of the Press. July Revolution. Abdication of Charles X; Duc d'Orléans accepts lieutenant-generalcy of France, afterwards becoming 'King of the French' as Louis-Philippe. New constitutional Charter. Comte begins publishing his *Cours de philosophie positive* (6 vols to 1842).

Anti-clerical riots in Paris. Casimir-Périer ministry. French expel Dutch from Belgium. Insurrection of Lyons silk-workers. Exhibition by painters of the Barbizon School. Cholera epidemic (to 1832).

Death of Duc de Reichstadt. Duchesse de Berry (mother of the legitimist heir, the Comte de Chambord) attempts to rouse Vendée. Death of Casimir-Périer. New ministry includes Broglie, Thiers and Guizot, with Marshal Soult as nominal head.

Guizot's education law.

Revolt in Lyons. Unrest in eastern Paris suppressed (rue Transnonain massacre).

Fieschi's assassination attempt on Louis-Philippe. Tocqueville's *La démocratie en Amérique* (vol. 1; vol. 2, 1840).

Attempted uprising by Louis Napoleon at Strasbourg. Government of Molé. Death of Charles X in exile.

DATE	AUTHOR'S LIFE	ARTISTIC CONTEXT
1837	*Grande Messe des Morts* commissioned by government for July celebrations. Performance cancelled, then given in December.	Balzac: *Illusions perdues* (1). Sand: *Mauprat*. Hugo: *Les voix intérieures*.
1838	*Cellini* performed three times at Opéra. Receives cheque for twenty thousand francs from Paganini after performance of *Harold* and the Fantastic Symphony.	Gautier: *La comédie de la mort*. Hugo: *Ruy Blas*. Delacroix: 'Portrait of Chopin'.
1839	Withdraws *Cellini*. Composes *Romeo and Juliet* symphony, dedicated to Paganini, and conducts three performances at Conservatoire (November–December). Appointed assistant librarian of Conservatoire. Meets Wagner.	Chopin: 24 Preludes (op. 28). Stendhal: *La Chartreuse de Parme*. Balzac: *Illusions perdues* (2). Daumier: *Les saltimbanques*.
1840	Composes Funeral and Triumphal Symphony to government commission.	Schumann: *Dichterliebe*. Chopin: opp. 35–42 published.
1841	Publishes *Les nuits d'été* (piano version). Supervises revival of *Der Freischütz* at Opéra. Begins composing *La nonne sanglante* for Opéra. Liaison with Marie Recio.	Adam: *Giselle*.
1842	Writes articles on orchestration which become the *Grand Traité d'instrumentation et d'orchestration modernes*. Gives concerts in Brussels (September). Leaves for tour of Germany (December), with Marie Recio.	Verdi: *Nabucco*. Wagner: *Rienzi*. Sand: *Consuelo*. Sue: *Les mystères de Paris*. Ingres: 'Cherubini and his Muse'.
1843	Concerts in Weimar, Dresden, Leipzig, Brunswick, Berlin, etc. Composes *Roman Carnival* overture.	Wagner: *Der fliegende Holländer*. Donizetti: *Don Pasquale*. Balzac: *Illusions perdues* (3). Hugo: *Les Burgraves*.
1844	Loses use of Conservatoire hall for his concerts. Publishes *Voyage musical en Allemagne et en Italie*. Composes *Hymne à la France* for Industrial Exhibition concert (August). Composes *Corsaire* overture during holiday in Nice. Separation from Harriet. Composes *Hamlet* funeral march.	Verdi: *Ernani*. Dumas: *The Count of Monte Cristo*; *The Three Musketeers*. Rousseau: 'Under the Birches, Evening'.

HISTORICAL BACKGROUND

Paris–Saint-Germain railway opened. Capture of Constantine (Algeria). Accession of Queen Victoria.

Death of Talleyrand. Rachel plays in Racine.

Revolt of Abd-el-Kader. Fall of Molé. Louis Blanc's *Organisation du travail.* Louis Napoleon's *Les idées napoléoniennes.*

Inauguration of Bastille Column. Napoleon's ashes returned to Paris. Attempt of Louis Napoleon at Boulogne. Government of Thiers (March–October). Mehemet Ali crisis. Guizot forms ministry. Proudhon's *Qu'est-ce que la propriété?*

Franco-British entente cordiale.

Duc d'Orléans killed in accident. Guizot's railway law. Railway mania in France (to 1846).

Pritchard affair in Tahiti (Franco–British dispute).

DATE	AUTHOR'S LIFE	ARTISTIC CONTEXT
1845	Concerts in Cirque Olympique and at Marseilles and Lyons. Visits Bonn for inauguration of Beethoven statue. Begins *The Damnation of Faust*. Leaves for tour of Austria-Hungary.	Wagner: *Tannhaüser.* Mérimée: 'Carmen'.
1846	Concerts in Vienna, Prague, Pest, Breslau and Brunswick. *Chant des chemins de fer* performed in Lille. Two performances of *Damnation* (December); heavy financial loss.	Mendelssohn: *Elijah.* Balzac: *La Cousine Bette.*
1847	Concerts in St Petersburg and Moscow. Abandons *La nonne sanglante.* Visits father at La Côte, with Louis (September). Appointed conductor of Jullien's Grand English Opera at Drury Lane.	Verdi: *Macbeth.*
1848	Concerts in London. Collapse of Jullien's enterprise. *Memoirs* begun. Visit to La Côte following father's death.	Sand: *La petite Fadette.* Millet: 'The Winnower'.
1849	Composes Te Deum.	Meyerbeer: *Le prophète.*
1850	Founds Société Philharmonique de Paris. Appointed librarian of Conservatoire. Composes *The Flight into Egypt.*	Wagner: *Lohengrin.* Delacroix: 'Michelangelo in his studio'. Courbet: 'Portrait of Berlioz'; 'Burial at Ornans'. Millet: 'The Sowers'.
1851	Second and final season of Société Philharmonique. Second visit to London, as juror at Great Exhibition.	Verdi: *Rigoletto.*
1852	Third visit to London as conductor of New Philharmonic. Publishes *Les soirées de l'orchestre.* Visits Weimar for Liszt's 'Berlioz Week', including *Benvenuto Cellini.*	Dumas *fils*: *La dame aux camélias.*

HISTORICAL BACKGROUND

Publication of Thiers' *Histoire du Consultat et de l'Empire* begins (to 1869).

Escape of Louis Napoleon from Ham, where he had been imprisoned since 1840. Marriage of Louis-Philippe's son, the Duc de Montpensier, with the sister of Queen Isabella of Spain. Bad harvests and potato blight affect most of western Europe.

Economic crisis in France. Capture of Abd-el-Kader. Teste trial: prosecution of former minister for corruption discredits government. Opposition launch campaign of banquets (July–December) at which government is denounced. First use of chloroform as an anaesthetic.

France: February Revolution in Paris. Resignation of Guizot. Abdication of Louis-Philippe. Provisional government proclaims universal suffrage. Slavery abolished. Demonstrations by National Guard (*bonnets à poil*); counter-demonstrations by Paris workers pacified by Minister of Interior, Ledru-Rollin (March). Election of Constituent Assembly (April). Unsuccessful left-wing 'push' (May). June Days: six days of street fighting in Paris as workers' rising put down by Cavaignac. Constitution of Second Republic (November). Election of Louis Napoleon as President (December). Government of Odilon Barrot.
Europe: Year of revolutions notably in Vienna, Prague, Berlin, Venice, Milan, Parma, Rome and Naples. Chartists' demonstration in London. Marx and Engels' *Communist Manifesto* published.

Election of Legislative Assembly (May). Attempted uprising in Paris fails (June). French restore Pius IX: fall of Roman republic (July). Dismissal of Barrot ministry (October). Austrians regain control of Venice. Kossuth declares a Hungarian republic.

Loi Falloux: clerical control of education extended. Left-wing victories in by-elections. Law restricting franchise. Hungarian republic defeated by Austria and Russia.

Legislative Assembly rejects constitutional reform. Louis Napoleon's *coup d'état* (2 December). Plebiscite. Victor Hugo goes into exile. Re-establishment of absolutism in Austria and Prussia. Great Exhibition in London.

New constitution. Plebiscite on Empire. Proclamation of Empire (1 December). Foundation of Crédit Foncier and Crédit Mobilier.

DATE	AUTHOR'S LIFE	ARTISTIC CONTEXT
1853	Fourth visit to London to conduct (old) Philharmonic and *Benvenuto Cellini* at Covent Garden (withdrawn after single performance). Concerts at Baden, Brunswick, Hanover, Bremen and Leipzig. Meets Brahms. Composes *The Arrival at Sais*.	Verdi: *Il Trovatore*; *La Traviata*. Liszt: B minor Sonata.
1854	Death of Harriet. Further concerts in Germany. Completes *The Childhood of Christ* and gives three performances (December). Completes *Memoirs*. Marries Marie Recio.	Heine: *Lutèce*.
1855	Second Berlioz Week in Weimar. Concerts in Brussels. Conducts Te Deum at St Eustache. Fifth visit to London, for concerts with New Philharmonic. Publishes *L'art du chef d'orchestre*. Gives three concerts at Palais de l'Industrie for Exposition Universelle. First signs of intestinal illness.	Verdi: *The Sicilian Vespers*.
1856	Visits Weimar, Gotha. Completes and publishes *Les nuits d'été* (orchestral version). Writes text of *The Trojans* and begins composition. Elected to the Institute. Conducts first of annual gala concerts in Baden.	Wagner: *Die Walküre*. Liszt: *Dante Symphony*. Ingres: 'Mme Moitessier'.
1857	Completes *Trojans* Acts I and IV and composes Acts II and III.	Liszt: *Faust Symphony*. Flaubert: *Madame Bovary*. Baudelaire: *Les fleurs du mal*.
1858	*Trojans* completed. Campaign to get it performed at Opéra. Chapters from *Memoirs* serialized in *Le Monde illustré*.	Brahms: First Piano Concerto. Offenbach: *Orphée aux enfers*.
1859	Publishes *Les grotesques de la musique*. Revives Gluck's *Orphée* for Théâtre-Lyrique, with Pauline Viardot.	Verdi: *Un ballo in maschera*. Gounod: *Faust*. Millet: 'The Angelus'.
1860	*The Trojans* accepted by Théâtre-Lyrique. *Tannhaüser* accepted by Opéra. Writes text and begins composition of *Beatrice and Benedict* (commissioned for Baden theatre). Arranges for private printing of *Trojans* vocal score.	

HISTORICAL BACKGROUND

Marriage of Napoleon III and Eugénie. France occupies New Caledonia. Haussmann made Prefect of the Seine (to 1870): embarks on reconstruction of Paris.

France enters Crimean War. Siege of Sebastopol. Faidherbe extends French control in Senegal (to 1865). Doctrine of the Immaculate Conception promulgated.

Exposition Universelle in Paris. Fall of Sebastopol. Nadar establishes photographic studio (rue St Lazare).

Peace conference in Paris. Tocqueville's *L'Ancien Régime.*

Prosecution of *Madame Bovary* and *Les fleurs du mal.* Port of Dakar founded.

Orisini bomb plot. Napoleon III and Cavour meet at Plombières. Vision at Lourdes.

Construction of Suez Canal begun. Napoleon III grants amnesty to political exiles. War of Italian Unification; battles of Magenta and Solferino; armistice of Villafranca. Darwin's *The Origin of Species* published.

France acquires Nice and Savoy. Free trade treaty with Britain. Anglo-French occupation of Peking. Expedition to Syria. First constitutional changes: Senate and Legislative body permitted annual debates on the speech from the throne.

DATE	AUTHOR'S LIFE	ARTISTIC CONTEXT
1861	Failure of *Tannhaüser.* Supervises revival of Gluck's *Alceste.* Opéra accepts *Trojans.*	Corot: 'The Lake'.
1862	Death of Marie Berlioz. Première of *Beatrice and Benedict.* Publishes *A travers chants.*	Verdi: *La forza del destino.* Flaubert: *Salammbô.* Hugo: *Les misérables.* Ingres: 'The Turkish Bath'.
1863	*Trojans* turned down by Opéra, accepted by Théâtre-Lyrique. Conducts *Beatrice* in Weimar. Concert in Loewenberg. Conducts *Childhood of Christ* in Strasbourg. Acts I and II of *Trojans* dropped, Acts III–V given twenty-one performances (as *The Trojans at Carthage*).	Bizet: *Les pêcheurs de perles.* Manet: 'Olympia'; 'Le déjeuner sur l'herbe'. Renan: *Vie de Jésus.*
1864	Adds Postface to *Memoirs.* Visits Dauphiné, meets Estelle and begins regular correspondence with her.	Offenbach: *La belle Hélène.* Rossini: *Petite Messe solennelle.* Corot: 'Souvenir of Mortefontaine'.
1865	*Memoirs* completed and printed for posthumous publication. Visits Estelle in Geneva.	Meyerbeer: *L'Africaine.* Wagner: *Tristan und Isolde*, première.
1866	Second visit to Geneva. *Alceste* revived at Opéra. Conducts *The Damnation of Faust* in Vienna.	Offenbach: *La vie Parisienne.*
1867	Conducts concerts in Cologne. Death of Louis Berlioz in Havana. Third visit to Estelle. Journey to Russia (December).	Verdi: *Don Carlos.* Manet: 'Massacre of Maximilian'.
1868	Conducts concerts in St Petersburg and Moscow. Injured in fall at Nice (March). Guest of honour at festival banquet in Grenoble (August).	Wagner: *Die Meistersinger*, première. Baudelaire: *Petits poèmes en prose.* Monet: 'The River'.
1869	Dies at 4 rue de Calais (8 March). Buried (11 March) in Montmartre Cemetery.	Wagner: *Das Rheingold*, première. Flaubert: *L'éducation sentimentale.* Verlaine: *Les fêtes galantes.* Daudet: *Lettres de mon moulin.*

HISTORICAL BACKGROUND

French intervention in Mexico. Work on Garnier's Paris Opéra (completed 1875). Victor Emmanuel King of Italy. American Civil War begins. First bicycles manufactured, in France.
France annexes Cochin-China.

Revolt of Poland. Salon des Refusés: founding of French Impressionist school. Legislative elections. Fall of Persigny. Rouher becomes Minister of State.

Schleswig-Holstein War. Maximilian proclaimed emperor in Mexico. Papal Syllabus of Errors (condemning liberalism).

Death of the Duc de Morny, leading influence on the Emperor's domestic policy since 1863. Duruy's educational reforms.

Austro-Prussian War. Austrians defeated at Sadowa. French troops evacuate Mexico.

Letter of Napoleon III announcing constitutional changes. Proposals for re-armament. Crisis of Crédit Mobilier. Exposition Universelle in Paris. Execution of Maximilian. Garibaldi repelled by French and papal troops at Mentana. Marx's *Das Kapital* (vol. 1).
French press laws relaxed.

Government of Ollivier. Suez Canal opens.

THE MEMOIRS OF

HECTOR BERLIOZ

1803–1869

MEMBER OF THE FRENCH INSTITUTE

INCLUDING HIS TRAVELS IN
ITALY, GERMANY, RUSSIA AND ENGLAND

Life's but a walking shadow; a poor player
That struts and frets his hour upon the stage
And then is heard no more; it is a tale
Told by an idiot, full of sound and fury
Signifying nothing.

SHAKESPEARE, *Macbeth*

PREFACE

LONDON, 21 March 1848

ACCOUNTS OF MY life have appeared, and from time to time still appear, so full of errors and inaccuracies that I have at length resolved to set down myself those things in my arduous and turbulent career which I believe may be of interest to lovers of art. Such an inquiry will, moreover, afford me the opportunity to give a clear idea of the difficulties confronting those who try to be composers at the present time and to offer them a few useful hints.

An earlier book of mine published several years ago and now out of print contained, along with short stories and pieces of musical criticism, the narrative of part of my travels.* Well-wishers have sometimes suggested that I should recast and complete these random notes.

If I now make the mistake of yielding to their friendly persuasion, it is not from any illusion as to the importance of such an undertaking. The public, I am aware, is little concerned with what I may have done or felt or thought. But a few artists and music-lovers having expressed the desire to know, I would rather they were given a true version than left to believe a false one. I do not have the least pretension to 'appear before God, book in hand', declaring myself the 'best of men', nor to write 'confessions'.† I shall tell only what I wish to tell; and the reader who refuses me his absolution must needs be harsh to the point of unorthodoxy, for I will admit none but venial sins.

But enough preamble: time is short. As I write, the juggernaut of Republicanism rolls across Europe. The art of music, long since dying, is now quite dead. They are about to bury it or rather throw it on the dung-heap. France and Germany have no further existence for me. Russia is too far away, I cannot go back there. England, since I have lived here, has treated me most warmly and hospitably; but now, with the first tremors from the

* [*Voyage musical en Allemagne et en Italie* (1844).]

† [The references are to the third paragraph of Rousseau's autobiography.]

Continent, flocks of frightened artists come hurrying from all points to seek refuge, as sea-birds fly landwards before great storms. Will the British capital be able to maintain so many exiles? Will it wish to listen to their tales of woe amid the vainglorious clamour of its neighbours—the noise of sovereign peoples crowning themselves king? May it not feel tempted by the example? *Jam proximus ardet Ucalegon!** Who knows what will have become of me in a few months—I have no sure means of support for myself and my dependants. Let me therefore make use of the time that is left, even though I may soon have to emulate the stoicism of those Indians of the Niagara who, after striving valiantly against the stream, recognize that their efforts are useless and, abandoning themselves to the current, contemplate with steadfast eye the short distance between them and the abyss, and sing, till the very moment the cataract seizes them and whirls them to infinity.

* ['Close by, Ucalegon's house is already ablaze!'—*Aeneid*, II, 311–12; from Aeneas' account of the fall of Troy.]

I

La Côte Saint-André—my first communion —first musical experience

I WAS BORN on 11 December 1803 in La Côte Saint-André, a very small French town in the department of Isère between Vienne, Grenoble and Lyons. During the months which preceded my birth my mother never dreamed, as Virgil's did, that she was about to bring forth a laurel branch. Nor, I must add—however painful the admission to my vanity—did she imagine she bore within her a flaming brand, like Olympias the mother of Alexander. This is extraordinary, I agree, but it is true. I came into the world quite normally, unheralded by any of the portents in use in poetic times to announce the arrival of those destined for glory. Can it be that our age is lacking in poetry?

La Côte Saint-André, as its name indicates, stands on the side of a hill. It overlooks a wide, rich plain, green and golden and in its stillness filled with a sense of dreamlike grandeur—a grandeur enhanced by the chain of mountains bounding the plain to the south and east, behind which, far off, gleaming with glaciers, rise the towering peaks of the Alps.

Needless to say, I was brought up in the Catholic and Apostolic Church of Rome. This charming religion (so attractive since it gave up burning people) was for seven whole years the joy of my life, and although we have long since fallen out I have always kept most tender memories of it. Indeed, such is its appeal for me that had I had the misfortune to be born into the bosom of one of those schisms ponderously hatched by Luther or Calvin I should undoubtedly have abjured it the moment I was able and flung myself into the arms of the fair Roman at the earliest promptings of poetic instinct. I took my first communion on the same day as my elder sister, at the Ursuline convent where she was a boarder. This unusual circumstance gave to my religious initiation a quality of sweetness which I recall even now with emotion. The almoner of the convent came to fetch me at six o'clock in the morning. It was spring; the sun was smiling, a breeze played among the whispering poplars; some delicious fragrance filled the air. Deeply moved, I crossed the sacred threshold and was admitted to the chapel.

There, in the midst of my sister's friends dressed in white, I prayed with them while I waited for the solemn ceremony. The priest came forward, the Mass began; I belonged to God. But I received a shock when the priest, with that boorish bias in favour of his own sex which certain men retain even at the Lord's table, beckoned me to come up to the altar first, ahead of those charming girls who, I felt, should go before me. However, I went up, blushing at the unmerited honour. As I took the sacrament a chorus of virginal voices broke into the eucharistic hymn, and I was filled with a mystic yet passionate unrest which I was powerless to hide from the congregation. I thought I saw heaven open, a heaven of love and chaste delight, a thousand times purer and more beautiful than the one I had so often been told about. Such is the magic power of true expression, the incomparable beauty of melody that comes from the heart! The tune was the romance 'When my sweetheart returns to me' from *Nina*, furnished with a text suitable for the occasion. I recognized it when I heard it ten years later. Oh, the ecstasy that possessed my young soul! Dear Dalayrac! Yet today the nation, forgetful of musicians, barely remembers your name!

It was my first musical experience.

Thus, at a blow, I became a saint—such a saint that I attended Mass every day and took communion every Sunday and went regularly to confession in order to say to my director, 'Father, I have done nothing.' To which the good man would answer, 'Carry on, my son.' I followed this counsel all too faithfully for a number of years.

2

My father—my literary education—my passion for travel —Virgil—first impact of poetry

MY FATHER, LOUIS Berlioz, was a doctor. It is not for me to appraise his abilities. I will say only that he was a highly respected figure not merely in our little town but in the neighbouring towns as well. He worked without respite; it was an article of faith with him that in a vocation as difficult and hazardous as medicine every moment should be devoted to improving one's skill, since the slightest negligence could cost the life of a fellow-creature. He was an ornament to his profession, which he pursued without regard to personal interest, behaving more as a benefactor of the poor and the peasantry than as a man who did it for a living. In 1810 he won a competition held by the Medical Society of Montpellier for the best monograph on an important new topic. I should add that the book was published in Paris* and that several well-known physicians borrowed its ideas without acknowledgement. My father, in his simplicity, was always surprised by this; but he only said, 'What does it matter, so long as truth prevails?' It is some time since he gave up his practice, which was getting beyond his strength. He now spends his time in reading and meditation.

He has a naturally liberal mind: that is, he is without any kind of social, political or religious prejudice. He had, however, so faithfully promised my mother to do nothing to wean me from the beliefs which she regarded as essential for my salvation that on several occasions, I remember, he even went so far as to hear my catechism—evidence of a degree of scrupulousness or philosophical impartiality of which I confess I should be incapable were my own son concerned. For some years my father has suffered from an incurable disease of the stomach. Many times he has nearly died of it. He is very weak; he eats practically nothing and keeps alive on constant and ever-increasing doses of opium. He has since told me that a few years ago, demoralized by the excruciating pain, he swallowed thirty-two grains at once. 'I will confess to you,' he said, 'that I did not take it as a cure.' Instead of killing him, as he had hoped, this colossal dose almost instantly relieved the pain and restored him temporarily to health.

When I was ten years old he sent me to the secondary school in La Côte, where I was to begin learning Latin. Soon afterwards he took me away again, having decided to look after my education himself.

Poor Father, with what tireless patience, with what perceptiveness and devotion he taught me languages, literature, history, geography and even, as will shortly be seen, music!

How much tenderness must a man feel for his son to undertake and carry through such a task, and how few fathers would be

* *Treatise on Chronic Diseases, Cupping and Acupuncture*. Croullebois, Paris.

capable of it! And yet I cannot think that in many respects a private education at home is as beneficial as ordinary school life. Children brought up in this way spend their time almost exclusively among relations, servants and a few chosen companions, instead of being early inured to the rough disciplines of human society. Life, the realities of the world, are a closed book to them. I am quite sure that, in this sense, I remained an awkward and untutored child till the age of twenty-five.

My father was a tolerant taskmaster. Try as he would, he could not inspire me with a real taste for classics. Above all I hated having to learn even a few lines of Horace or Virgil by heart each day. My brain memorized the splendid verse only with the most painful effort, and my thoughts, impatient of the beaten track, would fly off in all directions. Thus I would spend long hours poring over the atlas, examining the intricate system of islands, straits and promontories in the South Seas and the Indian Archipelago, pondering on the origins of those remote regions, their climate and vegetation and the people who lived there, and filled with an intense desire to visit them. It was the awakening of my passion for travel and adventure.

My father used to say of me, with reason, 'He knows the names of all the Molucca, Sandwich and Philippine Islands, he is familiar with the Torres Strait, with Timor, Java and Borneo, yet he could not tell you how many departments there are in France.' My curiosity about distant countries, especially those in the southern hemisphere, was sharpened by the accounts of voyages, modern and ancient, that I found in my father's library. I devoured them all; and had we lived in a port, sooner or later I would certainly have run away to sea and become a sailor, with or without my parents' consent. My son very early on showed the same inclination. He is now serving on a French ship. He chose the navy as a career before he had even seen the sea. I hope he will be an honour to it.

After I had chewed over Virgil and La Fontaine for some time, a feeling for the true beauties of poetry began to awake in me and my sea dreams took second place. The author of the *Fables* was, of the two, a later discovery than the Latin poet. Children are as a rule incapable of appreciating the profundities which underlie the simplicity of La Fontaine and the sheer skill concealed in that marvellously natural style. It was Virgil who first found the way to my heart and fired my nascent imagination, by speaking to me of epic passions for which instinct had prepared me. How often, as I construed the fourth book of the *Aeneid* for my father, did I feel my heart swell and my voice falter and break! One day, already disturbed from the very beginning of my oral translation by the line:

At regina gravi jamdudum saucia cura *

I arrived after a fashion at the turning-point of the drama. But when I came to the scene where Dido dies on the pyre, surrounded by the gifts and the weapons of the false-hearted Aeneas, and pours forth on the bed—'that bed with all its memories'—the angry stream of her life-blood, when I had to speak the despairing utterances of the dying queen, 'thrice raising herself on her elbow, thrice falling back', to describe her wound and the fatal love that convulsed her to the depths of her being, the cries of her sister, her nurse, her distracted women, and that agony so terrible that the gods themselves are moved and send Iris to end it, my lips trembled and the mumbled words would hardly come. At last, at the line

Quaesivit coelo lucem ingemuitque repertam

at that sublime image of Dido 'looking for light to the sky and moaning when she found it'—I was seized with a nervous shuddering and, in the impossibility of continuing, stopped dead.

It was one of the occasions when I was most grateful for my father's unutterable kindness. Seeing how embarrassed and confused I was by such an emotion, but pretending not to have noticed, he rose abruptly and shut the book. 'That's enough, my child,' he said; 'I'm tired.' And I ran off, out of sight of all, to give myself to my Virgilian grief.

3

Meylan—my uncle—the pink dancing shoes —the wood-nymph of Saint-Eynard—love in the life of a twelve-year-old

THE FACT IS I had already experienced the cruel passion so well described by the author of the *Aeneid*—a passion that is rare

* ['Now the Queen, for some time gnawed by the pangs of love . . .'—*Aeneid*, IV, 1.]

(whatever people may say about it), but very potent with certain natures. Love had been revealed to me at the same time as music, when I was twelve, and in the following manner.

My grandfather on my mother's side, whose name like that of the celebrated warrior in Walter Scott was Marmion, lived at Meylan in the country a few miles outside Grenoble, near the frontier of Savoy. The situation of this village and its surrounding hamlets at the conjunction of the Dauphiné mountains and the Basses Alpes, with the valley of the Isère spreading beneath it, is one of the most enchanting I know. My mother and my sisters and I usually went there for three weeks towards the end of the summer. Sometimes we were joined by my uncle, Félix Marmion. At that time he was following the glittering trail of the great Emperor and would arrive still hot from the breath of the cannon's mouth, decorated with a simple lance-thrust, a grape-shot wound in the foot, or a magnificent sabre-slash across the face. He was then only an adjutant in the Lancers; young, enamoured of Fame, ready to give his life for a glance from her, believing Napoleon's throne as unshakeable as Mont Blanc; gay, gallant, an enthusiastic amateur violinist and an accomplished singer of opéra-comique.

In the highest part of Meylan, right against the mountainside, is a small white house half hidden in gardens and vineyards with a wide prospect over the valley of the Isère far below; behind, a few craggy hillocks, an old tower in ruins, a wood, and the commanding bulk of the great rock-bastion of Saint-Eynard: in fact a spot clearly marked out to be the scene of some romantic drama. It was the villa of Madame Gautier. She lived there during the summer with her two nieces, the younger of whom was called Estelle. The name alone would have been enough to arouse my interest. It was already dear to me from Florian's pastorale *Estelle et Némorin*, which I had discovered in my father's library and secretly read and re-read a hundred times. This Estelle, however, was a girl of eighteen with a tall, elegant figure, large eyes primed for the attack (though they were always smiling), a head of hair that would have graced Achilles' helmet, and the feet, I will not say of an Andalusian, but of a pure-bred Parisian. And she wore pink dancing-shoes. I had never seen such things before. You may laugh; but although I have forgotten the colour of her hair (I believe it was black), I cannot think of her without seeing before me, dazzling as those great eyes of hers, the little pink shoes.

The moment I beheld her, I was conscious of an electric shock: I loved her. From then on I lived in a daze. I hoped for nothing, I knew nothing, and yet my heart felt weighed down by an immense sadness. I lay awake whole nights disconsolate. By day I hid myself in the maize Fields or in the secret corners of my grandfather's orchard, like a wounded bird, mute, suffering. Jealousy plagued me, pale companion of all true lovers. The least word addressed by any man to my divinity was torture to me. I can still hear—with the same shudder—the ring of my uncle's spurs as he danced with her. Everyone at home and in the neighbourhood laughed at the spectacle of a child of twelve broken on the wheel of a love beyond his years. She herself, who had been the first to realize the truth, was much amused, I am sure. One evening there was a large gathering at her aunt's house. Someone suggested a game of prisoner's base, which meant picking sides and dividing into two opposing camps. The gentlemen chose the ladies. They arranged it so that I should be the one to name his partner first. But I did not dare. My heart was beating too fast. I stood silent, with lowered eyes. They were all beginning to mock me, when Mlle Estelle, snatching my hand, cried, 'All right, I'll choose. I pick Monsieur Hector.' Oh the pain of that moment! She too was laughing, looking down at me from the remoteness of her unfeeling beauty.

Time is powerless. No other loves can efface the imprint of that first love. I was thirteen when I ceased to see her. I was thirty when I returned from Italy across the Alps and saw in the distance Saint-Eynard and the little white house and the old tower through a mist of tears. I still loved her. On reaching home I learnt that she was married—and all that follows; and it did not cure me. My mother, who used sometimes to tease me about my earliest passion, played me a trick which was perhaps more serious than she realized. A few days after I got back from Rome, she said, 'Could you take this letter for me? I have promised to deliver it to a lady who will shortly be passing through in the Vienne stage-coach. Go to the office and while the horses are being changed, ask for Madame F—— and give her the letter. I am sure you will recognize her, although you haven't met for seventeen years.' I went to the coach station, without any suspicion of what it meant. When the coach came in I went up to it with the letter in my hand, and asked which was Madame F——. 'I,' said a voice. 'She'—an answering cry reverberated deep within me. Estelle! Beautiful as ever! Estelle! the nymph, the hamadryad of Saint-Eynard and the green hills of Meylan. The same carriage of the head, the same splendid hair and dazzling smile (but alas—what had become of the little dancing-shoes?). The letter was taken. Was I recognized? I don't know. The coach drove off, and I went home, trembling from the shock of the encounter. 'Well,' my mother said, scrutinizing my face, 'I see that Némorin has not forgotten his Estelle.' His Estelle! Wicked mother!

4

First music lessons under the direction of my father —attempts at composition—studies in osteology —antipathy to medicine—I go to Paris

WHEN I SAID that music had been revealed to me at about the same time as love, at the age of twelve, I should have said composition; for I had already learnt to sing at sight and to play two instruments. It was my father, again, who started me off on my musical education.

One day I came upon a flageolet at the bottom of a drawer in which I was rummaging. I immediately wanted to play it and attempted to render the popular air 'Malbrouck', but to no purpose.

My father found these squeakings exceedingly disagreeable and begged me to leave him in peace until he had time to instruct me in the fingering of the instrument and the correct execution of the heroic strain I had chosen. This he did without much trouble. At the end of two days I was master of 'Malbrouck' and able to regale the whole family with it—an early manifestation of my remarkable feeling for wind instruments which will not, of course, escape the attention of the perceptive biographer.

The episode of the flageolet gave my father the notion of teaching me how to read music. He initiated me into its basic principles, explaining the meaning and function of musical notation. Not long afterwards he presented me with a flute, together with a copy of Devienne's *Method*, and again took the trouble to show me its mechanism. I worked so hard at it that in seven or eight months I could play pretty well. My father wished to encourage the talent I was showing and persuaded a few well-to-do families in La Côte to join with him and engage a music master from Lyons. The plan succeeded. A second violinist from the Théâtre des Célestins, who also played the clarinet, agreed to settle in our outlandish little town and try to musicalize its inhabitants, on condition they guaranteed him a certain number of pupils and a fixed salary for conducting the band of the National Guard. His name was Imbert.* He gave me lessons twice a day. I had an attractive treble voice and soon developed into a fearless reader and a fair singer, and could play Drouet's most intricate concertos on the flute. My master's son, who was a little older than I and already an accomplished horn-player, had taken a liking to me. One morning he came to see me as we were leaving for Meylan. 'What!' he said, 'you were going without saying good-bye? Embrace me; I might never see you again.' I was struck by my friend's strange manner and the unexpected solemnity of his leave-taking. But the overwhelming delight of seeing Meylan and my radiant *stella montis* again soon put him out of my mind. What sad news greeted my return! On the very day I left, young Imbert, taking advantage of his parents' momentary absence from the house, hanged himself. No one ever found out why.

I had discovered, among some old books, a copy of Rameau's *Treatise on Harmony*, annotated and simplified by d'Alembert. I sat up far into the night, puzzling over its abstruse doctrines. I could make no sense of them. Of course before you can grasp the author's meaning you need to have mastered the theory of chords and to be familiar with the branch of experimental physics on which the whole system is based. It is a treatise on harmony for those who already know harmony. All the same, I was determined to compose. I arranged two-part pieces for three and four parts without any idea how to achieve satisfactory basses and chords; but

* [The first contract with Imbert is dated 20 May 1817. Berlioz was then thirteen.]

at length, by dint of listening to the quartets of Pleyel, which our local amateurs played on Sundays, and with the aid of a copy of Catel's treatise on harmony which I had managed to procure, I suddenly found that the mysteries of chord formations and progressions had become clear to me. I immediately wrote a kind of medley in six parts on themes from a book of Italian airs in my possession. The harmony seemed tolerable, and I was emboldened by this first step to undertake the composition of a quintet for flute, two violins, viola and cello, which was performed by three of our amateurs, my teacher and myself.

It was a triumph. Only my father seemed not to share the general enthusiasm. Two months later another quintet followed. My father wanted to hear me try over the flute part before risking a full-scale performance (a characteristic attitude of provincial amateurs, who imagine they can judge a string quartet from the first violin part). I played it to him. At one particular passage he exclaimed, 'Ah, now that is what I call music.'

But this quintet, much more ambitious than its predecessor, was also considerably more difficult. Our amateurs were unable to give an adequate account of it. The viola and cello in particular floundered helplessly.

As this happened when I was twelve and a half years old, the biographers who still maintain that at the age of twenty I did not know the rudiments of music are strangely mistaken.

I destroyed the two quintets a few years later, but it is a curious fact that long afterwards in Paris, when I was writing my first orchestral work, the phrase my father approved of in the second of these early efforts came back to me and I adopted it. It is the theme in A flat which the first violins announce soon after the opening of the allegro of the *Francs-juges* overture.

After his son's tragic and unaccountable death, poor Imbert returned to Lyons, where I believe he died. His place at La Côte was taken almost at once by an altogether more accomplished musician called Dorant. Dorant, an Alsatian from Colmar, could play pretty well every instrument and excelled at clarinet, cello, violin and guitar. He gave guitar lessons to my elder sister, who had a good voice but absolutely no natural instinct for music (she is fond of it but has never been able to read music; she cannot even decipher a folk-song). I sat in on her lessons. Of course I had to have some too—until Dorant, an honest musician and an original, told my father bluntly, 'Sir, I can't go on giving guitar lessons to your son.'

'Indeed—why is that? Has he been rude to you, or is he so idle that you despair of his learning anything?'

'Certainly not; simply that it's absurd to go on teaching him when he already plays as well as I do.'

Behold me then, past master of those three magnificent instruments, the flageolet, the flute and the guitar. Can anyone fail to recognize in this judicious choice the hand of Nature urging me towards the grandest orchestral effects and the Michelangelesque in music? The flute, the guitar and the flageolet! I have never possessed any other skills as a performer; yet this seems to me already an impressive list. Indeed, I do myself an injustice: I could also play the drum.

My father would not let me take up the piano; otherwise I should no doubt have turned into a formidable pianist in company with forty thousand others. He had no intention of making me an artist, and he probably feared that the piano would take too strong a hold of me and that I would become more deeply involved in music than he wished. I have often felt the lack of this ability. On many occasions I would have found it useful. But when I think of the appalling quantity of platitudes for which the piano is daily responsible—flagrant platitudes which in most cases would never be written if their authors had only pen and paper to rely on and could not resort to their magic box—I can only offer up my gratitude to chance which taught me perforce to compose freely and in silence and thus saved me from the tyranny of keyboard habits, so dangerous to thought, and from the lure of conventional sonorities, to which all composers are to a greater or lesser extent prone. It is true that the numerous people who fancy such things are always lamenting their absence in me; but I cannot say it worries me.

My youthful essays in composition bore the stamp of a profound melancholy. Almost all my melodies were in the minor. I was aware of the limitation but could not help it. My romantic Meylan passion had edged my thoughts in permanent black crêpe. In this state of soul, reading *Estelle et Némorin* ceaselessly, it was not unlikely that I would end by setting to music some of its many ditties whose watery charms I then found sweet. And sure enough I did.

I wrote, among others, one intensely sad song to words which expressed my despair at leaving the woods and the haunts that had been 'graced by the footsteps and lighted by the eyes',* and by the pink dancing-shoes, of my cruel fair one. The pale verses come back to me now in a shaft of spring sunshine as I sit here in London, preoccupied with urgent affairs, racked by anxieties, raging at the absurd obstacles which beset me here as elsewhere. I quote the first stanza:

Je vais donc quitter pour jamais
Mon doux pays, ma douce amie.
Loin d'eux je vais traîner ma vie
Dans les pleurs et dans les regrets!
Fleuve dont j'ai vu l'eau limpide,
Pour réfléchir ses doux attraits,
Suspendre sa course rapide,
Je vais vous quitter pour jamais.†

As for the tune of this romance (which, along with the sextet and the quintets, I destroyed before leaving for Paris), it presented itself humbly to my mind when I began to write my Fantastic Symphony in 1829. It seemed to me suited to express the over-powering sadness of a young heart first tortured by a hopeless love, and I welcomed it. It is the theme played by the first violins at the beginning of the largo in the opening movement of the work, entitled 'Dreams, Passion'. I put it in unchanged.

All this time, amid these various musical activities, and absorbed as I was in reading, geography, religion and the alternate

* La Fontaine, 'Les deux pigeons'.

†['*Now must I leave for ever*
My dear country, my dear friend.
Far from them will my weary life be spent,
In sorrow and regret!
River, whose crystal stream
I have seen pause in its headlong course
To mirror their charms—
I am leaving you for ever.']

storms and serenities of first love, the moment was approaching when I must prepare to take up a career. My father intended me for his own, which he considered the finest in the world. For a long while he had made no secret of his intention.

I on my side had made no secret of what I thought of it, and my vigorous expressions of dissent on one or two occasions had not pleased him. Without being sure what I felt, I had a strong presentiment that my life was not going to be spent at the bedsides of the sick, in hospitals and dissecting-rooms. I dared not yet admit to myself what career it was I dreamed of, but I thought I knew for sure that no power on earth was going to make me a doctor. About this time I read the lives of Gluck and Haydn in the *Biographie universelle*. They excited me profoundly. As I contemplated the glorious careers of those illustrious men, I told myself that nothing could be finer and that to be able to live for such an art must be a supreme happiness. The effect of an apparently trivial incident on my impressionable mind intensified these feelings and gave me in a flash of illumination a glimpse of innumerable grand and mysterious musical horizons.

I had never seen a full score. The only pieces of music I knew were *solfèges* with figured bass, flute solos, or excerpts from operas with piano accompaniment. One day I came across a piece of paper with twenty-four staves ruled on it. The moment I saw that great array of lines I became aware of what a multitude of instrumental and vocal combinations lay open to an ingenious hand, and I exclaimed, 'What an orchestra one could write down on that!' From that moment my head was in a state of ever-increasing musical ferment, and my aversion to medicine grew accordingly. But I was too much in awe of my parents to dare breathe a word of these subversive thoughts. At this point my father determined on a coup d'état which would use music as a device to remove what he called my 'childish antipathies' and launch me on the study of medicine.

In order, he said, to get me accustomed without delay to the objects I would soon have to have constantly before my eyes, he had laid out in his study a copy of Monro's enormous treatise on osteology, with its life-size illustrations in which the various components of the human frame are meticulously reproduced. 'Here,' he said, 'is a work you will have to study. I cannot suppose you will persist in your hostility to medicine; it is unreasonable and wholly without foundation. If, on the other hand, you promise me to begin really seriously working at your osteology, I will send to Lyons and get you a splendid new flute with all the latest keys.' Such an instrument had long been the object of my dreams. What could I say? The impressive earnestness of the offer, the respect mingled with fear which, for all his kindness, my father inspired in me, and the temptation of the coveted flute, were more than I could resist. I stammered out a faint yes, went back to my room, and threw myself on my bed in utter dejection.

Become a doctor! Study anatomy! Dissect! Take part in horrible operations—instead of giving myself body and soul to music, sublime art whose grandeur I was beginning to perceive! Forsake the highest heaven for the wretchedest regions of earth, the immortal spirits of poetry and love and their divinely inspired strains for dirty hospital orderlies, dreadful dissecting-room attendants, hideous corpses, the screams of patients, the groans and rattling breath of the dying!

No, no! It seemed to me the reversal of the whole natural order of my existence. It was monstrous. It could not happen. Yet it did.

I began my osteological studies in company with a cousin, Alphonse Robert (now a distinguished Paris doctor), whom my father had undertaken to teach at the same time. Unfortunately Robert was a fine violinist (he had been one of the performers of my quintets), and our periods of study were devoted rather more energetically to music than to anatomy. But by working doggedly on his own at home he always knew far more about our demonstrations than I did. This brought many stern rebukes, and one or two terrible outbursts of paternal wrath.

Nevertheless, partly by my own efforts, partly by coercion, I managed after a fashion to learn all the anatomy my father could teach me from 'prepared specimens' (skeletons), and at nineteen, encouraged by my fellow-student, I resolved to attack my medical studies in earnest and to that end to go with him to Paris.*

* [Early November 1821; his passport is stamped 26 October, La Côte Saint-André. He was then a few weeks short of his eighteenth birthday.]

Here I pause for a moment before taking up the story of my Parisian life and the relentless struggle in which I became involved almost from the moment of arriving there, and which I have not ceased to carry on, against men, ideas and things. The reader will perhaps grant me a breathing-space.

Besides, today, the 10th April, the two hundred thousand English Chartists are to hold their demonstration. In a few hours, maybe, England will be engulfed like the rest of Europe and this refuge too will have failed me. I shall go out and see how the issue is decided.

(8 p.m.) Your Chartist is a very decent sort of revolutionary. Everything went off satisfactorily. The cannon, those eloquent orators and formidable logicians whose arguments appeal so powerfully to the Masses, were in the chair. They were not required to utter a word, their presence being enough to persuade everybody of the inexpediency of revolution, and the Chartists dispersed in perfect order.

My poor friends, you know as much about starting a riot as the Italians about writing a symphony. The Irish are doubtless the same, to judge from O'Connell's injunction: 'Agitate, agitate, but never act.'

(12 July) During the intervening three months I have had no opportunity to go on with these memoirs. And now I am returning to the unhappy country which is still called France and which is, after all, my country. I am going to see whether an artist can live there, or how long it takes him to die among the ruins beneath which art lies prostrate. England, farewell.

(France, 16 July 1848) I have come back. Paris is burying her dead. The pavements used for the barricades have been replaced—to be torn up again, perhaps, tomorrow. The moment I arrive I go straight to the Faubourg Saint-Antoine. A hateful scene of destruction; even the Spirit of Liberty on top of the Bastille column has a bullet through her body. Trees mutilated or overthrown, houses crumbling, squares, streets, quays—everything still seems to vibrate under the shock of bloody disorder. Who thinks of art at such a time of frenzy and carnage? Theatres shut, artists ruined, teachers unemployed, pupils scattered; pianists performing sonatas at street corners, historical painters sweeping the gutters, architects mixing mortar on public building sites. The Assembly has just voted a sum large enough to enable the theatres to reopen and to afford a little relief to the most hard-hit artists. Inadequate relief, above all to the musicians! A first violin at the Opéra was lucky if he earned nine hundred francs a year; he lived by giving lessons.* It is hardly to be supposed that he could have saved on a very brilliant scale. Now their pupils have gone, what is going to happen to such people? They won't be deported, though for many of them their only chance of making a living would be in America, India or Sydney. Deportation costs the government too much. To qualify, one must have deserved it, and our artists all made the mistake of attacking the barricades and fighting against the insurgents.

Surrounded by this ghastly confusion of justice and injustice, good and evil, truth and falsehood, hearing a language spoken whose words are perverted from their normal meaning, what is to prevent one from going completely mad?

I shall go on with my autobiography. I have nothing better to do; and scrutinizing the past will take my mind off the present.

5

A year of medical studies—Professor Amussat —a performance at the Opéra—the Conservatoire library— irresistible attraction towards music—my father refuses to let me take it up—family debates

On arriving in Paris in 1822† with my fellow-student Alphonse Robert, I gave myself up wholly to studying for the career which had been thrust upon me, and loyally kept the promise I had given my father on leaving. It was soon put to a somewhat severe test when Robert, having announced one morning that he had bought a 'subject' (a corpse), took me for

* [Cf. Hallé's account: 'In Paris by far the greatest part of a musician's income was invariably derived from teaching . . . but from the day after the Revolution the pupils disappeared, and at the end of a week I could only boast of one (he was an old Englishman) . . .' It was the Revolution that made him leave Paris and settle in England. *Life and Letters of Sir Charles Hallé.*]

† [1821. The two students lodged at 104 rue Saint-Jacques in the Latin quarter.]

the first time to the dissecting-room at the Hospice de la Pitié. At the sight of that terrible charnel-house—the disconnected limbs, the grinning faces and gaping skulls, the bloody quagmire underfoot and the atrocious smell it gave off, the swarms of sparrows wrangling over scraps of lung, the rats in their corner gnawing the bleeding vertebrae—such a feeling of revulsion possessed me that I leapt through the window of the dissecting-room and fled for home as though Death and all his hideous train were at my heels. The shock of that first impression lasted for twenty-four hours. I did not want to hear another word about anatomy, dissection or medicine, and I meditated a hundred mad schemes of escape from the future that hung over me.

Robert lavished his eloquence in a vain attempt to argue away my disgust and demonstrate the absurdity of my plans. In the end he got me to agree to make another effort. For the second time I accompanied him to the hospital and we entered the house of the dead. How strange! The objects which before had filled me with extreme horror had absolutely no effect upon me now. I felt nothing but a cold distaste; I was already as hardened to the scene as any seasoned medical student. The crisis was passed. I found I actually enjoyed groping about in a poor fellow's chest and feeding the winged inhabitants of that delightful place their ration of lung. 'Hallo!' Robert cried, laughing, 'you're getting civilized. "Thou giv'st the little birds their daily bread."' '"And o'er all nature's realm my bounty spread,"'* I retorted, tossing a shoulder-blade to a large rat staring at me with famished eyes.

So I went on with my anatomy course, feeling no enthusiasm, but stoically resigned. An instinctive affinity drew me to my teacher, Professor Amussat, who showed a passion for this science as great as I felt for music. Here was an artist in anatomy. Today his name is known throughout Europe as that of a daring innovator in surgery, and his discoveries arouse the admiration and hostility of the academic world. A twenty-four-hour working day is hardly long enough to satisfy him, and although the strain of such an existence tells, nothing can weaken the determination of this melancholy dreamer to pursue his hazardous researches to the

* [Racine, *Athalie*.]

end. Everything about him suggests a man of genius. I see him often; I love him.

Other powerful compensations were soon added. The lectures given by Thénard and Gay-Lussac at the Jardin des Plantes, the one in chemistry and the other in physics, and the literature course in which Andrieux's sly humour could hold a class enthralled, all delighted me; I followed them with growing interest. I was on my way to becoming just another student, destined to add one more obscure name to the lamentable catalogue of bad doctors, when one evening I went to the Opéra. They were giving *The Danaïds*, by Salieri. The pomp and brilliance of the spectacle, the massive sonority of orchestra and chorus, the inspired pathos of Mme Branchu, her extraordinary voice, the rugged grandeur of Dérivis, Hypermnestra's aria, in which I discerned, imitated by Salieri, all the characteristics of Gluck's style as I had conceived it from the pieces from his *Orphée* in my father's library, and finally the tremendous bacchanal and the sad, voluptuous ballet music that Spontini added to his old compatriot's score, disturbed and exalted me to an extent that I will not attempt to describe. It was as though a young man possessing all the instincts of a sailor, but knowing only the boats on the lakes of his native mountains, were suddenly to find himself on board a three-decker ship on the open sea. I hardly slept that night, and the anatomy lesson next morning suffered accordingly. I sang Danaüs' aria 'The kindly strokes of destiny' as I sawed my 'subject's' skull; and when Robert, impatient at my humming 'Descend into the sea-nymph's breast' when I should have been looking up the chapter in Bichat on nerve tissue, exclaimed, 'Oh come on, we're not getting anywhere, in three days our subject will have gone bad—eighteen francs down the drain. You really must be sensible,' I replied with the hymn to Nemesis, 'Goddess insatiable for blood', and the scalpel fell from his hand.

The following week I went to the Opéra again. This time I saw Méhul's *Stratonice*, and *Nina*, the ballet devised and composed by Persuis. The overture to *Stratonice* impressed me deeply; so did Seleucus' aria, 'Versez tous vos chagrins', and the consultation quartet. But on the whole I thought the work rather cold. The ballet, on the other hand, delighted me and I was profoundly moved to hear, played by Vogt on the cor anglais during a heart-rending mime scene by Mlle Bigottini, the tune of the hymn which my sister's companions had sung at the Ursuline convent on the day of my first communion. It was the romance 'Quand le bien-aimé reviendra'. A man sitting near me, who was murmuring the words to himself, told me the name of the composer and of the opera from which Persuis had taken it. I learnt that it was from Dalayrac's *Nina*. However remarkable the singer who created the role of Nina,* I find it hard to believe she can ever have made it sound as natural and touching as it did on Vogt's instrument, heightened as it was by the acting of the famous mime.

Notwithstanding all these distractions and the hours I spent every evening brooding over the melancholy discrepancy between my studies and my inclinations, I persisted in this double life for some time longer, without much benefit to my medical career and without being able to extend my meagre knowledge of music. I had given my word and I was holding to it. But when I learnt that the library of the Conservatoire with its wealth of scores was open to the public, the desire to go there and study the works of Gluck, for which I already had an instinctive passion but which were not then being performed at the Opéra, was too strong for me. Once admitted to that sanctuary, I never left it. It was the death-blow to my medical career. The dissecting-room was abandoned for good.

My thoughts were now so absorbed by music that I even neglected the course in experimental electricity, despite all my admiration for Gay-Lussac and the fascinations of the subject. I read and re-read Gluck's scores. I copied them and learnt them by heart. I went without sleep because of them and forgot to eat and drink. An ecstasy possessed me; and on the day when, after anxiously waiting, I was at last able to hear *Iphigénie en Tauride*, I vowed as I left the Opéra that in spite of father, mother, uncles, aunts, grandparents, friends, I would be a musician. I actually wrote off then and there to my father, acquainting him with the imperious and irresistible nature of my vocation and entreating him not to oppose it uselessly. He responded with friendly

* Mme Dugazon.

arguments, concluding that before long I would see the folly of my purpose and give up the pursuit of a chimera to return to a profession that was established and honourable. But my father deluded himself. Far from coming round to his point of view, I stuck tenaciously to mine, and from that moment we settled down to a steady exchange of letters which grew more and more stern and threatening on his side and more and more impassioned on mine, until all pretence of self-control was abandoned and anger raged without restraint.

6

I become one of Lesueur's pupils—his kindness—the Chapel Royal

WHILE THIS BITTER debate was going on, I had started to compose and had written, among other things, a cantata for full orchestra on a poem by Millevoye, 'The Arab Horse'. A pupil of Lesueur called Gerono, whom I often used to meet in the Conservatoire library, hinted at the possibility of my joining the master's composition class and offered to introduce me. I accepted with delight and, one morning, presented myself before Lesueur, armed with the score of my cantata and, as an auxiliary, a canon in three parts which I thought would be the right thing for the occasion. Lesueur had the kindness to read carefully through the first of these crude efforts and said, as he handed it back to me, 'There is plenty of feeling here, plenty of dramatic life, but you do not yet know how to write, and your harmony is riddled with mistakes—far too many for me to begin pointing them out to you now. Gerono will oblige by making you familiar with our principles of harmony, and as soon as you have grasped them sufficiently to be able to follow me, I shall be glad to have you as a pupil.' Gerono dutifully accepted his mission and in a few weeks took me through the whole system behind the master's theory of the formation and succession of chords—a system based on Rameau and his speculations about the resonance of a vibrating string.* I

* Which he calls the resonating body, as if vibrating strings were the only resonating bodies in the universe or rather, as if the theory of their vibrations could be applied to all other resonating bodies.

realized at once, from the way in which Gerono expounded these principles, that it would be idle to question their validity, since plainly in the school of Lesueur they constituted a kind of religion, to be deferred to blindly by everyone. In the end, such is the force of example, I came myself to believe sincerely in the doctrine, and by the time I was admitted to the circle of Lesueur's favourite pupils he could count me among his most fervent votaries.

I am far from ungrateful to that worthy and excellent man who watched over the outset of my career with so much sympathy and to the end of his life was a true friend. But what hours I wasted learning his antediluvian theories and putting them into practice, only to have to unlearn them and begin my education all over again from the beginning! I have reached the point of involuntarily averting my eyes when I come across one of his scores, in response to the same sort of impulse as we feel when we see the portrait of a friend who is no more. I had greatly admired those little oratorios which made up Lesueur's repertory at the Chapel Royal, and it grieved me to find my admiration waning. Besides, when I compare the present with the time when I used to go regularly every Sunday to the Tuileries to listen to them, how old and tired and empty of illusions I feel! How many of the renowned artists that I met at those high celebrations of religious art are dead, and how many others have fallen into the oblivion which is worse than death! What upheavals, what trials and tribulations have there been since that time! Those were days of profound enthusiasms, mighty musical passions, heroic day-dreams, boundless, unutterable joys! . . . When I got to the Chapel Royal I used to join Lesueur in the orchestra, and he would normally spend the few minutes before the service in telling me about the subject of the work to be performed and in outlining its general plan and explaining his intentions. A knowledge of what subject the composer had chosen was usually relevant, for it was rarely the text of the Mass. Lesueur had written a large number of Masses, but he was much more interested in setting those charming episodes in the Old Testament, the stories of Naomi, Ruth and Boaz, Rachel, Deborah and the like. He loved them, and the music he wrote for them had an antique flavour which was sometimes so true that in listening to it one forgot its thinness, its relentless imitation of the old-fashioned Italian dramatic style in the arias, duets and trios, and its feeble and rudimentary scoring. More than any other poetry with the possible exception of Macpherson's (which he persisted in attributing to Ossian), the Bible was unquestionably the greatest force in developing Lesueur's particular powers. At that time I shared his predilection; the East—the calm of its burning wildernesses, the grandeur of its immense ruins, its sense of the past, its legends—was the magnet which above all drew my imagination.

When the ceremony was over and, at the 'Ite, missa est', the King (Charles X) had withdrawn to a traditional fanfare in five-time performed on a fife and an enormous drum—a grotesque noise worthy of the barbarity of the Middle Ages which begot it—my master sometimes took me with him on his long walks. Those were days of precious counsel and curious confidences. Lesueur, to encourage me, was always telling me tales of his youth: his early struggles as choirmaster at Dijon; his admission to the Sainte-Chapelle in Paris; the examination for the conductorship at Notre-Dame; Méhul's bitter enmity; the snubs he had to endure from the mediocrities of the Conservatoire; the intrigues that went on against his opera *La caverne*, and Cherubini's generous behaviour on that occasion;* his friendship with Paisiello, his predecessor at the Imperial Chapel; the dizzy honours which Napoleon lavished on the composer of *The Bards*† and the great man's historic sayings about the work. My master would recount once again the endless trouble he had in getting his first opera performed, the fears and anxieties he felt before the opening night, the odd sense of sadness and emptiness that came over him after its success, the need to try his luck in the theatre again; the composition of *Télémaque* in three months; the superb beauty of Mme Scio when she appeared as Diana the huntress and her wonderful ardour and intensity in the role of Calypso. After that came the arguments: for I was allowed to argue with him when we were

* [Cherubini took the place of the absent prompter at the first three performances (1793).]

† The gold casket presented to Lesueur after the first performance of the opera bears the inscription, engraved on the inside: *From the Emperor Napoleon to the composer of* The Bards. [*Ossian, or The Bards*, first performed at the Opéra on 10 July 1804.]

alone, and I sometimes went further than I should. His theory of fundamental bass and his ideas on modulation were a natural subject for disagreement. When we ran out of musical topics he was always ready to put forward some religious or philosophical thesis, and here too more often than not we disagreed. But there were certain issues on which we were sure to find common ground, such as Gluck, Virgil and Napoleon; on them our enthusiasms coincided. After these long talks by the Seine or in the shade of the Tuileries gardens, he usually dismissed me so that he could devote himself for a few hours to the solitary meditation which had become a necessity to him.

7

First opera—M. Andrieux—first Mass—Chateaubriand

A FEW MONTHS after I had become one of Lesueur's private pupils, but before I had become a student at the Conservatoire, I decided I would write an opera. M. Andrieux was much in my thoughts at that time because of his literature course, which I still attended regularly; and I had the singular notion of asking the lively old man for a libretto. I don't remember what I wrote to him, but his reply was as follows:

17 June 1823

Sir,

Your letter interested me keenly. The zeal you demonstrate for the noble art of your choice will assuredly bring you success. I wish it for you with all my heart, and I should be only too glad to be able to help you obtain it. But the business you propose to me is not for a man of my age; my ideas and my studies lie in other directions. I should strike you as a barbarian were I to tell you how many years it is since I set foot in the Opéra or the Feydeau. I am sixty-four. To aspire to write love lyrics would ill become me; and as for music, I ought to be thinking only of requiems. I regret that you weren't born thirty or forty years earlier, or I later: we could have worked together. Please accept my excuses, which are only too real, and my sincere and affectionate greetings.

Andrieux

He was so good as to deliver his letter in person and stayed a long time chatting. As he left, he said, 'Ah, I too was a passionate lover of music in my youth. I was a great Piccinni man—and a Gluckist too.'

Foiled in my attempt to secure a literary celebrity, I turned instead to Gerono, who rather fancied himself as a poet, and asked him (you may well wonder at my ingenuousness) for a dramatization of Florian's *Estelle*. He agreed to tackle it, and I set his opus to music. Luckily no one ever heard a note of this composition prompted—to so little purpose—by my Meylan recollections. I will say only that my score was as absurd as Gerono's book and verses. This pallid performance was followed by something quite different, a very sombre and vigorous piece of work taken from Saurin's play *Beverley, or The Gambler.** I was enthusiastic about this fragment; I thought it very powerful stuff. It was written for solo bass and orchestra and I would have liked to hear it sung by Dérivis, to whom it seemed to me well suited. The difficulty was to discover an occasion. I thought I had found one when the Théâtre-Français announced a benefit for Talma, at which *Athalie* was to be given with Gossec's choruses. As they are going to have choruses, I reasoned, there will be an orchestra to accompany them. My score is quite easy and if Talma can only be persuaded to put it into the programme, Dérivis certainly won't refuse to sing it. I shall go and see Talma. But the mere idea of addressing the great tragedian, of seeing Nero face to face, filled me with fearful agitation. As I approached the house I could feel my heart beating with a violence that augured ill. At the sight of his door I began to tremble. I paused on the threshold, perplexed and irresolute. Dare I proceed any farther? Should I give up the idea? Twice my hand went up to the bell. Twice I let it fall. I blushed scarlet, there was a buzzing in my ears; I felt literally dizzy. Finally shyness prevailed and, abandoning all my hopes, I turned away, or rather fled headlong.

Who will understand this? Only a young semi-civilized enthusiast such as I was then.

* [An eighteenth-century adaptation by Bernard Saurin of *The Gamester* by Edward Moore. *Beverley* had been revived at the Odéon in March 1823.]

A short time afterwards M. Masson, choirmaster at the church of Saint-Roch, suggested that I write a solemn Mass; he would get it performed in the church on Innocents' Day, the feast day of the children of the choir. We should have an orchestra of a hundred picked musicians, and an even larger choir which would rehearse for a month. The parts would not cost me a penny, as they would be copied for nothing, and with due vigilance, by the Saint-Roch choirboys; and so on and so forth. Full of zeal, I set to work on my Mass, which in its arbitrariness and haphazardness of colour was nothing but a clumsy imitation of Lesueur. (As with most teachers, it was those passages in which his own style was most faithfully reproduced that he particularly approved of when he inspected the score.) The moment it was finished, I handed the manuscript to Masson and he passed it on to his young pupils to copy and learn. He kept on swearing by all that was sacred that the performance would be superb. All we lacked was a competent conductor, neither he nor I being in the habit of directing such 'huge forces' of singers and instrumentalists. Valentino was at that time in charge of the orchestra at the Opéra, and was hoping to be appointed conductor of the Chapel Royal orchestra as well. It was therefore unlikely he would refuse my master, who was director of the Chapel.* The letter which I delivered from Lesueur induced him, despite grave doubts about the means at our disposal, to promise his aid. On the day of the full rehearsal† our 'huge forces' assembled and proved to consist of a chorus of twenty (fifteen tenors and five basses), a dozen choirboys, nine violins, a viola, an oboe, a horn and a bassoon. My shame and despair at offering the celebrated conductor of one of the world's leading orchestras such a rabble of musicians may be imagined. 'It's all right,' Masson kept on saying, 'everybody will turn up for the performance tomorrow. Come along, start rehearsing!' Valentino, with a resigned air, gave the signal and they began; but after a few moments a halt had to be called. The parts were a Mass of mistakes and everyone was pointing them out at once: key signatures without flats and

* The director merely supervised the performance of his works and did not himself conduct.

† [27 December 1824.]

sharps, ten bars' rest missing, thirty bars of music left out. All was confusion. I suffered the torments of the damned; and my long-cherished vision of a full orchestral performance had, for the moment, to be abandoned.

But the lesson was not lost. The little I had heard of my unfortunate work had been enough to make me realize its more glaring faults. I made a radical resolve—in which Valentino backed me up by promising not to desert me when the time came to take my revenge—and rewrote almost the whole of the Mass. But while I was working at it my parents heard of the fiasco and seized on it as an argument to belittle my supposed vocation and ridicule my hopes. It was the dregs of my cup of bitterness. I swallowed them in silence, and went doggedly on.

When the score was finished, I set to work to copy the parts. Painful experience had taught me not to rely on others. I had no money to pay for professional copyists, so I wrote them out in duplicate, triplicate, quadruplicate myself. At the end of three months they were done. But now I was as stranded with my Mass as Robinson Crusoe with the great canoe he could not launch; I had no means whatever of getting it performed. To depend a second time on Masson's 'forces' would have been altogether too naïve. To appeal myself to the artists whom I needed was equally impractical: I knew none of them personally. Nor could I invoke the help of the Chapel Royal under Lesueur's aegis, for he had told me that it was quite out of the question.* At this point my friend Humbert Ferrand, of whom I shall have more to say presently, had the rather audacious idea that I should approach Chateaubriand, as being the only man capable of understanding such a request and agreeing to it, and ask him to help me put on a performance of my Mass by lending me twelve hundred francs. Chateaubriand replied as follows:

* I did not then appreciate why. Of course, if Lesueur had proposed that the choir and orchestra of the Chapel Royal remove to Saint-Roch or anywhere else to perform a work by one of his pupils, there would not have been the slightest objection. But presumably he was afraid that my fellow-students would claim the same privilege, which would have led to an impossible situation.

PARIS, *31 December 1824*

You ask me, sir, for twelve hundred francs. I have not got them. If I had, they would be yours. I have no means, either, of being useful to you with the Government.* I sympathize keenly with your difficulties. I love art and honour artists. But sometimes talent owes its success to the trials it has had to endure, and the hour of triumph compensates for all that one has suffered. My dear sir, please accept my regrets—they are very real.

Chateaubriand

8

Augustin de Pons—he lends me 1,200 francs —my Mass performed for the first time at Saint-Roch —second performance at Saint-Eustache—I burn it

I WAS NOW THOROUGHLY disheartened. I had no plausible answer to give my parents, who were bombarding me with letters. They were threatening to stop the modest allowance which enabled me to live in Paris when by good luck, at a performance of Piccinni's *Dido* at the Opéra, I ran into an acquaintance, a knowledgeable young music-lover and a man of generous and impulsive character who had been an enraged spectator of the Saint-Roch débâcle. He belonged to an aristocratic family of the Faubourg Saint-Germain and was fairly well off. Later he lost everything, having married, against his mother's wishes, a second-rate singer, a student from the Conservatoire. When she made her début he went on the stage too and trailed after her through France and Italy from one opera house to another. A few years later his prima donna abandoned him and he returned to Paris to vegetate and give singing lessons. I have occasionally been able to be of help to him in my articles in the *Journal des débats*; but I greatly regret that I have not been able to do more, for the spontaneous service he rendered me was of vital importance in my career and I shall never forget it. His name was Augustin de Pons. Last year he was finding it very hard to live on the proceeds of his lessons. I

* I must also have asked him to put in a word for me with the authorities, on the principle that one can't have too much of a good thing.

shudder to think what has become of him since the February Revolution, which must have deprived him of all his pupils.

When he saw me in the foyer of the Opéra he called out at the top of his very hearty voice, 'What news of the Mass? Is it rewritten? When are we going to perform it properly?'

'Oh yes, it's rewritten and what's more recopied, but how on earth am I to get it performed?'

'How? Damn it all, by paying the performers. What do you need? Let's see—twelve hundred francs? Fifteen hundred? Two thousand? I'll lend it to you.'

'Please—not so loud! If you really mean it, I'm delighted to accept your offer. Twelve hundred will do.'

'Then that's settled. Come and see me tomorrow morning, I'll have the money for you. We'll engage the Opéra chorus and a powerful orchestra. Valentino has got to be satisfied, we have got to be satisfied, and by God it's going to work!'

And it did. My Mass, conducted by Valentino, was splendidly performed at Saint-Roch before a large audience.* The papers were favourable; and so, thanks to the admirable de Pons, I succeeded for the first time in having my music heard and in hearing it myself. Every composer knows the importance of getting a foot in the stirrup, and the difficulty of doing so in Paris.

The work was performed again some years later (in 1827) in the church of Saint-Eustache, on the same day as the big riot in the rue Saint-Denis.† This time the orchestra and chorus of the Odéon came to my assistance by performing for nothing, and I decided to risk conducting the work myself. Apart from a few slips due to excitement, I did not do too badly. Yet how far I was from possessing the many varied qualities—precision, flexibility, sensitivity, intensity, presence of mind, combined with an indefinable instinct

* [10 July 1825. The work was evidently a success; and Berlioz, after being forced to listen to a long harangue by the curé of Saint-Roch who 'wished to demonstrate to me that Rousseau had perverted people's taste in music as well as in literature and that I was destined to bring the public back to the true way', had the satisfaction of hearing Lesueur declare that he would be 'no doctor or apothecary but a great composer'. (*Hector Berlioz: Correspondance générale*, I, 1803–1832, ed. P. Citron, 1972, 93 and 97.)]

† [22 November.]

—that go to make a really good conductor, and how much time and experience and heart-searching have I since put into acquiring two or three of them! We often complain of there being so few good singers, but good conductors are rarer still and in many cases far more important and potentially dangerous to the composer.

After this second trial I could not help seeing how little my Mass was worth; so, having extracted the Resurrexit, with which I was quite pleased,* I burnt the rest, together with *Beverley* (for which my enthusiasm had notably cooled), the opera *Estelle*, and an oratorio with Latin text, recently completed, called *The Crossing of the Red Sea*, a coldly impartial glance having shown me its inalienable right to a place in the auto-da-fé.

Mournful coincidence! Last night, after writing the above, I went to the Opéra-Comique and during an interval met a musician of my acquaintance who greeted me by saying, 'When did you get back from London?'

'A few weeks ago.'

'Then you know about de Pons?'

'No—what?'

'He poisoned himself last month.'

'Good God!'

'Yes, he wrote that he was tired of life; but I'm afraid the fact is life had become no longer possible for him: he had no more pupils—the Revolution had dispersed them all, and the sale of his furniture didn't even produce enough to pay the rent he owed.' Poor devil! Wretched artists, abandoned by this republic of pickpockets and costermongers!

'Horrible! horrible! most horrible!' Now the *Morning Post* has brought details of the death of Prince Lichnowsky, brutally murdered at the gates of Frankfurt by German peasants, worthy counterparts of our June heroes.† They stabbed him repeatedly with knives, hacked at him with scythes, tore his arms and legs to

* I subsequently destroyed it as well.

† [18 September 1848. Lichnowsky had incurred the hostility of republican and democratic opinion by his caustic right-wing speeches to the German National Assembly in Frankfurt. He was killed during the riots provoked by the signing of the Malmö Truce between Prussia and Denmark.]

shreds, shot him in more than twenty places but in such a way as *not to kill him*, stripped him and left him dying at the foot of a wall. He lived for five hours and died without a murmur. Noble, clever, generous, brave Lichnowsky! I knew him well in his Paris days, and saw him again in Berlin last year on my way back from Russia. He was then just beginning to make a name in the National Assembly. Vile human scum, a thousand times more bestial and brainless in your fatuous revolutionary antics than the baboons and orang-outangs of Borneo!

Oh, I must get out, walk, run, shout under the open sky!

9
First encounter with Cherubini—he chases me out of the Conservatoire library

LESUEUR, SEEING THE progress I had made, thought it time to regularize my position and have me enrolled in his class at the Conservatoire. He spoke to the director, Cherubini, and I was admitted. Mercifully no one suggested on this occasion that I should be introduced to the formidable composer of *Medea*, for the year before I had put him into one of his livid rages (as I shall now relate) and he could hardly have forgotten it.

The moment Cherubini took over the Conservatoire on the death of his predecessor, Perne, he determined to mark his accession by introducing revolutionary restrictions in the internal régime of the school, which had not been run on exactly puritan principles. In order that the two sexes should not mix except under the supervision of a teacher, he decreed that the men must use the door in the rue du Faubourg Poissonnière and the women the door in the rue Bergère, the two entrances being at opposite ends of the building.

One morning, knowing nothing of this moral edict, which had only just been promulgated, I proceeded to the Conservatoire and entered by the usual door in the rue Bergère—the *female* door. I was half-way to the library when a porter stopped me in the middle of the courtyard and tried to make me go back and return by the other entrance. I thought this so absurd that I sent the liveried Argus about his business and went on. The rogue, wishing to get in well with his new employer by showing that he could be just as strict, refused to admit defeat and hurried off to report the matter to the director. I had been absorbed in *Alceste* for a quarter of an hour and had thought no more of the incident, when Cherubini, with my accuser behind him, stumped into the reading-room, his face more cadaverous and basilisk-eyed, his hair bristling more angrily, than ever. They made the rounds of the table, where several students were reading. The porter scrutinized each in turn, then came to a halt in front of me.

'That's him,' he said. Cherubini was so angry that for a moment he could not speak.

'Eh! Eh! so it is you,' he cried at last, with a strong Italian accent made more grotesque by his fury, 'it is you who come een by the door that I weell not 'ave you use?'

'Sir, I was not aware of the new regulation. Another time I will conform to it.'

'Anothair time! Anothair time! What—what—what are you doeeng 'ere?'

'As you see, sir, I am studying Gluck's scores.'

'And what—what—what are Gluck's scores to you? Where deed you get pairmission to come to the library?'

'Sir' (I was beginning to lose my self-possession), 'Gluck's scores are the finest examples of dramatic music I know and I need no one's permission to come here and study them. The Conservatoire library is open to the public from ten till three and I have the right to use it.'

'The—the—the right?'

'Yes, sir.'

'I weell not allow you to return.'

'I shall return none the less.'

'What—what—what ees your name?' he yelled, shaking with rage.

'Sir,' I answered, growing pale in my turn, 'my name will perhaps be familiar to you one day—but you shall not have it now.'

'S-s-seize 'eem, Hottin,' he cried to the porter, 'I'll 'ave 'eem in preeson.'

Thereupon, to the stupefaction of the onlookers, the two of them, master and servant, began pursuing me round the table, knocking over stools and reading-desks in a vain attempt to catch me. In the end I made my escape, calling out with a laugh as I fled, 'You shan't have me or my name, and I shall soon be back again to study Gluck's scores.'

That was my first encounter with Cherubini. I do not know whether he remembered it when I was introduced to him in a more official manner. In any case it is a nice irony that twelve years later, in spite of him, I should have been appointed curator and then librarian of the very library from which he had tried to eject me. As for Hottin, he is now my most devoted orchestral attendant and a rabid admirer of my music. He even used to maintain, towards the end of Cherubini's life, that I was the great man's only possible successor as director of the Conservatoire. His opinion, however, was not shared by Auber.*

I shall have other similar stories to tell of Cherubini, from which the reader will see that if he chastised me with whips, I gave him a few scorpions in return whose sting he had cause to remember.

10

My father stops my allowance—I go back to La Côte—provincial ideas on art and artists—despair—my father's alarm—he agrees to my returning to Paris—my mother's fanatical opposition—her curse

THE FIRST PERFORMANCE of my Mass had been sufficiently successful to bring a momentary lull in the family hostilities which so distressed me. But now a fresh incident occurred to revive them and intensify my parents' displeasure.

I put my name down for the annual music competition at the Institute. Before being allowed to compete, candidates have to pass a preliminary exam which weeds out the weakest. I had the misfortune to be classed among them. My father heard about it and this time informed me unequivocally that if I persisted in remaining in Paris it would be without any further assistance from him, for he would stop my allowance. My kind master at once wrote begging him to reconsider his decision, assuring him that there

* [Auber became director of the Conservatoire on Cherubini's death in 1842.]

could be no possible doubt as to my future as a musician and that I 'oozed music at every pore'. Unluckily the weighty religious arguments which he advanced to prove that it was their duty to accept my vocation were the worst he could have chosen. My father's reply was curt and stiff, almost rude, and calculated to wound Lesueur's tenderest feelings and beliefs. It began, 'Sir—I am an unbeliever . . .' The rest may be imagined.

A vague hope that I might win my case by pleading it in person persuaded me that I should give way for the moment, and I returned to La Côte.

After a glacial reception, my parents left me to my own reflections for a few days. I was then called on to choose some other profession, as medicine did not appeal to me. I replied that my whole bent was for music and I simply could not believe I was not going back to Paris to devote myself to it. 'You had better get your mind straight on that point,' my father said, 'for I can assure you that you will never go back.'

From that moment I sank into almost total silence, barely answering when spoken to, not eating, spending part of the day wandering in the Fields and woods and the remainder shut up in my room. I had in truth no plans. The dull ferment of my thoughts and the constraint I was living under seemed to have numbed my brain. Even my rage had burnt itself out. I was dying for lack of air.

One morning early, my father came into my room and woke me. 'Get up,' he said, 'and as soon as you are dressed, come to my study. I want to talk to you.' I obeyed, without any presentiment of what was coming. My father's manner was grave and sad, not angry. All the same, as I went in I prepared myself for a new attack. What he said was utterly unexpected and overwhelmed me. 'After many sleepless nights, I have made up my mind. I am going to let you study music in Paris, but for a period only. If after further trial you should fail, I think you will do me the justice of acknowledging that I have done all that I reasonably could and you will accordingly choose another career. You know my opinion of second-rate poets. Second-rate artists of any kind are just as bad, and it would be an unspeakable grief and humiliation to me to see you numbered among such useless people.'

My father was unaware that he was more indulgent towards second-rate doctors, who are as numerous as bad artists and not merely useless but positively dangerous. But this is a general phenomenon, even among men of high intelligence: they use impeccable logic to combat other people's prejudices without realizing that such a two-edged weapon can be just as fatal to their own.

I waited no more but fell on his neck and promised all he asked. 'One thing further,' he continued; 'your mother's point of view differs radically from mine on this matter, and I have thought it better to say nothing to her of my new decision. So, to avoid any painful scenes, I insist you keep it to yourself and leave secretly for Paris.' I was careful throughout that day not to let slip any indiscreet word. But the change from silent gloom to a state of delirious happiness which I could not have concealed even if I had tried was too extraordinary not to excite the curiosity of my sisters. Nanci, the elder, badgered and begged me so eagerly to let her know the reason that in the end I told her everything, making her promise not to breathe a word to anyone. Of course she kept the secret as well as I had and before long the whole household, our friends and finally my mother knew all about it.

To appreciate what follows it should be understood that my mother, in addition to her religious convictions, which were fanatical, shared to the full the lamentable attitude to all arts in any way connected with the theatre that is held by a large number of French people to this day. In her eyes actors, actresses, singers, players, librettists and composers were creatures of abomination, marked by the Church's ban and as such predestined to everlasting fire.* An aunt of mine who is genuinely fond of me and who I trust still has a good opinion of me, but who had imbibed my mother's enlightened ideas, once made an astonishing reply. We were arguing on this very point, and I happened to observe that to

* [Prejudice against the theatre was not only a provincial attitude. Not many years before the time Berlioz is writing of, the curé of Saint-Roch had refused permission for the actress Françoise Raucourt to be buried there. In 1824, at the funeral of the actor Philippe, there were angry scenes at the church door. Two years later Talma brought off his last triumph when, by his own wish, his coffin was conveyed direct to Père-Lachaise cemetery and, to the intense annoyance of the clergy, buried without religious rites.]

hear her talk one would think she would be seriously put out if Racine were a member of her family. 'Well, my dear, you know,' she said, 'a good name matters more than anything.' Lesueur nearly choked with laughter when, back in Paris, I reported to him this typical remark; and whenever he was in high spirits he never failed to ask for news of Racine's enemy, my 'old aunt', though she was then young and radiantly pretty; he naturally attributed such an outlook to extreme old age.

My mother was therefore convinced that in deciding to become a composer (which to the French means the theatre) I was setting my feet on the broad road that leads to disgrace in this world and damnation in the next. The moment she got wind of what was happening her whole soul rose in righteous indignation. I could tell from her wrathful expression that she knew, so I thought it politic to avoid her and lie low until the time came for me to leave. But within a few minutes she followed me to my retreat and confronted me, her eyes blazing, every gesture betraying the intensity of the emotion that gripped her. 'Your father,' she said, addressing me by the formal you, 'has been so weak as to consent to your returning to Paris. He encourages you in your wicked, foolish ideas. I shall not have this sin to lay to my charge. I absolutely forbid you to go.'

'Mother!'

'Yes, I forbid you and, Hector, I implore you not to persist in this madness. Look, I kneel—I, your mother, I clasp your knees and humbly beg you to renounce it.'

'For God's sake, Mother, let me raise you to your feet, I can't bear it.'

'No, I will kneel.' Then, after a moment's silence: 'Wretched boy, you refuse? You can stand there unmoved while your mother kneels before you? Very well, go! Drag yourself through the gutters of Paris, besmirch our name, kill your father and me with shame and sorrow. I shall not set foot in this house again until you have left it. You are my son no longer. I curse you!'

One would hardly believe it possible that even the combination of religious fanaticism with the very grossest contempt for the artistic profession that provincial narrow-mindedness is capable of could lead to such a scene between so affectionate a mother as mine and so devoted a son as I had always been. It was a moment of horror, a scene of grotesque and exaggerated violence that I shall never forget, and to it more than to anything I owe my hatred of those crass medieval prejudices which still survive in most of the provinces of modern France.

The ordeal did not end there. My mother had gone; she had taken refuge at Le Chuzeau, a country house of ours near La Côte. When the time came for me to leave, my father decided we should make a last effort to get her to bid me goodbye and retract the bitter things she had said. He and I and my two sisters went to Le Chuzeau. My mother was sitting in the orchard under a tree, reading. When she saw us she got up and ran off. We waited for some time; we went after her; my father called out; my sisters and I were weeping. It was hopeless. I had to go away without embracing my mother, without a word or a look from her and with all the weight of her curse upon me.

II

Return to Paris—I give lessons—I join Reicha's class at the Conservatoire—dinners on the Pont Neuf —my father withdraws my allowance—implacable opposition—Humbert Ferrand—Kreutzer

THE MOMENT I was back in Paris (where I at once resumed my studies with Lesueur), I set myself to repay de Pons. The debt weighed on me. How was I going to settle it on a monthly allowance of a hundred and twenty francs? I was lucky enough to find some pupils in *solfège*, flute and guitar; and with the money from these lessons and also by economies in my personal spending I managed in a few months to put aside six hundred francs which I promptly handed over to my easy-going creditor.

It may be wondered what economies were possible on such an income. The answer is that I rented, very cheaply, a tiny fifth-floor room in the Ile de la Cité at the corner of the rue de Harlay and the quai des Orfèvres; and instead of eating at a restaurant, as I had been, I established an austere régime of meals which cost only seven or eight sous a time and generally consisted of bread with raisins, prunes or dates.

It was summer. I bought my delicacies at the nearby grocer's and usually took them to the little terrace on the Pont Neuf, at the foot of Henry IV's statue. There I sat and, while I tried not to think of the boiled chicken which the good king imagined his peasants having for their Sunday dinner, ate my frugal meal, watching the sun go down behind Mont Valérien, gazing entranced on the endless play of light and reflection on the waters of the shining Seine as it glided before me, my head full of splendid images from Thomas Moore's poetry, which I had just discovered in a translation and was devouring for the first time. But de Pons, doubtless worried at the privations I was undergoing because of my debt (for I could not hide them from him, we met too often), and perhaps himself in straits and in need of the rest of the money, wrote to my father, telling him the whole story and asking for the other six hundred francs. It was a disastrous disclosure. My father already bitterly regretted his leniency. Here I was after five months in Paris, with no change in my position, no evidence that my musical career had made any progress at all. No doubt he imagined that in that time I would get myself admitted to the Institute competition, win first prize, write an opera in three acts and have it performed with spectacular success, receive the Légion d'honneur and a pension from the government, and all the rest of it. Instead, here was news of a debt, half of which remained unpaid. The blow was a severe one, and it rebounded heavily on me. He paid de Pons the six hundred francs and notified me that if I refused to give up my musical wild-goose chase I must depend on myself alone, for he would not help me to stay in Paris a moment longer. But I had a few pupils; I was used to living cheaply; I was no longer in debt to de Pons. Why hesitate? I stayed. I was, in fact, actively and busily pursuing my musical studies. Cherubini, whose orderly mind showed itself in everything he did, knew that I had not been through the regular Conservatoire mill to get into Lesueur's composition class and had me enrolled in Reicha's class in counterpoint and fugue, which came before composition in the hierarchy of courses. So I was studying with both masters and taking both courses at once. In addition, I had lately made friends with a warm-hearted and intelligent young man named Humbert Ferrand (still, I am happy to say, one of my dearest friends). He had written me the poem for a grand opera, *Les francs-juges*, and I was working on the score with unparalleled enthusiasm. (This libretto was subsequently rejected by the board of the Opéra and my score simultaneously consigned to an oblivion from which it has never emerged. Only the overture has established itself. I have taken some of the best ideas in the opera and developed them in later works. What is left will probably go through the same process or else be thrown away.) Ferrand had also written a heroic scena for chorus on the Greek Revolution, a subject much in our minds at the time, and I had briefly interrupted my work on the *Francs-juges* to set it to music—music which on every page bore the stamp of Spontini's powerful influence. This work was the means of rudely awakening me to a commonplace fact of artistic life: the egoism of the celebrated composer and the aversion he generally feels for even the obscurest young aspirant.

Rodolphe Kreutzer was musical director of the Opéra, where the Holy Week *concerts spirituels* were shortly to take place. It lay with him to have my piece performed, so I went to see him about it. My visit had in fact been prepared by a letter from the Arts Secretary M. de La Rochefoucauld, who had been induced to write on my behalf on the strong recommendation of one of his staff, a friend of Ferrand's. In addition, Lesueur had spoken to his colleague and urged my claims in the warmest terms. There seemed good grounds for hope. My illusions were short-lived. Kreutzer, the eminent musician, composer of *The Death of Abel* (a fine work in my enthusiasm for which I had written him a positive panegyric a few months before)—Kreutzer who, because I admired him, I imagined to be as friendly and accessible as my master—received me with the utmost incivility and contempt. He barely acknowledged my greeting and addressed me over his shoulder without looking at me. 'My good friend' (he had never met me before), 'we can't perform new pieces at these concerts; we haven't time to prepare them. Lesueur knows that perfectly well.' I retired full of confusion. On the following Sunday he and Lesueur had it out at the Chapel Royal, where he was merely violinist. In the end, cornered by my master, he answered without concealing his ill humour, 'Damn it all! Where would we be if we were always helping the young?' At least he was frank.

12

I compete for a job in the chorus—I get it—
Antoine Charbonnel—our bachelor establishment

MEANWHILE WINTER WAS coming on. In my eagerness to write my opera, I had rather neglected my pupils. The Pont Neuf dining-room was no longer convenient for the old Lucullan feasts; the sun had gone and the air was raw and damp. I needed firewood and warmer clothes. Where was the money for these necessities to come from? My income from teaching at one franc a lesson, so far from sufficing, threatened to dry up altogether. Go back to my father, plead guilty, admit myself beaten—or perish from hunger: were these the only alternatives? The mere idea made me so furious that I felt new strength for the struggle, and I resolved to try anything and suffer whatever I had to suffer, even to leave Paris if I had to, rather than weakly return to La Côte to vegetate. My old passion for travel joining hands with music, I decided to apply to the agents for foreign theatres and obtain an engagement as first or second flute in an orchestra in New York, Mexico, Sydney or Calcutta. I would have gone to China or turned sailor, freebooter, pirate, savage, rather than give in. It is my nature to be thus. As useless and dangerous for another will to oppose mine when it is thoroughly roused as to try to prevent gunpowder from exploding by compression.

Happily, my negotiations with foreign theatre agents came to nothing. I do not know what I should have done had I not discovered that the Théâtre des Nouveautés was about to open with a repertoire which included, in addition to vaudeville, comic operas of a modest kind. I raced off to the manager's office to apply for a position as flute-player in the orchestra. The positions were already filled. I applied for the chorus. Again, no vacancy. Death and damnation! However, the manager took my address and promised to let me know if they decided to enlarge the chorus. It was a faint hope but it kept me going for several days, at the end of which a letter from the management informed me that I might compete for the desired appointment, for which auditions were being held at the Freemasons' Hall in the rue de Grenelle-Saint-Honoré. When I arrived, five or six poor devils in the same plight as myself were there already, waiting in nervous silence for their inquisitors to come.

They included a weaver, a blacksmith, an actor who had lost his job at one of the small boulevard theatres, and a chorister from Saint-Eustache. Basses were wanted. I was at best a second-rate baritone: but I thought the examiner might not go into that too closely.

It proved to be the general manager in person. He appeared, followed by a musician called Michel (who still plays today in the Vaudeville orchestra). Nothing had been done to provide a pianist or a piano. Michel's violin was to do for our accompaniment.

The session commenced. My rivals sang in turn, after their fashion, the particular piece that each had carefully prepared. Then it was my turn. The huge manager (rather pleasingly called Saint-Léger) asked me what I had brought.

'I? Why, nothing.'

'What do you mean, nothing? Then what do you propose to sing?'

'Whatever you want me to sing. Isn't there some score here, a *solfège*, a book of exercises?'

'No, we haven't anything like that. Besides,' he added with a touch of scorn, 'I don't imagine you can sing at sight.'

'Excuse me, I'll sing at sight anything that's put in front of me.'

'Ah, that is different. Well, then—but as we've no music, is there some well-known piece you can sing by heart?'

'Yes, there's *The Danaids*, *Stratonice*, *La Vestale*, *Cortez*, *Oedipe*, both *Iphigénies*, *Orphée*, *Armide*—'

'All right, all right! Deuce take it—what a memory! Well, since you're so ominiscient, give us "Elle m'a prodigué" from Sacchini's *Oedipe*.'

'With pleasure.'

'Can you accompany him, Michel?'

'Of course I can. Only, I've forgotten what key it's in.'

'E flat. Shall I sing the recitative?'

'Yes, let's hear the recitative.'

The accompanist gave me a chord of E flat and I began:

Antigone me reste, Antigone est ma fille,
Elle est tout pour mon coeur, seule elle est ma famille.
Elle m'a prodigué sa tendresse et ses soins,
Son zèle dans mes maux m'a fait trouver des charmes, etc.

As the grand melody rolled forth, the other candidates cast gloomy glances at each other, recognizing that in comparison with me (who was no Pischek or Lablache) they had sung not so much like cowherds as like cows. Indeed I saw by a sign from the big manager that they had 'got the bird.' Next day I was officially notified of my appointment. I had beaten the weaver, the blacksmith, the actor, even the lay clerk from Saint-Eustache. I was to begin work at once at a salary of fifty francs a month.*

So here I was, while waiting to become a damned dramatic composer, turned chorus-singer in a minor theatre—my good name discredited, and excommunicated cap-à-pie. Observe the success of my parents' efforts to snatch me from the bottomless pit.

Blessings seldom come singly. I was savouring my victory when two new pupils suddenly fell into my lap and I met a compatriot called Antoine Charbonnel, who was studying to be a pharmacist. He was looking for a room in the Latin quarter where he could be near his chemistry classes, and like me proposed to practise economies on a heroic scale. One glance at our respective fortunes and we were exclaiming almost simultaneously—adapting Walter in *The Life of a Gambler*—'What, no money either? My dear fellow, let's go into partnership.'† We rented two small rooms in the rue de la Harpe. Antoine, who was accustomed to handling furnaces and retorts, appointed himself chief cook and made me his pantry boy. Every morning we went to the market to buy our provisions, which to his acute embarrassment I would insist on carrying home under my arm, without bothering to conceal them from the passers-by. We actually had a serious scene about it. It offended his chemist's pride.

In this way we lived like two princes—exiled ones—for thirty francs a month apiece. I had not experienced such affluence since coming to Paris. I began to develop extravagant ideas. I bought a piano—if you could call it that.‡ I decorated the room with

* [The theatre opened, after several postponements, on 1 March 1827. Saint-Léger was general manager until 1829.]

† [*Trente ans, ou la vie d'un joueur* by Prosper Goubaux, one of the most successful melodramas of the period.]

‡ It cost me a hundred and ten francs. I have already remarked that I could not play the piano, but I like to have one and occasionally hammer out chords

framed portraits of my musical gods and presented myself with a copy of Moore's *The Loves of the Angels*. Antoine, who was as clever with his hands as a monkey (which is really a bad simile, as monkeys can only destroy), spent his spare moments knocking together innumerable useful gadgets. He made us each a pair of very competent clogs out of some of our firewood and, to vary our somewhat monotonously spartan fare, constructed a net and some decoy birds and, when spring came, trapped quail on the plain of Montrouge. The funniest part of it was that although I was regularly out in the evenings (for there was a performance at the Nouveautés every night), Antoine never knew during all the time we lived together that I had the misfortune to 'tread the boards'. I was not exactly proud of my humble position as a chorister and had no desire to enlighten him. While I was at the theatre I was supposed to be giving lessons at the other end of Paris. My pride equalled his. Just as he was embarrassed, and would blush scarlet and walk ahead of me on our shopping expeditions when I openly displayed the fruit of my labours, so it would have pained me to let him know how I had earned it. But to tell the truth, and to do myself justice, my silence was not mere foolish vanity. For all my parents' harshness in cutting me off as they had done, I would not for the world have caused them the anguish—and with their convictions it would have been extreme—of discovering the step I had taken; there was in any case no point in letting them discover it. I was afraid that the slightest indiscretion on my part might lead to the whole story coming out. So I kept quiet, and like Antoine Charbonnel himself they only found out about my theatrical career seven or eight years after it had come to an end, when they read the biographical sketches of me which appeared in various newspapers.*

---

on it. Besides, I enjoy the company of musical instruments. If I were rich, I would always have a grand piano, two or three Erard harps, some of Sax's trumpets and a collection of Stradivarius violins and cellos in the room with me as I worked.

* [An account-book kept by the Berlioz-Charbonnel ménage (quoted by Daniel Bernard, *Correspondance inédite de Hector Berlioz, 1819–68*, 1879) suggests that the economies were indeed heroic. The main items of expenditure seem to have been leeks, vinegar, mustard, cheese and lard; the worst days usually came at the end of the month: e.g. 29 September—only grapes, and 30 September—bread . . . 0 fr. 43 c. salt . . . 0 fr. 25 c. Total . . . 0 fr. 68 c.]

13

First orchestral compositions—my education at the Opéra —my two teachers, Lesueur and Reicha

IT WAS DURING this period that I wrote my first full-scale orchestral work, the overture to the *Francs-juges*. The *Waverley* overture followed soon afterwards. At the time I knew so little of the mechanism of certain instruments that, having written the trombone passage in D flat major in the introduction to the *Francs-juges*, I was struck by a sudden fear that it might prove extremely difficult to play, and I nervously took it to show to one of the trombone-players at the Opéra. His answer completely set my mind at rest. 'On the contrary,' he said, 'D flat is a particularly good key for the trombone; you can count on the passage having a splendid effect.'

I was so elated that I went home with my head in the clouds and, not looking where I was going, twisted my ankle. I get a pain in my foot whenever I hear the piece. Others, perhaps, get a pain in the head.

Neither of my masters taught me anything about instrumentation. Lesueur's notions on the subject were strictly limited. Reicha knew the individual scope and possibilities of most of the wind instruments, but I do not think he had more than rudimentary ideas about grouping them in varying numbers and combinations. In any case this aspect of musical training had nothing to do with his side of the business, which was counterpoint and fugue (it is still unrepresented at the Conservatoire). Some time before I was taken on at the Nouveautés I had got to know a friend of Gardel, the celebrated ballet-master. Thanks to him and the pit tickets he let me have for the Opéra, I went to everything that was given there. I took the score with me and followed it during the performance. In this way I began to grow familiar with the workings of an orchestra and to understand the character and tone of voice, if not the range and mechanism, of most of the instruments. By continually comparing the effect obtained with the means used to obtain it I came to appreciate the subtle connection between musical expression and the technique of instrumentation; but no one had let me into the secret. I analysed the methods of those three modern masters, Beethoven, Weber and Spontini, and made a scientific study of conventional systems of scoring and also of unusual forms and combinations; this and the company of virtuoso players of various instruments and the experiments I induced them to make, plus a dash of instinct, did the rest.

Reicha was an admirable teacher of counterpoint. He was extremely clear and never wasted words. I learnt a lot from him in a short time. Unlike most teachers, he hardly ever failed to give his pupils the reason for the rules he recommended to them, wherever that was possible.

He was neither an empiricist nor a reactionary. He was all for progress in certain branches of music, and his respect for tradition stopped well short of idolatry. Hence his constant disputes with Cherubini; for Cherubini carried his obeisance to the Law to the point of suppressing his own musical judgement—as when he says in his *Treatise on Counterpoint*, 'This harmonic setting seems to me preferable to that one, but the old masters thought otherwise and we must defer to them.'

In his own compositions, however, Reicha conformed to routine even while despising it. I once besought him to tell me candidly what he thought of those fugues vocalized on a single word or phrase, 'Amen' or 'Kyrie eleison', with which the Masses and Requiems of the greatest composers of every school are infested. His answer was unhesitating: 'Oh, they're barbarous!'

'In that case, sir, why do you write them?'

'Why, dear me—everybody does.' *Miseria!*

In this respect Lesueur was more consistent. Those unnatural fugues which, resembling as they do the bawling of a crowd of drunkards, give the impression of nothing so much as a blasphemous parody of ecclesiastical style and phraseology, he too regarded as relics of a barbarous age; he also took care not to write them. The fugues occasionally found in his sacred works have nothing in common with such abominations. One, indeed, which begins with the words 'Quis enarrabit coelorum gloriam', is a masterpiece of nobility of style, harmonic ingenuity and, even more important, expression, to which the fugal form is here very apt. The effect of the opening, with the broad and splendid subject announced on the dominant and then blazing out in answer on the tonic to the same words, 'Quis enarrabit' ('Who will tell the glories of the heavens?'), is as if one part of the choir, fired by the enthusiasm of the other, were leaping forward in its turn to sing with still greater exaltation of the wonders of the firmament. And how beautifully the vocal texture is coloured by the radiant orchestral writing: the massive tread of the cellos and basses and, high above them, the glittering network of violins shining like stars. The stretto on the pedal point is superb. In short, here is a fugue that is justified by the sense of the words, worthy of its subject, and of great beauty. It is the work of a musician who was inspired when he wrote it, an artist who thought about his art. As for the other kind, the low tavern fugues I discussed with Reicha, I could quote many examples signed by composers who are far greater than Lesueur but who, in writing them merely because it was the convention to do so, have none the less shamefully betrayed their intelligence and committed an unpardonable offence against musical expression.

Before coming to France, Reicha had been a fellow-student of Beethoven's in Bonn; but I do not think they were ever very close. Reicha set great store by his knowledge of mathematics. 'It was by studying it,' he told us during one of his classes, 'that I became master of my ideas. Thanks to mathematics I was able to tame my imagination, which had formerly run away with me. Now that it is subject to reason and reflection it has become twice as effective.' I rather doubt if Reicha's theory was as sound as he thought, or if his creative powers really benefited from a study of the exact sciences. It may well have given him his taste for abstract permutations and elaborate musical jokes. He loved solving problems; but this kind of thing can be the enemy of art by diverting it from the main purpose which it should always be striving to achieve. It is not impossible that the opposite of what Reicha supposed was true, and that his passion for calculating everything was in fact harmful to the success and value of his works, since what they gained in intricate combinations and difficulties ingeniously overcome—feats of technique addressed to the eye rather than to the ear—they lost in melodic and harmonic expression, in pure musicality. However, Reicha appeared equally indifferent to praise and to criticism. The success of the young Conservatoire musicians for whose education he was responsible was all he really seemed to care about, and his lessons were models of integrity and thoroughness. In the end he became very friendly to me; but when I first studied with him I could see that he was irked by my always asking him the reason for every rule he taught—a reason which in some cases he could not supply since there was none. His wind quintets enjoyed a certain vogue in Paris for a number of years. They are interesting pieces but a little cold. On the other hand I remember a magnificent duet full of fire and passion in *Sapho*, an opera of his which had a few performances.*

14

Examination at the Institute—my cantata declared unplayable—worship of Gluck and Spontini—the advent of Rossini—the dilettanti—my rage—Ingres

WHEN THE INSTITUTE examination came round, I put my name down again. This time I got through.† The successful candidates were set to write a scena for voice and full orchestra on the subject of 'Orpheus torn by the Bacchantes'. I think my final movement had its points. But the mediocre pianist‡ who was supposed to do duty for an orchestra under the incredible system obtaining at these contests (of which more presently) broke down in the Bacchanal, whereupon the music section of the Institute, consisting of Cherubini, Paër, Lesueur, Berton, Boïeldieu and Catel, pronounced my work 'unplayable' and disqualified me.

My education was progressing. I had seen something of egoism in high places, and how the young are cold-shouldered from fear of competition. Now I experienced the senseless tyranny of the institutions which muzzle them. Kreutzer had prevented me from possibly achieving a success which at that time would have been of considerable benefit to me. The academicians, by applying an absurd regulation to the letter, removed all chance of my winning a prize which, though not brilliant, at least represented a step forward. The effect of their snub was to leave me in a mood of despair and bitter resentment.

* [Opéra, 16 December 1822, for twelve nights only.]

† [27 July 1827.]

‡ [Louis-Victor-Etienne Rifaut, composer of opéras-comiques; two years later he was appointed professor of accompaniment at the Conservatoire.]

I had got a fortnight's leave from the Nouveautés to take part in the competition. The moment it was over I had to take up my burden again. But almost at once I fell seriously ill and was all but carried off by a severe quinsy. Antoine was out chasing *grisettes*, and I was left alone all day and half the night without either servant or nurse to look after me. I believe I would have died one evening had I not, in a moment of agony, stuck a penknife down my throat and lanced the abscess that was choking me. This somewhat unscientific operation was the turning-point. From that moment I began to get better. I had almost fully recovered when my father, who had been won over by my pertinacity and who must have wondered anxiously how I was managing to live, restored my allowance. Thanks to the unhoped-for revival of parental affection I was able to resign from the chorus. This was no small blessing; for quite apart from the physical grind of the work, the sheer stupidity of the music—blown-up vaudevilles which aped opera, terrible little operas that were indistinguishable from vaudeville—would have ended by bringing me down with cholera or turning me into a raving lunatic. Only a true musician, and one familiar with the pseudo-lyric theatre in France, will understand what I went through.*

I was free to resume my evenings at the Opéra, which had had to be sacrificed to the melancholy exigencies of the Nouveautés, and I did so with greater enthusiasm than ever. The study of high dramatic music was a religion to which I devoted myself body and soul. Instrumental music still meant nothing to me; the only concerts I had heard were those given at the Opéra, where the feebleness of the performances was not calculated to excite my interest. The symphonies of Haydn and Mozart (generally speaking, works of a rather intimate kind), when played by an inadequate orchestra on a stage far too large and acoustically unsuitable, produced about as much effect as if they had been performed on the Plaine de Grenelle; they sounded small, frigid and incoherent. Beethoven, I sensed, was a sun indeed, but a sun obscured by heavy clouds. I had seen two symphonies in score but had heard only an

* [The works performed at the Nouveautés in the first season had titles like *Grandma's Young Man*, *The Little Beggar Girl*, *The Man who Liked Widows*, etc. Shortly after Berlioz left the company, a *Faust*, after Goethe, was added to the repertoire, with music composed by one of the theatre's conductors.]

andante. Weber had not yet produced his masterpieces; even his name was unknown to us. As for Rossini and the Rossini cult which had lately become the rage of fashionable Paris, it incensed me. My wrath was all the greater because the whole style of the new school was diametrically opposed to that of Gluck and Spontini. I could imagine nothing more sublimely beautiful and true than the works of those great masters. By contrast, Rossini's melodic cynicism, his contempt for dramatic expression and good sense, his endless repetition of a single form of cadence, his eternal puerile crescendo and brutal bass drum, exasperated me to such a point that I was blind to the brilliant qualities of his genius even in his masterpiece, the *Barber*, exquisitely scored though it is.* More than once I debated with myself the possibility of mining the Théâtre-Italien and blowing it up one evening, along with all its congregation of Rossinians. Whenever I met one of the hated tribe of *dilettanti* I would glare at him with the eye of a Shylock and growl, 'Dog! Would that I might impale thee on a red-hot stake.' I must confess that my mentality, though no longer envisaging murder, is still at heart just as violent and intolerant. I would certainly not impale anyone on a red-hot stake, nor would I blow up the Théâtre-Italien even if the mine were laid and the match to hand; but I wholeheartedly agree with our great painter Ingres when he describes some of Rossini's works as 'the music of a dishonest man'.†

15

Evenings at the Opéra—missionary work—scandals exposed—a display of enthusiasm—deep feelings of a mathematician

MOST PERFORMANCES AT the Opéra were solemn ceremonies for which I prepared myself by reading and pondering the work in

* And without bass drum.

† I can pride myself on sharing my views with M. Ingres on other points besides Rossini's *opera seria*. This does not prevent the illustrious creator of *The Martyrdom of St Symphorian* from regarding me as a kind of monster, a brigand or antichrist of music. But I forgive him gladly because of his admiration for Gluck. Enthusiasm would thus seem to be the opposite of love; it makes us love those who love as we do, even when they hate us.

question. I and a few of the pit regulars were fanatics for our favourite composers. The admiration we professed for them was equalled only by our abomination of the rest. The Jove of our Olympus was Gluck. The most passionate music-lover of today can have no conception how fiercely we worshipped him. But if some of my companions were zealous adherents of the faith, I can say in all modesty that I was its high priest. Whenever I saw any weakening in their devotion I would revive it with sermons worthy of the disciples of Saint-Simon and drag them off to the Opéra, often paying for their tickets out of my own pocket while pretending that I had been given them by someone in the management. Having by this means lured my men into the theatre for the Gluck masterpiece that was being given that night, I would station them in a particular row in the pit with strict instructions not to change their seats: for not all places were equally good for hearing, I had tried them all and knew the defects or advantages of each. Thus in one you were on top of the horns, in another you could hardly hear them. On the right the trombones were too prominent, on the left you got an unpleasant effect from the sound bouncing off the stall boxes. At the front you were too near the orchestra, and the voices were drowned; on the other hand, at the back you were too far from the stage to make out the words or the expressions on the actors' faces. The orchestration of this work should be heard from here, the choruses in that work from there. In one act, where the scene was a sacred grove, the stage area was enormous, and the sound tended to disperse and lose itself about the theatre; in that case you had to go nearer. Another act took place in the interior of a palace, and the design was what is called a box set, an apparently unimportant change which doubled the power of the voices; so it became necessary to move a little farther back to allow voices and orchestra to find a better balance and a more harmonious ensemble.

Once these instructions had been laid down, I questioned my acolytes as to how well they knew the work they had come to hear. If they had not read the text, I produced a libretto from my pocket and while we waited for the curtain to go up I made them study it, to the accompaniment of copious explanations from myself on the composer's intentions in all the more important passages. We always got there early so that we could sit where we wanted to and so as not to risk missing the first notes of the overture, as well as for the pleasure that comes from savouring in anticipation a delightful experience that you know you are about to enjoy. We also loved watching the orchestra assemble. It was as empty as a piano without strings when we arrived; then it would gradually fill with players and music. The orchestral attendant came in first and put the parts on the desks. That was always an anxious moment. Something could have happened since our arrival to make them change the opera, and instead of Gluck's monumental work they might have substituted a *Nightingale* or an *Engaged Couple*, a *Caravan from Cairo*, a *Panurge*, a *Village Magician* or *Lasthènie*, all more or less spurious creations for which we declared our sovereign contempt.* The name of the work printed in large letters on the double bass parts, which were nearest to the pit, either relieved or confirmed our fears. In the latter case we would rise in a body and leave the theatre, swearing like marauding soldiers who discover water in what they had taken to be brandy casks, and including in our general execration the composer of the work substituted, the manager who had inflicted it on the public, and the government which allowed it to be performed. Poor Rousseau! He valued his music for *The Village Magician* as highly as all the great literary works by which his name lives, and firmly believed that he had eclipsed Rameau and his whole output (even the Trio of Fates†) with the sickly little songs, the feeble-minded little falalas, the vapid rondos, solos, pastorales and inanities of every description that his wretched little one-act opera is concocted of. Poor Rousseau, who was so persecuted, whose musical achievements the Holbachians‡ so begrudged him and whose tunes were sung by everyone in France from Jéliotte and Mlle Fel§ to Louis XV (who never tired of rendering 'J'ai perdu

* [Respectively by Lebrun, Lemoyne, Grétry, Grétry, Rousseau, and Hérold, and all in the Opéra's repertoire in 1824–5.]

† A curious and once famous piece from an opera by Rameau, *Hippolyte et Aricie*.

‡ [Disciples of Baron d'Holbach, eighteenth-century philosopher and one of the *encyclopédistes*.]

§ The performers at the Opéra who created the roles of Colin and Colette in *The Village Magician*.

mon serviteur' in the most villainously out-of-tune voice in his kingdom); Rousseau, whose pet work won every kind of success when it appeared—what would he have said if he could have heard our blasphemies? How could he have foreseen that his precious opera, which excited such enthusiasm, would one day be extinguished for ever beneath a huge powdered peruke, thrown at the heroine's feet by some irreverent joker? By pure chance I was present at that final performance of the *Magician*.* Many people, in consequence, attributed the production of the peruke to me. But I must protest my innocence. I even remember being quite as indignant as I was amused at the sacrilege, and can scarcely believe I would have been capable of it. But imagine Gluck of all people carrying irony a stage further and actually stating, some fifty years ago, apropos of this same unhappy *Magician*, in a published letter to Marie Antoinette, that 'France, which had not been greatly favoured in respect of music, could claim a few quite remarkable compositions, among which should be cited M. Rousseau's *Village Magician*'. Who would have credited Gluck with such a sense of humour? The German, by this thrust, outdid the Italians, the usual masters of concealed malice.

But to return to my narrative. When we saw from the name written on the band parts that there was to be no change in the opera, I went on with my exposition, singing the main passages and explaining how the more important orchestral effects were produced, until I had talked the members of our little club into a suitable state of advance enthusiasm. (Our excitement caused a good deal of astonishment among our neighbours in the pit, most of whom were visitors from the provinces and who, from the way I held forth on the marvels of the score, imagined they were going to be absolutely swept off their feet. In the event they generally found it more boring than pleasurable.) Next, I would make a point of naming each player as he entered the orchestra, adding a few comments on his ability and style of playing:

'That's Baillot. Unlike some solo violinists he doesn't save himself for the ballets; he doesn't consider it beneath him to

* *The Village Magician*, since that evening of blessed memory, has never reappeared at the Opéra. [By that time (1827) it had had more than four hundred performances there since its first appearance in 1753.]

accompany an opera by Gluck. In a moment you'll hear him play a passage on the G string which sounds right through the orchestra.

'That big red-faced man over there is the first double bass, old Chénié. A very lively old boy despite his age. He's as good as four normal basses, and you can be sure his part will be played exactly as the composer wrote it—he's not one of your simplifiers.

'The conductor should keep an eye on Guillou, the first flute, who's coming in now. He takes extraordinary liberties with Gluck: the sacred march in *Alceste*, for instance, where the composer has written for the bottom register of the flutes, precisely because he wants the special effect of their lowest notes. That doesn't suit Guillou. He has to dominate, his part has got to be heard—so he transposes the flute line up an octave, thus destroying the composer's intention and turning an imaginative idea into something feeble and obvious.'

My critical catalogue of the main personalities of the orchestra would be cut short by three loud knocks, the signal that the performance was about to begin. After that not another word: we sat in silence, waiting with palpitating hearts for Kreutzer or Valentino to raise his baton and give the beat. Once the overture had started, all talking, humming or beating time was strictly against the rules. If any of our neighbours did so, we silenced him with the well-known mot invented by a music-lover, which we had adopted for such occasions: 'Damn these musicians, they're depriving me of the pleasure of hearing what this chap's saying.'

It was just as unwise for the performers to change anything in the score, for I knew every note and would have died rather than let the slightest tampering with the great masters pass unchallenged. I had no intention of waiting until I could protest coldly in print at this crime against genius. No, indeed! I denounced the offenders then and there, publicly and in a loud, clear voice; and I can vouch for it that there is no form of criticism so effective. One day—to give an example—*Iphigénie en Tauride* was on. I had noticed at the previous performance that cymbals had been added to the Scythians' first dance in B minor, which Gluck wrote for strings alone, and also that in Orestes' great recitative in the third act the trombones, which are so superbly appropriate to the dramatic situation, had been omitted. I decided that if the same errors were repeated, I should point them out. When the Scythian ballet began I waited for the cymbals. They came in just as they had before. Although seething with rage, I managed to contain myself until the end of the piece: then, in the short pause which ensued, I yelled out, 'There are no cymbals there. Who has dared to correct Gluck?'*

There was a buzz of consternation. The public, who are very unclear about such artistic questions and do not care whether the composer's orchestration is altered or not, could not understand what this young lunatic in the pit was getting so angry about. But it was much worse in the third act. The trombones in Orestes' monologue were suppressed as I had feared they would be, and the same voice rang through the theatre: 'Why aren't the trombones playing? This is intolerable.'

The astonishment of both orchestra and audience was only equalled by the wrath—very natural, I admit—of Valentino, who was conducting that evening. It transpired that the trombones had only been obeying an express order not to play in that particular passage;† the orchestral parts complied exactly with the score.

As to the cymbals, which Gluck uses with such felicity in the first of the Scythian choruses, I do not know who had taken upon himself to put them into the dance music as well, thus altering the whole colour and disrupting the sinister stillness of that strange ballet. But I do know that at subsequent performances everything was in order. The cymbals were silent, the trombones spoke, and I contented myself with growling between my teeth, 'That's more like it.'

Not long afterwards de Pons, who was at least as fanatical as I, took exception to being subjected to someone else's ballet music in place of Sacchini's in the first act of *Oedipe à Colone*, and suggested that we deal with the interminable solos for horn and cello that had been substituted. I could hardly refuse my help in so laudable an enterprise. We went. The method used in *Iphigénie* proved equally successful in *Oedipe*. A few words shouted from the pit by de Pons and me, and the offending ballet music disappeared for ever.

* Cymbals are used only in the Scythian chorus 'Les dieux apaisent leur courroux'. The whole character of the ballet in question is different, so it is differently scored.

† So much the worse for whoever gave the order.

On one occasion only did we succeed in carrying the public with us. The playbills had announced that the solo violin part in the *Nina* ballet would be played by Baillot. Either because he was indisposed or for some other reason, the virtuoso was unable to perform; but the management saw fit to inform the audience only by means of a minute strip of paper pasted across the placard at the entrance of the Opéra, which is never read by anybody. The vast majority were therefore expecting to hear the great violinist.

We had reached the moment when Nina, supported on either side by her father and her betrothed, comes to her senses. Not even Mlle Bigottini's touching pantomime could make us forget Baillot. The scene was nearly over when: 'Wait a minute, what about the violin solo?' I said, in a voice loud enough to be heard. 'He's right,' someone said, 'it looks as if they're leaving it out. Baillot! Baillot! The violin solo!' At that the whole pit fired up. And then—something unheard of at the Opéra—the entire house rose and noisily demanded that the programme be carried out according to the bill. While this uproar was proceeding, the curtain came down. At that, the clamour redoubled. The players, alarmed by the fury of the pit, hastily abandoned the field; whereupon the enraged public invaded the orchestra, hurling chairs in all directions, overturning desks, bursting the drums. In vain I shouted, 'Gentlemen, gentlemen, what are you doing? You're breaking the instruments. This is madness. Can't you see that's old Chénié's double bass, a wonderful instrument with a superb black tone?' No one listened to me now. The rioters did not stop until they had laid waste the whole orchestra and left numerous instruments and chairs in ruins.

That was the bad side of the Draconian criticism-in-action that we exercised at the Opéra. The good side was our enthusiasm when everything was going right.

Then you should have seen how wildly we applauded the passages that no one else noticed—a fine bass, a felicitous modulation, an expressive line of recitative, a telling note on the oboe. The public took us for claqueurs, apprentice or part-time. The claque leader knew only too well that we were not. His delicate manœuvres were upset by our sudden storms of applause, and he would glare at us with a look worthy of Neptune uttering his

'Quos ego'.* When Mme Branchu was at her inspired best, the shouting and stamping that went on! Nothing like it happens nowadays, not even at the Conservatoire, the only place in France where real enthusiasm for music is still sometimes to be found.

The most curious scene of the sort that I recall occurred at a performance of *Oedipe*. Though Sacchini came far below Gluck in our estimation, we admired him greatly all the same. I had taken with me a friend, a student whose knowledge of art was confined to billiards, but whom I was determined to convert to music.† However, the sorrows of Antigone and her father made no impression on him and after the first act I gave him up as hopeless and sat in the row in front, out of reach of his maddening sang-froid. But chance, as if to preserve the contrast, had placed on his right another enthusiast, as deeply affected as he was impervious. I soon became aware of it. Dérivis had just had a wonderful burst of eloquence in the recitative:

Mon fils! tu ne l'es plus!
Va! ma haine est trop forte!

Engrossed as I was in the poetry and antique power of this fine passage, I could not help overhearing the dialogue which took place behind me between my man, who was peeling an orange, and his unknown neighbour, who was experiencing the most intense emotion.

'My dear sir, do be calm.'

'No, it's too much. It's tremendous, overwhelming.'

'Really, you know, you shouldn't get so worked up. You'll make yourself ill.'

'Leave me alone. . . . Ah!'

'Cheer up. After all, it's only a play. May I offer you a piece of this orange?'

'God, it's sublime!'

'It's Maltese.'

'Perfection!'

* [*Aeneid*, I, 135: the sea-god's rebuke to the winds for rousing, without his permission, the storm which wrecked the Trojan fleet on the coast of Carthage.]

† Léon de Boissieux, a fellow-pupil of mine at the little seminary in La Côte. He was for a short while one of the celebrated billiard-players of Paris.

'Do have some.'

'Ah, what music!'

'Yes, it's not bad.'

While this incongruous exchange was proceeding the opera had reached the lovely trio 'O doux moments' which follows the reconciliation scene. The extraordinary sweetness of the music, with its simple yet insidious melody, was too much for me. I hid my face in my hands and wept like a man overcome with grief. As the trio ended, two powerful arms lifted me bodily off my seat, nearly crushing my ribs. It was the unknown enthusiast. Unable to contain his emotion any longer, and having noticed one among all the audience round him who seemed to share it, he embraced me frantically, blurting out, 'B-b-b-by heaven, sir, isn't it beautiful?' Not the least taken aback, my face disfigured with crying, I answered by asking him, 'Are you a musician?'

'No, but I feel music as deeply as any man.'

'Yes. That's what matters. Give me your hand, sir. You're a splendid fellow.'

Thereupon regardless of the stares and sniggers of our neighbours and the blank astonishment of my orange-eating neophyte, we whispered together for a few moments; I gave him my name, he told me his* and his profession. He was an engineer, a mathematician! What strange habitation will true feeling choose next!

16

The advent of Weber at the Odéon—Castil-Blaze—Mozart—Lachnith—adapters and improvers—'Despair and die!'

IN THE MIDST of this ardent period of my musical education—the fever of my passion for Gluck and Spontini and of my aversion for the Rossinians and all their works then raging at its height—Weber appeared. *Der Freischütz* was performed at the Odéon: not the real thing but an insulting travesty, hacked and mutilated in the most wanton fashion by an arranger—*Freischütz* disguised as *Robin des bois*. The young orchestra was excellent, the chorus

* He was called le Tessier. I never saw him again.

second-rate, the soloists atrocious. Only one of them, the woman who played Agathe (re-christened 'Annette' by the translator), knew how to sing; but as she delivered the entire role without a glimmer of intelligence, passion or vitality, it went virtually for nothing. The great aria in the second act, sung with adamantine imperturbability, had the charm of one of Bordogni's exercises and passed almost unnoticed; it was long before I realized what a mine of inspiration it is.

The première was greeted with laughter and catcalls from all parts of the house. On the following evening the Waltz and the Huntsmen's Chorus, which had aroused interest from the first, created such a sensation that people were soon flocking to the Odéon to hear them. They made the rest of the work bearable. Later, the Bridesmaids' Chorus in the third act and Agathe's prayer (cut by half) were allowed to be quite pleasing, and it was also discovered that the overture had a certain bizarre vigour and that Max's aria was not without dramatic feeling. Finally, it became fashionable to find the devilry of the Wolf's Glen amusing, till in the end all Paris wanted to see this uncouth work. The Odéon made a fortune, and M. Castil-Blaze, the plunderer of the masterpiece, was richer by a good hundred thousand francs.*

In my exclusive worship of classical opera I had been intolerantly prepared to reject the new style; but to my surprise it delighted me, garbled though it was by incomplete or crude performance. Even in this ravaged form there was a wild fragrance,

* [After the failure of the opening night (7 December 1824) there was an interval of nine days before the second performance. In the meantime Castil-Blaze let it be known that he was refashioning the work radically to conform to Parisian taste. In fact it had been given from the first in mutilated form; but the Odéon public swallowed the bait. *Robin des bois, or The Three Balls* had more than a hundred performances. The version was published in full score as well as in vocal score (while the full score of *Der Freischütz* remained unpublished). Castil-Blaze's modifications included the reordering of several numbers in Act I; a certain amount of rescoring; the insertion of a love duet borrowed from *Euryanthe*, with a fresh accompaniment; various small cuts in Agathe's scena; the removal of the orchestral epilogue to the Bridesmaids' Chorus; numerous, often drastic, changes in the vocal line, some caused by the French text but many not; the action transferred to Yorkshire in the reign of Charles I, and a translation so free that it sometimes inverted the meaning of the original. In addition, about two hundred bars disappeared with the Hermit in the finale of Act III.]

a delicious freshness in the score that intoxicated me. I must admit I was getting a little tired of the tragic muse and her high solemnities. The swift movements and angular grace of this wood-nymph, her dreamy attitudes, the naïvety and purity of her passions, her virginal smile, her melancholy, overwhelmed me with a flood of undiscovered sensations.

I began to forsake the Opéra for the Odéon, where I had a pass to the pit. I never missed a performance, and soon knew *Freischütz*, or all of it that was given there, by heart.

Weber himself came to France about that time. It is twenty-one years now since he paid his first and last visit to Paris, on the way to London, to the near-failure of one of his masterpieces, *Oberon*, and his own death. How I longed to see him! How pantingly I pursued him that evening when, already a sick man, he went to hear the revival of Spontini's *Olympie** a few days before he left for England! But it was hopeless. The same morning Lesueur had greeted me with: 'Weber has just been here. If you had come five minutes earlier you would have heard him play me whole scenes from our operas; he knows them all.' A few hours later, in a music shop: 'Who do you think was sitting here a moment ago?'

'Who?'

'Weber!'

At the Opéra, when I arrived, everybody was talking about him. 'Weber's just walked through the foyer.' 'He's gone in.' 'He's in a box on the first tier.' I was in despair at never being able to catch up with him. But it was no use; no one there could point him out to me. He was like Shakespeare's apparitions in reverse—visible to all but one. Unknown as I was, I could not bring myself to write him a note, nor had I any friends there who were in a position to introduce me. So I never set eyes on him.

Oh! If great creative artists could only divine the grand passions their works inspire! If it were only given to them to perceive the enthusiasm of a hundred thousand hearts concentrated in a single heart, how they would grapple such secret devotion to their souls as a powerful consolation against the envy and hatred of some, the shallow-minded frivolity of others, the half-heartedness of all!

* [27 February 1826, with Mme Branchu.]

Despite his popularity, despite the glamour of *Freischütz* and the vogue it enjoyed, and conscious as he must have been of his own genius, Weber more than most might have been glad of such obscure but sincere adoration. He had written admirable things only to see them derided by performers and critics. His most recent opera, *Euryanthe*, had had only a limited success, and he had good reason to be anxious for *Oberon*, realizing that such a work, to be fully appreciated, requires an audience of poets and a pit full of intellectual aristocrats. Even Beethoven, the King of kings, had for long underrated him. One can see how at times (as he himself has written) he lost faith in what he was doing, and how it was that the failure of *Oberon* killed him.

If the fate of this marvellous score has been very different from that of its elder brother, *Freischütz*, which the public has seen fit to acclaim, this is not due to any vulgarity in the character of *Freischütz*, anything shoddy in its construction, anything sham in its brilliance or blatantly sensational in its style. In neither work has the composer made the least concession to passing fashion or to the even more imperious demands of singers and their vanity. He was as proudly himself, as true, as original, as hostile to formula, as resolute in integrity, as incapable of compromise for the sake of applause, as great, in *Freischütz* as in *Oberon*. The poetic invention of the former, however, is full of energy, passion and contrast; the supernatural element in it gives rise to strange and startling effects. Melody, harmony and rhythm alike are tremendously vivid and powerful; everything combines to arouse the listener. In addition the characters, being drawn from life, are more obviously appealing; the representation of their feelings and the world they live in has naturally prompted a less rarefied, more accessible style; yet it is treated with such exquisite skill that the most austere spirit cannot resist its charm, while for this same quality the Mass of the people deem it the very perfection of art and a miracle of invention.

In *Oberon*, on the other hand, though human emotion plays an important part, the fantastic is predominant—but the fantastic in a cool, serene, unassertive form. In place of monsters and fearful apparitions there are choirs of aerial spirits, sylphs, fairies, water-nymphs; and the musical idiom of these gentle, mild-eyed creatures—an idiom unlike any other—derives its chief attraction from the harmony. Melodically wayward and ambiguous, rhythmically fluid, unpredictable and often difficult to grasp, it is hardly likely to be understood by the general public when not even musicians can appreciate its subtleties without the most concentrated attention combined with the liveliest imagination. The romantic German temperament is presumably better attuned to this exquisite poetry. For the French, I fear, it could never be more than an object of curiosity; and we would very soon find ourselves getting bored with it.* The experience of 1828, when the Karlsruhe company gave some performances at the Théâtre Favart, was not reassuring. The Mermaids' Chorus—music that moves with the gentlest of pulses, breathing a mood of pure happiness—consists only of two quite short verses; but the tempo is slow and the softly undulating melody makes its points with the minimum of gesture. After a few bars the audience lost interest. At the end of the first couplet a perceptible restlessness spread through the house and people began talking. The second verse was barely audible; in consequence it was suppressed before the second performance.

Weber was naturally incensed when he discovered what Castil-Blaze, veterinary surgeon of music, had done with his *Freischütz*, and he aired his just grievance in a letter which was published in the Press before he left Paris. Castil-Blaze had the audacity to reply that it was precisely the changes of which the composer complained that had ensured the success of *Robin des bois*, and that it was most ungrateful of M. Weber to reproach the man who had popularized his music in France.

Villain! And a wretched sailor gets fifty lashes for a minor act of insubordination!†

* Since this was written, the production of *Oberon* at the Théâtre-Lyrique [1857] has proved me wrong. The work created a sensation and had an enormous success. The Parisian public must have made remarkable progress.

† [The public exchange of letters between Weber and Castil-Blaze took place a few weeks before Weber's visit to Paris. Weber had also tried, unsuccessfully, to prevent the incorporation of several numbers from *Euryanthe* in *La forêt de Sénart*, a Castil-Blazian concoction which opened at the Odéon on 14 January 1826. In his reply (*Journal des débats*, 25 January 1826) Castil-Blaze argued that it was 'common knowledge that foreign operas cannot succeed on the French stage unless they conform to our dramatic standards. The music must of necessity be cut and rearranged and the action adapted; one has in effect to take the score and compose

It was to ensure the success of *The Magic Flute* that the director of the Opéra, some twenty years earlier, commissioned the remarkable potpourri which under the title of *The Mysteries of Isis* has become part of our cultural heritage (the libretto is itself a mystery that no one to this day has ever fathomed). When the text had been suitably 'fixed', the director had the sagacity to send for a *German* musician to fix the music. The German musician did not flinch from his task. He tacked a few bars on to the end of the overture (the overture to *The Magic Flute*!), made a bass aria out of the soprano line of one of the choruses,* likewise adding a few bars of his own composition; removed the wind instruments from one scene and put them into another; altered the vocal line and the whole character of the accompaniment in Sarastro's sublime aria; manufactured a song out of the Slaves' Chorus 'O cara armonia'; converted a duet into a trio; and, as if *The Magic Flute* were not enough to sate his harpy's appetite, gorged himself on *Titus* and *Don Giovanni*: for the aria 'Quel charme à mes esprits rappelle' is taken from *Titus*, the andante at least; the allegro with which it ends not apparently satisfying our *uomo capace*, he ripped it out and stuck in another of his own fabrication, in which one may perceive only the frayed ends of Mozart's. After that, need one add that in the hands of this master the famous 'Fin ch'han del vino'—that explosion of licentious energy in which the whole character of the Don is summed up—duly reappeared as a trio for two sopranos and bass, singing, among other sweet nothings, the following lines:

Joy past all telling!
My heart is swelling!
How my lot is different from his!

---

a French opera from it. . . . M. Weber should really not feel outraged at the alterations we have introduced into his opera in order to ensure its enormous success. . . . The object of my endeavours has been to make his splendid masterpiece known in France, and to add to the laurels which Germany, Prussia, Holland and England have already laid upon the score of *Freischütz*.']

* The chorus 'Per voi risplende il giorno'. [Presumably Berlioz did not possess a German text of *The Magic Flute*. Both it and *Seraglio* were widely performed and published in Italian translations in the nineteenth century.]

What delight can equal my bliss?
Trust in thy friend, yes,
Until life's end, yes,
We'll be sharing our happiness.
Heav'ns, 'tis a blessing
Beyond all expressing!
Thy hand I'm pressing!
What joy it is!

When the whole lamentable concoction was complete, it was christened '*The Mysteries of Isis*, opera' and the said opera in that state performed, printed and published* in full score, in which, alongside Mozart's name, the arranger had condescended to place his own, the name of a fool and a vandal, the name of Lachnith,† which I append here as fit company for Castil-Blaze.

Thus, at an interval of twenty years, each of these beggars paraded in his rags and trampled the rich robes of a prince of music; and thus, dressed as apes, got up grotesquely in cheap finery, one eye gouged out, an arm withered, a leg broken, two men of genius were introduced to the French public! And their tormentors proclaimed, 'Look—Mozart! Weber!' and the public believed them. No one came forward to treat these criminals as they deserved, or at least to expose their crimes.

Alas, what if anyone had? The public is little troubled by such things. Not only in France but in Germany, England and elsewhere the greatest works of all kinds are suffered to be adapted, which means smirched and abused, by any nonentity. No one would in principle dispute that if such liberties are to be taken at all, only the very greatest artists ought to take them; any corrections made in a work, old or new, should come from above and

* *The Mysteries of Isis* and *Robin des bois* are both in print, and are in the library of the Paris Conservatoire.

† Lachnith, not Lachnitz: we must be careful not to misspell the name of so distinguished a man. [*Les mystères d'Isis* ('the recitative composed and the score compiled by Citizen Lachnith') was first produced on 20 August 1801. According to Loewenberg's *Annals of Opera*, it had a hundred and thirty-four performances, the last being on 2 May 1827. It was in the Opéra's repertoire throughout this period. An excerpt from it figured on the programme of a Conservatoire concert as late as 1847.]

never from below. Yet the reverse is allowed to happen all the time, without a voice being raised against it.

Mozart assassinated by Lachnith, Weber by Castil-Blaze; Gluck, Grétry, Mozart, Rossini, Beethoven, Vogel, mutilated by this same Castil-Blaze;* Beethoven's symphonies corrected by Fétis (as I shall describe), by Kreutzer and by Habeneck; Molière and Corneille cut down to size by unknown hacks at the Théâtre-Français; Shakespeare still performed in England as 'arranged' by Cibber and his kind.

Such corrections, I would suggest, come not from above but from below—perpendicularly!

Let no one argue that the adapters, in their operations among the great masters, have sometimes hit on a happy idea. Such discoveries are exceptions and cannot be used to justify inflicting on works of art so pernicious a principle.

No, no, no, a million times no! You musicians, you poets, prose-writers, actors, pianists, conductors, whether of third or second or even first rank, you do not have the right to meddle with a Shakespeare or a Beethoven, in order to bestow on them the blessings of your knowledge and taste.

No, no, no, ten million times no! No man, no matter who he is, has the right to compel another, no matter who he is, to give up his own face, wear a mask, speak in a manner that is not his, take a shape not of his choosing—to become while he lives a puppet, subject to an alien will, and to be galvanized when he is dead. If a man is mediocre, let him lie, undisturbed in his mediocrity. If he is great, a rare spirit, let his peers, his superiors even, respect him, and those who are less bow humbly before him.

I know that Garrick's dénouement to *Romeo and Juliet*, which he substituted for the less striking end that Shakespeare wrote, was an inspired discovery, incomparable in its pathos. But what of the miserable poetaster† who invented the dénouement which is quite often performed in place of the final scene of *King Lear*,

* There is hardly a work of these composers that he has not retouched in his own image. I believe he is mad.

† [Nahum Tate, whose *King Lear* (1681) was performed well into the nineteenth century.]

and in which Cordelia* is made to declaim coarse tirades full of passions utterly out of character with the gentle nobility of her nature? He should be made known and pointed out to all, so that every poet in the world, every artist, every father and lover, could heap blows on him and expose him in the pillory of public indignation, saying, 'You wretched fool! You have committed the most odious of crimes, for you are guilty of an offence against that combination of man's highest faculties which is called genius. May you be accursed! "Despair and die!"'

Richard III (from which I have borrowed this useful imprecation) is another that has been disfigured. *Hamlet* and *Romeo* doctored, new characters added to *The Tempest*—so it goes on. This is where Garrick's example has led. Everyone has been telling Shakespeare how he should have written.

And to return to music, we have the example of Kreutzer making numerous cuts in one of Beethoven's symphonies† at the time of the last *concerts spirituels* at the Opéra, after which we see Habeneck altering the orchestration of another.‡ In London you hear *Don Giovanni*, *Figaro* and *The Barber of Seville* with additional parts for bass drum, trombones and ophicleide supplied by M. Costa. But if conductors are free to tamper with works of this kind at will and add or subtract as they please, what is to stop a violin or a horn, or any back-desk player, from doing the same? It will be the translator and the editor next, even the copyist, the engraver and the printer, who will have a fine precedent for doing the same.§

Is this not the utter ruin and destruction of art? And ought not we, all of us who are in love with the glory of art and vigilant to protect the inalienable rights of the human spirit, ought we not, when we see them attacked, to rise up in our wrath and pursue and indict the malefactor, and cry aloud for all to hear, 'Your crime is contemptible—despair! Your stupidity is criminal—die! May you

* The youngest of Lear's daughters.

† No. 2 in D.

‡ For the last twenty years the C minor Symphony has been performed at the Conservatoire without double basses at the beginning of the scherzo. Habeneck thinks they do not sound effective. Telling Beethoven how he should have written!

§ That is just what is happening.

be scorned! May you be hissed and hooted! May you be accursed! Despair and die!'

17

Prejudice against operas written to an Italian text —it affects my reaction to some of Mozart's works

I HAVE SAID THAT at the time of my first examination at the Institute I was taken up exclusively with the study of great dramatic music. I should rather have said, of lyric tragedy; and it was for this reason that I regarded Mozart with a certain coolness.

Only Gluck and Spontini were allowed to inspire passion. There was, moreover, a practical reason why my admiration for the composer of *Don Giovanni* should have been lukewarm. *Don Giovanni* and *Figaro* were the two Mozart operas most often done in Paris, but they were always done at the Italian Opera, by Italians, in Italian. Therefore they belonged to the Italian school, and were guilty by association. That was more than enough to make me feel somewhat unsympathetic towards these masterpieces. Besides—and this was less unreasonable—I had been shocked by a passage in Donna Anna's music in which Mozart has unhappily written a most deplorable vocalise, a passage which lies like a stain on that glorious score. I refer to the allegro of the soprano aria (No. 22) in the second act. It is an aria of intense sadness, full of a heartbreaking sense of loss and sorrowing love, but towards the end degenerating into notes of such shocking unseemliness and absurdity that one can hardly believe it to be the work of the same man. One has the impression that Donna Anna has suddenly dried her tears and broken out in ribald clowning. The words at this point are: 'Forse un giorno il cielo ancora sentirà-a-a-a' (here an unbelievable succession of runs in the worst style) 'pietà di me.' It must be admitted that this is a strange fashion for the noble, outraged woman to express the hope that 'heaven will one day have pity on her'. I could not readily forgive Mozart for such a blunder. Today I feel that I would give some of my own blood to erase that shameful page and a few more of the same kind which one is forced to recognize among his works.*

* Even shameful seems to me too light a word to stigmatize this passage. Mozart here has committed one of the most odious and mindless crimes against passion, taste and common sense of which the history of art provides an example.

For this reason I could not help feeling that his dramatic principles were not to be trusted, and my enthusiasm sank almost to zero.

The religious splendours of *The Magic Flute* had, it is true, impressed me deeply; but my first experience of the work had been in the travestied form of *The Mysteries of Isis*, and it was not until later, in the Conservatoire library, that I got to know the original and could compare it with the miserable French hotchpotch performed at the Opéra.

As a whole, therefore, the dramatic works of this great composer had presented themselves in a bad light. It was some years before more favourable conditions enabled me to appreciate their charm and lovely perfection. The marvellous beauty of his quartets and quintets and of one or two of the sonatas was what first converted me to this celestial genius, which thenceforth I worshipped while regretting that his admitted association with Italians and learned contrapuntists had even slightly tarnished its purity.

18

The advent of Shakespeare—Miss Smithson —fatal passion—spiritual apathy—my first concert—comedy of Cherubini's opposition—his defeat—whips and scorpions

I COME NOW to the supreme drama of my life. I shall not recount all its sad vicissitudes. I will say only this: an English company came to Paris to give a season of Shakespeare at the Odéon, with a repertory of plays then quite unknown in France. I was at the first night of *Hamlet*.* In the role of Ophelia I saw Harriet Smithson, who five years later became my wife. The impression made on my heart and mind by her extraordinary talent, nay her dramatic genius, was equalled only by the havoc wrought in me by the poet she so nobly interpreted. That is all I can say.

Shakespeare, coming upon me unawares, struck me like a thunderbolt. The lightning flash of that sublime discovery opened before me at a stroke the whole heaven of art, illuminating it to its

* [11 September 1827. The company, directed by William Abbot, opened five nights earlier with *The Rivals* and Allingham's *Fortune's Frolic*. The first night of *Hamlet* had had to be postponed because the leading actor, Charles Kemble (younger brother of John), was delayed in England.]

remotest depths. I recognized the meaning of dramatic grandeur, beauty, truth. At the same time I saw the utter absurdity of the French view of Shakespeare which derives from Voltaire,

That ape of genius, sent
*By Satan among men to do his work**

and the pitiful narrowness of our own worn-out academic, cloistered traditions of poetry. I saw, I understood, I felt . . . that I was alive and that I must arise and walk.

But the shock was too strong, and it was long before I recovered from it. A feeling of intense, overpowering sadness came over me, accompanied by a nervous condition like a sickness, of which only a great writer on physiology could give any adequate idea.

I lost the power of sleep and with it all my former animation, all taste for my favourite studies, all ability to work. I wandered aimlessly about the Paris streets and the neighbouring plains. During that long period of affliction I recall only four occasions when I really slept—a deep death-like sleep brought on by physical exhaustion: one night on some sheaves of corn among the stubble near Ville-Juif; once during the daytime in a field outside Sceaux; once in the snow on the banks of the frozen Seine near Neuilly; and lastly at a table at the Café du Cardinal, on the corner of the boulevard des Italiens and the rue Richelieu, where I slept for five hours, to the great alarm of the waiters, who did not dare go near me in case they discovered I was dead.

It was on my return from one of these wanderings (during which I looked as if I were searching for my soul) that I came upon my copy of Moore's *Irish Melodies* lying open on the table at the poem which begins 'When he who adores thee' and, taking up my pen, wrote the music to that heartrending farewell straight off. It is the song called 'Elégie' which comes at the end of my collection *Irlande*. This is the sole occasion on which I was able to express a feeling of the sort directly in music while still under its active influence. But I think I have rarely found a melody of such truth and poignancy, steeped in such a surge of sombre harmony.

The piece is extremely difficult both to sing and to accompany. To catch its true meaning—that is to re-create more or less

* Victor Hugo, *Chants du crépuscule.*

faithfully the mood of pride and tenderness and dark despair which Moore must have experienced when he wrote the words, and which I felt when my music flooded out and took possession of them—two accomplished artists are needed, and especially a singer with a sympathetic voice and exceptional sensitivity.* To hear it poorly done would be inexpressibly painful for me. That is why, in all the twenty years of its existence, I have never asked anyone to sing it to me. Once, Alizard saw it in my room and tried it over without accompaniment, transposed down to B to suit his bass voice. I was so deeply moved that I interrupted him in the middle and begged him to stop. He understood the song. I saw that he would sing it perfectly, and this gave me the idea of arranging the piano part for orchestra. Then I reflected that works of this kind are not meant for the ordinary concert-going public; to expose them to its indifference would be a kind of sacrilege, and I broke off and destroyed as much as I had done.

By a fortunate piece of luck the French prose translation is so close to the original that I was able later to fit Moore's actual words to my music.

If this elegy ever becomes known in England or in Germany, it may strike some sympathetic chords; a sorrowing heart will find its own likeness. Such a piece, however, is incomprehensible to most French people and to the Italians simply nonsensical.

As I came out of *Hamlet*, shaken to the depths by the experience, I vowed not to expose myself a second time to the flame of Shakespeare's genius.

Next day the playbills announced *Romeo and Juliet*. I had my pass to the pit; but to make doubly sure of getting in, just in case the doorkeeper at the Odéon might have had orders to suspend the free list, I rushed round to the box office the moment I saw the posters and bought a stall. My fate was doubly sealed.

After the melancholy of *Hamlet*, after the agonizing sorrows, the love 'all tears', the cruel ironies and black meditations, the heartbreak, the madness, the weeping, the bereavements, the disasters and fatal accidents, after Denmark's sombre clouds and icy winds, to

* Pischek accompanying himself would realize my ideal of how this elegy should be performed.

be exposed to the fiery sun and balmy nights of Italy, to witness the drama of that passion swift as thought, burning as lava, radiantly pure as an angel's glance, imperious, irresistible, the raging vendettas, the desperate kisses, the frantic strife of love and death, was more than I could bear. By the third act, scarcely able to breathe—it was as though an iron hand had gripped me by the heart—I knew that I was lost. I may add that at that time I did not know a word of English; I could only glimpse Shakespeare darkly through the mists of Letourneur's translation; the splendour of the poetry which gives a whole new glowing dimension to his glorious works was lost on me. Even now I labour to some extent under this disadvantage.* It is much harder for a Frenchman to sound the depths of Shakespeare's style than it is for an Englishman to catch the individual flavour and subtlety of La Fontaine or Molière. They are continents, Shakespeare is a world. But the power of the acting, especially that of Juliet herself, the rapid flow of the scenes, the play of expression and voice and gesture, told me more and gave me a far richer awareness of the ideas and passions of the original than the words of my pale and garbled translation could do. An English critic stated in the *Illustrated London News* last winter† that after seeing Miss Smithson as Juliet I exclaimed, 'I shall marry that woman and write my biggest symphony on the play.' I did both, but I never said anything of the sort. My biographer credited me with ambitions larger than life. I was too overwhelmed even to dream of such things. This narrative will show how and in what strange circumstances they became realities.

The success of Shakespeare—to which the enthusiastic support of the new school of writers led by Victor Hugo, Alexandre Dumas and Alfred de Vigny contributed—took Paris by storm. But it was surpassed by Miss Smithson's. No dramatic artist in France ever touched and excited the public as she did. No press notices ever equalled the eulogies which the French papers published in her honour.

* [Even now, that is, that he understands the language. In 1828 we hear of Berlioz attending an evening class in English. He became a fluent reader, and able to speak it tolerably well.]

† [12 February 1848. The writer was Charles Gruneisen, music critic of the *Illustrated London News*, the *Morning Chronicle* and *Britannia*.]

After these two performances I had no further difficulty in keeping away from the English company. Another such ordeal would have felled me. The mere thought of laying myself open to it made me shudder. I dreaded it as one dreads acute physical pain.

I had spent several months in the kind of dull despair whose causes and symptoms I have touched on, dreaming ceaselessly of Shakespeare and of the actress of genius, the 'fair Ophelia' who had become the rage of Paris, and contrasting her dazzling reputation and my own miserable obscurity, when at last I roused myself. I resolved that though my name was unknown to her I would by a supreme effort make it shine so that even she caught a gleam of it. I would dare to attempt what no composer had attempted in France before: I would give a concert exclusively of my works, at the Conservatoire. Yes, I thought, I will show her that 'I too am a painter.'* To achieve it I needed three things: copies of my music, people to perform it, and a hall to perform it in.

Once the decision was taken, I set about it and, working sixteen hours out of twenty-four, copied every part, orchestral and choral, of the pieces which I had chosen.

My programme consisted of the *Waverley* and *Francs-juges* overtures, an aria and a trio with chorus from the *Francs-juges*, the heroic scena on the Greek Revolution, and the cantata on the death of Orpheus which the Institute jury had declared unplayable. While copying away without respite I had practised even stricter economies and had managed to add a few hundred francs to my store of savings. With this I intended to pay my chorus. For the players, I knew I could count on the generous help of the Odéon orchestra as well as of certain members of the Opéra and the Nouveautés.

That left the hall; and here, as always in Paris, lay the chief obstacle. In order to obtain the use of the Conservatoire auditorium, the only really good one, it was necessary to have the permission of the Secretary of Fine Arts, M. Sosthène de La Rochefoucauld, and the consent of Cherubini.

M. de La Rochefoucauld readily granted the application; but Cherubini, at the mention of my plan, flew into a rage.

* [Correggio's remark, on his seeing Raphael's *St Cecilia*.]

'So you wish to geeve a concert?' he said, with his usual suavity.

'Yes, sir.'

'For that you will 'ave to 'ave the pairmission of the Secretary of Fine Arts.'

'I have got it.'

'What, M. Rossefoucauld agrees?'

'Yes, sir.'

'But—but—but I—I do not agree. And—and—and I object to your 'aveeng the 'all.'

'But sir, what reason can you have for refusing? The Conservatoire is not using it—there is nothing on there for a fortnight.'

'I tell you I do not wish you to geeve this concert. Everybody is in the country, you will not make a profit.'

'I am not expecting to make a profit. The object of giving this concert is simply to get myself known.'

'There is no necessity at all for you to be known. Also, for the expenses you needa some money. I don't suppose you 'ave it?'

'Yes, sir.'

'Ah, you 'ave some. And what will you play at this concert?'

'Two overtures, some pieces from an opera, my cantata *The Death of Orpheus*, and——'

'Thatta competeetion cantata? No, that I will not 'ave. It is bad, it—it is not possible to play it.'

'That was how you judged it, sir, and now it is my turn to judge. If a bad pianist couldn't accompany it, does this prove that it's unplayable by a good orchestra?'

'So you are planneeng an insult for the Academy?'

'No, sir, simply an experiment. If—as is probable—the Academy was right in declaring my score unplayable, clearly it won't be played. If on the other hand the Academy was mistaken, it will be said that I took its advice and that I have corrected the work since the competition.'

'You can only geeve your concert on a Sunday.'

'Very well, I will give it on a Sunday.'

'But the staff of the 'all, the attendants and ushers employed by the Conservatoire, it is their only free day. You don't want to keell these poor people with overwork—to—to—to keell them?'

'You must be joking, sir. Those poor people you feel so sorry for are only too glad of a chance to earn a little extra money. You would be doing them a positive disservice if you took it away from them.'

'I will not 'ave it, I will not. I will write to the Secretary to ask heem to withdraw his pairmission.'

'You're very kind, sir; but M. de La Rochefoucauld will not go back on his word. I too shall write to him and send him an exact account of our conversation. This will enable him to weigh up the arguments on both sides.'

And I did send it, as it appears above. I heard some years later from an official in the Fine Arts department that my letter in dialogue form made the Secretary laugh till he cried. Cherubini's consideration for the Conservatoire staff whom I wanted to 'kill with overwork' appealed to him particularly. He wrote back at once and, as any man of good sense would, confirmed the authorization, adding, 'You will be so kind as to show this letter to M. Cherubini, who has received the necessary orders concerning you'—an expression for which I shall always feel exquisitely grateful to him. The moment the official document arrived, I galloped off to the Conservatoire and handed it to the director, saying, 'Sir, would you please read this?' Cherubini took the letter, read it carefully, re-read it, turned green under his habitual pallor, and handed it back without a word.

That was the first scorpion I gave him in return for the whip he had chastised me with in driving me out of the library on the occasion of our first meeting.

I came away not without a certain sense of satisfaction, murmuring to myself in irreverent imitation of his dulcet tones, 'Come, sir, it's only a leetle steeng, it won't hurt much. Gently now! There may be othairs like it, eef you don't let me alone.'

19

An ineffective concert—a conductor who can't conduct—a chorus which doesn't sing

THE PLAYERS I was counting on for my orchestra having promised their aid, the chorus being engaged, the parts copied, and the hall extorted from *il burbero direttore*, I had only to find soloists and a conductor. Bloc, the conductor at the Odéon, kindly said he would direct the concert, a task I did not feel equal to myself. Duprez, who was then almost unknown (he had recently graduated from Choron's school), agreed to sing an aria from the *Francs-juges*. Alexis Dupont, although unwell, again took under his wing *The Death of Orpheus*, for which he had tried to obtain a hearing from the jury of the Institute. For the soprano and bass in the *Francs-juges* trio I had to make do with two minor singers from the Opéra who possessed neither voice nor talent.*

The general rehearsal followed the pattern of all such occasions when the orchestra plays for nothing. Many players were missing at the start and an even greater number vanished before the end. However, the two overtures, the aria and the cantata went fairly well. The introduction to the *Francs-juges* was warmly applauded by the orchestra, and the final section of the cantata made an even greater impression. Here, in a passage which had not been prescribed by the terms of the competition but which the sense of the words seemed to suggest, I had made the wind instruments, after the Bacchanal, recall the theme of Orpheus' hymn to love, accompanied by a vague murmur in the rest of the orchestra like the sound of the Hebrus 'bearing the pallid visage on its eddying flood', while a faint expiring voice uttered at long intervals the mournful cry which the river bank re-echoed: 'Eurydice! Eurydice! wretched Eurydice!'

I had had in my mind those splendid lines in the *Georgics*:

> *Tum quoque, marmorea caput a cervice revulsum,*
> *Gurgite quum medio portans Œagrius Hebrus*
> *Volveret, Eurydicen, vox ipsa et frigida lingua*
> *Ah! miseram Eurydicen, anima fugiente vocabat.*
> *Eurydicen! toto referebant flumine ripae.*†

* [Mme Lebrun, and Ferdinand Prévost. The piece was the Mélodie Pastorale from Act II.]

† [IV, 523–7: 'Even then, while the head torn from the flawless neck rolled in midstream down the paternal Hebrus, the bare voice and death-cold tongue still called with faint breath, "Eurydice, wretched Eurydice," and "Eurydice" echoed from the banks along the whole river.']

The poetic idea contained in this tone picture was inevitably lost on nine-tenths of the rather philistine audience at the rehearsal; but its strange sadness sent a shiver through the whole orchestra and it was greeted at the end with a storm of bravos. I am sorry now that I destroyed the score of the cantata; the final pages ought to have made me keep it. Apart from the Bacchanal, which the orchestra brought off with admirable verve,* the rest of the work did not go well. Dupont was hoarse and had to strain badly to produce his high notes; so much so that that evening he warned me not to count on him for the following day.

I was thus to my great disgust deprived of the satisfaction of stating in the programme: '*The Death of Orpheus*, scena for voice and orchestra, declared unplayable by the Academy of Fine Arts, played on —— May 1828.' Cherubini no doubt declined to believe the reason for my withdrawing the work and preferred to say it was because the orchestra could not get through it.

During the rehearsal of this unfortunate cantata I discovered how incompetent conductors can be who lack practical experience of grand opera, when confronted with the free rhythms and fluid style of recitative. This was Bloc's trouble. At the Odéon they performed only operas with spoken dialogue. After Orpheus' first aria there was a recitative, interspersed with recurring phrases in the orchestra, which he could not get right; certain orchestral entries defeated him every time. This prompted a periwigged old music-lover present at the rehearsal to exclaim, 'Oh, give me the old Italian cantatas any day. There's music that doesn't confuse the conductor. It plays itself.'

'Yes,' I said, 'like an old donkey that finds its own way round the treadmill.'

That was how I was beginning to make friends.

At all events the cantata was replaced by the Resurrexit from my Mass, which both chorus and orchestra knew, and the concert took place.† The two overtures and the Resurrexit were on the whole well received and were applauded. So was the aria, an

* The very passage in which the Institute's pianist had come to grief.

† [26 May 1828. The programme also included a Sacred March of the Magi.]

invocation to sleep, which Duprez, whose voice was at that time small and sweet-toned, displayed to advantage. But the trio with chorus was wretchedly sung and *without chorus*, for the choir, having missed its first entry, remained discreetly silent throughout the remainder of the piece. *The Greek Revolution*, whose style presupposes large vocal forces, left the audience cold. It was never performed again, and I eventually destroyed it.

Yet in the final account the concert proved of real use to me: first, by helping to make me known among the public and the musical profession—which, Cherubini's opinion to the contrary notwithstanding, was beginning to become 'necessary'; and secondly, by bringing me face to face with the many difficulties that confront the composer who wishes to organize performances of his music. The experience made me realize how much more I would have to do if I was fully to overcome them. It is unnecessary to add that the receipts barely covered the expense of lighting, advertising, the *poor-tax*, and my priceless chorus which had preserved such a masterly silence.

Several papers spoke enthusiastically of the concert. Fétis, who later . . . Fétis said some extremely flattering things about me at somebody's salon, hailing my appearance on the scene as a notable event.

But had these repercussions been enough to reach Miss Smithson and make her pause for an instant in the whirl of her triumphs? Alas, I learnt later that, engrossed in her brilliant task, of me and my concert, my struggles, my success, she never heard a word.*

* [The concert does not seem to have been very well attended (the *Revue musicale* reported that the hall was 'almost empty', and Berlioz—in a letter to his father—that it was 'only two-thirds full'). None the less, as he remarks, it achieved one of its main objects. Those who came included many of the important musical personalities of the day, and the players were enthusiastic. Fétis, editor of the *Revue musicale*, published a favourable notice (III, 1828, 422–4): the young composer sometimes went too far in the ardour of his originality, but 'he has great natural talent, his style is virile and energetic, and his ideas are often felicitous'. The *Figaro*, though counselling greater moderation, was full of encouragement (and especially impressed by *Waverley*), and the *Voleur* urged him to 'live up to the brilliant expectations that we have of him'.]

20

The advent of Beethoven at the Conservatoire—jealous reservations on the part of French composers—impression produced on Lesueur by the Symphony in C minor—he sticks to his system

IN AN ARTIST'S life one thunderclap sometimes follows swiftly on another, as in those outsize storms in which the clouds, charged to bursting with electric energy, seem to hurl the lightning back and forth and blow the whirlwind.

I had just had the successive revelations of Shakespeare and Weber. Now at another point on the horizon I saw the giant form of Beethoven rear up. The shock was almost as great as that of Shakespeare had been. Beethoven opened before me a new world of music, as Shakespeare had revealed a new universe of poetry.

The Conservatoire Concert Society had recently been founded* under the fervent and vigorous direction of Habeneck. With all his serious defects as a musician and his shortcomings in the service of his idol, he was a sincere and even an able conductor; and it is only just to acknowledge that his alone is the glory of having popularized Beethoven's works in Paris. It is thanks to him that this great institution, today famous throughout the civilized world, was founded at all. It was a hard struggle; and before he could secure adequate performances, he had to persuade a large body of players to share his enthusiasm for totally unfamiliar music which had the reputation of being eccentric and difficult to play; he had to overcome an indifference which turned to hostility at the prospect of endless rehearsals and unremunerative toil stretching ahead.

Not the least of Habeneck's troubles was the steady undercurrent of opposition from French and Italian composers, who regarded the whole idea with malicious and ill-concealed disapproval. They had no desire to see official homage paid to a German whose works seemed to them misbegotten monstrosities and yet at the same time a threat to their own style of composition. I have

* [15 February 1828, by decree of the Secretary of Fine Arts. The first concert (9 March) opened with the Eroica, which was repeated on 23 March. The Fifth Symphony followed on 13 April.]

heard them airing the most abominable nonsense about those marvels of inspiration and technical skill.

In this connection my teacher, Lesueur, an honest man without envy in his nature and devoted to his art, but the prisoner of musical dogmas which I must be allowed to describe as sheer delusion, let slip a significant remark. Although he lived a somewhat retired life, buried in his work, it was not long before he became aware of the stir which the inauguration of the Conservatoire concerts and the performances of Beethoven's symphonies was causing in the Paris musical world. His surprise was all the greater because like most of his fellow-academicians he considered instrumental music an inferior branch of the art, respectable certainly but of limited importance, in which Haydn and Mozart had in any case gone as far as it was possible to go.

Like the rest of them—like Berton, who regarded the whole of modern German music with pitying contempt; like Boïeldieu, who did not know what to think of it all and expressed a childlike astonishment at any harmonic progression beyond the three chords he had been using all his life; like Cherubini, who choked back his bile and did not openly vent it on a composer whose success exasperated him and undermined his most cherished theories; like Paër, the crafty Italian, who claimed to have known Beethoven, and told stories about him more or less discreditable to the great man and favourable to himself; like Catel, who had disagreed with music, and lived only for his garden and his collection of rose-trees; like Kreutzer, who shared Berton's contempt for everything that originated beyond the Rhine—Lesueur took no notice. Confronted with the immense enthusiasm of musicians in general and of me in particular, he shut his ears and carefully avoided the Conservatoire concerts. To have gone would have meant committing himself to a personal opinion of Beethoven; it would have meant being physically involved in the tremendous excitement which Beethoven aroused. This was just what Lesueur, without admitting it, did not wish to happen. However, I kept on at him, solemnly pointing out that when something as important as this occurred in our art—a completely new style on an unprecedented scale—it was his duty to find out about it and judge for himself; and in the end he yielded and let himself be dragged off to the Conservatoire one day when the C minor Symphony was being performed. He wanted to give it an unbiased hearing, without distractions of any kind, so he dismissed me and sat by himself at the back of one of the ground-floor boxes, among people he did not know. When it was over I came down from the floor above, eager to know what effect this extraordinary work had had on him and what he thought of it.

I found him in the corridor, striding along with flushed face. 'Well, master?'

'Ouf! I'm going outside—I need some air. It's unbelievable, wonderful! It so moved and disturbed me and turned me upside down that when I came out of my box and went to put my hat on, for a moment I didn't know where my head was. Leave me alone. I'll see you tomorrow.'

I was triumphant. The next day I hurried round to see him. The conversation at once turned to the masterpiece which had stirred us so profoundly. Lesueur let me talk on for some time, assenting in a rather constrained manner to my exclamations of enthusiasm. But it was easy to see that my companion was no longer the man who had spoken to me the day before, and that he found the subject painful. I persisted, however, until I had dragged from him a further acknowledgement of how deeply Beethoven's symphony had moved him; at which he suddenly shook his head and smiled in a curious way and said, 'All the same, that sort of music should not be written.'

'Don't worry, master,' I retorted, 'there is not much danger that it will.'

Poor human nature! Poor master! What a world of regret, of stubborn resentment, jealousy, dread of the unknown, confession of incapacity lies behind it and all such remarks made by countless men in similar situations! To say, 'That sort of music should not be written,' after having felt its power and been forced to recognize its beauty, is as much as to say that you yourself would never do such a thing—because you know you couldn't even if you wanted to.

Haydn said much the same of Beethoven, whom he insisted on calling a 'great pianist'. Grétry wrote silly aphorisms of a similar kind about Mozart, accusing him of placing the statue in the orchestra pit and the pedestal on the stage. Handel claimed that his cook was more of a musician than Gluck. Rossini's comment on Weber is that his music gives him colic.

In the case of Handel and Rossini, their antipathy to Gluck and Weber comes not, I think, from any motive of envy but simply from the natural inability of those great pot-bellies to understand men of such feeling. But the fierce opposition that Spontini aroused, which for long ranged the whole French school and the majority of Italian musicians against him, was certainly a fruit of that complex emotion whose meanness and absurdity La Fontaine fixed once and for all in the fable of 'The Fox and the Grapes'.

Lesueur's dogged refusal to accept the evidence of his senses finally convinced me of the hollowness of the theories he had been striving to instil into me; and from that moment I abandoned the old high road and made my own way across country, over hills and valleys and through woods and Fields. But I did my best to hide my 'apostasy' from him. He did not find out till much later, when he heard the new works which I had carefully avoided showing him.

I shall come back to Habeneck and the Conservatoire Society when I have occasion to speak of my relations with that able but limited and unreliable conductor.

21
Calamity—I become a critic

I MUST NOW DESCRIBE the circumstances by which I came to be caught in the toils of criticism. Humbert Ferrand, with Cazalès and Carné—names quite well known in the political world of the time—had recently founded the *Revue européenne*, a periodical designed to uphold their religious and monarchical views. To complete their staff, they needed a few more people to join them.

Humbert Ferrand suggested that I should look after the musical criticism. I told him I was no writer and my prose would be terrible. I would never have the face to do it. 'You're wrong,' he replied. 'I know from your letters how you write. You'll soon get the hang of it. Besides, we'll go over your articles before they're printed, and point out anything that needs altering. Come and see Carné; he'll discuss it with you and tell you what terms we can offer.'

I began to see the attractions of the idea. What a weapon I would have for defending the beautiful and attacking whatever seemed to me opposed to it! There was also the consideration that it would add a little to my income, which was still very meagre. I decided I would do it. Ferrand took me to see Carné and it was all arranged.

I have never had much confidence in myself until I have actually tried my strength; but in this case the feeling had been intensified by an unfortunate foray which I had already made into the field of musical polemics. It was at the time when the journals which represented Rossini were in full cry, blaspheming against Gluck and Spontini and the whole school of dramatic expression and good sense. The lengths to which they went to vaunt Rossini and his purely sensuous art, the unbelievably preposterous arguments used to demonstrate that music, dramatic or otherwise, has only one purpose, to charm the ear, and is in no way concerned with the expression of feelings and passions, and a whole host of arrogant fatuities pronounced by people who did not know the first thing about music, threw me into a paroxysm of rage.

One day, reading the ramblings of one of these lunatics, I was seized by the desire to answer them.

I needed a reputable platform. I wrote to Michaud, editor and proprietor of the *Quotidienne*, a paper then rather fashionable, and explained what I wanted, what my opinions were and what I hoped to achieve, promising to fight cleanly as well as hard. My letter, half-serious, half-playful, pleased him and his reply was prompt and favourable: my proposal was accepted and my first article awaited with impatience. I leapt for joy and thought, 'I've got you now, you wretches.' But I was wrong. I had not got anybody or anything. My ignorance of the art of writing, of the ways of the world and the conventions of journalism, coupled with the violence of my musical passions, was too much for me. I blundered hopelessly. The article which I took to Michaud, besides being inadequately thought out and badly put together, went far beyond the bounds of newspaper warfare, uninhibited though it is reckoned to be. Michaud listened while I read it to him. He was aghast at my extravagance. 'All this may be true,' he said, 'but you've gone quite mad. I couldn't possibly publish a piece like that in the

Quotidienne.' I went away, promising to rewrite it. Then a reaction set in. I felt too lazy and disgusted at the thought of all the evasions and compromises required, and I did nothing more about it.

When I speak of laziness, I mean the apathy which always comes over me at the prospect of writing prose. I have sat up many nights over a score. I can stay at my writing-table for eight hours at a stretch, engrossed in the labour of instrumentation, without even wanting to change my position. But it is a struggle to get myself to begin to write a page of prose, and before I have done a dozen lines (except on very rare occasions) I get up, pace the room, stare out of the window into the street, pick up the first book that comes to hand, in short do anything to fight off the boredom and fatigue which rapidly descend on me. It can take eight or nine attempts before I am rid of an article for the *Journal des débats*. I have to set aside two days for it, even when the subject excites or amuses me. And then, the blots and the scratchings-out! The first draft is like a battlefield.

Musical composition is a natural activity for me and a pleasure, prose-writing a burden.

Nevertheless, prodded and egged on by Ferrand, I wrote some pieces for the *Revue européenne*, enthusiastic appraisals of Gluck, Spontini and Beethoven. After I had gone over them with Carné's help, they were published and were quite well received.* Thus I began to discover the difficulties of this hazardous trade which has come to play such a large and lamentable part in my life. The reader will see how impossible it has become for me to extricate myself, and in how many ways, in France and elsewhere, it has affected my career as an artist.

22

The composition prize—the regulations of the Academy of Fine Arts—I come second

RAVAGED NIGHT AND day by my Shakespearean love, which the discovery of Beethoven's music, so far from alleviating, seemed only to make more painfully intense; my sole occupation

* [The first appeared on 21 April 1829. About the same time he became a contributor to the *Berliner allgemeine musikalische Zeitung*.]

an occasional piece of musical journalism, laborious and half-formed; perpetually in a dream, silent to the point of dumbness, unsociable, unkempt in appearance, unbearable alike to myself and my friends, I reached the month of June in the year 1828 and for the third time put my name down for the examination at the Institute. I was again admitted, and won second prize.

The advantages which this distinction confers are a laureate crown publicly presented, a gold medal of modest value, a free pass to all the opera houses, and a good chance of winning first prize the following year.

The first prize carries far more substantial privileges. The winner is guaranteed an annual grant of three thousand francs for a period of five years on condition that he spends the first two of them at the French Academy in Rome and the third in visiting Germany; the remainder he receives in Paris while he does what he can to establish himself and keep the wolf from the door. The description which follows is a condensed version of what I wrote in various papers, fifteen or sixteen years ago, about the curious organization of this competition.

The government which instituted the Prix de Rome* had a double purpose: to ascertain who were the most promising young composers, and to foster their talent by enabling them, by means of a grant, to devote themselves for five years exclusively to the study of composition. These were the objects. As for the methods used to achieve them, the system described below was still in force a few years ago. Things have changed a little since then, but only very slightly.†

To most readers the facts I am about to cite will no doubt appear highly improbable; but having obtained the second and subsequently the first prize, I set down nothing that I did not see for myself and am not perfectly sure of the truth of. The fact that I was a prizewinner entitles me to speak my mind fully without fear of people's attributing to bitterness and wounded vanity opinions which spring from deep personal conviction and love of art.

* [In 1803.]

† They are now quite different. The Emperor has lately rescinded that particular clause in the statutes of the Institute. It is no longer the Academy of Fine Arts which awards the music prize (1865).

The freedom with which I have already expressed myself on the subject has drawn a rebuke from Cherubini—most academic of academicians past, present or future, and consequently the most irked by my remarks—who claims that in attacking the Academy I am 'biting the hand that fed me'. Had I not won the prize he could not have accused me of ingratitude; but he, and many others, would have set me down as a failure avenging my own defeat. The conclusion would seem to be that there is no way for me to approach this sacred topic. Yet I do approach it, and I shall treat it like any other, without equivocation.

The competition, as established in the statutes, was (and is) open to any native-born or naturalized Frenchman under the age of thirty.

When the date had been fixed, would-be candidates entered their names at the Institute office. They had first to sit a preliminary examination, the object of which was to pick out the five or six most advanced pupils.

The subject of the competition proper was required to be a large-scale scena on some serious theme for one or two voices and orchestra. In order to show that they possessed the feeling for melody and dramatic expression, the practical knowledge of orchestration and the other skills needed to make a reasonable attempt at a work of this kind, the candidates were asked to write a vocal fugue. Each fugue had to be signed.

On the following day the music section of the Institute met, considered the fugues, and made their choice—not always a strictly impartial one, seeing that a certain number of the papers, duly signed, were the work of their own pupils.

The votes having been counted and the competitors nominated, the latter were summoned back soon afterwards to receive the text they were to set to music. The Permanent Secretary of the Academy dictated the classical poem, which usually began:

'E'en now the rosy-fingered dawn appears'
or 'E'en now doth Nature greet returning day'
or 'E'en now with lustre soft th' horizon glows'
or 'E'en now blond Phoebus' shining car draws near'
or 'E'en now in purple pomp the mountains decked'...

Armed with this luminous effusion the candidates were then shut up, with a piano, in separate rooms known as boxes, until such time as they had completed their scores. At eleven in the morning and six in the evening the porter who had charge of the keys of all the boxes let them out, and they reassembled and took their meals together; but they were forbidden to leave the Institute building.

Everything sent from the outside world—letters, documents, books, clean clothes—was meticulously searched, to prevent the slightest aid or advice from reaching the candidates. Yet they were officially permitted to receive visitors in the courtyard of the Institute every evening from six till eight and even to invite their friends to convivial dinners at which any amount of communication could go on, verbal or written, between the claret and the champagne. The time allowed for the competition was three weeks, but any candidate who finished earlier was free to go, after handing in his manuscript, signed as always and with the pages numbered.

When all the scores had been delivered, the grave and reverend signors of the jury met once again, this time with the addition of two members from the other sections of the Institute: a sculptor and a painter, for example, or a sculptor and an engraver, or an architect and a painter, or even two engravers or two painters or two architects or two sculptors: the important thing was that they should not be musicians. They had votes and were there to pronounce on an art that was not their own.

The scenas—written, as I have indicated, for orchestra—were performed one after the other, *reduced for piano*, by a solitary accompanist; a practice which remains in force to this day.

Does anyone seriously maintain that one can judge the true quality of an orchestral work emasculated in this fashion? Nothing could be further from the truth. The piano can give an impression of the orchestra when one has already heard the work complete; memory, set off by the act of hearing it again, supplies what is missing; the music affects you by recollection. But with a new work, and in music's present state of development, this is impossible. A score like Sacchini's *Oedipe* or any other work of that school, innocent of orchestration as it is, might lose little in such an encounter. But any modern piece—assuming the composer has made use of the resources at his disposal—comes into a different category altogether. Try performing the Communion March from Cherubini's Coronation Mass on the piano. What happens to those exquisite long-drawn notes on the wind instruments which induce in the listener a strange ecstasy, the marvellous interweaving of flutes and clarinets on which practically the whole effect depends? They disappear completely, the piano being able neither to sustain nor to swell a note. Try accompanying Agamemnon's aria from *Iphigénie en Aulide* on the piano. At the words:

J'entends retentir dans mon sein
Le cri plaintif de la nature

there is a wonderfully touching solo for the oboe. Play it on the piano, and in place of the poignant, plaintive effect Gluck intended, you hear so many disconnected notes like the separate strokes of a bell. The whole idea, the essence and genius of the passage in fact, is destroyed or falsified. I am not even speaking of large-scale orchestral effects—the piquant contrasts produced by strings and wind in juxtaposition, the characteristic tone-colours which distinguish brass from woodwind, the mysterious power and grandeur of percussion instruments played softly and the tremendous impact of their forte, the striking sonorities achieved when two sources of sound are placed at some distance from each other, and hundreds of other examples, superfluous to enumerate, in which the fallacy of the system stands revealed in all its absurdity and injustice. The piano, in short, by destroying all sense of instrumentation, places every composer on the same level. The master of the orchestra is shrunk to the size of the fumbling incompetent who lacks the first idea of that branch of his art. The fumbler can write trombones for clarinets and ophicleides for bassoons, can make huge blunders and not even know the compass of the various instruments, and the expert can produce a splendid orchestral work, without it being possible from such a rendering to tell the difference. The piano, for the orchestral composer, is a guillotine which chops off the aristocrat's head and from which only the poor have nothing to fear.

At all events, when the scores have been thus performed, the voting takes place (I use the present tense since nothing has changed in that respect) and the prize is awarded. You imagine that concludes the matter? Not a bit! A week later all sections of the Academy of Fine Arts assemble to pronounce the definitive verdict. This time an imposing jury of from thirty to thirty-five members sits in judgment, made up of painters, sculptors, architects, engravers of medals and engravers in copper. Nor are the six musicians excluded. They are able to compensate for the shortcomings of the piano accompaniment to a certain extent by going through the score; but this is a crutch not available to the other academicians, who cannot read music.

When the performers—singer and pianist—have once again discharged each piece in the same fashion as before, the urn of destiny is handed round, the ballots are counted, and the judgment which the music section arrived at a week before is either confirmed, modified or quashed by majority vote.

Thus the prize for music is awarded by men who are not musicians and who have not even had the chance of hearing an adequate performance of the works from among which, by a grotesque regulation, they are required to make their choice.

Justice compels me to add that if the painters, engravers and the rest pronounce on music, the musicians get their own back by turning up to judge the painting and engraving competitions, at which the prizes are again awarded by the majority decision of all sections of the Academy of Fine Arts combined. But I know in my heart that had I the honour to belong to that learned body, I should find it hard to give my reasons for voting for a particular engraver or architect, and would be able to show my impartiality only in choosing the most deserving candidate by lot.

On the day of the prize-giving the cantata chosen by painters, sculptors and engravers is performed complete and in its entirety. It seems just a trifle late. It might perhaps have been better to convene the orchestra before giving judgment. The money spent on this belated performance is used to little purpose, for the decision, once taken, cannot be reversed. But the Academy is curious: it would like to hear the work which it has dignified with the prize. A thoroughly natural desire!

23
The Institute usher—his revelations

In my time there was an old porter at the Institute called Pingard, whose indignation at all this harlequinade was most comical. It was the duty of this excellent fellow, while the competition was on, to lock us up in our boxes and let us out again, morning and evening, and to supervise our activities during visiting hours. He also fulfilled the function of usher to the academicians and was therefore present at every session, public and private, where he had made a number of interesting observations.

At the age of sixteen he had embarked as a cabin-boy on a frigate and had visited most of the Sunda Islands. On Java, where they had to put in for some time, he had, he said, thanks to a strong constitution—ninth in the family though he was—survived a virulent epidemic of fever which carried off the rest of the crew.

I have always liked old travellers, provided they have tales of far-off countries to tell me. When they do I can listen to them for hours in perfect contentment and without ever tiring of their digressions. I gladly follow them right to the end of their most intricate episodes within episodes; and when the narrator at length attempts to pick up the thread again but cannot find it and strikes his forehead and cries, 'God damn it, where was I?', I love putting him back on the right course and supplying him with the name he was looking for or the date he had forgotten; I get a real satisfaction from hearing him exclaim delightedly, 'Ah yes, that was it—well, as I was saying.' So old Pingard and I were firm friends. He approved of me in the first place because of the pleasure I found in talking to him about Batavia, the Celebes, Amboyna, Coromandel, Borneo and Sumatra, and because I questioned him closely about Javanese women, whose love is fatal to Europeans and whose society the young dog cultivated with such vigour that at one point it seemed sheer exhaustion would do what Asiatic cholera had failed to accomplish. I went up further in his estimation one day, when we were talking of Syria, by mentioning

Volney.* 'Oh, that was a fine man. Count de Volney, so natural —he always wore blue woollen stockings.' But his delight knew no bounds when I happened to ask him if he had known the famous explorer Levaillant.

'Mr Levaillant?' he cried eagerly. 'Know him? I should think I did. Look here: one day at the Cape of Good Hope I was strolling about, whistling to myself; as a matter of fact I was waiting for a little negress, she'd agreed to meet me on the shore because, between ourselves, there were reasons why it was better for her not to come to my place. I'll tell you why. You see——'

'Quite, quite, but go on about Levaillant.'

'Yes, of course. Well, one day at the Cape of Good Hope I was strolling about, whistling, when a big man, sunburnt and with a beard like a sapper, turned round and stared at me. He'd heard me whistling in French, that must have been how he knew me. "Hey, you young rogue," says he, "are you French?" "I should bloody well think I am," say I. "I'm from Givet, in the Ardennes. Mr Méhul's part of the country."† "Ah, you're a Frenchman." "Yes." "Ah..." and he turned away. It was Mr Levaillant. Oh yes, I knew him all right.'

So old Pingard was my friend, and he treated me as his by telling me things that he would have never dreamed of disclosing to anyone else. I remember a very spirited conversation we had the day I won the second prize.‡ That year the subject was an episode from Tasso: Herminia putting on Clorinda's armour and, under cover of the disguise, leaving the walls of Jerusalem behind her to seek out the wounded Tancred and nurse him with the devotion of her loyal and tragic love.§

* [Well-known traveller whose *Voyage en Egypte et Syrie* (1787), with its meticulous observation of topography and local culture, served as a kind of guide-book for Napoleon's Middle Eastern expedition.]

† Méhul was from Givet, though I doubt if he was born at the time Pingard claimed to have spoken of him with Levaillant.

‡ [2 August 1828.]

§ [The French text was by Vieillard. Fétis in the *Revue musicale* complained of 'ces cantates usées et décrépites' and pointed out that it was the fifth time that this particular subject had been set in the twenty-five years of the competition's existence.]

The third aria—there are always three arias in these Institute cantatas (to begin with, the inevitable dawn, then the first recitative followed by the first aria, the second recitative followed by the second aria, the third recitative followed by the third aria, all for the same character)—the third aria included these four lines:

God of the Christians, whom I seek to ignore,
Thou whom I once disdainfully did spurn,
Thy might acknowledging I Thee implore,
Upon my feeble plaint Thy pity turn.

I had the effrontery to suppose that although the aria was marked agitato these four lines ought to be treated as a prayer, since the trembling Queen of Antioch would hardly be expected to implore the God of the Christians with melodramatic cries to the accompaniment of a raging orchestra. So I made it a prayer; and without doubt if there was anything good in my score, it was that andante.

When I arrived at the Institute on the evening of Judgment Day to learn my fate and discover if the painters, sculptors, engravers of medals and engravers in copper had settled whether I was a good musician or a bad one, I met Pingard on the stairs.

'Well,' I asked, 'what have they decided?'

'Oh, hallo, Berlioz. Heavens, I'm glad you're here. I've been looking for you.'

'What have I got? Hurry up and tell me. First, second, honourable mention, or nothing at all?'

'Look here. Oh, I'm still feeling quite shaken. Would you believe it, you were only two votes short of the first prize.'

'What! That's the first I've heard of it.'

'Wait till I tell you. You've got second prize all right; another two votes and you'd have had first. Look here, it's really upset me—because, you know, I'm not a painter or an architect or an engraver of medals so of course I know nothing about music, but I'll be damned if that "God of the Christians" of yours didn't fair churn me up inside. And, by thunder—look here, if I'd run into you just then, I'd—I'd have stood you a small coffee.'

'Thanks awfully, Pingard. You're very kind. I admire your taste. Besides, haven't you been on the Coromandel coast?'

'I certainly have. Why?'

'And to Java?'

'Yes, but——'

'And Sumatra?'

'Yes.'

'Borneo?'

'Yes.'

'You knew Levaillant well?'

'I should say I did—hand in glove with him.'

'You've often talked with Volney?'

'The Count de Volney who wore blue stockings?'

'That's the one.'

'Absolutely.'

'Well, then, you're an excellent judge of music.'

'How's that?'

'What a question! Simply that if anyone happens to say to you, "What right have you to judge between one composer and another, are you a painter, an engraver in copper, an architect or a sculptor?" you can reply, "No, I am a—er—a traveller, a sailor, a friend of Levaillant and Volney. What more do you want?" But tell me, what happened at the session?'

'Oh well, look here, don't speak to me of it. It's always the same thing. If I had thirty children, devil take me if I'd let one of them be an artist. You see, I watch what goes on. You don't know what a bloody bazaar it is in there. They get together and bargain over their votes; they even sell 'em. Look here, once when it was the painting competition, I heard Mr Lethière asking Mr Cherubini to vote for one of his pupils. "Come," says he, "you won't refuse an old comrade. Besides, this pupil of mine is really talented, his picture's very good." "No," says the other, "I won't. Your pupil promised me an album of drawings that my wife very much wanted, and he's not done her so much as a tree. I'm not voting for him."

' "That's very wrong of you," says Mr Lethière, "I vote for your people and you won't vote for mine." "No, I won't." "Look, I'll do you the album myself; there, I can't say more than that." "That's different. What's your pupil called? I never can remember. Let me have his first name as well and the number of the picture, so I won't go and make a mistake. Let me write it all down." "Pingard!" "Sir?" "A pencil and some paper." "Here, sir!" They go off into the recess by the window and write down something, and as they come back I hear the musician say, "All right, I'll vote for him." Well now, isn't that shocking? If I had a son in that competition and they played him tricks like that, it would be enough to make me throw myself out of the window.'

'Come on, Pingard, calm down and tell me what happened today.'

'Well, as I was saying, you've got second prize and you were only two votes off first. When Mr Dupont had finished singing your cantata, they started to write down their verdicts and I brought the hurn.* A musician near me was whispering to an architect, "Don't vote for him—he's a hopeless case. That depraved fellow Beethoven is all he cares about. They'll never get him back on to the right path."

'"You think so?" says the architect. "All the same——"

'"Oh, I'm certain. Go and ask Cherubini. You'll surely accept the great man's opinion. He'll tell you, just as I have, that the young man is mad—Beethoven has disturbed his brain."

'Excuse me a moment,' said Pingard, breaking off his story, 'but who is this Mr Beethoven? He's not a member of the Institute, but everybody's talking about him.'

'No, he's not a member of the Institute. He's a German. Go on.'

'Ah well, it was soon over. When I handed the hurn to the architect I saw that he voted for No. 4 and not for you, so there you are. Suddenly one of the musicians gets up and says, "Gentlemen, before we go any further I must tell you that in the second part of the work we have just heard there is some very ingenious orchestration; the piano can't give any idea of it, but it should make an excellent effect."

'"What are you babbling about?" retorts another musician. "Your pupil hasn't kept to the instructions. He has written two agitatos instead of one, and in the middle he's stuck in a prayer that has no business there. Our regulations can't be disregarded like this. We must make an example of him."

* This was how old Pingard always referred to the sacred vessel used on these occasions.

'"That's not fair. What does the Permanent Secretary say?"

'"I think our friend is a little severe, and we may forgive your pupil the liberties he has taken. But it is important the jury should know what these qualities are which you say could not be realized on the piano."

'"No, no," says Mr Cherubini, "it's quite untrue. This alleged triumph of orchestration doesn't exist. It's just a muddle, it doesn't begin to make sense, and would sound frightful with the orchestra."

'"Well, you hear that, gentlemen," say all the painters, sculptors, architects and engravers. "We can only go by what we hear, and if you can't agree——" "Yes!" "No!" "But for heaven's sake!" "What the devil——" "I tell you that——" "Nonsense!" They were all shouting at once, and Mr Regnault and two other painters got bored and went off, saying they declined to give an opinion and weren't going to vote at all. Then the votes in the hurn were counted, and you were two short. That's why you've only got second prize.'

'Thank you, my dear Pingard. But tell me, was it like that in the Academy at the Cape of Good Hope?'

'Go on with you, you're joking. An Academy at the Cape? A Hottentot Institute? You know quite well there isn't one.'

'Really? Nor among the Indians of Coromandel?'

'None there neither.'

'Nor among the Malayans?'

'No.'

'What, no Academy in the East at all?'

'Certainly not.'

'The Orientals are much to be pitied.'

'It doesn't worry them.'

'The barbarians!'

Thereupon I parted from the old porter, usher and pillar of the Institute, thinking what a good thing it would be to send the Academy to civilize the island of Borneo. I was already ruminating a plan which I wanted to lay before the academicians themselves, which would commit them, like Pingard, to a short stroll on the Cape of Good Hope. But we Westerners are such egoists, with so little feeling for humanity, that those poor Hottentots and

Malayans without an Academy of their own occupied me seriously for only an hour or two; by the next day I had forgotten all about them. Two years later, as will be seen, I won first prize. In the meantime old Pingard had died. It was a great pity. If he had heard my 'Burning of the Palace of Sardanapalus' he might have stood me a large coffee.

24

Still Miss Smithson—a benefit performance —cruel accidents of fate

AFTER THE COMPETITION and the subsequent distribution of prizes,* I relapsed into the gloomy inertia which had become my normal state. I was still the same dark planet revolving obscurely round its sun—so radiant then, so sadly destined to burn out. (The beautiful Estelle, the *stella montis*, star of my dawn, had vanished without trace, lost in the infinities of space and the high noon of her dazzling rival. I never dreamed she would appear above my horizon again.) I avoided going near the English theatre and averted my gaze from the pictures of Miss Smithson that were displayed in all the bookshop windows. I wrote to her, however, but without getting a word in reply. After the first few letters, which had not so much touched as alarmed her, she told her maid not to accept any more, and nothing would alter her decision. The English season was now nearing its end. There was talk of the whole company going to Holland, and Miss Smithson's final appearances were advertised. I deliberately kept away. To see her play Juliet or Ophelia again would, as I have said, have been more than I could bear. But when I heard that two acts of *Romeo*, with Miss Smithson and Abbot, were to figure in a benefit performance organized for the French actor Huet, I had a sudden fancy to have my name on the playbill alongside that of the great tragédienne. I hoped to score a success under her very eyes; and, full of this childish idea, I went to see the manager of the Opéra-Comique to ask him to add an overture of mine† to the programme. The conductor was agreeable and the manager consented. When I

* [4 October 1828. In the interval, he had spent three weeks with his family.]

† [*Waverley*.]

got to the theatre for the rehearsal, the English actors were just finishing; they had reached the tomb scene. I came in just as the frantic Romeo was bearing Juliet in his arms. My glance fell involuntarily on the Shakespearean scene. I gave a shriek and fled, wringing my hands. Juliet saw me and heard my cry. She was afraid. Pointing me out to the actors who were on the stage with her, she warned them to beware of that 'gentleman with the eyes that bode no good'.

When I came back an hour later the stage was empty. The orchestra assembled and my overture was rehearsed. I listened like one in a dream, without making the least comment. But the players applauded the work, and this revived my hopes that the public would like it, which would in turn have an effect upon Miss Smithson. Fool that I was! It is hardly to be believed that I could have been so profoundly ignorant of the world I lived in.

At a benefit performance in France an overture—be it the overture to *Freischütz* or *The Magic Flute*—is regarded as a curtain-raiser, and the audience takes not the slightest notice of it. Besides, even if it received an attentive hearing, it could not be expected to make much impression, performed out of context by a small theatre orchestra like that of the Opéra-Comique. In any case, the great actors who play for a fellow-actor's benefit turn up at the theatre when they are needed and not before; they barely know what the rest of the programme consists of and are not in the least interested. Far from hanging about in the wings listening to something which cannot concern them, they go straight in and get dressed. It had not occurred to me that even if the improbable happened and my overture, despite the odds against it, made a hit and was loudly encored, Miss Smithson in her dressing-room, thinking over her part while the dresser got her ready, would not even be aware of it. Or supposing she was, what then? Hearing the applause, she would ask what it was for. 'It's nothing, madame, it's an overture—they're going to play it again.' Besides, whether or not she found out who the composer was, a success on this exiguous scale was not going to transform indifference into love. Nothing could be more obvious.

My overture was well played and quite well received but not encored; and Miss Smithson remained in entire ignorance of it.

After a fresh triumph in her favourite role, she left for Holland the next day. By pure chance (though she could never believe it) I had taken lodgings in the rue Richelieu, at No. 96, almost opposite her apartment at the corner of the rue Neuve-Saint-Marc.

I had been lying since the previous evening crushed, moribund on my bed, when at three in the afternoon I got up and went mechanically to the window and looked out. By one of those malignant freaks of fate, at that precise moment I saw Miss Smithson get into her carriage and drive off on her way to Amsterdam.

It is difficult to put into words what I suffered—the longing that was tearing my heart out by the roots, the dreadful loneliness in an empty universe, the agonies that thrilled through me as if the blood were running ice-cold in my veins, the disgust with living, the impossibility of dying. Shakespeare himself never described this torture; but he counts it, in *Hamlet*, among the most terrible of all the evils of existence.

I had stopped composing; my mind seemed to become feebler as my feelings grew more intense. I did nothing. One power was left me—to suffer.

25

My third competition at the Institute—no first prize awarded—a curious conversation with Boïeldieu—soothing music

WHEN JUNE CAME round I once more entered the academic lists. This time I had hopes of being finally done with it. My success was generally predicted. Even the members of the music section were saying that I was sure to get first prize. I had a great advantage over my fellow-competitors. None of them had done anything of note. I, on the other hand, had obtained a second prize. I was like a crowned head among so many bourgeois. I told myself that I was bound to win, and I reasoned—disastrously, as experience soon showed—that since they had already decided to give me the prize, there was no point in cramping my style as I had done the year before and writing their kind of music. Why not let myself go and write my own kind—something from the heart? I would take my task seriously and compose a really good cantata.

The subject was 'Cleopatra after the Battle of Actium'. The Queen of Egypt clasps the asp to her bosom and dies in convulsions; but before dying, she invokes the spirits of the Pharaohs and in holy fear demands to know if she, a queen of crimes and dissipations, may hope to enter those mighty vaults erected to the shades of monarchs distinguished for their fame and virtue.

Here was an idea worth expressing in music. I had often in my imagination conceived a musical equivalent of Juliet's wonderful monologue, 'How if, when I am laid into the tomb', a passage that had something in common, at least in its sense of dread, with the feelings contained in the invocation which our French rhymester had put into the mouth of Cleopatra. I was mad enough to write the line, in English, at the head of my score. This for a start was an unpardonable crime to Voltairean academicians like my examiners.

The music for this scene came easily to me. I wrote what I believe was an imposing piece, the rhythm strikingly original, the enharmonic progressions creating a rich and sombre effect, and the melody unfolding slowly and dramatically in a long sustained crescendo. I afterwards used it unchanged for the unison Chorus of Shades in my monodrama *Lélio*.

I have performed it at my concerts in Germany and know how it sounds. I cannot now remember what the rest of the cantata was like, but on the strength of this piece alone I think it deserved first prize. That was precisely why it did not get it. None of the other cantatas got it either.

The jury decided to award no first prize at all that year rather than give official encouragement to a young composer who 'betrayed such dangerous tendencies'. The day following this verdict, I met Boïeldieu on the boulevard.* I give the conversation word for word; it was too remarkable for me to have forgotten it.

When he saw me, he cried out, 'My dear boy, what have you done? You had the prize in your hands and you simply threw it away.'

'I assure you, sir, I did my best.'

'That is exactly what we have against you. You should not have done your best. Your best is the enemy of the good. How can I be

* [2 August 1829.]

expected to approve of such things when you know that what I like most is soothing music?'

'Sir, it's a little difficult to write soothing music for an Egyptian queen who has been bitten by a poisonous snake and is dying a painful death in an agony of remorse.'

'Oh, I know you have an answer—you always do. But that proves nothing. It is always possible to be graceful.'

'Gladiators could die gracefully, but not Cleopatra. She hadn't the knack—it was not her way. Besides, she wasn't dying in public.'

'You exaggerate. We were not asking you to make her sing a quadrille. Then, what need was there to go and use such extraordinary harmonies in your invocation to the Pharaohs? I'm not much of a harmonist, you know, and I must own that those unearthly chords of yours were beyond me.'

I bowed silently; I could hardly make the obvious rejoinder: 'Is it my fault that you are not much of a harmonist?'

'And then,' he went on, 'why do you bring that absolutely unheard-of rhythm into your accompaniment?'

'I was not aware, sir, that one should avoid using new procedures when one had the good luck to hit on one, and it suited the character of the piece.'

'But my dear fellow, Madame Dabadie is a very fine musician, and yet one could see it took all her intelligence and powers of concentration to get through your cantata safely.'

'I see. This is also new to me. Music is meant to be performed without intelligence or concentration?'

'Ah, well, you've always got an answer, haven't you? Goodbye, take this lesson to heart and be more sensible next year, and meanwhile come and see me and we'll talk it over. I shall take you on again—like a good "French gentleman".' And he went off, very pleased with his exit line, as the comedy writers say. (To appreciate its subtlety, which was worthy of Elleviou himself,* it should be realized that he was, as it were, quoting from one of his own works, *Jean de Paris*, in which this courtly phrase is set to music.)

* A famous actor at the Opéra-Comique who played the typical French gentleman of the Empire.

The artless Boïeldieu had merely been expressing current French ideas about the art of music. Yes, that was it, soothing music was what the general public in Paris wanted, even in the most violent situations; music that was not too dramatic, but lucid, rather colourless, safely predictable, innocent of unheard-of rhythms or harmonies or new procedures of any sort, modest in its demands on the intelligence and concentration of performer and listener alike: a 'French gentleman's' art, dressed in tights and top boots, never carried away, always correct, lively, urbane, chivalrous, pleasure-loving, Parisian.

A few years ago they wanted something different and not much better. Now they don't know what they want, or rather they don't want anything at all.

What the devil was the good Lord thinking of when he had me born in 'this pleasant land of France'? Yet I love our absurd country, whenever I can forget art and the impossibly unstable politics. What gaiety there is, how amusing things are, between whiles! What a hotbed of ideas it is (verbally, at least)! How they tear the universe to pieces with their fine white teeth and scratch its Creator with their exquisite nails! How they dance on the pin-point of a good phrase! How royally they play the fool—and republicanly! The latter style, however, is rather less entertaining.

26

First reading of Goethe's Faust—I write my Fantastic Symphony—unsuccessful attempt to get it performed

ANOTHER LANDMARK IN my life that I must mention was my first encounter with Goethe's *Faust*, which I read in Gérard de Nerval's translation, and which made a strange and deep impression on me. The marvellous book fascinated me from the first. I could not put it down; I read it incessantly, at meals, at the theatre, in the street, wherever I happened to be.

The translation was in prose but contained a number of ballads, hymns and other pieces in verse. I was unable to resist setting them to music; and, this hazardous undertaking completed, I had the foolhardiness to get it printed without having heard a note of the work. It was published in Paris, at my expense, under the title *Eight Scenes from Faust*, and a few copies circulated here and there. One of them was seen by Marx, the well-known Berlin theorist and critic, who wrote me a friendly letter about it. Coming from Germany, this unexpected encouragement naturally delighted me; but it did not long delude me as to the many and grave defects of the work. I still think the ideas were good; indeed I used them again, very differently developed, in my dramatic legend *The Damnation of Faust*. But the work as a whole was crude and badly written. As soon as I had made up my mind on this point, I rounded up all the copies I could get hold of and destroyed them.

I remember now that I included one of the *Eight Scenes*, the one for six voices called Concert of Sylphs, in the programme of my first concert.* It was sung by six students from the Conservatoire, and produced no effect at all. No one could see any point in it, the whole thing seemed formless, empty, and completely 'without any tune'.† Eighteen years later, with a few minor changes in harmony and orchestration, the same piece became a favourite all over Europe. Wherever I have performed it, in St Petersburg, Moscow, Berlin, London, Paris, I have never known it not to be encored. The music seems quite clear in form and delightfully tuneful. It is true, of course, that it is now sung by a chorus. Being unable to find six good soloists, I used a choir of eighty instead, and the whole point of the piece suddenly became intelligible; the colour and shape were apparent, and the effect was tripled. A good many pieces of this kind which lose all their character and charm because of feeble soloists would be transformed simply by being sung by a well-trained chorus of adequate size. Where one mediocre voice is odious, fifty can sound enchanting. One soulless singer can make a composer's most passionate music seem cold and even ridiculous. Conversely, the warmth of feeling collectively located in a really musical body can suffice to set the flame at the

* [The concert was given at the Conservatoire on 1 November 1829 and also included the *Francs-juges* and *Waverley* overtures, the Resurrexit, and the first Paris performance of Beethoven's 'Emperor' concerto, with Ferdinand Hiller as soloist. Habeneck conducted.]

† [Cf. the comment on this piece in the *Revue musicale*, VI, 1830: 'Is there no melodic element in M. Berlioz's head?']

heart of a work ablaze so that it lives, where a virtuoso with no spark in him would extinguish it utterly.

Immediately after the composition of the *Faust* pieces, and still under the influence of Goethe's poem, I wrote my Fantastic Symphony: very slowly and laboriously in some parts, with extraordinary ease in others. The adagio (the Scene in the Fields), which always affects the public and myself so keenly, cost me nearly a month's arduous toil; two or three times I gave it up. On the other hand, the March to the Scaffold was written in one night. But I continued to make considerable changes to both movements, and to the rest of the work, over the course of several years.

The Théâtre des Nouveautés had for some time been performing opéras-comiques, and now had a reasonably good orchestra under the command of Bloc. He persuaded me to offer my new work to the directors of the theatre; we should jointly organize a concert and give the work a hearing. The directors consented, for the sole reason that the symphony's unusual programme had caught their fancy; they thought a lot of people would come out of curiosity. But I wanted a performance on a really grand scale, so I engaged a further eighty players. When added to Bloc's, they formed an orchestra of a hundred and thirty. The theatre had no normal provision for an army of performers on this scale; the necessary physical conditions, the platforms for the different levels, even the desks, were lacking. To all my inquiries the directors replied with the imperturbable calm of men who have no conception of the difficulties involved: I had no need to worry, everything would be seen to, they had a scene-shifter who was a clever fellow. But when the day came for the rehearsal,* and my orchestra of a hundred and thirty tried to arrange themselves on the stage, there was nowhere to put them. The tiny pit, when pressed into service, barely accommodated the violins. From all over the theatre an uproar arose that would have driven a much more sanguine composer demented. People were calling for desks, while the carpenters strove to knock together something that would do instead. The scene-shifter† went about swearing

* [Mid-May, 1830.]

† [Whose name was Poulet.]

and searching for his flats and his struts. There were cries for chairs, for instruments, for candles; the double basses were short of strings; there was no room anywhere for the drums. The orchestral attendant did not know where to begin. Bloc and I were in thirty-seven different places at once; but it was all to no avail. The situation had got beyond control. It was a rout, a musical Crossing of the Beresina.

However, despite the confusion, Bloc insisted on trying a couple of movements, 'to give the directors an idea of the symphony'. We rehearsed the Ball and the March to the Scaffold as well as was possible with our forces in disarray; and the March created a perfect furore among the players. But the concert never took place. The directors recoiled before the tumult, and the enterprise was abandoned. It would involve, they said, too many elaborate preparations; they 'had no idea so much was required for a symphony'.

My plan had been wrecked for want of desks and a few benches. The extreme care which I now take over the practical details of concert-giving dates from then. I know too well what disasters the least negligence in this respect can lead to.

27
I compose a fantasy on The Tempest—its performance at the Opéra

GIRARD WAS AT that time conductor at the Théâtre-Italien. To console me for this reverse he suggested that I should compose another piece, shorter than the Fantastic Symphony. If I did, he would see that it received a proper performance, free from all complications. I set to work to write a dramatic fantasy, with chorus, on Shakespeare's *Tempest*. But the moment Girard saw the completed score, he exclaimed, 'This is too big for us; it needs large forces. We can't perform a work on this scale at the Théâtre-Italien. The Opéra's the only place for it.' I immediately went to see Lubbert, the director of the Opéra, and offered it to him. To my great surprise he agreed to include the work in the programme of a benefit performance which was shortly to take place in aid of the Artists' Pension Fund. My name, it seemed, was not unknown to him. My first concert at the Conservatoire had made quite a stir, he had seen what the papers said about it. In short, he had confidence in me; he would not even ask me to submit to any humiliating examination of my score. He gave his word and kept it punctiliously (he was, it will be agreed, a somewhat unusual director). As soon as the parts were copied, the Opéra chorus set about learning it. At the final rehearsal everything went splendidly. Fétis, who had been tremendously encouraging, was present and said some flattering things about the work and its author. But imagine my luck! The following day,* an hour before the Opéra opened its doors, the worst storm in fifty years broke over Paris. A mighty cloudburst turned the streets into veritable rivers and lakes; all traffic, wheeled or on foot, became virtually impossible. During the whole of the first half of the evening, just when my own little tempest was supposed to be raging, the Opéra was almost deserted. Two or three hundred people at the most were there, performers included. All that effort 'down the drain'!

28

A violent distraction—F—— H——
Mademoiselle M——

THESE MUSICAL SKIRMISHES were not my only source of excitement. The German composer and pianist H——, with whom I had been on intimate terms since his arrival in Paris, had become passionately attached to a young lady who is today our most celebrated virtuoso by reason of her musical and other talents. H—— knew all about my great Shakespearean passion and was distressed at the pangs it caused me. He was naïve enough to talk about it quite often to Mlle M——, telling her that he had never seen an infatuation like it. He actually said to her one day that he would 'never be jealous of him, for it's certain *he* will never fall in love with you'. The effect of this rash statement on a true Parisian may be imagined. She became possessed with a desire to prove her excessively trusting and platonic admirer wrong.

During that summer the headmistress of a girls' boarding school, a Madame d'Aubré, had proposed my teaching the guitar

* [7 November 1830.]

at her school,* and I had accepted. (Curiously enough, I still figure on the prospectus of the d'Aubré establishment as teacher of that noble instrument.) Mlle M—— also taught there; she gave piano lessons. She teased me on my melancholy air and told me there was someone who 'took the deepest interest in me'. She talked about H—— who, she said, was very fond of her, but it would 'never come to anything'.

One morning I got a letter from Mlle M——. Under the pretext of speaking to me further about H——, she made a secret rendezvous for the following day. When the moment came, I forgot to turn up. A stroke worthy of the great masters of intrigue—if I had done it intentionally! But I really did forget, and remembered only some hours later. This lordly indifference completed the work so well begun; and after rather brutally playing Joseph to her Potiphar's wife for a few days, I yielded and let myself find consolation for all my sorrows in a new passion, into which I threw myself with an enthusiasm not at all surprising when one considers my age and ardent disposition and the eighteen years and maddening beauty of Mlle M——.

If I were to describe the whole affair and the incredible incidents of every kind that it gave rise to, the reader would no doubt be entertained in an unexpected and interesting fashion. But, as I have stated before, I am not writing confessions. Suffice it to say that Mlle M—— set my senses on fire till all the devils of hell danced in my veins. Poor H—— when I told him the truth, as I felt I had to, wept bitterly at first. Then, realizing that I had not fundamentally been guilty of treachery towards him, he put a brave and dignified face on it, clasped my hand convulsively, wished me every joy, and left for Frankfurt. I have always admired the way he behaved on that occasion.

That is all I have to say about this violent interlude which, by awakening me to the pleasures of the senses, distracted me briefly from the great passion that absorbed me heart and soul. It remains to show, in the account of my Italian travels, how dramatically the affair ended and how nearly and in what terrible manner Mlle

* [The school was an orthopaedic institution in the rue Harlay-Marais.]

M—— had cause to feel the force of the proverb: 'It is dangerous to play with fire.'*

29

Fourth competition at the Institute—I obtain the prize—the July Revolution—the capture of Babylon—the Marseillaise—Rouget de Lisle

THE INSTITUTE COMPETITION took place a little later than usual that year. The date fixed was 15 July. For the fifth time I went up, resolved that whatever happened I would not go in for it again. It was the year 1830. I was finishing my cantata when the Revolution broke out.

And as the sun upon bare pavements beat
Of empty bridges and deserted quays,
How all the bellowing bells did shout, a rain
Of bullets whistled on the sultry air;
Through Paris an awakened people's roar

* [Mlle M—— was Camille Moke, later famous as Marie Pleyel, one of the most distinguished pianists of the mid-nineteenth century. H—— was the German pianist and composer Ferdinand Hiller. In his *Künstlerleben* Hiller, who lived in Paris from 1828 to 1835, gives a similar account of the origins of the affair, adding that the 'German musician of his acquaintance' (i.e. himself) used Berlioz as a go-between to carry notes to Camille at Mme d'Aubré's school. Camille's German mother, a shrewd business-woman who opened a Dutch lingerie shop in the Faubourg Montmartre when her Belgian husband, a professor of linguistics at Ghent University, lost his money in speculation, was out to make the most advantageous possible match for her extremely pretty daughter. Berlioz, the heir to a decent estate and a young man with good connections and brilliant if uncertain prospects, was certainly not to be turned down out of hand; and, impressed by his Prix de Rome and the success of the Fantastic Symphony, she went so far as to agree to the young couple getting engaged on the eve of Berlioz's departure for Italy in December 1830. They exchanged rings, and a date conveniently far ahead—Easter 1832—was fixed for their marriage. But meanwhile another, more desirable suitor had appeared—the middle-aged M. Pleyel, son of the composer Ignaz Pleyel and head of the powerful firm of piano-manufacturers; and within a few months of Berlioz's leaving for Italy, Mlle Moke had married him. Though the *Memoirs* makes light of the affair, the blow clearly cut deep. Berlioz was very much in love with Camille. Harriet Smithson was eclipsed.]

Was like the sound of an approaching sea,
And to the ancient cannon's surly growl
*The Marseillaise replied . . .**

The Palais de l'Institut presented a curious sight. A number of families had taken refuge there. Grapeshot rattled on the barricaded doors, cannon-balls thudded against the façade, women screamed, and in the brief lulls in the firing the swallows filled the air with their shrill sweet cry. I dashed off the final pages of my orchestral score to the sound of stray bullets coming over the roofs and pattering on the wall outside my window. On the 29th I had finished and was free to go out and roam about Paris till morning, pistol in hand, with Barbier's 'holy rabble'.

I shall never forget how Paris looked during those famous days: the fantastic bravery of the guttersnipes, the enthusiasm of the men, the wild excitement of the whores, the grim resignation of the Swiss and the Royal Guard, the strange pride of the working class in being, as they said, masters of Paris and stealing nothing; the young men bragging of preposterous exploits, based on feats of genuine courage but so thickly embellished in the telling as to sound ludicrous. It was not enough to have stormed the cavalry barracks in the rue de Babylone with quite heavy losses; they had to announce, with a gravity worthy of Alexander's veterans, 'We were at the capture of Babylon.' The full title was too long for convenience; and the event was so much talked about that the abbreviation stuck. The portentous way they delivered the word 'Babylon' with a prodigious lengthening of the *o* was ripe comedy. Parisians! Charlatans—charlatans of genius, if you like, but charlatans!

And the music that there was then, the songs, the harsh voices resounding through the streets—nobody who did not hear it can have any idea what it was like.†

It was a day or two after this harmonious revolution that I had a musical experience—shock would almost be a better word—of extraordinary intensity. I was crossing the courtyard of the Palais

* August Barbier, *Iambes*.

† [Louis-Philippe had to come out every few hours and beat time to the Marseillaise.]

Royal when I thought I heard a tune I knew well; it seemed to be coming from a group of people on the far side. I went towards them and perceived that a dozen or so young men were engaged in singing a battle hymn of my composition, the words of which, translated from Moore's *Irish Melodies*, happened to suit the situation exactly.* Unused as I was to this kind of popularity, the discovery delighted me and I pushed my way through to the circle of singers and requested permission to join them. It was granted and I was handed a copy of the bass part—which in the case of this particular chorus was quite superfluous. I was careful, however, not to betray my identity, though I remember having a lively argument with the conductor over the tempo at which he was taking my piece. Happily I redeemed myself in his eyes by correctly singing my part in Béranger's 'Vieux Drapeau', which he himself had set to music and which came next in the programme. During the intervals in this improvised concert three National Guardsmen, who were keeping the crowd clear of the singers, handed round their shakos and made a collection for the people wounded during the Three Days. The idea appealed to the Parisian sense of the bizarre and there was soon a deluge of five-franc pieces which our music by itself would hardly have been enough to charm from their owners' pockets. The audience grew steadily and the space round the little patriotic band got smaller and smaller. Our military escort began to lose all hope of stemming the tide. We barely escaped, and fled with the crowd streaming behind us till we reached the Galerie Colbert which leads to the rue Vivienne. There, surrounded and hemmed in like bears at a fair, we were invited to resume our singing. A haberdasher, whose shop opened off the glass-covered central area of the arcade, asked us up to the first floor, where we could 'rain down our music on our admirers' without risk of being suffocated. The offer was accepted, and we struck up the Marseillaise. Almost at once the seething Mass at our feet grew quiet and a holy stillness fell upon them. It was like the silence in St Peter's Square when the Pope gives his blessing, *urbi et orbi*, from the pontifical balcony. At the end of the second verse, at the point where the refrain enters, there

* ['Chant guerrier', No. 3 of *Neuf mélodies* (published in February 1830).]

was again a profound silence. It was the same after the third. This was not at all what I had expected. On beholding that vast concourse of people I recalled that I had just arranged Rouget de Lisle's song for double chorus and full orchestra, and that where one normally writes 'tenors and basses' I had written instead 'everyone with a voice, a soul, and blood in his veins'. Here was just the occasion for it; so it was all the more mortifying to be met with a stubborn silence. The fourth time, unable to contain myself, I yelled, 'Confound it all—sing!' And the great crowd launched into its 'Aux armes, citoyens!' with the energy and precision of a trained choir. Picture it—the arcade leading to the rue Vivienne full of people, as was the arcade that gives on to the rue Neuve-des-Petits-Champs and the central area beneath the dome, and these four or five thousand voices crammed into a reverberant space bounded to right and left by the clapboards of the shops' shutters, overhead by the glass roof and beneath by the resonant paving-stones, and most of them moreover, men, women and children, still throbbing with the emotion of the recent struggle—and then imagine the effect of that stupendous refrain. I literally sank to the floor; and our little band, awestruck at the explosion, stood dumbfounded, silent as birds after a thunderclap.

I said a moment ago that I had arranged the Marseillaise for double chorus and full orchestra. I dedicated it to the author of that immortal hymn, and I have always treasured the letter that he wrote to me about it.

CHOISY-LE-ROI, *20 December 1830*

My dear Monsieur Berlioz,

We have never met; but it would give me so much pleasure if we could. Your mind seems a veritable volcano in continual eruption. Mine never produced more than a flash in the pan; the fire's going out now, though there's still some smoke. But the richness of your volcano and the remains of my little fire combined might do something. In saying this I am thinking of one, possibly two proposals that I should like to make to you. But we would have to meet and get to know one another first. If you feel like it, suggest a day when I could see you, or come to Choisy and have lunch with me or dinner. It won't be much, but you are a poet and will not mind, and the country air will season it. Forgive me for waiting until now before attempting to thank you for the honour you did me and this poor child of mine when you clothed its nakedness in the riches of your imagination; but I am nothing but a miserable lame old recluse who hardly ever comes near your great city and for nine-tenths of his life does none of the things he would like to do. May I dare to hope you will not refuse my request, little though there may be in it to tempt you, but will in one way or another allow me to thank you personally and to tell you how wholeheartedly I share the expectations which all true lovers of music have formed of your audacious talent?

Rouget de Lisle

I heard later that Rouget de Lisle—who incidentally wrote many fine songs besides the Marseillaise—had an unpublished libretto on *Othello* that he wished to offer me. Being obliged to leave Paris on the day after I received his letter, I sent my apologies and explained that my visit would have to wait until after my return from Italy. The poor man died in the interval. I never met him.*

When calm had after a fashion been restored to Paris, when Lafayette had presented Louis-Philippe to the people† as the best of all possible republics, and the trick had worked and the wheels of society had begun to turn again, then the Academy of Fine Arts once more took up its tasks. Our cantatas were played—on the piano, as always—before the two Areopagi whose constitution I explained earlier. And since both of them clearly recognized that I was converted to truth and sanity (on the strength of a piece which I have since destroyed), they bestowed on me, at long last, the prize.‡ I had been deeply disappointed in previous years when I had won nothing. Now I felt little pleasure when Pradier, the sculptor, who had left the conference hall to look for me, came up to me in the library where I awaited my fate and, shaking me

* [Berlioz's letter is dated 29 December 1830 (*Correspondance générale*, I, 394). He left Paris the following morning. A manuscript copy of a libretto on *Othello* was found among Rouget de Lisle's papers.]

† [On 3 August 1830, from a balcony of the Hôtel de Ville.]

‡ [On 21 August 1830.]

warmly by the hand, said, 'You have got it.' To see him so delighted and me so unconcerned, one would have thought he was the laureate and I the academician.* But I soon began to appreciate the advantages of the award. I might not be able to take much pride in it, holding the views I did on the way the competition was run, but it represented official success and would undoubtedly gratify my parents. It gave me an annuity of a thousand crowns as well as free entry to every opera house. It was a diploma, a certificate of ability, and it meant a degree of financial independence, almost of affluence, for the next five years.

30

The Institute prize-giving—the academicians —my Sardanapalus cantata—its performance —the conflagration that will not catch fire —rage—consternation of Mme Malibran

TWO MONTHS LATER came the usual Institute prize-giving and the performance of the winning cantata by a large orchestra. The ceremony is still carried out in precisely the same fashion. Year after year the same players perform the same sort of piece and the prizes, awarded with the same discrimination, are handed out with the same imposing ritual. Year after year, on the same day, at the same time, the same academician, standing on the same step of the same staircase, makes the same speech to the successful candidate. Day, the first Saturday in October; time, 4 p.m.; step, the third; academician, no need to say who;† speech, as follows: 'Now, young man, *macte animo* . . . about to set forth on a splendid journey . . . ancestral home of the arts . . . celebrated land, with its Piccinnis and its Pergolesis . . . the stimulus of its skies . . . no doubt return with some magnificent new work . . . launched upon your career . . .'

In honour of the great day the academicians don their ceremonial best and sit resplendent in green embroidery. They are about to crown with due solemnity a painter, a sculptor, an

* [Pradier had supported Berlioz's candidature the year before.]

† [Quatremère de Quincy, archaeologist, one-time deputy, author of many learned works, of which Larousse's *Dictionnaire du XIX siècle* says, 'On y remarque une érudition vaste mais mal digérée, et une prolixité trop grande.']

architect, an engraver, and a musician. Great on Parnassus is the Muses' joy. But what am I saying? That last sentence was in verse. The truth is, my mind was miles from the Academy. I was thinking, for some reason, of that stanza of Victor Hugo's:

Eagle they followed day and night, our army's star,
Whose blood-stained plumes are scattered on a hundred Fields,
Whose lightnings were one night extinguished in the flood;
Thou who in the maternal eyrie guarded them,
Look on them, be contented; croak and flap thy wings.
*Mother, thy eaglets now are hatched!**

To return to our laureates—some of whom are less like eagles than owls (La Fontaine's 'surly little monsters') but all of whom share equally in the mother-love of the Academy—on the first Saturday in October the great mother 'flaps her wings' and the winning cantata is at last performed in earnest. A full orchestra is assembled, with nothing missing: strings, two flutes, two oboes, two clarinets (though to be strictly accurate, in my day when the Prix de Rome launched me upon my career there was only a clarinet and a half, the old man who had done duty as first clarinet since time immemorial having lost nearly all his teeth and being in consequence unable to sound more than half the notes of his aristocratic instrument; it was not until recently that this vital section was brought up to full strength), four horns, three trombones, and even cornets—modern instruments! You are incredulous? It is true. The Academy doesn't know itself; it goes mad and lashes out in all directions. The mother bird 'is contented, croaks and flaps her wings, her owlets (or rather, eaglets) now are hatched'. Everyone is at his post. The conductor raises his bow and gives the signal.

The sun rises: cello solo, un poco crescendo.

The little birds awake: flute solo, violin trills.

The little brooks murmur: viola solo.

The little lambs bleat: oboe solo.

And, as the crescendo goes on, it so happens that by the time the little birds and the little brooks and the little lambs have had

* [From *Les chants du crépuscule* (1835). 'Dicté après juillet 1830'.]

their say, the sun is high in the sky and it is at least midday. The recitative commences:

E'en now returning day, etc.

Then comes the aria, followed by the second recitative, the second aria, the third recitative, and the third aria, which usually kills off the hero but revives the singer and the audience; whereupon the Permanent Secretary, holding in one hand the wreath of artificial laurels which will crown the victor's brow and in the other the solid gold medal which will pay his rent until he leaves for Rome (it is worth a hundred and fifty francs, as I discovered), reads out in a loud and clear voice the surname and first names of the composer. The laureate rises:

Upon his candid forehead freshly shorn
*A blush of manly modesty appearing.**

He embraces the Permanent Secretary (polite applause). The laureate's distinguished master is sitting a few feet from the Permanent Secretary's rostrum. The pupil embraces his distinguished master (more polite applause). On a bench at the back, behind the academicians, the laureate's parents sit weeping tears of silent joy. The laureate vaults over the intervening benches, treading on someone's toe, trampling another's coat and, reaching the top, flings himself into the arms of his father and mother, who by now are sobbing unashamedly (no applause; but people are beginning to laugh). To the right of this touching group a young person is signalling to the hero of the hour. He responds by leaping in her direction and, after tearing a woman's dress and crushing a dandy's hat, contrives to reach his cousin. He embraces his cousin. Sometimes he embraces his cousin's neighbour (loud laughter). Another lady, sitting by herself in a distant corner of the hall, makes discreet signs of affection which our hero affects not to notice. Then he turns and flies to embrace his mistress—his betrothed, the woman who is to share his life and fame. This time, in his haste and confusion and blindness to all other women, he kicks one of them over, trips over a bench, falls with a crash, abandons all

* [Boileau, *Le lutrin* ('The Lectern').]

hope of greeting the hapless girl, and regains his seat, bathed in perspiration (loud and prolonged laughter and applause). This is the crowning moment of the academic year, and I know many people who go along solely to witness it. I say this without any rancour against these jokers; for when my time came there was no father, mother, cousin, master or mistress for me to embrace. My master was ill, my parents disgruntled and elsewhere, and my mistress . . . So I embraced only the Permanent Secretary, and I doubt that anyone noticed the blush of modesty on my forehead as I did so, for so far from being freshly shorn it was buried beneath a forest of red hair—a feature which, in conjunction with other characteristic points, tended to place me unmistakably in the owl category.

I was, besides, in no mood to embrace anybody. I do not believe I have ever been in such a black fury in my life. The reason was this. Our subject that year was 'The Last Night of Sardanapalus'. The poem ended at the moment when the vanquished potentate gathers his most beautiful slaves round him and mounts the funeral pyre. My first impulse had been to write a kind of symphonic description of the scene: the wails of the reluctant victims, the great sensualist defying death in the midst of the encircling flames, the crash of the falling palace. Then I thought of the means that would be required in a purely orchestral piece to suggest a scene of this kind, and I restrained myself. The music section of the Academy would certainly have condemned the whole cantata after one look at such a finale, quite apart from the fact that, boiled down for the piano, it would have sounded nonsensical. So I waited. When the prize had been awarded and I was sure of not losing it, and sure of performance by a full orchestra, I wrote my conflagration. At the final rehearsal the piece produced such an effect that several academicians, who had been caught unawares, came up and congratulated me warmly and without any resentment at the trick I had played on their sacred beliefs.

The rehearsal in the Institute assembly hall was attended by a large number of artists and music-lovers who had come to hear this cantata by a young composer already notorious for his eccentricity. Most of them went away full of the extraordinary impression the conflagration had made on them. As a result of their enthusiastic accounts, the audience arrived next day in an unusual state of curiosity and expectation.

I was not altogether confident of the abilities of Grasset, ex-conductor at the Théâtre-Italien, who was in charge of the performance, and before it began I went and sat near him, manuscript in hand. Mme Malibran, whose interest had been aroused by the reports of the day before, but who had not been able to find a seat in the hall, was also accommodated nearby on a stool, sandwiched between two double basses. It was the last time I saw her.*

My decrescendo began (for the first words of the cantata were 'E'en now Nature in darkest night lies veiled', and I had therefore been obliged to compose a sunset in place of the traditional dawn; it seems I am doomed to be different, forever at odds with life and the Academy!). All went smoothly; Sardanapalus learnt of his defeat, resolved to die and summoned his women, and the pyre was kindled. Everyone listened intently. Those who had been at the rehearsal whispered to their neighbours, 'Now it's coming. Wait till you hear it—it's fantastic.'

Ten million curses on all musicians who do not count their rests! In my score the horn was supposed to give the cue to the timpani, the timpani to the cymbals, the cymbals to the bass drum; the first stroke of the bass drum was the signal for the final explosion. But the damnable horn-player failed to play his note. Without it, the timpanist was afraid to come in. In consequence, cymbals and bass drum also kept silent. Absolutely nothing happened. The violins and cellos went on with their futile tremolo; no explosion: the fire went out without so much as a pop; the much-heralded holocaust had turned into a damp squib—*ridiculus mus*. Only a composer who has himself been through such an experience can conceive the fury that possessed me. I could hardly breathe. A cry of horror burst from me. I hurled my score into the middle of the orchestra and sent the two nearest desks flying. Mme Malibran sprang back as if a mine had gone off at her feet. The whole place was in an uproar—the orchestra in confusion, the academicians scandalized, the audience mystified, the composer's

* [Saturday, 30 October. The prizegiving was held four weeks later than usual that year.]

friends in high indignation. Another musical catastrophe had overtaken me, the cruellest I had yet experienced. Would that it had been the last!

31

I give my second concert—the Fantastic Symphony—
Liszt pays me a visit—beginning of our friendship
—the Paris critics—Cherubini's remark—I leave for Italy

IN SPITE OF my earnest request to the Ministry of the Interior for a dispensation, there was no getting out of going to Rome. For all laureates it was obligatory; and I prepared to leave.*

I did not want to go away, however, without giving a public performance of my *Sardanapalus* cantata, whose finale had come to so inglorious an end at the Institute prize-giving. So I organized a concert at the Conservatoire at which the academic offering figured along with the Fantastic Symphony, a work that had not yet been heard. Habeneck undertook to conduct and all the players, with a generosity for which I shall always be profoundly grateful, for the third time gave their services.

On the day before the concert, Liszt called on me. It was our first meeting. I spoke of Goethe's *Faust*, which he confessed he had not read, but which he soon came to love as much as I. We felt an immediate affinity, and from that moment our friendship has grown ever closer and stronger. He came to the concert and was conspicuous for his applause and his enthusiastic demonstrations.†

* [Berlioz campaigned for several months to obtain exemption. His letter of 28 October to the Minister of the Interior, François Guizot (*Correspondance générale*, I, 376–8), enclosed eloquent testimonials from Fétis, Spontini, Meyerbeer and Lesueur, and a medical certificate stating that the Italian climate would be injurious to someone in his highly strung nervous condition. In the margin, next to his request to be allowed to receive his grant in Paris, someone has written, in pencil, 'impossible'. The Minister's refusal was sent on 14 December. Berlioz's extreme unwillingness to leave the Parisian scene was personal as well as professional. He was in love with Camille Moke; at the same time an enforced absence of a couple of years was the last thing he wanted at this stage of his career. The two motives interacted, for Mme Moke had made her consent to the marriage dependent on his scoring a success in the opera house.]

† ['Liszt, the well-known pianist, literally dragged me off to have dinner at his house and overwhelmed me with the vigour of his enthusiasm.' (Berlioz to his

The performance was by no means perfect—it could hardly be, with works of such difficulty and after only two rehearsals. But it was good enough to give a reasonable idea of the music. Three of the movements of the symphony, the Waltz, the March to the Scaffold and the Witches' Sabbath, created a sensation; the March especially took the audience by storm. The Scene in the Fields made no impression at all. True, it bore little resemblance to the present version. I made up my mind at once to rewrite it. Ferdinand Hiller, who was then in Paris, gave me some excellent advice which I endeavoured to profit by.

The cantata was well performed; the conflagration caught fire at the appointed time and the palace crashed in ruins. Altogether it was a great success. A few days later the watchdogs of the Press pronounced their verdicts, some for, some against, both equally vehement. The hostile critics nearly all blamed me for the wrong things. Instead of pointing out the palpable defects in both works—serious defects which in the case of the symphony it took me several years of the most diligent labour to expunge—they attacked the absurd ideas I was supposed to have, though I had never had them, the crudeness of certain modulations which were not there at all, the systematic failure to observe certain fundamental rules of music which I had faithfully observed, and the neglect of certain musical procedures which I had employed precisely in those passages where their absence was deplored. I must confess my partisans too have often been given to crediting me with ridiculous and totally alien intentions. The amount of fatuous theorizing and sheer foolishness lavished by French critics in praise as well as execration of my music since that time beggars description.* Two or three men at the most had the sense and

---

father, 6 December 1830, *Correspondance générale*, I, 385.) At nineteen Liszt was already a virtuoso of repute. Berlioz's concert took place on 5 December, at 2 p.m., and included—in addition to *Sardanapalus* and the symphony—the *Francs-juges* overture, 'Chant sacré' and 'Chant guerrier' from *Neuf mélodies*, and an unspecified violin solo played by Chrétien Urhan. The same evening, at the Opéra, Harriet Smithson played the mute role of the heroine Fenella in an act from Auber's *La muette de Portici*.]

* [Cf. Verdi on the Press notices of *Aida*: 'Stupid criticism, and still more stupid praise'; and Britten: 'I can say with honesty that in every piece I have written, in

intelligence, when I appeared on the scene, to reserve judgment and write about me with moderation. But critics who are both knowledgeable and perceptive, who combine imagination, sensitivity and an unprejudiced mind and are capable of assessing me sanely and of understanding what I am aiming at, are few and far between even now. In the early years of my career they did not exist at all; and even had they existed, the rare and far from expert performances of my works to be heard then would have left a great deal to their imaginations.

Any young man in Paris then who was at all musical and who had that sixth sense which is called artistic feeling, whether musician or not, understood me better and quicker than those arid scribes, the critics, whose only authority was their own vanity and pretentious ignorance. The official composers had already begun to abhor me. Their own staid productions were insulted by certain features of my style. Above all, my blasphemies against various hallowed articles of faith exasperated them. And God knows there is nothing in the world more violent and implacable than bigotry of this kind. Cherubini's reaction to the heretical ideas provoked by my music and to the general commotion I was causing may be imagined. His spies had given him a report on the final rehearsal of that 'abomination' of a symphony. The following day he happened to pass the door of the hall just as the audience was going in. Someone stopped him and said, 'Hallo, aren't you coming to hear this new thing of Berlioz's?'

'I do not need to know 'ow music ought not to be wreetten,' he retorted, with the air of a cat about to be given a dose of mustard. It was worse after the success of the concert: he looked as if he had swallowed mustard; he didn't say a word, but only sneezed. A few days later he sent for me. 'So you are leaving for Italy?' he said.

'Yes, sir.'

'Your name will no longer be on the regeester of Conservatoire students; your studies are at an end. But I theenk you ought to 'ave

---

spite of hard work, there are still passages where I have not quite solved problems. Not once have these passages been noticed, nor of course suggestions made as to how I could have improved them.']

come and seen me before goeeng. One does not go out of the Conservatoire as eef it were a stable.' I nearly replied, 'Why not, since we are treated like horses?' but I had the sense not to. Instead, I assured our genial director that I had had no intention of leaving Paris without coming to say goodbye to him and thanking him for his many kindnesses.

There was nothing for it, then, but to repair to the French Academy in Rome and there forget at my leisure the amiable Cherubini, Boïeldieu the French gentleman with his rapier thrusts, the antics of the Press, the vigorous enthusiasm and partisanship of my friends, the abuse of my enemies, the musical world, and music itself.

In theory, no doubt, the French Academy in Rome was designed to serve a useful artistic purpose. It is not for me to judge how far its founder's aims have been achieved in the case of the painters, sculptors, engravers and architects who go there. For the musicians, however, the time spent in Italy is so much time lost. The country's wealth of artistic treasures, its scenery and associations can hardly fail to enrich the mind and deepen the imagination; but so far as opportunities for specialized study are concerned, it is quite useless. This will become clear from the faithful account I shall give of the life which French students lead in Rome.

Before embarking on their epic journey, the five or six laureates usually meet and arrange to travel together. An Italian coachman contracts for a fairly modest sum to convey his cargo of great men to Italy, and packs them into a large wagon, like so many bourgeois from the Marais.* As he never changes horses, it takes him a considerable time to get across France, over the Alps, and down through northern Italy to the Roman States. But such a progress, with its endless short stages, must be rich in incidents when the passengers are half a dozen far from melancholy young men at the most completely carefree period of their lives. I say 'must' because I did not make it myself. Various causes combined to keep me in Paris until the middle of January, after which, having

* [A district in the second (today the fourth) arrondissement of Paris. The Marais had drastically declined in status since its fashionable heyday in the seventeenth century.]

spent a few weeks at La Côte Saint-André—where my parents, very proud of my academic distinction, received me with the utmost warmth—I bent my step towards Italy, alone and somewhat dejected.*

* [Berlioz spent a month at La Côte—part of it ill in bed. He had left Paris formally engaged to Camille, and he received at least one letter from her and from her mother during his stay in Dauphiné. But Hiller wrote warning him that Camille seemed to be taking his absence very calmly, and hinted that worse news might follow. Berlioz was already in a state of jealous anxiety when he resumed his journey in February.]

TRAVELS IN ITALY

32

Marseilles to Leghorn—a storm—Leghorn to Rome—the French Academy in Rome

A JOURNEY ACROSS the Alps was not an inviting prospect at that time of year, so I decided to outflank them, and made for Marseilles. It was my first encounter with the sea. I spent some time trying to find a reasonably clean-looking ship sailing for Leghorn; but I could discover only the most squalid little boats, smelling vilely and piled high with cargoes of wool, oil-casks, or bones for the manufacture of bone-black, with nowhere on board for a civilized human being to berth and no question of food or shelter: I would have to bring my own provisions and at night curl up like a dog in whatever corner they were prepared to give me. My sole companions would be four sailors with faces like bulldogs and an air of doubtful honesty. I decided against it, and killed time for a few days exploring the rocks near Notre-Dame de la Garde, a type of occupation which has always greatly appealed to me.

At last I heard of a Sardinian brig that was on the point of sailing for Leghorn. Some pleasant-looking young men whom I met in the Cannebière* told me they had booked passages on her, and suggested we mess together. The captain would not undertake to feed us, so it was up to us to make our own arrangements. We took provisions for a week, reckoning that we should have some left over, since in fair weather the crossing took three or four days at the most. Few things are so delightful as one's first experience of the Mediterranean when the weather is fine, the ship tolerable, and one is not seasick. I congratulated myself on my good fortune in being spared the pangs which afflicted my fellow-passengers for the first two days of the voyage, and revelled in my surroundings. Our meals on deck, under a splendid sun and in sight of the Sardinian coast,† were memorable occasions. All my companions

* [The main street of Marseilles, running down to the port.]

† [The Kingdom of Sardinia included a large area of the mainland, between Nice and La Spezia, and extending northwards almost to the Rhone.]

were Italians and were full of good stories, some rather far-fetched and all fascinating. One had fought for the cause of liberty in Greece and had known Canaris, and we never tired of questioning him about that heroic figure whose career had blazed across the world with the meteoric brilliance of one of his own fire-ships but now seemed on the point of extinction. A Venetian, a somewhat dubious-looking character who spoke atrocious French, claimed to have commanded Byron's corvette during the poet's forays down the Adriatic coast and through the Greek archipelago. He described in minute detail the glittering uniform which Byron had insisted on his wearing and the orgies they took part in together; he made a great point of the tribute which the celebrated traveller had paid to his daring. In the middle of a storm Byron had invited him to his cabin for a game of écarté. The captain, rather than decline the invitation, left the bridge and went below. The game had begun when the ship gave a violent lurch, and cards and players were sent flying.

'Pick up the cards—we continue,' cried Byron.

'With pleasure, my lord.'

'Captain, you're a brave fellow.'

It is possible there was not a word of truth in it; but one must admit that the gold-lace uniform and the game of écarté are quite in character with the author of *Lara*. Besides, the narrator did not have enough wit to invent such convincing local colour; and I was much too pleased at meeting someone who had been with Childe Harold on his pilgrimage not to believe it all implicitly.

Time went on and we were getting no nearer Leghorn. For three days we lay becalmed in sight of Nice. The light breeze that got up every evening took us forward a few miles, but after a couple of hours it fell again, and during the night the current prevailing on that part of the coast carried us imperceptibly back to the same point. Every morning when I came up on deck I asked the sailors the name of the town visible on the coast, and every morning I received the same answer: '*È Nizza, signore. Ancora Nizza. È sempre Nizza.*' I began to think that the charming city of Nice possessed a magnetic attraction sufficient, if not to draw out every particle of iron in the ship (as happens, according to sailors, when you approach the poles), at least to keep her there indefinitely. I found out my mistake when a raging north wind straight off the Alps fell upon us like an avalanche. The captain, seizing the opportunity to make up for lost time, crowded on sail and the ship, struck full on her beam, went over at a horrifying angle. After a while I got used to the alarming slope of the deck. But towards midnight, as we entered the Gulf of Spezia, the *tramontana* blew so violently that the sailors themselves began to be frightened at the captain's refusal to take in sail. It was now a real tempest (I shall give a description of it in the best academic style some other time). I clutched one of the iron rails of the bridge and surveyed the scene with pounding heart, while the Venetian stood with his eyes fixed on the captain, from time to time exclaiming darkly, 'The obstinate old fool—he'll have us all drowned. He's mad. Fifteen sails set in a wind like this!' The captain held the wheel and never said a word. All at once a terrific gust caught the ship and sent her staggering over on her beam-ends. It was a ghastly moment. Our improvident captain went down like a log. While he lay rolling about among the barrels which the sudden shock had thrown up onto the bridge, the Venetian sprang forward and, seizing the wheel, took command—an illicit assumption of authority, but one justified by the extremity of the danger, as the sailors instinctively recognized. Some of them had already given themselves up for lost and were calling on the Madonna to rescue them. 'Never mind the Madonna—for God's sake get those sails in—all of you!' In an instant the masts were swarming with men and the sails were taken in. The ship half righted herself; control was gradually re-established. We were saved.

Next day we reached Leghorn under a single sail, so strong was the wind. A few hours after we had installed ourselves in the Hotel Aquila Nera, the sailors came in a body to see us; not, as might have been thought, from any ulterior motive, but simply out of fellow-feeling for the dangers we had shared and to congratulate us on our escape. These poor devils hardly make enough to pay for the ration of salted cod and ship's biscuit that is their normal fare, but they absolutely refused to accept any money from us, and we had the utmost difficulty in persuading them to stay with us and share in an improvised meal—a degree of delicacy of feeling that is rare, especially in Italy, and deserves to be recorded.

During the crossing my companions had revealed that they were on their way to join the revolt which had lately broken out against the Duke of Modena. They were full of enthusiasm and believed the hour of their country's liberation was at hand. Modena once taken, Tuscany would rise; then they would march on Rome; France meanwhile would surely come to their aid; and so on and so forth. Alas, two of them were arrested by the Grand Ducal police before they reached Florence and flung into gaol, where they may well be rotting still. I heard later that the others had distinguished themselves fighting with the patriots at Modena and Bologna but that, as members of Menotti's forces, they had shared the fate of that brave, ill-starred commander. So ended their dreams of liberty.

At Florence I said goodbye to them, never imagining it would be for ever, and made arrangements for my departure for Rome. It was a bad moment to enter the Papal States, particularly for a Frenchman coming from Paris. The authorities refused to endorse my passport. Academy students were strongly suspected of having been behind the disturbances in the Piazza Colonna, and no doubt the Papacy was not anxious to see this little enclave of revolutionaries grow any bigger. I wrote to the director, Horace Vernet. After some energetic protests he prevailed on Cardinal Bernetti to issue the necessary permit, and I was free to continue.*

It happened that I had left Paris on my own; I had been the sole Frenchman on board during the crossing from Marseilles to Leghorn; I was the only passenger the Florence coachman could find who wanted to go to Rome; and thus I travelled there in solitary

* [About 8 March 1831. The July Revolution, which brought Italian discontent to a head, had made Frenchmen suspect to the Italian authorities and correspondingly popular with the insurgents (the president of the revolutionary government in Bologna likened the Three Days to the six days of creation). Paris had since 1820 been the headquarters of the Carbonari, the secret society which fomented resistance to Austrian and Papal rule in Italy. But the government of Louis-Philippe prudently refrained from action and, after a few weeks of heady success, the revolution was easily crushed by Austrian troops. Menotti, one of the leaders of the Modenese Liberals, was double-crossed by the Duke of Modena (who had been negotiating with him in the hope of using him against the Austrians) and beheaded on 6 March. A month later the exiled Mazzini settled in Marseilles and set up a printing-press, from which appeals for independence and freedom were sent out in the name of Young Italy.]

state. Two volumes of a life of the Empress Josephine which I had picked up at a bookstall in Siena helped me kill time while the old four-wheeler jogged gently along. My Jehu could speak no word of French, and my Italian was confined to a few phrases such as '*Fa molto caldo*', '*Piove*', '*Quando lo pranzo?*', which made any significant interchange of ideas difficult. The scenery was dull. The complete lack of anything approaching comfort in the towns and villages we stopped in depressed me further, and I cursed Italy and the ridiculous system that had brought me there. One morning, about ten o'clock, we came to a small cluster of houses called La Storta. The *vetturino* poured himself a glass of wine and remarked casually, '*Ecco Roma, signore*'; and without turning round indicated with a jerk of his thumb the cross of St Peter's. This terse statement brought about a complete reversal of feeling in me. How can I describe the sudden shock that went through me at the sight of the Eternal City, lying far off in the midst of that wide and desolate plain? At once everything took on an aura of the poetic and the sublime. My sense of awe deepened, a short while later, at the grandeur of the Piazza del Popolo through which the traveller from France passes on his way into Rome; and I was lost in dreamy contemplation when the horses, whose slow progress had ceased to irritate me, came to a halt in front of an austere and imposing palace. It was the Academy.

The Villa Medici, the home of the students and the director of the French Academy, was built in 1557 by Annibale Lippi, a wing and various embellishments being added later by Michelangelo. It stands on the slope of the Pincian Hill which overlooks the city. The view is one of the most splendid in the world. To the right stretches the Pincian Way, the Champs-Elysées of Rome. There each evening when the heat of the day begins to abate, people come out in hundreds and parade up and down on foot, on horseback and, most of all, in open carriages. On the stroke of seven they hurry in again, vanishing like a cloud of gnats on the breeze, and the great plateau, which a moment before was swarming with humanity, is still and deserted: such is the Romans' almost superstitious dread of 'harmful air'; and if you see a few figures lingering on after the crowd has gone and rashly braving the injurious effects of *l'aria cattiva* to admire the glories of the landscape spread out in the light of the sun going down behind Monte Mario, you may be sure they are foreigners.

To the left, the Pincian Way leads into the little Piazza della Trinità del Monte, with its ornamental obelisk; from there a wide flight of marble steps runs down into the city, providing a direct route from the summit of the hill to the Piazza di Spagna.

On its other side the palace looks out over magnificent gardens, laid out in the style of Le Nôtre, as all good institute gardens should be. They include a patch of woodland—laurels and ilex trees—on high terraced ground, bounded at one end by the ramparts of Rome and at the other by the convent of the French Ursulines, whose land adjoins the grounds of the Villa Medici.

Opposite, Raphael's country house, derelict and sad, can be made out among the waste lands of the Villa Borghese. To complete the desolate character of the view in this direction, the horizon beyond defines itself as a long, melancholy line of umbrella pines, black with crows that roost there at all times of the year.

Such, or near enough, are the truly regal surroundings provided by a generous government for its young artists during their stay in Rome. The director's quarters are superb; many ambassadors would be glad to possess anything like them. The students' rooms, on the other hand, are with one or two exceptions small, inconvenient and badly furnished; I should be surprised if a quartermaster-sergeant at the Poppincourt Barracks in Paris were not better off in this respect than I was at the Accademia di Francia. Most of the painters' and sculptors' studios are situated in the grounds; the remainder are scattered about the palace, a few of them in a kind of gallery built out from it, overlooking the garden of the Ursuline convent, with a prospect of the Sabine Hills, Monte Cavo and Hannibal's camp. A library, totally devoid of modern works but quite well stocked with standard classics, is open till three for the studiously-minded to work in; for those who are not, it provides a useful resort where they can browse away the time when they have nothing else to do. For it is only fair to say that the freedom the students enjoy is virtually complete. They are supposed to send back a sample of their work, a painting or drawing or engraving or piece of music, once a year to the Academy in Paris. Apart from that they can work as they like or not work at all, without anybody's being the wiser. The director's duties are limited to running the establishment and seeing that its rules are observed; he has nothing directly to do with the students' work. It could hardly be otherwise. The twenty-two students are concerned with five related but quite different branches of art. One man cannot be master of all of them, and it would be foolish of him to offer advice on those with which he is unfamiliar.

33

The students at the Academy—Felix Mendelssohn

THE AVE MARIA had just rung when I alighted at the door of the Academy. On entering, I was informed that it was dinner time and that all my new comrades were in the refectory, so I had myself taken straight there. My arrival, as I have said, had been delayed for various reasons, and I was the only one still to come. The moment I appeared in the doorway of the large hall, where some twenty diners were seated noisily round a table groaning with food, a roar went up sufficient to have shattered the windows had there been any:

'Look who's here! The great Berlioz in person! Gad sir, what a head! What hair! My dear, the nose! Admit it, Jalay, your nose has lost face.'

'What about your hair? He makes you look bald.'

'Ye gods, what a mop!'

'Hey, Berlioz? Don't you recognize me? Remember? Sardanapalus—the ceremony at the Institute—those damned drums of yours that wouldn't start the conflagration? Was he mad! By Jove, he had a right to be! Now don't you recognize me?'

'Yes, I do recognize you, but your name——'

'I say, listen to this—he addresses me as "vous". We're getting affected in our old age. Everybody's "tu" here straight away.'

'All right. What's your name?'

'His name's Signol.'

'Rossignol, you mean.'

'That's a vile pun. Rossignol is a vile pun.'

'Beneath contempt.'

'Let the poor thing be.'

'What, the pun?'

'Ass, no—Berlioz.'

'Not puns but punch, I say. Here, Fleury, bring some of your best. We need it to take away the taste.'

'So our music section is complete at last.'

'Here, Montfort,* allow me to introduce your colleague.'

'Montfort!'

'Montforte!'

'Montfortissimo!'

'Shake hands.'

'Let's shake hands.'

'They shall not shake hands.'

'Shake hands they shall.'

'Shake hands they shall not.'

'Here, you idiots, while you're carrying on like this he's hogging all the macaroni. Would you be so good as to leave me a little?'

'Well, let's all shake hands with him, and then call a truce.'

'Truce be damned. Let battle commence. Here comes the punch. Don't bother with your wine, Berlioz.'

'No more wine!'

'Down with the wine!'

'Come on, who'll break a bottle with me? Look out, Fleury!'

Crash!

'Gentlemen, gentlemen! At least you might spare the glasses—you'll need them for the punch. Unless you would rather have it in small glasses?'

'Perish the thought!'

'Good man, Fleury. Well stopped. The whole lot nearly went that time.'

Fleury is the resident factotum, an admirable fellow who fully deserves the trust which successive directors have placed in him. He has waited on the inmates for as long as anyone can remember and has witnessed so many scenes of the sort that he has learnt to take no notice of them; and the contrast between his impassive demeanour and the tumult raging round him adds to the fun.

* The other laureate that year. The Academy, not having awarded the first prize in 1829, awarded two in 1830. Montfort got the deferred prize, which entitled him to a grant for four years.

When I had recovered from the shock of my reception, I looked round the hall. It was a curious sight. Down the length of one wall hung framed portraits of about fifty former laureates. The opposite wall was covered with a kind of fresco consisting of a series of indescribably grotesque life-size caricatures, the originals of which had also been residents of the Academy. Unluckily the space had run out and the great work had had to be discontinued. Newcomers whose appearance lent itself to treatment no longer had the honour of being exhibited there.

That evening, after paying my respects to M. Vernet, I joined my companions at their usual haunt, the Café Greco. The Café Greco is the most odious place imaginable—dark, dirty and ill-lit—and there is nothing to justify its extraordinary popularity with artists of every nationality except its convenient situation, near the Piazza di Spagna with the Restaurant Lepri opposite, which brings it a considerable clientèle. One sits there killing time, smoking abominable cigars and drinking cups of coffee which are none the better for being served not on the usual marble-topped surface that you find everywhere else but on squalid little wooden tables the width of a small hat and as grimy and grease-stained as the walls. Yet it is so much frequented by foreign artists that most of them have their letters sent there; and if a new arrival wants to find his compatriots, he cannot do better than go to the Café Greco.

Next day I met Felix Mendelssohn, who had been in Rome for several weeks. I shall write of this encounter and the episodes it gave rise to when I come to describe my first visit to Germany.

34

Drama—I leave Rome—Florence to Nice —I return to Rome—no deaths

> One has heard of guns going off without having been loaded; but I believe there are more pistols that are loaded but do not go off.

I SPENT SOME TIME trying to adjust myself to this unfamiliar existence. But I could take no interest either in my surroundings or in the circle into which I had been suddenly thrust. A profound uneasiness possessed me. I had felt it the moment I saw that the letters from Paris which I expected to find on my arrival in Rome had not come. For three weeks I waited in ever-increasing anxiety. At length the desire to discover what lay behind this mysterious silence became too much for me, and despite the friendly warnings of Horace Vernet, who tried to restrain me by telling me that he would be forced to remove my name from the register of students if I left Italy, I insisted on returning to France.*

On my way through Florence I was confined to bed for a week with a sharp attack of quinsy. It was at this time that I met the Danish architect Schlick, an engaging fellow and an artist very highly thought of by connoisseurs. During my illness I occupied myself in rescoring the Ball Scene of my Fantastic Symphony (and in adding the present coda). I had not finished when I was allowed out for the first time and went to the post-office to see if there were any letters. The packet which was handed to me contained one, written with such vulgar effrontery and so wounding to a man of my age and disposition, that a terrible change came over me as I read it. Two tears of rage started from my eyes, and instantly I knew my course. I must go post-haste to Paris and there kill without compunction two guilty women and one innocent man.† As for subsequently killing myself, after a coup on this scale it was the least I could do. My plan of campaign was formed in a few minutes. They knew me, they would be expecting me to come back. Therefore I must take every precaution and go in disguise. I went to see Schlick, to whom the cause of this great drama was not unknown.

'Good God! What's happened?' he exclaimed, at the sight of my white face.

'Read this,' I said, and handed him the letter.

'Oh, it's monstrous,' he said, when he had read it. 'What are you going to do?'

At that moment it occurred to me that if I wanted to act freely I must not tell him.

'What am I going to do? I'm still going back, but I shall go to my father's house and not to Paris.'

* [He left Rome 1 April 1831.]

† All this, the reader will surmise, relates to my fair consoler. Her good mother, though perfectly well aware of the true state of the case, accused me of being 'destined to bring trouble' to her family, and announced her daughter's marriage to M. P——. [Pleyel. Berlioz received Mme Moke's letter in mid-April.]

'Yes, that's right, my dear fellow—go home, stay with your family for a while. It's only there that you'll be able to forget. You need time and rest. You're terribly upset, I can see. Come on, cheer up.'

'Don't worry—only, I must leave at once. I can't answer for myself tomorrow.'

'Nothing easier—we'll get you off this evening. I know the police and post-office people here. In a couple of hours I'll have your passport ready and in five I'll have a seat for you in the mail coach. I shall go and see to it. You go back to your hotel and get ready, and I'll join you there.'

Instead of going back, I repaired to the embankment of the Arno where there was a French milliner's. I entered the shop and, having consulted my watch, spoke as follows: 'Madam, it is now midday. I am leaving by tonight's mail. I need a complete lady's maid's outfit—dress, hat, green veil, and the rest—by five o'clock. Can you do it for me? I will pay you whatever you want. Money is no object.'

The milliner thought for a moment and then assured me it would all be ready by the appointed time. I paid a deposit, returned across the river to the Hôtel des Quatre Nations, where I was staying, and summoned the head porter.

'Antoine, I'm leaving for France at six o'clock. I can't take my trunk with me, the mail coach hasn't room, so can you look after it and send it on to my father at the first reliable opportunity? The address is here.' Next I took the score of the Ball Scene and, as the coda was not completely orchestrated, wrote across it, 'I have not had time to finish this. If the Conservatoire Concert Society should happen to want to perform the work during the composer's *absence*, I beg Habeneck to double the flute passage at the last entry of the theme with clarinets and horns at the lower octave and to score the chords which follow for full orchestra. That will suffice for the ending.'*

Then I wrapped up the score of the symphony, addressed it to Habeneck, and threw it into a valise with a few clothes; ceremoniously loaded a pair of double-barrelled pistols which I had

* This manuscript, with the inscription crossed out, is in the possession of my friend Joseph d'Ortigue.

with me; examined and replaced in my pocket two small bottles of those invaluable cordials, laudanum and strychnine; and, reassured as to my arsenal, went out again and spent the remainder of the time aimlessly wandering the streets of Florence with the restless, sickly air of a mad dog.

At five I went back to the milliner's and tried on my finery. It fitted perfectly. In paying the agreed sum, I gave twenty francs too much. The young assistant at the cash desk noticed and tried to point out my mistake; but her mistress interposed and pushed her aside, sweeping the money briskly into the till. 'Leave the gentleman alone, you silly goose. Do you think he has time to listen to your chatter?' And as I smiled ironically, she bowed with a singular grace and added, 'A thousand thanks, sir. You will be quite charming. I predict a great success for your little comedy.'

At last six o'clock struck. I said goodbye to the valiant Schlick (who regarded me as a lost sheep returning, somewhat the worse for wear, to the fold), stowed away my female apparel safely in a side pocket of the coach, threw a farewell glance at Benvenuto Cellini's Perseus, with its famous inscription: *Si quis te laeserit, ego tuus ultor ero*,* and we were off.

Mile after mile went by, and between the courier and me a profound silence reigned. My throat was dry and tight, my teeth clenched. I neither ate nor said anything. Towards midnight we exchanged a few words about the pistols I was carrying, which he prudently uncapped and concealed under the cushions; for he was afraid that we might be attacked, in which case we must not even look as though we meant to defend ourselves if we did not want to be murdered.

'As you wish,' I said. 'I should hate to compromise us, and I have no quarrel with the brigands.'

On our arrival at Genoa—I meanwhile having had nothing but a little orange juice since we started, to the astonishment of the courier, who could not make out whether I belonged to this world or the next—a fresh disaster was revealed. I had lost my female attire. We had changed coaches at a village called Pietra Santa, and

* 'If any man offend thee, I myself will be thy avenger.' The celebrated statue is in the Piazza della Signoria, from which the mail coach starts.

I had left it behind. 'Damnation take it,' I thought; 'some cursed guardian angel must be trying to foil my plan. Well, we shall see.'

I at once got hold of a manservant who could speak both French and Genoese. He took me off to a milliner's. It was almost midday; the coach left again at six. I demanded another set of clothes but was told that it was impossible to fit me out in so short a time. Three other milliners refused for the same reason. Finally, we found one who said she would summon some more seamstresses and do her best to have it ready in time.

She was as good as her word. I was re-equipped. But while I had been chasing after dressmakers, the Sardinian police had been examining my passport and had concluded that I was a dangerous character, an emissary of the July Revolution, a *co-carbonaro* working for liberation. They refused to give me a visa for Turin and informed me that I must go by Nice.

'Then for God's sake give me a visa for Nice. What difference does it make? I will go by the infernal regions if you wish, so long as I go.'

Which of us was the more splendidly idiotic: the police, who saw in every Frenchman an agent of the revolution, or I, who imagined I must not set foot in Paris without having first disguised myself as a woman, as though everyone who met me would instantly read my intentions in my face, or as though I could not easily have lain up in a hotel for twenty-four hours and found fifty milliners ready to accoutre me to perfection?

There is something fascinating about people in the grip of a passion: their unquestioning belief that the whole world is engrossed in it too, and the touching faith with which they act on that assumption.

I set out accordingly along the road to Nice. Far from having cooled off, I rehearsed in my mind every detail of the little comedy I intended to enact when I reached Paris. I go to my 'friend's' house at nine in the evening just when the family has assembled for tea. I say I am the Countess M——'s personal maid with an urgent message. I am shown into the drawing-room, where I deliver a letter. While it is being read I draw my double-barrelled pistols, blow out the brains of number one and number two, seize number three by the hair, reveal myself and, disregarding her screams, pay my respects to her in similar fashion, after which, before this cantata for voices and orchestra has had time to attract attention, I present my right temple with the unanswerable argument of the remaining barrel; or should the gun by any chance misfire, I have recourse to my cordials. What a fine scene it would have made. It really is a pity it had to be dropped.

And yet, despite my rage, I began to think other thoughts. It would of course be a moment of intense gratification. But to have to kill myself immediately afterwards was not so satisfactory. To say farewell to life and art, to leave behind me the reputation of a boor, a savage who did not know how to live, to leave my first symphony unfinished, to have other, greater works in my head, unwritten: no, it was—but then my almost blunted purpose would reassert itself and I would exclaim, 'No, no, no, I must destroy them, I must blow their brains out, they must all die—they must and they shall.' And the horses trotted on, bearing me towards France. Night fell. We were on the Corniche, where the Alps come down to the coast and the road is cut out of the rock more than six hundred feet above the sea. For the last hour, love of life and love of art had been whispering a thousand promises, nor had I checked them but had listened with a certain wistful fascination, when suddenly the driver stopped to attach the drag to the wheels. In the silence which followed I heard the dull crash of the waves foaming at the foot of the precipice. The sound struck a terrible chord within me, and a tempest of rage and grief swept over me, more violent than any that I had yet experienced. I raged like the sea and, clutching the seat with both hands, made a convulsive movement as if to cast myself headlong, at the same time letting out a wild 'Ha!' of such hoarseness and ferocity that the unfortunate driver, as he sprang back, must have definitely decided that his passenger was some demon compelled to wander the earth with a piece of the true cross on his person.

Yet, it had to be recognized, the fever was only intermittent; life was contending with death. As soon as I saw this, I reasoned with myself as follows—not altogether absurdly, I think, considering the hour and the place: supposing, in one of my lucid intervals (that is, the moments when life began to seem inviting—I was, in fact, on the point of surrender), supposing I had something to rely on, something solid to attach myself to, which would help me weather the next bout of fever when it came, I might perhaps succeed in reaching a decision—to live. Why not see? We had come to a little Sardinian village* standing right by the sea (which no longer roared so loudly). Here we stopped to change horses. I asked the driver for time to write a letter, and went into a small café where I seized a scrap of paper and wrote to M. Vernet, begging him not to strike my name off the register of students if he had not already done so, assuring him that I had not yet transgressed the Academy's ruling against leaving Italy, and promising on my honour not to cross the frontier before I had received his answer, which I would await at Nice.

Protected by my word of honour yet free to resume my Huron schemes should the Academy take away my grant and cast me forth without a penny, I got back more composedly into the coach. And then I realized that I was hungry, having eaten nothing since Florence. Oh blessed, base human nature! It was clear that I was cured.

I reached Nice, still growling at intervals. I waited a few days. Then M. Vernet's letter came—a friendly, sympathetic, paternal letter which touched me profoundly. The great man, though ignorant of the cause of my troubles, gave me the best advice possible. He pointed out that work and art were the two sovereign remedies for an afflicted mind. He told me that my name was still on the register, that the Minister should never hear of my escapade; in short, that I could return to Rome, where I would be received with open arms.

'So, they are saved!' I said, with a deep sigh. 'Suppose I live too? Live peacefully, contentedly, for music? What a farce! Why not try?'

So I lived, and drank deep draughts of the balmy air of Nice. Life and joy came running, music embraced me, the future smiled at me. I stayed in Nice for a month, wandering in the orange groves, immersing myself in the sea, dozing in the heather among the hills of Villefranche and watching from their splendid heights the silent traffic of ships coming and going across the shining water. I was

* I think it was Ventimiglia.

entirely on my own. I wrote the overture to *King Lear*. I breathed, I sang, I believed in God. A convalescence indeed.

They were the three happiest weeks of my life. *O Nizza!*

The King of Sardinia's police, crossing my path for the second time, put an end to this idyllic existence.

I had taken to exchanging an occasional word with two officers of the Piedmontese garrison who frequented the same café. One day I went so far as to join them in a game of billiards. This was sufficient to arouse the darkest suspicions of the chief of police.

'Now clearly,' he reasoned, 'this young French musician has not come to Nice to see *Matilde di Shabran*'* (the only opera being given at the time), 'since he never goes to the theatre. He spends whole days on the rocks at Villefranche; he must be waiting for a signal from some revolutionary vessel. He never dines at the table d'hôte. Of course—because he does not wish to be drawn into conversation by our agents. And now he is surreptitiously entering into relations with the officers of our regiments—undoubtedly in order to open negotiations with them—negotiations with which he has been entrusted by the leaders of Young Italy. A flagrant case of conspiracy!'

O man of great wisdom, sublime politician—thou ravest!

I was summoned to police headquarters and formally interrogated:

'What are you doing here?'

'Recovering from a painful illness. I compose, I dream, I thank God for the glorious sun, the blue sea and the great green hills.'

'You are not a painter?'

'No, sir.'

'Yet you are seen everywhere, sketch-book in hand, drawing. Are you by any chance making plans?'

'Yes, I am making plans for an overture on *King Lear*: in fact I have made them. The drafting and the instrumentation are complete. In fact I believe he will cause quite a stir when he appears.'

'Appears? Who is this King Lear?'

'Alas, a poor old English king.'

'English!'

* [An opera by Rossini, first heard in 1821 (conducted by Paganini) in Rome.]

'Yes. According to Shakespeare he lived some eighteen hundred years ago and was silly enough to divide his kingdom between two wicked daughters, who kicked him out when he had nothing more to give them. You will appreciate that few kings—'

'Never mind the king. This word instrumentation?'

'A musical term.'

'The same excuse again. Now, sir, I know quite well that's not the way people compose, without a piano, simply wandering about the beach with a sketch-book and a pencil. Tell me where you wish to go, and your passport will be made out. You can't stay in Nice any longer.'

'Very well, I'll return to Rome, and by your leave continue to compose without a piano.'

And that was that. Next day I left Nice,* very reluctantly but with a light heart and in the highest spirits. I was alive and cured. Thus was one more example provided of 'pistols that are loaded but do not go off'.

All the same, I think my little comedy had a certain interest. It really is a pity it was not performed.

35

The theatres of Genoa and Florence—Bellini's I Montecchi ed i Capuleti—Romeo played by a woman —Pacini's La Vestale—Licinius played by a woman —the Florentine organist—the Feast of Corpus Christi —I return to the Academy

ON MY WAY back through Genoa I went to hear Paër's *Agnese*, which had been a famous opera in the dark ages before the dawn of Rossini.†

It left me unmoved and bored; no doubt its beauties were obscured by the performance, which was appalling. I noticed at once that, in accordance with the charming practice of certain persons who, though incapable of writing anything themselves, see it as their mission to rewrite or touch up everything, and who

* [About 21 May. He spent a fortnight on the journey back to Rome, during which he sketched the monologues for *Lélio*.]

† [*Agnese di Fitz-Henry*, first heard in 1809.]

can tell at a glance of their eagle eye what a work lacks, someone had strengthened the score by the addition of a bass drum; with the result that Paër's modest and sensible orchestration, not being designed to stand the shock of such an encounter, disappeared without trace. Mme Ferlotti sang—she was careful not to act—the role of Agnes. She was one of those economical singers who know to the nearest franc how much a year their throats are worth to them. In the scene where Agnes' father goes mad, she bore herself with unruffled composure; one would have supposed her rehearsing the part, merely sketching the gestures, and singing without expression for fear of tiring her voice.

The orchestra struck me as tolerable: small but innocuous. The violins played in tune and the wind kept fairly well together. But it only served to remind me that while I was wasting my time in his native city, Paganini was electrifying Paris. Cursing the ill luck which prevented me from hearing him, I tried at least to find out more about him from his fellow-Genoese; but with the indifference to art characteristic of commercial cities they displayed no interest in the extraordinary figure who had been acclaimed all over Germany, France and England. When I asked where his father lived, no one seemed to know. Neither could I find any trace of the memorial I felt sure there must be to Columbus—no temple, no building of any kind, no column. In all my wanderings through the streets I never saw so much as a bust of the discoverer of the New World who immortalized the city of his birth.

Of all the great Italian cities, I have happiest memories of Florence. Untroubled by the spleen which assailed me later in Rome and Naples, completely on my own, knowing no one, equipped with a sufficient supply of piastres (despite the large hole which the trip to Nice had made in my funds), and in consequence quite free, I spent delightful days wandering about the many churches and palaces and musing on Dante and Michelangelo, or reading Shakespeare in the delicious silence of the woods along the right bank of the Arno, where the solitude permitted me to express my admiration in uninhibited terms. I hardly thought of hearing any music, for I took it as a matter of course that the capital of Tuscany was not the place to expect what Naples and Milan alone might provide if I was lucky. But at dinner in the hotel I learnt that Bellini's latest opera, *I Montecchi ed i Capuleti*, was being performed. Everyone was saying how good the music was; but the libretto too was well spoken of. This surprised me; the Italians as a rule pay little attention to the words of an opera. Here was something new! Perhaps I was about to hear a real *Romeo* at last, after all the lamentable attempts that had been made, a *Romeo* worthy of Shakespeare's genius. What a subject for an opera! How it lent itself to music! To begin with, the dazzling ball at the Capulets', where amid a whirling cloud of beauties the young Montague first sets eyes on 'sweet Juliet', whose constant love will bring her to the grave; then those furious battles in the streets of Verona, with the fiery Tybalt presiding like the personification of Revenge; the glorious night scene on Juliet's balcony, the lovers' voices 'like softest music to attending ears', uttering an ecstasy as radiant as the watchful moon shining its benediction upon them; the dashing Mercutio and his sharp-tongued, fantastical humour; the cackling nurse; the stately hermit, even in his cell caught up in the tragic conflict of love and hate and vainly striving to resolve it; and then the catastrophe, extremes of joy and despair drained to the dregs in the same instant, passion's heat chilled in the rigour of death; and, at the last, the solemn oath sworn by the warring houses, too late, on the bodies of their children, to abjure the feud which shed so much blood, so many tears. I hurried to the Pergola Theatre. A large chorus was in possession of the stage, singing, I thought, tolerably well, with full-bodied, incisive tone, among them a dozen boys of fourteen or fifteen whose alto voices were particularly effective. In due course the principals appeared. Of these, all sang out of tune with the exception of two women, one of whom, who was tall and beefy, played Juliet. The other, who was short and thin, played Romeo. What! After all these years, after Vaccai and Zingarelli,* to do it again, and write

* [Both of whom wrote a *Giulietta e Romeo* (1825 and 1796 respectively). Vaccai's librettist was Romani, who adapted the text for Bellini a few years later. Bellini's opera was first produced on 11 March 1830 in Venice, at the Fenice. On its first performance at the Paris Opéra in 1859, Berlioz wrote an article in the *Journal des débats* comparing the *Romeo* settings of Steibelt, Dalayrac, Zingarelli, Vaccai and Bellini (13 September 1859, reprinted in *A travers Chants*). By that time it had become an established custom to replace Bellini's final act with Vaccai's, on the

Romeo's part for a woman—as though there were some law that Juliet's lover must always appear shorn of his manhood; as if the Romeo who in three strokes pierces the 'furious Tybalt', the master swordsman, to the heart and later bursts the gates of Juliet's tomb and with disdainful arm lays County Paris lifeless on the steps of the monument were but a child, and the passions which consume him—his despair when he is exiled, his terrible numb resignation at the news of Juliet's death, his frenzy as the poison begins to work—were the common attribute of eunuchs!

Or was there some idea that the musical effect of two women's voices is best? Then why not do away with tenors, baritones and basses altogether, and have all roles played by sopranos and contraltos? Moses or Othello discharged in a piping treble would hardly be more incongruous than a female Romeo. Then I reflected that I had better make the best of it; the work itself would compensate.

Bitter disappointment! The opera contained no ball at the Capulets', no Mercutio, no garrulous nurse, no grave and tranquil hermit, no balcony scene, no sublime soliloquy for Juliet as she takes the hermit's phial, no duet in the cell between the banished Romeo and the disconsolate friar, no Shakespeare, nothing—a squandered opportunity. Yet this wretched libretto carved out of Shakespeare's great play is the work of a distinguished poet, Felice Romani; such is the dominance of mediocre ideas and shoddy traditions on the Italian operatic stage.

The composer has, however, contrived at one important point to extract something memorable. It comes at the conclusion of an act, when the lovers, dragged apart by their infuriated parents, tear themselves free for an instant and rush into each other's arms with the cry 'We shall meet again in heaven.' Bellini has set this passage to a phrase of wonderful élan and intensity, delivered by the two characters in unison. The two voices singing as one, as though in perfect union, give the melody an extraordinary force and bold impetus; and whether it was the context in which the phrase occurred and the manner in which it was then brought back and repeated, or the sudden effect of the unison, so unexpected and so

---

grounds that the former was 'too weak'. By a curious coincidence Vaccai's opera had its Paris première, at the Théâtre-Italien, on the same night as the first performance of *Romeo and Juliet* by the English company, 15 September 1827.]

apt, or the beauty of the tune itself, I was carried away in spite of myself and applauded enthusiastically. Since those days, duets in unison have been worked to death.

Having resolved to drink the cup to the lees, I went back a few days later to see Pacini's *La Vestale*.* From what I knew of it already, I gathered that it had nothing in common with Spontini's opera except the name; but I had not expected anything quite so bad. Licinius, too, was played by a woman. After a few painful minutes I was exclaiming, with Hamlet, 'Wormwood, wormwood'; and in the middle of the second act, feeling that I could swallow no more, I left, giving the wall such a kick that my big toe was sore for three days. Poor Italy! At least in the churches, I shall be told, the music is on a par with the grandeur of the ceremonial. Poor Italy! The reader will see what kind of music was practised in Rome, capital of the Christian world. Meanwhile, this is what I heard with my own ears while I was in Florence.

It was not long after the uprisings at Modena and Bologna. Louis Bonaparte's two sons had been actively involved. One of them had escaped with their mother, Queen Hortense; the other had died in his father's arms. His funeral service was being celebrated in a church draped entirely in black, with catafalques, flaring torches, and a host of priests in attendance. It was a sight to conjure with, yet not as awe-inspiring as the thought of who it was that lay there: the very name set great echoes ringing in my mind. A Bonaparte! *His* nephew, almost his grandson—now dead at twenty, and his mother fled to England, snatching her last surviving son† from the reactionaries' axe, and debarred from returning to France, the scene of her splendid youth. My mind, travelling back over the years, pictured the young creole child dancing on the deck of the ship that brought her from the New World to the Old, the obscure offspring of Madame Beauharnais who became the adopted daughter of the master of Europe, Queen of Holland—and now

* [First performed in 1830.]

† Now President of the French Republic, which melancholy task he discharges conscientiously and with vigour and good sense. I was presented to him in London at Count d'Orsay's last year. [Early 1848. Louis Napoleon was elected President of the Second Republic in December 1848. Four years later he became the Emperor Napoleon III.]

forgotten, orphaned, bereft, without a kingdom, without a home. Oh, Beethoven! Where was the Homeric mind that created the Eroica, the Funeral March for the death of a hero, and all those great epics of affliction that wring the heart and exalt the soul? The organist had pulled out the piccolo stop and was hopping about at the top of the keyboard, twittering little snatches of song, as wrens do when they perch on a garden wall and preen themselves in the pale winter sunshine. . . .

The Feast of Corpus Christi was due to be celebrated in Rome. For the last few days I had heard constant talk of what a tremendous affair it was, and I decided to return at once in company with several Florentines who were going there for the same reason. On the way they spoke of nothing but the wonders we would see, and painted me a scene of mitred glory, with tiaras and chasubles, crosses studded with gems, and golden vestments glowing in a mist of incense.

'*Ma la musica?*'

'*Oh! signore, lei sentirà un coro immenso!*' And they would return to their clouds of incense, golden vestments and crosses studded with gems, and the splendid noise of all the bells and the cannon. But old prejudices die hard, and I persisted with my question.

'*La musica? La musica di questa ceremonia?*'

'*Oh! signore, lei sentirà un coro immenso!*'

Well, at any rate, there was going to be . . . an immense chorus. Perhaps it really would be something remarkable. I thought of the musical rites in the temple of Solomon. As my imagination took fire I began to hope for some modern equivalent of the colossal splendours of ancient Egypt. Accursed faculty that makes our life a perpetual mirage! But for it, I might have been delighted by the acrid falsetto in which the *castrati* regaled me with their insipid counterpoint. But for it, no doubt I should not have been in the least astonished at a Corpus Christi procession with no train of white-clad girls in attendance, chanting sweet hymns to heaven, the music of their fresh young voices rising from them like a perfume of living roses. But for this fatal imagination of mine I might not have taken quite such violent exception to the twin groups of quacking clarinets, bellowing trombones, rampant bass drums and circus trumpets spewing forth their ungodly noise—

though, admittedly, in that case I would have had to suppress the faculty of hearing as well. The Romans have a name for it: they call it 'military music'. Had it heralded old Silenus riding on an ass, with a ribald company of satyrs and lewd bacchantes in attendance, nothing could have been more appropriate. But the sacrament, the Pope, the statues of the Virgin!* However, this was only the beginning of my initiation into the holy mysteries. But I will come to that later.

Here I was, then, back at the Villa Medici,† kindly received by the director and welcomed with open arms by my comrades, who must have been curious to know the object of my pilgrimage but who with exemplary tact never once alluded to it.

I had gone away; I had had my reasons for going; now I was back, and that was splendid. No comments were made and no questions asked.

36

Life at the Academy—wanderings in the Abruzzi —St Peter's—spleen—excursions in the Roman Campagna —the Carnival—the Piazza Navona

I WAS ALREADY familiar with the routine of life at the Academy, both within the precincts and outside. At mealtimes a bell was rung in the passages and along the garden paths, and we went straight in as we were, in our straw hats, slippered feet, tunics torn or plastered with clay, no ties—the tattered uniform of the studio. Afterwards we generally lounged about the garden for an hour or two, playing quoits or tennis, firing pistols and potting at the unfortunate blackbirds in the laurel wood, or training puppies—in all of which activities Horace Vernet, whose relations with us were more those of a boon companion than of an orthodox director, often joined. In the evening we sallied forth down the hill to the inevitable Café Greco and smoked the cigar of peace and drank the patriotic punchbowl with the lower orders, as we called the French artists who were not attached to the Academy. After

* Barbarous! The Pope is a barbarian, like most other sovereigns. The Roman people are barbarians, like all other peoples.

† [About 3 June 1831.]

which, the company dispersed. . . . Those who returned virtuously to academic barracks sometimes forgathered in the large portico which gives onto the garden. When I happened to be one of the party my bad voice and wretched guitar were pressed into service. We sat round the marble basin of the little fountain as it splashed and glinted in the moonlight, tempering the heat, and sang the dreamy tunes of *Freischütz* and *Oberon*, the rousing choruses of *Euryanthe*, or whole acts of *Iphigénie en Tauride*, *La Vestale* or *Don Giovanni*; for I must say, to the credit of my messmates, their musical taste was anything but low.

There was also another kind of music-making which we called 'English Concerts'. This too had its attractions, after a somewhat riotous dinner. The drinkers, whether they could sing or not, would each choose some favourite air that they could remember after a fashion. No two people could have the same tune; and to ensure the greatest possible variety, each sang in a key different from that of the man next to him. Duc, the lively and gifted architect, had his special number, 'La colonne' and Dantan his 'Sultan Saladin'. Montfort was sensational in the march from *La Vestale*, Signol gave a charming rendering of the romance 'La fleuve du Tage', and I enjoyed a certain success with that simple but heart-easing strain 'Il pleut bergère'. At a given signal the performers would start off, one after the other; and as this vast ensemble in twenty-four parts rose to a climax, all the dogs of the Pincian Way would set up a mournful howling, while the barbers in the Piazza di Spagna came out onto their door-steps and winked at each other and exclaimed, '*Musica francese!*'

Every Thursday there was a reception at the director's, presided over with grace and distinction by Mme Vernet and her daughter. These soirées were very fashionable, and the brightest lights of Roman society were to be seen there. Of course we students always went along too. Sunday, on the other hand, was usually the day for expeditions into the country round Rome, either to Ponte Molle, where you get Orvieto wine, a thick, sweetish stuff rather like medicine—a favourite drink of the Romans—or to the Villa Pamphili, or to San Lorenzo-fuori-le-mure, or best of all to the splendid tomb of Cecilia Metella, where there is a remarkable echo which it is obligatory to cross-examine at length until you have shouted yourself hoarse and worked up an excuse for repairing to the nearby tavern and drinking its coarse dark wine, thick with midges.

With the director's permission, students can go off on much longer trips and be away for indefinite periods, the sole proviso being that they do not stray beyond the Roman States—that is, until the moment during their stay when the regulations permit them to travel all over Italy. For this reason it is very unusual for all the students to be in residence at any one time. There are almost always at least two of them off on trips to Naples, Venice, Florence, Palermo or Milan. The painters and sculptors are normally the least impatient to leave Rome, where they have Raphael and Michelangelo, but the architects are always eager to see Paestum, Pompeii and Sicily, and the landscape artists spend the greater part of their time in the mountains. As for the musicians, since the various centres of Italy are all about equally inviting, they have no more precise motive for leaving Rome than a general 'restlessness and the desire to see things';* where they go and for how long depends entirely on personal inclination. I liked exploring, and made use of the freedom accorded us to escape to the Abruzzi whenever I felt the boredom of Rome begin to stifle me. Had I not done so, I doubt whether I could have stood the monotony of our existence; for neither the jovial company of my fellow-artists nor the brilliant balls at the Academy and the Embassy nor the freemasonry of the bistro could make me forget that I had come from Paris, the centre of civilization, and now found myself at a stroke cut off from music, from the theatre, which in Rome functions for only four months a year, from literature (most of the books I admired being at that time on the Papal Index), from all the events and questions of the hour; in fact from everything which to me meant life.

Not all the great relics of classical Rome, which alone give glamour to the modern city, could compensate me for what I was missing. Nor is that so surprising. The objects one has constantly before one's eyes soon become so familiar that eventually they cease to arouse any but the most commonplace ideas and impressions. I must however except the Colosseum, which day or night I

* [La Fontaine, 'Les deux pigeons'.]

never looked on unmoved. St Peter's too always thrilled me. It is so vast, so nobly beautiful, so serene and majestic. I liked spending the day there when the summer's heat became unbearable. I would take a volume of Byron and, settling myself comfortably in a confessional, enjoy the cool air of the cathedral and, in a religious silence unbroken by any sound but the murmur of the two fountains in the square outside wafting in as the wind stirred momentarily, would sit there absorbed in that burning verse, following the Corsair across the sea on his audacious journeys, adoring the extraordinary nature of the man, at once ruthless and of great tenderness, generous-hearted and without pity, a strange amalgam of two feelings seemingly opposed: love of a woman, hatred of his kind.

Occasionally, laying down the book to meditate, I let my gaze wander round. Attracted by the light, my eyes would look upwards to Michelangelo's glorious dome and my thoughts accomplish an abrupt transformation. From roaring pirates and bloody execution I passed in an instant to the music of the spheres, the quiring seraphim, goodness, serenity, and the infinite peace of heaven. Then, coming down to earth a little, I fancied some palpable imprint of the poet still lingered in the place. He must have stood there, I thought, and looked at those figures of Canova's. His feet trod this marble, his hands explored that bronze. He breathed this air, his words vibrated in this stillness—words, perhaps, of tenderness and love. Of course, for he must have come here with his friend the Countess Guiccioli*—rare and admirable woman, who understood him so completely, by whom he was so profoundly loved. Yes, loved, a poet, free, rich—he was all those things. And in the silence of the confessional I ground my teeth till the damned must have heard it and trembled.

One day, in a mood of similar frustration, I got up on a sudden impulse, but stopped and stood still in the middle of the church. A peasant came in and, going quietly up, kissed St Peter's big toe.

'Lucky creature,' I thought with bitterness, 'what do you lack? You believe, you have hope. The statue you adore was formerly Jupiter Tonans; its right hand held thunderbolts instead of the keys

* I saw her one evening at M. Vernet's, with her golden hair falling about her sad face like the branches of a weeping willow. Three days later, in Dantan's studio, I saw a rough sketch in clay that he had made of her.

of paradise. You don't know this and are not disillusioned. When you go out of here, what will you be looking for? A patch of shade to sleep in. The wayside shrines are yours, you will find it there. What are your dreams of wealth? The handful of piastres necessary to buy a donkey or get married; three years' saving will achieve it. What is a wife in your eyes? Someone of a different sex. What do you look for in art? A means of giving tangible form to the objects of your worship, making you laugh, and providing something to dance to. For you, painting means the Virgin in red and green; drama means puppets and Punch and Judy; music means the bagpipe and the tambourine—whereas for me it means hatred and despair, since I lack everything I am looking for and have given up hope of finding it.'

After I had stood there listening for some time to the storm raging within me, I realized that it was evening. The peasant had gone; I was alone in St Peter's. I went out. Some German painters whom I met took me off to a tavern outside the city where we drank innumerable bottles of Orvieto, held forth extravagantly, smoked, and ate raw some small birds which we had bought from a sportsman. My companions found them delicious, and I was soon agreeing with them, despite the revulsion I had felt at first.

We returned to Rome singing choruses from Weber—a reminder of musical delights that would not be ours for many months to come. At midnight I went to the ball at the Ambassador's. I saw an English girl there, as beautiful as Diana. It appeared that, in addition to possessing a fortune of fifty thousand pounds a year, she had a superb voice and was an excellent pianist. Further evidence of the impartiality with which Providence bestows its favours! I encountered old women with faces like the witches in *Macbeth*, bent over the écarté table, eyes flaming with greed. I watched some simpering coquettes. Two elegant young girls were pointed out to me, making what their mothers call their 'first appearance in the world': expensive, delicate flowers whom its blasts would soon wither. These sights delighted me. Near where I stood, three amateurs held forth on enthusiasm, poetry, music. They drew comparisons between Beethoven and M. Vaccai, Shakespeare and M. Ducis,*

* [Eighteenth-century poet whose pallid adaptations of Shakespeare held the Paris stage for half a century.]

said had I read Goethe and didn't I think *Faust* charming, and many other happy notions of the sort. I left the room wishing a meteorite the size of a mountain could fall on the Embassy, obliterating it and everything it contained.

On our way back to the Academy up the steps of the Trinità del Monte, we were obliged to draw our long Roman knives. Some wretches were in ambush on the terrace, waiting to ask passers-by for their money or their lives. But there were two of us to their three, and the click of our knives as we snapped them open showed them, for the moment, the error of their ways.

Often, after these pale functions, where the sound of vapid cavatinas vapidly sung to the piano served only to tantalize my thirst for music and sharpen my ill humour, I found sleep impossible. Then I would go down into the garden, wrapped in a large hooded coat, and seated on a marble slab, listening to the sound of the owls of the Villa Borghese and pursuing the dark misanthropic current of my thoughts, stay there till the sun came up. If my comrades had found out about these aimless starlight vigils, they would certainly have accused me of affectation (the time-honoured word), and there would have been a stream of witticisms on the subject. But I kept quiet about it.

This, then, with shooting and riding,* made up the elegant round of ideas and activities within which I revolved unceasingly during my stay in Rome. Add the enervating effect of the sirocco, the craving, imperious but never satisfied, for the pleasures of my art, painful memories, the misery of knowing that I was exiled for two years from the musical world, and the inexplicable but genuine impossibility of working at the Academy, and the reader will understand how intense was the spleen that consumed me.

I was as surly as a chained dog. My companions' attempts to include me in their diversions only made me more irritable. The

* It was on a riding excursion in the Roman Campagna with Felix Mendelssohn that I mentioned my surprise that no one had ever thought of writing a scherzo on Shakespeare's glittering little poem, 'Queen Mab'. He was equally surprised, and I instantly regretted having put the idea into his head. For several years afterwards I dreaded hearing that he had used the subject. Had he done so it would have been impossible, or at any rate very unwise, to make the double attempt (a vocal scherzetto and an orchestral scherzo) that I made in my *Romeo and Juliet* symphony. Happily for me he thought no more of it.

attraction they found in the 'delights' of the Carnival particularly exasperated me. I could not conceive (I still cannot) what pleasure anyone could take in the festivities connected with what are appropriately called, in Rome as in Paris, the fat days, *i giorni grassi*. Bloated days, greasy with mire and sweat and grinning painted faces, gross with brutalities and foul-mouthed abuse, drunken informers, whores, half-wits gaping and guffawing, broken-down horses, the reek of the streets, the boredom and degradation of humanity! In Rome, where they preserved the great traditions of the ancient world, a human victim was sacrificed during the festival. I do not know whether this charming practice, redolent of the poetry of the arena, is still extant. No doubt it is; ideas of such grandeur do not disappear so quickly. In those days some poor devil under sentence of death was kept for the purpose and fattened so as to be a worthy offering to the sacred people of Rome; and in due time, when this rabble of fools of every nation (for in justice it must be said, the foreigners are as eager for the sport), when this horde of apes in the likeness of men grew bored with watching the horse-racing and pelting each other in the face with plaster pellets, to the accompaniment of shrieks of witty merriment, they went off to see 'the man' die. The worms, they do well to call him that. Generally it is some luckless bandit who, weakened by his wounds, is taken half dead by the valiant soldiers of the Pope, carefully patched up, nursed back to health, and fattened and shriven for Shrovetide: and to my mind this wretched prisoner is a thousand times more truly a man than the gloating multitude for whose amusement the Church's spiritual and temporal head (*abhorrens a sanguine*) and the representative of God on earth is obliged from time to time to provide the spectacle of a severed head.*

* The Parisians still maintain the standards set by the Romans in 1831. M. Léon Halévy, brother of the well-known composer, has just written a thoroughly sensible and right-minded letter to the *Journal des débats*, demanding the suppression of the disgusting rites celebrated during the Carnival, when the Shrovetide bull is paraded through the streets of Paris for three days and finally driven exhausted to the slaughterhouse, where its throat is cut amid scenes of great pomp.

His eloquent protest stirred me to send him the following letter:

'*Sir*—permit me to congratulate you most warmly on the admirable letter published in the *Journal des débats* this morning. No, do not believe you have

It is true that soon afterwards the fastidious crowd repairs to the Piazza Navona to wash itself free of any stains which the blood may have left on its clothes. The square is completely flooded; the vegetable market disappears and is replaced by a stagnant pond, upon whose bosom float not water-lilies but cabbage stalks, lettuce leaves, melon peel, straw and the husks of almonds. On a platform erected towards one side of the enchanted lake a small band of musicians, with a couple of bass drums, tenor drum, side drum, triangle, Turkish crescent and two pairs of cymbals, supported for appearance's sake by a few horns or clarinets, discourse music in a style as pure as the water lapping round the supports of their stage, while the carriages of the great process slowly through the pool, cheered on with ironic shouts by the sovereign people from the safety of the bank.

'*Mirate, mirate!* There's the Austrian Ambassador.'

'No it's not, it's the English Envoy.'

'Can't you see his coat of arms, a sort of eagle?'

'No, I make it some other animal, and anyway there's the famous motto: *Dieu et mon droit.*'

'Look, the Spanish Consul with his faithful Sancho. Rosinante doesn't seem to care much for this water excursion.'

'Good heavens! The French Ambassador as well?'

'Of course. The old one behind him in the cardinal's hat must be Napoleon's uncle.'

'Who's that pot-bellied little man with the mischievous smile, trying to look solemn?'

That is a very clever man who writes imaginatively about the arts.* He is consul at Cività Vecchia, but feels in duty bound to leave his post on the Mediterranean and tour the sewage of the Piazza Navona in his barouche—it is the thing to do. Just now he is thinking up a new chapter for his novel *Rouge et Noir.*

---

made yourself look foolish. In any case, to be thought foolish by trivial minds is far better than to be thought callous and insensitive by men of feeling for remaining indifferent to the scenes you so justly stigmatize, which turn so-called civilized man into the nastiest of all predatory animals.— *7 March 1865.*'

* M. Beile or Bayle or Baile, who wrote a life of Rossini under the name of Stendhal, full of the most tiresome nonsense about music, for which he fancied he had a feeling.

'*Mirate, mirate!* There's our precious Vittoria in person, our small-footed Fornarina* (perhaps not so small), posing as a Princess of the Church—a relaxation after her hard work in the studios at the Academy. Look at her on her chariot, like Venus rising from the sea. Watch out, the tritons of the Piazza Navona all know her and are lifting up their horns to give her a triumphal march. Quick, get away while there's time!'

'What's all that shouting? What's going on over there? A private carriage has overturned! Do you see who it is? It's our fat tobacconist from the Via Condotti. Good for her! She's striking out like Agrippina in the Bay of Pozzuoli. Look, while she takes the whip to her little boy to console him for his ducking, the horses, not being used to such sport, plunge madly about in the muddy water. Oh, this is really splendid: one of them has been drowned. Agrippina's tearing her hair. The audience are beside themselves. They're pelting her with orange peel, the naughty things.'

Good people! There is something very touching in your simple sport, a kind of poetry and natural dignity in your pleasures. How right they are, the great critics, when they say, Art is for all. If Raphael painted his divine madonnas, it was because he understood the exalted passion of the Masses for the pure, the beautiful, the ideal. If Michelangelo wrested his immortal Moses from the bowels of the marble and raised up with his mighty hands a glorious temple, it was of course to satisfy their souls' yearning for profound emotions. It was to feed the sacred flame which burns in the hearts of the people that Tasso and Dante sang. Let all works not admired by the mob be anathema! For if it scorns them, it is because they are worthless. If it holds them in contempt, it is because they are contemptible. And if it formally rejects them with catcalls, let the author too be rejected! He has shown a want of proper respect for the public, he has outraged its intelligence and wounded its deepest sensibilities. Away with him to the mines!

* [Fornarina was Raphael's model and mistress.]

37

Shooting in the mountains—the Campagna again —Virgilian recollections—wild Italy—regrets —tavern balls—my guitar

LIFE IN THE city had become unbearable for me. I seized every opportunity to leave it and escape to the mountains, until such time as I should be allowed to return to France.

As a stepping-stone for longer expeditions into that part of Italy, a region normally visited only by landscape painters, I often went to Subiaco, a large village some miles from Tivoli, in the Papal States.

The trip was my regular remedy for spleen—a sovereign remedy which seemed to restore me to life. Wearing a straw hat and an old grey tunic, with half a dozen piastres in my pocket and gun or guitar in hand, I would set off, not caring where I spent the night, knowing I could always find shelter if need be in one of the countless wayside caves or shrines. Sometimes I went at a great pace, sometimes I would stop to examine an old tomb or, from the top of one of those melancholy hillocks that dot the dusty Roman plain, listen to the boom of the bells of St Peter's, whose golden cross gleamed on the horizon, or break off the pursuit of a flock of lapwing to jot down in my notebook some symphonic idea that had just occurred to me; always, whatever I did, drinking to the full the unutterable delight of complete and absolute freedom.

Sometimes, when I had my guitar with me instead of my gun, I would station myself in the midst of a landscape in harmony with my mood, and some passage from the *Aeneid*, dormant in my memory since childhood, would come back to me, set off by the character of the country into which I had wandered. Then, improvising a strange recitative to stranger harmonies, I would sing of Pallas' death and the despair of the good Evander, the young warrior's funeral procession, his horse Aethon unharnessed and with flowing mane and great tears following the body, the terror of good King Latinus; the siege of Latium, whose dust I trod, Amata's sad end and the cruel death of Lavinia's noble lover.

Under the combined influence of poetry, music and association I would work myself up into an incredible state of excitement.

The triple intoxication always ended in floods of tears and uncontrollable sobbing. The most curious part of it was that I was able to analyse my feelings. I wept for poor Turnus, robbed by the hypocrite Aeneas of kingdom, mistress and life; I wept for the beautiful and pathetic Lavinia, forced to wed an unknown brigand with her lover's blood still fresh upon him. I longed for those poetic days when the heroes, sons of the gods, walked the earth in glittering armour, casting delicate javelins, their points set in a ring of gleaming gold. Quitting the past for the present, I wept for my own private disappointments, my uncertain future, my interrupted career; until, collapsing amid this maelstrom of poetry, and murmuring snatches of Shakespeare, Virgil and Dante—*Nessun maggior dolore . . . che ricordarsi . . .* Oh poor Ophelia. . . . Good night, sweet ladies. . . . *Vitaque cum gemitu . . . fugit indignata . . . sub umbras*—I fell asleep.

What madness, many will say. Yes, but what happiness. Sensible people have no idea what it is to have this intense consciousness simply of being alive. One's heart dilates, one's imagination expands and soars, one exists with a kind of frenzy; under the influence of extreme nervous stimulation, one's very body seems made of iron. I took countless risks and did things then that perhaps would kill me now.

Once I left Tivoli in pouring rain, taking my gun with hammers which made shooting possible despite the wet. I did my twenty-five miles, shot fifteen head of game on the way, and arrived at Subiaco in the evening, having spent the whole day soaked to the skin.

Now, immersed again in the Parisian vortex, how clearly and vividly I recall that wild Abruzzi country where I wandered far and wide. Mysterious villages, thinly populated by thinly dressed inhabitants with distrustful eyes and ancient battered guns that shoot far and find their mark only too often; curious lonely corners where the utter stillness of the place possessed me—a host of forgotten impressions come crowding back. Subiaco, Alatri, Civitella, Isola di Sora, San Germano, Arce; the old monasteries, neglected and abandoned, their chapels standing wide open; the monks are gone, a profound silence reigns. . . . Later, monks and bandits will return together. Rich abbeys, splendid foundations

AUSTRIAN EMPIRE
SWITZERLAND
FRANCE
Geneva
La Côte Saint-André
SAVOY
M. Cenis
Grenoble
Turin
Milan
Lodi
LOMBARDY
VENETIA
Piacenza
Parma
PARMA
PIEDMONT
MODENA
Modena
Bologna
ISTRIA
Adriatic Sea
LIGURIA
Genoa
La Spezia
Diano Marina
Pietra Santa
R. Arno
Pisa
Leghorn
Florence
Nice
Ventimiglia
The Corniche
Marseilles
KINGDOM OF SARDINIA
TUSCANY
PAPAL STATES
Perugia
L. Trasimeno
Foligno
Radicoffani
Elba
Spoleto
Terni
CORSICA (to France)
Rome
Tivoli
Subiaco
Arce
M. Cassino
Capua
Naples
Pozzuoli
I. of Nisida
Castellamare
SARDINIA
Tyrrhenian Sea
KINGDOM OF THE TWO SICILIES
SICILY
Miles
0 50 100 150
Rome and its environs
Isola Farnese
R. Tiber
Vico-var
Arsoli
Anticoli
Tivoli
R. Aniene
Subiaco
Rome
Lago di Gabia
Olevano
Civitella Roveto
Genesano
Arcinasso
TUSCULUM
Palestrina
Castelgandolfo
Isola di Sora
Albano
Alatri
Veroli
Arce
Ceprano
Monte Cassino
Miles
0 10 20 30 40 50

inhabited by pious, benevolent men who receive travellers with the utmost courtesy and surprise them by the charm, vivacity and learning of their conversation; the Benedictine palace of Monte Cassino with its wealth of dazzling mosaics, its wood-carvings and its shrines; the other monastery of San Benedetto at Subiaco, where you can see the cave in which St Benedict took refuge and the rose trees that he planted still grow. Farther up the same mountain, on the edge of a precipice high above the murmuring Anio, stream beloved of Horace and Virgil, Beato Lorenzo's cell clinging to the sun-baked rock, a place where I have seen swallows shelter in January; great woods of dark-leaved chestnut trees, and rising among them ruins, sometimes at dusk crowned by the sudden figure of a man, herdsman or brigand, appearing for an instant and vanishing without a sound. Opposite, on the farther bank of the Anio, a big hill like a whale's back and on it, visible to this day, the little pyramid of stones I set myself to build one day when the spleen was on me, and which the French painters, faithful frequenters of those solitudes, ceremoniously baptized in my honour. Below it, a cave that one can reach only by dropping down from the rock just above and crawling in, at the risk of arriving battered to pieces at the bottom, five hundred feet below.

To the right, a field where some reapers stopped me, astonished at my being there, and after bombarding me with questions, only allowed me to proceed with the ascent on my assuring them several times that I was on my way to fulfil a vow to the Madonna. A long way from there, standing in a narrow plain on the banks of the inevitable Anio, the lonely house of La Piagia, where I used to take shelter and have my clothes dried after long hours of shooting on rainy autumn days; the proprietress, an admirable woman, had a remarkably beautiful daughter who later married our friend Flacheron, the painter from Lyons; I can still see that young scalliwag Crispino, half bandit, half irregular soldier, who used to bring us gunpowder and cigars. Then the rows of shrines to the Madonna along the tops of the high hills where at evening, returning late from the plain, the reapers pass, chanting their litanies, while from somewhere comes the sad jangle of a monastery bell—pine forests resounding to the rustic tunes of the *pifferari*—great girls with raven hair and swarthy skin and raucous laughs, whose passion for dancing so often taxed the patience and the fingers *di questo signore chi suona la chitarra francese**—the traditional tambourine beating time to my improvised saltarellos—the *carabinieri*'s insistence on forcing their way in and joining our tavern ball—indignation of the dancers, French and Abruzzian—Flacheron's prodigious fists flailing—humiliating expulsion of the soldiers of the Pope—dark threats of ambuscades and long knives—Flacheron, without a word, slipping off to his midnight tryst, armed only with a stick—total absence of *carabinieri*—wild delight of Crispino.

And then Albano, Castelgandolfo, Tusculum, Cicero's little theatre, the frescoes in his ruined villa, the lake of Gabia, the marsh where I slept at midday without thought of fever, the remains of the gardens where the noble Zenobia lived, beautiful dethroned queen of Palmyra, the long lines of ancient aqueducts vanishing into the distance.

Poignant memories of days of freedom long ago! Freedom of the heart, of the mind, of the soul, of everything. Freedom to do nothing, not even think; freedom to forget time, to despise ambition, to laugh at fame, to dismiss love; freedom to go north, south, east or west, to sleep in the open, to live on little, to wander at large, without premeditation, to dream, to drowse away whole days immobile in the breath of the *sirocco*. Oh great, strong Italy, wild Italy, heedless of your sister, the Italy of art:

The lovely Juliet stretched upon her bier.†

38

Subiaco—the convent of St Benedict—a serenade —Civitella—my gun—my friend Crispino

SUBIACO IS A small market town of four thousand inhabitants, bizarrely constructed round the slopes of a sugar-loaf hill. The Anio, which farther downstream forms the famous waterfalls of Tivoli, gives it what prosperity it has by supplying the power for a few rather dilapidated mills.

* ['The gentleman that plays the French guitar.']

† [From Auguste Barbier's *Il Pianto*.]

The river's course in places runs through a narrow gorge. Nero had it dammed up by an enormous wall (the remains of which are still visible), which created a deep lake above the village; hence the name, *Sub-lacu*. The monastery of San Benedetto, two or three miles upstream, is virtually the only building of interest anywhere around and is much visited. The chapel altar stands before the entrance to the little cave where the founder of the Benedictine order once took refuge.

The interior of the church has a most unusual design, being on two levels connected by a flight of ten steps.

After the monks have made you admire the *santa spelunca* and the grotesque pictures on its walls, they take you down to the lower floor. Here they store great heaps of petals from the rose bushes in the convent garden. These flowers possess the miraculous property of curing convulsions and the monks do a flourishing trade in them. Three bent rusty old muskets hang near the fragrant nostrum, testifying to a no less remarkable miracle: some sportsmen, who had rashly overloaded their guns, realized *in the act of firing* the danger they were in and, while their weapons were going off, called upon St Benedict (in abbreviated form, no doubt) and were duly preserved not merely from death but from the slightest scratch. Continuing up the mountain for a couple of miles you reach the hermitage of Beato Lorenzo, now uninhabited. The awful solitude of the place, a wilderness of bare red rock, is enhanced by the almost total neglect in which it has been left since the hermit's death. A huge dog was its solitary guardian when I visited it. He lay crouched and motionless in the sun, following me about with his eyes. I must confess that, unarmed as I was, and on the brink of a precipice, the presence of that silent, distrustful Argus—who could easily hurl headlong or bury his teeth in any stranger who aroused his suspicions by an unguarded movement—persuaded me to keep my meditations brief. Subiaco is not so deep in the mountains as to be beyond the reach of civilization. There is a café where the politicians of the district meet. There is even a philharmonic society. The musician who conducts it also fulfils the functions of parish organist. At Mass on Palm Sunday he treated us to the overture to *La Cenerentola*. This so discouraged me that I decided to steer clear of his choral union for fear of betraying my revulsion and thus hurting the feelings of those excellent *dilettanti*. I confined my attentions to the peasants' music, which was at any rate fresh and original. One night the strangest serenade I had yet heard woke me. A *ragazzo* with a formidable pair of lungs was roaring out a love song under the window of his *ragazza*, accompanied by an immense mandolin, a bagpipe, and a small iron instrument like a triangle which they call *stimbalo*. His song, or rather bellow, consisted of a series of four or five descending notes culminating, without pause for breath, on a long sustained moan from the leading note back to the tonic. The bagpipe, the mandolin and the *stimbalo* struck two chords in regular and practically unvaried succession. After a brief pause at the end of each stanza, during which the accompaniment continued to sound, the singer would begin again at the top of his voice, just as the spirit moved him, without caring whether or not the notes he attacked so confidently were in harmony with the chords of his accompanists, who were equally unconcerned. He might have been singing to the sea or to the roar of a cataract. Despite its uncouthness, the whole performance gave me extraordinary pleasure. Distance and the intervening buildings reduced the discordance and softened the impact of that crude mountain voice. Bit by bit the monotonous sequence of short stanzas, with their doleful conclusion followed by silence, lulled me into a half-waking dream full of pleasing fancies; and when the gallant *ragazzo* finished what he had to say to his fair one and concluded his song, I felt that something essential had in that moment been taken from me, and I continued to listen for it. My thoughts had flowed so gently on the sounds, had been so seductively entwined with them. When one ceased, the thread of the other was broken, and I lay till morning, wakeful, dreamless, empty of thoughts.*

The same melodic phrase recurs all over the Abruzzi. I have heard it sung from Subiaco to Arce in the Kingdom of Naples,

* [In *Italie pittoresque* (1836), an illustrated travel book by various writers which contains the earliest published version of this part of the *Memoirs*, Berlioz quotes the serenade in full, with accompaniment for guitar. With small though significant modifications, the tune and its accompaniment became the foundryworkers' chorus 'Bienheureux les matelots' in the last act of *Benvenuto Cellini*. Crispino's war-cry (see below) is a more distant relative.]

modified according to the emotions of the particular singer and the tempo at which he sang it. I swear it sounded positively beautiful one night at Alatri, sung slowly and softly, without accompaniment; it took on an almost religious feeling, quite different from the qualities I normally associated with it. The number of bars in this sort of melodic cry is not necessarily the same in each stanza, but varies with the words improvised by the singer, the accompanists adapting themselves as best they can. Such improvisation calls for no great poetic effort from the mountain Orpheus; the language is vernacular prose, used exactly as in ordinary conversation.

Crispino, the lad I mentioned, who had the audacity to claim he had been a brigand on the strength of having spent two years in the galleys, never failed to greet me on my arrival in Subiaco with this tune, which he shouted out like a madman:

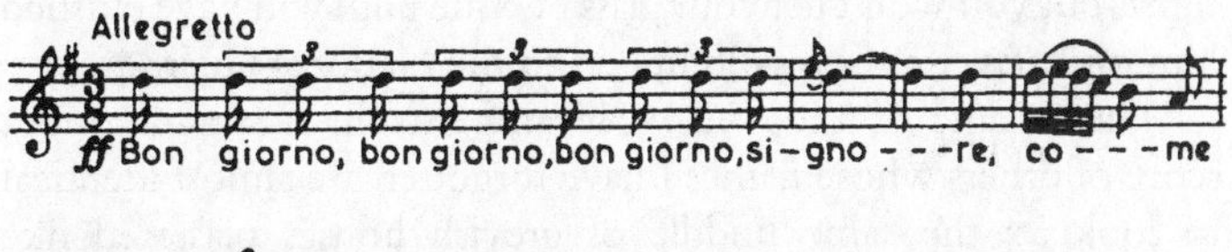

The repetition of the final vowel at the bar marked ═══ is obligatory. It is produced with a kind of gulp, rather like a sob, the effect of which is most curious.

I picked up nothing, not so much as a crumb of music, in the other near-by villages (of which Subiaco seems to be the capital). The most interesting, Civitella—a veritable eagle's nest, perched on the summit of an almost inaccessible rock—is a wretched, foul-smelling place. The climb up to it is exhausting but worth while for the superb view from the top. The extraordinary formation of the rocks, piled fantastically on one another, has a particular attraction for artists; a painter friend of mine stayed there for six months. One flank of the village rests on superimposed slabs of stone so huge that one cannot imagine how human beings ever managed to move them at all. It is like a Titan's battlement, and stands in the same ratio to Cyclopean architecture as that does to modern public buildings. Yet its existence seems quite unknown;

and though habitually in the company of architects I had never heard it mentioned.

Civitella has, besides, one priceless advantage for the traveller which none of the other similar villages can boast: an inn—or something approaching one—where you can put up and eat quite decently. It is run by the rich man of the district, *il signor* Vincenzo. He does his best to entertain strangers hospitably, especially the French, for whom he professes a commendable partiality but whom he plagues with endless questions about politics. The good man, unassuming in all his other demands, is insatiable in this. Swathed in a frock coat which he has worn continuously for the last ten years, and ensconced beneath his smoke-blackened chimneypiece, he begins his interrogation the moment you come in. You may be at your last gasp and exhausted with hunger or thirst, but you won't get your glass of wine until you have satisfied him on Lafayette, Louis-Philippe and the National Guard.*

The villages of Vico-Var, Olevano, Arsoli, Genesano and a score of others whose names I have forgotten are almost identical to look at: the same huddle of greyish houses plastered like swallows' nests against the same barren and almost sheer mountainside, the same half-naked children running up at the sight of strangers with cries of *Pittore! pittore! Inglese! mezzo baiocco!* † (To them every stranger who visits the place is a painter or an Englishman.) Streets or paths, where they exist, are mere ledges in the rock, barely discernible from the rest. You encounter men loafing about, who stare oddly at you; women driving pigs, which, with maize, form the entire wealth of the region; girls carrying heavy copper vessels or bundles of dry sticks on their heads; and all so wretched, downtrodden and squalidly dirty that in spite of the natural beauty of the people and the picturesque cut of the native dress it is hard to look at them and experience any feeling but pity.

* That was the topic in 1832. Today, I imagine, his researches are divided between Louis-Napoleon, Changarnier and, of course, the National Guard. [In January 1851 Louis-Napoleon dismissed the republican general Changarnier, commander of the National Guard in Paris. Twenty years earlier Louis-Philippe, concerned to ensure its loyal support of the régime, rejected Lafayette's proposal to throw membership open to all classes of the population.]

† A small Roman coin.

And yet I keenly enjoyed exploring these fastnesses, on foot, gun in hand—or without it. Indeed, when it came to scaling some remote peak, I took care to leave this splendid weapon behind. The Abruzzians coveted it and were quite capable of lying in wait for its owner behind some wall and dispatching him with a few shots from their villainous old carbines.

In the end, by often visiting their villages, I came to be on friendly terms with those worthy people. Crispino in particular grew attached to me. He did me all sorts of good turns; he procured me not only perfumed pipe stems of a most exquisite flavour,* and powder and shot, but even firing-caps, which was quite a feat in that benighted place where neither art nor industrialism had penetrated. In addition, Crispino knew all the smart *ragazze* for twenty-five miles around—their predilections, their affairs, their ambitions and obsessions, and those of their families and friends. He kept a note of the virtue and temperature of each to the nearest degree—a thermometer which I sometimes enjoyed testing.

His affection for me really went back to the night I directed a serenade to his mistress. I sang a duet with him to the young she-wolf (it was a song much in vogue at the time among the gallants of Tivoli) and accompanied it on the *chitarra francese*. The attachment was cemented by my presenting him with two shirts, a pair of trousers, and three splendid kicks in the pants one day when he treated me with disrespect.† Crispino had not had time to master the art of reading, and never wrote to me. When he had some interesting piece of news to give me from the mountains, he came to Rome. What were seventy miles *per un bravo* like him? At the Academy we were in the habit of leaving our doors open. One January morning (I had not been in the mountains since October, and had in consequence had three months of boredom), on turning over in bed I found myself staring at a great sun-bronzed rapscallion with pointed hat and twisted leggings, politely waiting for me to wake.

* I was a smoker in those days, not yet having discovered how much the stimulation produced by tobacco disagreed with me.

† That is quite untrue, and an example of the proneness of artists to write for effect. I never kicked Crispino. Flacheron was the only one of us who allowed himself such a liberty.

'Hallo, Crispino—what are you doing in Rome?'

'*Sono venuto . . . per vederlo.*'

'To see me, yes—and what else?'

'*Crederei mancare al più preciso mio debito, se in questa occasione . . .*'

'What occasion?'

'*Per dire la verità . . . mi manca . . . il danaro.*'

'Ah, that is more like it. That's what I call speaking *la verità*. So you haven't got any money? And what do you expect me to do about it, *birbonaccio*?'

'*Per Bacco, non sono birbone!*'

I will translate the rest of his reply:

'If you call me a rogue because I'm penniless, it is right; but if it's because I was two years at Cività Vecchia it is not right. I wasn't sent to the galleys for stealing but for good honest shots and mighty knife-thrusts at strangers (*forestieri*) in the mountains.' My friend was doubtless indulging in fantasy; he had probably not killed so much as a monk. But after all he had his honour to think of; and in his indignation he would only accept three piastres, a shirt, and a silk handkerchief, and would not wait till I had put on my boots to give him . . . the rest. The poor fellow is dead now: he was hit on the head with a stone in a brawl two years ago.

Shall we meet again in a better world?

39

The life of a musician in Rome—music in St Peter's —the Sistine Chapel—prejudice against Palestrina —modern religious music in the church of Saint-Louis —the opera houses—Mozart and Vaccai—the pifferari —compositions at Rome

YET ALWAYS I HAD to return to that eternal city of Rome and learn each time more thoroughly the melancholy truth that of all existences an artist can lead, there is none more depressing than that of a foreign musician condemned to live there, if he has a true passion for his art. Life when one first arrives is a continual mortification as one's romantic illusions are successively shattered and the musical treasure-house of one's imagination crumbles before the hopelessness of the reality. Every day fresh experiences bring fresh disappointments. You see the other arts spread out in all their splendour, arrayed in their manifest genius, recognized, honoured, and in the midst of them music sunk to the status of the lowest slave, dulled by long misery, singing cheap songs in a cracked voice for a crust of bread. It did not take me many weeks to discover it. I had hardly arrived before I was rushing off to St Peter's. Sublime, overpowering! Michelangelo, Raphael, Canova on this side and that; underfoot precious marbles and rare and beautiful mosaics. And the intense stillness, the solemnity, the cool atmosphere, the bright, clear colours, rich and harmonious; an aged pilgrim, kneeling alone in the immense space; a faint rumbling from some distant corner of the church, reverberating around the great vaults like far-off thunder. A sudden fear seized me. It seemed to me that this really was the temple of God, that I had no right to be here. Then I reflected that it was weak creatures like myself that had dared to conceive and build this tremendous thing, and I felt a thrill of pride; and as I thought of the glorious role that my own art must play there, my heart began to beat with excitement. Yes, of course—these paintings and statues, those great pillars, all this giant architecture, are but the body of the building. Music is its soul, the supreme manifestation of its existence. Music is the sum of all the other arts; it is music that gives utterance to their eternal hymn of praise, uplifting it as song to the throne of the Almighty. Where then was the organ? The organ was slightly larger than the one in use at the Paris Opéra. It was on wheels. A pillar had concealed it from me. Well, never mind; no doubt this puny instrument was only there to give the choir its note and was the best that could be expected in the circumstances, all instrumental effects being proscribed. How many singers were there? I recalled the small auditorium of the Conservatoire, which St Peter's could accommodate fifty times over, and reckoned that if a choir of ninety regularly sang there, the choir of St Peter's should be numbered in thousands.

There are eighteen for normal occasions and thirty-two for important feast-days. I even heard a 'Miserere' in the Sistine Chapel sung by five voices. A very able German critic has recently taken it upon himself to defend the Sistine Chapel:*

* [Joseph Mainzer, an ex-priest turned music critic; at first well-disposed towards Berlioz's music, later, as critic of the *National*, a vigorous opponent.]

Most travellers [he writes] go there expecting to hear a more inspiring, one might even say a more entertaining, version of the music of the Italian operas they have enjoyed in their own countries; instead of which they find the Papal Choir singing an ancient, dignified plainsong of the utmost simplicity and devoid of all accompaniment. In their disappointment these *dilettanti* go back home declaring that the Sistine Chapel has nothing to offer in the way of musical interest, and that the glowing accounts people give of it are quite unfounded.

We would not go quite so far as those superficial observers of whom the writer speaks. This music of the distant past, which has come down to us unchanged in style or form, affords a musician the same interest as the frescoes at Pompeii possess for a painter. Far from missing the accompaniment of trumpets and bass drum which Italian composers have made so fashionable that no singer or dancer believes he can attain his due success without it, we freely acknowledge the Sistine Chapel to be the one musical institution in Italy where this abuse has not penetrated. One is grateful for the refuge it provides from the heavy artillery of the cavatina-manufacturers. We grant that the papal choir of thirty-two voices, while incapable of producing any effect or even of making itself heard in the largest church in the world, is adequate for performing the works of Palestrina in the limited space of the pontifical chapel. We would agree with the German critic that the music's purity and tranquillity lulls one into a state of suspended animation which has a charm of its own. But the charm is in the style, in the harmony itself, and is quite independent of the alleged genius of the composer—if indeed one can give that title to musicians who spent their lives compiling successions of chords like these which form part of Palestrina's *Improperia*:

Po-pu-le me-e, quid fe-ci ti — — bi aut in quo contristavi te, res-

Although these psalmodies in four parts contain neither melody nor rhythm, and the harmony is confined to common chords interspersed with a few suspensions, one may concede taste and a certain skill to the musician who wrote them. But genius! They must be joking.

It is also a delusion to suppose that Palestrina set his sacred texts in this way with the deliberate purpose of attaining as nearly as possible to a kind of ideal sanctity of expression. Those who believe so cannot be familiar with his madrigals, in which a very similar style is yoked to the most light-hearted and suggestive texts. For instance, 'On the banks of the Tiber I saw a fair shepherd boy and listened to his amorous complaining', etc. has inspired him to a measured chorus whose harmony and general effect are indistinguishable from those of his so-called religious compositions. The truth is, he could not write any other sort of music; and he was so far from aspiring to an unearthly perfection that his works are full of formulas and conundrums taken over from the contrapuntists who preceded him, whose great antagonist he is supposed to have been. For proof, look at his *Missa ad fugam*.

Granted that such contrapuntal problems are ingeniously solved, has this anything to do with the expression of religious feeling? Granted that the compiler of chords is a patient and diligent craftsman, what does it prove of his dedication to the true object of his work? Surely the answer is, nothing. The expressive character of a piece of music is no more valid or cogent because the piece is written in strict canon; it has no bearing on the truth and beauty of the result that the composer has solved some quite extraneous problem, any more than it would if he had been handicapped by physical pain or by some material obstacle while writing it.

If Palestrina had lost both his hands and been obliged to write with his feet, and had contrived to do so, his works would not thereby gain in value nor be either more or less sacred.

Nevertheless the German critic does not hesitate to call Palestrina's *Improperia* sublime:

> The whole ritual [he goes on], the event it commemorates, the appearance of the Pope surrounded by the college of cardinals, the quality of the singing, which is admirably precise and sensitive—all this combines to make the ceremony one of the most impressive and moving in Holy Week.

Certainly; but all this does not combine to turn the music into a work of genius and inspiration.

On one of those dark days towards the end of the year, made more dismal still by the blasts of a chill north wind, try listening, while you read your 'Ossian', to the fantastic harmonies of an aeolian harp hung from the top of a leafless tree, and you will experience a feeling of profound sadness, a vague but overmastering desire for another existence and a disgust with this one, in short a powerful access of spleen combined with an inclination to suicide. The effect is even more striking than that of the harmonies of the Sistine Chapel; yet no one has ever thought of numbering the makers of aeolian harps among the great composers.

At least, however, the music of the Sistine Chapel has preserved a suitable dignity and solemnity, whereas the other churches in Rome, by neglecting their old traditions, have lapsed into an incredible state of decay, one might even say degradation. Several French priests have been moved to anger at the spectacle of sacred art so debased.

I was present, on the King's feast-day,* at a celebration of High Mass with full chorus and orchestra. Our ambassador, M. de Sainte-Aulaire, had asked for the best musicians in Rome. There were about sixty performers, accommodated on a large tiered platform erected in front of the organ. They began by tuning up as noisily as if it had been the green-room of a theatre. The pitch of the organ was so flat that, because of the wind instruments, there

* [1 May 1832.]

could be no question of combining it with the orchestra; the only possible course was to leave it out. However, the organist did not see the matter in that light. He was going to take part, if the ears of the audience had to bleed with the agony of it. The good man wanted to earn his pay, and I must say he earned it well; I never laughed so heartily in my life. Throughout the service he kept to the upper register of the instrument, in accordance with the admirable practice of Italian organists. So long as the orchestra was in action, its *tutti* more or less covered the noise of his piccolo stops. But whenever there was a short chord followed by silence, the organ, which always drags slightly and cannot cut off a sound as quickly as other instruments, was left exposed on a chord a quarter of a tone lower, with the most atrociously comical wailing effect.

In between, while the priests chanted their plainsong, the performers, unable to contain the demon of music that possessed them, tuned up loudly, with unbelievable sangfroid. The flute executed little flourishes up and down the scale of D major; the horn blew fanfares in E flat; the violins practised elegant *gruppetti*; the bassoon rattled its large keys and self-importantly displayed its bottom notes; and the organ, warbling over all, added the final touch to a gallimaufry reminiscent of Callot.* And all this took place before an audience of civilized human beings, among whom were the French Ambassador, the director of the Academy, a large body of cardinals and priests, and a gathering of artists of every nationality. The music was worthy of the performers: cavatinas furnished with the routine apparatus of crescendos, cabalettas, pedal points and florid embellishments, the whole a nameless monster with a passage from Vaccai for a head, limbs articulated from selected scraps of Pacini, and a ballet by Gallenberg† bringing up the body and tail. To crown all, the solos were dispatched in a soprano voice by a vigorous-looking gentleman with florid complexion and enormous black side-whiskers. 'Good God,' I exclaimed to my neighbour, who was choking with suppressed laughter, 'is everything miraculous in this favoured country? Have you ever seen a bearded castrato before?'

* [French seventeenth-century painter and engraver, a master of the grotesque.]

† [Bohemian composer of ballets and operettas, who settled in Italy and married Beethoven's friend Countess Giulietta Guicciardi.]

'*Castrato!*' An Italian lady in front of us had overheard our comments, and shot round indignantly. '*D'avvero non è castrato!*'*

'You know him, madam?'

'*Per Bacco! non burlate. Imparate, pezzi d'asino, che quel virtuoso meraviglioso è il marito mio.*'†

I often heard in other churches the overtures to *The Barber of Seville*, *La Cenerentola* and *Otello*. These pieces seemed to be particular favourites of the organists. They gave an unusual flavour to divine service.

Music in the theatres is in an equally flourishing state—as dramatic as the church music is religious. You find the same degree of originality and integrity, the same charm of style, the same seriousness. Most of the singers that I heard during the theatre season had good voices and sang with that natural facility which is characteristic of the Italians;‡ but apart from Mme Ungher, the German prima donna (much admired in Paris recently), and Salvator, a reasonably good baritone, none of them rose above mediocrity. The choruses are rather below that of the Opéra-Comique in point of warmth, intonation, and ensemble; the orchestras are formidable and imposing in the manner of the Monégasque army, possessing every single quality which is normally considered a defect. At the Valle Theatre the cellos number precisely one, a goldsmith by trade, in which respect he is more fortunate than a colleague of his, who earns his living by repairing cane-bottomed chairs.§ In Rome the word 'symphony', like the

* ['Castrato, my foot!']

† ['Good God! Don't be funny, you great idiots. That splendid singer's my husband.']

‡ Which *was* characteristic of the Italians.

§ [Cf. Mendelssohn, writing to his family from Rome in January 1831: 'The orchestras are worse than anyone can believe. . . . The few violinists play according to their individual tastes, and make their entrances as and when they please; the wind instruments are tuned either too high or too low, and they execute flourishes like those we are accustomed to hear in farm-yards . . . everyone seems so indifferent about it that there is not the slightest prospect [of improvement]. . . . I heard a flute solo in which the flute was more than a quarter of a tone sharp; it set my teeth on edge, but no one noticed it, and as there was a trill at the end they applauded. If the singing were even a shade better! . . .' (Mendelssohn, *Letters*, ed. G. Selden-Goth.)]

word 'overture', is used to designate a certain kind of noise which theatre orchestras produce before the rise of the curtain, and to which no one pays any attention. The names of Weber and Beethoven are virtually unknown. A learned priest of the Sistine Chapel told Mendelssohn that he had heard mention of 'a young man of great promise called Mozart'. It is true that the worthy cleric lives away from the world and has devoted his life to the works of Palestrina, so neither his opinions nor his personal habits can be regarded as typical. Although Mozart is never performed, there are undeniably quite a number of people who have heard more of him than that he is a young man of great promise. The smarter *dilettanti* know that he is dead and that, without approaching Donizetti, he wrote one or two remarkable things. I knew one who had got hold of a score of *Don Giovanni*. After studying it for some time at the piano he told me frankly, in confidence, that this 'old music' seemed to him to surpass M. Vaccai's *Zadig e Astartea*, which had lately been staged at the Apollo Theatre. Instrumental music is a closed book to the Romans. What we call a symphony means nothing to them.

In Rome I was struck by one type of music only, and that (as I am inclined to think) a relic of antiquity: the folk music of the *pifferari*. These are strolling musicians who, towards Christmas, come down from the mountains in groups of four or five, armed with bagpipes and *pifferi* (a sort of oboe), to play in pious homage before the statues of the Madonna. They are generally dressed in large brown woollen coats and the pointed hats that brigands sport, and their whole appearance is instinct with a sort of mystic savagery that is most striking. I spent hours at a time watching them in the streets of Rome as they stood, heads inclined to one side, bright eyes alight with faith and fixed adoringly on the holy mother, almost as still as the image they worshipped. The bagpipe sustains a harmony of two or three notes, supported by a large *piffero* doubling the lowest; above it, a double *piffero* of medium size gives out the melody, and above that two very small *pifferi* played by children of from twelve to fifteen years of age execute trills and rhythmic figures, drenching the rustic tune in a shower of the weirdest ornamentation. After a lot of lively, cheerful tunes, which they repeat over and over again, the concert concludes with a slow, grave piece like a prayer, deeply felt, full of solemn patriarchal dignity (the melody has been printed in various Neapolitan collections, so I will not reproduce it here). Close to, the sound is overpoweringly loud, but at a certain distance the effect of this strange orchestra is haunting, and few are unmoved by it. Later I heard the *pifferari* in their own surroundings, and if I was impressed by them in Rome, it may be imagined what I felt when I encountered them, wandering where my fancy led me, in the untamed mountains of the Abruzzi. Volcanic rocks and dark pine forests are the natural setting and complement of such primordial music. When the scene also included some great Cyclopean Mass of masonry, monument of a vanished age, and a few shepherds dressed in rough sheepskins with the whole fleece worn outside (the garment of the Sabine herdsmen), I could believe myself back in the time of the ancient peoples among whom Evander the Arcadian settled, the liberal host of Aeneas.

One must virtually resign oneself therefore to hearing no music while one is in Rome. For me the anti-musical atmosphere was so uncongenial that I was no longer able to compose. My entire output at the Academy consisted of three or four pieces: (1) An overture, *Rob Roy*, long and diffuse, performed a year later in Paris* and very badly received; I destroyed it immediately after the concert. (2) The Scene in the Fields from my Fantastic Symphony, which I recast almost completely while roaming about the Villa Borghese. (3) The Chant de bonheur from my monodrama *Lélio*,† which came to me one day as I lay on the flat top of the thick clipped box hedge in our formal Academy garden, lulled by the soft, insidious airs of my enemy the south wind. (4) The song called 'La captive', a piece whose popularity I never foresaw when I wrote it. I am wrong, however, to say it was composed in Rome; it dates from one of my visits to Subiaco.‡ I remember the occasion. I was in the inn where we used to stay; I was watching my friend Lefebvre, the architect, drawing at a table, when a sudden

* [14 April 1833, by the Conservatoire Concert Society.]

† I had written the words (spoken and sung) of this work, which forms a sequel to the Fantastic Symphony, on the road back from Nice and during the journey I made on foot from Siena to Montefiascone.

‡ [Early February 1832.]

movement of his elbow knocked a book onto the floor. I picked it up. It was a copy of Hugo's *Orientales*; it had fallen open at that enchanting poem 'La captive'. I read the poem, then turning to Lefebvre, said, 'If I had some manuscript paper I would set this to music—I can *hear* it.'

'Don't let that deter you—I'll make you some'; and taking a pen and a ruler, he rapidly drew a few staves, on which I jotted down the tune and the bass. I put it away among my papers and thought no more of it. A fortnight later, in Rome, during some music at the director's, I remembered 'La captive'. 'I must show you a song that I thought up in Subiaco,' I said to Mlle Vernet; 'I'm curious to know if it's any good, I have no idea.' I scribbled the piano accompaniment and we performed it there and then; and so well did it catch on that a month later the desperate Vernet admonished me, 'Look here, Berlioz, next time you go up to the mountains please don't bring back any more songs. That "Captive" of yours is beginning to make my life at the Villa a misery. It's everywhere—in the palace, the gardens, the wood, the terrace, in all the passages. One can't move a yard without hearing someone bawling or grunting "Le long du mur sombre . . . le sabre du Spahis . . . je ne suis pas Tartare . . . l'eunuque noir," and the rest of it. It's driving me mad. Tomorrow I'm getting rid of one of my servants, and I shall engage another on the strict understanding that he does not sing "La captive".'

I later developed and orchestrated the song. To my mind it is one of the most colourful I have written.

To conclude this brief catalogue of Roman works I must mention the six-part 'Méditation religieuse' with orchestral accompaniment, on a prose translation of a poem by Moore ('This world is all a fleeting show'). It forms the first number of my Op. 18, *Tristia*.*

As to the Resurrexit for full orchestra and chorus which, obedient to the regulation, I sent back to the academicians in Paris, and in which those gentlemen were pleased to discover clear evidence that Rome was having a beneficial effect on me and that I had abandoned my 'unfortunate tendencies' and was making remarkable progress, it was simply a piece from the Mass

* [The autograph is dated 4 August 1831. The piece was 'composed in Rome, one day when the spleen was killing me' (*Correspondance générale*, I, 516).]

performed at Saint-Roch and Saint-Eustache (as already related) several years before I won the Institute prize. So much for the judgment of the Immortals.

40
Varieties of spleen—isolation

IT WAS ABOUT this time in my academic career that I again became prey to that frightful affliction—psychological, nervous, imaginary, what you will—that I will call the disease of isolation. I had first had an attack when I was sixteen. One fine May morning I was sitting in a field in the shade of a clump of large oak trees, at La Côte Saint-André, reading a novel by Montjoie called *Manuscript Found on Mount Posilippo*. Absorbed as I was in my book, my attention was distracted by the faint plaintive sounds of singing coming across the plain at regular intervals. The Rogation procession was passing nearby; the voices I heard were the peasants', chanting the litany of the saints. This time-honoured visitation of the hillsides and plains in springtime to ask for heaven's blessing on the fruits of the earth has something poetic and touching about it that moves me inexpressibly. The procession halted at the foot of a wooden cross decorated with leaves; I saw the people kneel while the priest blessed the land. Then it moved slowly off and the melancholy chanting resumed.

From time to time our old curé's quavering tones were clearly audible, with snatches of phrase:

. . . Conservare digneris.
(The peasants)
Te rogamus, audi nos!

And the pious throng passed on, further and further into the distance.

. . . (Decrescendo)
Sancte Barnaba,
Ora pro nobis!
(Perdendo)
Sancta Magdalena,
Ora pro . . .

Sancta Maria,
Ora . . .
Sancta . . .
. . . nobis.

Silence . . . rustle of the young wheat stirring in the light morning wind . . . cry of quail calling to their mates . . . a bunting pouring forth its song from the top of a poplar . . . profound peace . . . a dead leaf drifting down from one of the oak trees . . . the dull beating of my own heart. . . . Life seemed so very far away, a thing apart from me. On the horizon the glaciers of the Alps flashed and glinted in the mounting sun. Over there lay Meylan, and beyond the Alps Italy, Naples, Posilippo . . . the characters in my book . . . burning passions . . . a secret unfathomable happiness. Oh for wings, devouring distance: I want to see, to admire, I want to know love, rapture, the fire of an embrace, I want life in all its grandeur and richness. But my earth-bound body drags me down. These people, who never lived, or live no more—nothing exists of all that love and pride and greatness of spirit . . . and my star, my *stella montis*—gone, perhaps for ever. When shall I see Italy?

And the fit burst forth in all its fury. I suffered agonies and lay on the ground groaning, stretching out abandoned arms, convulsively tearing up handfuls of grass and wide-eyed innocent daisies, struggling against *absence*, against a mortal isolation.

Yet such an attack is not to be compared with the tortures that I have known since then in ever-increasing measure.

What can I say that will give some idea of the action of this abominable disease? I can think only of an analogy from physics. If you place two cups, one full of water and the other containing sulphuric acid, side by side under the glass jar of an air-pump and create a vacuum, you will see the water seethe, begin to boil, and finally evaporate. The sulphuric acid absorbs the water vapour as it is given off; and because it is the property of the molecules of vapour to draw off heat while vaporizing, the temperature of the water at the bottom of the vessel drops to the point where it forms a small lump of ice.

Something comparable occurs when this sense of isolation and feeling of absence take possession of me. A vacuum forms round my panting breast, and it is as if my heart, subject to an irresistible force of suction, were evaporating and about to dissolve by expansion. The skin smarts and burns all over my body; I flush from head to foot. I have an impulse to cry out, to call my friends or even strangers to comfort and protect me, defend me, save me from destruction, catch hold of my life, which is rushing from me to the four points of the compass. During these crises one has no thought of death; the very notion of suicide is intolerable. Far from desiring death you yearn for life; you long to live it with a thousand times greater energy. It is a prodigious capacity for happiness, which is exasperated for want of use and which can be satisfied only by immense, all-consuming delights equal to the superabundance of sensibility you feel endowed with.

This state is not spleen, though it precipitates it: it is the boiling and evaporation of heart, senses, brain and nervous system. Spleen is the congealing of all that, the lump of ice. Even in a calm state I am always conscious of a little of this 'isolation' on Sundays in summer, because the city is inactive and everyone has gone to the country—because they are happy a long way off, because they are absent. The adagios of Beethoven's symphonies, certain scenes in Gluck's *Alceste* and *Armide*, an aria in his Italian opera *Telemaco* and the Elysian Fields in his *Orphée* also produce quite strong attacks of the disease, but these masterpieces carry their own antidote: they stimulate tears and tears bring relief. The adagios of one or two Beethoven sonatas and Gluck's *Iphigénie en Tauride*, on the other hand, are provokers of spleen and irrevocably associated with it. It's cold in those works, the air dark, the sky overcast, the north wind moaning.

There are moreover two kinds of spleen: one active, mocking, passionate, malignant, the other morose and wholly passive, when your one desire is to be left alone in silence to do nothing but sleep. For anyone possessed by this latter kind, nothing has any more meaning—the destruction of a world would hardly stir you. At such times I could wish the earth were a shell filled with gunpowder, which I should put a match to for my amusement.

One day when the spleen (the passive variety) was on me, I was lying asleep in the laurel wood at the Academy, rolled up on a heap of dry leaves like a hedgehog, when I felt feet prodding me awake.

I opened my eyes. Two figures were standing over me. It was Constant Dufeu, the architect, and the elder Dantan, the sculptor.

'Come on, Old Father Jollity, do you want to come to Naples? We're going.'

'Go to hell! You know I've no money left.'

'Idiot! We have, we'll lend you some. Here, Dantan, help me up with this great baby or we'll never get anywhere. There! Now brush yourself down and go and ask Vernet for a month's leave, and when you've packed your bag we'll go. All right?'

We went.*

Apart from an amusing but unprintable scandal that we caused in the little town of Ceprano after dinner one evening, I recall no particularly striking incident from our journey, which was made prosaically by coach. But Naples . . .!

41

Naples—the enthusiastic soldier—a trip to Nisida —the lazzaroni—an invitation to dinner—a crack of the whip—the Teatro San Carlo—return to Rome on foot through the Abruzzi—Tivoli—Virgil again

NAPLES—THE PURE, translucent sky, the festive sun and fecund earth!

Everybody has described, and better than I could hope to, that enchanted garden. What traveller has looked unmoved on its splendour? Midday and the wide blue stillness of the sleeping sea, the swish of its quiet swell, making long slow folds in the silky water; midnight on the crater of Vesuvius—a vague thrill of fear at the rumble of its subterranean thunders, the roar forced up from its vitals, the explosion hurling heavenwards like flaming blasphemies great lumps of molten rock which, falling, roll down till they form a huge fiery necklace round the throat of the volcano; the melancholy fascination of Pompeii, the bones of the ruined town where, standing on the steps of the amphitheatre, a solitary spectator, you can half imagine a tragedy of Euripides or Sophocles about to begin on the stage below you; the charm

* [Late September 1831.]

of the *lazzaroni*, those childlike creatures whom one cannot help condoning, with their high spirits, their profound instinct for stealing, their wit, and their moments of sheer spontaneous goodness.

I shall not try to compete with the many writers who have described it before me; but I cannot resist recounting an incident which illustrates to perfection the character of the Neapolitan fishermen. It concerns a feast that the *lazzaroni* treated me to, a few days after my arrival, and a present they made me during dessert. It was one of those fine autumn days with a cool, crisp breeze and the atmosphere so clear you feel you could reach across and pick the oranges on Capri. I was walking by myself at the Villa Reale (having begged my companions to let me spend the day on my own). As I passed a small pavilion which I had not noticed, a soldier on guard at the entrance called out abruptly in French, 'Take your hat off, sir.'

'What for?'

'Look'—and he pointed to a marble statue in the centre of the pavilion. The two words that I read on the pedestal made me hasten to pay the respect which the pious sentry demanded. It said: *Torquato Tasso*. Yes, of course, how right, and touching—though I still wonder how the man guessed that I was a Frenchman and an artist and would instantly obey his injunction. A clever physiognomist! But to return to my *lazzaroni*, I walked idly on along the shore, lost in sad reflection on the fate of Tasso, whose humble tomb I had visited with Mendelssohn in Rome at the Convent of Sant'Onofrio a few months earlier, and meditating on the woes of poets who are poets of the heart, with all the other appropriate sentiments. From Tasso my mind jumped to Cervantes, from Cervantes to his delightful pastorale *Galatea*, from *Galatea* to the dazzling creature with the charming name of Nisida who figures in the same story, and from Nisida to the island of that name in the Bay of Pozzuoli—whereupon I am seized with an irresistible desire to visit it.*

I rush off, through the grotto of Posilippo, and reach the shore still running. There I see a fishing boat. I decide to hire it. I ask for

* The correct name is Nisita, as I later discovered. [The modern name is Nisida.]

four rowers; six appear. I offer them a reasonable sum, pointing out that I do not require six men to ferry me across to Nisida in a cockleshell. They smilingly insist and name a figure equivalent to about thirty francs, the journey being worth five at the most. Two boys are standing a little way off; they say nothing, and watch with wistful eyes; I feel in a good humour and am amused by my oarsmen's outrageous demands; so, indicating the two *lazzaronetti*, I call out, 'All right, then, thirty francs, but all eight of you come, and you've jolly well got to row.'

Yells of delight; young and old leap for joy. We pile into the boat and reach Nisida in a few minutes. Leaving my well-built ship in charge of her trusty crew, I ascend the island and explore it thoroughly. I watch the sun go down behind Cape Misenum, immortalized by the author of the *Aeneid*, while the sea, which remembers neither Virgil nor Aeneas nor Ascanius nor Misenus nor Palinurus, sings its own gay music in a major key.

While I wandered aimlessly about, a soldier speaking excellent French came up and offered to show me the principal curiosities of the island, the finest views, etc.—a proposal which I accepted with alacrity. At the end of an hour, as I was about to leave him, I reached for my purse to give the customary *buona mano*, but he stepped back, looking almost offended, and waving my hand away said, 'What is that for, sir? I don't want anything—except . . . that you pray for me.'

'I'll do it,' I thought, as I replaced my purse; 'what a queer idea. But I'll be damned if I don't.'

And that evening, as I was going to bed, I solemnly said a Paternoster for the excellent sergeant. I began a second, but burst out laughing. So I very much fear the poor fellow never got on, but remained a sergeant.

I should probably have stayed on Nisida until the following day, but one of the crew, who had been deputed by the captain of our vessel to seek me out, hailed me with the information that the wind was getting up and that if we did not weigh anchor and set sail at once, we would have difficulty in making the mainland. I defer to this sage counsel and return to the ship. Each man takes his appointed place on the stout-built thwarts; the captain, like to the Trojan hero himself,

. . . eripit ensem
Fulmineum
(takes out his knife)
strictoque ferit retinacula ferro
(and cuts the rope).
Idem omnes simul ardor habet; rapiuntque, ruuntque,
Litora deseruere; latet sub classibus aequor;
*Adnixi torquent spumas, et caerula verrunt.**

(Full of zeal yet not without anxiety, we all leap in. The shore is left behind. Our blades churn the water, the sea disappears beneath our . . . boat.—Free translation.)

But now we really were in danger. The cockleshell was tossing about on the white crests of alarmingly large waves. My sly dogs had stopped laughing and were looking for their rosaries. The damnable absurdity of the whole situation struck me. Here I was, about to be drowned, and for what? For a soldier with literary leanings who admired Tasso. No, not even for that: for a hat; for had I been bareheaded, he would hardly have challenged me. I would not have thought of the sweet singer of Armida's woes, nor of the author of *Galatea*, nor of Nisida. I would never have made this idiotic expedition. At this very minute I should have been sitting peacefully in the San Carlo, listening to la Brambilla and Tamburini. With these reflections and the movement of the stricken vessel, I began to feel very sick. But the sea-god relented, deciding the sport had gone far enough, and suffered us to land safely; and the sailors, till then silent as clams, started chattering like jackdaws. They were in such high spirits that when I handed over the thirty francs which I had agreed to let them rob me of, they felt a twinge of remorse and begged me with genuine cordiality to have dinner with them. I accepted. They took me quite a long way off along the road to Pozzuoli, into the middle of a plantation of poplars miles from anywhere, and I was beginning to suspect their intentions (poor *lazzaroni*!), when we came upon a thatched cottage, where my amphitryons at once made themselves at home and gave orders for the feast.

Soon a small mountain of smoking macaroni appeared, into which I was invited to plunge my right hand with the rest. A

* [*Aeneid*, IV, 579–83: the Trojans' departure from Carthage.]

large jar of Posilippo wine was placed on the table and we drank from it in turn, beginning with a toothless old man, the only one allowed to take precedence over me; respect for age ranking in their eyes even higher than courtesy to one's guest. After an interminable draught, the old man launched into a discussion of politics and became very emotional on the subject of King Joachim, to whom he had been devoted. To distract him and give me some entertainment, the young *lazzaroni* pressed him to tell the story of his famous voyage.

Thereupon, while we listened open-mouthed, the old *lazzarone* recalled how at the age of twenty, embarking on a *speronara*,* he had spent three days and two nights at sea, constantly driven towards unknown shores, and how at last he had been washed up on a far-distant island where it is said Napoleon was afterwards exiled, and which the inhabitants call the island of Elba. I showed the keenest emotion at this amazing tale and congratulated the brave sailor on his escape from such formidable perils. My reaction greatly endeared me to the *lazzaroni*; they looked delighted, and a good deal of whispering and mysterious comings and goings ensued in the cottage. I gathered that some surprise was being prepared for me. Sure enough, as I rose to say goodbye, the tallest of the young *lazzaroni* came up to me with an embarrassed air and begged me on behalf of his friends and out of the love I bore them to accept a souvenir, the finest they had to offer and one calculated to bring a tear to the most unfeeling eye. It was a monstrous onion, a shallot of preternatural size, which I received with a modest gravity appropriate to the occasion and carried off in triumph to the top of Posilippo, after numerous farewells, hand-shakings and protestations of eternal friendship.

It was almost dark when I left my hosts and began limping back along the road. I had bruised my right foot coming down from Nisida, and when a handsome-looking carriage passed me with no footman on the box I saw a chance of an easy if unceremonious ride back to Naples and jumped up. But I reckoned without the pretty little Parisian inside, lording it in a cloud of muslin, who called out to her coachman in a sharp, shrill voice, 'Louis, there's

* [A small, narrow-prowed coaster equipped with single triangular sail and oars.]

someone behind!' at which I received a liberal cut from the whip across my face—a souvenir from my charming compatriot. French doll! If Crispino had only been there we would have given you an interesting ten minutes.

So I hobbled back, reflecting on the attractions of the brigand's life and thinking that despite the hardships it would be the only really decent career left for an honest man, if there were not so many wretched subnormal and vile-smelling creatures even in the smallest gangs.

To drown my sorrows and rest my legs I went to the San Carlo and there, for the first time since coming to Italy, heard music. The orchestra, compared with those I had encountered until then, struck me as excellent. One could safely listen to the wind instruments. The violins were competent and the cellos played with a good singing tone, though there were too few of them (the common practice in Italy of having fewer cellos than double basses has no justification, not even in the kind of music that Italian orchestras normally play). The highly disagreeable noise made by the conductor tapping with his bow on the desk was another point I was disposed to criticize; but I was told that without it his musicians would sometimes have been hard put to play in time. This was unanswerable: and in any case one cannot expect orchestras of the quality of those of Berlin, Dresden or Paris in a country where instrumental music is almost unknown. The chorus was indescribably feeble. A composer who writes for the San Carlo assured me that it is extremely difficult if not impossible to get a decent performance of music written in four parts. The sopranos find it very hard to keep a separate line from the tenors, so one is more or less obliged to write the two parts in octaves.

At the Fondo, opera buffa is given with a zest and fire and brio that make it incomparably superior to most opéra-comique theatres. While I was there they were performing a very amusing farce by Donizetti, *Le convenienze ed inconvenienze teatrali*.*

For all that, the operatic attractions of Naples could hardly compete with the delights of exploring the surroundings, and I was more often out of town than in.

* [A one-act farce first produced at the Teatro Nuovo, Naples, on 21 November 1827.]

One morning I was having breakfast at Castellamare with Munier the marine painter (whom we had nicknamed Neptune), when he said, throwing down his napkin, 'What shall we do? I'm sick of Naples. Let's not go back there.'

'What about going to Sicily?'

'Excellent idea. Just let me finish a sketch I've begun, and at five o'clock we'll go and book our places on the steamer.'

'All right—but how much money have we got left?'

On examination of our purses it turned out that we had enough to take us as far as Palermo, but for our return we would have to trust to God, as the monks say: and being French and therefore totally devoid of the virtue which moves mountains we decided not to tempt providence, and parted, he to paint the sea and I to return to Rome on foot.

This plan had been in my mind for several days. The same evening, back in Naples, having said goodbye to Dufeu and Dantan, I ran into two Swedish officers of my acquaintance, who told me they intended walking to Rome.

'Well I'm damned: I'm starting for Subiaco tomorrow. My idea is to go straight over the mountains, "o'er flood and field", like the chamois-hunters. We ought to make the journey together.'

Despite the oddity of the idea, they accepted it. Our belongings were dispatched by *vetturino*. We agreed to make for Subiaco as the crow flies and then, after resting there for a day, take the main road back to Rome. And so we did. We all three wore the regulation grey linen. B—— had his sketch-book and pencils. A couple of walking-sticks were our only weapons.

It was harvest time in the vineyards, and for most of the first day* we lived on delicious grapes (though not as good as the ones on Vesuvius). The peasants would not always accept our money, and we sometimes omitted to consult the owners.

That evening, at Capua, we found a meal, a bed, and an extemporizer. The fellow executed a few brilliant flourishes on a large mandolin and then asked what country we came from.

'France,' said Kl——rn.

* [14 October 1831.]

I had come across this local Tyrtaeus a month before and had heard his 'improvisations'. He had put the same question; my companions had replied 'Poland', whereupon he declaimed with glowing enthusiasm, 'All the world over have I travelled: Italy, Spain, France, Germany, England, Poland and Russia; but the bravest of all are the Poles, are the Poles.' Now without a second's hesitation, extemporizing both words and music, he addressed the three self-styled Frenchmen in the following remarkable fashion:

Allegretto
Ho gi – ra-to per tutto il mondo, ho gi – ra-to per tutto il mondo, per la
Francià, per l'Is-pa-nia, per l'I — ta-lia, per la Ger-ma-nia, per l'Inghil-
ter-ra, ma li più bra-vi, ma li più bel-li so-no i Fran-ce-si, so-no i Fran-ce-si.

The reader can imagine my pride, and the mortification of the Swedes.

Before striking into the Abruzzi we stopped for a day at San Germano, in order to see the famous monastery of Monte Cassino.

This Benedictine foundation, like the one at Subiaco, is built on a hill, but in every other respect it could not be more different. Whereas the charm of San Benedetto is in its freshness and rough simplicity, at Monte Cassino you find the scale and sumptuousness of a palace. The mind boggles at the sums which must have been spent on the treasures in the church alone. There is an organ decorated with the most absurd little figures of angels which blow trumpets and clash cymbals when the instrument is set in motion. The entire pavement is made of the finest marble; and those with a taste for such things may admire the exquisitely carved choirstalls, representing various scenes of monastic life.

Next day by a forced march we reached Isola di Sora, a village on the northern boundary of the Kingdom of Naples, remarkable for the little river which forms some rather pretty falls and farther upstream works a number of mills. There a problem awaited us. Both Kl——rn and I had badly blistered feet; all three of us were hot, dusty, worn out, and frantic with thirst. The moment we arrived we asked for *la locanda* (the inn).

'*E . . . locanda . . . non ce n'è*,'* replied the peasants, with an air of jeering concern.

'*Ma però per la notte dove si va?*'†

'*E . . . chi lo sa?*'‡

We asked if we could spend the night in a tumble-down coach-house, but there was no straw in it and in any case the owner refused. By now we were fuming, and the derisive indifference of the yokels only increased our exasperation. To arrive in a trading centre such as this and have to sleep in the streets for want of a single inn or a house willing to give us shelter was too much! However, we should certainly have had to, had I not suddenly remembered the name of a Frenchman, M. Courrier, the proprietor of a paper mill, whom I had met when spending some time at Isola di Sora once before. His brother was pointed out to us among a knot of people. I explained our predicament, and after a moment's consideration he answered calmly, in French, or rather in Dauphinois—for the accent is so strong as to make it virtually a separate dialect—'Certainly, we'll give you a bed.'

'We're saved! M. Courrier is a Dauphinois, I am a Dauphinois, and as Charlet would say, agreement is possible.'§

And so it was. The paper manufacturer remembered me and entertained us most hospitably. After an excellent supper, we all three retired to one vast bed (such as I have seen only in Italy) and slept very comfortably. But we agreed that for the remainder of our journey we had better find out which villages had inns, in order not to run any further risk of the kind we had just escaped. Our host encouraged us a little next morning with the assurance that two days' march would bring us to Subiaco; so there would be only one more night when we might have to take our chance. A small boy showed us the way through vineyards and woods for the

* ['Inn? There isn't one.']

† ['But where can we spend the night?']

‡ ['How should we know?']

§ [Title of a well-known lithograph by the French graphic artist Nicolas-Toussaint Charlet.]

first hour; after which, following his rather vague directions, we continued on our own.

Veroli is a large hill-top village; from a distance it looks like a town. We dined there, badly, off bread and unsmoked ham, but it gave us strength to push on before nightfall to the next inhabited rock, an even wilder and more desolate place called Alatri. As soon as we appeared in the main street, a small crowd of women and children materialized behind us and followed us with the liveliest curiosity to the market place. There we were shown a kind of glorified dog-house, with an ancient signboard indicating that it was the *locanda*; and there, despite all our repugnance, we had to spend the night. God, what a night! There was no question of sleep. Our sheets were crawling with insects of every description; rest was impossible. For my part I was so badly bitten that by morning I had developed a raging fever.

What was to be done? My companions did not want to leave me behind at Alatri. We had to get to Subiaco. To stay in this hole was unthinkable. On the other hand, I was shivering so badly that nothing would make me warm, and I felt hardly capable of moving a step. While I lay shaking with the ague, there was a council of war, in Swedish; but I understood all too well from their expressions the extreme inconvenience I was causing them. A special effort was clearly called for. I made it; and by the end of two hours' rapid walking, the fever had gone.

Before we left Alatri a conference of local geographers was held in the main square to determine our route. Various theories having been put forward and argued, the one that took us to Subiaco by way of Arcino and Anticoli eventually prevailed, and we adopted it. That day was the most strenuous we had had since we started. There were no proper paths. We made our way laboriously along the rock-strewn beds of streams. In this fashion we came to a hideous village, whose name I never discovered. The appalling hovels—one could not call them houses—stood open but deserted. The only inhabitants we saw were a pair of young pigs wallowing in black mud on the rough boulders which served the wretched place for streets. Where was the population? It was a case of '*Chi lo sa?*'

Several times we lost our way in the labyrinth of rocks. When that happened there was nothing for it but to clamber back up the hill we had descended, or shout up from the bottom to some peasant, '*Ohe!!! la strada d'Anticoli?*'*

At which he would roar with laughter, or shout back, '*Via, via,*'† neither of which was very encouraging. However, we got to Anticoli; I remember we even found eggs and ham and maize in large quantities, which we ate roasted after the manner of the inhabitants of this barren region; the strange, pungent flavour was rather agreeable. The local surgeon, a big red-faced man who looked like a butcher, was good enough to question us about the National Guard and to offer us a 'printed book' that he had for sale.

There was still a large stretch of pasture land to be covered before nightfall, and a guide was essential. We engaged one, but he did not seem at all sure of the route and often stopped in doubt. An old shepherd sitting by a pool, who had probably not heard a human voice for weeks and who was unaware of our approach, our feet making no sound on the soft turf, nearly fell into the water when we asked him the way to Arcinasso—a pretty village (according to our guide) where we would find refreshments of every kind.

His terror abated somewhat at the sight of a few *baiocchi*, which proved our intentions were friendly; but it was almost impossible to make out a word he said: his guttural speech was more like a gargle than any language known to man. The pretty village of Arcinasso resolved itself into a solitary *osteria* (tavern) standing in the middle of a wide, deserted landscape and tenanted by an old woman who sold wine and fresh water. B——'s sketch-book attracted her attention. We told her it was a Bible, and she jumped up delightedly and examined the drawings one by one; then, having warmly embraced him, she gave us all three her blessing.

No words can describe the utter stillness of that great plateau. We saw no sign of life apart from the old shepherd and his flock, and a crow stalking about with an air of melancholy dignity. It flew off in a northerly direction as we approached. I followed it for a long time with my eyes. Then my thoughts took wing after it, towards England, and I plunged deep in Shakespearean reverie.

* ['Hey! Which is the way to Anticoli?']
† ['Clear off!']

But it was no time for day-dreaming and gawping at crows; Subiaco had to be reached that evening. Our guide had turned back and it was rapidly getting dark. We had been walking along for about three hours, silent as ghosts, when I recognized a bush on which I had shot a thrush six months before, and realized where we were.

'Come on,' I said to the Swedes, 'one more effort. I know this part of the world—we'll be there within two hours.'

Forty minutes later we saw lights far below us. It was Subiaco. There I found Gibert,* who lent me a badly needed change of clothes. I had intended going to bed, but before long there were cries of, '*Oh! Signor Sidoro!*† *Ecco questo signore francese chi suona la chitarra!*' (as they always called me, not being able to pronounce my name). And Flacheron came running, with his beautiful Mariucia,‡ clutching a tambourine, and willy-nilly it was dancing and the saltarello till midnight.

On leaving Subiaco two days later, I had the brilliant idea for the experiment, a description of which now follows.

My two Swedish companions, Bennet and Klinksporn, were walking very fast, and I was getting exhausted. Unable to persuade them to halt from time to time or else to walk more slowly, I let them go and stretched myself out luxuriously in the shade, with the intention of catching them up later, like the hare in the fable. They were a long way ahead by the time I got to my feet again. As I did so I thought: would it be possible to run without stopping all the way to Tivoli (a good fifteen miles)? Why not try? Whereupon I set off like someone in mad pursuit of an abducted mistress. I catch up and overtake the Swedes. I storm through first one village, then another, pursued by the barking of every dog in the neighbourhood, while panic-stricken pigs scatter in all directions and the inhabitants look on benevolently, concluding that I must have 'got into trouble'.§

* [Jean-Baptiste-Adolphe Gibert (1802–89). French landscape painter; Prix de Rome in 1829.]

† Isidore Flacheron.

‡ Now Madame Flacheron.

§ Murdered someone.

After a while I feel a sharp pain in the knee joint and find I can no longer bend my right leg. I have to let it trail, while I continue hopping on the left. It is devilish, but I keep going and reach Tivoli without having once interrupted my grotesque marathon. I ought by rights to have died of heart failure when I got there. In fact I suffered no ill effects. I must have a tough heart.

The Swedes, on reaching Tivoli an hour later, found me asleep. When I awoke and they saw that I was quite sound in body and mind (which I forgive them for doubting), they asked me to be their guide on a tour of the local sights. So we visited the charming little temple of Vesta (which is more like a temple of Love), the large falls and the smaller ones, Neptune's grotto and, of course, the immense stalactite a hundred feet high below which Horace's famous Tibur villa lies buried. I left my companions to rest for an hour in the olive grove above the poet's house and climbed alone to the top of the near-by hill to pick a spray of young myrtle; for, like a goat, I cannot see a green hill without feeling an irresistible itch to climb it. On our way down to the plain we got them to open Maecenas' villa for us and inspected the large vaulted room, where a branch of the Anio now flows through, supplying the power for an iron foundry, and the air is clangorous with the measured beat of great hammers thudding on enormous anvils. That same room once rang to the Epicurean Odes of Horace and Virgil's melancholy voice reciting, at a feast presided over by the minister of Augustus, some splendid fragment from his country poems:

Hactenus arvorum cultus et sidera coeli:
Nunc te, Bacche, canam, nec non silvestria tecum
*Virgulta, et prolem tarde crescentis olivae.**

Farther down, we saw over the Villa d'Este, whose name recalls the Princess Eleonora, immortalized by Tasso, and the unhappy love she inspired in him.

Below, where the plain begins, I took them round the maze in Hadrian's villa. We examined what remains of its gardens, the little valley where the caprice of the master of the world created a tiny

* [*Georgics*, II, 1–3: 'Thus far I have told of the cultivation of the fields and of the starry sky. Now I will sing of thee, Bacchus, and with thee of the young forest trees and the fruit of the slow-growing olive.']

replica of the Vale of Tempe, the guardroom, where birds of prey now keep watch, and the site of the Emperor's private theatre, ignobly given over to the cultivation of cabbages.

How Time and Death must laugh at these bizarre transformations!

42

Influenza in Rome—a new system of philosophy —shooting—domestic trouble—I leave for France

BACK IN ACADEMIC barracks, boredom again takes possession. A severe form of influenza rages in the city; people die with alacrity, in hundreds, in thousands. Dressed (to the amusement of the Roman loafers) in a hooded cloak of the kind that painters give Petrarch, I accompany the cartloads of dead to the Trasteverine Church where a spacious burial chamber is waiting to receive them. A flagstone is lifted in the inner courtyard and the corpses, lowered on iron hooks, gently deposited on the floor of this palace of putrefaction. In a few cases the cranium has been opened by doctors curious to discover why the invalids refused to get well, and the brains have run out over the bottom of the cart. The Roman equivalent of the gravedigger in other countries scrapes up the fragments of grey matter with a trowel and flips them dexterously into the abyss. Not even Shakespeare's gravedigger, that mason who built to 'last till doomsday', thought of using a trowel or resorting to human mortar.

Garrez, one of the architects at the Academy, does a drawing of this agreeable scene, in which I figure in my hooded cloak. Intensification of spleen.

Bézard the artist, Gibert the landscape painter, Delanoie the architect, and I form ourselves into a society called The Four. Its object: to extend and perfect the grand new system of philosophy the foundations of which I laid down six months before. It is known as the 'System of Absolute Indifference in all that pertains to Matter', a transcendental doctrine which aims to produce in man the sensitivity and rounded perfection of a stone. Our system does not catch on. Objections are raised: the existence of pain and pleasure, feelings, sensations. We are regarded as mad. In vain we reply with exemplary unworldliness:

'These gentlemen say we are mad. How does that affect you, Bézard? What do you think, Gibert? And you, Delanoie?'

'It doesn't affect any of us at all.'

'But I tell you these gentlemen regard us as mad.'

'Very well, they regard us as mad.'

We are simply laughed at. Great philosophers have always been misunderstood.

I go shooting one night with Debay, the sculptor. We rouse the watchman at the Porta del Popolo; thanks to a papal regulation in favour of sportsmen he is compelled to get up and open the gate for us, on our presenting our gun licences. Walk till two in the morning. We see a movement in the long grass at the side of the road, think it must be a hare, and fire simultaneously. We get it; but it's a fellow-sportsman, a rival who now lies bleeding and consigning his soul to his maker—a wretched cat, shot in the act of stalking a covey of quail. We are overcome with sleep and stretch out in a field for a few hours. After that we separate. It comes on to rain heavily. See a clump of oaks in a dip in the plain and try to shelter. Useless. There I shoot a porcupine and take several fine quills as trophies. A lonely village looms up through the rain, occupied, so far as I can see, by a solitary old woman washing her clothes in a narrow stream. Learn from her that this silent spot is called Isola Farnese. Isola Farnese is said to be the ancient Veii, capital of those proud warriors and legendary foes of Rome, the Volscians. So Aufidius drew up his army here, and the fiery Marcius Coriolanus came to lend an impious hand in the destruction of his own country. Perhaps just where the old woman squats by the stream, the sublime Veturia,* at the head of a deputation of Roman matrons, knelt before her son. All morning I've been walking over the sites of many splendid battles whose fame Plutarch preserved and Shakespeare immortalized; though they must have been pretty small-scale affairs—rather as if war were to break out between Versailles and Saint-Cloud. Stand still, lost in reverie. The rain beats down: my dogs, half blinded, bury their noses in the

* Whom Shakespeare calls Volumnia.

undergrowth. I shoot a snake; the silly fellow should have stayed in its hole on a day like this. Hear shots; it is Debay summoning me. Reunite for breakfast: slices of ham, which we place in a skull I have with me in my game bag (I picked it up in the cemetery at Radicoffani on my way back from Nice the year before—it now holds my writing sand) and dip in a stream to soak some of the salt out of it. It makes a somewhat frugal meal, seasoned with cold rain. Wine conspicuous by its absence, cigars ditto. Debay's bag is worse than mine; he has shot nothing. I have sent only a harmless robin to join the cat, the porcupine and the snake. We make for the inn at La Storta, the sole doss-house for miles around. Go to bed and sleep for three hours while my clothes are drying. When I wake up, the rain has stopped; the sun comes out. Manage to drag on my still-damp garments and set off. Debay, keen as ever, has gone on ahead. Come upon a flock of most beautiful birds, said to come from the coast of Africa; I've never discovered what they're called. They resemble swallows in their perpetually soaring, skimming flight, and have a thin, faint cry rather like partridge. The plumage is a mottled greeny-yellow. Bring down half a dozen. Honour saved. Catch sight of Debay in the distance, firing at a hare; he misses. We return to Rome caked with mud, as Marius must have been when he emerged from the Minturnan marshes.

Week of stagnation.

At last some signs of life at the Academy. We have to thank our friend L——. His terror is comical to behold. It seems he has been caught by Vernet's Italian footman in the act of making love to the man's wife and lives in constant fear of being murdered. He daren't leave his room. At mealtimes we go in a body and escort him to the refectory. He imagines he sees knives gleaming in every corner of the palace. He's wasting away; has turned pale, then yellow, and now a delicate shade of blue. The other day at lunch Delanoie greeted him with this charming remark: 'Well, my poor friend, still suffering from domestic trouble?'*

The mot has become famous, and is much quoted.

* L—— was a great seducer of housemaids. He claimed that an infallible technique for getting them to fall for you was 'always look sad and wear white trousers'.

But boredom creeps on inexorably. My thoughts are now turned entirely towards Paris. I have finished my monodrama and revised my Fantastic Symphony; I want to have them performed. I obtain Vernet's permission to leave before my term of exile runs out. I sit for my portrait—which, according to custom, is painted by the senior artist and hung in the refectory gallery. I make a last brief trip to Tivoli, Albano and Palestrina, sell my gun, break my guitar, write in various albums, treat my comrades to a farewell punch, and spend a long time stroking M. Vernet's two dogs, companions on many shooting expeditions. I experience a moment of profound sadness at the thought that I am leaving this poetic land and may never see it again. My friends accompany me as far as Ponte Molle. I jump into a battered old wagon and am gone.*

43

Florence—a funeral scene—la bella sposina —the cheerful Florentine—Lodi—Milan—the Teatro Cannobiana—the public—thoughts on the musical life of the Italians—their incorrigible taste for showy platitudes and vocal display—return to France

FOR ALL THAT my passionate desire to see France again was about to be satisfied, I felt oppressed. There was something solemn and irrevocable in saying farewell to Italy, and without being fully able to account for my feelings I was conscious of a heavy cloud over them. Florence in particular, which I was visiting for the fourth time, made an overwhelming impression on me. During the two days that I spent in that queen of the arts among cities I was told that Chenavard, the painter—that great head bursting with intelligence—was hunting for me everywhere. He had missed me

* [2 May 1832. He took four weeks over the journey to Grenoble, making a long detour via Terni, Spoleto, Foligno, Perugia, and Lake Trasimene and not reaching Florence until the 12th. The stages of his journey were noted in a pocket-book, together with details of expenses—theatre tickets, lodgings, straw hats for his two sisters, etc.—and ideas stimulated by what he saw. (See D. Kern Holoman, 'The Berlioz Sketchbook Recovered', in *19th Century Music*, Vol. VII, no. 3, April 1984.)]

twice at the Pitti Palace, had asked for me at my hotel, and was bent on seeing me. Flattered at this sign of interest from so distinguished an artist, I in turn tried to find him, with equal lack of success. I left without making his acquaintance, and it was not until five years later that we finally met in Paris and I was able to admire the extraordinary acuteness and lucidity of his mind even when applied to fundamental problems of arts such as music and poetry which are quite different from his own.

One evening, when I had gone to look for him in the cathedral and was sitting by a pillar watching the tiny motes of dust dancing in a great shaft of gold from the setting sun that slanted across the darkening church, a group of priests and candle-bearers appeared in the nave. A funeral service was about to begin. I went nearer and asked a Florentine whose funeral it was. '*È una sposina, morta al mezzo giorno*,'* he replied cheerfully. The prayers were of a brevity that astonished me; the priests seemed in a hurry to get it over. Presently the body was placed in a sort of covered barrow and the cortège set out for the place where the dead girl was to lie until the following day, before being finally interred. I followed. While they walked, the cantors mumbled some vague litany for form's sake; but their occupation was to melt as much as possible of the wax from the candles provided by the family of the deceased. This was the reason. Any stump of candle left over at the end of the ceremony reverted to the Church; and it being too risky to steal whole pieces, the ingenious torch-bearers had made an arrangement with a gang of urchins. They kept opening out the wicks and tilting the candles so that the melted wax dropped on the pavement. At the same time the boys, who were watching them like hawks, scrabbled eagerly on the ground and scraped up the wax with their knives, rolling it into a ball as they did so. By the time the procession reached the morgue, which was on the outskirts of Florence, the ball had grown into a respectable chunk of mortuary wax. In this way they passed the time while the poor *sposina* was borne to her last resting-place.

At the entrance to the morgue the same cheerful Florentine to whom I had spoken in the cathedral, and who had been in the

* ['It's a young wife—died at noon.']

procession, seeing me an anxious spectator of the scene, came up and addressed me in a species of French.

'You like go in?'

'Yes. Is it possible?'

'Give me *tre paoli*.'

I slipped the coins into his hand, he had a word with the porter, and I was ushered in. The dead girl had been laid on a table. A long white cotton garment tied at the neck and below her feet covered her almost completely. Her black hair, partly braided, flowed down over her shoulders. The large blue eyes were half shut. She had a small mouth, a sad smile, a neck of alabaster, and an air—how shall I describe it? noble and candid, and young—so young, and so dead. The Italian, still smiling, spoke out loud: '*È bella!*'; and, to let me see her features better, raised the beautiful young head and with his grubby hands pushed back the hair which had seemed from modesty to cling to her cheeks and forehead, as if to hide the inexpressible charm that still glowed there; which done, he let go and the head fell back onto the table with a thud. The room echoed with the sound. I felt my heart stop dead at the brutality, the impiety of it. I fell on my knees, unable to contain myself, I seized her hand and covered it with kisses in expiation of the blasphemy against such loveliness, while an anguish as intense as I have ever known welled up in me. The Florentine continued to grin.

Then abruptly the thought occurred to me: what would the husband say if he could see that pure cold hand, once dear to him, warmed by the kisses of an unknown young man? In his horror and indignation would he not jump to the conclusion that I was his wife's lover who, more faithful than he, had come to prostrate himself in Shakespearean despair on her body? How wrong! Yet he almost deserved the unspeakable distress such a mistake would have caused him. Phlegmatic spouse! Does one suffer the beloved dead to be snatched from one's arms while one still has life?

*Addio! addio! bella sposa abbandonata! ombra dolente! adesso, forse, consolata! perdona ad un straniero le pie lagrime sulla pallida mano. Almen colui non ignora l'amore ostinato ne la religione della beltà.**

* ['Farewell, farewell, beautiful forsaken wife, sad shade—now perhaps comforted! Forgive the tribute of a stranger's tears on your pale hand. At least he knows what it is to worship beauty and to love unalterably.']

And I went out utterly overcome.

What a lot of mortuary tales! The fine ladies who will read me—if any of them read me—will be entitled to ask if it is to tease them that I thrust these horrid images beneath their noses. God forbid! I don't have the least desire to vex them in this way, nor to repeat Hamlet's ironical admonition. I don't even have any marked taste for death; I love life a thousand times more. I am describing some of the things which struck me. A few of them are sombre in character; that is all. I can, however, reassure those of my fair readers who do not laugh when they are reminded that 'to this favour they must come' that I have no further unpleasantness to recount; they may set their minds at rest and read on without fear—unless, as is highly probable, they would rather titivate themselves, listen to bad music, dance the polka, gossip, or torment their lovers.

On my way through Lodi I made a point of visiting the famous bridge, and fancied I could still hear the crash of Napoleon's grape-shot and the cries of the retreating Austrians. It was a glorious day. The bridge was deserted, except for an old man sitting on the footpath, fishing . . . St Helena!

On arriving in Milan,* out of a sense of duty I made myself go to hear the latest opera. Donizetti's *L'elisir d'amore* was being given at the Cannobiana. I found the theatre full of people talking in normal voices, with their backs to the stage. The singers, undeterred, gesticulated and yelled their lungs out in the strictest spirit of rivalry. At least I presumed they did, from their wide-open mouths; but the noise of the audience was such that no sound penetrated except the bass drum. People were gambling, eating supper in their boxes, etc. etc. Consequently, perceiving it was useless to expect to hear anything of the score, which was then new to me, I left. It appears that the Italians do sometimes listen. I have been assured by several people that it is so. The fact remains that music to the Milanese, as to the Neapolitans, the Romans, the Florentines and the Genoese, means arias, duets, trios, well sung; anything beyond that provokes only aversion or indifference. It may be that such antipathies are mere prejudice, due above all to the feebleness of their orchestras and choruses, which prevents them from appre-

* [On 20 May 1832, after crossing the Apennines to Bologna, and thence via Modena, Parma and Piacenza.]

ciating any great music outside the narrow circuit they have ploughed for so long. It may also be that they are capable to some extent of rising to the challenge of genius, provided the composer is careful not to disturb entrenched habits of mind too rudely. The striking success of *William Tell* in Florence supports this view; even the sublime *Vestale* of Spontini had a series of brilliantly successful performances in Naples twenty-five years ago. Again, if you observe people in towns under Austrian domination, you will see them flock to hear a military band and listen avidly to its rich German harmonies, so unlike the pale cavatinas they are normally fed on. Nevertheless, in general there is no denying that the Italians as a nation appreciate music solely for its physical effect and are alive only to what is on the surface.

Of all the nations of Europe, I am strongly inclined to think them the most impervious to the evocative, poetic side of music, as well as to any conception at all lofty and out of the common run. Music for the Italians is a sensual pleasure and nothing more. For this noble expression of the mind they have hardly more respect than for the art of cooking. They want a score that, like a plate of macaroni, can be assimilated immediately without their having to think about it or even to pay attention to it.

We French, so paltry and mean-minded in musical matters, are as capable as the Italians of roaring our heads off at the trill or chromatic run of a fashionable *cantatrice*, while a fine dramatic chorus or an accompanied recitative in the grandest style passes us by; but at least we listen (if we don't understand the composer's ideas, it is *never* our fault). The behaviour of audiences beyond the Alps is so humiliating to art and to artists that I confess I would as soon sell pepper and cinnamon in a grocer's shop in the rue Saint-Denis as write for the Italians.* Add that they are bigoted and reactionary to a degree no longer known even at the Academy, and that the slightest innovation in melody, harmony, rhythm or orchestration throws them into a fury, to the point that when Rossini's *Barber of Seville* first appeared, Italian though it is through and through, the Roman *dilettanti* were ready to lynch the insolent young composer for presuming to go beyond Paisiello.

But what finally makes all hope of improvement vain, and

* I would *sooner.*

forces one to the conclusion that the peculiar musical tastes of the Italians are a natural and immutable consequence of the national physiology (as Gall and Spurzheim have argued),* is their exclusive appetite for everything that dances and is gay and brilliant, in defiance of all the diverse passions by which the characters are moved, in defiance of time and place—in a word, in defiance of sense. Their music is always laughing;† and if the composer, forgetting himself so far as to let the drama dictate the style, becomes sensible for an instant, he quickly returns to the *gruppetti* and trills and melodic trivialities, vocal and orchestral, of the approved style—the effect of which, following immediately on a few bars of true expression, is to give to *opera seria* an irresistible air of burlesque.‡

I could quote some famous examples; but, simply arguing in general terms and leaving aside all higher aesthetic questions, where but in Italy did those conventional, stereotyped formulas of composition originate which have been adopted by more than one French composer, and which Cherubini and Spontini alone among their fellow-countrymen have resisted, although the German school is quite uncorrupted by them? Would a nation with any real feeling for musical expression happily accept a style of ensemble-writing in which four characters, moved in totally opposing ways, can in turn declare their passions to an identical phrase, the same tune doing duty for 'Oh thou whom I adore,' 'What terror chills my blood,' 'My heart with pleasure beats' and

* [German-born phrenologists active in Paris in the first quarter of the nineteenth century. They collaborated on a number of books and pamphlets. The first society of phrenology in Europe was founded by Spurzheim in Edinburgh in 1823. Gall took a plaster cast of the young Liszt's skull at a concert in Paris in the same year.]

† An exception must to some extent be made of Bellini's style and that of his imitators, which goes to the other extreme. Here the predominant mood is mournful: the music sighs and wails. These composers revert only occasionally to the inanities of the brilliant style, and in order that the old traditions should not be entirely lost. It would also be unjust to exclude from the category of music that is false in expression certain passages in Donizetti's *Lucia di Lammermoor.* The great ensemble in the finale of the second act and the scene of Edgardo's death have an admirable pathos. I do not yet know Verdi's works.

‡ [Even Stendhal conceded that Rossini had 'infinite wit and little or no passion. . . . Love in his music is never more than a form of voluptuousness, and his style is never more than amusing and vivacious' (Geoffrey Strickland, *Selected Journalism by Stendhal*).]

'With rage I am consumed'? There are indeed people who seriously believe music to be a language of such vagueness that the vocabulary of rage will do as well for fear, joy and love. This only proves that they are devoid of that faculty which to others makes the expressive variety of music a fact as incontrovertible as the existence of the sun. The question, however, has been endlessly debated and I must have done with it. I will add only this. Having given the Italian musical sensibility a long and unbiased scrutiny, I conclude that their composers write as they do because the natural taste of the public wills it, with the rider that the natural taste of the composers shows every sign of sympathizing. These tendencies were already apparent in the time of Pergolesi, and were responsible for his setting one of the verses in his overrated *Stabat*:

Et maerebat
Et tremebat,
Cum videbat
Nati poenas inclyti

as a sort of bravura aria. They were deplored by the learned Martini,* by Beccaria† and Calzabigi‡ and many other intelligent and serious-minded people; yet not even Gluck, with all his genius and the prodigious success of *Orfeo* behind him, was able to get the better of them. They are actively supported by the singers; and certain composers have in turn fostered them in the public. In short, such qualities are as native to the Italians and as indestructible as the passion for vaudeville to the French.

As for their alleged feeling for harmony, I can vouch for its being at the very least exaggerated. True, I heard ordinary working people in Tivoli and Subiaco singing tolerably well in two parts; but this is a commonplace in the south of France, which enjoys no such reputation. In Rome I never once detected a musical sound on the lips of the populace. The *pecorari* (herdsmen) of the plain have a kind of strange grunting song which corresponds to no known scale and defies notation. It is believed to

* [The most celebrated musical theorist of the mid-eighteenth century.]

† [Famous economist and criminologist, influential advocate of penal reform and the abolition of the death penalty, a key figure in the Enlightenment.]

‡ [Librettist of Gluck's 'reform' operas, *Orfeo*, *Alceste* and *Paride e Elena*.]

present many points of comparison with the music of the Turks.

Not until I reached Turin, the capital of Piedmont, did I hear people singing in chorus in the streets. But these open-air choristers were usually music-lovers, educated to a certain degree of sophistication by regular visits to the opera. Paris is, in this respect, just as well provided; often in the middle of the night I have heard the rue Richelieu resounding with quite respectable harmonies. I must also say that the Piedmontese performers laced their harmonies with consecutive fifths, obnoxious to a trained ear *when introduced in this way*.

As for the villages whose churches have no organ and whose population no contact with the big cities, it would be pointless to look there for any trace of the boasted Italian instinct for harmony—there is none. Even at Tivoli, where I heard two young men singing some attractive duets with quite a good sense of thirds and sixths, I was astonished a few months later to hear the whole congregation bawling out the litany of the Blessed Virgin *in unison*.

Without wishing to father any reputation of the kind on the people of Dauphiné, who on the contrary I believe to be entirely innocent in all things connected with the art of music, I must point out that with them the melody of this same litany is gentle and pleading, as befits a prayer addressed to the Mother of God, whereas the Tivoli variety suggests a posse of nightwatchmen.

I quote them both; the reader may judge between them.

Tune from Tivoli

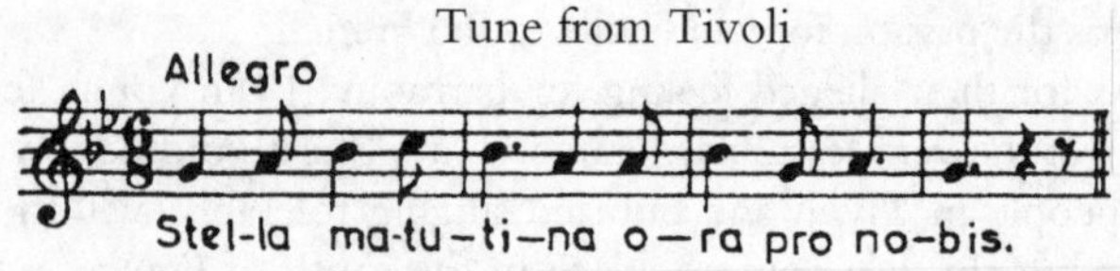

Tune* from La Côte Saint-André, Dauphiné (with the bad Latin prosody customary in France)

* [Used in *The Damnation of Faust* (Ride to the Abyss), where it is sung by a chorus of peasants kneeling at a wayside cross.]

What are undoubtedly more common in Italy than anywhere else are good voices, voices that are not only full and incisive but agile and flexible as well. But the prevalence of voices lending themselves naturally to vocalization and the public's instinctive love of glitter and display react on each other. Hence the mania for *fioriture* which debases the finest melodies; hence those convenient vocal formulas which make all Italian phrases sound alike; hence that eternal device of the final cadence, which leaves the singer free to embroider at will but maddens many listeners by its perfunctoriness and dreadful inevitability; hence the constant tendency to break into buffo style which lurks even in the tenderest scenes of pathos; hence, in short, all those abuses which have made of melody, harmony, tempo, rhythm, orchestration, modulation, plot, staging, poetry, the poet, and the composer the abject slaves and playthings of the singer.

Thus it was that on 12 May 1832, as I came down the Mont Cenis, I saw again in all its spring beauty the lovely valley of the Grésivaudan where the Isère winds, where I had spent the most idyllic hours of my childhood and the first intimations of passion had come to disturb me. There was the old rock of Saint-Eynard, and the magic retreat where the *stella montis* had shone. Down there in that blue haze lay my grandfather's house; it seemed to be welcoming me home. All that enchanted landscape, the smiling houses, the green, rich land—how beautiful it was! Italy had nothing to equal it. I felt an upsurge of pure delight—abruptly cut short by a sudden pain stabbing at my heart. I fancied I heard the distant roar of Paris.

44

The papal censorship—concert preparations —the new English company—Fétis—his corrections to Beethoven's symphonies—I am introduced to Miss Smithson —she is bankrupt—she breaks her leg—I marry her

A SPECIAL DISPENSATION from Horace Vernet having permitted me to leave Rome six months before the end of the statutory two years, I went to my father's house for the first half of the time. My intention was to use the second half to organize one or two concerts in Paris before setting out for Germany, where I was required by the rules of the Institute to go for a further year. My leisure at La Côte Saint-André was spent in copying the orchestral parts of the monodrama which I had written during my wanderings in Italy and which I now wished to have performed. I had had the chorus parts copied in Rome, where I had become embroiled in a dispute with the papal censorship over one of the movements, the Chorus of Shades. The text of this piece (which I mentioned earlier) was in an 'unknown tongue'—the language of the dead, unintelligible to the living.* When I applied to the censor for a licence to print it, the question of the precise meaning to be attached to the words caused consternation among the philologists. What was this language and how was this strange speech to be interpreted? A German was sent for, but declared he could make no sense of it; after him, an Englishman, with no better luck. Then a Dane, a Swede, a Russian, a Spaniard, an Irishman, and a Bohemian—each confessed himself mystified. Confusion in the censor's office, the printer unable to proceed, the publication in abeyance until further notice. At last one of the censors hit upon an argument the soundness of which impressed all his colleagues. 'Since none of the interpreters, English, Russian, Spanish, Danish, Swedish, Irish or Bohemian, can understand this mysterious language,' said he, 'it is very probable that the Roman people will not understand it either. It seems to me therefore that we can safely authorize the publication without serious risk to morals or religion.' So the Chorus of Shades was printed. Rash censors! It might have been in Sanskrit.

On my arrival in Paris,† one of the first people I went to see was Cherubini. I found him sadly aged and enfeebled. He greeted me with a warmth that I had not observed in his character before. The contrast with his former attitude touched and quite disarmed me. 'Good God,' I thought, 'this Cherubini is so unlike the one I used to know, I believe the poor man is about to leave us.' As the reader will see, it was not long before I received evidence of life which completely reassured me on that score.

* I later substituted ordinary speech, and reserved the device for the Pandemonium scene in *The Damnation of Faust*.

† [7 November 1832.]

My old apartment in the rue Richelieu where I lived before going to Rome had, I found, been let. A hidden impulse moved me to take rooms in the house opposite, 1 rue Neuve Saint-Marc, which Miss Smithson had at one time occupied. Next day, meeting the old servant who had for many years been housekeeper to the establishment, I asked what had become of Miss Smithson and whether she had heard any news of her. 'But sir, didn't you . . . She's in Paris, she was staying here only a few days ago. She left the day before yesterday and moved to the rue de Rivoli. She was in the apartment that you have now. She is director of an English company that's opening next week.' I stood aghast at the extraordinary series of coincidences. It was fate. I saw it was no longer possible for me to struggle against it. For two years I had heard nothing of the fair Ophelia; I had had no idea where she was, whether in England, Scotland or America; and here I was, arriving from Italy at exactly the moment when she reappeared after a tour of northern Europe. We had just missed meeting each other in the same house; I had taken the apartment that she had left just before.

A believer in the magnetic attractions and secret affinities of the heart would find in all this some fine arguments to support his theories. Without going so far, I reasoned as follows: I had come to Paris to have my new work (the monodrama) performed. If I went to the English theatre and saw her again before I had given my concert, the old delirium tremens would inevitably seize me. As before, I would lose all independence of will and be incapable of the attention and concentrated effort which the enterprise demanded. Let me first give my concert. Afterwards I would see her, whether as Ophelia or as Juliet, even if it killed me; I would give myself up to the destiny which seemed to pursue me, and not struggle any more.

Therefore, though the dread Shakespearean names beckoned to me daily from the walls of Paris, I resisted their blandishments and the concert was arranged.

The programme consisted of my Fantastic Symphony followed by its sequel *Lélio* or *The Return to Life*, the monodrama which forms the second part of the 'Episode in an Artist's Life'. The subject of this musical drama, as is known, was none other than my love for Miss Smithson and the anguish and 'bad dreams' it had brought me. Now consider the incredible chain of accidents which follows.

Two days before the concert—which I thought of as a farewell to art and life—I was in Schlesinger's music shop when an Englishman came in and almost immediately went out again. 'Who was that?' I asked Schlesinger, moved by a curiosity for which there was no rational motive. 'That's Schutter, who writes for *Galignani's Messenger.* Wait a moment,' he added, striking his forehead, 'I have an idea. Let me have a box for your concert. Schutter knows Miss Smithson. I'll ask him to take her the tickets and persuade her to come.' The suggestion made me shudder, but I lacked the strength of mind to reject it. I gave him the tickets. Schlesinger ran after Schutter, caught him up, and doubtless explained what a stir the presence of the famous actress would create. Schutter promised to do everything he could to get her there.

While I was occupied with the rehearsals and all the other preparations, the unfortunate director of the English company was busy ruining herself.* The guileless actress had been counting on the continued enthusiasm of the Parisians and on the support of the new school of writers who three years earlier had lauded both Shakespeare and his interpreter to the skies. But Shakespeare was no longer a novelty to the feckless and frivolous public. The literary revolution demanded by the Romantics had been achieved; and not only were the leaders of the movement not eager for any further demonstration of the power of the greatest of all dramatic poets: unconsciously, they feared it. It was not in their interests that the public should become too familiar with works from which they had borrowed so extensively.

The result was that the English company excited little response and receipts were low. It had been an expensive venture. The season showed a deficit which swallowed up the imprudent director's entire capital. That was the situation when Schutter called

* [The short season, at the Théâtre-Italien, opened on 21 November 1832 and had a cool response from Press and public; it ran for only a few weeks. The company reappeared at a minor theatre (rue Chantereine) in January 1833, and in March closed down for good.]

on Miss Smithson and offered her a box for my concert, and this is what ensued. She herself told me long afterwards.

Schutter found her in a state of profound despondency, and his proposal was at first badly received. At such a moment it was hardly to be expected she should have time for music. But Miss Smithson's sister joined with him in urging her to accept it: it would be a distraction for her; and an English actor, who was with them, on his side appeared anxious to take advantage of the offer. A cab was summoned and Miss Smithson allowed herself, half willingly, half forcibly, to be escorted into it. The triumphant Schutter gave the address: 'The Conservatoire', and they were off. On the way the unhappy creature glanced at the programme. My name had not been mentioned. She now learnt that I was the originator of the proceedings. The title of the symphony and the headings of the various movements somewhat astonished her; but it never so much as occurred to her that the heroine of this strange and doleful drama might be herself.

On entering the stage box above a sea of musicians (for I had collected an immense orchestra), she was aware of a buzz of interest all over the hall. Everyone seemed to be staring in her direction; a thrill of emotion went through her, half excitement, half fear, which she could not clearly account for. Habeneck was conducting. When I came in and sat breathlessly down behind him, Miss Smithson, who until then had supposed she might have mistaken the name at the head of the programme, recognized me. 'Yes, it is he,' she thought; 'poor young man, I expect he has forgotten me; at least . . . I hope he has.' The symphony began and produced a tremendous effect. (Those were days of great public fervour in that hall from which I am now excluded.) The brilliant reception, the passionate character of the work, its ardent, exalted melodies, its protestations of love, its sudden outbursts of violence, and the sensation of hearing an orchestra of that size close to, could not fail to make an impression—an impression as profound as it was totally unexpected—on her nervous system and poetic imagination, and in her heart of hearts she thought, 'Ah, if he still loved me!' During the interval which followed the performance of the symphony the ambiguous remarks of Schutter, and of Schlesinger too—for he had been unable to resist coming into her box—and their transparent allusions to the cause of this young composer's well-known troubles of the heart, began to make her suspect the truth, and she heard them in growing agitation. But when Bocage, the actor who spoke the part of Lélio* (that is, myself), declaimed these lines:

Oh, if I could only find her, the Juliet, the Ophelia that my heart cries out for! If I could drink deep of the mingled joy and sadness that real love offers us, and one autumn evening on some wild heath with the north wind blowing over it, lie in her arms and sleep a last, long, sorrowful sleep!

'God!' she thought: 'Juliet—Ophelia! Am I dreaming? I can no longer doubt. It is of me he speaks. He loves me still.' From that moment, so she has often told me, she felt the room reel about her; she heard no more but sat in a dream, and at the end returned home like a sleepwalker, hardly aware what was happening.

The date was 9 December 1832.†

While this private drama was going on in one part of the hall, another was brewing on the opposite side—a drama in which the wounded vanity of a music critic was to play the leading role, arousing in him a bitter animosity whose effects I felt until my own emergence as a critic (and therefore as a man to be feared) counselled prudence and opened his eyes wonderfully to the injustice. That person was M. Fétis, and the occasion a scathing rebuke unmistakably addressed to him in one of the scenes of the monodrama. A very natural indignation had prompted me.

Before I went to Italy one of my sources of livelihood was proof-reading. Among other works that the publisher, Troupenas, gave me to read were Beethoven's symphonies, the proofs of which had already been gone through by Fétis. I found them littered with impertinent emendations affecting the composer's thought itself, and with even more presumptuous remarks

* *Lélio* was not performed dramatically, as it was later in Germany (a theatre is required for that), but only as a concert work interspersed with spoken monologues.

† [The programme was repeated on 30 December, with the addition of the *Francs-juges* overture and 'La captive' (first performance, in a version for voice, cello and piano).]

scribbled in the margin. Anything in Beethoven's harmony which did not conform to the doctrines of Fétis had been altered with unbelievable aplomb. Opposite the E flat which the clarinet sustains over a chord of the sixth (D flat, F, B flat) in the andante of the C minor Symphony, Fétis had naïvely written, 'This E flat must be an F. Beethoven could not possibly have made so gross a blunder.' In other words, a man like Beethoven could not possibly fail to be in entire agreement with the harmonic theories of M. Fétis. Consequently Fétis had replaced the highly characteristic E flat with an F, thereby frustrating the clear intention behind the pedal note, which does not rise to F until later, and after passing through E natural, producing a little ascending chromatic progression, with crescendo, of striking effect. I was already in a state of irritation over other similar corrections which I need not mention here; but this exasperated me. 'What!' I thought, 'bring out a French edition of the greatest instrumental works the human mind has ever created and emasculate them, make Beethoven submit to corrections like a student in a harmony class, because the publisher has had the idea of recruiting a self-opinionated professor no more capable of advancing beyond the narrow circle of his own theories than a caged squirrel on a treadmill? No indeed! It must be stopped!' I went straight to Troupenas and told him so. Fétis' corrections were a crime, I said, and an insult to Beethoven and common intelligence. The E flat which he wanted removed from the andante of the C minor Symphony was a magical touch, familiar to every orchestra in Europe, whereas the F was a platitude. I promised that I would expose the inaccuracy of his edition and the activities of Fétis to every player at the Concert Society and the Opéra; his professor would get the treatment he deserved from everyone who valued genius and despised pretentious mediocrity. And I did. The musicians, when they heard of this profanation, were incensed—not least Habeneck (for all that he too was in the habit of correcting Beethoven by removing an entire repeat in the finale when performing the same symphony and leaving out the double bass part at the beginning of the scherzo). There was such an outcry that Troupenas was obliged to remove the corrections and restore the original text, and Fétis thought it advisable to publish in his *Revue musicale* a barefaced denial that there was the slightest foundation in the rumour which accused him of correcting Beethoven's symphonies.*

Fétis saw it as an act of insubordination by a pupil to whom he had from the beginning given encouragement. Quite apart from the dangerous inclination towards musical heresy it revealed, the ingratitude was unforgivable.

Many people are like this. Because they were once good enough to acknowledge that you are not untalented, you are bound henceforth to admire them unreservedly whatever they choose to do, or undo, on pain of being considered 'ungrateful'. Many a hack who has shown a more or less sincere enthusiasm for my works concludes that I must be a very unpleasant person when, some time later, I express myself half-heartedly about some ruinous banality, comic opera or Mass (equally comic) that he has perpetrated.

Thus on my departure for Italy I left behind me in Paris a dedicated opponent—the first personal enemy I had made. I already had a certain number of others, but through no virtue of mine; they had sprung into being as spontaneously as the infusoria which multiply in stagnant water. Neither kind worried me much. I was Fétis' enemy even more than he was mine. Although it had come to nothing I could not think of his attempt on Beethoven without an access of rage. I did not forget it when I wrote the spoken part of the monodrama; there was an allusion to it in one of Lélio's monologues:

But the deadliest enemies of genius are those lost souls who worship in the temple of Routine, high priests of reaction who would sacrifice to their stupid goddess the most original new idea—if it were ever given to them to have one: beardless professors of eighty, living in an ocean of prejudice yet persuaded that the world is bounded by the shores of their desert island; worn-out sensualists of every age, for whom music's sole function is to amuse and titillate, and who have no conception that the chaste muse might have a higher purpose. But worse than any of these are the vandals who presume to lay profane hands on original works, subjecting them to mutilations which they call corrections and improvements and represent as valuable work requiring

* [*Revue musicale*, V, 1829, 136.]

considerable taste.* To hell with them! Their crimes make a mockery of art. Such are the birds that infest public gardens, perching proudly on the most splendid statues. They bespatter the brow of Jupiter, Hercules' forearm or the breast of Venus, and then preen and strut as though they had laid a golden egg.

The burst of laughter and applause which greeted this tirade was all the louder because most of the orchestra and many of the audience understood the allusion, which Bocage emphasized when he came to 'requiring considerable taste' by pronouncing the phrase in a capital imitation of Fétis' affected voice. Fétis was present at the concert, in a prominent position in the balcony, and received my broadside full in the face. Needless to say, he was not pleased and, as the reader will readily surmise, honoured me henceforth with his most intimate hatred.†

The bitter-sweet satisfaction I felt at having avenged Beethoven was, however, completely forgotten the following day. I had obtained Miss Smithson's leave to be introduced to her. From then on I knew no peace. I was alternately elated with wild hopes and racked with fearful apprehensions. The strain I was subjected to during that whole period, which lasted for more than a year, may be imagined but cannot be described. Her mother and sister formally opposed our marriage. My parents, on their side,

* I had heard Fétis use this very expression.

† [Fétis wrote in the *Revue musicale*, on 15 December 1832: '... Before one can be an innovator in music, one has to be a musician. This is something that M. Berlioz does not appear to have realized.... His melody—if indeed I can use the word at all—is ill-shaped, clumsy, wanting in proportion, and—to make matters even worse—nearly always closes on a note which has no logical connection with what precedes it.' The *idée fixe* could not be less poetic and more ordinary....'His harmony is wrong; the chords are unrelated to each other or fit awkwardly together. Yet at the same time it lacks originality. It is not too much to say that when it is not grotesque it is commonplace.' Nor can he be considered a successful innovator in rhythm. He can be said, however, to have a natural feeling for orchestration. As Adolphe Jullien remarks, the review embodies virtually all the main points of criticism subsequently made against Berlioz. Fétis attacked the Fantastic Symphony on several occasions—with particular bitterness when reviewing Liszt's piano transcription on 1 February 1835—and moved Schumann to protest that 'if ever a criticism has seemed to me totally unjust, it is M. Fétis' claim that the symphony is "lacking in melodic and harmonic invention"'.]

would not hear of it. Hence wrath and displeasure on the part of the two families, and all the usual scenes which such opposition gives rise to in a situation of this kind. In the midst of it all, the English company was forced to close down. Miss Smithson was left without a penny, her entire fortune being insufficient to pay the debts which the disastrous enterprise had brought upon her.

Shortly afterwards a cruel accident added a crowning touch to her misfortunes. Stepping down from a carriage outside her door, one day when she had been preparing for a benefit performance which she had arranged, she missed her footing on the pavement and broke a leg. Two passers-by caught her as she fell and carried her half-conscious into the house.*

In England no one took the accident seriously; they thought it a stratagem on the part of the director of the English company to soften her creditors. But it was only too real; and in Paris it aroused the liveliest sympathy of the artistic world and the public. Mlle Mars behaved splendidly on this occasion:† she gave money, rallied her friends, and did everything in her power to help 'poor Ophelia' who had lost all she possessed (yet who, when she found out from her sister that I had brought a few hundred francs, wept copious tears and forced me to take it back, threatening never to see me again if I refused). She responded very slowly to our care. The two bones of the leg had broken just above the ankle. Time alone would mend it completely; there was even a fear that she might always be lame. While the invalid lay despondently on her bed, I managed to carry through the arrangements for that fatal benefit performance which had occasioned the accident. Liszt and Chopin performed during an entr'acte‡ and the evening produced a sizeable sum of money. It was used at once to settle the most pressing debts. At length, in the summer of 1833, Harriet Smithson being bankrupt and still weak, I married her in the face of the violent opposition of her family and after having had to resort to

* [1 March 1833.]

† [Possibly a reference to the famous actress's reputation for jealousy of her colleagues.]

‡ [Playing a duet. The two Grisis, Rubini, Tamburini, the viola player Chrétien Urhan, Mlle Mars, Mlle Duchesnois and the Vaudeville company also took part (Théâtre-Italien, 2 April 1833).]

legal action with regard to mine. On our wedding day she had nothing in the world but her debts and the dread that because of her accident she would never be able to make a successful return to the stage. I on my side possessed the total sum of three hundred francs, lent me by my friend Gounet; and once again I had quarrelled with my parents.

But she was mine, and I defied the world.*

45

Benefit performance and concert at the Théâtre-Italien —the fourth act of Hamlet—Antony—defection of the orchestra—the tables turned—a visit from Paganini —his viola—composition of Harold in Italy —Girard's deficiencies as a conductor—I resolve always to conduct my works myself—an anonymous letter

I STILL HAD, in addition, a small but regular source of income in my grant as winner of the Prix de Rome, which had another year and a half to run. The Minister of the Interior had exempted me from the regulation period in Germany. I was beginning to win support in Paris† and was confident of the future. To finish paying off my wife's debts I once more set about the laborious business of arranging a benefit, and after a great deal of exhausting effort succeeded in organizing a joint theatrical and musical evening at the Théâtre-Italien.‡ My friends again came to the rescue, among them Alexandre Dumas, who has always been very cordial towards me.

* [The wedding took place, in the chapel of the British Embassy, on 3 October 1833. Liszt was one of the witnesses. The honeymoon was spent at Vincennes, after which the couple set up house in the now familiar 1 rue Neuve Saint-Marc, before moving, in April 1834, to Montmartre.]

† [Once again he had no wish to leave Paris just when his music, aided by an energetic publicity campaign conducted by journalists like Janin and d'Ortigue, was beginning to win him a reputation as a brilliant innovator. The immense success of Meyerbeer's *Robert le diable* during his absence in Rome had only sharpened his determination to secure an operatic commission—the one certain road to success. Harriet's reappearance in his life added a personal motive for staying. By the beginning of 1834 she was expecting a child (their son Louis was born on 14 August 1834). But Berlioz never regarded the visit to Germany as anything more than put off; the extensive tour of 1842–3 described in the *Memoirs* was long meditated.]

‡ [24 November 1833.]

The programme consisted of Dumas' *Antony** with Firmin and Madame Dorval, the fourth act of *Hamlet* with Harriet and a few English amateurs whom we had ended by recruiting, and a concert, conducted by me, which was to include the Fantastic Symphony, the *Francs-juges* overture, *Sardanapalus*, Weber's Concertstück played by the incomparable Liszt, and a Weber chorus.† There was, in fact, far too much of both drama and music. The concert, had it ended, would have gone on until one in the morning.

Painful though it will be I must give an exact account of the whole unhappy occasion, as an example to other young artists.

Being somewhat ignorant of the ways of theatre musicians, I had come to an arrangement with the director of the Italian Opera whereby he leased me his theatre and his orchestra, to which I added a few players from the Opéra. It was the most dangerous possible combination. Players who are bound by the terms of their contract to take part in all concerts given in their theatre regard them as an imposition and approach them in a spirit of boredom and ill will. If, on top of that, they have to play alongside musicians who are getting paid while they are not, their sense of grievance is all the greater, and the artist who gives the concert is very soon aware of it.

My wife and I were unfamiliar with all the little behind-the-scenes manœuvrings which go on in the French theatre, and had neglected to take the usual precautions to 'ensure the success' of the heroine of the evening. We had not provided a single ticket for the claque. Madame Dorval, on the other hand, assuming as a matter of course that there would be a formidable faction working for my wife, with all the usual arrangements to ensure a brilliant reception, had naturally taken steps to defend her interests and had garrisoned the pit, using her own allocation of tickets and Dumas', as well as some she had bought herself for the purpose. In consequence she was loudly applauded (she was in any case admirable in the role of Adèle) and recalled many times. The fourth act of *Hamlet* which followed proved a meaningless fragment, especially

* [A contemporary drama of adultery and social taboos, *Antony* (first performed at the Théâtre Porte-Saint-Martin on 3 May 1831, with Dorval and Bocage) was one of the most influential plays of its time.]

† [*Lützow's wilde Jagt.*]

to a French audience, without the preceding acts to prepare and explain it; the sublime role of Ophelia, so poetic and harrowing in its effect a few years earlier, lost three-quarters of its glamour; the great play itself seemed uninteresting. And although the actress was as superb as ever, people noticed how difficult she found it to stand up at the end of the scene where Ophelia kneels beside her black veil (believing it to be her father's shroud); she had to support herself on one hand. For her it was a grim discovery. She had recovered sufficiently to walk without a limp, but the ease and certainty of some of her movements had gone. And then, when the curtain came down and the public, whose idol she had been and who had just accorded Madame Dorval an ovation, did not recall her once—it was a cruel blow. Every woman and every artist will understand what she felt. I grieved for her. Poor Ophelia! Your star was setting.

The concert began. The *Francs-juges* overture, poorly played, was received to my surprise with rounds of applause. Weber's Concertstück, played with the irresistible fire that Liszt always brings to it, scored a triumph. I was so carried away by my enthusiasm that I embraced him publicly on the stage—a foolish solecism which could have brought ridicule on us both; but the audience were kind enough not to make fun of it.

In the orchestral introduction to *Sardanapalus* my lack of conducting experience was responsible for the second violins missing an entry. The whole orchestra lost its place. To restore order, I had to give the final chord and skip the rest. Alexis Dupont sang the cantata well enough, but the famous conflagration, underrehearsed and feebly played, made little impression. Nothing was going right. I could hear only the dull thudding of my own pulse; I felt as if I were slowly sinking into the ground. It was late; there were still the Weber chorus and the Fantastic Symphony to be performed. The rules of the Théâtre-Italien apparently do not require the musicians to play after midnight. Being ill-disposed towards me (for the reasons stated), they were waiting impatiently for the moment of escape; it was no concern of theirs what happened if they went. Sure enough, on the stroke of midnight my worthy artists slipped out furtively under cover of the Weber chorus. Only the extra players, who were being paid, remained at their posts. When I turned round to begin the symphony, I found I had an orchestra of five violins, two violas, four cellos and a trombone. In my consternation I did not know what to do. The audience showed no sign of wanting to go. They grew restless and began clamouring for the symphony. But it was out of the question. In the midst of the confusion a voice shouted from the gallery, 'Give us the March to the Scaffold!' I replied, 'I cannot perform the March to the Scaffold with five violins, it is not my fault, the orchestra has disappeared, I hope the audience . . .' I was crimson with anger and mortification. The disappointed audience rose, and the concert came to an abrupt end—a fact which my enemies did not fail to cite as evidence that my music 'drove the players away'.*

I do not believe there was ever a comparable action inspired by such ignoble motives. I wish I had kept the names of those damnable players; but their obscurity wraps them in oblivion.

This melancholy evening brought me in about seven thousand francs. Within a few days the whole sum had disappeared into the gulf of my wife's debts—alas, without filling it; that I achieved only after several years more and by dint of imposing cruel hardships on us both.

I would have liked to give Harriet the opportunity for a splendid retaliation; but there was no English actor in Paris whose aid she could enlist. She would have had again to resort to wholly inadequate amateurs and appear only in mutilated fragments of Shakespeare—a worse than useless thing, as events had shown. So we had to give up the idea. But I at least could try to answer all the adverse talk with a resounding success. I at once engaged—at a price—a first-rate orchestra made up of the élite of Paris musicians, many of whom were my friends or at the very least impartial judges of my music, and announced a concert in the Conservatoire Hall. I was taking a big risk; there was every possibility that the expenses would not be covered. But my wife herself encouraged me to do it and proved herself, as from then on she always did, the sworn enemy of all half-measures and timid methods and, where the interest of art or the reputation of an

* [E.g. Fétis in the *Revue musicale*, 30 November 1833.]

artist was at stake, bold to the point of recklessness in the face of penury and privation.

I was afraid to jeopardize the performance by conducting it myself. Habeneck flatly refused; but Girard, at that time one of my staunch friends, agreed to take it on and acquitted himself well. The Fantastic Symphony again figured in the programme and from the first took the hall by storm. The success was complete. I was rehabilitated.* The players, none of whom came from the Théâtre-Italien, were radiant with enthusiasm as they left the platform. To crown my good fortune, one member of the audience stayed behind in the empty hall, a man with flowing hair, piercing eyes and a strange, ravaged countenance, a creature haunted by genius, a Titan among giants, whom I had never seen before, the first sight of whom stirred me to the depths. He stopped me as I was leaving and seizing my hand uttered such glowing eulogies that my heart and brain were set on fire. It was Paganini. The date was 22 December 1833.

That was the beginning of my friendship with the great artist who exerted such a happy influence on my career and whose princely generosity gave rise, as will shortly be seen, to so much malicious and absurd comment.

A few weeks after the concert which had re-established me, Paganini came to see me.† He told me he had a Stradivarius viola, a marvellous instrument, which he wanted to play in public; but he lacked the right music. Would I write him a piece for it? 'You are the only one I would trust with such a commission,' he said. I replied that I was more flattered than I could say but that to live up to his expectations and write a work that showed off a virtuoso such as he in a suitably brilliant light one should be able to play the viola, which I could not. 'No, no, I insist,' he said; 'you will manage. I can't possibly do it—I am too ill just now to compose.'

So, to please the great man, I attempted to write a solo for the viola, but a solo combined with orchestral accompaniment in such

* [The programme also included Weber's Concertstück played by Liszt, a violin fantasy by Théodore Hauman, two Berlioz songs, and the first performance of the overture *King Lear*.]

† [Mid-January 1834.]

a way as to leave the orchestra full freedom of action; for I was confident that, by the incomparable power of his playing, Paganini would be able to maintain the supremacy of the soloist. The concept struck me as new; and before long a rather happy scheme for the work had formed itself in my mind which I was eager to carry out. No sooner was the first movement written than Paganini wanted to see it. At the sight of so many rests in the viola part in the allegro he exclaimed: 'That's no good. There's not enough for me to do here. I should be playing all the time.' 'That's exactly what I said,' I replied. 'What you want is a viola concerto, and in this case only you can write it.' He did not answer; he looked disappointed, and went away without referring to my symphonic fragment again. A few days later, already suffering from the disease of the throat which killed him, he left for Nice. It was three years before he returned.

Realizing that my scheme would never suit him, I set to work to carry it out with a different emphasis and without troubling myself any more about how to show off the viola in a brilliant light. My idea was to write a series of orchestral scenes in which the solo viola would be involved, to a greater or lesser extent, like an actual person, retaining the same character throughout. I decided to give it as a setting the poetic impressions recollected from my wanderings in the Abruzzi and to make it a kind of melancholy dreamer in the style of Byron's Childe Harold. Hence the title of the symphony, *Harold in Italy*. As in the Fantastic Symphony, a motto (the viola's first theme) recurs throughout the work, but with the difference that whereas the theme of the Fantastic Symphony, the *idée fixe*, keeps obtruding like an obsessive idea on scenes that are alien to it and deflects the current of the music, the Harold theme is superimposed on the other orchestral voices so as to contrast with them in character and tempo without interrupting their development. Despite its complex harmonic organization, the symphony took me as little time to compose as my other works have usually done; but once again I spent a considerable time revising it. The Pilgrims' March itself—which I sketched in a couple of hours one evening, musing by the fire—underwent many changes of detail during the next six years or more which I think greatly improved it. As it was, the original version had an immediate success when the work was performed for the first time at a concert that I gave on 23 November 1834 at the Conservatoire.*

Only the first movement received little applause. The fault was Girard's. He could never work it up sufficiently in the coda, where the tempo should gradually increase until it is twice as fast. Without this progressive animation the end of the movement sounds feeble and uninteresting. It was torture to me to hear it dragged in this way. The Pilgrims' March was encored. The second time through, at the point in the latter half of the movement where the sound of the monastery bells (represented by two notes on the harp doubled by flutes, oboes and horns) is heard again after a short interruption, the harpist miscounted his bars and got lost. Instead of putting him right, as I have had to do a dozen times (three players out of four go wrong at this point), Girard shouted out, 'Last chord!'; which the orchestra accordingly gave, skipping the intervening fifty-odd bars. It was a massacre. Fortunately the March had been well performed the first time, and the audience were under no illusion as to the cause of the disaster. Had it occurred at the outset, the composer would have been held responsible for the cacophony that ensued. Though I knew this, the catastrophe at the Théâtre-Italien had made me so distrustful of my abilities as a conductor that I left it to Girard to direct my concerts for some time longer. But at the fourth performance of *Harold*† he made a serious mistake at the end of the Serenade (where, unless the tempo of one part of the orchestra is exactly halved, the other cannot proceed, since each whole bar of the latter corresponds to half a bar of the former); and as it was clear that he was incapable of galvanizing the orchestra at the end of the first allegro, I resolved in future to conduct my works myself and not rely on anyone else to convey my intentions to the players. Only once did I fail to keep the promise I had made myself. The reader will see what nearly happened as a result.

After the first performance of the symphony a musical journal in Paris published an article abusing me violently. The article

* [Together with the Fantastic Symphony, and some vocal pieces sung by Mlle Falcon. The viola soloist in *Harold* was Urhan.]

† [22 November 1835.]

began, in the wittiest fashion: 'Ha! ha! ha!—*haro*! *haro*! *Harold*!* A day after it appeared I got an anonymous letter which, after a stream of even cruder insults, accused me of 'not having the courage to blow my brains out'.

46

M. de Gasparin commissions me to write a Requiem Mass—the Directors of Fine Arts—their views on music —a breach of faith—the capture of Constantine —Cherubini's intrigues—a boa constrictor —my Requiem is performed—Habeneck's snuff-box —I am not paid—attempts to fob me off with the Légion d'honneur—skulduggery of every description —rage—threats—I am paid

IN 1836 M. DE GASPARIN was Minister of the Interior. He belonged to that small minority of French politicians who are interested in music, and to the still more select company who have a feeling for it. Wishing to restore sacred music to the prestige which it had long ago lost in France, he proposed that a sum of three thousand francs be allocated annually out of the reserves of the Department of Fine Arts for a large-scale Mass or oratorio by a French composer, to be nominated by the Minister. Under this scheme the Minister would also be responsible for having the work performed at government expense. 'I shall begin with Berlioz,' he said. 'He ought to write a Requiem Mass. I am sure he will do it well.' This was told me by a friend of M. de Gasparin's son whom I knew. I was as astonished as I was delighted. To make sure it was true, I requested an audience with the Minister, who confirmed what I had been told. 'I am about to leave office,' he added. 'It will be my musical legacy. You have of course received the commission for the Requiem?' 'No, sir. It was pure chance that I heard of your generous intentions.' 'What! I gave instructions for it to be sent to you a week ago. This must be some bureaucratic oversight. I will look into it.'

* ['*Haro*' is a term, or rather shout, of denunciation: '*clameur dont on se servait autrefois pour arrêter quelqu'un ou quelque chose et procéder sur-le-champ en justice*' (*Larousse*).]

Several days passed and still the commission did not come. Full of anxiety, I appealed to M. de Gasparin's son, who put me wise to a plot that I had not had the least suspicion of. X, the Director of Fine Arts,* did not at all approve of the Minister's plan to foster sacred music, still less of his choice of me as the composer to point the way. He knew that in a few days M. de Gasparin would have left the Ministry.† If he could delay the drafting of the decree establishing the award and commissioning me to write a Requiem until the Minister had gone, it would be a simple matter to quash the whole project by dissuading the next Minister from going on with it. Such was the director's intention. M. de Gasparin, however, was not a man to be trifled with and when, on the day before he was due to leave the Ministry, he learnt from his son that nothing had been done, he issued a sharply worded order to X to draft the decree and send it to me at once, and it was duly done—a rebuff which did not make X feel any more amiably disposed towards me.

This arbiter of artistic destinies was not prepared to concede real merit to any music except Rossini's. True, I did once hear him, after he had dismissed almost every major European composer past and present, suddenly stop and say, 'But wait a moment, isn't there someone else? What's his name—that German fellow whose symphonies they play at the Conservatoire? You ought to know, M. Berlioz.' 'You mean Beethoven?' 'That's it, Beethoven. Yes, he was not devoid of talent.' With my own ears I heard the Director of Fine Arts acknowledge that Beethoven was not devoid of talent.

Yet in this he was merely the most prominent exponent of musical attitudes that were common to the whole civil service of the period. Hundreds of similar connoisseurs blocked the routes along which artists had to pass, and worked the cogs of the great governmental machine that drove the musical institutions of France. Today . . .

The moment I was armed with my commission, I set to work. The text of the Requiem was a quarry that I had long coveted. Now at last it was mine, and I fell upon it with a kind of fury. My

* He has been dead for ten years, but why name him? [Edmond Cavé.]

† [He was replaced by the Comte de Montalivet in Molé's cabinet reshuffle in April 1837.]

brain felt as though it would explode with the pressure of ideas. The outline of one piece was barely sketched before the next formed itself in my mind. It was impossible to write fast enough, and I devised a sort of musical shorthand which was a great help to me, especially in the Lacrymosa. All composers know the agony of forgetting ideas and of finding that they have vanished for ever, for want of time to set them down.

As a result I wrote this work very quickly, and made few changes in it, and only much later; they are to be found in the second edition of the score published by Ricordi in Milan.*

The ministerial decree laid down that my Requiem was to be performed at government expense on the day of the annual service commemorating the dead of the 1830 Revolution. As July, the month of the ceremony, approached, I had the separate orchestral and choral parts copied; and, at the word from the Director of Fine Arts, the rehearsals began. Almost at once an official letter from the Ministry informed me that the memorial service would be taking place without music. I was requested to discontinue my preparations.† That did not make the new Minister any less indebted for a considerable sum to the copyist and to the two hundred choristers who, under contract, had been attending my rehearsals. For five months I sought in vain for the payment of these debts. As to what was owing to myself, I hardly liked to mention it: it seemed completely to have slipped their minds. My patience had almost run out when one day, as I left X's office after a very lively interview, the Invalides cannon proclaimed the capture of Constantine. Two hours later I was summoned hastily back to the Ministry. X had found a way of getting rid of me; or so he thought. General Damrémont had perished under the walls of Constantine.‡ A

* Strange that just at this time, while I was composing the work, and after I had married Miss Smithson, I should have twice dreamed the identical dream: I was sitting in Madame Gautier's little garden at Meylan, under a beautiful umbrella-acacia, alone; Estelle was not there, and I kept saying, 'Where is she? Where is she?' Who can explain such things? Sailors, perhaps, and scientists, who study the phenomenon of the magnetic needle and who know that the hearts of some men are moved in the same mysterious way.

† [Mid-July 1837.]

‡ [Hill-top town in Algeria captured on 12 October 1837. General Damrémont was wounded in the early stages of the assault and died shortly afterwards.]

solemn service for him and for the other French soldiers slain during the siege was to be held in the chapel of the Invalides. The ceremony came under the jurisdiction of the Ministry of War; and the Minister, General Bernard, had consented to have my Requiem performed as part of the service. Such was the surprising intelligence which greeted me on my arrival.

At this point, however, the plot becomes complicated and one dramatic incident follows closely on another. I counsel all struggling artists who read this account to profit by my experience and ponder what befell me. They will learn the useful if melancholy lesson that in such situations one must trust nobody and nothing, put no more faith in written undertakings than in spoken ones, and arm oneself against heaven and hell.

The news that my Requiem was to be performed at a state ceremony of this magnitude was communicated to Cherubini and threw him into a fever of resentment. It had long been the custom on such occasions to perform one of his two Masses. To be passed over in favour of a young man only just beginning his career and known to have introduced heresy into the school was an affront to his dignity, reputation and acknowledged superiority, and an exasperating infringement of his rights. His friends and pupils, headed by Halévy, shared this sense of outrage and tried to raise a storm, the object of which was to oust the young man in favour of the old. I was actually in the office of the *Journal des débats* (whose staff I had lately joined, and whose editor, Bertin, was an active and generous supporter of mine) one evening when Halévy came in. I realized at once the purpose of his visit: it was to enlist the powerful Bertin influence on Cherubini's side. He was a little disconcerted at finding me there and still more by the cool reception he got from Bertin and his son Armand, and he promptly switched his fire. He followed Bertin into the adjoining room and, through the open door I heard him say that Cherubini had been 'terribly upset, was positively ill and had had to go to bed and that he, Halévy, had come to entreat M. Bertin to use his authority to see that the great man was made a commander of the Legion of Honour to make up for it'. At this point the stern voice of Bertin interrupted him: 'My dear Halévy, we will do what you ask to help Cherubini get the decoration; he thoroughly deserves it. But so far as the Requiem is concerned, if they propose some kind of compromise to Berlioz and he yields an inch, I shall never speak to him again.' Halévy withdrew in some confusion; and the good Cherubini, who had already tried to treat me to some very pretty scorpions, had to submit to a veritable boa constrictor in return—an insult he never swallowed.

This plot was followed by another, more skilfully contrived and of such black villainy that I prefer not to dredge too deeply into it. I incriminate no one. I give the unvarnished facts, without comment, exactly as they occurred.

General Bernard having himself informed me that my Requiem was to be performed, with certain conditions which I shall state presently, I was about to begin rehearsals when X sent for me. 'You are aware,' he said, 'that Habeneck is officially in charge of all important state musical occasions.' ('There we go,' I thought, 'here comes another catch.') 'It is true that you are now in the habit of conducting your works yourself, but Habeneck is an old man' (look out!) 'and I happen to know that he would be deeply hurt if he did not direct the performance of your Requiem. How do you get on with him?'

'We're on bad terms, I have no idea why. He hasn't spoken to me for the last three years. I don't know what his motives are and I confess I haven't bothered to find out. He began by curtly refusing to conduct one of my concerts. His behaviour towards me is rude and incomprehensible. However, as I can see that he feels he should figure at Marshal Damrémont's service and as it would clearly gratify you, I agree to let him conduct; but I reserve the right to take one rehearsal myself.'

'No difficulty at all,' X replied; 'I shall tell him so.'

Both sectional and general rehearsals proceeded smoothly, great care being taken over them. Habeneck treated me as if relations had never been interrupted. All seemed likely to go well.

On the day of the performance, royalty, ministers, peers, deputies, the entire French Press, the correspondents of the foreign newspapers, and an immense crowd of people, thronged the chapel of the Invalides. A success was absolutely vital for me; a mediocre result would be fatal; by the same token a failure would destroy me utterly.

Now mark what follows.

My forces had been divided into several groups spread over a wide area; necessarily so because of the four brass bands which I use in the Tuba mirum, and which have to be placed beyond the main body of performers, one at each corner. At the point where they enter, at the beginning of the Tuba mirum—which follows the Dies irae without a pause—the music broadens to a tempo twice as slow. First, all four groups break in simultaneously—at the new tempo—then successively, challenging and answering one another from a distance, the entries piling up, each a third higher than the one before. It is therefore of the utmost importance to indicate the four beats of the slower tempo very clearly the moment it is reached; otherwise the great cataclysm, a musical representation of the Last Judgment, prepared for with such deliberation and employing an exceptional combination of forces in a manner at the time unprecedented and not attempted since—a passage which will, I hope, endure as something great in our art—is mere noise and pandemonium, a monstrosity.

With my habitual mistrust I had stayed just behind Habeneck. Standing with my back to him, I supervised the group of timpani (which he could not see), as the moment approached for them to join in the general tumult. There are perhaps a thousand bars in my Requiem. In the very bar I have been speaking of, in which the tempo broadens and the brass proclaim their tremendous fanfare—the one bar, in fact, in which the conductor's direction is absolutely indispensable—Habeneck laid down his baton and, calmly producing his snuff-box, proceeded to take a pinch of snuff. I had been keeping my eye on him. In a flash I turned on my heel, sprang forward in front of him and, stretching out my arm, marked out the four large beats of the new tempo. The bands followed me and everything went off in order. I conducted the piece to the end. The effect I had dreamed of was attained. When, at the final words of the chorus, Habeneck saw that the Tuba mirum was saved, he said, 'God! I was in a cold sweat. Without you we would have been lost.' 'I know,' I replied, looking him straight in the eye. I did not say another word. Had he done it deliberately? Was it possible that this man, in collusion with X (who hated me) and with Cherubini's friends, had actually planned and attempted to carry out an act of such base treachery? I would rather not think so. Yet I cannot doubt it. God forgive me if I do him an injustice!

The success of the Requiem was complete, despite all the intrigues and stratagems, blatant or underhand, official and unofficial, which had been resorted to to stop it.

I alluded just now to the conditions under which the Minister of War had agreed to have it performed. The scrupulous General Bernard promised to produce ten thousand francs for the performance of the Requiem, but this sum was only to be handed to me on my presenting a letter from his colleague the Minister of the Interior undertaking to pay me what was due for the composition of the work under the terms of M. de Gasparin's edict, together with what was owed to the chorus for their rehearsals in July and to the copyist.

The Minister of the Interior had given General Bernard a verbal assurance that this triple debt would be discharged. The letter was already drawn up and only wanted his signature. To obtain it I waited in his ante-room, with one of his secretaries, who was armed with the letter and a pen, from ten in the morning until four in the afternoon. At four o'clock the Minister finally emerged and the secretary caught him on his way out and got him to append his precious signature to the document. Without a moment's delay I went straight to General Bernard. After carefully reading what his colleague had written, he had the ten thousand francs handed over to me.

I devoted the whole of this sum to paying the performers; and I gave three hundred francs to Duprez, who had sung the solo part in the Sanctus, and three hundred to Habeneck, the great snuff-man who had had such timely recourse to his snuff-box. When this had been done, nothing was left. I assumed that I was at last about to be paid by the Minister of the Interior, who was doubly bound, by his predecessor's decree and by the formal undertaking he had just given personally to the Minister of War. *Sancta simplicitas*, as Mephistopheles would say. A month passed, two months, three, four, eight months, without my being able to extort a penny from him. Eventually, by dint of endless errands, applications, petitions, intercessions by friends of the Minister, and complaints verbal and in writing, the chorus rehearsals and the copying were paid for and I ceased to be harried and importuned by all those people who had grown tired of waiting for the money that was due to them and who no doubt had their suspicions about my honesty—though the mere thought still makes me go hot with indignation.

But that I, the composer of the Requiem, could possibly attach any importance to filthy lucre! An insulting suggestion! Accordingly they studiously refrained from paying me. I was none the less tactless enough to insist on all the ministerial promises being redeemed in full. I was in fact in urgent need of money. Once more I had to gird myself and lay siege to the office of the Director of Fine Arts. Several weeks passed in futile applications. I was getting more and more angry and losing sleep and weight. At length one morning,* white with rage, I arrived at the Ministry, resolved to make a scene, to stop at nothing. I stormed into X's room: 'Now look here, are they or are they not going to pay me?' 'My dear Berlioz, I assure you it's not my fault. I have made stringent inquiries, I've investigated the whole thing very thoroughly. The money intended for you has disappeared; it was spent on something else. I'm not clear which office was responsible for the error. My goodness, if anything like that happened in mine!'

'I see—so money intended for the Fine Arts can be disposed of outside your department without your knowledge. Anybody can come along and appropriate your funds. But such things are no concern of mine. A Requiem was commissioned from me by the Ministry of the Interior for an agreed sum of three thousand francs. I want my three thousand francs.'

'Tut, tut, just be patient a little longer. It will be seen to. In any case, there's some talk of giving you the cross of the Legion of Honour.'

'Damn your cross. Give me my money.'

'But——'

'There is no but,' I yelled, knocking over an armchair. 'I give you till twelve tomorrow morning. If I haven't got the money by

* [17 January 1838 (see the letter of 18 January to his mother in *Correspondance générale*, II, 406–7, which gives a similar account of the ensuing conversation).]

then, I will raise a scandal about you and the Minister the like of which has never been seen. You are aware that I have means of doing so.' Whereupon the director in consternation, forgetting his hat, rushed down the staircase that led to the Ministry, with me at his heels shouting, 'Tell him from me I should be ashamed to treat my shoemaker as he treats me, and I'll see that everyone knows about it.'*

This time I had found the chink in the Minister's armour. Ten minutes later X returned with a bond for three thousand francs, payable by the treasury of the Department of Fine Arts. The money had been found. I cite this as an example of what artists sometimes have to do to get justice in Paris. There are also other, more violent methods which I advise them not to overlook.

Some time later the excellent Gasparin, having again been made Minister of the Interior and apparently wishing to compensate me for the injustices I had suffered over the Requiem, had me awarded the famous cross of the Legion of Honour which they had virtually tried to sell me for three thousand francs and for which, when offered then and in that way, I would not have given thirty sous. This banal decoration was conferred upon me at the same time as on the great Duponchel, then director of the Opéra, and on Bordogni, the most imposing singing-teacher of the epoch.

Later still, when the Requiem was published, I dedicated it to M. de Gasparin, all the more naturally as he was no longer in power.

What made the Minister's behaviour peculiarly piquant was that after the performance of the Requiem, when I had paid the orchestra, the chorus, the carpenters who constructed the special orchestral platform, Habeneck, Duprez and the rest, but was only at the beginning of the campaign to extract my three thousand francs, certain opposition newspapers represented me as a favourite of the régime, a sort of silkworm feeding on the revenue, and solemnly stated that I had been paid thirty thousand francs for the Requiem.

They merely added a nought to the sum which I had not received. That is how history is written.

* And yet he was an admirable man, full of good intentions. [The Comte de Montalivet.]

47

The Lacrymosa from my Requiem performed in Lille —a small scorpion for Cherubini—a neat trick—a stinging reprisal—I join the staff of the Journal des débats —the painful business of being a critic

A FEW YEARS after the ceremony whose curious history I related in the previous chapter, the city of Lille held its first festival. Habeneck was engaged to direct the musical side. With one of those sudden impulses of generosity which were not uncharacteristic of him in spite of everything, and perhaps also in an attempt to make me forget—if such a thing were possible—his precious pinch of snuff, he had proposed to the festival committee, among other items, the Lacrymosa from my Requiem. The Credo from a Mass by Cherubini figured in the same programme. Habeneck rehearsed my piece with the greatest care, and the performance,* it seemed, left nothing to be desired. The Lacrymosa apparently made a profound impression and despite its huge scale was encored by the enthusiastic audience. Some of them were moved to tears. The Lille committee had not done me the honour of inviting me and I remained in Paris; but after the concert Habeneck, delighted to have brought off such a difficult piece so well, wrote to me briefly in some such terms as these:

My dear Berlioz

I cannot resist the pleasure of writing to tell you that your Lacrymosa was performed quite perfectly and produced a tremendous effect.

Yours ever *Habeneck*

The letter was published in Paris by the *Gazette musicale.*† On his return Habeneck went to see Cherubini to assure him that the Credo had been given an excellent performance. 'Yes,' replied Cherubini tersely, 'but you deed not write to me.'‡

* [25 June 1838, repeated on the 26th.]

† [1 July 1838.]

‡ I had spoken truly when I said that he would know my name one day.

That was quite an innocent little scorpion. To him, however, it was yet another affront that he owed to that damnable Requiem; and it provoked a reprisal in the following amusing circumstances.

A professorship of harmony at the Conservatoire had fallen vacant,* and one of my friends persuaded me to put in for it. Without nursing any great hopes, I nevertheless wrote to our good director, Cherubini. On receipt of my letter he sent for me.

'You are applyeeng for the 'armony class?' he said, in the most honeyed voice and winning manner he could muster.

'Yes, sir, I am.'

'Then you will get it. The reputation you 'ave acquired, your connections . . .'

'Good. I applied because I wanted to get it.'

'Yes, but . . . but that is what bothairs me: I want to give it to anothair.'

'In that case, I'll withdraw my application.'

'No, no, that is no good—because, you see, people would say that I was the cause of your withdraweeng.'

'Then I'll remain a candidate.'

'But I tell you you will get it if you do, and I deed not intend it for you.'

'Then what are we to do?'

'You know that—er—that it is necessary to be a pianist to teach 'armony at the Conservatoire—you know that, my dear fellow?'

'It is necessary to be a pianist, is it? Ah, that hadn't occurred to me. Of course! An admirable excuse! I'll write to you that, not being a pianist, I cannot aspire to be a professor of harmony at the Conservatoire, and that I am therefore withdrawing my application.'

'Exactly, my dear fellow—but it is not I who am the cause of your——'

'No, no, certainly not. Of course I must withdraw. It was stupid of me to forget that only pianists can teach harmony.'

'Just so, my dear fellow. Come, embrace me. You know how fond I am of you.'

'Oh yes, I know.'

* [In March 1838, with the death of Rifaut.]

And embrace me he did, with an almost paternal tenderness. I went away and wrote informing him that I was standing down. A week later he had the post given to a certain Bienaimé, who is no more a pianist than I.

That is what I call a neatly executed trick, and I was the first to laugh, very heartily, at it.

The reader will admire my restraint in not replying to Cherubini, 'But then you yourself wouldn't be able to teach harmony, sir, would you?'—for the great man himself was no pianist.

It is very much on my conscience that soon afterwards, and quite involuntarily, I wounded my illustrious friend in the cruellest fashion. I was at the Opéra, in the pit, for the first performance of his *Ali Baba**—one of the feeblest things Cherubini ever wrote, as was generally agreed at the time. Towards the end of the first act, weary of hearing nothing of the slightest interest, I could not help exclaiming, loudly enough to be heard by the people sitting near me, 'Twenty francs for an idea!' In the middle of the second act, still pursuing the same chimera, I raised my bid: 'Forty francs for an idea!' The finale commenced: 'Eighty francs!' The finale reached its appointed end. I rose, calling out as I went, 'I give up! I'm not rich enough.'

Two or three young men sitting near me in the same row stared at me indignantly. They were Conservatoire students who had been given seats so that they could usefully admire their director. I heard later that they went straight off next day and told him of my insolent bids and the still more insolent way I had abandoned them as hopeless. Cherubini was all the more outraged, having just told me that I 'knew how fond he was of me'. He must have thought me horribly 'ungrateful' as usual. This time, I agree, it was no mere scorpion but one of those venomous asps whose bite is so painful to one's self-esteem. Somehow it slipped out.

I think I should now explain how I had come to join the staff of the *Journal des débats*. Since returning from Italy I had had a fair number of articles published in the *Revue européenne*, *L'Europe littéraire* and the *Monde dramatique* (all short-lived magazines), the *Gazette musicale* and the *Correspondant*, and one or two other

* [22 July 1833.]

papers now forgotten. But these various labours were on a fairly modest scale and of small importance. They brought me in very little and did next to nothing to relieve my financial embarrassment.

One day, desperate for a few francs, I wrote a kind of short story called 'Rubini at Calais' which appeared in the *Gazette musicale*.* Although I was in very low spirits when I wrote it, the story was particularly gay and light-hearted (a familiar contradiction). A few days later the *Journal des débats* reprinted it† with a few lines of introduction by the editor, M. Bertin, who said some nice things about me. I went at once and thanked him. He suggested that I take over the musical feuilleton in the *Débats*; the throne, a much-coveted position, had become vacant through the retirement of Castil-Blaze. I occupied part of it only, to begin with. For a time I wrote only the reviews of concerts and new works. Later, opera was added,‡ though the Théâtre-Italien remained the province of M. Delécluse (as it still is), and Jules Janin retained his *jus primae noctis* over the ballets at the Opéra; at the same time I stopped writing for the *Correspondant* and confined my criticism to what the *Journal des débats* and the weekly *Gazette musicale* were prepared to take. I have now virtually given up my position even on the latter paper, in spite of the favourable terms I enjoyed there, and I write in the *Débats* only when absolutely forced to by the events of the musical world.§ Such is my aversion to all work of this nature. I cannot hear of a forthcoming performance at one of our opera houses without a feeling of malaise which goes on getting worse until my article is finished.

This self-perpetuating task poisons my life. And yet, quite apart from the income I get from it, which I cannot do without, I see no prospect of being able to give it up. To do so would leave me without weapons, exposed to all the rancour and hatred that I have incurred by it. For in one sense the Press is a more useful weapon than the spear of Achilles. Not only can it heal the wounds it has

* [5 October 1834.]
† [10 October 1834.]
‡ [1836. Berlioz's first notice as critic of the *Débats* appeared on 25 January 1835.]
§ They pay me a hundred francs an article; that is, about fourteen hundred francs during the year.

inflicted; it also serves the user as a shield. Oh, but the manœuvrings, the abject subterfuges I am obliged to practise! the circumventions in order to avoid telling the truth, the concessions to society and even to public opinion, the rage repressed, the shame swallowed! Yet there are those who think me violent, scathing, supercilious in what I write. Fools! If I really spoke my mind, you would find the nettles you complain of a bed of roses compared with the gridiron on which I would roast you.

In justice to myself I can at least say that never for any consideration whatever have I been put off expressing, ungrudgingly, what I feel about works or artists I admire. I have warmly praised men who have done me a lot of harm and with whom I am no longer on speaking terms. Indeed, the sole compensation that journalism offers me for all its torments is the scope it gives my passion for the true, the great, the beautiful, wherever they exist. It is sweet to me to praise an enemy who has merit—as well as being a duty which any honest man takes pride in fulfilling. On the other hand every untrue word on behalf of an untalented friend causes me acute unhappiness. But, as every critic knows, the result is the same in both cases. Your enemy, annoyed at the credit you acquire for your generous impartiality, dislikes you all the more, while your friend, dissatisfied with the laboured eulogies that are the best you can do for him, likes you rather less in consequence.

When you have the misfortune, as I have, to be both critic and creative artist, you have to put up with endless Lilliputian trivia of one sort or another, the most unpleasant of all being the cringing flattery of those who have or are going to have need of you. I often amuse myself by following the subterranean operations of certain gentlemen as they burrow a tunnel fifty miles long to arrive at what they call a 'good notice'. Nothing is so laughable as the tireless activity of their picks, unless it is the care with which they hollow out the gallery and construct the vaulting: until the moment when the critic, wearying of this mole-work, opens a sluice which inundates the mine and sometimes the miner.

Therefore where the assessment of my own works is concerned I attach importance only to the opinions of those who are immune to the influence of a feuilleton. Among musicians the only people whose approval really gratifies me are orchestral players and members of the chorus. As their individual abilities are seldom exposed to a critic's scrutiny, I know they have no interest in currying favour with him. As for the eulogies that from time to time are extorted from me, they can hardly afford the recipient much satisfaction. It costs me such violent efforts to bring myself to praise certain works that the truth comes out between the lines, as in the action of a hydraulic press the water seeps through the pores of the metal.

Balzac, in a score of places in his splendid *Comédie humaine*, has said some admirable things about contemporary criticism; but while anatomizing the errors and follies of the profession he has not, to my mind, sufficiently emphasized the achievements of those who keep their integrity, nor done justice to their secret miseries. Even in his *Monograph on the Press*, although written in collaboration with his friend Laurent-Jan (also a friend of mine and one of the keenest minds I know), he has not illuminated every side of the question. Laurent-Jan contributed to a number of papers, but not regularly, and more as a writer of fantasies than as a critic; no more than Balzac was he in a position to see and appreciate everything.

One day Armand Bertin, who was worried at my being so badly off, greeted me with a piece of news which delighted me all the more for being completely unexpected.

'My dear fellow,' he said, 'you're made. I have spoken to the Minister of the Interior, and he has decided that in spite of Cherubini's opposition you shall have a professorship in composition at the Conservatoire, with a salary of fifteen hundred francs, and on top of that a grant of four thousand five hundred out of the Ministry's fund for the encouragement of the arts. With six thousand a year you'll be rid of all anxieties and free to devote yourself to composing.'

The following evening I happened to be backstage at the Opéra when X, whose attitude towards me has been discussed and who was still in charge of the Fine Arts department of the Ministry, caught sight of me, came over, and repeated in more or less identical terms what Armand Bertin had said. I thanked him and asked him to express my warmest gratitude to the Minister. *This undertaking, made gratuitously to a man who had not solicited it, was* *no better kept than so many others had been, and that was the last that was heard of it.**

48

Mademoiselle Bertin's Esmeralda—rehearsals for my opera Benvenuto Cellini—its resounding failure —the Roman Carnival overture—Habeneck —Duprez—Ernest Legouvé

THE ONLY THING I did get—as always in spite of Cherubini—was the post of librarian at the Conservatoire, which I still hold at a salary of 118 francs a month.† Some years later, when I was in England and the Republic had been proclaimed in France, several good patriots who fancied the position took the opportunity to apply for it, claiming that it should not be left in the hands of a man who was so often away. On my return from London I heard that I was going to be relieved of it. Fortunately Victor Hugo, who was then a people's representative, enjoyed a certain amount of authority in the Chamber, despite his genius; and he intervened to preserve me my modest situation. At about the same time Charles Blanc, brother of the well-known socialist, a cultivated man and a true friend of the arts, became Director of Fine Arts. On several occasions he did me a good turn with a warmth and alacrity that I shall not forget.

The narrative which follows will provide an example of the hostility to which journalists who write about politics or the arts are exposed—a relentless hostility that is unleashed the moment they give the slightest occasion for it, even indirectly.

Mlle Louise Bertin, daughter of the founder and proprietor of the *Journal des débats* and sister of the editor, is a writer and a musician of considerable distinction and one of the most intelligent women of our time. Her musical talent is, to my mind, more

* [This démarche belongs to late 1838. The departure from office of the Minister in question, Montalivet, shortly afterwards no doubt explains its failure.]

† [He was appointed assistant curator on 9 February 1839, the appointment taking effect from 1 January 1839. The curator, Bottée de Toulmon, was unpaid and his salary went to Berlioz. When Bottée died, Berlioz became curator (1850) and remained so until his death.]

intellectual than instinctive, but it is a genuine talent; and though her opera *Esmeralda* (written to a libretto by Victor Hugo)* suffers from a certain indecisiveness of style and from the rather naïve character of some of its melodies, it contains some fine things and passages of great interest. Since Mlle Bertin could not herself direct or supervise the rehearsals in the theatre, her father entrusted the task to me (and compensated me very generously for the time I spent on it). The main parts—Phoebus, Frollo, Esmeralda and Quasimodo—were taken respectively by Nourrit, Levasseur, Mlle Falcon and Massol: in other words by the best actor-singers at the Opéra.

Several numbers, including the big duet for the Priest and the Gipsy in the second act, a ballad, and the extremely striking aria for Quasimodo, were loudly applauded at the dress rehearsal. Nevertheless this work by a woman who had never written a line of criticism, who had never been guilty of attacking anybody nor of praising them insufficiently, and whose sole crime was that she belonged to a family which owned a powerful newspaper whose political views were detested by a section of the community—this work, though greatly superior to many ephemeral pieces that are successful or at least tolerated, failed utterly and catastrophically. On the opening night it was greeted by a barrage of boos, groans and catcalls, the like of which had never been seen.† On the second night they had to bring down the curtain in the middle of an act. It was impossible to finish the performance.

Quasimodo's aria, well known under the name of the 'Bell Song', was none the less applauded and encored by the whole house. As its success could not be denied or challenged, one or two people who were particularly hostile to the Bertin family shouted out quite shamelessly, 'It's not by Mlle Bertin, it's by Berlioz,' and actively fostered the rumour that I had written the piece in the style of the rest of the score. It was no more mine than anything

* [After his novel *Notre-Dame de Paris*.]

† [14 November 1836. The *Journal des débats*, as an enthusiastic supporter of the July Monarchy, was unpopular in many circles. *Esmeralda* had a few more performances in 1837, latterly in shortened form and followed by a ballet—a hallowed recipe at the Opéra, later resorted to with *Benvenuto Cellini* and *Freischütz*.]

else in the work, and I swear on my honour that I did not write a note of it. But the anti-Bertin faction was too deeply committed against the composer not to make all the capital it could out of the part I was known to have taken in the rehearsing and staging of the work, and the 'Bell Song' was generally attributed to me.

This gave me an idea of what I could expect from my enemies—those whom I had made directly by my criticism as well as the opponents of the *Journal des débats*—when my turn should come to make an appearance at the Opéra, where cowardly acts of assassination are so often committed with impunity.

My turn came and my failure was resounding. This is how it happened.

I had been greatly struck by certain episodes in the life of Benvenuto Cellini. I had the misfortune to believe they would make an interesting and dramatic subject for an opera, and I asked Léon de Wailly and Auguste Barbier—the powerful poet of the *Iambes*—to write a libretto around them.

The result, according to even our mutual friends, lacked the essential ingredients of what is known as a well-made drama, but I liked it, and I still do not see in what way it is worse than many that are performed daily. The then director of the Opéra, Duponchel, regarded me as a kind of lunatic whose music was a conglomeration of absurdities, beyond human redemption; but in order to keep in with the *Journal des débats* he consented to listen to a reading of the libretto of *Benvenuto*, and appeared to like it, for he went about saying that he was putting on the opera not because of the music, which he knew would be preposterous, but because of the book, which he found charming.

Accordingly he had it put into rehearsal. I shall never forget the horror of those three months.* The indifference, the distaste manifested by most of the singers (who were already convinced that it would be a fiasco); Habeneck's ill-humour, and the vague rumours that went round the theatre; the crass objections raised by that whole crowd of illiterates to certain turns of phrase in a libretto so different in style from the empty, mechanical rhyming prose of the Scribe school—all this was eloquent of an atmosphere

* [May–August 1838.]

of general hostility against which I was powerless, but which I had to pretend not to notice.

Auguste Barbier, here and there in the recitatives, may have let slip a word or phrase unashamedly deriving from the vocabulary of the people and therefore unacceptable to the niceness of modern taste; but it is hardly credible that the following lines, which occur in a duet written by Léon de Wailly, should have struck most of the singers as ridiculous:

> *When I came to my senses,*
> *The rooftops were shining in the first light of dawn,*
> *The cocks were crowing, etc., etc.*

'Ah, the cocks!' they said, 'ha! ha! ha! The cocks! It'll be the hens next!' and so on in the same vein. What could one say to such idiots?

When we came to the orchestral rehearsals, the players, seeing Habeneck's surly manner, held aloof and treated me with cold reserve. They did their duty, however, which can hardly be said of Habeneck. He could not catch the lively pace of the saltarello that is danced and sung in the Piazza Colonna in the second act. The dancers, put out by his sluggish tempo, complained to me. I kept on urging him, 'Faster, faster! Put more life into it!' Habeneck struck the desk in his annoyance and broke his bow. In the end, after witnessing four or five similar outbursts, I remarked with a coolness that infuriated him, 'My dear sir, breaking fifty bows won't prevent your tempo from being twice as slow as it ought to be. This is a saltarello.'

At which Habeneck stopped and, turning round to the orchestra, said, 'Since I am unfortunately unable to satisfy M. Berlioz, we will leave it at that for today. You may go, gentlemen.'

And there the rehearsal ended.*

A few years later, when I wrote the *Roman Carnival* overture—the main theme of the allegro of which is this same saltarello that he could never get right—Habeneck was in the artists' room at the Salle Herz on the evening of the first performance.† He had heard

* I could not conduct the rehearsals of *Cellini* myself. Composers are not *entitled* to direct their own works in the French theatre.

† [3 February 1844.]

that at the morning rehearsal we had played it through without the wind instruments (the National Guard having relieved me of part of my orchestra), and he had come to witness the catastrophe. Indeed, when I arrived in the orchestra, all the wind players crowded round me, appalled at the thought of giving a public performance of an overture that was completely unknown to them.

'Don't worry,' I said. 'The parts are correct and you are all excellent players. Watch my stick as often as you can, count your rests carefully, and everything will be all right.'

Not a single mistake occurred. I started the allegro at the right tempo, the whirlwind tempo of the Roman dancers. The audience encored it; we played it again; it went even better the second time. On my return to the artists' room I saw Habeneck standing with a slightly crestfallen air, and said casually as I went past, 'That's how it goes.' He did not reply.

I was never more blessedly aware of the advantages of being able to conduct my music myself. My delight was the greater for the thought of what Habeneck had made me endure.

Unhappy composers! Learn to conduct yourselves (in both senses of the word); for conductors, never forget, are the most dangerous of all your interpreters.

To return to *Benvenuto*. The orchestra had been prudently holding aloof, lest their attitude should seem at variance with their conductor's veiled hostility; but by the time the final rehearsals were reached they were openly enthusiastic about several numbers. One or two pronounced my score one of the most original they had heard. This reached the ears of Duponchel. I heard him one evening deriding the 'curious change of front': 'We're now told that Berlioz's music is charming. It seems our ridiculous orchestra is lauding it to the skies.' Some of them had, however, preserved their independence, like the two who were discovered during the finale of the second act playing that well-known air 'J'ai du bon tabac' instead of their own parts; they hoped it would ingratiate them with the conductor. I met the equal of this skulduggery on the stage. In the same finale, where the stage is darkened, representing the Piazza Colonna at night with an immense crowd in masks, the male dancers amused themselves by pinching the female dancers and, when they screamed, screaming too, to the discomfiture of the chorus, who were attempting to sing. When I indignantly appealed to the director to put an end to this insolent and undisciplined behaviour, Duponchel was nowhere to be found: he did not deign to attend rehearsals.

Briefly, the performance took place. The overture was extravagantly applauded; the rest was hissed with exemplary precision and energy. It was performed three times, however,* after which Duprez saw fit to abandon the role of Benvenuto and the work disappeared from the bills, not to reappear until much later—Alexis Dupont having taken five months to learn the part which he had been furious at not being given in the first place.

Duprez was splendid in the vigorous music, such as the passage in the sextet where Cellini threatens to smash the statue. But already his voice had coarsened to the point where smoothly produced tone and quiet or reflective music no longer came naturally to him. In the aria 'Sur les monts les plus sauvages', for example, he could not sustain the high G at the end of the phrase 'Je chanterais gaiement'; instead of holding it for three bars, as is written, he sang a short note, and the whole effect was lost. Madame Dorus-Gras and Madame Stoltz were delightful in the roles of Teresa and Ascanio. They had throughout been very conscientious and co-operative. Madame Stoltz's striking success with her rondo in the second act, 'Mais qu'ai-je donc?', may even be seen as the first step in her rise to that exaggerated position which she later acquired at the Opéra and from which she has been so rudely dethroned.†

It is fourteen years since I was stretched on the rack at the Opéra. I have just re-read my poor score carefully and with the strictest impartiality, and I cannot help recognizing that it contains a variety of ideas, a verve and impetus and a brilliance of musical colour that I shall perhaps never find again and that deserved a better fate.‡

* [10, 12 and 14 September 1838.]

† [Rosine Stoltz became the mistress of Duponchel's successor, Léon Pillet, and the power behind the throne at the Opéra.]

‡ N.B. That was written in 1850. Since then *Benvenuto Cellini*, with certain changes in the libretto, has been successfully staged at Weimar. It is often

The composition of *Benvenuto* occupied a good deal of time. But for a friend who came to my rescue I would not have been able to finish it by the appointed date. One must be free of all other work when writing an opera; that is, one's livelihood must be assured for a certain period. This was very far from being the case with me. I was living from hand to mouth on the proceeds of the articles that I contributed to various papers. Writing them was practically my sole occupation. In the first access of excitement over my score I did attempt to keep two months clear for working uninterruptedly at it. But brutal necessity soon forced me to stop playing the composer and turn critic again. It was an agonizing decision; but there was no alternative. I had a wife and child; how could I leave them with nothing to live on? Yet, in my dejection, harassed on one side by poverty and on the other by musical ideas I was obliged to repress, I no longer had the heart to do my usual scribbling, so abhorrent had it become.

I was plunged in gloomy thoughts when Ernest Legouvé came to see me. 'How are you getting on with your opera?' he asked.

'I haven't finished the first act yet. I can't get time to work on it.'

'Supposing you had time?'

'Don't—I would write from dawn till dusk.'

'What would you need to make you independent?'

'Two thousand francs—which I haven't got.'

'And if someone . . . supposing you were . . . come on, help me.'

'What? What do you mean?'

'All right—supposing one of your friends lent it to you?'

'What friend could I possibly ask to lend me such an amount?'

'You don't have to ask. I am offering it to you.'

I leave the reader to imagine how I felt. Next day Legouvé duly lent me the two thousand francs, thanks to which I was able to finish *Benvenuto*. This good and charming man, a distinguished writer, an artist himself, had in the generosity of his heart understood my misery and resolved to put an end to it, but with

---

performed there, under the direction of Liszt. The vocal score, with French and German text, was published in 1858 by Mayer of Brunswick.

It was even published in Paris, by Choudens, in 1865.

exquisite tact had feared to offend me by a straightforward offer of money. Artists are virtually alone in having this kind of mutual understanding. I have had the good luck to know several who have come to my aid in the same way.

49

Concert of 16 December 1838—Paganini's letter and gift—my wife's holy enthusiasm—a furore—congratulation and calumny—I visit Paganini—his departure—I write Romeo and Juliet—criticisms provoked by that work

PAGANINI RETURNED FROM Sardinia* in time to see *Benvenuto* slaughtered. He was present at that terrible first night, and came away appalled. Afterwards he boldly stated that if he were director of the Opéra he would 'immediately commission that young man to write three more operas, pay him for them in advance, and get a very good bargain out of it'.

The failure of the work, and still more the strain of the interminable rehearsals and the state of repressed rage in which I had been living, brought on an attack of bronchitis. I was forced to stay in bed and do nothing. Yet something had to be done; we had to live. I roused myself and put on two concerts at the Conservatoire. The first† barely covered expenses. To stimulate receipts I announced that the programme of the second would include my two symphonies, the Fantastic and *Harold*. Though still suffering from bronchitis, I felt strong enough to conduct the concert, which took place on 16 December 1838.‡

Paganini was present. This was the occasion of the famous incident around which so much controversy and malicious gossip have collected. I have described how Paganini, before leaving Paris, had been the cause of my writing *Harold*. The symphony had been performed several times during his absence but had not figured in any of my programmes since his return;

* [I.e. from the Kingdom of Sardinia: in this case, Nice.]

† [Sunday 25 November 1838.]

‡ [In addition to the two symphonies, the programme included the Act III finale and the great Act I aria from Gluck's *Alceste* (with Stoltz and Alizard) and some shorter solo pieces.]

consequently he did not know the work, and heard it that day for the first time.

The concert had just ended; I was worn out, lathered in sweat and shaking all over, when Paganini, followed by his son Achille, came up to me at the orchestra door, gesticulating violently. He was already suffering from the disease of the larynx which killed him and had completely lost his voice, so that unless it was absolutely quiet only his son could hear or rather divine what he was saying. He made a sign to the boy, who stood on a chair and put his ear close to his father's mouth. Achille listened carefully, then got down again and addressed me: 'My father bids me tell you, sir, that never in all his life has he been so affected by any concert. Your music has overwhelmed him, and it is all he can do not to go down on his knees to thank you.' At these astonishing words I made a gesture of embarrassment and incredulity; but Paganini, seizing me by the arm and hoarsely whispering with what was left of his voice, 'Yes, yes,' dragged me back onto the platform, where many of the players still lingered, knelt down and kissed my hand. No need to describe my feelings: the facts speak for themselves.

Coming out in a state of fever-heat, I met Armand Bertin on the boulevard. I stood for some time in the bitter air, telling him of the scene that had just taken place, and caught a chill. When I got home, I retired to bed, iller than ever. Two days later I was alone in my room when the door opened and little Achille came in. 'My father will be very sorry to hear that you are still unwell,' he said. 'If he were not so ill himself he would have come to see you. Here is a letter he told me to bring.' I was about to open it when the child stopped me. 'There is no answer; my father said you would read it when you were by yourself.' With that, he left.

I supposed it to be a letter of congratulation. I opened it and read:

PARIGI, *18 dicembre 1838*

Mio caro amico,

Beethoven spento non c'era che Berlioz che potesse farlo rivivere; ed io che ho gustato le vostre divine composizioni degne d'un genio qual siete, credo mio dovere di pregarvi a voler accettare, in segno del mio omaggio, venti mila franchi, i quali vi saranno rimessi dal signor baron de Rothschild dopo che gli avrete presentato l'acclusa. Credete me sempre il vostro affezionatissimo amico

*Nicolò Paganini**

I know enough Italian to understand a letter like that; but the contents took me so completely by surprise that my mind became confused and I failed to grasp their meaning. A note, however, addressed to M. de Rothschild, was enclosed. Without thinking I was acting improperly, I tore it open. It said:

My dear Baron,

Please be so good as to remit to M. Berlioz the twenty thousand francs which I deposited with you yesterday.

Yours, etc. *Paganini*

It was only then that light dawned. I must have turned very pale, for my wife, coming in at that moment, and seeing me in apparent consternation with a letter in my hand, exclaimed, 'What is it? Has something else gone wrong? Don't despair. We have borne it before.'

'No, no, it's not that at all.'

'What is it then?'

'Paganini——'

'Yes?'

'He's sent me—twenty thousand francs.'

'Louis! Louis!' cried Harriet distractedly, rushing to fetch our son, who was playing in the next room; 'come here, come with your mother, come and thank God for what He has done for your father!' And my wife and son ran back into the room and fell on their knees by the bed, the mother praying, the wondering child

* [*My dear friend,*

Beethoven being dead, only Berlioz can make him live again; and I who have heard your divine compositions, so worthy of your genius, humbly beg you to accept, as a token of my homage, twenty thousand francs, which Baron de Rothschild will remit to you on your presenting the enclosed.

Believe me ever your most affectionate friend,

Nicolò Paganini]

beside her joining his little hands together. Oh Paganini! If only he could have witnessed it!

My first act was, naturally, to answer his letter, it being impossible for me to leave the house. The reply I wrote* has always seemed to me so inadequate, so far from expressing what I felt, that I cannot bring myself to reproduce it here. There are some feelings and situations which leave one overwhelmed.

The rumour of Paganini's noble action soon got round, and for two days my apartment was visited by a constant stream of artists who wanted to see the famous letter and to hear the full details of this extraordinary event. I was congratulated on all sides. One showed a slight resentment, not against me but against Paganini. 'I'm not a rich man,' he said, 'or I would have done as much myself.' He was, it must be said, a violinist. It is the only instance I know of an impulse of honourable envy. After that the floodgates were open. My opponents, in their annoyance, spread lies and disparaging comments. My friends were triumphant. Janin wrote to me, unforgettably, and published a magnificent article in the *Journal des débats*. I was abused by a few ill-natured individuals, and slanderous insinuations were made against Paganini. In short, a clamour of conflicting passions, generous and ignoble, was unleashed.

In the midst of all this agitation I lay impatiently in bed, a prey to intense emotion. At length at the end of the sixth day, feeling a little better and unable to contain myself any longer, I dressed and hurried round to the Néothermes in the rue de la Victoire where Paganini was staying. There I was informed that he was in the billiard room, alone. I went in; we embraced without a word. After a few minutes, as I was stammering out I know not what in the way of thanks, Paganini—whose words I could hear in the silence of the empty room—stopped me and said, 'Don't speak of it. No, please say no more. It has given me the greatest satisfaction of my life. You cannot imagine how deeply your music has moved me. It is many years since I felt anything like it. Ah! but now,' he went on, banging his fist on the billiard table, 'all those people who intrigue against you will not dare say another word. They know that I understand what is what, and that I am not easy.'

* [See *Correspondance générale*, II, 489.]

What did he mean by this last expression? Did he mean, 'I am not easily moved by music,' or, 'I don't easily part with my money,' or, 'I am not a rich man'?

The sardonic tone of voice in which he said it rules out, I rather think, the third interpretation.

In any case the great man was mistaken. His authority was enormous; but it was not enough to silence all the fools and knaves. He did not know the Parisian rabble intimately. Before long they were yapping at my heels more viciously than ever. According to a naturalist, some dogs aspire to the condition of man; I believe the opposite is much more common.

My debts paid, I still had a handsome sum of money. My one idea was to put it to a musical purpose. I would give up everything else and write a really important work, something splendid on a grand and original plan, full of passion and imagination, worthy to be dedicated to the glorious artist to whom I owed so much. While I was turning it over in my mind, Paganini, whose health had been deteriorating, was obliged to leave Paris and go first to Marseilles and from there to Nice—never, alas, to return. I wrote to him, submitting various subjects for the work which I had told him I was planning to compose; but his reply was, 'I cannot advise you about it. You know best what will suit you.'

In the end, after hesitating for some time, I settled on the idea of a symphony with chorus, soloists and choral recitative on the sublime and perennial theme of Shakespeare's *Romeo and Juliet*. I wrote out in prose the text which was to be sung between the instrumental movements; Emile Deschamps, with his usual kindness and most unusual facility, put it into verse, and I began.

This time, no more newspaper articles, or very few. I had money. Paganini had given it to me to write music, and I did. I worked for seven months at my symphony* without breaking off for more than three or four days in thirty on any pretext whatsoever.

Oh, the ardent existence I lived during that time! I struck out boldly across that great ocean of poetry, caressed by the wild, sweet breeze of fancy, under that fiery sun of love that Shakespeare kindled. I felt within me the strength to reach the enchanted isle where the temple of pure art stands serene under a clear sky.

* [Late January to early September 1839.]

It is not for me to determine whether I succeeded. The work as it was then was performed three times at the Conservatoire under my direction* and, each time, appeared to be a genuine success. But I felt at once that much would have to be changed, and I went over it carefully and critically from every point of view. To my keen regret Paganini never heard the score nor read it. I kept hoping he would return to Paris; moreover I was waiting until the symphony was finally complete and published before sending it to him. In the meantime he died in Nice,† and to add to my sadness I had the chagrin of not knowing whether he would have been satisfied with this work undertaken above all to please him and with the object of justifying in his eyes what he had done for me. He too seemed greatly to regret that he did not know *Romeo and Juliet*, as he said in a letter from Nice, dated 7 January 1840. The letter also contained the phrase: 'Now that all is done, envy cannot but be silent.' Dear, noble friend! Happily he never read the scarifying nonsense that appeared in several Paris newspapers: about the scheme of the work, the introduction, the adagio, Queen Mab, Friar Laurence's narration. One taunted me with the absurdity of attempting this new form of symphony; another dismissed the Queen Mab scherzo as a ridiculous little noise reminiscent of 'a badly oiled syringe'; a third, passing judgment on the love scene, the adagio—the movement which three-quarters of the musicians in Europe that know it rate above everything I have written—announced that I had 'failed to understand Shakespeare'. Toad, swollen with wind and crapulous stupidity! Let him prove it!

I had not been prepared for such criticism and was deeply wounded by it.‡ Yet as usual none of the pundits who pronounced for or against the work deigned to point out a single one of its specific faults, which I corrected later as and when I recognized them.

M. Frankoski, Ernst's secretary, drew my attention in Vienna to the weak and much too abrupt ending of the Queen Mab scherzo, and I wrote the present coda in its place. On the advice of (I think)

* [24 November, 1 and 15 December 1839.]

† [27 May 1840.]

‡ [Cf. Verdi's reaction to similar criticism from Paris: 'Perhaps I have not succeeded in rendering *Macbeth*; but to say that I don't know, that I don't feel and understand Shakespeare—no, by heaven, no!']

d'Ortigue, a cut was contrived in Friar Laurence's narration which greatly improved it; I had made it too long, led astray by the excessive number of lines furnished by the librettist. All the other modifications, additions and suppressions I made on my own initiative, by dint of observing the effect of the work as a whole and in detail when I heard it in Paris, Berlin, Vienna and Prague. If there are other blemishes that I have missed, at least I have tried sincerely and with what judgment I posses to detect them.

After which, what can a composer do but admit candidly that he has done his best, and resign himself to the work's imperfections? When I had reached that point, and only then, the *Romeo and Juliet* symphony was published.*

The work is enormously difficult to perform. It poses problems of every kind, problems inherent in the form and in the style and only to be solved by long and patient rehearsal, impeccably directed. To be well done, it needs first-rate performers—players, singers, conductor—intent on preparing it with as much care as a new opera is prepared in a good opera house, in fact almost as if it were to be performed by heart.

For this reason it will never be given in London, where the necessary rehearsals are not to be had. In that country musicians do not have time for music.†

50

M. de Rémusat commissions the Funeral and Triumphal Symphony—its performance—its popularity in Paris —Habeneck's remark—epithet invented for the work by Spontini—his mistake about the Requiem

IN 1840, AS THE month of July drew near, the government proposed to celebrate the tenth anniversary of the 1830 Revolution

* [1847. Berlioz was frequently urged to publish his symphonies or to send copies of them to various cities in Germany, but refused to do so until he had himself conducted them there, on the grounds that they were 'too young to travel without him'. See his open letter to Schumann in the *Gazette musicale* of 19 February 1837, reproduced in *Correspondance générale*, II, 327–32.]

† Since this was written the first four parts of *Romeo and Juliet* have been given in London under my direction, with a reception as brilliant as they have had anywhere. [24 March 1852, at Exeter Hall.]

with public ceremonies on an imposing scale. The relics of the more or less heroic victims were to be translated to the monument that had been erected to them in the Place de la Bastille. M. de Rémusat, who was the Minister of the Interior at the time, happens by a remarkable coincidence to be, like M. de Gasparin, a lover of music. He decided to commission me to write a symphony for the occasion, leaving the choice of the form of the work and the forces entirely to me. In return I would receive ten thousand francs, out of which I was to pay the expenses of copying and performance.

It seemed to me that for such a work the simpler the plan the better, and that only a large body of wind instruments would be suitable for a symphony that was to be heard—the first time at any rate—in the open air. I wished, to begin with, to recall the conflicts of the famous Three Days amid the mourning strains of a bleak but awe-inspiring march, to be played during the procession; to follow this with a kind of funeral oration or farewell address to the illustrious dead, while the bodies were lowered into the cenotaph; and to conclude with a hymn of praise at the moment when, the tomb being sealed, all eyes were fixed on the high column on which Liberty with wings outspread seemed soaring towards heaven like the souls of those who had given their lives for her.

I had almost completed the funeral march when a rumour went round that the July ceremonies would not take place. 'Ah-ha,' I thought, 'this is the Requiem all over again; this is as far as I go: I know these people.' And I stopped. A few days later I was strolling through Paris, when the Minister passed me in his carriage and, catching sight of me, beckoned me over. He wanted to know how far I had got with the symphony. I told him bluntly the reason which had led me to stop work on it, adding that I had not forgotten what I suffered over Marshal Damrémont's funeral and the Requiem.

'But the rumour which has alarmed you is completely false,' he said. 'Nothing has changed; the inauguration of the Bastille column, the translation of the July dead—everything stands. I'm counting on you. Hurry up and finish the work.'

Although my mistrust had been all too natural, this assurance set my mind at rest and I resumed work at once. The march and the funeral oration were completed and the theme found for the

Apotheosis; but I was held up for quite a long time over the fanfare which I wanted to bring gradually up from the depths of the orchestra to the high note on which the song of triumph bursts in. I wrote version after version. None of them satisfied me. The effect was either commonplace, or it was insufficiently spacious or too light-hearted, or it lacked sonority, or the transition was badly managed. I imagined a trumpet-call of archangels, simple but sublime, boundless, glittering, an immense radiance swelling and resounding, proclaiming to earth and heaven the opening of the Empyrean gates. In the end I settled, not without anxiety, on the version which is familiar, and the rest was soon done. Later, after I had made the usual corrections and modifications, I added strings and chorus. Though not absolutely necessary they greatly enhance the effect.

I engaged for the occasion a military band of two hundred. Habeneck would again have liked to conduct, but I prudently reserved that function for myself. I had not forgotten the episode of the snuff-box.

Happily it occurred to me to invite a large audience to the final rehearsal, for it was impossible to get any idea of the work on the day of the performance.* Despite the volume of sound produced by a wind band of that size very little was heard during the procession. The only exception was the music played as we went along the Boulevard Poissonnière, where the big trees—still standing at that date—acted as reflectors. The rest was lost.

In the open spaces of the Place de la Bastille it was worse. Almost nothing could be made out more than ten yards away. To cap it all, the National Guard, growing tired of standing so long at the slope in the blazing sun, began to march off before the end to the accompaniment of some fifty side-drums maintaining a relentless barrage throughout the Apotheosis, not a note of which survived. That is how they regard the role of music on public occasions in France: by all means let it figure as an attraction—for the eye.

This I knew. The final rehearsal in the Salle Vivienne was the real performance. It made such an impression that the impresario

* [28 July 1840. The final rehearsal took place two days earlier.]

in charge of the hall engaged me for four evening concerts,* at which the new symphony was the main work in the programme and a lot of money was taken.

On the way out of one of these performances Habeneck, with whom I had had a fresh quarrel (I do not remember why), remarked, 'One must admit the b—— has some damned fine ideas.' A week later he was probably saying the opposite. This time I had no bone to pick with the Minister. M. de Rémusat behaved like a gentleman; the ten thousand francs were sent forthwith. When I had paid the bill for the band and the copyist I had two thousand eight hundred francs left. It was not much; but the Minister was pleased and, as each performance made clear, the work appealed to the public more than all its predecessors. People became wildly excited by it. One evening at the Salle Vivienne, after the Apotheosis, some young men were moved to pick up their chairs and pound them against the floor, yelling as they did so. The management promptly gave orders that at subsequent performances patrons would kindly express their enthusiasm in more customary ways.

Spontini wrote me a long and curious letter on the subject of this symphony when it was performed much later at the Conservatoire, with strings as well as wind but without chorus.† I am sorry not to be able to reproduce it here: I foolishly gave it to a collector of autographs. I remember only that it began: 'I write still being under the impression of your shaking [*sic*] music.'

Despite his friendship for me this was the only time he praised a composition of mine. He always went to hear them but never spoke of them to me. However, I am forgetting one other occasion, after a performance of my Requiem at Saint-Eustache,‡ when he said to me, 'You know, you're wrong to say the Institute prize-winners shouldn't be sent to Rome. Without Michelangelo's "Last Judgment" you would never have conceived a Requiem like that.'

In this he was strangely mistaken, for the only reaction that the famous Sistine fresco produced in me was a feeling of acute

* [7 and 14 August 1840, 1 and 15 February 1842.]

† [19 November 1843.]

‡ [29 August 1846.]

disappointment. I see the torments of the damned depicted there but nothing that suggests mankind gathered together on the last day. However, I know nothing about painting and have little feeling for conventional beauty.

51

Expedition to Brussels and concerts there—a word about my domestic life and its storms—the Belgians—Zani de Ferranti—Fétis—serious error of the latter—festival organized and conducted by me at the Paris Opéra —plot by Habeneck's supporters foiled—a scene in M. de Girardin's box—how to make a fortune —I leave for Germany

IT WAS TOWARDS the end of the same year (1840) that I made my first musical expedition outside France; that is, began giving concerts abroad. M. Snel of Brussels invited me to perform a few of my works in the Salle de la Grande Harmonie, where the society of that name (whose director he was) held their concerts, and I decided to try my luck and go.

Before I could do so, however, nothing short of a coup d'état was required in my domestic life. On one pretext or another my wife had always opposed my plans for travelling. Had I listened to her, to this day I would not have left Paris. An insane jealousy, for which I had long given absolutely no grounds, was her underlying motive. To carry out my plan I had to keep it secret and smuggle my bundles of music and a trunk out of the house and set off without warning, leaving behind a letter explaining my disappearance. But I did not go alone. I had a travelling companion* who since that time has accompanied me on my various expeditions. By dint of being accused and tortured in countless ways, always unjustly, until I could find no peace or rest at home, in the end I came, by accident, to enjoy in actual fact the position wrongly imputed to me, and my life was transformed.

In a word, to cut short this part of my tale and not to go into some extremely painful details, I will say only that from that

* [Marie Recio, a minor opera singer of mixed French and Spanish parentage; Berlioz's mistress for about twelve years, later his wife.]

moment, after a period of protracted bitterness, an amicable separation took place between me and my wife. I see her often, my affection for her is in no way diminished; the wretched state of her health only makes her more dear to me.

This brief summary must suffice as explanation of my subsequent conduct for those who have known me only since that time. I shall add nothing more; for, I repeat, I am not writing confessions.

I gave two concerts in Brussels, one in the Salle de la Grande Harmonie, the other in the Augustinian church (which has long since ceased to be used for Catholic worship).* Both halls are excessively resonant; so much so that any music at all quick and strenuously scored inevitably becomes a blur. Slow, quiet pieces, particularly in the Salle de la Grande Harmonie, are the only kind which are not distorted by the reverberation and so make their proper effect.

Opinions on my music were at least as sharply divided in Brussels as in Paris. A curious debate ensued, I was told, between Fétis, who was still hostile to me, and another critic, M. Zani de Ferranti, an artist and writer of note who set up as my champion. When the latter singled out, among the items that I had performed, the Pilgrims' March in *Harold* as one of the most interesting things he had ever heard, Fétis answered, 'How can I be expected to approve of a piece in which one is constantly hearing two notes that are not part of the harmony?' (He was referring to the C and B which recur at the end of each stanza, like a slow tolling of bells.)

'Indeed?' de Ferranti replied. 'Well, I don't believe in this anomaly of yours. Or rather, if a composer has managed to write a piece which delights me from beginning to end as this has done, with two notes that are not part of the harmony, then I can only say he must be a god, not a man.'

Alas, I would have replied to my Italian enthusiast, I am but an ordinary man and M. Fétis a poor musician, for those famous notes are part of the harmony. Fétis had not observed that it is precisely through their addition to the chord that the various keys in which

* [The two concerts were on 26 September and 9 October 1842. Among the pieces performed were the Funeral Symphony, the Fantastic, and the Pilgrims' March, with Ernst playing the viola part.]

the stanzas end are resolved into the main key, as no real musician should or could for a moment fail to see. In fact from a technical point of view that is precisely the curious and novel thing about the March. When I heard of this strange misapprehension I was tempted to publish an open letter to Zani de Ferranti in one of the papers, pointing out Fétis' error. Then I thought better of it and withdrew behind my rule, which I believe to be a sound one, of never replying to criticism no matter how absurd.

When the score of *Harold* was published a few years later,* Fétis was able to see for himself that the two notes invariably form part of the harmony.

This journey beyond the frontier was merely an experiment. I planned to make a tour of Germany and to take five or six months over it. I therefore returned to Paris to get ready and to bid Paris farewell with a gigantic concert—an idea which I had for some time been meditating.

M. Pillet, then director of the Opéra, welcomed the proposal I put to him that I should organize a festival† in the theatre, and I set to work, without letting any news of the project leak out. The problem lay in not giving Habeneck time to act against it. He was bound to take a jaundiced view of my directing a great musical enterprise of the kind, the greatest yet seen in Paris, in the theatre where he was conductor. So I prepared secretly all the music needed for my chosen programme and engaged the players without revealing where the concert was being held. When everything was ready and I could safely show my hand, I asked Pillet to inform Habeneck that I was in charge of the proceedings. But he could not bring himself to do it, such was his dread of the formidable old man. The awkward task was left to me. So I wrote to Habeneck and told him what arrangements I had made, with Pillet's approval, and added that as I was in the habit of conducting my own concerts I hoped he would not take it amiss if I conducted this one as well.

* [1848.]

† This word, which I was the first to employ on the posters in Paris, is now used indiscriminately in the most ludicrous contexts. We have 'festivals' of music and dancing in the least pleasure garden, with three violins, a bass drum and two cornets.

Habeneck received my letter at the Opéra, in the middle of a rehearsal. He read it several times, paced gloomily about the stage for a long time and then, suddenly making up his mind, went down to the manager's office and announced that the whole thing suited him admirably, as he had intended in any case to spend that day in the country. But his annoyance was obvious and it was soon shared by many of his players, all the more vehemently because they knew they would flatter him by showing it. Under the agreement I had made with Pillet, the whole orchestra was to be at my disposal, together with the players whom I had recruited from outside.

The concert was a benefit for the director of the Opéra; he guaranteed me a mere five hundred francs for my pains and a free hand with all the arrangements. Consequently, Habeneck's players were bound to take part and would not be paid for it. I remembered the gentlemen of the Théâtre-Italien and the way they had made a fool of me in very similar circumstances. This time, indeed, I was in an even more delicate position with regard to the players at the Opéra. Every evening I could see private meetings going on in the orchestra during the intervals. The air was electric. Habeneck, with a bodyguard of supporters in angry attendance, was cold and impenetrable. Copies of the *Charivari*, in which I was torn to pieces, were distributed on the desks.* The storm was clearly gathering: a few of Habeneck's henchmen had announced that they would not march 'without their old general'; and now that the full rehearsals were due to begin I tried to get Pillet to agree that the Opéra players should be paid like the others. When he refused I said, 'I fully appreciate your reasons. Only, in this way you're endangering the whole performance. I have no choice but to use the five hundred francs which you're giving me to pay those Opéra musicians who don't actually refuse to play.'

'What!' he said. 'Get nothing out of it, after all that frightful effort?'

* [E.g. 'This concert, grandiloquently announced under the imposing title of "festival", is nothing more nor less than a means of satisfying the self-esteem of the critic of the *Journal des débats*' (25 October 1840). 'The performance will terminate, by general demand, with the ascension by M. Hector Berlioz in a bass drum' (1 November 1840).]

'That is not important. The great thing is that it should go well. My five hundred francs will keep the less mutinous quiet. For the others, I would rather you didn't use your authority to force them to play. We'll leave them to their old general.'

So it was arranged. I had a combined orchestra and chorus of six hundred. The programme consisted of the first act of Gluck's *Iphigénie en Tauride*, a scene from Handel's *Athalia*, the Dies irae and Lacrymosa from my Requiem, the Apotheosis from my Funeral and Triumphal Symphony, the adagio, scherzo and finale from *Romeo and Juliet*, and an unaccompanied chorus by Palestrina. Considering how my army of performers was put together I cannot imagine how I contrived to teach them such a difficult programme in so short a time as a week; but I did. I would go straight from the Opéra to the Théâtre-Italien (where I had engaged the chorus only), and from the Théâtre-Italien to the Opéra-Comique and the Conservatoire, taking a chorus practice in one place, a sectional rehearsal of the orchestra in another; supervising the entire work myself, not leaving anything to anybody else. After that I took the combined instrumental forces, in two halves one after the other, in the foyer of the Opéra: the strings from eight in the morning till midday, the wind from midday till four. I was on my feet, baton in hand, all day. My throat was on fire, my voice had gone, my arm was dropping off. I felt ready to faint with thirst and exhaustion, when a compassionate member of the chorus brought me a large glass of mulled wine; it gave me the strength to carry through this gruelling session to the end.

Fresh demands by the Opéra musicians had added to its natural trials. Discovering that I was paying some of the outside players twenty francs, they considered that this gave them the right to come up in the middle, one after the other, and demand to be paid the same amount.

'It's not the money,' they said, 'but you can't have Opéra artists getting less than players from minor theatres.'

'All right,' I said, 'you shall have your twenty francs—I guarantee it; only, for God's sake get on with your job and stop bothering me.'

Next day the final rehearsal took place on the stage of the Opéra and was satisfactory. Everything went reasonably well except the Queen Mab scherzo, which I had rashly included in the programme. The piece is too swift and delicate to be performed by an orchestra of this size, nor should it be. With so short a bar, it is virtually impossible to keep the extremities of such a huge body of players together. Those farthest from the conductor soon get behind because they cannot quite keep up with the very rapid beat. I was in such a state of agitation that it never occurred to me to form a small picked orchestra which, concentrated near me in the middle of the stage, could have carried out my intentions without difficulty. After the most fearful struggles we had to abandon the scherzo, and it was removed from the programme. I noticed on this occasion how difficult, indeed impossible, it is to prevent the little cymbals in B flat and F from dragging when the players are a long way from the conductor. I had stupidly left them at the back of the stage, next to the drums, and despite everything I could do they were sometimes as much as a bar behind. Since then I have been careful to place them right beside me, and the difficulty has vanished.

I had counted on resting the following day, at any rate until the evening; but a friend* warned me that Habeneck's partisans were planning to spoil if not wreck the whole enterprise: the drums, he wrote, were to be slit and the bows of the double basses greased, and in the middle of the concert they were going to call for the Marseillaise.

This information, the reader will surmise, somewhat disturbed my much-needed rest. Instead of spending the day asleep, I paced feverishly up and down outside the Opéra. As I was prowling about on the boulevard I had the luck to meet Habeneck in person. I went straight up to him and took his arm.

'I've been warned that your players have some foul play planned for tonight. But I've got my eye on them.'

'Oh, you've nothing to fear,' the old hypocrite answered; 'they won't do anything. I've made them listen to reason.'

'My dear man, it's not I who need reassuring. I'm trying to reassure you. You see, if anything happened it would fall pretty heavily on you. But don't worry: as you say, they won't do anything.'

* Léon Gatayes. [(1805–77); harpist, composer and critic.]

All the same, when evening came I was not without anxiety. I had stationed my copyist in the orchestra all day to stand guard over the drums and the double basses. The instruments were untouched. But there was something else that I was afraid of. The four small brass bands in the pieces from the Requiem contain trumpets and cornets in various keys (B flat, F, and E flat). Now the crook of a trumpet in F, as it happens, differs little from the crook of a trumpet in B flat, and it is easy to confuse them. In the Tuba mirum some sly dog could slip me a fanfare in F instead of B flat. His excuse would be that he had used the wrong crook. Meanwhile he would have engineered a fearsome cacophony.

Just before the Dies irae began, I left my desk and went round the orchestra, asking each trumpet- and cornet-player to let me see his instrument. I inspected them carefully, scrutinizing the inscriptions on the various crooks, 'in F', 'in E♭', 'in B♭', until I reached the band which included the Dauverné brothers (who played in the Opéra orchestra), when the elder made me blush by saying, 'Oh Berlioz, how could you? Surely you don't suspect us? We would never do a thing like that. And we're your friends.' The reproach stung me (though what I had done was only too excusable) and I stopped my investigations.

My worthy trumpeters made no mistakes, everything went well, and the Requiem pieces produced their due effect.

Immediately after this part of the concert there was an interval. During the ensuing lull the Habeneckists tried to explode their remaining bombshell, the simplest and the least dangerous to themselves. Several voices from the pit shouted, 'The Marseillaise, the Marseillaise!', hoping to stir up the audience and upset the whole arrangement of the evening. A number of spectators, attracted by the idea of hearing the famous hymn declaimed by such a chorus and orchestra, were already joining in the cry when I came forward to the front of the stage and roared out at the top of my voice, 'We will not play the Marseillaise. That is not what we are here for'; and calm was instantly restored.

It did not last long. A moment later another incident, this time quite unconnected with me, set the house in a greater commotion. Cries of 'Murder! It's an outrage! Arrest him!' were heard coming from the amphitheatre, and the audience rose in confusion. A dishevelled Madame de Girardin was waving her arms about in her box and calling for help. Her husband had just had his face slapped by Bergeron, one of the editors of the *Charivari*, a notorious lampooner of Louis-Philippe, and the man popularly supposed to have fired the pistol shot at the King from the Pont Royal a few years before.*

Such a fracas could not but be damaging to the rest of the concert, which passed without incident but in a general atmosphere of abstractedness.

Be that as it may, I had overcome my difficulties and frustrated the enemy general staff. The receipts came to eight thousand five hundred francs. As the sum which I had surrendered in order to pay the Opéra players was not enough, owing to my having promised them all twenty francs, I was obliged to present the cashier of the theatre with three hundred and sixty francs. He accepted it, indicating the source in his book with an entry in red ink: *Surplus handed over by M. Berlioz.*

Thus I succeeded, alone and unaided, in organizing the largest concert that had yet been given in Paris, despite Habeneck and his men, and by giving up the modest amount allocated to me. The takings were eight thousand five hundred francs, while my part in the proceedings cost me three hundred and sixty francs.

That is the way to get rich! I have often employed this method during my career. So I too must have made my fortune. . . . How was it that Pillet, who is a gentleman, allowed it? I could never understand. Perhaps the cashier did not tell him.

A few days later I left for Germany. The following series of letters, which I addressed on my return to various friends (and to two individuals who cannot claim that title),† will show the reader what I did and saw on that first journey. It was admittedly an

* [19 November 1832. Bergeron had been arrested on suspicion but released owing to lack of evidence. In 1840, when Emile de Girardin's paper, the *Presse*, repeated the insinuation, Bergeron (who was on the editorial staff of the rival *Siècle*) challenged him to a duel; but since killing Armand Carrel, editor of the *National*, Girardin had refused to fight duels. Bergeron sought him out at the Opéra in the hope of provoking him. He was sentenced to three months' imprisonment for assault.]

† Habeneck and Girard.

arduous voyage of discovery; but it was a musical one. From the pecuniary point of view it was quite profitable; and I had the happiness of living in a congenial atmosphere, out of reach of the squalid intrigues and the platitudes of Paris.

I give the letters here, more or less as they were published at the time under the title *Musical Travels in Germany.**

* [*Journal des débats*, August–November 1843 and January 1844, and then in book form later in 1844. Berlioz had long meditated a tour of Germany. Its object was partly, as always, to make a flank attack on Paris and force the authorities to give him the official recognition they had so far withheld; and the bulletins which he sent back to the Press were propaganda directed to that end. But Germany was also an end in itself—the spiritual home of music, which had lately shown signs of developing a healthy curiosity about him. In 1835 in the *Neue Zeitschrift für Musik* Schumann analysed the Fantastic Symphony (from Liszt's piano transcription) at great length and on the whole very favourably. During the last few years there had been a number of performances, in Leipzig, Weimar and elsewhere, of the *Francs-juges*, *Waverley* and *King Lear* overtures (the only orchestral works that Berlioz had yet ventured to publish); and since early 1840 the *Neue Zeitschrift* had been regularly reproducing articles of his from the *Débats*. The time was ripe for him to go there in person, taking with him manuscript scores and parts of his major works, the Fantastic, *Harold*, the Requiem, *Romeo* and the Funeral Symphony. He left in early December 1842, having obtained a publisher's advance on his newly completed *Treatise on Modern Orchestration* to pay for the journey. Marie Recio accompanied him, and proved a very mixed blessing owing to her insistence on singing at his concerts.]

TRAVELS IN GERMANY—I
1841–2

First Letter

Brussels, Mainz, Frankfurt

TO AUGUSTE MOREL*

Well, my dear Morel, here I am back from this long trip to Germany, in the course of which I gave fifteen concerts and took nearly fifty rehearsals. You may suppose that after such exertions I am in need of rest and inactivity and you will be right; but you can hardly imagine how strange it seems. Often in the morning, half waking, I leap out of bed and get dressed under the firm impression that I am late and the orchestra is waiting for me. Then, after a moment's reflection, reality reasserts itself and I think, 'What orchestra? I am in Paris, where they order things differently and it's the orchestra that keeps you waiting. What is more, I am not giving a concert, I have no chorus to rehearse, no symphony to conduct, no morning appointment with Meyerbeer or Mendelssohn or Lipinski or Marschner, Anton Bohrer, Schloesser, Mangold, the brothers Müller, or with any of those excellent German artists who welcomed me so courteously and gave me so many proofs of respect and devotion.' There is scarcely any music to be heard in France at the moment, and you, my friend, whom I was so delighted to see again, look so doleful and dejected when I question you about what has been happening in Paris during my absence that I feel a chill at heart together with a powerful desire to go back to Germany, where enthusiasm is still to be found. Yet consider what immense resources we possess in this maelstrom that is Paris, to which the hopes and restless ambitions of all Europe turn. Think what splendid results might be achieved if all the means at the disposal of the Conservatoire, the Gymnase, the three opera houses, the churches and the schools of singing were combined! With judicious selection one could create from

* One of my closest friends and one of the finest musicians I know. His compositions have real merit. He is now director of the Marseilles Conservatoire.

all these separate elements, if not an ideal choir (the voices are not sufficiently trained), at any rate an incomparable orchestra. To give Parisians a superb ensemble of eight or nine hundred musicians, two things alone are required: somewhere to put them and a little love of art to get them there. We have not got a single large concert hall. The Opéra might serve the purpose if the stage were not occupied almost every day with scenery and all the routine activities of a repertory theatre, which would make the preparations necessary for such a grand affair virtually impossible to carry out. Then, would one ever find the collective enthusiasm, the single-mindedness, the ability to act together, the disinterested devotion, the patience, without which nothing worth while can be accomplished in this field? It is to be hoped; but one can only hope. The exceptional discipline which prevails at the rehearsals of the Conservatoire Society, and the zeal displayed by the members of that famous body, are universally admired. Yes; but it is the rarest things that are prized so highly. On the other hand, almost everywhere I went in Germany I found discipline and alertness combined with a genuine respect for the maestro. I should say 'maestros', for there are several: the composer, who nearly always directs both rehearsals and performance of his work, without the conductor's pride being in the least offended; the kapellmeister, generally a competent composer, who is in charge of the large operas in the repertoire—all the important works of composers who are dead or elsewhere; and the leader, who looks after the smaller operas and the ballets and, when not conducting, plays the first violin part and conveys the kapellmeister's instructions and comments to the back desks of the orchestra, keeps an eye on all the material side of the orchestra's work, sees that nothing is missing with regard to instruments or music, and sometimes demonstrates the bowing or the correct way of phrasing a passage—which the kapellmeister cannot do, as he always conducts with a baton.

No doubt in Germany, too, among all the hordes of musicians of varying abilities, there are plenty of cases of obscure, unsatisfied vanity and stored-up resentment, but with one solitary exception I do not remember an occasion when it openly declared itself. Perhaps this was because I do not understand German.

I came across very few good chorus-masters. Most of them are poor pianists. I met one who could not play the piano at all, and who gave the notes by striking the keyboard with two fingers of the right hand. Moreover, in Germany, as here, they still rehearse all the voices together in the same place under one conductor, instead of having three practice rooms and three chorus-masters for the preliminary rehearsals and keeping sopranos and altos, tenors, and basses in separate groups for a few days—a method which saves time and ensures that each part is thoroughly learnt. In general the voices, tenors especially, are fresher and of better quality than we hear in our theatres. But it would be rash to conclude that German choruses are superior to ours, and you will shortly see, if you care to follow me through the various towns that I visited, that with the exception of Berlin, Frankfurt and possibly Dresden the theatre choruses are all either bad or very mediocre. On the other hand the choral societies are among the glories of Germany. We shall attempt later on to discover the reason for this contradiction.

My journey began under alarming auspices. I suffered one mishap after another, and I assure you it required the persistence of a mule to go on with it and bring it to a successful conclusion. I left Paris in the firm belief that my first three concerts had definitely been arranged. One was to be in Brussels, where I had been engaged by the Société de la Grande Harmonie. The other two were to be in Frankfurt; they had already been announced by the director of the theatre, who appeared to attach considerable importance to them and to be taking the greatest pains to make them a success. What was the outcome of all this zeal and all these fine promises? Absolutely nothing. This is what happened. Madame Nathan-Treillet had kindly promised to come from Paris expressly to sing at the Brussels concert. Just as rehearsals were about to begin and the evening had been advertised in the most resounding fashion, we learnt that the diva was stricken with a serious illness and in consequence could not leave Paris. Madame Nathan-Treillet is a sacred name to the Belgians, from the days when she was prima donna at the opera house; it is no exaggeration to say they worship her. To them all the symphonies in the world are not worth a romance by Loisa Puget sung by Madame Nathan-Treillet. At the news of this catastrophe the entire Grande Harmonie expired in a wail, the smoking-room adjoining the concert hall became deserted, all the pipes went out as if suddenly deprived of air and the Grand Harmonists dispersed with groans. In vain I sought to console them: 'Be calm, there isn't going to be any concert, you will be spared the unpleasantness of listening to my music; that is surely compensation enough.' It was no use—

Their eyes dissolved in beery tears, and nolebant consolari*

—Madame Nathan-Treillet was not coming. So there was my concert in ruins. The conductor of that grandly harmonic society, a man of real talent, full of devotion to his art, when all is said an eminent musician, a man not normally given to despair, even when robbed of Mlle Puget's romances—in a word, Snel, who had invited me to come to Brussels, in shame and embarrassment

Swore, somewhat late, he'd not be caught again.†

What was I to do? Apply to the rival society, the Philharmonic, conducted by Bender, head of the admirable Musique des Guides?‡ Collect a brilliant orchestra by combining the players from the theatre with the students from the Conservatoire? There would be no difficulty in doing so, thanks to the good will of Messrs Henssens, Mertz and Wéry, who had all three on a previous occasion been eager to use their influence with their pupils and friends on my behalf. But this would have meant starting again from scratch, and time was lacking: I believed that I was expected in Frankfurt for the two concerts mentioned above. There was nothing for it but to leave,§ full of anxiety and self-reproach for the grievous affliction I had in all innocence and to my own detriment brought upon the *dilettanti* of Belgium. Happily, remorse of this kind does not last, the smoke goeth over it and it is gone, and I had not been an hour on the Rhine steamer,

* [The Latin phrase is an adaptation of *Jeremiah XXXI*, 15: 'they refused to be comforted'.]

† [La Fontaine, 'Le corbeau et le renard'.]

‡ [The band of the regiment of that name, which Valentine Bender had directed since 1832.]

§ [About 19 December 1842.]

admiring the river and the passing scene upon its banks, before I had ceased to think about it. The Rhine! It's beautiful, so beautiful! Perhaps you imagine, my dear Morel, that I shall seize the opportunity to expatiate in grand poetic terms. God forbid! I know too well that my poetic expatiation would be but prosaic diminution of such a subject. Besides, I like to think for your reputation's sake that you are familiar with Victor Hugo's splendid book.*

On reaching Mainz I made inquiries about the Austrian military band which had been there the previous year and which, according to Strauss (the Paris Strauss),† had performed several

* [*Le Rhin*, published earlier that year (1842) in the form of thirty-nine letters and an epilogue, describing a journey made in 1838–9.]

† The name of Strauss is famous throughout Europe wherever people dance. It is associated with innumerable piquant and fanciful waltzes whose novel rhythms and characteristic lilt have taken them round the world. It may indeed be supposed one would have no wish to see such waltzes pirated or so great a name forged.

But look what is happening. There is a Strauss in Paris, who has a brother. There is a Strauss in Vienna, who has none. Therein lies the sole difference between them. Hence some highly disagreeable misapprehensions and cross-purposes for our Strauss, who conducts the balls at the Opéra-Comique and all the private balls given by the aristocracy, with a verve worthy of his name. The other day at the Austrian Embassy, a Viennese—clearly a bogus one—accosted Strauss, in Austrian: 'Hello, delighted to see you, my dear Strauss. Don't you recognize me?' 'No, sir.' 'Oh, I recognize you all right, though I am bound to say you're a little stouter. But in any case no one else writes waltzes like this. Only you know how a dance orchestra should be handled. There's only one Strauss.' 'You are very kind, but I assure you the Vienna Strauss is also talented.' 'Eh? The Vienna Strauss? But you are the Vienna Strauss! There isn't any other. I know you well. You're pale, he's pale. You speak Austrian, he speaks Austrian. You write the most exquisite dance tunes.' 'That is true.' 'You always accent the weak beat of the bar in waltz rhythm.' 'Ah, the weak beat, that is my strong point.' 'Didn't you write a waltz called *The Diamond*?' 'Sparkling.' 'You speak Hebrew?' 'Very well.' [In English in the original.] 'English?' 'Not at all.' [In English in the original.] 'There you are, I told you, you're Strauss. Besides, your name is on the poster.' 'Sir, once again, I am not the Vienna Strauss. He is not the only one who knows how to syncopate a waltz and accent a tune across the beat. I am the Paris Strauss. My brother, an excellent violinist whom you see over there, is also Strauss. The Vienna Strauss is Strauss. That makes three Strausses.' 'No, no, you're having me on. I mean to say, there's only one Strauss.' Whereupon the Viennese walks off, leaving our Strauss very annoyed and at a loss how to establish his identity: so much so that he has asked me to extricate him from this double entanglement. I accordingly declare that the Paris Strauss, a very pale man who speaks perfect Austrian and Hebrew, rather bad French, and English not at of my overtures with verve and power and immense success; but the regiment had left: no more band music (that really would have been a Grande Harmonie), no possibility of giving the concert which I had fancied I might spring on the unsuspecting inhabitants of Mainz. Still, there was no harm in trying. I went to see Schott, the patriarch of music publishers. The worthy man gives the impression of having been, like the Sleeping Beauty, in a coma for the past hundred years. To all my questions he answered very slowly, interspersing his words with profound silences: 'I do not think . . . you can . . . give a concert . . . here . . . there is no . . . orchestra . . . there is no . . . audience . . . we haven't got any . . . money!'

As I haven't got an unlimited quantity of . . . patience, I made straight for the railway station and left for Frankfurt. To complete my irritation—as if I needed anything!—the train had also gone to sleep. It refused to be hurried, and ambled along, choosing this of all days to make interminable pedal points at each station along the route. But every adagio has an end, and before nightfall I was in Frankfurt. Frankfurt is a delightful town, very much awake, pervaded by an air of activity and wealth, solidly built, clean and bright as a brand-new hundred-sou piece and girdled with a ring of green and fragrant boulevards planted with shrubs and flowers in the style of an English garden. Although it was December, and greenery and flowers had long since vanished, a cheerful sun glinted among the wintry branches; and whether because of the contrast between these gleaming, airy avenues and the dark streets

---

all, who writes the most spirited waltzes full of delicious subtleties of rhythm and impeccably scored, and conducts his mettlesome dance orchestra with a melancholy air but incontestable skill—I declare that this Strauss has long been resident in Paris, has for the last ten years played viola at all my concerts, is a member of the orchestra of the Théâtre-Italien, and goes off every summer to earn large sums of money in Aix, Geneva, Mainz, Munich, in fact everywhere except Vienna, which he avoids out of consideration for the other Strauss (who, for all that, once came to Paris).

In other words, the Viennese have only to take this lesson to heart, and keep their Strauss and leave us ours. Let each one render unto Strauss the things which are not Strauss's, and cease to attribute what is Strauss's to Strauss. Otherwise—such is the force of prejudice—it will end by people saying that Strauss paste [*Stras*] is worth more than Strauss diamond and that Strauss diamond is only paste.

of Mainz, or because of my hopes of being at last about to begin on my Frankfurt concerts, or from some quite different reason not to be analysed, a chorus of joy rose up within me and for two hours I walked in a state of delicious happiness. 'Important matters can wait till tomorrow,' I thought as I went back to the hotel.

Next day I set out in high spirits for the theatre, where I imagined I would find everything in readiness for my rehearsals. As I was crossing the square in which the theatre stands I saw some young men carrying wind instruments and asked them, since they seemed to be members of the orchestra, if they would present my card to their director and kapellmeister, Guhr. The expression of respectful alacrity which instantly appeared on the faces of those excellent artists at the sight of my name did me a lot of good. One of them, who knew French, spoke for his colleagues.

'We are very happy to see you at last. M. Guhr has long been telling us that you were coming, we have twice performed your *King Lear* overture. You will not find your Conservatoire orchestra here, but we think that all the same you may not be too displeased.' At this point Guhr appeared. He is a small man with a rather mischievous face and bright, piercing eyes, his movements rapid and his speech curt and incisive. It is clear he does not err on the side of indulgence when he directs his orchestra. Everything about him suggests musical intelligence and purpose: he is a leader. He speaks French, but not quickly enough for his natural impatience, and he interlards each sentence with great oaths pronounced with a German accent, the effect of which is most bizarre. I shall indicate them by their initials. The moment he saw me:

'Ah! S.N.T.T.*—it's you, my dear! Then you didn't get my letter?'

'What letter?'

'I wrote to Brussels to tell you—S.N.T.T.—wait, I don't speak properly. A misfortune, a great misfortune. Ah, here is our stage manager, he can act as my interpreter.'

And continuing to speak in French:

'Tell M. Berlioz how upset I am, that I wrote to tell him not to come yet, that the little Milanollo girls are filling the theatre every

* ['Sacré nom te Tieu.']

evening, that we've never known the public get so excited about anything, S.N.T.T., and that serious music and concerts on a large scale will have to wait till some other time.'

The stage manager: 'M. Guhr wishes me to tell you, sir, that——'

I: 'Please don't bother to repeat it. I understood all too well; you see, he didn't speak in German.'

Guhr: 'Ah! ah! I spoke French, S.N.T.T., without knowing it.'

I: 'You know it very well, and I know that I shall have to go back, or else take a chance and go on with my journey at the risk of being checkmated by infant prodigies somewhere else.'

Guhr: 'What can one do, my dear, the infants make money, S.N.T.T., French romances make money, French vaudeville draws the crowds. What would you have me do? S.N.T.T., I am director, I cannot refuse money. But stay till tomorrow at any rate and you can hear *Fidelio* with Pischek and Mlle Capitaine and, S.N.T.T., you shall tell me what you think of our artists.'

I: 'I am sure they are excellent, especially when you conduct them. But my dear Guhr, why do you swear so much? Do you think it consoles me?'

'Ah! ah! S.N.T.T., that's just speaking in a family way' (he meant to say familiarly).

At that I was seized with uncontrollable laughter, my ill-humour vanished and, taking his hand, I said, 'All right, since I am one of the family, come and drink some Rhine wine with me. I'll forgive you your little Milanollo girls and stay to hear *Fidelio* and Mlle Capitaine, whose lieutenant you seem to want to be.'

We settled that I would leave in two days for Stuttgart (not that I was expected there) and try my fortunes with Lindpaintner and the King of Württemberg. The Frankfurters should be given time to recover their composure and forget some of the frantic emotions aroused in their breasts by those two charming sisters with their violins, whom I had been among the first to applaud in Paris but whose presence in Frankfurt at this precise moment I found strangely inconvenient.*

* [Teresa and Maria Milanollo, daughters of a Lombard carpenter, gave twelve concerts in Frankfurt in late 1842; they were then aged fifteen and ten

Next day I heard *Fidelio*. The performance was one of the finest I saw in Germany. Guhr had been right to propose it as compensation for my disappointment. I have rarely known a more completely enjoyable musical experience.

Mlle Capitaine, in the role of Fidelio (Leonore), to my mind possesses the essential musical and dramatic characteristics for Beethoven's splendid creation. The timbre of her voice has a peculiar quality which makes it ideal for expressing the profound feelings—feelings suppressed but always on the point of exploding—which inspire and impel the heroic wife of Florestan. She sings without affectation and perfectly in tune and her acting is consistently true to life. In the famous scene with the pistol she does not electrify the house, as Madame Schroeder-Devrient used to with her convulsive laugh, sixteen or so years ago in Paris when she was still young, but she grips your attention; she moves you by other means. Mlle Capitaine is no prima donna in the spectacular sense of the word; but of all the women whom I heard in Germany in genre opera she is certainly the one I liked best. Yet until then I had never heard of her. One or two who had been mentioned to me as exceptional struck me as quite detestable.

Unhappily I do not remember the name of the tenor who played Florestan. He has good points, without possessing a voice that you would call remarkable. He delivered the extremely difficult prison aria, not indeed so well as to make me forget Haitzinger * and the sublimities he achieved in it, but well enough to have earned the applause of an audience less frigid than that of Frankfurt. As for Pischek, whose qualities I was able to assess even better a few months later when I saw him in Spohr's *Faust*, he made me really understand the full significance of the Governor's part, which we never appreciated in Paris. For that alone I would owe him my gratitude. Pischek is an artist. He has obviously

---

respectively. They toured Europe with their parents and their numerous brothers and sisters, and were so successful that in 1847 their father was able to buy a large property near Nancy.]

* [The great Florestan of his day, who had first sung the part in 1822 in Vienna, in the presence of Beethoven. Berlioz heard him in Paris in 1829–30.]

studied hard; but nature has richly endowed him. He has a magnificent baritone voice, penetrating, flexible, true and of good range, a noble face and a tall, commanding figure, and he is young and full of fire and energy. It is a great misfortune that he knows only German. I was impressed with the chorus, which is well drilled and punctilious. Their voices are fresh and they hardly ever sing out of tune. I wish merely that there were more of them. There is always a certain roughness of tone about these choruses of forty or so singers which you do not find in large bodies. Not having seen them rehearsing a new work, I cannot say whether the Frankfurt choristers are good readers and musicians. I can only record that they gave a very satisfying account of the first Prisoners' Chorus—quiet, restrained music which absolutely must be *sung*—and an even better one of the great finale, in which fervour and energy are all-important. As for the orchestra, judging it simply as a theatre orchestra I thought it first-rate. Not a nuance escapes it, the various timbres blend into a harmonious body of sound free from all trace of harshness, it never falters, its ensemble is precise; it plays like one instrument. Guhr's exceptional skill as a conductor and his strictness at rehearsals no doubt have a great deal to do with this happy state of affairs. The orchestra is made up as follows: eight first violins, eight seconds, four violas, five cellos, four basses, two flutes, two oboes, two clarinets, two bassoons, four horns, two trumpets, three trombones, and timpani. The identical force of forty-seven players is, with minor variations, found in every German town of the second rank. So is the arrangement of the orchestra: violins, violas and cellos together on the right, basses in a straight line in the middle against the footlights, flutes, oboes, clarinets, bassoons, horns and trumpets grouped on the left opposite the strings, and drums and trombones by themselves at the back on the right.* Not having been able to test the orchestra in symphonic work, I have no means of telling how quickly it can grasp an idea, how well it adapts itself to

* [In Berlin and Dresden, as at the Paris Opéra, the strings extended across the orchestra, with the first and second violins on either side of the conductor. This general system was commonly found in concert halls as well, and was advocated by Berlioz (see *Traité*, 310). But the precise arrangement of the orchestra seems to have been quite as varied in the mid-nineteenth century as it is today. See Carse, *The Orchestra from Beethoven to Berlioz*.]

an irregular or humorous style of music, how strong its sense of rhythm is, and so on, but Guhr assured me that it is just as good in the concert hall as it is in the theatre, and I believe him; for Guhr is not one of those fathers given to undue admiration of their children. The violins belong to an excellent school. The cellos play with a big tone. I do not know how good the violas are; they have a fairly unobtrusive role in the operas that I saw. The wind instruments as a whole play beautifully; I would only criticize the horns for the brassy sound they often produce by forcing the tone, especially on high notes (a fault very common in Germany). This kind of tone-production debases the natural quality of the horn. It can on occasion be effective but I do not see it becoming part of the generally accepted technique of the instrument.

At the conclusion of this admirable performance of *Fidelio*, ten or twelve members of the audience condescended to give a little applause as they went out; and that was all. I was indignant at such coldness. As someone was trying to persuade me that even though the audience had not applauded much it none the less appreciated the beauties of the work, Guhr interrupted:

'No, they understand nothing, nothing at all, S.N.T.T. He's right, they're a bourgeois public.'

That evening I had spied my old friend Ferdinand Hiller in a box. He lived for a long time in Paris, where connoisseurs still talk about him and his great musical abilities. We renewed acquaintance and were soon back on our old friendly footing. Hiller is working on an opera for the Frankfurt theatre. Two years ago he wrote an oratorio, *The Fall of Jerusalem*, which was performed several times with great success. By ill luck, whenever I visit Frankfurt it invariably seems to happen that Hiller gives a concert on the day after I have to leave, so that I can only quote other people's opinions of his music—which exonerates me from any charge of partisanship. At his last concert the new works included an overture, warmly received, and various pieces for soprano and four male voices which, I am told, made an impression of great piquancy and originality.

A Frankfurt institution of which I heard several people speak very highly is the Saint Cecilia Choral Society. It has the reputation of being a large and very capable body; but as I was not invited to hear it, I have nothing to say on the subject.

The Frankfurt public may be predominantly bourgeois, but in view of the large number of people in the upper classes who are genuinely interested in music I cannot believe that one could not muster an intelligent audience capable of responding to serious works of art. At all events, I did not have the time to make the experiment.

Now, my dear Morel, I must recollect my impressions of Lindpaintner and the Stuttgart chorus and orchestra. It will provide material for a second letter, but I shall not address it to you; for I must satisfy those of our friends who are as eager as you to hear all about my German expedition. So, goodbye.

P.S. Have you published any new songs? Everyone is talking of the success of your latest tunes. I heard yesterday the rondo 'Page et mari' that you wrote to words by Alexandre Dumas fils. I tell you it's an enchantingly delicate and witty piece, the best thing you've ever done in that line. It is going to be unbearably popular. Every barrel organ will grind you out, and it will serve you right.

Second Letter

Stuttgart, Hechingen

TO NARCISSE GIRARD

My first concern before leaving Frankfurt and venturing into the kingdom of Württemberg was to establish exactly what forces I would find in Stuttgart, devise a programme that would suit them, and take with me only the music that was necessary for the purpose. You see, my dear Girard, one of my greatest problems in travelling about Germany, and the one least easily foreseeable, was the enormous cost of transporting my music. You will readily appreciate this when I tell you that the total collection of orchestral and choral parts, manuscript, lithographed or engraved, weighed a prodigious amount and that almost everywhere I went I was obliged to have it follow me at great expense, by mail coach.* On this one occasion,

* The network of railways that now covers Germany did not exist at that time. [Cf. Berlioz's letter to his father from Brunswick (*Correspondance générale*, II, 79), in which he refers to 'the ruinous cost of transporting my music, which weighs 500 lb. Without this expense my tour would be quite profitable.']

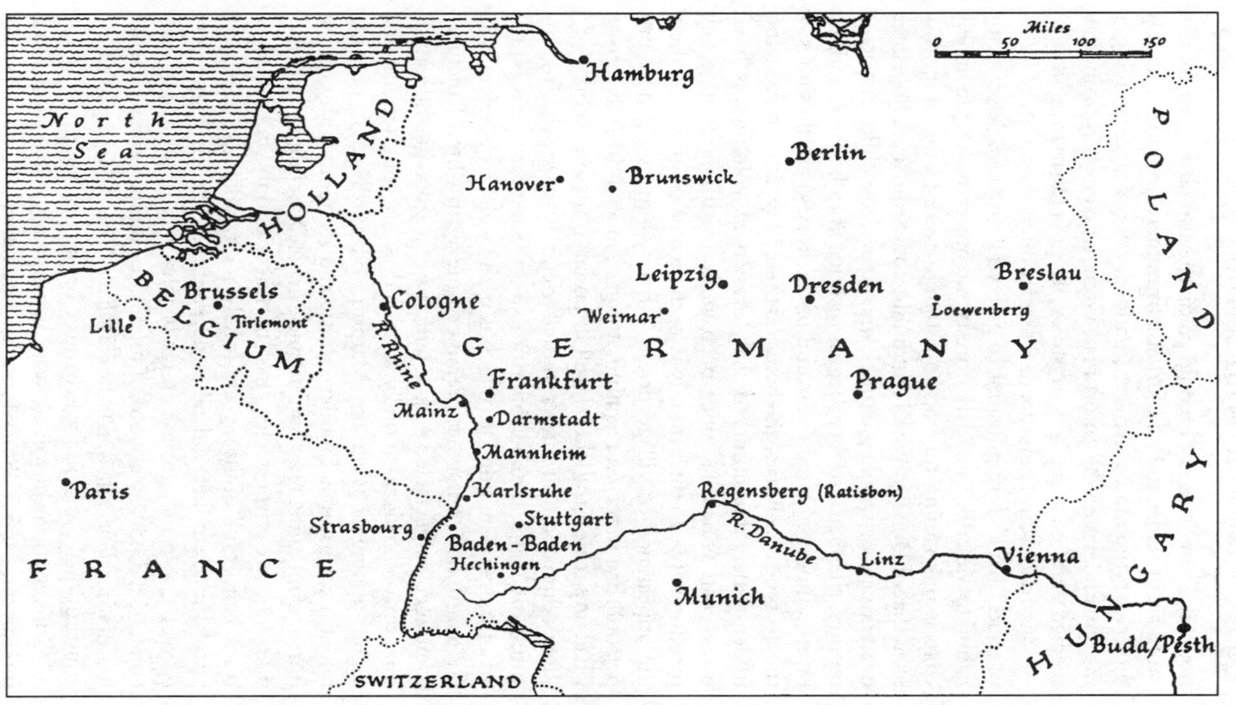
Miles
0
50
100
150
North Sea
HOLLAND
Hamburg
Hanover
Brunswick
Berlin
POLAND
BELGIUM
Brussels
Tirlemont
Lille
Cologne
R. Rhine
Leipzig
Weimar
Dresden
Breslau
Loewenberg
GERMANY
Frankfurt
Prague
Mainz
Darmstadt
Mannheim
Paris
Karlsruhe
Regensberg (Ratisbon)
Strasbourg
Stuttgart
Baden-Baden
Hechingen
R. Danube
Linz
Vienna
FRANCE
Munich
HUNGARY
Buda/Pesth
SWITZERLAND

not being sure whether I would go on to Munich after my stay in Stuttgart or return to Frankfurt and from there go north, I merely took two symphonies, an overture and a few vocal pieces, leaving all the remainder with the unfortunate Guhr, who one way or another seemed destined to find my music a source of embarrassment.

The road from Frankfurt to Stuttgart offers no points of interest, and I have no impressions to give you: not a single romantic haunt to describe, no dark forests, no monasteries, no lonely chapels or foaming torrents, no strange noise in the night, not even that of Don Quixote's windmills; not so much as a huntsman or milkmaid or weeping damsel, stray heifer, lost child, distracted mother, shepherd, robber, beggar or brigand to be seen; nothing but the moonlight and the sound of the horses and the snores of the sleeping coachman, and here and there a few uncouth peasants under wide three-cornered hats, dressed in voluminous linen frock-coats which had once been white, with long trailing tails meeting between their muddy legs, the whole outfit giving them the appearance of village priests off duty—that's all! The first person I had to see on reaching Stuttgart, indeed the only person I had any reason to believe well disposed to me on account of a slight connection through a mutual friend, was Dr Schilling, the author of a large number of critical and theoretical works on the art of music. The title Dr (which is used by almost everybody in Germany) had somewhat prejudiced me against him. I pictured some aged bespectacled pedant with russet wig and gigantic snuff-box, an old codger eternally straddled at his counterpoint and fugue, prating of Bach and Marpurg; outwardly civil, perhaps, but at heart hating all modern music and recoiling with peculiar horror from mine. How wrong one can be! Dr Schilling is not old, does not wear spectacles, has an uncommonly fine head of black hair, is full of life, speaks loudly and rapidly, like a series of pistol shots; smokes and takes no snuff; and received me very cordially, told me at once precisely what I must do to put on a concert, did not say a word of fugues or canons, expressed scorn for neither *The Huguenots* nor *William Tell*, and displayed no constitutional aversion for my music before hearing it.

Conversation, however, was far from easy when we had no interpreter, Dr Schilling's French being rather like my German.

One day, impatient at not being able to make himself understood, he said, 'Do you speak English?'

'I know a little. What about you?'

'Me? No. But Italian, do you know Italian?'

'*Si, un poco. Come si chiama il direttore del teatro?*'*

'Oh damn! No speak Italian either.'

I have an idea—God forgive me—that had I said I understood neither English nor Italian, the ebullient doctor had a mind to play the scene in the *Médecin malgré lui* with me in those two languages: '*Archituram, catalamus, nominativo, singulariter; estne oratio latinas?*'

In the end we tried Latin and understood one another after a fashion, though not without a certain amount of 'archituram, catalamus'. But it may be imagined that the discussion was a little exhausting and did not exactly turn on Herder's *Ideas* or Kant's *Critique of Pure Reason*. Dr Schilling was at length able to convey to me that I could give my concert either in the theatre or in the Redoutensaal, the hall used for musical occasions of this sort. In the former case I would have the advantage—enormous in a town like Stuttgart—of the presence of the King and the court, which he thought I was sure of obtaining, and the performance would not cost me a penny, nor would I have to concern myself with tickets, advertising or any other such arrangements. In the latter case I should have to pay the orchestra and see to everything myself, and the King would not come; he never went near the concert hall. Accordingly, I followed the doctor's advice and hastened to lay my request before Baron von Topenheim, Grand Marshal of the court and intendant of the theatre. He received me with charming courtesy, assuring me that he would speak to the King about my petition that same evening, and that he believed it would be granted.

'I would, however, draw your attention', he added, 'to the fact that the Redoutensaal is the only suitable place for concerts, and that the theatre, on the contrary, has such a bad acoustic that they have long since given up performing instrumental works of any importance in it.'

I hardly knew what to answer or what decision to take. Go and see Lindpaintner, I thought: he must be the final arbiter. I cannot

* ['A little. What is the name of the director of the theatre?']

tell you, my dear Girard, how much good my first meeting with that admirable artist did me. By the end of five minutes we felt as if we had known each other ten years. Lindpaintner quickly put me wise to the position.

'To begin with,' he said, 'I must undeceive you as to the musical importance of our town. It's true that it is a royal residence, but there is no money and no public.' (I thought of Mainz and old Schott.) 'However, since you are here, it's certainly not going to be said that we let you leave without performing some of your works, which we are so curious to know. This is what we have to do. The theatre is useless for music, absolutely useless. The question of the King's presence is irrelevant. His Majesty never goes to concerts, so he won't go to yours, no matter where you hold it. So take the Redoutensaal, which has excellent acoustics and is ideal for orchestral sound, and so far as the players are concerned you need only donate the modest sum of eighty francs to their pension fund, and to a man they will consider it an honour as well as a duty to perform your works under your direction and to devote several rehearsals to them. Come and hear *Freischütz* this evening; during one of the intervals I will present you to the band, and you will see if I am wrong in vouching for their good will.'

I duly followed this advice. Lindpaintner introduced me to the players, and after he had translated a short speech which I thought it right to address to them, my doubts and anxieties vanished. I had an orchestra.

I had an orchestra constituted more or less like the orchestra at Frankfurt, and young and full of fire and energy. This I could clearly tell from the manner in which the whole of Weber's masterpiece was played. The chorus struck me as very ordinary, small in number and neglecting even the most obvious nuances in this splendid score, familiar though it is. They sang at a constant mezzo forte and could not conceal their boredom with the proceedings. The principals attained a level of decent mediocrity. I do not remember any of their names. The prima donna, who sang Agathe, has a powerful but hard, rather inflexible voice. The second soprano (Aennchen) is a more supple vocalist but is inclined to sing out of tune. To my mind the baritone (Caspar) is the best singer in the Stuttgart company. I subsequently heard the same performers in *La muette de Portici* without revising my opinion of them. Lindpaintner, in his conducting of both operas, surprised me by the rapidity of some of his tempos. I noticed that many German kapellmeisters, among others Mendelssohn, Krebs and Guhr, showed the same tendency. Where *Freischütz* is concerned I dare say they know the authentic traditions far better than I do; but as regards *La muette*, *La Vestale*, *Moses* and *The Huguenots*, all of which were produced in Paris under their composers' supervision, the tempos of which have been preserved as they were established at the original performances, I must positively state that the extreme speed at which certain parts of those works are taken in Stuttgart, Leipzig, Hamburg and Frankfurt amounts, however unwittingly, to a serious distortion of the music. And yet in France we think the Germans take all our tempos too slowly.*

The Stuttgart orchestra consists of sixteen violins, four violas, four cellos, four basses, and the wind and percussion necessary for performing most modern operas. There is also an excellent harpist (Krüger)—a great rarity in Germany. The practice of this splendid instrument is absurdly, not to say barbarously, neglected, and for no discoverable reason. I am inclined to think it must always have been so, for none of the composers of the German school has made use of it. There is no harp anywhere in Mozart's works; neither in *Don Giovanni*, *Figaro*, *The Magic Flute*, *Seraglio*, *Idomeneo*, *Così fan tutte*, nor in his Masses, nor in his symphonies. Weber never wrote for it, Haydn and Beethoven likewise. Gluck went so far as to compose a very simple part for one hand in *Orphée*, an opera which in any case was written and performed in Italy. There is something in this that I find both irritating and extraordinary. It is a blot on the orchestras of Germany, every one of which should have at least two harps, especially now that they perform French and Italian operas, in which harps are so often used.

The Stuttgart violins are excellent. You can tell that most of them are pupils of the leader, Molique, whose vigorous playing, large, austere, if slightly monotonous style and skilful compositions we admired at the Paris Conservatoire a few years ago. Molique is first violin for both operas and concerts; and the fact

* [Wagner too complained of the excessively rapid tempos commonly adopted by German conductors.]

that nearly all the violinists under him are his own pupils, with a very proper respect and admiration for him, is responsible for the unusual precision with which they play—a precision due to uniformity of technique and feeling as well as to the alertness of the players themselves.

Among them I must single out the deputy leader, Habenheim, a fine artist in every respect. I heard a cantata of his, written in an expressive melodic style, simple and unaffected in harmony and admirably scored.

The other strings, if not the equal of the violins, are still to be reckoned good. So, I would say, are the wind instruments. The first clarinet and first oboe are excellent. The first flute, Krüger senior, unfortunately plays on an ancient instrument that leaves much to be desired in purity of tone and unhampered execution of the higher notes. M. Krüger should also be on his guard against a tendency to introduce trills and *gruppetti* where the composer has refrained from writing them.

The first bassoon, Neukirchner, is a master of the instrument, but is perhaps too inclined to make a parade of difficulties, and he plays on such an excruciatingly bad bassoon that the effect of even his best phrases is marred by poor intonation. Schunke is the most remarkable of the horns; but he too, like his colleagues at Frankfurt, produces a little too brassy a sound on the high notes. Cylinder, or chromatic, horns are the only kind in use in Stuttgart. That able instrument-maker Adolphe Sax, who has now settled in Paris, has conclusively demonstrated the superiority of this system to the piston method. The latter has been virtually abandoned all over Germany, and the cylinder method is becoming generally used for horns, trumpets, bombardons and bass tubas. The German term for instruments made with this mechanism is valve (*Ventil*) instruments: thus *Ventilhorn*, *Ventiltrompetten*. I was surprised to find the Stuttgart military band, which is rather a good one, still using the two-piston trumpet, a very unsatisfactory instrument, in sonority and tone quality far behind the cylinder trumpet which has been adopted almost everywhere else. I do not, of course, include Paris. We shall discover it some ten years from now.

The trombones are extremely good. The first, Schrade, who was in the Vivienne concert orchestra four years ago, is a most gifted player, a complete master of his instrument who makes light of the most formidable difficulties and produces a magnificent tone from the tenor trombone—I should rather say tones, for by some process not yet explained he can play three or four notes at the same time, like the young horn-player whom the musical Press of Paris has been so taken up with lately.* During a fantasia which he performed at a public concert in Stuttgart, Schrade paused at a pedal point and to the astonishment of all present sounded simultaneously the four notes of the chord of the dominant seventh in the key of B flat, pitched as follows: E flat, A, C, F. It is for the acousticians to account for this new phenomenon of natural resonance and for us musicians to study it and profit by it if the occasion arises.

Another great quality of the Stuttgart orchestra is that the players are fearless sight-readers. Nothing disconcerts them; they read not only the note but the nuance as well; from the first, not a *p* or an *f*, a mezzo forte or a smorzando, escapes them. Furthermore they are attuned to every device and quirk of rhythm and metre; there is none of that dogged clinging to the strong beat that one so often hears; they accent the weak beat unhesitatingly and change from one syncopation to another without effort and with no sense of executing a laborious tour de force. In a word, their musical education is complete. I could see this the moment I began rehearsing them for my concert. I had chosen the Fantastic Symphony and the overture to the *Francs-juges*. You know what rhythmical problems they contain: syncopated phrases, cross-rhythms, groups of four notes superimposed on groups of three, and so on—all of which we give the public hot and strong at the Conservatoire nowadays but which required a great deal of hard work from us over a long period. So I had reason to expect a Mass of mistakes at various points in the overture and in the finale of the symphony. Yet I did not have to point out a single error. It was all seen and read and conquered the first time through. I was astounded. So will you

* Vivier; ingenious practical joker and eccentric artist, but artist of genuine talent and rare musical ability. [In his *Histoire de la Société des Concerts*, Elwart recounts a contretemps between Vivier and a Bonn innkeeper who heard him playing the horn one night and tried to charge him for the three extra guests staying in his room.]

be when I tell you that we put on that damned symphony and the rest of the programme in two rehearsals. Indeed it would all have gone off very satisfactorily if illness, real or feigned, had not relieved me of half the violins on the day of the concert.* Imagine it: four first violins and four seconds to pit against all that force of wind and percussion instruments! The epidemic had spared the rest of the orchestra, and nothing was wanting—nothing except violins. I would have done as Max does in *Freischütz* and signed a pact with all the devils in hell, if I could only have got some. It was the more maddening because, for all Lindpaintner's predictions, the King and the court did come. Despite the gaps in our ranks, the performances if not very powerful—that was impossible—were at least intelligent, precise and vital. The movements of the Fantastic Symphony which made the greatest impression were the adagio (Scene in the Fields) and the finale (Witches' Sabbath). The overture was warmly received. But the Pilgrims' March from *Harold*, which also figured in the programme, passed almost unnoticed. The same thing happened on another occasion when I was rash enough to perform it on its own; whereas, whenever I gave the symphony complete, or at any rate the first three movements of it, the March was received as it is in Paris and frequently encored—fresh proof that certain works ought never to be dismembered and should be produced only at the right moment and in their true guise.

Must I now tell you that when the concert was over I received all sorts of congratulations on behalf of the King, Count Neiperg and Prince Jérôme Bonaparte?† Why not? Princes are known to be graciously disposed towards foreign artists; and I should really be failing in modesty only if I were to repeat what some of the players said to me on the evening of the concert and subsequently. For that matter, why should one not fail in modesty? So as to avoid being growled at by one or two evil-minded watchdogs who want to bite anyone passing their kennels in freedom? What is the point of solemnly acting out an old comedy which imposes on nobody?

* [29 December 1842.]

† [Son of the youngest of Napoleon's four brothers (the one-time King of Westphalia) and of Princess Catherine of Württemberg.]

True modesty would consist not merely in not talking about oneself but in not getting oneself talked about, in not attracting the attention of the public in any way, in not saying, writing or doing anything, in secreting oneself out of sight of the world, in not living—which you will agree is an absurd proposition. In any case I decided to tell everything, the good and the bad; I began doing so in my last letter and am prepared to continue in this one. Thus, I am very much afraid that Lindpaintner, a master whose approval I was eager to win, liked only the overture and absolutely abominated the symphony. I would wager that Molique did not like anything. As for Dr Schilling, I am sure he found it all detestable and was ashamed at having been responsible for introducing into Stuttgart a brigand of my description—a man strongly suspected of having violated the art of music and quite capable, should he succeed in infecting her with his passion for the open air and the vagabond's life, of turning the chaste muse into a sort of gipsy, less Esmeralda than Helen Macgregor,* an armed virago bounding barefoot over the rocks, her hair streaming to the winds, dark cloak flashing with gaudy trinkets, or dreaming to the roar of the elements, terrifying the women with her baleful glance and maddening the men, but not to love.

Schilling, in his capacity as counsellor to the Prince of Hohenzollern-Hechingen, duly wrote off to His Highness recommending this curious savage for his diversion—a creature more at home in the Black Forest than in a sophisticated community; and the savage, curious to see everything, upon receipt of an invitation from Baron von Billing, another of the Prince's intimate counsellors, couched in terms as civil as they were superior, set forth through the snow and the great pine-woods towards the little town of Hechingen, not worrying too much about what he would do when he got there.

This trip to the Black Forest has left a confusion of impressions in my memory, gay, melancholy, disagreeable, delightful, which I cannot recall without an almost inexplicable pang. The cold, the mantle of white and black on the mountains in double mourning, the wind moaning among the shuddering pines, the secret gnawing sorrows of the heart, so active in solitude, a sad episode in a

* [Wife of Scott's Rob Roy—'an incarnate devil when her bluid's up'.]

harrowing novel read during the journey; then the arrival at Hechingen, the cheerful faces, the friendliness of the Prince, New Year festivities, ball, concert, laughter, high spirits, plans for meeting again in Paris—then goodbyes, departure, and once again . . . What devil possessed me to tell you this? There is, as you will see, no touching or romantic incident to recommend it. But I am so constituted that I sometimes suffer without apparent cause, just as in certain electric conditions of the atmosphere the leaves stir when there is no breath of wind to shake them.

Fortunately, my dear Girard, you have known me a long time and will not find anything too ridiculous in this exposition with no development, this introduction without allegro, this subject sans fugue. A subject without a fugue! Now that, you will admit, is a rare piece of good fortune. You and I have read innumerable fugues that have no subject at all, not to speak of fugues with bad subjects.* There—my depression is lifting, thanks for once to the intervention of fugue (the old crone who so often spreads gloom and despondency); I've recovered my good humour and will tell you about Hechingen.

When I described it a moment ago as a small town, I exaggerated its geographical status. Hechingen is no more than a large village, at most a little market town, built on a steepish hillside, not unlike the hilly part of Montmartre or, better still, the village of Subiaco in the Roman States. Above, placed so as to dominate it completely, is the Villa Eugenia, the residence of the Prince. To the right of this miniature palace lies a deep valley and, just beyond, a bare, rugged peak crowned by the old castle of the Hohenzollerns, now used only as a hunting lodge but for long the feudal domicile of the Prince's forebears.

The present ruler of this picturesque domain is a clever, lively and generous-hearted young man who appears to have only two abiding interests in life, a desire to make the inhabitants of his little realm as happy as possible and a passion for music. Can you imagine a more agreeable existence? He sees everyone around him contented. His subjects adore him. He has a natural gift for

* [A play on the word *sujet*, which has the double meaning of 'subject' and 'reason, object'; with a further pun implied by *mauvais sujet* = 'bad lot'.]

music and an understanding of it both as poet and as musician. He composes charming songs; two of them, 'Der Fischerknabe' and 'Schiffers Abendlied', really moved me by their melodic expressiveness. He sings them in a composer's voice but with infectious enthusiasm and intense feeling and conviction. His musical establishment may not boast a theatre but it has an orchestra directed by an admirable musician, Täglichsbeck (the Paris Conservatoire has had the honour of performing his symphonies), who puts on modest but carefully rehearsed performances of the simpler orchestral masterpieces for the Prince's benefit. Such is the amiable monarch whose invitation I had received with such pleasure and who now welcomed me in the most cordial manner.

On my arrival in Hechingen I renewed acquaintance with Täglichsbeck. I had known him in Paris five years before. Now, in his own home, he overwhelmed me with the sort of warmth and true consideration that one never forgets. He quickly apprised me of the musical forces at our disposal. We would have eight violins (of whom three were very weak), three violas, two cellos and two basses. The first violin, Stern, is a gifted player; so is Oswald, the first cello. The chaplain (and Hechingen archivist) plays the double bass well enough to satisfy the most exacting composer. The first flute, the first oboe and the first clarinet are all excellent (though the first flute has the same tendency to embellish the music that I criticized in the Stuttgart player), and the seconds are adequate. The two bassoons and the two horns leave, it must be confessed, a little to be desired. As to the trumpets, the trombone (there is only one) and the timpanist, whenever they play they make you wish you had asked them not to; their incapacity is total.

I see you laughing, my dear Girard. You are about to ask what I could possibly perform with such a minute orchestra. Well, by dint of much patience and good will, by arranging here and modifying there and holding five rehearsals in three days, we put on the *King Lear* overture, the Pilgrims' March, the Ball from the Fantastic Symphony, and various other pieces of a size suitable to the scale of the performance.* And it all went off very well, with precision and even with verve.

* [Marie Recio sang Berlioz's romance 'Le jeune pâtre breton' (1 January 1843).]

I had pencilled the essential, exposed notes of the third and fourth horn parts into the viola parts (since we had only a first and a second horn). Täglichsbeck played the first harp part in the Ball on the piano and kindly undertook the viola solo in the March from *Harold*. The Prince stood beside the timpanist to count his rests for him and see that he came in in the right place. I suppressed all the trumpet passages which were clearly beyond the players' grasp. The solitary trombone was left to his own devices; but as he wisely confined himself to the notes with which he was thoroughly familiar, such as A flat, D and F, and was careful to avoid all others, his success in the role was almost entirely a silent one. You should have seen the vital currents of the music spreading and flickering among the large audience that His Highness had collected in his delightful concert hall. And yet, as you may imagine, the pleasure I took in all these signs of enthusiasm was not unmixed with impatience; and when the Prince came up and shook me by the hand, I could not help saying, 'Ah, Your Highness, I swear I would give two of the remaining years of my life to have my Conservatoire orchestra with me now, so that you could hear it at work on these scores which you treat with such indulgence.'

'Yes, yes, I know,' he answered. 'You have an imperial orchestra which calls you Sire. I am a mere Highness. But I shall go and hear it in Paris, I shall, I shall.'

May he keep his promise! His congratulations stuck in my throat, they were so little merited.

After the concert there was a supper party in the Villa Eugenia. Everyone was infected by the Prince's delightful high spirits. He insisted on my hearing a piece he had written for tenor, cello and pianoforte. Täglichsbeck seated himself at the piano, the composer assumed responsibility for the vocal line, while I, amid the acclamations of the entire company, was chosen to sing the cello part. There was loud applause for the work and almost as much laughter for the remarkable quality of my top string. The ladies in particular were electrified by my high A.

Two days later* I had to return to Stuttgart, after many fond farewells. The snow was melting on the weeping pines, great black

* [3 January 1843.]

stains gashed the whiteness of the mountains. It was utterly dismal; the heartache could resume its work . . .

'The rest is silence . . . Farewell.'

Third Letter

Mannheim, Weimar

TO LISZT

After my return from Hechingen, I stayed a few more days in Stuttgart, a prey to fresh uncertainty. To all questions about my plans and about the next stage of this journey barely begun, I could have truthfully answered like the character in Molière:

No, I am not returning for I never went,
Nor go I hence, for I am here detained,
But stay here neither, since 'tis my intent
*At every moment to be gone . . .**

To be gone—where? I hardly knew. True, I had written to Weimar, but the answer had not come and until it did I could reach no decision. You, my dear Liszt, know nothing of such perplexities. It is of small interest to you whether the town you propose to pass through has a decent musical establishment, let alone whether the theatre is available, the intendant willing to let you use it, etc. etc. How should such information concern you? You can confidently say, adapting Louis XIV:

'I am the orchestra! I am the chorus and the conductor as well. My piano sings, broods, flashes, thunders. It rivals the keenest bows in swiftness; it has its own brazen harmonies and can conjure on the evening air its veiled enchantment of insubstantial chords and fairy melodies, just as the orchestra can and without all the paraphernalia. I need no theatre, no special carpentry, no elaborate construction of ramps and tiers. I don't have to wear myself out taking interminable rehearsals. I don't require a hundred musicians or even twenty—I require none at all. I don't even require any

* [*Le dépit amoureux*, Act I scene 4.]

music. A large room with a grand piano in it, and I have a great audience at my command. I simply appear, amid applause, and sit down. My memory awakens. At once dazzling inventions spring to life beneath my fingers and rapturous exclamations greet them in response. I play Schubert's "Ave Maria" and Beethoven's "Adelaide", and all hearts reach out to me as one. No one breathes; a passionate silence reigns, a deep, still hush of wonder. Then come the explosions, the glittering set-piece that crowns the firework display, the cheers of the audience, the hail of flowers and bouquets raining round the high priest of music, rapt and quivering on his tripod, the lovely girls in their holy frenzy kissing the hem of his garment and moistening it with their tears, the sincere tributes of the serious-minded, the feverish applause wrung from the envious, the great intellects bowed in admiration, the narrow hearts expanding in spite of themselves.' And next day the young god, having dispensed as much as he wished of his inexhaustible inspiration, departs and is gone, leaving behind him a radiant afterglow of luminous enthusiasm and fame. What a dream! A golden dream such as one dreams when one's name is Liszt or Paganini.

For the composer who would attempt, as I have done, to travel in order to perform his works, how different! The never-ending toil he must endure, the torture that rehearsals can be—no one who has not experienced it can have an idea what it is like. To begin with he has to face the whole orchestra, who resent being put to this unexpected inconvenience and extra work on his account. The looks say plainly, 'What does he want, this Frenchman? Why can't he stay where he belongs?' However, each man takes his place. But the moment the composer glances round the assembled company he is aware of alarming gaps. He asks the kapellmeister to explain. 'The first clarinet is ill, the oboe's wife is in labour, the first violin's child has the croup, the trombones are on parade, they forgot to ask for exemption from their military duties, the timpanist has sprained his wrist, the harp isn't coming, he needs time to study his part,' etc., etc. Nevertheless one begins. The notes are read after a fashion, at a tempo more than twice too slow (nothing is so dreadful as this devitalizing of the rhythm!). Gradually your instinct gets the better of you, your blood begins to glow, you get carried away and involuntarily quicken the beat until you are giving the correct tempo. The result: chaos, a raucous confusion to split your ears and break your spirit. You have to stop and resume the original pace, and work your way laboriously, piecemeal, through the long phrases which so often before, with other orchestras, you were wont to sail through swiftly, without hindrance. Even then it is not enough; despite the slow tempo, strange discords are discernible among the wind instruments. You try to discover the reason. 'Let me hear the trumpets by themselves . . . What are you doing? I should be hearing a third, you're playing a second. The second trumpet in C has a D, give me your D. . . . Good. Now, the first trumpet has a C which sounds F. Let me hear your C. . . . Hey! What the devil! You've given me an E flat.'

'Excuse me, I'm playing what's written.'

'You're not, you're a tone out.'

'I'm sorry, I'm playing a C.'

'What key is your trumpet in?'

'E flat.'

'That's what it is—you should be playing an F trumpet.'

'Oh yes, I hadn't looked properly. Sorry, you're quite right.'

'Timpani, why are you making such a frightful din over there?'

'I have fortissimo, sir.'

'You haven't, it's mezzo forte—*mf*, not *ff*. In any case you're playing with wooden sticks when you should be using sponge-headed ones. It's the difference between black and white.'

'We don't know them,' the kapellmeister interposes. 'What do you mean by sponge-headed sticks? We only know the one kind.'

'I suspected as much, so I brought some with me from Paris. Take the pair on the table there. Now, are we all ready? . . . For heaven's sake—it's ten times too loud. And why aren't you using mutes?'

'The orchestral attendant forgot to put them out on the desks. We will have them tomorrow,' etc. etc.

After three or four hours of this antimusical tug of war they have not been able to make sense of a single piece. Everything is fragmentary, disjointed, out of tune, cold, dull, loud, discordant, detestable. And this is the impression you leave on sixty or eighty musicians, who finish the rehearsal exhausted and disgruntled and go around saying they have no idea what it's all about, it's a chaotic, heathenish music, they have never had to put up with anything like it before. Next day little progress is visible. It is only on the third day that the thing takes shape. Only then does the poor composer begin to breathe. The harmonies, correctly pitched, become clear, the rhythms leap to life, the melodies sigh and smile; the whole ensemble acquires confidence, cohesion, attack. The stumbling and stammering are forgotten: the orchestra has grown up, it can walk and talk, it has become a man. With comprehension, courage returns to the astonished players. The composer asks for a fourth trial of skill, and his interpreters—who when all is said are the best fellows in the world—grant it with alacrity. This time, *fiat lux*! 'Watch out for the expression. You're not afraid now?'

'No—give us the right tempo.'

Via! And there is light! Art is born, the whole conception becomes manifest; the work is understood. And the orchestra rises to its feet, applauding and acclaiming the composer, the kapellmeister congratulates him, the inquisitive people lurking in the hall emerge and come up onto the platform and exchange exclamations of pleasure and surprise with the players, with many a wondering glance at the foreign maestro whom at first they took for a madman or a barbarian. At this point you would like to relax. Do no such thing! It is now that you must intensify your vigilance. You must return before the concert to supervise the arrangement of the desks and inspect the orchestral parts to make sure none of them has got misplaced. You must go meticulously along the ranks, red pencil in hand, writing German key-indications for French in the wind parts, altering *ut*, *ré*, *ré bémol*, *fa dièse*, to *C*, *D*, *Des*, *Fis*. You have to transpose a cor anglais solo for the oboe; the orchestra does not possess the instrument in question and the oboist is inclined to be nervous about transposing it himself. If the chorus or the soloists are still unsure of themselves, you must rehearse them separately. But the audience is arriving, it is time; and you stagger to the conductor's desk, a physical and mental wreck, weary, stale, flat and unprofitable, scarcely able to stand—until that magical moment when the applause of the audience, the zest of the players, and your own love for the work transform you in an instant into a dynamo of energy, radiating invisible, irresistible rays of light and power. And then the recompense begins. Then, I grant you, the composer-conductor lives on a plane of existence unknown to the virtuoso. With what ecstasy he abandons himself to the delights of 'playing' the orchestra! How he hugs and clasps and sways this immense and fiery instrument! Once more he is all vigilance. His eyes are everywhere. He indicates with a glance each vocal and orchestral entry. His right arm unleashes tremendous chords which seem to explode like harmonious projectiles. At the pauses he brings the whole accumulated impetus to a sudden halt, rivets every eye, arrests every arm, every breath; listens for an instant to the silence—then gives freer rein than ever to the harnessed whirlwind:

Luctantes ventos tempestatesque sonoras
*Imperio premit, ac vinclis et carcere frenat.**

And in the long adagios, the bliss of floating cradled on a lake of serene harmony while a hundred soft voices intertwined chant his love songs or seem to confide his present sorrows and past regrets to solitude and the stillness of the night! Then often, though only then, the composer-conductor becomes oblivious of the public. He listens to himself and judges his own handiwork; and if he is moved and the same emotion shared by the artists around him, he takes no further heed of the reaction of the audience: they are remote from him. If he has felt his heart thrill to the touch of the poetry and melody of the music and has sensed within him the secret fire which is the signal of the soul's incandescence, his goal is attained, the heaven of art is opened to him, and what signifies earth?

When the concert is over and he has triumphed, his joy is multiplied a hundred times, shared as it is with the gratified pride of every member of his army. You, the great virtuosos, are princes and kings by the grace of God; you are born on the steps of the throne. We composers must fight and overcome and conquer to

* ['The wrestling winds and roaring tempests
He subdues to his dominion, and curbs and confines them.'
Aeneid, I, 53–4; from the passage describing Aeolus, ruler of the winds.]

reign. But the very dangers and hardships of the struggle make our victories the more intoxicating, and we would perhaps be more fortunate than you—if we always had soldiers.

That, my dear Liszt, was a long digression. I had almost forgotten the sober record of my travels in the pleasure of talking to you. Let me now return to it.

During the few days that I spent in Stuttgart waiting for letters from Weimar, the Redoutengesellschaft under Lindpaintner's direction gave a brilliant concert at which I again had occasion to observe the indifference of the bulk of the public in Germany to the mightiest conceptions of Beethoven's genius. The *Leonore* overture, a truly gigantic piece, played with rare precision and verve, was received with only the feeblest applause, and I later heard a gentleman at dinner complain at their not doing Haydn's symphonies instead of this 'uncivilized music with no tunes in it'!! Even in Paris we do not have that kind of bourgeois any more.

A favourable reply having come at last from Weimar, I set off. I would have liked to give a concert on my way through Karlsruhe; but the kapellmeister, Strauss,* informed me that I would have to wait a week or ten days, the theatre having entered into a contract with a flautist from Piedmont; so, full of wholesome respect for the great man and his flute, I pressed on to Mannheim. Mannheim is a very placid, cold, horizontal, rectangular town. I doubt whether the inhabitants are ever kept awake by their passion for music. However, it has a large choral society, a reasonably good theatre company, and a lively little orchestra. The choral society and the orchestra are directed by the younger Lachner, brother of the well-known composer—a gentle, diffident artist, modest and talented. He soon arranged a concert for me. I forget exactly how the programme was made up; I remember only that I wanted to give my second symphony (*Harold*) complete but that at the first rehearsal I had to suppress the finale (the Orgy) because the trombones were manifestly unequal to it. Lachner was most upset, being, as he said, eager to get to know the whole picture. I had to insist and assure him that, quite apart from the inadequacy of the trombones, it would be madness to expect the finale to

* Yet another. But this one does not write waltzes.

make its effect with an orchestra so weak in violins. The first three movements were well performed and produced a vivid impression on the audience. The Grand Duchess Amelia, who was present at the concert, remarked (so I was told) on the evocative colour of the Pilgrims' March and even more on the Serenade in the Abruzzi, which she said recalled for her the beauty and serenity of the Italian night. One of the violas in the orchestra, though a player with no pretensions to virtuosity, gave a capable account of the solo part.*

In Mannheim I found a reasonably good harpist, a first-rate oboist who plays the cor anglais rather poorly, an able cellist, Heinefetter (cousin of the singers of the same name), and an intrepid pair of trumpets. There is no ophicleide; Lachner had attempted to devise a substitute for this instrument, which is used in all modern scores, by having a valve trombone made with a compass extending to bottom C or B. In my opinion it would have been simpler to send for an ophicleide and much better from the musical point of view, as the two instruments have little in common. I was able to hear only one rehearsal of the choral society. The members, who are amateurs, have reasonably good voices on the whole, but by no means all are musicians and readers.

During my stay in Mannheim Mlle Heinefetter gave a performance of *Norma*. I had not heard her since she left the Théâtre-Italien. Her voice is still powerful and fairly agile but she is a little inclined to force it and her high notes are now often difficult to bear. For all that, Mlle Heinefetter has few rivals among German prima donnas. She is a real singer.

I found Mannheim very boring, despite the kindness and solicitude of a Frenchman, M. Désiré Lemire, whom I had met occasionally in Paris eight or ten years ago. The fact is one need only look at the inhabitants, or indeed at the town itself, to see that all real artistic interest is foreign to them and that music is regarded as an agreeable pastime to which one is happy to resort in the leisure moments left by business. Moreover, it rained continuously; and my hotel adjoined a clock whose chime has a resonance

* [13 January 1843, in the theatre. Marie Recio sang—unbearably badly, according to a letter from Berlioz to Morel; 'but at the mere idea of another singer, she is up in arms' (*Correspondance générale*, III, 55).]

of a minor third,* and a tower inhabited by a villainous sparrow-hawk whose shrill, harsh cries bored into my brain from morning till night. Finally, I was impatient to reach the city of poets, whither I was urged to proceed in letters that I received from the kapellmeister—my fellow-countryman Chélard—and from Lobe, that quintessential German musician whose abilities and generosity of spirit you have, I know, had occasion to appreciate.

So once more the Rhine! Embark—Frankfurt—meet Guhr—he begins swearing again—leave him—see our friend Hiller for a moment—he informs me he is about to perform his oratorio *The Fall of Jerusalem*—depart, with splendid sore throat—have frightful dream which I won't repeat—sleep—wake up—there's Weimar—feel very ill—vain attempts of Lobe and Chélard to set me up—preparations for concert—first rehearsal announced—spirits revive—cured!

Yes, this is different! Here I can breathe! I feel something in the very air that proclaims Weimar a cultivated, artistic town. It is just as I imagined: calm, luminous, airy, contemplative, at peace, in a landscape of streams and wooded hills and charming valleys. How my heart beats as I walk through it. So that was Goethe's summer-house, where the late Grand Duke liked to go and take part in the learned discussions of Schiller, Herder and Wieland. This Latin inscription was carved in the rock by the author of *Faust*. And those two little windows, did they really light the garret where Schiller lived? Was it in that humble abode that the poet of the noblest passions of the human heart wrote *Don Carlos*, *Maria Stuart*, *The Robbers*, *Wallenstein*? He lived there like a mere student! I do not like Goethe for allowing that. He, a rich man, a

* In Germany I was able to make many observations as to the different resonances of bells, and it is clear to me that once again nature makes mock of the experts. Some theoreticians maintain that all resonating bodies without exception have a resonance of a major third. A mathematician has lately come forward declaring that, on the contrary, all bells produce a minor third. The fact is, they create all sorts of intervals. Some produce a minor third, others a fourth. One of the bells at Weimar sounds a minor seventh and an octave in succession (fundamental F, resonance octave F and E flat). There are those that even produce an augmented fourth. Clearly the harmonic resonance of a bell depends on the shape given to it by the bell-founder, on the varying degrees of thickness at certain points in the curve of the metal, and on the chance irregularities of casting.

minister of state, could surely have transformed his friend's existence. Was that famous friendship only a pretence? I fear it was real only on Schiller's side. Goethe loved himself too well, was too closely attached to his accursed son Mephisto; he lived too long and feared death too keenly.

Schiller! you deserved a less human friend. I cannot take my eyes from the narrow windows, the obscure house, the mean black roof. One in the morning, a brilliant moon, the cold intense; all quiet in that city of the dead. As I stand watching, my heart swells, a trembling seizes me. Overwhelmed by respect and regret and by that infinite sympathy that genius can inspire from beyond the grave in the lowliest of the living, I kneel by the humble threshold and repeat over and over again in love and grief and admiration, 'Schiller! Schiller!'

What can I tell you now of the real subject of this letter? How am I to come back to earth and prosaic reality? Only by thinking of another former inhabitant of Weimar, a man of the highest talent, who wrote Masses and fine septets and played the piano with great severity—Hummel. . . . Enough—I am rational again!

Chélard, like a true artist and also as compatriot and old friend, did everything possible to help me achieve my ends. The intendant, Baron von Spiegel, was equally friendly and co-operative and put the theatre and the orchestra at my disposal. Not the chorus, however: he probably could not bring himself to mention them. I had heard them soon after I arrived, in Marschner's *Vampire*, and knew them for a rabble of unimaginable incompetents, bawling their way through the score with a contempt for the conventions of pitch and rhythm such as I have never heard equalled. As for the female soloists—but gallantry compels me to draw a veil over those unhappy women. On the other hand, the bass who took the part of the Vampire: you can guess whom I mean—Genast! Don't you agree that there is an artist in the full sense of the word? He is particularly fine in tragedy, and I greatly regret that I could not stay long enough in Weimar to see him as Lear in Shakespeare's play, which they were putting on just as I left.*

* [Eduard Genast, later stage manager at the Weimar theatre, was, like many German actors of the period, a singer as well. A baritone of evidently exceptional

The Weimar orchestra is a good one. But in my honour Chélard and Lobe had hunted up all the extra string players they could find to augment its normal strength, and they presented me with an active force of twenty-two violins, seven violas, seven cellos and seven double basses. There was a full muster of wind players, among whom I especially noticed an excellent first clarinet and a superb valve trumpet (Sachse). There was no cor anglais (I had to transpose the part for clarinet), no harp—a very pleasant young man called Montag, a good pianist and an impeccable musician, agreed to arrange the harp parts for the piano and play them himself—and no ophicleide, a tolerably powerful bombardon being substituted. This done, we were complete and rehearsals began. I must tell you that I discovered among the Weimar musicians a well developed passion for my *Francs-juges* overture, which they had performed several times; so they could not have been better disposed towards me, and contrary to my usual experience I really enjoyed rehearsing the Fantastic Symphony, which I had again chosen, at their request. To be understood immediately like this is a rare joy. I remember the impression that the first movement (Reverie, Passion) and the third (Scene in the Fields) made on the players and on a few music-lovers who were present at the rehearsal. The conclusion of the latter movement, in particular, seemed to hold everyone spellbound; and when, after the final rumble of thunder, the solitary shepherd having ended his tune, the orchestra entered like a deep sigh and then faded into silence, before the exclamations broke forth I heard the players near me sigh in sympathy. Chélard declared that for him the March to the Scaffold came before everything else, but the public appeared to like the Ball and the Scene in the Fields best. The *Francs-juges* overture was received like an old acquaintance whom one is delighted to meet again.* There I go, you see, on the point of failing in modesty again; and if I tell you of the packed hall, the prolonged applause, the recalls, the chamber-

---

range, he sang roles like Caspar (under Weber at Dresden), Don Giovanni, Rossini's Figaro, and even Fra Diavolo at one end of the scale and Sarastro at the other.]

* [The date of the concert was 25 January.]

lains coming up to congratulate the composer on behalf of Their Highnesses, the new friends waiting at the stage door to shake his hand and forcibly keep him up till three in the morning—if, in short, I chronicle a success, I shall be set down as a vulgarian, an indelicate person, a buffoon, a —— enough: despite my stoicism, the thought horrifies me, so I shall say no more. Goodbye.

Fourth Letter

Leipzig

TO STEPHEN HELLER

You must have laughed, my dear Heller, at the gaffe I committed in my last letter when I referred to the Grand Duchess Stephanie as Amelia. Very well—but I cannot say I am greatly disturbed at the strictures I shall incur on my ignorance and frivolity. Now, if I had called the Emperor Napoleon Francis or George! But it is permissible, at a pinch, to alter the name of the sovereign lady of Mannheim, charming though it be. Shakespeare has said it:

What's in a name? That which we call a rose
By any other name would smell as sweet.

At all events I humbly beg Her Highness's pardon, and if she grants it, as I trust she will, then a fig for your derision.

From Weimar, the town most easily visited next was Leipzig; yet I hesitated to go there, for all that Felix Mendelssohn was musical dictator of the place. We had been on friendly terms in Rome in 1831; since then, however, our artistic paths had diverged so far that frankly I feared I would not find him sympathetic. Chélard, who knows him, made me feel ashamed of my misgivings, so I wrote to him. His reply was prompt and as follows:

My dear Berlioz,

I thank you most warmly for your kind letter, and for still remembering our Rome friendship. For my part I shall never forget it so long as I live, and I am delighted that I shall soon be able to tell you so in person. It will be both a duty and a pleasure for me to do all I can to make your stay in Leipzig agreeable and profitable. I think I can promise you that you will be satisfied with the town—with the musicians and the public, that is. Before writing to you I consulted several people who know Leipzig better than I, and all agree with me that you should be able to give a first-rate concert. The expenses of orchestra, hall, advertising, etc. will be a hundred and ten crowns; the receipts could be as much as six hundred or eight hundred. You should be here to arrange the programme and everything else that may be necessary a good ten days beforehand. In addition, the directors of the Subscription Concerts Society have instructed me to ask you whether you will agree to one of your works being performed at the concert to be held in aid of the poor of Leipzig on 22 February—that is, after the concert which you will yourself have given. I hope you will accept this proposal. So, I recommend that you come here as soon as you are able to leave Weimar. I am delighted that I can shake you by the hand and say *willkommen* to Germany. Please don't laugh at my bad French, as you used to in Rome, and remain my friend, as you were then, as I shall always be yours.*

Felix Mendelssohn-Bartholdy

Could I resist an invitation couched in such terms? Accordingly I set out for Leipzig,† not without regrets for Weimar and the new friends I was leaving there.

My relationship with Mendelssohn had begun in Rome in a somewhat curious fashion. At our first meeting he mentioned my *Sardanapalus* cantata, which had won the Institute prize and parts of which my fellow-laureate Montfort had played to him. On my revealing a positive aversion for the opening allegro, he exclaimed delightedly, 'Thank heavens for that! I congratulate you . . . on

* I now see, from reading the volume of Felix Mendelssohn's letters recently published by his brother, what his 'Rome friendship' for me amounted to. He writes to his mother, in a passage which plainly refers to me: '—— is a real grotesque, without a spark of talent,' etc., etc. 'Sometimes I would like to strangle him.' At the time that he wrote this letter Mendelssohn was twenty-one and did not know a single score of mine. I had produced only the first draft of my Fantastic Symphony, which he had not seen; and it was not until a few days before he left Rome that I showed him the overture *King Lear* which I had just completed. (25 May 1864.)

† [28 January 1843.]

your taste. I was afraid you might be pleased with it. Frankly, it's pretty awful.'

We nearly quarrelled the following day. When I spoke with enthusiasm of Gluck, he replied in a tone of quizzical surprise, 'Oh—you like Gluck?'

The implication seemed to be, 'How can a musician of your sort possibly have the loftiness of ideas and the feeling for grandeur of style and truth of expression required to like Gluck?' It was not long before I had an opportunity of avenging myself for this little slight. I had brought with me, from Paris, Asteria's aria from Gluck's Italian opera *Telemaco*—a fine but little-known piece—and I placed a manuscript copy, without the composer's name on it, on Montfort's piano one day when we were expecting a visit from Mendelssohn. He came, noticed the music, and at once sat down and began playing it. He had reached the last four bars—where, at the words 'O giorno! o dolce sguardo! o rimembranza! o amor!' the music becomes truly sublime—and was parodying it extravagantly in imitation of Rubini, when I stopped him and said, with an air of blank astonishment, 'Oh, don't you like Gluck, then?'

'Gluck?'

'Alas, my dear friend: this piece is by Gluck, and not by Bellini as you thought. You see, I know him better than you do and am of the same opinion as you—more than you are yourself.'

One day, when I spoke of the metronome and its usefulness, Mendelssohn said sharply, 'What on earth is the point of a metronome? It's a futile device. Any musician who cannot tell the tempo of a piece by looking at it is a duffer.'

I could have replied that in that case there were a good many duffers, but I held my peace.

At that time I had hardly published anything. Mendelssohn knew only my *Irish Melodies*, with piano accompaniment. One day he asked to see the score of the *King Lear* overture, which I had just composed in Nice. He read it through slowly and carefully, and was about to begin playing it on the piano (which he did, with incomparable skill) when he stopped and said, 'Give me the right tempo.'

'What on earth for? I thought you said that any musician who couldn't guess the tempo was a duffer?'

He would not admit it, but these ripostes, or rather unexpected thrusts, annoyed him intensely.*

He never mentioned Sebastian Bach without adding ironically, 'Your pupil.' In short, he was as prickly as a porcupine when the talk was of music; you never knew where to take hold of him without getting hurt. But being very good-natured and of a sweet and charming disposition, he never minded being contradicted on any other subject, and I on my side used to abuse his forbearance during the religious and philosophical arguments that we sometimes engaged in.

One evening we were exploring the Baths of Caracalla together, while debating the question of merit or demerit in human behaviour and its reward in this life. As I was propounding some outrageous thesis or other in answer to the strictly orthodox and pious views put forward by him, his foot slipped and the next moment he was lying in a bruised condition at the bottom of a steep ruined staircase.

'Look at that for divine justice,' I said, helping him onto his feet. 'I blaspheme, you fall.'

This irreverence, accompanied by roars of laughter, apparently went too far, and thenceforth all religious arguments were banned. It was in Rome that I first got to know that fine-spun yet richly coloured work, the overture *Fingal's Cave*. Mendelssohn had just completed the piece, and he gave me a remarkably exact idea of it; such was his amazing capacity for rendering the most elaborate scores on the piano. Often, on days of oppressive heat when the sirocco blew, I would interrupt him at his work (he is an indefatigably prolific worker). With the greatest good humour he would put down his pen and, seeing me positively dropsical with spleen, would seek to assuage it by playing anything I cared to name from the works of composers we both admired. How many times, stretched morosely on his sofa, did I sing the aria from *Iphigénie en Tauride*, 'D'une image, hélas! trop chérie,' while he accompanied, soberly seated at the piano. And he would exclaim, 'It's beautiful, so beautiful! I could go on hearing that all day, always, and never grow tired of it.' And we would begin all over again. He

* Perhaps that is why he would have liked to strangle me. (1864.)

was also fond of getting me to hum, in my plaintive voice and in the same horizontal position, two or three of the tunes which I had written to poems by Moore, and which he liked. (Mendelssohn always thought quite highly of my *songs*.) After a month of this sort of relations—which had come to have an intense interest for me—he vanished without saying goodbye and I did not see him again. Consequently I could not help being very agreeably surprised by his letter. It suggested a warmth of heart and an ease of manners that I had not associated with him; and I soon discovered when I got to Leipzig that these admirable qualities had indeed become his. His artistic principles are as strict and unbending as ever but he no longer seeks to impose them forcibly on other people. As kapellmeister his policy is to produce only what he considers good and to leave anything that seems to him poor or a bad influence severely alone. He is still, it must be said, a little too fond of the dead.

The Subscription Concerts Society which he had mentioned in his letter is a large and flourishing organization with a magnificent choir, a first-rate orchestra, and a hall, the Gewandhaus, which has perfect acoustics. It was in this spacious and splendid building that I was to give my concert. I went straight there on alighting from the coach and came in in the middle of the final rehearsal of Mendelssohn's new work, which is a kind of oratorio on Goethe's *Walpurgisnacht*.* I was at once quite astounded by the quality of the voices, the responsiveness of the singers, and above all the grandeur of the work.

I am strongly inclined to regard it as the finest thing that Mendelssohn has done.† The poem has no connection with the Witches' Sabbath in *Faust*. Its subject is the nocturnal meetings held in the hills in the early days of Christianity by a religious sect which had stayed faithful to the old observances, although these mountain sacrifices were by then forbidden. It was their custom, on nights marked out for the celebration of their rites, to post armed sentinels in considerable numbers, wearing strange robes and masks, at the approaches to the mountain. Upon a given signal

* [The first performance of *Die erste Walpurgisnacht* took place the following day, 2 February 1843.]

† I had not then heard his ravishing *Midsummer Night's Dream*.

and as the priest, having ascended the altar, was intoning the sacred hymn, this devilish-looking band would begin brandishing torches and pitchforks and uttering all manner of gruesome shouts, shrieks and groans in order to obscure the sound of chanting and discourage any of the profane who might feel tempted to disturb the holy mysteries. This is no doubt the origin of the word 'Sabbath' as a synonym for 'a loud noise in the night'. One must hear Mendelssohn's music to realize what scope the poem offers a skilful composer. He has made admirable use of his opportunities. The score is of impeccable clarity, notwithstanding the complexity of the writing. Voices and instruments are completely integrated, and interwoven with an apparent confusion which is the perfection of art. I would especially single out, as superb examples of two diametrically opposite genres, the mysterious scene of the posting of the sentinels and the final chorus in which the voice of the priest rises solemnly and serenely at intervals above the din of the decoy demons and sorcerers. One does not know which to praise most in this finale, the orchestral or the choral writing or the whirling momentum and sweep of the whole.

As Mendelssohn stepped down from the rostrum, radiant with the sense of achievement, I came forward, thrilled at having heard it. The moment could not have been better chosen. Yet, after the first exchange of greetings, the same melancholy thought struck us both.

'What! Twelve years? Can it really be twelve years since we daydreamed together in the Campagna?'

'And in the Baths of Caracalla.'

'Ah, still the same scoffer, I see, always ready to mock me!'

'No, no, my mocking days are over. I said it to test your memory and to see whether you had forgiven me for my irreverence. In fact I mock so little that I'm going to ask you on the spot, in all seriousness, to make me a present of something of great value to me.'

'What is that?'

'The baton with which you have just been rehearsing your new work.'

'With the greatest pleasure, on condition that you let me have yours.'

'It will be copper for gold. Still, it's a bargain.'

And Mendelssohn's sceptre was brought to me forthwith. Next day I sent him my heavy oak cudgel, together with the following letter (which the Last of the Mohicans would not, I hope, have disowned):

To Chief Mendelssohn—Great chief! We are pledged to exchange tomahawks. Here is mine. It is rough-hewn. Yours is plain. Only squaws and palefaces like ornate weapons. Be my brother; and when the Great Spirit sends us to hunt in the land of souls, may our warriors hang our tomahawks side by side at the entrance to the council chamber.

Such are the simple facts out of which the gossips, in all innocence of course, thought to create an absurd dramatic incident. When it came to arranging my concert, a few days later, Mendelssohn did indeed behave like a brother towards me. The first artist he introduced me to—presenting him as his *fidus Achates**—was David, the leader of the orchestra, a distinguished musician, talented composer and violinist of repute. David, who in addition speaks perfect French, was of the greatest help to me.

The Leipzig orchestra is no larger than those of Frankfurt and Stuttgart. But the town is rich in instrumentalists, so I thought I would augment it a little. The number of violins was accordingly raised to twenty-four—an innovation which, I heard later, aroused the indignation of two or three critics who had already determined their attitude towards me. (The insolence and presumption of it! Twenty-four violins, when sixteen had always been quite enough for performing the symphonies of Mozart and Beethoven!) We tried in vain to procure three additional instruments, cor anglais, ophicleide and harp, which are used in several of my scores (another crime!). The cor anglais—the instrument, that is—was of such poor quality and in such bad condition and, in consequence, so remarkably out of tune that despite the skill of the player we had to abandon all idea of using it and entrust the solo to the first clarinet.

* [Aeneas' faithful companion.]

The ophicleide, or rather the meagre brass object masquerading under that name, bore no resemblance to the French variety, having practically no tone. It was therefore declared null and void and replaced, after a fashion, by a fourth trombone. As for the harp, it was apparently out of the question. Six months earlier Mendelssohn had had to send to Berlin for harps when he wanted to perform some pieces from his *Antigone*. As I was told that he had not found them very satisfactory, I wrote to Dresden, and Lipinski (a splendid artist of whom I shall shortly have occasion to speak) sent me the theatre harpist. It was then merely a question of finding an instrument. After a fruitless quest among various manufacturers and music-dealers, Mendelssohn eventually heard of an amateur who owned a harp and got him to agree to lend it to us for a few days. Imagine my wretched luck! The harp having been duly fetched and furnished with a set of brand-new strings, it was discovered that Richter, the Dresden harpist who had so obligingly come to Leipzig on Lipinski's request, was an expert pianist and a more than competent performer on the violin but scarcely played the harp at all. He had been studying it for only eighteen months, in order to be able to play the simple arpeggios which are commonly used to accompany the tunes in Italian operas. At the sight of the numerous scale passages and melodic phrases which occur in my symphony * his courage failed him, and at the concert Mendelssohn himself had to play them on the piano in order that the part should be heard and the entries made in the right places. What a lot of fuss for so little!

At all events, once I had decided on a solution to these problems, rehearsals began. The orchestral arrangement in this admirable hall is so good, communication between the conductor and each member of the orchestra is so easy, and the players, besides being capital musicans, have been trained by Mendelssohn and David to such a pitch of discipline and concentration that two rehearsals sufficed for putting on a long programme which included, among other difficult works, the *King Lear* and *Francs-juges* overtures and the Fantastic Symphony. In addition, David had agreed to play the violin solo that I wrote two years ago for Artot, which has quite an elaborate orchestral part; he gave a

* [The Fantastic.]

masterly performance and was acclaimed by the whole audience.*

To state that the orchestra played the above-mentioned pieces faultlessly after only two rehearsals is praise indeed, as every Paris musician and many other besides would, I think, agree.

The concert threw musical Leipzig into a state of agitation, and so far as I was able to judge from the dispute that raged in the newspapers the ensuing controversy was at least as violent as the same works had aroused in Paris ten years before. While Leipzig debated the morality of my actions, some representing them as noble deeds, others as crimes with malice aforethought, I went off to Dresden, as I shall shortly describe. So as not to divide the narrative of my Leipzig experiences, however, I shall recount what happened on my return, in connection with the concert for the benefit of the poor which Mendelssohn had mentioned in his letter and in which I had promised to take part.

The whole evening was being organized by the Concerts Society, so I had at my disposal the splendid choir whose just praises I sang a little earlier. As you can imagine, I was not going to let such a chance slip and I proposed to the directors of the society that we do the finale of *Romeo and Juliet*, which is written for triple chorus. A German translation had been made in Paris by Professor Duesberg. All that was required was to fit it to the notes in the voice parts. This proved a long and laborious task; furthermore, the copyists failed to observe the rules of German prosody in the allocation of long and short syllables, with the result that the singers were often confused and Mendelssohn was obliged to waste time in revising the text so as to correct the more glaring mistakes. He had, in addition, to rehearse the choir for nearly a week. (In Paris that number of rehearsals with a choir of this size would cost four thousand eight hundred francs—and I am sometimes asked why I do not give *Romeo and Juliet* at my concerts!) The choir includes a few people from the theatre and the boys of the Thomaskirche, but it is almost wholly made up of amateurs

* [The work was *Rêverie et caprice*. The concert took place on 4 February 1843. Marie sang the fourth song from *Les nuits d'été*, 'Absence', with piano accompaniment; Berlioz's notebook of the tour (preserved in the museum at La Côte Saint-André) quotes the first sixteen bars, dated 'Leipzig, 3 February 1843, after the rehearsal at which Marie sang very well'.]

drawn from the upper ranks of Leipzig society. That is why it is relatively easy to obtain a large number of rehearsals when there is an exacting work to be learned. There was still a fair amount to be done, however, when I got back from Dresden, the men in particular leaving much to be desired. It grieved me to see a great composer and performing artist like Mendelssohn saddled with the subordinate job of chorus-master—a job which, it must be said, he discharges with unfailing patience. His criticisms are invariably good-humoured and polite. The choir would be more grateful for their good fortune if they knew how rare these qualities are among chorus-masters. I have often been accused by the ladies of the Opéra of a want of gallantry; I have a terrible reputation in this respect, and I admit I deserve it. The moment there is a question of taking a large chorus, before rehearsals have even begun, a sort of anticipatory rage possesses me, my throat tightens, and although nothing has yet occurred to make me lose my temper I glare at the singers in a manner reminiscent of the Gascon who kicked an inoffensive small boy passing near him, and on the latter's protesting that he had not 'done anything', replied, 'Just think if you had!'

However, after two further sessions the three chorus parts were learnt; and the whole finale, with the orchestra in support, would undoubtedly have gone very well if a singer from the theatre, who had been chosen for the role of Friar Laurence and who had for some days been complaining of its difficulty, had not at a stroke demolished the entire edifice constructed with such effort.

I had already noticed at the piano rehearsals that this gentleman (I forget his name) belonged to that large and flourishing class of musicians who are ignorant of music. He could not count his rests, came in in the wrong place, failed to pitch the note correctly, and so on. But I said to myself, 'Perhaps he has not had time to study the part. He learns difficult roles at the theatre, surely he should be able to manage this one.' All the same I often thought longingly of Alizard, who is always so good in this scene, and wished he knew German and had not been in Brussels. At the final rehearsal on the eve of the concert, as our friend had still made no progress and kept muttering gross Teutonic imprecations whenever the orchestra had to be stopped on his account or whenever Mendelssohn or I sang his part for him, my patience finally gave out and I thanked the choir and the orchestra, begging them not to bother any more with the work, since owing to the bass part it was obviously impossible to perform it. On my way back to the hotel I indulged in some melancholy reflections. Two composers who for years had devoted all the intelligence and imagination they possessed to the study of their art, and two hundred performers, skilled and conscientious singers and instrumentalists, had laboured fruitlessly for a week and had had to abandon the work they had undertaken, because of the incompetence of one man. Were all singers gods, even those who did not sing? The society was in great perplexity, wondering how to replace this finale, which lasts half an hour. In the event orchestra and choir agreed to hold an extra rehearsal on the morning of the concert,* and the situation was saved. The *King Lear* overture, a work the orchestra had already mastered, and the Offertorium from my Requiem, in which the choir have only a few notes to sing, were chosen instead and performed very satisfactorily. I may add that the movement from the Requiem surprised me by the impression it made and won me the priceless approval of Robert Schumann, one of the most justly renowned composer-critics in Germany.†

A few days later this same piece earned me an even more unexpected compliment. During my stay in Leipzig I had again been taken ill. As I was leaving I asked the doctor who had looked after me how much I owed him.

'Write me the theme of your Offertorium on this sheet of paper, with your signature, and I shall still be indebted to you,' he replied. 'Never have I been so struck by any piece of music.' I was a little hesistant to be rid of my obligation to the doctor so easily, but he insisted. And then, would you believe it, I had the chance to cap his compliment with one better deserved, and failed to take it. I had written at the head of the page: *To Dr Clarus*.

* [22 February 1843.]

† At the rehearsal Schumann, breaking his habitual taciturnity, said to me, 'This Offertorium surpasses everything.' Mendelssohn himself congratulated me on a *double-bass entry* in my song 'Absence', which was sung at the same concert. [Again by Marie; Berlioz had meanwhile orchestrated it. Mendelssohn made a similar comment after a performance of *Tannhäuser*, assuring Wagner that he had been impressed by a canonic passage in the finale of the second act.]

'"Carus,"' he said; 'you have given me an *l*.'

I immediately thought, '*Patientibus Carus sed Clarus inter doctos*,'* but did not have the gumption to write it.

There are times when I am quite exceptionally stupid.

A highly cultivated composer such as you, my dear Heller, takes a keen interest in everything that concerns his art, so I find it very natural that you should have asked me so many questions about Leipzig's rich musical life. I shall reply briefly to a few of them:

Does that great pianist Madame Clara Schumann have any rival in Germany who can properly be compared with her?

I believe not.

Can I tell you if the musical taste among Leipzeg intellectuals is good, or at least inclined towards what you and I would call beautiful?

I would rather not.

If it is true that the solemn oath taken by all who profess to love lofty and serious art is, 'There is no God but Bach, and Mendelssohn is his prophet'?

I ought not.

If the theatre is good, and if the public is very wrong to enjoy the operettas of Lortzing that are often given there?

I cannot.

If I have read or heard any of those ancient five-part Masses with basso continuo that are so highly thought of in Leipzig?

I know not.

Goodbye, go on writing splendid capriccios like your last two, and may God preserve you from quadruple fugues on a chorale.

Fifth Letter

Dresden

TO ERNST

You particularly advised me, my dear Ernst, not to stop in the small towns when I visited Germany, assuring me that only the capitals would provide me with the forces I needed.

* 'Beloved by the sick, famous among the learned.'

Others besides you, and one or two German critics as well, said the same thing and later blamed me for not doing as they had recommended and going straight to Berlin or Vienna. But, as you know, it is always easier to give advice than to follow it, and if I didn't pursue what everyone considered the most sensible plan of campaign it was because I couldn't. For one thing, I was not my own master, free to choose when to travel. Having made a fruitless visit to Frankfurt (as described) I could not simply return to Paris with my tail between my legs. I would have liked to go on to Munich, but a letter from Bärmann* informed me that my concerts there would have to wait for a month. At the same time Meyerbeer wrote to say that as the Berlin theatre would be busy with several important revivals there was no point in my coming to Prussia for the moment. I could not remain inactive, however; and so, being desirous of finding out all about your musical country and its institutions, I formed the resolve to see everything, hear everything, and so far reduce my choral and orchestral demands that my music could be performed almost anywhere. I was well aware that in towns of the second rank I would not find the lavish resources which the scale and character of one or two of my works require. But I would keep these pieces to the end, they would be the forte to my crescendo; and I thought that, all things considered, this gradual and cumulative progress would be both prudent and not without a certain interest. And I don't regret it at all.

But now, to speak of Dresden, where I had been engaged to give two concerts. I was to find choir, orchestra, military band, and a famous tenor to boot, together making up the richest combination of musical resources that I had encountered since coming to Germany; and on top of that a loyal, active and enthusiastic friend in Karl Lipinski. I had known him previously in Paris. I cannot tell you with what ardour this excellent man devoted himself to helping me.

* [The virtuoso clarinettist for whom Weber wrote his two clarinet concertos and his concertino; he was a prominent member of the Munich orchestra until his death. Berlioz never went to Munich. A visit arranged for August 1854 was cancelled at the last minute when a vacancy at the French Institute occurred, causing new elections to be held, for which he felt bound to enter (though he was not elected). Munich remained the one important musical centre in Germany not visited by him.]

His position as principal leader of the orchestra and the general esteem in which he is held both personally and professionally give him great authority over his fellow-artists, and he was certainly not slow to use it. The intendant Baron von Lüttichau having promised me two evenings, the entire theatre was at my disposal and I had nothing to do but see to it that the performance was good. It was magnificent; and yet our programme was a formidable one. It included the overture *King Lear*, the Fantastic Symphony, the Offertorium, Sanctus and Quaerens me from my Requiem, the last two movements of my Funeral Symphony—scored, as you know, for a double orchestra and chorus—and a few vocal pieces.* I did not have a translation of the chorus part in the symphony, but the stage manager, Winkler, a man of wit and intelligence, very obligingly extemporized the German verses that we needed, and rehearsals for the finale could begin. The solos were sung in Latin, German and French. Tichatschek, the tenor whom I mentioned a moment ago, has a pure and charming voice which in the theatre, under the stimulus of dramatic action, takes on uncommon warmth and energy. His style is simple and tasteful; he is a most accomplished musician and reader. He at once agreed to sing the tenor solo in the Sanctus without even asking to see it, and without frowning or making excuses or generally acting the god. He could, as so many do in such circumstances, have accepted the Sanctus on condition that he be allowed to throw in some pet cavatina to ensure a personal success, but he refrained. What about that!

On the other hand the cavatina from *Benvenuto*, which I had taken it into my head to add to the programme, gave me more trouble than the whole of the rest of the concert. It could not be offered to the prima donna, Madame Devrient, the tessitura of the piece lying too high for her and the florid passages requiring a lighter, more flexible voice. Mlle Wüst, the second soprano, to whom Lipinski proposed it, declared the German translation bad, the andante too high and too long, the allegro too low and too short; she wanted cuts and alterations, she was suffering from a cold, etc., etc.—you know the whole comedy by heart: the *cantatrice* who can't and won't.

* [Including the first performance of the newly orchestrated 'Absence', sung by Marie (17 February 1843).]

Eventually Madame Schubert, the wife of the able violinist and excellent leader whom you know, came to my rescue and undertook the unfortunate cavatina—not without misgivings, for her modesty made her exaggerate its difficulty—and scored a great success with it. Really, it can be almost harder to get 'Fleuve du Tage' sung than to do a performance of the C minor Symphony.

Lipinski had put the Dresden musicians thoroughly on their mettle. They were fired with the ambition to do well and above all to do better than Leipzig (there is a tacit rivalry between the two towns), and we worked immensely hard. Four long rehearsals were barely enough to satisfy them; they would themselves have willingly asked for a fifth had there been time. All this bore fruit in an excellent performance. At the final rehearsal only the chorus caused me anxiety; but two further practices before the concert gave them the confidence they lacked, and the Requiem pieces were as well performed as the rest of the programme. The Funeral Symphony produced the same effect as in Paris. Next morning the bandsmen, in high spirits, blew me out of bed with a reveille and, though badly in need of sleep and suffering from a headache and my eternal sore throat, I was obliged to empty a small vat of punch with them.

It was at this Dresden concert that the German public's partiality for my Requiem first showed itself—although on this occasion, the choir not being large enough, we had not ventured to do the bigger movements (Dies irae, Lacrymosa, etc.). The Fantastic Symphony was much less well received by one section of the audience. The smart elements, headed by the King of Saxony and the court, were not amused (so I was told) by the violence of its passions and the sadness of its reveries and all the horrid phantasmagoria of the finale; I believe the Ball and the Scene in the Fields alone found any favour with them. The ordinary public simply let itself be carried along by the current of the music, and it applauded the March to the Scaffold and the Witches' Sabbath more warmly than the other three movements. But it was quite clear that this work, so well received in Stuttgart, so perfectly understood in Weimar, so keenly debated in Leipzig, was in its whole musical and poetic ethos largely alien to the inhabitants of Dresden and disconcerted them by being so unlike the symphonies they were used to. They were more surprised than charmed—not so much moved as dazed.

The Dresden kapelle, for long under the command of the Italian Morlacchi and the illustrious composer of *Freischütz*, is now directed by Messrs Reissiger and Richard Wagner. We know almost nothing of Reissiger's in Paris, apart from the mild and wistful waltz published under the title 'Weber's Last Thoughts'. During my stay in Dresden one of his sacred works was performed and was highly praised. I was unfortunately unable to add my tribute; a severe bout of illness kept me in bed on the day of the ceremony in which it figured, and so prevented me from hearing it. The young kapellmeister Richard Wagner spent a long time in Paris without succeeding in making a name for himself except as the author of a few articles in the *Gazette musicale*. His first act of authority was to help me with my rehearsals, which he did with energy and good will. The ceremony of installation and formal oath-taking was held on the day after my arrival, and when I met him he was glowing with understandable pleasure and satisfaction. Having endured in France untold hardships and all the frustrations and mortifications that come when one is obscure, he returned to his native Saxony and had the audacity to embark on the composition of the words and the music of a five-act opera, *Rienzi*, and the good fortune to accomplish it. The work had a brilliant success in Dresden. It was soon followed by *The Flying Dutchman*, a three-act opera for which he again wrote both words and music. Whatever one's opinion of these works, it will be conceded that there are not many men who could twice bring off a double feat of this kind, and that at the very least it reveals him as a figure of unusual interest and ability. This is what the King of Saxony clearly appreciated; and when he guaranteed Richard Wagner a livelihood by making him assistant to his senior kapellmeister, lovers of art could have echoed the words with which Jean Bart replied to Louis XIV when the king informed the intrepid sea-dog that he had appointed him commodore: 'Sire, you have done well.'

As *Rienzi* far exceeds the length normally given to operas in Germany it is no longer performed in one piece: they play the first two acts on one evening and the remaining three on another. It was this second part that I saw. I cannot claim to know it well enough after one hearing to express a definite opinion about it; I remember only a fine prayer sung by Rienzi (Tichatschek) in the last act and a triumphal march modelled, though in no spirit of slavish imitation, on the superb march in Spontini's *Olympie*. *The Flying Dutchman* impressed me by the sombre colouring of the music and by some remarkable effects of storm and wind which are an integral part of the dramatic character of the work. But I also noticed an abuse of tremolo, all the more annoying because I had already been struck by it in *Rienzi* and because it suggests a certain laziness of mind, against which he should be more on his guard. A sustained tremolo is of all orchestral devices the one that the ear tires of most quickly. It calls for no invention on the part of the composer when there is no striking idea accompanying it above or below.

Be that as it may, I repeat, all honour to the enlightened King who, by taking him so decisively under his protection, has in effect saved a young artist of rare talents.

The management of the Dresden theatre has spared no pains to give Wagner's two works as brilliant a performance as possible. Scenery, costumes and production approach the best standards achieved in Paris in works of this kind. Madame Devrient, of whom I shall have more to say in connection with her performances in Berlin, plays the part of a young man in *Rienzi*, an impersonation which no longer goes with her somewhat matronly figure. I thought her much better cast in *The Flying Dutchman*, in spite of one or two affected poses and the spoken phrases that she finds it necessary to interject throughout the role. But the singer who excited and impressed me as a really remarkable and unspoiled talent was Wächter, who plays the doomed Dutchman. He has one of the finest baritone voices I have heard and he uses it with complete mastery. The timbre is of that smooth and at the same time vibrant kind that can be so expressive if the artist sings with any warmth and sensitivity—and Wächter has both qualities in abundance. Tichatschek is brilliant and irresistible as Rienzi—elegant, impassioned, heroic, his fine voice and great lustrous eyes marvellously effective in the part. Mlle Wüst plays Rienzi's sister, a role which gives her almost nothing to sing. The composer, in devising it, has gauged her powers to perfection.

Now, my dear Ernst, I should like to talk about Lipinski; but what can I tell you—the violinist admired and applauded from one end of Europe to the other, the conscientious and knowledgeable artist—about your great predecessor's talents? You know his singing tone and the power and pathos of his playing in music of the grand style as well as I do, indeed better, and the beauties of his concertos have long been fixed in your infallible memory. Besides, Lipinski was so good to me during my stay in Dresden, so loyal and energetic on my behalf, that many people would consider my tributes wanting in impartiality. They would be ascribed (quite wrongly, I may say) to gratitude rather than to genuine and spontaneous admiration. He received immense applause at my concert for his playing of the violin romance (which had been played a few days before in Leipzig by David) and for his account of the viola solo in my second symphony, *Harold*.

This latter concert was even more successful than the first had been. The melancholy passages and the scenes of religious life in *Harold* seemed to appeal immediately to the audience, and it was the same with the pieces from *Romeo and Juliet*, the adagio and the Capulets' Feast. But the work which impressed both the public and the artists of Dresden most vividly was the cantata *The Fifth of May*, admirably sung by Wächter and the chorus to a translation kindly made for the occasion by the indefatigable Winkler. Napoleon's memory is cherished today by the people of Germany almost as much as it is in France, which no doubt explains the profound effect that the piece produced in every town where I subsequently gave it. The end in particular—

Far from this rock in silent awe we fled;
The sun is gone, the light of heav'n's put out

—often provoked extraordinary demonstrations.*

In Dresden I met the prodigious English harpist Parish-Alvars, a name not yet as renowned as it ought to be. He had just come from Vienna. The man is the Liszt of the harp. You cannot

* [Berlioz's second Dresden concert, on 17 February 1843, also included the Offertorium and Sanctus from the Requiem and the finale of the Funeral Symphony (all repeated from the first programme), and the overture to *Benvenuto Cellini*.]

conceive all the delicate and powerful effects, the novel touches and unprecedented sonorities, that he manages to produce from an instrument in many respects so limited. His fantasy on *Moses* (imitated and adapted for the piano with such happy results by Thalberg), his variations for harmonic notes on the Mermaids' Chorus from *Oberon*, and a score of similar pieces, delighted me more than I can say. The advantage the new harps possess of being able to sound two strings in unison, by means of the double action of the pedals, has stimulated him to invent combinations which on paper look quite impossible.

Their difficulty, however, consists solely in the skilful use of the pedals to produce the doubled notes known as synonyms. Thus he can play with astounding rapidity a series of four-part chords moving by leaps of a minor third, because by means of synonyms the strings of the harp, instead of sounding the diatonic scale of C flat as they normally do, can give in descending order the sequence C natural, C natural, A natural, G flat, G flat, E flat, E flat. Parish-Alvars left a few very promising pupils behind him in Vienna after his stay there. He has now been heard in Dresden, Leipzig, Berlin and many other towns where his extraordinary talent invariably aroused enthusiasm. When is he coming to Paris?

In addition to the distinguished artists I have mentioned, the Dresden orchestra includes the excellent teacher Dotzauer. He leads the cellos and has also to be acting leader of the double basses, for the ancient bass-player who shares the desk with him can no longer play some of the notes and indeed can barely support the weight of his instrument. I came across many instances in Germany of this mistaken regard for the old. Kapellmeisters tend to let them keep their jobs long after their physical strength has failed, and even to leave them there till death itself supervenes. More than once I had to harden my heart and ruthlessly insist on the replacement of one of these poor invalids.* There is a very good cor

* [Cf. Wagner's account of a rehearsal of the Dresden orchestra under Spontini in 1844. Spontini, objecting to the way the violas played a passage in the second act of *La Vestale*, asked 'in sepulchral tones: "Are the violas dying?", at which the two pale and hopelessly melancholy old dotards at the first desk who, to my sorrow, stuck tenaciously to their jobs (notwithstanding their right to a pension), stared in

anglais in the Dresden orchestra. The first oboe has a fine tone but an antiquated style and a mania for inserting trills and grace-notes which outraged my deepest convictions. He indulged in some particularly disgusting embellishments at the beginning of the Scene in the Fields. I expressed myself on the subject in vigorous terms at the second rehearsal. The sly dog refrained at the two subsequent rehearsals, but it was a feint. At the concert, knowing that I would not stop the orchestra and arraign him personally in the presence of the court, he treacherously resumed his little tricks, eyeing me with a quizzical air the while. I nearly collapsed with indignation.

The horns include Levy, a virtuoso player with a great reputation in Saxony. Like his colleagues he plays on a cylinder or rotary-valve horn. Nearly all orchestras in North Germany have adopted it, Leipzig being virtually the only one that still resists the innovation. The Dresden trumpets too are rotary-valve instruments; they can profitably be substituted for our piston cornets, which are not known there.

The military band is very good. Even the drummers are musicians. But the reed instruments that I heard struck me as unsatisfactory, their intonation leaving something to be desired; and the bandmasters of these regiments would do well to apply to our incomparable Adolphe Sax for a few of his clarinets. There are no ophicleides; the bottom line is taken by Russian bassoons, serpents and tubas.

I often thought of Weber while conducting the Dresden orchestra. He directed it for a few years. It was larger then than it is now.

Weber trained it so well that sometimes in the overture to *Freischütz* he would give the tempo of the allegro, beat the first four bars, and then leave the orchestra to proceed on its own until it reached the pause bars at the end. It must make players feel very proud to see their conductor fold his arms and let them play by themselves.

---

alarm at Spontini, thinking he was threatening them . . .' (*Mein Leben*, Part 2). The practice of placing front-desk cellos and basses together, one each to a desk, lasted well into the nineteenth century.]

Would you believe it, my dear Ernst, during the three weeks that I spent in this intensely musical city no one thought of mentioning to me that Weber's family were living there? I would have been so happy to meet them and express something of my respect and admiration for the great composer who made their name illustrious. I discovered too late what a precious chance I had lost. Let me at least take this opportunity to assure Madame Weber and her children of my keen regret.

In Dresden I was shown some scores by the famous Hasse, known as the Saxon, who also at one time had charge of the company and for many years* controlled its destinies. I must admit I found nothing of much interest apart from a Te Deum, written for some splendid celebration at the Court, which has the ceremonial brilliance of a great peal of bells. For those who demand nothing more than sheer sonority on these occasions, it would pass for a fine work; to my mind this quality is not enough. What I would particularly like to hear—in good performances—would be a few of the many operas which Hasse wrote for the theatres of Italy, Germany and England and on which his immense reputation was based. Why not try to revive at least one of them in Dresden? It would be an interesting experiment and might even be a revelation. Hasse's life must have been an extremely contentious one, but I tried in vain to find out about it. The only books I could discover were commonplace biographies which told me what I already knew and said nothing of what I wanted to know. He travelled widely and lived much in the torrid zone and the regions of the pole, that is to say in Italy and England. There should be a curious tale to tell of his relations with the Venetian composer Marcello and of his love affair with Faustina, whom he married and who sang the leading roles in his operas—a tale of conjugal rivalry, war between composer and prima donna, in which the master was the slave and right always wrong. Or perhaps it was not like that at all. Who knows? Faustina could have lived the life of a civilized diva, a singer of irreproachable modesty, a good wife and a virtuous musician, faithful to her husband, faithful to her roles, telling her beads and knitting stockings

* [1734–64.]

when she had nothing to do—Hasse composing, Faustina singing, both making a great deal of money and not spending it. Stranger things have happened. If you get married, it is what I wish for you.

When I left Dresden to return to Leipzig, Lipinski, on hearing that Mendelssohn was putting on the finale from my *Romeo and Juliet* at the concert in aid of the poor, announced his intention of coming to hear it if the intendant would give him two or three days' leave. I took this as a polite gesture. Imagine my dismay when on the day of the concert—at which, because of the business described in my last letter, the finale was not performed after all—Lipinski turned up. He had come nearly ninety miles to hear the piece. There is a musician devoted to music! But you are the last man to be astonished by such an attitude. You would do the same, I know—artist that you are!

Farewell, farewell.

Sixth Letter

Brunswick, Hamburg

TO HEINRICH HEINE

I had every kind of good fortune in the excellent town of Brunswick. Accordingly my first thought in preparing this account was to select some favourite enemy to regale with it on the grounds that it would give him pleasure, and not address it to you, my dear Heine, who might be pained by such a spectacle of musical merrymaking. The anti-moralists maintain that in every happiness that befalls us there is something essentially disagreeable for our closest friends. But I refuse to believe such an unpleasing aspersion. I can think of friends who have had sudden phenomenal strokes of luck without its making the slightest difference to me.

But enough! Let us not venture on the prickly ground of irony, a territory inhabited by toads and vipers, where spurge and wormwood flourish in the shade of the nettle tree, lake-water heaves and hisses, the earth shifts beneath your feet, the night wind scorches, and lightning flickers among the western clouds. To what end the curling lip, the jaundiced eye leering between half-closed lids, the gentle grinding of teeth, the well-placed banana skin, when, far from being bitter, one's thoughts are wholly absorbed with delightful recollections and one's heart overflows with gratitude and innocent pleasure, and one wishes one had a hundred trumpet tongues to tell all those dear to one: that day I was entirely happy. It was nothing but an impulse of childish vanity that made me begin as I did. Without realizing it, I wanted to imitate you—you, the inimitable ironist! It won't happen to me again. I have too often regretted, in our conversations together, that I could not get you to be serious and restrain the convulsive action of your claws even in moments when you fancy yourself purring, tiger-cat that you are, *leo quaerens quem devorat*! Yet what feeling, what wealth of imagination untouched by malice, lies scattered about your works. How you sing in the major mode when you want to! How splendidly reckless and ungrudging your enthusiasm when admiration catches you unawares and you forget yourself! What depths of tenderness lurk in the corners of your heart for the country you have so long mocked, for that Germany, teeming land of poets, birthplace of brooding geniuses, whom you call your old grandmother—and who loves you in spite of everything!

I saw this clearly by the fond, regretful way you were spoken of during my travels. Without doubt she loves you. All her affection is now concentrated upon you. Her elder sons, her great sons and great men, are dead. She looks only to you, whom she calls with a smile the naughty one of the family. It is she and the high romantic songs she sang over your cradle that have given you so true and exalted a feeling for music; and it was when you left her and wandered the world and suffered that you became mocking and pitiless.

It would be simple for you, I know, to make a monstrous parody of the account I am about to give you of my visit to Brunswick. But see what confidence I have in our friendship (or how I am no longer afraid of irony): it's to you that I address it and to no one else.

Just as I was leaving Leipzig I received a letter from Meyerbeer telling me that it would be another month before they could do anything about my concerts. The great man recommended that I make use of this delay to go to Brunswick, where I would find a 'vintage orchestra'. I followed his advice, never suspecting how much cause I would have to congratulate myself on having done so. I knew no one in Brunswick and had no notion what the attitude of the artists or the public's taste might be. But the thought that the four Müller brothers were at the head of the orchestra would have been enough by itself to give me confidence even without Meyerbeer's advocacy. I had heard them on their last visit to Paris* and regarded their performances of Beethoven's quartets as among the marvels of our time.

The Müllers represent the ideal of Beethoven quartet-playing (as the Bohrers do of Beethoven trio-playing). Nowhere else have precision of ensemble, unanimity of feeling, depth of expression, purity of style, grandeur, power, vitality and passion been brought to such a pitch. Their interpretations of those sublime works give us, I believe, an exact idea of what Beethoven thought and felt in writing them. It's an echo of the original inspiration, a by-product of the creative act.

The musical Müllers are even more numerous than I had supposed. I counted seven of them, brothers, sons and nephews, in the Brunswick orchestra. Georg Müller is kapellmeister. His elder brother Carl, though only the leader, is a highly respected figure, as head of the famous quartet. You can see this from the deferential way everybody listens whenever he makes a remark. The deputy leader is Freudenthal, an accomplished violinist and composer. I had written to tell Carl Müller that I was coming. On alighting from the coach I was accosted by a very agreeable young man, M. Zinkeisen, one of the first violins, who speaks French like you or me and who had come so that he could take me to the kapellmeister the moment I arrived—a degree of zeal and consideration which I thought augured well. Zinkeisen had seen me once or twice in Paris and he recognized me now despite the pitiable state I was reduced to by the cold—for I had spent the night in the open compartment, virtually exposed to the four winds, in order to escape the smoke and stench of six abominable pipes going full blast inside. I am lost in admiration of the police regulations in Germany. It is forbidden on pain of a fine to smoke on the public highway, where the practice of the gentle art

* [In 1837.]

inconveniences nobody; but go into a café, and people are smoking; a restaurant—smoking again; a stagecoach—smoking. Wherever you go, the revolting pipe pursues you. You, my dear Heine, are a German yet you do not smoke. Believe me it is not the least of your virtues. Posterity may not record it but in your own time many men and all women will owe you a signal debt of gratitude.

Carl Müller received me with that grave, impassive air which sometimes alarmed me in Germany, for I took it for a sign of coldness and indifference; but there is less to fear from it than from our French effusiveness—those flowery speeches and smiling assurances with which we greet a foreigner whom we have forgotten five minutes later. Indeed the very opposite was the case. Having asked me what I wanted in the way of orchestral forces, the *Konzertmeister* went straight off to make arrangements with his brother for mustering the necessary strings and to apply to those amateurs and professionals not attached to the ducal establishment who were competent to play with it. By the following day they had assembled a splendid orchestra, slightly bigger than that of the Paris Opéra and made up of players who were not only highly skilled but full of unrivalled fire and enthusiasm. The case of the harp, the ophicleide and the cor anglais reared its head again, as it had done in Weimar, Leipzig and Dresden. (I tell you all this that you may acquire the reputation of being a musician.) A member of the orchestra, Leibrock,* a fine artist with a wide knowledge of the literature of music, played the harp, but having been studying it for only a year he was extremely nervous of being put to the test of my second symphony; his harp, too, is an old one with a rudimentary pedal action and therefore unable to play all the music written nowadays for the instrument. Fortunately the harp part in *Harold* is very easy and he worked so hard for five or six days that he acquitted himself admirably—at the final rehearsal. On the evening of the concert he was seized with panic at the crucial moment and stopped short in the introduction, leaving Carl Müller, who was playing the viola solo, to continue on his own.

That was the only serious mishap we suffered. The audience was quite unaware of it, but M. Leibrock was still reproaching

* [A cellist.]

himself bitterly several days later in spite of my efforts to make him forget it. As to the ophicleide, there was none of any kind in Brunswick. I was offered as substitutes a bass tuba (a magnificent low instrument of which I shall be speaking in connection with the military bands of Berlin)—but the young man who played it did not seem to have thoroughly grasped its mechanism, being uncertain even of the true range—and after that a Russian bassoon, which the player persisted in calling a double bassoon. I had great difficulty in undeceiving him as to the name and nature of his instrument, which sounds as it is written and, like the ophicleide, is played with a mouthpiece, whereas the double bassoon, a transposing reed instrument, is simply a large bassoon which reproduces most of the bassoon's compass an octave lower. Anyway, the Russian bassoon was chosen to do the best it could in place of the missing ophicleide. There being no cor anglais either, its solos were arranged for the oboe, and we began the orchestral rehearsals, while the choir rehearsed in another hall. I must here state that never have I met a body of established artists, in France, Belgium or Germany, so conscientiously and passionately dedicated to the task in hand. After the first encounter, which gave them an idea of the chief difficulties in my symphonies, the word was given. For all the ensuing sessions it was agreed to deceive me as to the time of starting. An hour before I arrived each morning (I discovered later) the orchestra met to practise the most hazardous phrases and rhythms. I was more and more astonished at the rapid change I found from one day to the next and at the confidence with which they attacked difficult passages which even my Paris orchestra, that Young Guard of the Grand Army, had approached warily. Only one piece worried Carl Müller: this was the scherzo from *Romeo and Juliet* (Queen Mab). For the first time since coming to Germany I had ventured to include it in the programme, at the urgent request of Zinkeisen who had heard it in Paris.

'We'll work at it until we get it right,' he had said to me, and in fact he did not overestimate the orchestra. Queen Mab in her microscopic chariot, drawn at full gallop by her team of little atomies and driven by the murmuring gnat that buzzes and hovers on summer eves, danced her mad revels to the admiration of the Brunswick audience. You, poet of sprites and fairies, blood-brother to all those delicate and mordant creatures, will realize my misgivings. You know only too well from what gossamer thread their gauzy wings are spun and how serene the sky must be before that inconstant swarm can sport without fear under the pale light of the stars. Well! The orchestra, defying our doubts, identifying itself completely with Shakespeare's exquisite fancy, made itself so small and fine and nimble that never, I think, did the insubstantial queen dart more gleefully among her noiseless harmonies.

When we came to the finale of *Harold*, what a contrast! In that brigands' orgy, where wine, blood, joy and rage mingle in mutual intoxication and make music together, and the rhythm seems now to stumble, now to rush furiously forward, and the mouths of the brass to spew forth curses, answering prayer with blasphemy, and they laugh and swill and strike, smash, kill, rape, and generally enjoy themselves, the orchestra played as though a devil possessed them. There was something uncanny and awe-inspiring in their frantic exhilaration. Violins, cellos, trombones, drums, cymbals, roared and leapt and sang with incredible accuracy and precision, while from the viola, the pensive Harold fleeing in dismay, a few faint echoes of his evening hymn still hovered on the vibrant air. My heart was beating like a drum roll. I shuddered as I conducted this astounding orchestra. I thought all my young Paris warriors were with me, more ardent than ever. You poets, you have no conception what it is like to be seized and swept along by these living hurricanes. I longed to embrace the entire band, and I could not help crying out—in French, it's true, but the tone of voice must have made my meaning clear—'Sublime! stupendous! Thank you, gentlemen, I congratulate you. You are perfect brigands!'

It was the same when they played the overture to *Benvenuto*. Yet the introduction to *Harold*, the Pilgrims' March and the Serenade—pieces of a quite different character—have never been performed with more untroubled grandeur and holy serenity. As for the Feast at the Capulets' from *Romeo*, it approximates to the whirlwind category, so it too was given a stunning performance, as we say in Paris.

You should have seen all those flushed faces when we paused for a break during rehearsals. Schmidt, the prodigious first double bass, tore the skin off his right forefinger at the beginning of the pizzicato passage in the Orgy, but not thinking to stop for such a trifle he ignored the blood and went on playing, merely changing to another finger. That is what is known in military parlance as steadiness under fire.

While we were indulging in these gentle pursuits the chorus on its side had been toiling away, though with different results, at the pieces from my Requiem. The Offertorium and the Quaerens me went well enough in the end but the Sanctus, the solo part in which was to have been sung by Schmetzer, the first tenor at the theatre and an excellent artist, encountered an impassable obstacle. The andante for women's voices in three parts contains a few enharmonic modulations which the Dresden chorus had managed perfectly well but which were apparently beyond the capacity of the Brunswick chorus to master. After vainly grappling with the passage for three days, at the end of which the sense and pitch still eluded them, the poor creatures in despair sent a deputation to beg me not to expose them to public ignominy and to obtain the removal of the terrible Sanctus from the programme. I was forced to agree, though with regret, especially on account of Schmetzer, whose high tenor voice is ideally suited to this seraphic hymn and who, besides, was enjoying singing it.

Everything was now ready, and despite the fears of Carl Müller, who would have liked to rehearse the scherzo once again, we were about to try conclusions at the concert and see what impression the music created. I should tell you that, on the advice of the kapellmeister, I had invited some twenty of the leading Brunswick music-lovers to the rehearsals. They became in effect a kind of live puff; their daily reports spread the word and aroused general curiosity throughout the town. Even the man in the street began to take an interest in the preparations for this concert, and the players and privileged listeners were plied with questions. 'What happened this morning?—Is he pleased?—Is he really French?—Surely the French only write comic operas?—I hear the chorus find him awful.—He said the women sang like dancers.—Then he knows the sopranos come from the corps de ballet?—Is it true he stopped in the middle of a movement to congratulate the trombones?—The orchestral attendant is positive that at yesterday's rehearsal he drank two jugs of water, a bottle of white wine and three glasses of brandy.—Why does he keep saying to the leader, "César! César!"? (C'est ça, c'est ça!),' etc.

The result was that long before the appointed hour the theatre was crammed to the rafters with an impatient crowd already predisposed in my favour. (At this point, my dear Heine, you must draw in your claws, for it is here that you may be tempted to make me feel them.) When the time came and the orchestra were assembled, I entered and made my way through the ranks of the violins to the conductor's desk. Imagine my alarm on seeing it swathed from top to bottom in a kind of candelabrum of greenery. I thought, 'This is the players' doing. They have compromised me. How could they be so rash? Counting their chickens before they're hatched! I shall be in a fine mess if the audience doesn't agree with them. In Paris a demonstration like this would doom an artist twenty times over.' However, the overture was greeted with loud applause, the Pilgrims' March had to be repeated, the Orgy set the hall ablaze, the Offertorium, with its chorus on two notes, and the Quaerens me seemed greatly to affect the pious-minded, Carl Müller scored a success in the Romance for violin, Queen Mab caused utter astonishment, a song with orchestra was encored, and the Feast at the Capulets' brought the evening to a glowing conclusion. Hardly had the last chord sounded when an appalling hubbub engulfed the hall. The entire audience were shouting, in the stalls, in the boxes, everywhere, and trombones, horns and trumpets blaring out fanfares in a selection of keys, energetically accompanied by the clatter of bows on the wood of the stringed instruments and the din of percussion.

The German language has a word to designate this peculiar way of applauding.* My first reaction was one of anger and abhorrence: they were spoiling the musical experience I had just been enjoying. For a moment I almost hated the players for choosing such a deafening method of showing me their appreciation. But it was impossible not to feel deeply touched by their tributes when the kapellmeister, Georg Müller, advancing upon me laden with flowers, addressed me, in French:

* [*Tusch*. The concert was given on 9 March 1843.]

'Permit me to offer you these wreaths in the name of the whole ducal establishment, and allow me to lay them on your scores.'

At these words the audience shouted louder than ever, the orchestra resumed its fanfares, and the baton dropped from my hand: I no longer knew what was happening. (All right, laugh then, don't mind me. It will do you good and cannot do me any harm. Besides, I have not done yet, and it would be too much of a strain for you to hear my dithyramb through to the end without a single scratch. . . . But I see you are quite well behaved today. I continue.) I had barely left the theatre, sweating and steaming as though I had been dipped in the Styx, and in a daze of delight, not knowing whom to pay attention to among all that crowd pressing round me and congratulating me, when I was informed that supper for a hundred and fifty had been ordered at my hotel by a society of artists and music-lovers and that I was invited to join them. Of course I had to go. Upon my arrival, fresh applause, renewed acclamations; a succession of toasts, speeches in French and German. I reply as best I can to those that I understand; and as each health is proposed a hundred and fifty voices reply with a magnificent choral hurrah. The basses start, on D, the tenors answer with A, the women add F sharp to make the chord of D major, which is followed by the four chords of subdominant, tonic, dominant, tonic, forming successively a plagal and a perfect cadence, the whole grand salvo going off in measured style with resounding and majestic effect. I found it beautiful; this kind of applause at least is worthy of a musical nation.

Yes, my dear Heine, though you should think me naïve and callow in the extreme I cannot conceal that all this sonorous show of approval made me very happy. The pleasure a composer feels at such demonstrations may not be comparable with the delight of conducting a superb orchestra in an inspired performance of his favourite works; but the two go very well together, and after such a concert an evening of this sort does not come amiss. So you see, I am much indebted to the artists and music-lovers of Brunswick. I owe a great deal too to the leading music critic, Robert Griepenkerl, who in an erudite pamphlet* vehemently took issue with a

* [*Ritter Berlioz in Braunschweig: zur Charakteristik dieses Tondichters*. Brunswick, 1843.]

Leipzig journal and gave what seems to me a very accurate idea of my music and of the force and direction of the musical impulses that drive me on.

Take my hand, then, and let us sing a loud hurrah for Brunswick, using its own favourite chords:

Long live all artistic towns!

It grieves me, dear poet, but your reputation as a musician is now compromised.

Now for your native town, Hamburg—a city as devastated as ancient Pompeii, but heroically patching up its wounds and rising renewed from its own ashes.* Here, too, I have nothing but praise to bestow. Hamburg has rich musical resources: choral societies, philharmonic societies, military bands and all the rest. The theatre orchestra has admittedly been cut down to the bone for the sake of economy, but I had stated my terms in advance to the director and the orchestra that I was presented with was admirable in point of both numbers and quality thanks to a generous reinforcement of strings and the leave of absence I obtained for two or three practically centenarian old dodderers to whom the theatre is devoted. A strange fact which I must mention at once is Hamburg's possession of an excellent harpist with a first-rate instrument to his name. I had begun to despair of meeting with either in Germany. I also found a vigorous ophicleide, but was obliged to dispense with the services of the cor anglais-player.

* [Hamburg had suffered a disastrous fire the previous May.]

Both the first flute, Canthal, and the first violin, Lindenau, are outstandingly fine players. The kapellmeister, Krebs, does his job efficiently and with a strictness of discipline that I like to see in a conductor. He gave me most friendly assistance during the long rehearsals that we held. The company, when I was there, was tolerably good and included three talented singers: a tenor who, though not endowed with an exceptional voice, has taste and a sound technique; an agile soprano, Mlle . . . Mlle—damn it, I have forgotten her name (and the young goddess would have done me the honour of singing at my concert had I been better known—Hosanna in excelsis!); and the formidable bass, Reichel, who in addition to a voice of enormous volume and splendid timbre has a range of two and a half octaves and is a magnificent-looking man to boot, playing such parts as Sarastro, Moses and Bertram to perfection. Madame Cornet, wife of the director, an accomplished musician and a soprano with a wide compass, whose voice must have had unusual brilliance, was not a member of the company, appearing only occasionally when she was required. I was impressed by her performance as the Queen of Night in *The Magic Flute*, a difficult role written in the upper register which few singers possess. The chorus, though rather small and weak, did well in the pieces that I had given them.

The opera house is enormous. I feared its size, having seen it empty three times in a row at performances of *The Magic Flute*, *Moses* and *Linda di Chamounix*; so it was an agreeable surprise to find it full when the day came for my appearance before the Hamburg public.

An excellent performance and a large, intelligent and animated audience made this concert one of the best I gave in Germany. *Harold* and the cantata *The Fifth of May*, sung with profound feeling by Reichel, carried off the honours.* I was greatly touched, at the end of the cantata, by two players near me addressing me in low tones and halting French: 'Ah, sir! Our respects! our respects!' It

* [The programme, given on 22 March 1843, also included the cavatina from *Benvenuto* sung by Madame Cornet, *Rêverie et Caprice* (with the leader of the orchestra, Lindenau), Berlioz's orchestration of Weber's *Invitation to the Waltz*, the *Francs-juges* overture, two songs sung by Marie Recio, and the Offertorium and Quaerens me from the Requiem.]

was all they knew how to say. In sum, I am proud to state that I made staunch friends of the Hamburg orchestra. Only Krebs' approval was strangely qualified. 'My dear fellow,' he said, 'in a few years your music will be all over Germany. It will become popular, and that will be a disaster. Think how it will be imitated! Think of the style it will breed, the extravagances! It would be better for art if you had never been born!'

One can but hope that these poor symphonies are not so contagious as he likes to think and that no one will catch cholera or yellow fever from them.

And now, Heine, Heinrich Heine, celebrated financier of the imagination, nephew of Mr Solomon Heine, the author of so many priceless poems in ingots, I have no more to say, so I humbly take my leave of you.

Seventh Letter

Berlin

TO MADEMOISELLE LOUISE BERTIN

Before I do anything else, dear Mlle Bertin, I must crave your indulgence for the letter I am presuming to write to you. I cannot but feel apprehensive about it in my present state of mind. For the last few days I have been in the grip of the black philosophy, and God alone knows what dark imaginings, strange tales and grotesque conclusions I shall be led into if it goes on. You may not perhaps be sure what the black philosophy is? It is simply white magic in reverse.

White magic is the power by which we divine that Victor Hugo is a great poet; that Beethoven is a great musician; that you are both musician and poet; that Janin is a witty man; that if a fine opera, well performed, is a failure, the public has not understood a word of it; that if it is a success, the public has not understood a word of it; that the beautiful is unusual; that the unusual is not always beautiful; that might is right; that Abd-el-Kader is wrong, and O'Connell too; that Arabs indisputably are not Frenchmen; that passive resistance is an absurdity; and other equally knotty propositions.

Black philosophy makes one question and stare in astonishment at everything, see fair things as foul and foul things as they are. One is full of grievance, blaspheming life, railing against death. Like Hamlet, one feels a sense of outrage that 'Imperious Caesar, dead and turned to clay,/Might stop a hole to keep the wind away'. (One would feel a much greater sense of outrage if the humble and meek were alone fit for such base uses.) One grieves that poor Yorick cannot so much as laugh at the foolish face he pulls after fifteen years under the ground, and one shrinks from his skull in disgust—or one takes it and saws it in half to make a cup, and poor Yorick, who can no longer drink, is employed to slake the thirst and draw the wit of a company of jeering Rhenish-swillers.

Thus, in your sanctuary at Les Roches, where you peacefully pursue your meditations, I for my part in my present state would experience only a mortal weariness and frustration.* If you made me admire a splendid sunset, I would be quite capable of preferring the gas lamps in the Champs-Elysées. If you pointed out the graceful shapes of your swans gliding on the lake, I would declare the swan a stupid creature which thinks of nothing but dabbling and eating, its only song a hideous, meaningless rattle. If you sat down at the piano to play me something from your favourite Mozart or Cimarosa, I might well peevishly interrupt you and announce that it was time to have done with this adulation of Mozart, with his operas that are all alike and his maddening imperturbability, and that as for Cimarosa, his eternal *Secret Marriage* is beyond redemption, being nearly as boring as *The Marriage of Figaro* and not nearly as musical. I would prove to you that the comedy of the work consists exclusively in the wit of the actors; that its melodic invention is circumscribed; that those perfect cadences, recurring every minute, account by themselves for some two-thirds of the score; in short, that it is an opera fit only for fairs and

* Yesterday, when the fit was on me, I was at a house where they have a mania for autograph-collecting. Inevitably, my hostess begged me for something for her album. 'Mind though, nothing commonplace,' she warned. The injunction irritated me, and I immediately wrote: *The death penalty is a great evil, since but for it I should probably have murdered a large number of people and we would now be plagued by fewer of those pernicious fools who are the bane of art and artists.* They laughed a great deal at my aphorism, thinking I had not meant it seriously.

carnivals.* If you then tried something in a contrasting style and had recourse to some work by Sebastian Bach, I might well flee at the first whiff of his fugues and leave you alone with his Passion.

You see the consequences of this dread disease! When one is in its power one loses all one's manners, amiability, circumspection, proportion, canniness, and common sense; one says all sorts of frightful things; and what is worse, one believes them, one commits oneself, one goes too far.

But a fig for black philosophy! The fit has passed: I am sane enough to talk rationally to you now and tell you what I saw and heard in Berlin. About my own performances I shall speak later. I begin with grand opera. Honour to whom honour is due.

The German Opera, which was burnt to the ground only three months ago,† was a rather gloomy and ramshackle place, but well designed from the point of view of musical effect, with fine resonant acoustics. The orchestra pit did not come so far out into the auditorium as in Paris; it extended much farther on either side, and the more vehement instruments—trombones, trumpets, timpani, bass drum—were partly overhung by the first row of boxes, which cut off their extreme reverberations. For important performances the orchestra—one of the best I heard—is made up as follows: fourteen first violins, fourteen seconds, eight violas, ten cellos, eight double basses, four flutes, four oboes, four clarinets, four bassoons, four horns, four trumpets, four trombones, timpani, bass drum, cymbals and two harps.

The strings are nearly all first-rate, but one should particularly single out the brothers Ganz (the admirable first violin and first cello) and the able violinist Ries. The woodwind are also very good and, as you see, double the number of the woodwind at the Paris Opéra—a great advantage, since it provides a ripieno force of two flutes, two oboes, two clarinets and two bassoons for use at climaxes. This is remarkably effective in softening the stridency of the brass (without it they are always too prominent). The horns are

* Mlle Bertin assured me the other day that I libelled her when I included Cimarosa among her favourite composers. I hereby acknowledge my error and regret having committed it. However, the libel is not perhaps a very serious one, and I think one may survive it.

† [On 18 August 1843.]

splendid, and all of the rotary-valve variety—much to the regret of Meyerbeer, who thinks as I did until recently about the new mechanism. A number of composers object to the rotary-valve horn because, they maintain, its timbre is inferior to that of the natural horn. I have several times experimented by listening to the open notes of the natural horn and of the chromatic or rotary-valve horn one after the other, and I must confess I could not detect the slightest difference in timbre or volume. There is at first sight more substance in another objection that has been raised against the new horns, but it can be easily disposed of. Since this instrument (now perfected, in my opinion) was introduced into orchestras, certain cornists who play natural-horn parts on rotary-valve horns find it less trouble to produce the stopped notes indicated by the composer, as open notes. This is certainly a serious abuse, but the fault lies in the player and not in the instrument. Far from it, indeed, for in the hands of a skilful artist the rotary-valve horn not merely produces all the stopped notes which the natural horn produces but can actually play the entire compass without resorting to a single open note. The conclusion is simply that horn-players should know the technique of hand-stopping as if the rotary-valve mechanism did not exist, and that composers should henceforth indicate by some special sign the notes that are to be played stopped, the player producing as open sounds only those notes which carry no such indication.

The same prejudice for some time opposed the use of rotary-valve trumpets (now general throughout Germany), but less violently than in the case of the new horns. The question of stopped notes naturally did not apply, since no composer wrote them for the trumpet. Opposition has been confined to the argument that the tone of the trumpet loses much of its brilliance with the rotary-valve mechanism. This is not true, to my ear at least. Even if a more sensitive ear than mine can perceive a difference between the two instruments, it will surely be admitted that the disadvantage resulting from such a difference is not to be compared with the advantage of being able to play up and down the chromatic scale easily and without the smallest unevenness of tone over a range of two and a half octaves. For this reason I can only rejoice that the natural trumpet has been almost completely superseded in

Germany today. In France we still have practically no chromatic or rotary-valve trumpets. Up till now the incredible popularity of the cornet has stood in their way—quite wrongly, in my view, for the cornet has nothing like the trumpet's nobility and splendour of timbre. It is not that we lack the instruments. Adolphe Sax is now making rotary-valve trumpets, large and small, in all possible keys, familiar and unfamiliar, instruments whose excellent tone-quality and finished workmanship are indisputable. It is scarcely to be believed that this gifted young artist should be finding it difficult to maintain his position and make a career in Paris. The persecutions he suffers are worthy of the Middle Ages and recall the antics of the enemies of Benvenuto, the Florentine sculptor. They lure away his workmen, steal his designs, accuse him of insanity, and bring legal proceedings against him. With a little more dash they would assassinate him. Such is the hatred inventors inspire in rivals who are incapable of inventing anything themselves. Fortunately he has been able to count on the protection and friendship of General de Rumigny, and until now this has helped him to endure the sordid struggle. But how much longer will it suffice? It ought to be the Minister of War's responsibility to see that a man of such rare and useful accomplishments is given the position his ability and exertions entitle him to. Our military bands are still without either rotary-valve trumpets or bass tubas (the most powerful of the lower instruments). If French military music is to achieve the standard of Prussian and Austrian, we will have to manufacture these instruments. A government order to Adolphe Sax for three hundred trumpets and a hundred bass tubas would be the salvation of him.

Berlin is the only German city I visited where you find the true bass trombone, in E flat. We have not yet got any; Parisian musicians refuse to play an instrument that is so tiring to the chest. Prussian lungs are evidently more robust than ours. The Berlin Opera orchestra has two bass trombones. Their combined volume of tone is so great as to obliterate the alto and tenor trombones playing the two upper parts. The aggressive tone of one bass trombone would be enough to upset the balance of the three trombone parts as written by composers nowadays. But, there being no ophicleide at the Berlin Opera, instead of replacing it with a bass tuba in works of French origin, which nearly all have an ophicleide part, they give the part to a second bass trombone. The effect of having two of these formidable instruments, one above the other (the ophicleide part being frequently written an octave below the third trombone), is disastrous. You hear nothing but the bottom line; even the trumpets are all but drowned. When I came to give my concerts I found that the bass trombone was much too prominent—although in the symphonies I was using only one—and I had to ask the player to sit so that the bell of the instrument was laid against the surface of the desk, which acted as a sort of mute, while the alto and tenor trombonists stood up to play. Only in this way could all three parts be heard. Having made repeated observations of the kind in Berlin, I now believe that the best solution in the opera house is after all the solution adopted at the Paris Opéra, which is to use three tenor trombones. The tone of the small, alto trombone is thin and its high notes are poor; I would vote to exclude it too from theatre orchestras. The bass trombone I would use only when the trombones are in four parts and there are three tenors capable of standing up to it.

If my words are not golden, at least you will grant they are rich in brass. But I feel confident that all this technical stuff about instruments will interest you far more than my misanthropic tirades and death's head tales. You are melodist and harmonist but not, so far as I am aware, a student of osteology. So I will continue my survey of the musical resources of the Berlin Opera.

The timpanist is a good musician but his wrists lack suppleness; his rolls are not sufficiently rapid. In addition, the drums he plays are too small; their tone is feeble, and he is familiar with only one sort of stick, an ineffective kind half-way between our leather-headed sticks and the sponge-headed variety. In this respect the Germans as a whole are far behind the French. Even as regards technique, with the exception of Wiprecht, the director of military bands in Berlin who plays the drums with the force of a thunderclap, I heard no player to compare in point of precision, rapidity of roll and delicacy of nuance with Poussard, the admirable timpanist at the Paris Opéra. Should I also mention the cymbals? Yes, if only to tell you that a whole and unblemished pair, neither cracked nor chipped, is extremely rare; I did not find one in Weimar, Leipzig, Dresden, Hamburg or Berlin. This always made me very angry, and I have kept an orchestra waiting half an hour and refused to start the rehearsal until they brought me two brand-new cymbals, suitably vibrant and Turkish, to show the kapellmeister whether I was wrong to object so strongly to the ludicrous fragments of broken plate offered to me under that name. There is no denying that certain parts of the orchestra are still maintained at a shockingly low standard in Germany. They do not seem to realize what can be done with them and what is done in other places; the actual instruments are poor and the players have no conception of their full possibilities. This is true of timpani, cymbals and even bass drum, as well as of cor anglais, ophicleide and harp. But the real responsibility lies with the composers and their style of writing. By never demanding anything of significance from these instruments they make it almost impossible for their successors who write in a different style to achieve anything with them.

We, on the other hand, have no conception how far superior the Germans are to us in brass instruments, especially trumpets. Their clarinets too are better than ours, but not their oboes: here, I think, there is nothing to choose between the two schools. In flutes we surpass them; nowhere do you hear the flute played as it is in Paris. Their double basses are more powerful, but their cellos, violas and violins, though splendid, are not seriously to be ranked with our younger school of string players; the violins, violas and cellos of the Paris Conservatoire Orchestra have no rivals. I think I have sufficiently proved the scarcity of good harps in Germany. Those of Berlin are no exception to the general rule; the city is in dire need of a few Parish-Alvars pupils. This magnificent orchestra, so remarkable for its precision, ensemble, vigour and refinement, is under the command of Meyerbeer, director-general of music to the King of Prussia, composer and—but I believe you know him. He is assisted by Henning, first kapellmeister, an able man, whose qualities are much admired among artists, and by the assistant kapellmeister, Taubert, a brilliant pianist and composer; I heard a trio of his performed by him and the brothers Ganz, an admirably written piece, original in style and full of vitality. Taubert has recently composed and successfully performed some choruses for a production of the Greek tragedy *Medea* in Berlin.

The office and title of leader of the orchestra are shared between Messrs Ganz and Ries.

Now let us go up onto the stage.

The chorus, for ordinary performances, is made up of only sixty singers; but when they give grand opera in the presence of the King it is doubled by the addition of another sixty from outside. All have excellent voices, fresh and resonant. Most of them, men, women and children, are musicians; not such quick readers as the choristers at the Paris Opéra, perhaps, but much more highly trained in the art of singing, more alert and conscientious, and better paid. It is the finest theatre chorus I have ever heard. The director is Eissler, brother of the famous dancer. This clever and painstaking artist would save himself a good deal of trouble and find that the chorus parts were learnt more quickly if, instead of taking all hundred and twenty singers together in the same hall, he divided them to begin with into three groups—sopranos and altos, tenors, basses—and had them rehearse separately and simultaneously in three different rooms under three assistant conductors chosen and supervised by himself. Opera houses may refuse to adopt it, for low reasons of economy and ingrained routine, but this sectional method is the only one that enables each part to be learnt really thoroughly and sung with the requisite precision and subtlety of expression. I have said it before and I shall go on saying it.

The Berlin actor-singers do not have the same high position in the European hierarchy as the chorus and the orchestra have achieved in their respective Fields. None the less the company contains some notable talents, among whom I would single out the following:

Mlle Marx, soprano; attractive and expressive voice, regrettably already beginning to show signs of wear at the top and bottom of its range.

Mlle Tutchek, soprano; light and flexible voice, reasonably pure in quality.

Mlle Hähnel, contralto; full of character.

Boeticher, bass; first-rate, of large range and splendid quality; accomplished singer, fine actor, admirable musician and reader.

Zsische, basso cantante; a genuine talent—voice and style appear to be even more suited to the concert platform than to the opera house.

Mantius, first tenor; voice a little lacking in flexibility and of limited range.

Madame Schroeder-Devrient, soprano (joined the company only a few months ago); upper register threadbare, voice somewhat unwieldy, but powerful and dramatic; now sings flat when not able to attack the note vigorously; her ornaments in very poor taste and her vocal line interlarded with spoken words and phrases in the manner of vaudeville singers, with execrable effect, the whole amounting to an anti-musical style of singing and an awful example for students to guard against.

I am told that Pischek, the excellent baritone whom I mentioned in connection with the Frankfurt opera, has just been engaged by Meyerbeer. The Berlin management should be congratulated on a valuable acquisition.

There, Mademoiselle, is all I know about the resources at the disposal of dramatic music in Berlin. As I did not hear a single performance at the Italian Opera I shall refrain from speaking of it.

In a subsequent letter, before giving an account of my concerts, I must marshal my impressions of the performances of *Armide* and *The Huguenots* which I attended, and also describe the choral society and the military bands—two quite different institutions, both of first-rate importance and both of such splendour beside anything we possess in the same line that one's national pride can only feel humiliated by the comparison.

Eighth Letter

Berlin (continued)

TO HABENECK

I lately gave Mlle Louise Bertin (whose knowledge of music and devotion to art you are familiar with) an account of the riches, vocal and instrumental, of the Berlin Grand Opera. I should now go on to speak of the choral society and the military bands; but as you are particularly keen to hear what I thought of the performances I attended, I am transposing the order of my narrative so as to tell you about the work of the Prussian artists as I saw it displayed in operas by Meyerbeer, Gluck, Mozart and Weber.

In Berlin, unhappily, as in Paris and everywhere else, there are days when there seems to be a kind of tacit agreement between artists and public that the performance shall be in greater or lesser degree trifling and perfunctory. Many seats in the house are empty and many desks in the orchestra unoccupied. These are the nights when the leading singers dine out, give balls, go shooting, etc. The musicians, half asleep, merely play the notes. One or two do not even do that; they snooze, read, draw caricatures, indulge in crude tricks at the expense of their neighbours, chat to each other in normal voices—but I don't need to tell you what goes on in an orchestra on those occasions.

The actors are too exposed to take such liberties (though even that can sometimes happen), but the chorus really let themselves go. They come on sporadically, in twos and threes. Some, having arrived late at the theatre, are not yet in costume; a few, who have been on duty in church during the day, shuffle on exhausted, determined not to sing a note. Everyone relaxes. High notes are put down an octave or 'marked'. All expression disappears; a steady mezzo forte is established for the evening. No one looks at the conductor's beat, and as a result there are several wrong entries and as many ragged phrases. What does it matter? The public never notices. The director knows nothing about it. If the composer complains he is laughed at and waved aside as an interfering busybody. The ladies have a particularly delightful time, keeping up a constant exchange of semaphored messages with members of the orchestra or with the regulars in the circle. This morning they went to see their colleague Mlle ——'s baby christened. One of them has brought back some sugared almonds, and as they munch they have a good laugh and chatter away about the godfather's ridiculous expression, the affected behaviour of the godmother, and the curé's beaming face—administering a few clouts the while to the chorus-boys, who are getting above themselves.

'Any more of that, you little beggar, and I'll tell the chorus-master.'

'Do look, dear—the lovely rose M——'s got in his buttonhole. Florence gave it to him.'

'So she's still mad about her advocate?'

'Yes, only it's a secret. We can't all have solicitors.'

'Oh, what a clever pun! Are you going to the court concert?'

'No, I've something on that day.'

'What?'

'I'm getting married.'

'Well, whatever next?'

'Look out, here's the curtain.'

And the act is duly brought to an end, the public imposed on, and the work ruined. Well, what of it? One must relax sometimes, we cannot always be sublime; and these slovenly performances serve to emphasize more vividly the performances which are the product of skill, enthusiasm and application. I don't dispute it; but you will admit that there is something melancholy in the spectacle of a great work treated with such gross familiarity. Granted that no one burns incense night and day before the images of the masters; but wouldn't it anger you to see a bust of Beethoven or Gluck used for a barber's block?

However, I mustn't start philosophizing; that, I know, would really annoy you.

I do not wish to imply that they unbutton to quite the same extent at the Berlin Opera; they go about it with greater restraint. In this field, as in one or two others, we are supreme. The Prussians would never go so far as to get up a masterpiece in the negligent style that is sometimes seen in Paris. *Figaro* and *Freischütz*, when I saw them, were in nothing worse than informal dress. It was not positively bad. Neither was it good. There was a certain slackness in ensemble, a certain blurring of outline, a modified vivacity, a grudging warmth; it merely wanted the colour and animation which show that a performance is alive, and that abundance, that amplitude without which good music cannot truly exist; above all, the breath of inspiration.

When it came to *Armide* and *The Huguenots* the transformation was complete. I felt as though I were at one of those first nights in Paris when you arrive early so as to have time to glance round your forces and give your final instructions, and everyone is at his post beforehand, every mind keyed up, every face alert with a grave and lively concentration—in short, all the signs of a momentous musical event about to come to fruition.

Chorus and orchestra were at full strength—a hundred and twenty voices, twenty-eight violins, double wind—and Meyerbeer in command at the first desk. I was eager to see him conduct, especially to see him conduct his own work. He does it as a man would a job he has been doing for twenty years; he holds the orchestra in the hollow of his hand and does with it as he pleases. As for his tempos, they are the same as yours, except that the entry of the monks in the fourth act and the march at the end of the third are both a little slower. I thought the more deliberate pace took something of the life out of the monks' music but was a clear gain in the case of the march—which, by the way, is played by the military band on the stage.

It is not possible for me to analyse the orchestral playing scene by scene. I can only say that from beginning to end I found it superb in its beauty and refinement and incomparably lucid and precise even in the most intricate passages. The finale of the second act, for example, with its stream of scales over a series of diminished sevenths and its enharmonic modulations, was done with flawless intonation and with a clarity of detail which extended to the obscurest subsidiary part. The choir was equally remarkable. The rapid runs, the antiphonal double choruses, the entries in imitation, the sudden transitions from forte to piano and all the gradations in between—everything was punctiliously and energetically rendered, with an uncommon warmth of feeling and a sense of dramatic expression that is even rarer. The stretto in the Blessing of the Daggers was an overwhelming moment; it was some time before I recovered from it. The richness of texture in the Pré-aux-Clercs scene, with the women quarrelling, the Catholics intoning the prayer to the Virgin, and the Huguenot soldiers bawling out the Rataplan, was extraordinary, yet the ear could follow it with such ease that every strand in the composer's complex thought was continually apparent—a marvel of dramatic counterpoint realized by the finest choral singing I have heard. I do not believe Meyerbeer could find better anywhere else in Europe. I should add that the staging has been most ingeniously devised. In the Rataplan the chorus mime a kind of drum march, stepping backwards and forwards, which enlivens the scene and enhances the effect of the music.

The military band, instead of being placed, as it is in Paris, at the back of the stage—in which position the immense throng of people prevents it from following the conductor's beat—begins playing in the wings at the front of the stage to the audience's right, then proceeds across the stage, passing close to the footlights through the groups of choristers. In this way the players remain in close touch with the conductor almost to the end of the piece and there is no discrepancy in tempo and rhythm between the two sources of sound.

Boeticher is an excellent Saint-Bris, and Zsische a very capable Marcel without possessing that gift of dramatic humour which makes our Levasseur so distinctive and convincing in the part. Mlle Marx plays Valentine sensitively and with a certain quiet dignity, qualities fundamental to the character; but I have to reproach her for two or three spoken monosyllables wantonly inserted after the manner of Madame Devrient. I saw the latter as Valentine a few days later, and since my vigorous and unconcealed objections to her style of playing the role astonished and even shocked several highly intelligent persons who, no doubt from sheer force of habit, admired the celebrated artist without reservation, I must here state my reasons for so radically disagreeing with them. I had no bias nor predisposition for or against Madame Devrient. I remembered only that I thought her admirable in Beethoven's *Fidelio* in Paris many years ago, whereas in Dresden recently I had noticed some very bad habits in her singing and a tendency to overemphasis and affectation in her acting. In *The Huguenots* I found these defects all the more striking because the dramatic situations are more vivid and the music correspondingly grander and truer. I therefore criticized the singer and the actress, on the following grounds. In the conjuration scene Valentine, though horrified when her father reveals to Nevers and his friends his plan to massacre the Huguenots, is careful not to show her feelings, Saint-Bris being hardly the man to tolerate such an attitude in his daughter. Thus her sudden involuntary gesture towards her husband, Nevers, the instant he breaks his sword and refuses to have anything to do with the conspiracy, is a fine dramatic stroke which depends for its effect on the timid woman having until then suffered her agonies of spirit in silence. Madame Devrient, instead of concealing her agitation and remaining to all appearances impassive, as sense clearly requires in such a scene, seizes hold of Nevers and drags him to the back of the stage where, pacing masterfully at his side, she appears to be dictating his plan of action and instructing him as to how he shall answer Saint-Bris. Consequently Nevers' exclamation, 'I count soldiers among my proud ancestors but never a murderer,' loses all its merit as an impulse of bold opposition; the gesture ceases to be spontaneous, Nevers having the air of a submissive husband dutifully repeating what his wife has told him. When Saint-Bris delivers the famous theme 'A cette cause sainte', Madame Devrient actually forgets herself so far as to spring into his arms (although Saint-Bris is supposed to be still unaware of his daughter's feelings) and importune him with a dumb show of such vehemence that Boeticher, visibly taken aback by this unseasonable outburst, the first time it occurred, and hard put to preserve freedom of wind and limb, executed frantic movements with his head and right arm, as though to say, 'For God's sake leave me be, woman, and allow me to sing my role to the end.' The incident demonstrates the extent to which Madame Devrient has succumbed to the demon of personality; she would consider herself to have failed if she did not monopolize the attention of the house, rightly or wrongly and by whatever piece of stage business, in every scene she appears in. Her whole manner suggests that she sees herself as the focus of the drama, the only character with whom the audience need concern itself. 'What? Listening to that fellow? Admiring the composer? Interested in that chorus? How can you be so misguided? Look over here, this is what you should be attending to. I am the libretto, I am the poetry, I am the music. The one object of interest this evening is me. The sole reason for your coming to the theatre is me!' During the tremendous duet which follows this great scene, while Raoul abandons himself to the frenzy of his despair, Madame Devrient rests her hands decorously on a settee and inclines her head to the left so as to let her fine blond hair fall free. She sings a phrase or two and then, while Raoul replies, changes her pose, to allow the audience to admire the soft glow and play of her ringlets from a different angle. I take leave to question whether it is with such considerations of coquettish personal vanity that Valentine's mind is occupied at that moment.

Her singing, as I have said, is often wanting in accuracy of intonation and taste. The cadenzas and the numerous alterations which she now inserts into her roles are in poor style and clumsily managed. But her spoken interjections are in a class apart. Madame Devrient never *sings* the words, 'Dieu! o mon Dieu! oui! non! est-il vrai? est-il possible?' etc. She speaks the whole passage, or rather shouts it at the top of her voice. I cannot attempt to do justice to what I feel on the subject of this anti-musical style of declamation. I would far rather hear tragedy sung than opera spoken.

There is no suggestion that the notes marked *canto parlato* in certain scores are meant to be roared out by the singer in this way. In serious dramatic music, at least, they demand a quality of voice which preserves the pitch of the note, that is, remains within the sphere of music. No one who ever heard it can have forgotten the effect that Mlle Falcon used to produce at the end of the duet with the words 'Raoul, ils te tueront!' delivered in a *canto parlato* that was at once natural and musical.

When, on the contrary, Madame Devrient, in response to Raoul's entreaties, breaks into speech and shouts out three times, 'Nein! Nein! Nein!' with increasing force and vehemence, I am reminded of Madame Dorval or Mlle Georges in some melodrama, and for a moment wonder that the orchestra should still be playing since the opera has come to an end. The effect is grotesque. I was so indignant at seeing a masterpiece like the fourth act disfigured in this fashion that I did not stay to hear the fifth. Am I wrong in believing you would have done the same, my dear Habeneck? I know how you react to music. When the performance of a fine work is uniformly bad you put a stoical face on it; the worse it is, the more heroic your fortitude. But when everything is going perfectly with one solitary exception, this exception irks and jars and frets you until you are seized by a kind of cold fury in which you would watch not merely with composure but with deep satisfaction the annihilation of the individual in question, and while the bourgeois marvel at your rage all true artists share it, and I grind my teeth in sympathy.

Madame Devrient undoubtedly possesses striking qualities. She has fire and energy. But even supposing these qualities enough by themselves, she does not always succeed in containing them within the natural limits of the roles she plays. For example, Valentine: quite apart from the above criticisms, the character of this noble-hearted but reticent young bride, who admits her chaste and secret love to Raoul solely in order to save his life, is better served by restrained passion, disciplined acting and expressive singing than by all Madame Devrient's powerful broadsides and demonic egoism.

A few days later I saw a performance of *Armide*. The revival of this famous work had been undertaken with due care and respect; the staging was magnificent; and the public showed itself worthy of the compliment. Of all the old masters it is Gluck—as I see it—whose greatness has least to fear from the constant revolutions of art. He never made concessions to singers and their whims or to the tyrannies of fashion or to those deeply entrenched habits of mind that he had to contend with when he arrived in France, still weary from his struggles with equally reactionary forces in the Italian theatre. The war against the *dilettanti* of Milan, Naples and Parma, instead of weakening him, must have actually given him fresh strength by making him fully conscious of his powers; for despite all our bigotry in artistic matters at that time, he crushed the obstacles in his path and trampled them underfoot with almost contemptuous ease. Once only did he allow the critics' bleatings to sting him to a reply.* This outburst of anger was the sole imprudence with which he could reproach himself. Thereafter, as before, he moved silently and undeviatingly towards his goal. What that goal was, and whether it has ever been given to any man to attain it more fully, you know. With less steadfastness or less conviction it is likely that with all his natural gifts his works, thus debased, would not have long survived his mediocre rivals', now so totally forgotten. But truth of expression and the purity of style and grandeur of form which follow from it are for all time. The fine things in Gluck will always remain so. As Victor Hugo has said, 'the heart knows no wrinkles'.†

* [*Journal de Paris*, 12 October 1777: a reply to La Harpe's criticism of *Armide*.]
† [*Hernani*, Act III scene I.]

I thought Mlle Marx noble and impassioned as Armide but at the same time a trifle overburdened by her epic responsibilities. To play Gluck's heroines it is not enough to have genuine talent. As with Shakespeare's, such exceptional qualities of soul, heart, voice, physiognomy and movement are involved that nothing less than beauty and genius will do.

I spent a blissful evening at that performance of *Armide*, which Meyerbeer conducted. Orchestra and chorus, fired by the double inspiration of composer and conductor, did not fail either of them. The famous finale, 'Poursuivons jusqu'au trépas', was positively explosive; but I thought the Hatred scene, with admirable dances devised (I think) by Paul Taglioni, ballet master of the Berlin Grand Opera,* equally remarkable, full of sinuous animation, at first sight shapeless but woven into an intricate pattern, a dark, diabolical order and symmetry. In this act they cut the A major ballet music in six-eight which we include, and instead restored the great B flat Chaconne (never heard in Paris)—an extended movement, vivid and passionate. What a conception this whole act is! I had never understood or admired it so deeply. That wonderful passage in the invocation:

Sauvez-moi de l'amour,
Rien n'est si redoutable!

made me shudder. At the end of the first half-line the oboes sound a harsh dissonance of a major seventh—a woman's cry, instinct with fear and anguish. But in the next line:

Contre un ennemi trop aimable

how tenderly do those same two voices languish and sigh in thirds! How much regret is in those few notes, and how one senses that a love thus regretted will prove too strong! And so it does, for hardly have Hatred and her hideous crew begun their work than Armide interrupts them and rejects their aid. There follows the chorus:

Suis l'amour, puisque tu le veux,
Infortunée Armide,
Suis l'amour qui te guide
Dans un abîme affreux!

* [Brother of the famous dancer Marie Taglioni.]

In Quinault's poem the act ends there; Armide, without another word, goes out with the chorus. To Gluck this made for a crude and implausible ending. He wanted the enchantress to be left for a moment and then to go out alone, musing on what she has just heard; and one day at the Opéra after a rehearsal he improvised the scene, both words and music. The text is:

O ciel! quelle horrible menace!
Je frémis! tout mon sang se glace!
Amour, puissant amour, viens calmer mon effroi,
Et prends pitié d'un coeur qui s'abandonne à toi!

The music is beautiful—melodically and harmonically and in its sense of sweet languor and vague disquiet—as only a masterpiece of dramatic and musical inspiration can be. In the first two lines, after each exclamation, while the second violins play a kind of intermittent tremolo, the cellos unfold a long chromatic phrase like a warning voice, with a hint of menace in it; until, at the beginning of the third line, at the word 'Amour', a ravishing melody, grave, tender, lucid, sensuous, steals in, dispelling the shadows of the previous bars. Then it fades into silence, and Armide moves away, her eyes fixed on the ground, while the second violins (the rest of the orchestra having ceased) continue their soft, almost imperceptible pulsations. Immense the genius that created such a scene!

But here I am, naïvely treating you to a rhapsodical analysis of Gluck's score as if I were initiating you, Habeneck, into its beauties! Forgive me: I could not help myself. I feel I am talking to you now as we sometimes do in the street after a Conservatoire concert, when our enthusiasm simply has to find an outlet.

I have one criticism to make of the Berlin staging of this scene: the stage manager brings the curtain down too soon. He should wait until after the last bar of the music. Otherwise we do not see Armide moving slowly away up the whole length of the stage as the sighings and flutterings in the orchestra grow fainter and fainter. (The effect was very fine at the Paris Opéra when *Armide* used to be performed there; the curtain was not lowered at all.) On the other hand, although I am as you know no great believer in the conductor's altering music not his own—his business being simply to secure a good performance—I must compliment Meyerbeer on his happy idea with regard to the aforesaid tremolo passage on the low D. To bring it out he has it played on two strings in unison, open D and D on the G string. This of course gives the impression that the number of second violins has suddenly been doubled; at the same time the two strings combined produce a particular resonance which is most effective in the context. So long as it is only a question of this sort of correction being made to Gluck, one may legitimately approve.* It is like your idea of having the famous tremolo in the oracle scene in *Alceste* played close to the bridge, flattening the string: Gluck did not actually specify it but he *must* have meant it.

But for sheer beauty and subtlety of expression nothing equalled the scenes in the Garden of Delights. A gliding, voluptuous languor, a kind of hypnotic ease, seemed to waft me inside the enchanted palace of love (dream picture of two poets, Gluck and Tasso) and to offer it to me for my own. I closed my eyes and let that divine gavotte lap over me with its caressing melody and the hum of its soft, unchanging harmonies, and heard the chorus murmuring of endless felicity: 'Jamais dans ces beaux lieux'; and as I listened saw around me arms coiled in seductive arms, delicious feet entwined, the ripple of perfumed hair, and everywhere bewitching smiles and the gleam of sparkling eyes. Pleasure seemed to open like a flower at the soft insistence of the music, loosing a stream of harmonious sounds and scents and colours from its luxuriant corolla. And Gluck wrote this: Gluck—the mighty composer who sang the griefs of mankind and made Tartarus roar and evoked the harsh shores of Tauris and the savagery of its inhabitants—found music to catch this vision of an ideal sensuality, a love without care! Why not? Was it not he

* Indeed one may *not*. I should not have written that. Gluck knew the effect of two strings in unison quite as well as Meyerbeer and, if he did not wish to use it, it is not for anyone else to do it for him. Meyerbeer, as a matter of fact, introduced other effects into *Armide* which cannot be too strongly deplored, such as the use of trombones in the duet 'Esprits de haine et de rage'—an unbelievable blunder. Spontini mentioned them to me one day and reproved me for not having pointed them out. Yet he himself added certain wind instruments to the score of *Iphigénie en Tauride*—a lapse that he had evidently forgotten when he exclaimed, on another occasion: 'It's appalling! Shall I too be reorchestrated when I am dead?'

who unlocked the gates of the Elysian Fields and wrote the immortal strains of the chorus of the blessed spirits:

Torna, o bella, al tuo consorte
Che non vuol che più diviso,
Sia da te pietoso il ciel!

And, as our great modern poet has also said, is it not the strong that are generally the most gentle? *

But I see that in the enjoyment of talking with you about all these delights I have gone on too long and have no room left to tell you about the other musical institutions, not connected with the theatre, which flourish in Berlin. They must be the subject of a further letter. They will give me a pretext for boring someone else with my inexhaustible garrulity.

You don't hold this one against me, do you? In any case, goodbye!

Ninth Letter

Berlin (concluded)

TO M. DESMAREST†

Were I to describe in detail all the musical riches of the royal city of Berlin I should never have done with it. Few if any capitals can boast comparable resources. Music is part of the air you breathe; you absorb it through the very pores of your skin. One meets it everywhere, in concert hall, church, theatre, in the streets, in the public gardens, everywhere: strong, proud, vigorous, youthful, noble, like an angel in dazzling armour deigning to walk the earth but with wings quivering to take flight again towards heaven.

For music is universally respected in Berlin. Rich and poor, professional and amateur, clergy and army, people and king, hold it in equal veneration. The King‡ in particular worships it with the

* [I have failed to identify this allusion to Victor Hugo.]
† [One of the leading French cellists of the mid-nineteenth century.]
‡ [Frederick William IV. He reigned from 1840 to 1861.]

same genuine passion that he shows for science and for the other arts, which is saying a great deal. He follows with a lively curiosity the forward march, or rather the sudden leaps and lunges, of modern music without neglecting the preservation of the great works of the past. He has a prodigious memory; this can be embarrassing for his kapellmeisters when he suddenly asks for the performance of a piece by some forgotten old master. Nothing escapes him, old or new; he wants to hear everything and explore everything. Hence the attraction of Berlin for leading artists and the extraordinary prestige of music in Prussia; and hence the great choral and instrumental institutions of its capital which so impressed me.

One of these is the Choral Society. Like its equivalent in Leipzig and like all similar societies throughout Germany it is made up almost entirely of amateurs; but several artists from the theatres belong to it, and fashionable women see no objection to singing a Bach oratorio next to Mantius, Boeticher or Mlle Hähnel. Most of the members of the Berlin Choral Society are competent musicians and nearly all have fresh strong voices; I thought the sopranos and the basses particularly good. They rehearse long and thoroughly under the able direction of M. Rungenhagen. In consequence the results, when a great work is performed, are magnificent and far beyond anything we ever hear in Paris.

When I went to hear them, at the invitation of their director, they were performing Sebastian Bach's Passion.* This famous work, which you have no doubt looked at, is written for double chorus and double orchestra. The singers—at least three hundred in number—were arranged in tiers on a huge amphitheatre exactly like the one in the chemistry lecture-hall at the Jardin des Plantes, the two choruses being separated by a space of only three or four feet. The two orchestras, both small, occupied the top tiers, accompanying the voices from behind, and were consequently some distance from the conductor who was stationed at the bottom, next to the piano. I say piano, but harpsichord would be a better name, for it hardly differed in tone from the wretched instruments used in Bach's time. Whether such a choice is made

* [The *St Matthew.*]

deliberately I cannot say; but I observed that in practice halls, theatre rehearsal rooms, wherever voices have to be accompanied, the piano is invariably quite the worst that can be procured. The only exception was the piano used by Mendelssohn in the Gewandhaus in Leipzig.

You will ask me what a piano/harpsichord can have to do during the actual performance of a work in which the composer has not employed the instrument.* It plays the accompaniment with the strings, flutes and oboes, and probably serves to keep the front rows of the chorus in tune, the assumption being that they are too far from the orchestra to hear it well in the tuttis. At any rate it is the custom. The constant jangling of the chords from this villainous keyboard has a most depressing effect, laying an unnecessary veneer of monotony over the whole texture; but that is no doubt all the more reason for not getting rid of it. Tradition is so sacred when it is bad!

The chorus sit when they are not singing and get up just before their entries. I am sure there is a genuine advantage from the point of view of good vocal production in singing standing up. It is merely unfortunate that they give way so readily to fatigue that they are obliged to sit down again the moment a particular passage is finished; for it means that in a work such as Bach's, where the two choirs, in addition to engaging in frequent dialogue with one another, are constantly cut short by solo recitatives, there always seems to be one group getting up or another sitting down, and in the long run these eternal risings and subsidings take on an air of absurdity—quite apart from the fact that certain choral entries lose their unexpectedness when one can, so to speak, see them coming. For myself I would rather have the chorus seated throughout if they cannot remain standing. This kind of obstacle disappears miraculously, however, when the director is a man who insists on getting what he wants.

For all that, I was impressed by the performance of this great body of voices. The first tutti of the two choirs took my breath away; I was quite unprepared for such a burst of sound. Yet it cannot be denied that such sonority, with all its splendour, palls

* [The keyboard continuo part is for organ.]

much more quickly than that of an orchestra, choral timbre being naturally less varied than instrumental, with only about four distinct types of voice as against more than thirty different kinds of instrument.

I imagine, my dear Desmarest, that you will not expect me to give an analysis of Bach's great work. Such a task would far exceed the limits I have had to set myself. In any case the extract performed at the Conservatoire three years ago may be considered as representative of the composer's style in this work.* The Germans profess boundless admiration for his recitatives, but their distinctiveness was necessarily lost on me since, not understanding the language in which they are set, I could not appreciate their expressive qualities.

For the visitor from Paris, accustomed to the way we do things there, the reverence with which a German audience listens to such a work has to be seen to be believed. Each person follows from a copy of the text; not a movement anywhere, no whisper of approval or criticism, no applause. One is not at a concert but at divine service; one is in church, hearing the Evangelist—which is really how this music ought to be listened to. They believe in Bach, they worship him. It never for a moment occurs to them that his divinity could be questioned. A heretic would horrify them; the very idea is unthinkable. God is God and Bach is Bach.

A few days after the performance of Bach's masterpiece the Choral Society announced Graun's *Death of Jesus*.† This is another piece of holy writ; but the faithful are mainly to be found in Berlin, whereas the religion of Sebastian Bach is professed all over North Germany. You can imagine how interested I was in this second evening, especially after the impression made on me by the first, and how delighted I would have been to hear the favourite work of the great Frederick's kapellmeister. Behold my misfortune! On the day of the performance I fell ill. My doctor (the able and charming Dr Gaspard), keen amateur of music though he was, absolutely forbade me to leave my room. Later, I was urged to

* [The tenor aria with oboe obbligato and chorus, 'Ich will bei meinem Jesu wachen', given at the concert of 12 January 1840.]

† [Graun's *Der Tod Jesu* (1755) was performed annually in Berlin during Passion Week until late in the nineteenth century.]

come and admire a famous organist, but in vain: the doctor was inexorable, and it was not until Holy Week was at an end, and there were no more oratorios, fugues, or chorales, that the good Lord restored me to health. That and none other is the reason for my silence on the subject of Berlin church music, which is said to be so remarkable. If I ever go back to Prussia, well or not I shall hear Graun's music, and you may rest assured that I will, even if it kills me—though in that case too I wouldn't be able to tell you about it. . . . Well, it seems clear you will never hear of it from me, so you must go there yourself; then you will have the pleasure of telling me.

To turn to the military bands: here one would have to be exceedingly cross-grained to avoid hearing any, for they parade about the streets at all hours of the day, on foot or on horseback. Not that these small independent troupes give one any idea of the majesty of the great armies which the trainer-director of the Berlin and Potsdam military bands, Wiprecht, can mobilize whenever he wishes. Think of it: he has a corps of more than six hundred players under his command (not so much regimental musicians as musical regiments), all good readers, masters of their instruments, playing in tune, and blessed by nature with lips of leather and indefatigable lungs; hence the ease with which the trumpets, horns and cornets produce high notes that our players cannot reach at all. The Crown Prince,* anticipating my desire to hear his forces in action and to study them at close quarters, graciously invited me to a matinée arranged in my honour at his palace and gave Wiprecht orders accordingly.

The audience was tiny: ten or fifteen at the most. I was wondering where the orchestra had got to—for no sound betrayed its presence—when a measured phrase in F minor that you and I know well made me turn my head in the direction of the main hall of the palace, which a large curtain concealed from view. His Royal Highness had had the courtesy to begin the concert with the *Francs-juges* overture. I had never heard it arranged for wind instruments. There were three hundred and twenty of them. Under Wiprecht's direction they performed this difficult piece

* [The future King William I of Prussia and Emperor of Germany.]

with superb precision and with that same furious gusto which you Conservatoire players display in it on days of special enthusiasm.

The brass passage in the introduction was tremendous, intoned by fifteen bass trombones, eighteen or twenty tenors and altos, twelve bass tubas and a swarm of trumpets.

The bass tuba, which I have mentioned several times in previous letters, has completely dislodged the ophicleide in Prussia, if indeed the latter was ever prevalent there, which I doubt. It is a large brass instrument derived from the bombardon and fitted with a mechanism of five rotary valves which gives it an enormous range in the lower register.

The lowest notes of all are a little blurred, it is true; but when doubled an octave higher by another bass tuba, they take on amazing richness and resonance; and in the middle and upper registers the tone is impressively noble and not at all dull like the ophicleide's but full and vibrant and well matched with the timbre of trombones and trumpets, to which it serves as a true bass, blending perfectly with them. Wiprecht is the man who popularized the instrument in Prussia. Adolphe Sax now makes admirable tubas in Paris.

The clarinets, I thought, were as good as the brass. They were particularly imposing in a battle symphony for double wind band written by the English Ambassador, the Earl of Westmorland.

After that came a splendidly showy piece for brass instruments alone, composed by Meyerbeer for use at court festivities under the title of Torchlight Dance, in the course of which eighteen trumpets sustained a trill on D for sixteen bars, executing it with the rapidity of clarinets.

The concert concluded with an impressive and admirably written funeral march by Wiprecht. And for all this they had had only one rehearsal!

During the intervals in the music, while this prodigious band paused for breath, I had the privilege of exchanging a few words with the Crown Princess of Prussia,* a woman whose rare taste and knowledge of composition make her good opinion very

* [Augusta of Saxe-Weimar-Eisenach, wife of Crown Prince William and future Empress of Germany.]

precious. Her Royal Highness, besides, speaks our language with a purity and elegance that made me feel positively nervous conversing with her. I wish I could attempt a Shakespearean portrait of the Princess, or even convey to you a vague idea of her delicate beauty. But one would need to be a great poet.

I attended one of the court concerts. Meyerbeer was at the piano (there was no orchestra); the singers were members of the opera company—the same that I have already mentioned. Towards the end of the evening Meyerbeer, fine pianist though he is—or perhaps because of it—grew tired, and made way for—can you guess whom?—the King's head chamberlain, Count Redern, who accompanied Madame Devrient in Schubert's 'Erl-King' with the greatest technical and artistic assurance! Proof, if you like, of an astounding pervasiveness of musical culture. The count, it may be added, has other accomplishments, as he brilliantly demonstrated last winter when he organized the famous masked ball on the theme of 'The Court of Ferrara' which was the talk of Berlin. Meyerbeer wrote a whole host of pieces for the event.

There is always something frigid and unreal about these formal concerts, but one enjoys them once they are over, as the audience usually contains one or two people with whom it is an honour and a pleasure to have a few moments' conversation. Thus at the King of Prussia's soirée I renewed acquaintance with that great ornament of scientific scholarship and anatomist of the terrestrial globe, Alexander von Humboldt.

Several times during the evening the King and Queen and the Crown Princess came and talked to me about the concert I had just given at the Grand Theatre, asking my opinion of the leading Prussian artists, questioning me about my methods of instrumentation and so on. The King claimed that I had put a demon into every member of his orchestra. After supper His Majesty was about to return to his apartments when, as if on a sudden impulse, he turned to me and said, 'By the way, M. Berlioz, what are you giving us at your next concert?'

'Sire, I shall repeat half the previous programme and add five pieces from my *Romeo and Juliet* symphony.'

'*Romeo and Juliet*—and I am going away! We must hear that. I shall come back.'

And sure enough, five minutes before the concert was due to begin, the King alighted from his carriage and a moment later entered the royal box.

Now I suppose I must give you an account of these two evenings. They caused me great trouble, I can tell you. And yet the performers were skilled artists full of good will towards me, and Meyerbeer did everything possible and more to help. The fact is that the day-to-day responsibilities of a great theatre like the Berlin Opera are so demanding as to be incompatible with concert-giving, and without doubt it cost Meyerbeer greater energy and ingenuity to surmount or circumvent the difficulties that were constantly arising than he required to put on *The Huguenots* for the first time. Then I was determined that Berlin should hear the big pieces from the Requiem, those from the Sequence (Dies irae, Lacrymosa, etc.), which I had not been able to tackle anywhere else in Germany; and you know what vocal and instrumental equipment they involve. Fortunately I had forewarned Meyerbeer and he had already begun his search for the necessary forces before I arrived. The four little brass orchestras were easy to come by: we could have had thirty if we had wanted them; but finding the drums and the men to play them was a problem. Eventually both were mustered with the help of the excellent Wiprecht.

For the early orchestral rehearsals we were put in a concert hall attached to the second theatre—a splendid-looking place but so excessively resonant that the moment I entered I saw we were in for trouble. Everything was a blur, and we found it exceedingly difficult to rehearse. One piece, the scherzo from *Romeo and Juliet*, had to be abandoned; after an hour's work we were half-way through it. Yet the orchestra, as I have said, was absolutely first-rate. Time being short, however, the scherzo was put off until the second concert. In the end I hardened myself to the hubbub and learnt to detect whether a passage was well or badly played, and we stuck heroically to our work without worrying what it sounded like. I am happy to say that it sounded very different in the Opera. The overture to *Benvenuto*, *Harold*, Weber's 'Invitation to the Waltz', and the pieces from the Requiem were duly mastered by the orchestra, the choir meanwhile rehearsing separately in another place.

At the special session that I had called for the four brass bands which play in the Dies irae and Lacrymosa I observed for the third time a phenomenon which I have never been able to account for. In the middle of the Tuba mirum there is a fanfare for the four groups of trombones on the four notes of the chord of G major. The first group sounds G on the first beat, the second group B on the second, the third D on the third, the fourth the octave G on the fourth, at a broad and measured tempo. A simpler sequence of notes could not be conceived, and nothing could be easier to play than each of them individually. Yet when the Requiem was performed for the first time in Paris at the church of the Invalides it was impossible to get the passage right. Later, when I gave parts of the work at the Opéra, I spent a quarter of an hour fruitlessly rehearsing this one bar and finally gave up the struggle; one group or another invariably failed to come in—always the B or the D or both. Now, when my eye fell on the page in question, I remembered the reluctant trombones of Paris and wondered whether the Prussian players would succeed in triumphing over this non-existent obstacle. Alas! futile attempt! Patient perseverance and rage equally unavailing; impossible to get the second and third groups to come in; even the fourth, not receiving its cue, refuses to budge. I take them separately. I ask No. 2 for its B. Excellent. Now, No. 3: let me have your D. No difficulty there either. Good. Now let us take the four notes one after another in the order in which they occur.... Impossible! Quite impossible! We have to give up the attempt. Can you imagine it? It's enough to make one batter one's head against the wall. Yet when I asked the Paris and the Berlin trombonists why they didn't play in the fatal bar they could not answer. Those two notes hypnotized them.*

I must write to Romberg, who put on the work in St Petersburg, and find out whether the Russian trombones have been able to break the spell.

So far as all the rest of the programme was concerned the orchestra grasped and carried out my intentions admirably. Before long we were ready to hold our general rehearsal at the Opera,

* At the last two performances of the Requiem in the church of Saint-Eustache the passage has been correctly played. [There were performances at Saint-Eustache in 1846, 1850 and 1852.]

where the stage had been built up in tiers in readiness for the concert. Symphony, overture, cantata, all went perfectly; but when it came to the movements from the Requiem there was general panic. I had not been able to rehearse the chorus myself. They had learnt their music at tempos different from mine, and when they found themselves suddenly at grips with the orchestra, at the correct tempos, they went to pieces. Entries were wrong or made hesitantly, without conviction. In the Lacrymosa the tenors stopped singing altogether. I was at my wits' end. Meyerbeer, who was not at all well, had had to stay in bed. Elssler, the chorus-master, was ill too. The orchestra faltered, demoralized by the failure of the choir. For an instant I sat down, feeling exhausted and quite helpless and wondering whether I shouldn't just walk out, leaving them all there, and quit Berlin that evening; and at this moment of crisis I thought of you, and said to myself, 'It's madness to go on. Now if Desmarest were here—Desmarest who is never satisfied with our rehearsals at the Conservatoire—and he realized I intended to let the concert be announced for tomorrow, I know just what he would do: he'd lock me in my room, put the key in his pocket, and go straight off and tell the intendant the concert had been cancelled.' You would have, wouldn't you? Well, you would have been wrong, as you will see. When the first spasm had passed, I wiped the cold sweat from my forehead, pulled myself together, and said, 'We have got to get this right.'

I turned to Ries and Ganz, the two leaders—who were hovering round, not knowing what to say to rally me—and asked briskly, 'Are you sure of the orchestra?'

'Yes. You've nothing to be afraid of there. We're very tired, but we have got the hang of your music; we won't let you down tomorrow.'

'All right, there's only one thing to be done: the chorus must be called for the morning. As Elssler is ill, I shall want a good accompanist; and you, Ganz, or rather you, Ries, bring your violin, and we'll go through the chorus part, if need be for three hours.'

'Very well—we'll be there, instructions will be given.'

Next morning we set to work, Ries, the accompanist and I. We took separately, in succession, the children, the women—first sopranos, second sopranos—first tenors, second tenors, and first and second basses. We made them sing in groups of ten, then of twenty. Next we combined two parts, then three, then four, finally all voices together; until I could exclaim like the Jehu in the fable:

*Why, what is this? The cart moves on apace.**

I made a little speech to the chorus, which Ries conveyed to them sentence by sentence in German. And there we were, with our troops re-formed and in fighting spirits and overjoyed not to have lost this great battle in which their honour and mine were at stake. Far from it, indeed; we had won it in a brilliant and decisive fashion. That evening† overture, symphony and cantata (*The Fifth of May*) were royally performed as they could hardly fail to be with such an orchestra and with a singer like Boeticher. Then came the Requiem. Everyone alert and with me to a man, orchestras and chorus drawn up in perfect order, each one at his post, nothing wanting, we began the Dies irae. Not a mistake, not a moment's hesitation. The chorus received the orchestral onslaught without flinching; the fourfold fanfare pealed forth from the four corners of the stage, the air shook with the roll of ten pairs of drumsticks and the tremolo of fifty bows unleashed, and in the midst of the tumult of baleful harmonies, the blast from beyond the grave, a hundred and twenty voices proclaimed their tremendous prophecy:

Judex ergo cum sedebit
Quidquid latet apparebit!

The applause and shouts of the audience momentarily obscured the entry of the 'Liber scriptus', and we arrived at the final sotto voce chords of the 'Mors stupebit' palpitating but victorious. Then, the delight of the performers, the glances that flashed from one end of the stage to the other! As for me, my heart was going like a bell, my knees shaking, my head spinning like a mill-wheel; I dug my nails into the desk; and had I not forced myself, the moment the music was over, to talk loud and fast to Ries, who played up to me, I have no doubt that for the first time

* [La Fontaine, 'Le chartier embourbé' (The carter stuck in the mud).]
† [8 April 1843.]

in my life I would have disgraced myself by 'passing out on parade', as they say in the army. . . . Once the first barrage had been survived, the rest was child's play; and the Lacrymosa brought this apocalyptic evening to a close to the entire satisfaction of the composer.

At the conclusion of the concert a great many people spoke to me and congratulated me and wrung me by the hand, but I could only stand there dazed, not comprehending, feeling nothing. My brain and nervous system had over-taxed themselves and craved rest, I was stupid with fatigue. Only Wiprecht managed to bring me to myself with a hug like a cuirassier's. The good man made my ribs crack, interspersing his exclamations with Teutonic oaths besides which Guhr's were Ave Marias.

Then my happiness was not to be measured, it was fathomless. So you see, it is sometimes wise to act foolishly. But for my recklessness the concert could not have taken place, for the theatre's schedule of work was so arranged that there was no possibility of taking up the Requiem again for a long time ahead.

For the second concert, as already said, I announced five pieces from *Romeo and Juliet*, among them Queen Mab. During the fortnight that separated the two events, Ganz and Taubert went carefully through the score. When they saw me determined to give the scherzo it was their turn to be alarmed.

'We'll never manage it,' they said. 'You know we have only two rehearsals. It needs five or six. It's as difficult and dangerous as any piece in existence, it's a spider's web of sound, and without an exceptionally light and delicate touch it'll be torn to shreds.'

'Nonsense! I'm sure it will be all right. I know we have only two rehearsals, but there are only five pieces to learn, four of them not particularly difficult. Besides, the orchestra already has some idea of the scherzo from the first time, when we went through part of it. And Meyerbeer has spoken about it to the King, who wants to hear it, and I want the players to get to know it too. It will go all right.'

And it did, almost as well as at Brunswick. Much may be dared with such an orchestra—an orchestra which, before Meyerbeer conducted it, was for many years under the powerful baton of Spontini.

This second concert* was as successful as the first. The pieces from *Romeo* were extremely well played. Queen Mab greatly puzzled the audience, even those with a knowledge of music; witness the Crown Princess, who was agog to know how I had produced the effect of the accompaniment in the allegretto, and had no idea that it was with violin and harp harmonics in several parts. The King preferred the Capulets' Feast and asked for a copy of it. But I think the orchestra's favourite was the Love Scene; if so, the Berlin players feel the same as their Paris colleagues. Mlle Hähnel sang the contralto's song from the Prologue simply and unaffectedly at the rehearsal, but at the concert felt obliged to embellish the pause at the end of the phrase

Where the nightingale pines
In long-drawn sighs

with a long-drawn trill in imitation of the nightingale. My dear young lady, how could you be so treacherous? And you looked such a nice person!

Would you believe it?—there were people who, out of all the music that I performed in Berlin, the Requiem pieces—Dies irae, Tuba mirum, Lacrymosa and Offertorium—the *Benvenuto* and *King Lear* overtures, *Harold*, its Serenade, its Pilgrims, its Orgy, the festivities at the Capulets', the frolics of Queen Mab—honestly preferred *The Fifth of May*. Human beings' reactions are as varied as their physiognomies, I know. But when I was told that, I had to make a face. Happily this opinion was quite exceptional.

Goodbye, my dear Desmarest. Don't forget we have an anthem to recite to the public at the Conservatoire in a few days' time,† so assemble your sixteen cellos; I am looking forward to hearing those noble singers again, and to seeing you at their head. It is so long since we made music together! To whet their appetites, tell them I shall conduct with Mendelssohn's baton.

* [23 April 1843.]

† [This letter appeared in the *Débats* on 8 November 1843; the concert in question took place on the 19th. It proved the last that Berlioz was allowed to give in the Conservatoire hall.]

Tenth Letter

Hanover, Darmstadt

TO M. GEORGE OSBORNE

Alas, my dear Osborne, my journey is nearing its end. I leave Prussia, full of gratitude for the welcome I have received, the warmth of sympathy which the artists have shown me and the indulgence of critics and public, but absolutely worn out by this unnaturally hectic life, the strain of rehearsing new orchestras all the time—so worn out that I shall give up Breslau, Vienna and Munich for the present. I am returning to France; and already I can feel, from a kind of restlessness in the blood, a vague sense of unease permeating my heart and mind, that I have come in contact once more with the electric currents of Paris—Paris, which our great poet Auguste Barbier has all too accurately described as

. . . that pit of hell,
That quarry of monstrous circumference,
Looped three times by a sallow, livid river,
That great volcano churning ceaselessly
A turgid stream of human lava . . .
There no man sleeps, there like a bow drawn taut
*The mind bends labouring and never loosens.**

Paris is where music one moment lies moribund and the next moment seethes with life; where it is sublime and second-rate, lordly and cringing, beggar and king; where it is both glorified and despised, worshipped and insulted. In Paris music has its loyal and intelligent followers; in Paris music too often speaks to morons, barbarians and the deaf. You see it now walking freely and without restraint, now barely able to move for the clammy fetters with which the witch Routine shackles its powerful limbs. In Paris music is a god—so long as only the skinniest sacrifices are required to feed its altars. The god is granted temples laden with splendid trophies—on condition that he turn man, and clown too on occasion. In Paris you see Art's scrofulous bastard brother, Commerce, flaunting his bourgeois finery in the public eye, and Art,

* ['La Cuve' (The Vat), from *Iambes*.]

naked and unadorned as the Pythian Apollo, lost in contemplation, hardly deigning to glance down on him with a smile of remote contempt. You may even see Commerce obtain unbelievable favours from his too unworldly brother, creeping into the great chariot of the sun, seizing the reins and attempting to turn the immortal car round; whereupon the true driver, startled into activity by such mad presumption, tears him off the seat and hurls him from his presence.

These unsavoury, if short-lived, alliances are always brought about by money—the greed for rapid gain that can corrupt the most high-minded people:

Money, the last cruel god of human kind,
Seizes, enslaves, deforms them, drives them blind,
Goads them to evil, till from sordid lust
*For gold they'd tread their fathers in the dust.**

And when the high-minded fall it is usually through a simple failure to recognize the melancholy but incontestable truth that with our culture as it is, and under our form of government, the more of an artist a man is the more he will have to endure; the grander and more original his work, the harsher the penalty he must pay; the loftier his inspiration soars, the harder for the blear-eyed multitude to discern it.

The Medici are dead. If anyone is to replace them it will not be our deputies. You recall the sage comment of that provincial Lycurgus who listened to some lines by one of our greatest poets (the poet who wrote *The Fall of an Angel*)† and then remarked, as he opened his snuff-box with a benevolent air, 'Aye, I've a nephew that writes b——ls like that.' As good as your bloody poets any day! Try asking him to support the arts.

You virtuosos, who do not deal in massed forces and have no need of large halls and voluminous choirs, and write only for the orchestra of your two hands, may have less to fear from contact with a bourgeois culture; but you too feel its effect. Scribble off some glittering trifle, and the publishers will scramble for the

* ['Melpomène', from Barbier's *Iambes*.]
† [Lamartine.]

honour of investing their gold in it. But be guilty of a genuine idea and of developing it seriously on a large scale, and you know what to expect: the work sits on your shelf, unpublished; or, if published, sells only a handful of copies.

In justice to Paris and constitutional monarchy, it must be said that the same situation prevails almost everywhere else. In Vienna, as here, a fashionable tunesmith receives a thousand francs for a waltz or a romance, where Beethoven was forced to sell the C minor Symphony for less than a hundred crowns.

Consider some of the trios or the pieces for piano solo that you have had published in London—music lofty in style and spacious in design; or even, setting aside your large-scale works, those charming songs of yours: 'The beating of my own heart', 'My lonely home', or 'Such things were', which your sister, Mrs Hampton, sings so evocatively. Nothing stimulates my imagination more than those pure, fresh melodies, so original yet so natural, which take one straight to the green hills of Ireland and seem to come carried on the evening breeze softly across the rippling lakes of Killarney—those odes to long-suffering love which move one without one's knowing why and turn one's thoughts to solitude and the grandeur of nature, loved ones who are no more, heroes of old, a country's woes, and death itself, 'holy and calm as the night', to quote your national poet Thomas Moore.* Weigh all that inspiration, all that sad, sweet poetry in the scale against some wild and whirling capriccio or other piece of heartless, brainless flummery such as the music-mongers regularly commission from you on the more vulgar themes from the latest opera, with the notes cascading and jangling about like a fistful of hand-bells shaken in a sack, and then see where the money is.

No, one must simply resign oneself to the fact that except in rare circumstances which are the result of chance, and in association with lesser arts whose company always debases it to a greater or lesser extent, music is unproductive in the commercial sense of the word. It appeals too exclusively to a small minority of civilized society; it requires too many resources and too much preparation in order to exist in outward form. Those who cultivate it must

* [From *Irish Melodies*: 'Oh! had we some bright little isle of our own'.]

therefore of necessity live in a kind of dignified ostracism, cutting themselves off from all interests that are hostile to it. The very greatest nations, in their relation to the pure artist, are like our friend the deputy: alongside the giants of the human spirit, they can all put their 'nephews that write', etc.

In the archives of one of London's theatres there is a letter to Queen Elizabeth signed by a troupe of twenty actors describing themselves collectively as 'your poor players'. One of them is William Shakespeare. Yet drama was a more truly popular art in Shakespeare's time than music is today even in countries which most pride themselves on their feeling for it. Music is essentially aristocratic. The muse is a girl of pedigree whose dowry only princes can provide nowadays; and she had better learn to live in virgin poverty than marry beneath herself.

No doubt all these considerations have occurred to you a thousand times, and you will thank me to have done with them and get on with the account of the last two concerts that I gave in Germany, after I had left Berlin. But I am afraid it will not offer you anything of much interest so far as my own activities are concerned. I shall have once more to speak of works that have perhaps already been more than sufficiently discussed in previous letters: the inevitable *Fifth of May*, *Harold*, excerpts from *Romeo and Juliet*, and the rest; the same difficulties in procuring certain instruments; the same high quality in all other departments, constituting what may be called the traditional or Mozart orchestra; the same mistakes recurring at the same points in the same pieces the first time through, to disappear at length after a few diligent rehearsals.

I did not stop in Magdeburg—where, however, an unusual success awaited me. I was practically assaulted for having the audacity to call myself by my own name, and by a mail-office clerk at that: on registering my luggage and examining the labels on it, he said with a suspicious air, '*Berlioz? Komponist?*'

'*Ja*.'

Whereupon, righteous rage of the clerk at my impertinence in masquerading as the composer of that name. No doubt the good man had supposed that this fabulous musician would be bound to travel, if not mounted on a hippogriff in a whirlwind of flame, at least with a sumptuous baggage-train and a small army of flunkeys in attendance; instead of which, here was a man who looked like any other man who has been at once smoked and chilled in a railway carriage and who saw to the weighing of his own trunk, walked by himself unaided, did his own talking, in French, spoke no word of German but '*Ja*', and was clearly an impostor. As you can imagine, his shruggings and grumblings delighted me. The more sceptical he became in gesture and tone of voice, the more I preened myself. I should certainly have ended by embracing him but for the intervention of another clerk who spoke my language fluently and was more disposed to grant me the right to be myself. I found his honeyed words far less flattering than his colleague's splendidly churlish disbelief. And a mere half-million francs would have robbed me of this success! In future I shall make a point of not carrying them about with me, and of always travelling in the same fashion—although this conflicts with the dictum propounded by our genial theatrical censor, Perpignan, when told of a man who owed his life in a duel to a five-franc piece in his waistcoat pocket: 'The rich have all the luck. I would have been killed stone dead.'

I reached Hanover, where Anton Bohrer was awaiting me. The intendant, von Meding, had kindly put the chorus and orchestra at my disposal, and I was about to begin my rehearsals when the Duke of Sussex,* a relative of the King, died, the court went into mourning, and the concert was postponed for a week. This gave me a little more time to get to know the principal artists who were about to have my contentious compositions thrust upon them.

I did not get very far with the kapellmeister, Marschner. He finds it so difficult to express himself in French that our conversations were laborious affairs; and he is an extremely busy man. Marschner is one of the leading composers in Germany today. You admire, as we all do, those admirable works, *The Vampire* and *The Templar.* Bohrer I knew already; the trios and quartets of Beethoven had brought us together in Paris, and our common enthusiasm had not cooled since then. To my mind Anton Bohrer feels and understands the popularly supposed eccentric and unintelligible works among Beethoven's output as few men do. I can

* [Augustus Frederick, sixth son of George III.]

see him now at quartet rehearsals, with his brother Max (the well-known cellist, now in America), Claudel, second violin, and Urhan, viola, in ardent support. Max, at the strains of that transcendental music, would smile with the sheer pride and delight of playing it; he had the relaxed, contented air that comes from breathing one's native element. Urhan worshipped in silence, eyes averted as though from the radiance of the sun; he seemed to be saying, 'God willed that there should be a man as great as Beethoven, and that we should be allowed to contemplate him. God willed it!' Claudel admired the others for the depth of their admirations. But with Anton Bohrer, the first violin, it was a sublime passion, an ecstasy of love. One evening, in one of those unearthly adagios where Beethoven's spirit soars vast and solitary like the huge bird above the snows of Chimborazo,* Bohrer's violin as it sang the heavenly melody seemed to become possessed with the divine fire and, suddenly taking on a new force and eloquence of expression, broke into accents unknown even to it, while his face lit up with the light of pure inspiration. We held our breath, our hearts swelled—when he abruptly stopped, put down his bow and rushed from the room. Madame Bohrer, worried, went after him, but Max, still smiling, said, 'It's nothing—he couldn't contain his feelings. Leave him to calm down a little, then we'll start again. You must forgive him.'

We forgive you—dear, great artist.

In Hanover Anton Bohrer leads the orchestra. He composes little now; his greatest interest is in supervising the musical education of his daughter, a fascinating girl of twelve whose astounding abilities are not surprisingly an object of constant and anxious concern to all around her. In the first place she is a quite extraordinarily gifted pianist. Secondly, she has such a phenomenal memory that for the concerts which she gave in Vienna last year her father, in place of the normal printed programme, distributed a list of seventy-two pieces—sonatas, concertos, fantasies, fugues, variations, studies, by Beethoven, Weber, Cramer, Bach, Handel, Liszt, Thalberg, Chopin, Döhler, etc.—which the little Sophie

* [An allusion to Humboldt's account of the condor in the Andes (*Tableaux de la nature*).]

knew by heart and from which she was able to perform without a moment's hesitation whichever her audience cared to name. She has only to play a piece three or four times to have it firmly fixed in her head, no matter how long and complicated it is. All those permutations engraved on one youthful brain! Don't you find something uncanny in it, calculated to arouse awe as well as admiration?

It is to be hoped that in a few years' time, when little Sophie has become Mlle Bohrer, she will return among us; at present the Parisian public has only a faint idea of her astonishing talent.*

The Hanover orchestra is good, but weak in strings. There are only seven first violins, seven seconds, three violas, four cellos and three double basses; and one or two of the violins are infirm. The cellos are skilled players and the violas and basses are good. For the woodwind I have nothing but praise, especially the first flute, the first oboe (Eduard Rose), a player with a marvellous pianissimo, and the first clarinet, who has an exquisite tone. The two bassoons—there are only two—play in tune, which is sadly rare. The horns, though not first-rate, are adequate and the natural trumpets quite good. There is one superb valve-trumpet, with the same name as his Weimar rival, Sachse; I would not like to say which is the better. The first oboe can play the cor anglais, but his instrument is badly out of tune. There is no ophicleide; the bass tubas from the military band may be used to advantage. The timpanist is mediocre; the musician entrusted with the bass drum is no musician; the cymbal player is unreliable and the cymbals are so cracked and chipped that hardly a third of each one is left.

There is a harp, quite well played by one of the ladies of the chorus. She is no virtuoso but she has learnt to play the instrument. She and the Stuttgart, Berlin and Hamburg players were the only exceptions I found to the general rule that harpists in Germany do not know how to play the harp. Unfortunately she is very timid and a rather weak musician; but if you give her several days to study her part her accuracy can be depended on. She executes harmonics admirably; her harp is a fine double-action instrument.

* [Sophie Bohrer played in Paris in 1845 with enormous success, but died six years later, aged twenty.]

The chorus is small, numbering only about forty voices, but far from negligible. They all sing in tune and the tenors have an unusually good tone into the bargain. The resident company of singers is worse than second-rate. With the exception of the bass, Steinmüller, an excellent musician with a fine voice which he uses well (apart from a slight tendency to force the tone), I heard nothing that I thought worth mentioning.

We were able to have only two rehearsals. Even that was considered extraordinary, and some of the players grumbled openly about it. It was the sole occasion on which I had this trouble in Germany, where the artists constantly received me as a friend and never complained of all the time and labour involved in preparing my concerts. Anton Bohrer was in despair. He would have liked four rehearsals or at the very least three, but it was out of the question. The performance, however, was competent, though quite lacking in warmth and energy. Imagine—three double basses, six and a half violins a side!* The audience was polite but no more. I have no doubt they are still wondering what the devil it was all about. Dr Griepenkerl, who had come from Brunswick to hear the concert, was struck as he could not fail to be by the difference in the whole artistic spirit of the two towns. He and I and a few Brunswick officers amused ourselves by tormenting poor Bohrer with a detailed description of the musical feast I had been treated to in Brunswick three months before. It nearly broke his heart. Griepenkerl presented me with a copy of the book he had written about me,† and in turn requested the baton with which I had just conducted *The Fifth of May*.‡

Let us hope these batons planted in France and Germany will take root and grow into trees, beneath which I may one day find shade. . . .

The Crown Prince of Hanover was at the concert. I had the honour of speaking with him for a few moments before I left, and

* [Cf. Berlioz's German notebook: 'Depressing concert; orchestra wretchedly short of strings—3 double basses!! The players inclined to put on airs, and not prepared to rehearse more than twice; they dispatched *Harold* in really priceless style; the excellent Bohrer ashamed for his orchestra; the audience not bad.']

† [See above, p. 322 and n.]

‡ [6 May 1843.]

am happy to have met a man of such distinguished mind and charmingly affable demeanour. The frightful misfortune of losing his sight has in no way affected his serenity of spirit.

Now for Darmstadt. I pass through Kassel at seven in the morning.

Spohr is asleep and not to be disturbed.*

Continuing on my way, I reach Frankfurt—my fourth visit. There I meet Parish-Alvars again and am mesmerized by his playing his fantasia for harmonics on the mermaids' chorus from *Oberon*. The man is a magician. In his hands the harp becomes a siren, lovely neck inclined and wild hair flowing, stirred by his passionate embrace to utter the music of another world. Guhr is there too, up to his eyes in scaffolding: workmen are restoring his theatre—which reminds me that I have something I must say to that dread kapellmeister, if you will excuse me a moment, Osborne; I will be back directly.

My dear Guhr,

Do you know—I was afraid, from what several people had told me, that you might be offended by the mild pleasantries I indulged in when describing our first encounter? I could hardly credit it, knowing your sense of humour, but the thought that it might be so distressed me. I am delighted to hear that far from being annoyed at the dissonances I imputed to your euphonious style of speech you were the first to laugh, and that you have had a translation of the relevant letter published in one of the Frankfurt newspapers. Splendid! You can take a joke; and besides, no one is damned for a little mild swearing. Vivat! Terque quaterque vivat! S.N.T.T. Seriously, please count me among your most devoted friends and allow me to offer you once more my warmest compliments on your Frankfurt company, which is worthy to be directed by an artist of your distinction. Goodbye. S.N.T.T.

Where was I? Oh yes, Darmstadt. We shall find some friends there, among them Louis Schloesser, the leader of the orchestra, who was a fellow-pupil of mine in Lesueur's class in the days when

* Spohr is kapellmeister at Kassel.

he lived in Paris. I had also brought letters from M. de Rothschild of Frankfurt to Prince Emile, who gave me the most charming welcome and prevailed on the Grand Duke to offer me more than I had dared to hope for for my concert. In most German towns that I visited the terms fixed with the local intendant were virtually the same: the management undertook nearly all the expenses and I received half the takings. The Weimar theatre had been alone in courteously allowing me the entire receipts (I have said before, Weimar is an artistic town where the ducal dynasty knows how to honour the arts). But in Darmstadt the Grand Duke not only granted me the same generous concession but also insisted on my being relieved of all expense. Evidently this liberal monarch has no 'nephews that write . . .'.

The concert was soon arranged. Far from having to be begged to rehearse, the orchestra would have been only too happy if I could have worked with them for another week. We had five rehearsals. At the concert* everything went off well except the double chorus of the 'young Capulets leaving the fête', at the beginning of the Love Scene in *Romeo and Juliet*. This passage was a vocal débâcle, the tenors of the second chorus dropping nearly a semitone and the tenors of the first missing their entry at the return of the theme. The chorus-master's rage was all the more understandable because he had spent a week instructing his choristers and had taken infinite trouble.

The Darmstadt orchestra is slightly bigger than the one at Hanover and exceptional in possessing a first-rate ophicleide. The harp is entrusted to a painter, a willing man who does his best without succeeding in putting much colour into his playing. For the rest it is an efficient, well-balanced and very lively orchestra. It contains one really remarkable player called Müller (no relation of the famous Brunswick Müllers), a giant of a man who plays the genuine four-stringed double bass with extraordinary facility. Instead of exploiting it for the execution of vulgar feats of technique, scales and arpeggios which astonish by their difficulty and pointlessness, he makes this enormous instrument an expressive vehicle of great dignity and nobility, drawing the most

* [24 May 1843.]

beautiful and subtly varied sounds from it. I heard him play a fine adagio by the younger Mangold, brother of the kapellmeister, in such a way that a critical audience was deeply moved. This was at a soirée given by Dr Huth, the leading Darmstadt amateur, whose contribution to the musical life and atmosphere of the town is as important and influential in its way as Mr Alsager's to that of London.* Müller is a prize that many composers and conductors must covet; but the Grand Duke will certainly do all he can to keep him.

The able kapellmeister, Mangold, an excellent man, received a good deal of his musical education in Paris, where he was one of Reicha's best pupils. For me, therefore, he was a fellow-student and he treated me as such. As for Schloesser, the aforementioned leader of the orchestra, he was such a good friend and helped me so wholeheartedly that I find it impossible to speak as I should like of those of his compositions that he let me see; it would look as though I were repaying him for his hospitality when I would only be giving him the credit he deserves. Fresh proof of the truth of the antiproverb that 'a good turn is always wasted'!

Darmstadt also has a military band of about thirty players which I greatly envied the Grand Duke. The whole band plays stylishly and in tune and with a sense of rhythm that makes even the side-drum parts full of interest.

Reichel, the prodigious bass who was of such service to me in Hamburg, had been in Darmstadt for some time when I arrived, and had had a triumphant success as Marcel in *The Huguenots*. He kindly sang *The Fifth of May* again, and with a much greater mastery and sensitivity than on the first occasion. He was particularly fine in the last verse—the most difficult to sing with the right expression:

Wie? Sterben er? O Ruhm, wie verwaist bist du!
(What! He die? Then, Fame, thou art orphaned!)

A brilliant account of 'Non più andrai' from Mozart's *Figaro*, which we had added to the programme, revealed another side of his versatile gifts. It earned him an encore from the whole

* [Thomas Alsager, financial editor of *The Times*, organized concerts at his house in Queen's Square and founded the Beethoven Quartet Society.]

audience and next day a highly favourable engagement at the Darmstadt theatre. I refrain from retailing the rest of the proceedings; but if you go there they will tell you that in my egoism and simplicity I thought the public and the artists most intelligent.

With that, my dear Osborne, I come to the end of my pilgrimage—perhaps the most arduous ever undertaken by a musician, the memory of which will surely cast its influence over me for the rest of my life. Meanwhile, like the priests of ancient Greece, I have been consulting the Delphic oracle. Have I correctly grasped the sense of its reply? Should I believe it when it seems to hold out the promise of fair things flattering to my hopes? May not oracles deceive? The future alone will show.* However that may be, I have now to return to France and say goodbye at last to Germany, bounteous second mother to all the sons of harmony. But how can I find words to express the depth of my gratitude, admiration and regret? What paean would be worthy of her glory and greatness? As I leave I can only bow in profound respect and utter a heartfelt

Vale, Germania, alma parens!

52

I produce Freischütz at the Opéra—my recitatives—the singers—Dessauer—Léon Pillet—havoc wrought by his successors on Weber's score

I WAS ON MY WAY back from this long tour of Germany when Léon Pillet, the director of the Opéra, decided that he would like to put on *Freischütz*. But in *Freischütz* the musical numbers are interspersed with prose dialogue, as in our opéras-comiques, whereas the conventions of the Opéra require every word of the dramas or lyric tragedies performed there to be sung. It was therefore necessary to put the spoken text into recitative. M. Pillet suggested that I do it.

I replied that I did not think one ought to add recitatives to *Freischütz*, but that since this was the condition of its being performed at the Opéra and if I did not write them the job would be

* [This evidently refers to Berlioz's hopes that, through his influence on the director, Pillet, he might be appointed conductor at the Opéra.]

given to someone possibly less familiar with Weber and certainly less dedicated to the glorification of his masterpiece, I would accept his offer, but on condition that the work was performed in its entirety without a word or a note being changed.

'That is precisely what I have in mind,' he said. 'Do you think me capable of perpetrating another *Robin des bois*?'

'Splendid. Then I'll do it. How are you going to cast the opera?'

'I shall have Madame Stoltz as Agathe and Mlle Dobré as Annette. Duprez will sing Max.'

'I'm sure he won't,' I interrupted.

'Why not?'

'You'll soon see.'

'Bouché will make an excellent Caspar.'

'Who have you got for the Hermit?'

'Well,' he said awkwardly, 'it's a superfluous role, really—it slows up the action. I thought I would leave out the part of the opera that he appears in.'

'You don't say! So that is your idea of respecting *Freischütz* and not doing a Castil-Blaze? I'm afraid we don't see it in quite the same way. If you don't mind, I shall withdraw. I can't possibly be a party to this latest improvement.'

'Well, well, you're very consistent in your opinions, to be sure. All right, we'll keep the Hermit, we'll preserve everything, I give you my word.'

Emilien Paccini, who was to translate the libretto, gave the same assurance, and I agreed, not without misgivings, to undertake the composition of the recitatives. By insisting on the preservation of the work in its pristine integrity—an attitude which many called fetishism—I forestalled all the cutting and altering, the tampering and improving which would otherwise have been enthusiastically resorted to. But my inflexibility had one serious disadvantage. Despite the care I took to make it flow as swiftly as possible, the spoken dialogue, when set complete to music, seemed too long. I could not get the actors to abandon their slow emphatic style of singing recitative. In the exchanges between Max and Caspar especially, the homely, colloquial phrases took on the ceremonious gravity of a scene from classical opera. This spoiled the general effect of *Freischütz* a little. None the less the work had a brilliant success. I had decided not to be officially named as the author of these recitatives, but according to artists and critics they were not only dramatically conceived but also perfectly attuned to Weber's style, as well as being orchestrated with a restraint that even my enemies were forced to recognize.*

As I had foreseen, Duprez, who ten years before when his voice was small and light had sung Tony (Max) in *Robin des bois*, could not now adjust his big heroic tenor to the part (which admittedly lies on the whole rather low). He proposed the strangest transpositions, necessitating grotesque joins and insane modulations. I cut this nonsense short by pointing out to Pillet that Duprez on his own admission was incapable of singing the role without distorting it, and it was given to the second tenor, Marie, a fine musician with a voice not without character in the lower register but a dull and ungainly singer.

Madame Stoltz was equally unable to sing Agathe without transposing both her arias. I had to put the first (which is in E) into D, and lower the A flat major prayer in Act III by a minor third, which took away three-quarters of its enchanting colour. She was, however, able to retain the original key (B) of the final sextet, and sang the top line with a fire and energy that invariably brought the house down.

In all such cases of singers refusing to perform a part as it is written, a quarter is genuine difficulty, a quarter ignorance, and a good half caprice.

I remember Duprez obstinately declining to sing a middle G in the romance 'La gloire était ma seule idole' in my opera *Benvenuto Cellini*, although an easier note for his voice or for anyone else's could not be conceived. The word 'protège' is sung to the notes G-D, which make a lively and pleasing preliminary to the final cadence. Duprez preferred D-D, which is a vulgar commonplace. In the aria 'Asile héréditaire' in *William Tell* he could never sing

* [*Freischütz*, conducted by Habeneck's assistant Pantaléon Battu, had its première at the Opéra on 7 June 1841. Berlioz received two hundred and thirty francs a performance; by 1846, when it was dropped from the repertoire for a few years, there had been sixty-one.]

the G flat, the enharmonic of F sharp which Rossini has shrewdly and aptly put there to prepare for the return of the theme in the tonic key. He always substituted an F, the effect of which was both crude and insipid and destroyed the whole charm of the modulation.

One day I was returning from the country with Duprez. As I sat beside him in the carriage something prompted me to hum the phrase in question—with the G flat—right in his ear. He turned and looked straight at me, blushing slightly, and said, 'You're criticizing me!'

'Yes—I am. Why on earth don't you sing the passage as it's written?'

'I don't know—that note bothers me; it makes me nervous.'

'Come, come, you're not being serious. How can it bother you when it doesn't bother singers with half your voice and ability?'

'You may be right.'

'I'm quite sure I'm right.'

'Very well, in future I'll sing the G flat—for your sake.'

'No—do it for your own sake and the composer's and for the sake of ordinary musical common sense, which it is so odd to see an artist like you violating.'

Pshaw! Neither for my sake nor for his nor for Rossini's, nor for music nor common sense, has Duprez ever sung the G flat at any subsequent performance of *William Tell*. Saints, or devils, could not get him to give up his damnable F. He will die unrepentant.

Serda, the bass who sang the role of the Cardinal in *Benvenuto Cellini*, maintained that he could not manage the high E flat in his aria 'A tous péchés pleine indulgence', and transposed it to the lower octave, making a downward leap of a sixth instead of an upward leap of a third, which completely falsified the phrase. On one occasion he had to miss a rehearsal, and Alizard was asked to take his place. Alizard, with his superb voice (the beauty and expressive power of which had yet to be recognized), sang the aria, at sight, without any alteration and to such effect that the chorus standing round him broke into enthusiastic applause. Serda heard of his success. Next day he discovered the E flat. Note that this same Serda, who claimed that the E flat was too high for him, sang E natural and even F sharp in the role of Saint-Bris in *The Huguenots*.

Singers! What a race!

To return to *Freischütz*. Naturally there had to be a ballet. When all my efforts to stop it proved useless, I proposed devising a dance scene along the lines indicated by Weber himself in his rondo for piano, 'Invitation to the Waltz', and I arranged this delightful piece for orchestra. But instead of following the music's own clearly marked scheme, the choreographer could only produce a string of hackneyed dance steps and balletic clichés, calculated to leave the audience cold. So it was decided to make up in quantity what was lacking in quality, and three more numbers were asked for. At this point the dancers had the happy notion that some of the movements in my symphonies were suitable for the purpose and would round the ballet off very nicely. They mentioned it to Pillet; he agreed that it was a splendid idea and asked me to take the ball scene from the Fantastic Symphony and the fête from *Romeo and Juliet* and work them into the score of the opera.

The German composer Dessauer was in Paris at the time, and was often to be found backstage at the Opéra. When Pillet put his proposal to me I restrained myself and merely replied that I could not agree to inserting music not by Weber into *Freischütz*, but that for proof that this was not simply exaggerated and unreasonable respect for the Master, he could ask Dessauer, up there at the back of the stage, and see what he thought. If he approved, I would do what the director asked; if not, he would be so good as not to mention it to me again.

As soon as Pillet began speaking, Dessauer looked sharply round at me and said, 'Berlioz, you can't do it!'

I turned to Pillet. 'You heard what he said.'

And that was that. We took some of the dance numbers from *Oberon* and *Preciosa*, and so the ballet was completed with music composed by Weber himself. After a few performances, however, the *Oberon* and *Preciosa* pieces disappeared. Then random cuts appeared in the 'Invitation to the Waltz', although it had been a great success as an orchestral piece. When Pillet ceased to be director of the Opéra, and while I was in Russia, they began to trim *Freischütz* itself, removing part of the finale of the third act and then actually suppressing the entire first scene of this act, including Agathe's sublime prayer, the music for the young girls and Aennchen's picturesque air with solo viola; in which degrading condition *Freischütz* is today performed at the Paris Opéra. This masterpiece of originality, passion and poetic imagination now serves as a curtain-raiser for the most insignificant ballets and must accordingly be tailored to fit the space available. If some new choreographic creation should arise, more ambitious than its predecessors, *Freischütz* will be cut again to make room for it. And then, the way they perform what is left of it! the singers! the conductor! the indolence and sluggishness of the tempos and the helpless incoherence of the ensembles! the appalling inanity and insipidity pervading every aspect of the interpretation! If you want to be smirched, reviled, persecuted, be an innovator, a standard-bearer, a poet, a man of genius. Pedlars and money-changers! Pending the advent of a new Christ to scourge you from the temple, be assured that everyone in Europe with the slightest feeling for art holds you in bottomless contempt.*

53

I am forced to write articles—despair—impulse to suicide—Festival of Industry—1,022 performers—receipts, 32,000 francs—profit, 800 francs—M. Delessert, Commissioner of Police—censorship of concert programmes set up—the poor-house tax-collectors—Dr Amussat—I go to Nice—concerts in the Champs-Elysées Circus

MY LIFE IN the period which followed offers no musical event worth mentioning. I remained in Paris, occupied almost exclusively with my trade, I will not say of critic, but of feuilletonist—a very different thing. The critic—let us suppose him intelligent and honest—writes only when he has something to say: when he

* [In 1853 a Polish nobleman, Count Tyczkiewicz, brought an action for false pretences against the director of the Opéra on the grounds that the performance of Weber's *Freischütz* for which he had bought a ticket in good faith did not correspond to the score of that name. Before the case was dismissed, counsel for the Opéra tried to shift the responsibility onto Berlioz.]

wishes to illuminate some question, challenge some theory, bestow well-merited praise or blame. He always has reasons, to him genuine, for airing his opinions and dispensing his accolades or his thunderbolts. The wretched feuilletonist, obliged to write on anything and everything within the domain of his feuilleton (gloomy domain, bog-ridden, infested with toads and grasshoppers), wishes one thing only—to be done with the labour that weighs upon him. More often than not he has no opinion about the objects on which he is compelled to give an opinion; they stir him to neither anger nor admiration; they do not exist. Yet he has to behave as if he believed in their existence and felt strongly about them and had powerful motives for bringing his whole mind to bear upon them. Most of my colleagues can extricate themselves without difficulty and often with a dexterity which it is a pleasure to watch. But for me it is a long and painful struggle to keep up the pretence. Once, when I had to write a feuilleton about the Opéra-Comique, I spent three days immured in my room, unable to begin. I don't remember what opus I was supposed to be discussing (within a week of the opening night its name had faded from my mind for ever), but the torture I went through during those three days before I could write the first three lines of my article—that I have not forgotten. The lobes of my brain seemed about to disintegrate; I felt as if burning embers were scorching my veins. Sometimes I stayed sitting with my elbows on the table, holding my head in my hands. Sometimes I strode up and down like a sentry on duty in twenty-five degrees of frost. I stood at the window and looked out at the neighbouring gardens and the heights of Montmartre and the setting sun—and at once my thoughts flew off and I was carried a thousand miles from that hideous opéra-comique. Then I turned back and my eye fell once more on the accursed sheet of paper, blank except for the accursed title at the top and waiting obstinately for the other words to cover it—and a feeling of despair surged over me. There was a guitar propped up against the table. With a kick I stove it in. Two pistols stared down at me from the chimney-piece with round, dark eyes. For a long time I stood contemplating them. I beat with my fists against my skull. At last, like a schoolboy who cannot do his composition, I tore my hair and wept in a fury of rage and vexation. The salt tears seemed to relieve me a little. I took the pistols, which still stared at me, and turned their barrels to the wall. I had pity on my innocent guitar and, picking it up, tried a few chords, which it gave me without resentment. At that moment my six-year-old son, with whom I had unjustly lost my temper that morning, knocked at the door. When I did not open it, he called out, 'Father, will you be friends?'

I ran to the door to let him in.

'Yes, my boy, let's be friends. Come!'

I took him on my lap and rested his fair head against my breast and we both went to sleep. The evening of the third day! And I had just given up trying to find a beginning for my article. Next day I managed at last, somehow or other, to write I know not what about I know not what.

That was fifteen years ago and the rack still turns. Ruin and destruction! To be always at it! Give me scores to compose, orchestras to conduct, rehearsals to direct; make me stay on my feet eight or ten hours at a stretch, baton in hand, training choirs, without an instrument to accompany them, giving the leads myself while I beat time, until I cough blood and my arm is rigid with cramp; let me be made to carry desks, double basses, harps, to shift platforms, nail planks, like a porter or a carpenter; and then force me, as a relaxation, to sit up all night correcting the mistakes of engravers and copyists: I have done it, I do it, I will do it again; it is part of my life as a musician, and I bear it without complaint, without even a thought, as a sportsman endures cold, heat, hunger, thirst, sunshine and downpour, mud, dust and all the countless exertions of the chase. But eternally to scratch feuilletons for a living! to write nothing about nothing! to give tepid approval to insufferable insipidities! to speak one evening of a great master and the next of an idiot in the same language, with the same gravity of utterance! to expend your time, your intelligence, your spirit and patient endeavour on this drudgery, without even the compensation of knowing that you are at least serving a useful artistic purpose by helping to abolish a few abuses, eradicate prejudices, enlighten opinion, refine public taste and put men and things in their true place and perspective—oh, it is utter humiliation! Better to be—to be finance minister in a republic!

If only I had the choice!

I was feeling less resigned than ever to the disadvantages of my position when the Exhibition of Industrial Products took place in Paris, in 1844. Shortly before it ended, chance, the unpredictable spirit who plays such a large part in my life, decreed that I should meet Strauss, maestro of the fashionable balls, in a café. Conversation turned to the impending closure of the exhibition and the possibility of putting on a great festival in honour of the manufacturers who had exhibited there, in the immense building shortly to become vacant. I told Strauss that I had been thinking of doing so for some time but, after working out the musical statistics of the enterprise, had been brought up short by the problem of actually securing the hall. He promptly replied that we could get round that, for he knew Sénac, secretary to the Minister of Trade, very well; Sénac was in charge of everything to do with French industry and would see that we were able to carry out our project.

Despite Strauss's enthusiasm I still wanted convincing. It was merely agreed, before we parted, that we would both call on M. Sénac the following day and if there seemed any likelihood of our having the use of the building we would go more carefully into the whole question. Without absolutely committing himself, M. Sénac said nothing to discourage us when we unfolded our plan. He promised an immediate reply. The letter came a few days later and was favourable. It remained to get the permission of the Commissioner of Police, M. Delessert.

We saw him and explained our idea, which was to give a three-day festival consisting of a concert, a ball, and a banquet for the exhibitors. Strauss's plan of following the concert with eating, drinking and dancing would undoubtedly have brought in a great deal of money; but Delessert, his commissioner's mind perpetually running on riots and conspiracies, would not hear of it. Indeed, he would sanction neither music nor ball nor banquet, and flatly prohibited the festival.

This seemed to me carrying prudence to absurd lengths, and I mentioned it to M. Bertin. He agreed, and succeeded in persuading the Minister of the Interior, Duchâtel, to see it in the same light. The latter at once sent an order instructing the commissioner that the music at least must be allowed, and Delessert was obliged to authorize us to put on a grand concert of serious music, to be held on the opening day, and a so-called popular concert under the direction of Strauss a day later—a promenade concert at which dance music—waltzes, polkas and galops—would be played, though there would be no dancing.

Such an arrangement would of course lose us our guaranteed profit on the enterprise; but M. Delessert still feared danger to the state from our choirs and orchestras and from all the music-lovers pouring into the Champs-Elysées in broad daylight to listen to them. How could one be sure that Strauss and I were not conspirators disguised as musicians? Nevertheless I felt content to be able to organize and direct a concert on this gigantic scale, and limited my ambitions to achieving a musical success without losing everything I possessed.

My plans were soon formed. Leaving Strauss to look after his dance orchestra—to which no one was going to dance—I engaged for my concert virtually every orchestral player and chorister of any ability in Paris. I succeeded in mustering a body of a thousand and twenty-two performers. All were to be paid except the singers (non-chorus, that is) from the opera houses, to whom I had appealed in a letter begging them to take part as leaders of my choral multitude and 'inspire them with heart and soul and voice'.

Only Duprez, Madame Stoltz and Chollet declined. Their absence was commented upon at the concert and openly criticized in the Press next day. Almost all the members of the Conservatoire Concert Society likewise felt obliged to hold aloof and sulk once again with their 'old general'. Habeneck quite naturally regarded this great ceremony which he was 'not himself conducting' with a jaundiced eye.

So as not to be committed to exorbitant expenses, I engaged the performers for only two rehearsals, one sectional and one general. We hired the Salle Herz, and I took separately, one after the other, violins, violas and cellos, basses, woodwind, brass, harps, percussion, women and children of the chorus, and men. These nine rehearsals, of which no player took part in more than one, produced marvellous results—results which would certainly not have been obtained from as many as five full rehearsals. The session with the thirty-six double basses was particularly interesting. When we tried the scale passage in the scherzo of Beethoven's C minor Symphony, it sounded like the grunting of a herd of stampeding pigs, the playing was so ragged and out of tune. But little by little it improved, ensemble was achieved and the passage emerged clearly in all its rough-hewn energy:

At first all went awry, then slowly better,
*Then well, till it was perfect to the letter.**

We must have gone back over it eighteen or twenty times. This would not have been possible if the whole orchestra had been there. That is the beauty of sectional rehearsals: you pass rapidly over anything that presents no problem to the particular section of chorus or orchestra in question, and contrariwise give all the time and concentration required to getting the awkward and difficult things right. The only disadvantage is that by the end the conductor is absolutely exhausted. However, as I think I have said, in that sort of situation I become gifted with exceptional energy and rival a cart-horse in stamina.

In selecting my programme I had naturally confined myself to music which was broad in style or which the performers knew already. It consisted of the following:

Overture to *La Vestale* (Spontini)
Prayer from *La muette* (Auber)
Scherzo and finale from Symphony in C minor (Beethoven)
Prayer from *Moses* (Rossini)
Hymn to France, which I had composed for the occasion†
Overture to *Freischütz* (Weber)
Hymn to Bacchus from *Antigone* (Mendelssohn)
March to the Scaffold from my Fantastic Symphony
Song of the Manufacturers, also written expressly for the festival, with text by Adolphe Dumas and music by Méraux
A chorus from *Charles VI* (Halévy)
Chorus of the Blessing of the Daggers from *The Huguenots* (Meyerbeer)

* [La Fontaine, 'Le renard et le loup'.]
† [To a poem by Barbier.]

Garden of Delights scene from *Armide* (Gluck)
Apotheosis from my Funeral and Triumphal Symphony

We planned to hold the general rehearsal in the great central area of the exhibition building, known as the Hall of Machinery, which I had chosen for the concert. Yet on the eve of this crucial trial, while the carpenters were constructing the platform, the hall had yet to be vacated. A large number of heavy iron machines lay encamped on the space intended for the audience. No arrangements had been made to have these monsters removed.

I will not attempt to describe what I felt.

The walls of Paris were covered with posters announcing the festival, I was committed for a considerable sum of money, and I now found my efforts blocked by an obstacle as unforeseen as it was insurmountable. We could not delay the concert by a single day. An order for the demolition of the building by 5 August at the latest had already been issued. The contractors who owned the material used to construct it were empowered to begin pulling it down on the 1st and had had to be bribed to let it stand a few hours longer. They were the real masters of the premises and they left us in no doubt that the Minister of Trade had lent us something that did not belong to him. I had a moment of panic and rushed frantically off to have a poster put up cancelling the festival. Strauss almost forcibly restrained me, assuring me that fifty carts were coming next day and the ground would then be freed. I felt I was done for whatever happened, so I let matters take their course. Next day my thousand performers appeared for the general rehearsal, which took place amid the din of bawling carters, cracking whips and neighing horses. But at any rate the carters had come. Gradually the horses hauled away the machines, the space was cleared, and I breathed more freely. When the rehearsal was over, a new nightmare was revealed. The many people who had been listening came up and unanimously declared that the platform would have to be rebuilt; it was impossible to hear a sound from the instruments, with the chorus placed in front of them. The idea of an orchestra of five hundred which could not be heard was a novel one. But sixty workmen set to work; the platform, which did not slope sufficiently, was cut in two, and the front half (the part occupied by the chorus) lowered ten feet. This exposed the orchestra, the back rows of which were then raised still higher. With the new arrangement it would be possible to hear the orchestra, even in a hall of such unresonant acoustics (a defect we could no longer fail to recognize but could do nothing to remedy). No sooner had this second alarm died down than a third, equally serious, arose. Strauss and I, taking advantage of a few hours' lull in the battle, had jumped into a cab and made a tour of the various music shops which were selling tickets for the concert, to see what kind of business they had done. On adding everything together we were appalled to discover that the total amount, twelve thousand francs, would not cover half the general expenses. We must rely on taking an exceptionally large sum at the door; or, failing that, prepare to pay the deficit ourselves.

What a night we spent after this reconnaissance! But it was too late to withdraw now.

On the following day, 1 August, I went to the exhibition building shortly before noon. The concert was due to begin at one. To my joy (though I did not dare give way to it), the first thing I noticed was the remarkable number of carriages converging on the centre of the Champs-Elysées. On entering I found everything in perfect order; my instructions had been followed to the letter. Players, choristers, and sub-conductors of orchestra and chorus were quietly and calmly taking up their appointed positions. I glanced inquiringly at my librarian, M. Rocquemont (a man of uncommon intelligence and a tireless worker who out of his regard for me—as sincere as mine for him—has rendered me unforgettable services on many such occasions). He assured me that the music was set out and nothing missing. The fever of musical action began to flow in my veins and I thought no more of the public, the receipts or the deficit. I was about to signal the attack when there was a loud splintering sound, accompanied by a sustained roar. It was the crowd, which had burst through the wooden barrier and, armed with tickets just purchased at the box office, now surged into the hall with shouts of satisfaction.

'Look at that—it's a tidal wave!' said a player, pointing to the rapidly filling hall.

'We're saved!' I exclaimed, giving the desk as joyous a rap with my baton as I have given in my life. 'Now we shall do something really good.'

We began. The broad phrases of the prelude to *La Vestale* rolled forth; and from that moment the grandeur and power and exactitude of that enormous multitude of instruments and voices grew progressively more astonishing. My thousand and twenty-two performers moved with the unanimity of a first-rate quartet. I had two assistant conductors: Tilmant, conductor at the Opéra-Comique, who directed the wind instruments, and my friend Auguste Morel (now director of the Marseilles Conservatoire), who was in charge of the percussion. There were also five chorus-masters, one at the centre and the others at the four corners of the immense chorus; their task was to transmit my beat to the singers, who could not see it because they had their backs to me. There were thus seven additional time-beaters, whose eyes never left me for an instant; and despite the distance between us our arms rose and fell with incredible precision. Hence the miraculous ensemble which so astonished the audience.

The pieces which made the greatest impression were the *Freischütz* overture, with the andante given by twenty-four horns; the prayer from *Moses*, which was encored, and in which the twenty-five harps sounded like a hundred, because they played the arpeggios in four-part chords instead of in single notes, thus quadrupling the number of strings in vibration; the Hymn to France, encored like the first two but not repeated; and the Blessing of the Daggers from *The Huguenots*, which staggered the audience. Here I had multiplied the solo voices by twenty, so that Saint-Bris and the three monks were sung by eighty basses. The effect of this sublime piece on the performers and on those listeners nearest to the orchestra was quite extraordinary. As for me, I was seized with such a fit of nervous trembling that my teeth chattered as though I had a raging fever. Despite the non-resonance of the hall I do not think anything like this can often have been experienced, and I regretted that Meyerbeer was not there to witness it. It was as if the whole tremendous piece—written, one might have said, in electric current by a giant galvanic pile—were accompanied by claps of thunder and roared out by the winds of heaven.

I was in such a state at the end of this scene that there had to be a fairly lengthy interruption while they brought me punch and a change of clothes. There on the platform a miniature dressing-room was constructed out of a dozen harps with their covers replaced; by stooping slightly I was able to undress and change my shirt in front of the audience without being seen.

Of the remaining pieces the most successful were the Funeral Oration and Apotheosis from my Funeral and Triumphal Symphony (with the trombone solo impressively played by Dieppo) and the scene from *Armide*, which enchanted everyone by its voluptuous serenity.

My March to the Scaffold, which sounds so vigorous and powerfully scored in a normal concert hall, appeared muted and feeble. It was the same with the scherzo and finale of Beethoven's C minor Symphony. Mendelssohn's hymn seemed heavy and uninteresting; one paper remarked a few days afterwards that the priests of this Bacchus must have drunk beer instead of Cyprus wine.

The Song of the Manufacturers was very badly received, above all by the performers. I had undertaken to write the music for Adolphe Dumas' text myself but found it impossible to do so; and so that his poem should not be wasted, and for the sake of good will, I had to agree to let it be set by a composer of his choice. He chose his brother-in-law, a piano teacher in Rouen.

The overture to *La Vestale* was warmly applauded. So was the unaccompanied chorus from *La muette*. But a special success was reserved for the excerpt from *Charles VI*, which had been included at the pressing request of Schlesinger, the publisher of Halévy's opera. The piece stirred up the brute instincts of opposition that always lurk in the breast of the Parisian populace; and at the well-known refrain

Fight we the tyrant, never shall
The English dog be lord in France!

three-quarters of the audience gave tongue and joined in with the chorus. It was a crudely nationalistic protest by the common man against the policy which Louis-Philippe was following at the time.* It seemed only to vindicate the commissioner's prejudice. The incident had a sequel, which I shall come to in a moment.

In short, my Musical Exhibition was brought off not only without mishap but with brilliant success and the hearty approbation of the immense audience attending it. On my way out I had the unspeakable satisfaction of seeing the proceeds being busily counted at a huge table by the poor-house tax-collectors. The sum came to thirty-two thousand francs, of which the tax-collectors took an eighth—four thousand francs. The proceeds of the concert of dance music, which my partner Strauss conducted two days later and which was not a success, were meagre in the extreme; the deficit had to be made up from the profit on the big concert. In the final reckoning I had a grand net profit of eight hundred francs and a receipt for four thousand francs, signed personally by the chief collector, to show for all the difficulties endured, the risks run and the endeavours accomplished.

The delights of living in a free country, where artists are serfs, humbly paying their heartfelt tribute to its liberal and equitable laws!

Hardly had Strauss and I finished paying the musicians, copyists, printers, instrument-makers, masons, roofers, joiners, carpenters, upholsterers, clerks and hall superintendents, when the Commissioner of Police—who had charged us the modest sum of one thousand two hundred and thirty-eight francs for the services of his constables and municipal watchmen (police surveillance at the Opéra costs eighty francs)—summoned us to his office on urgent business.

'What can it be about?' I said to Strauss. 'Have you any idea?'

'None at all.'

'Can Delessert have been smitten with remorse for charging us so much for his useless constables?'

'Of course—that must be what it is!'

We reached police headquarters.

'Sir,' said M. Delessert, addressing me, 'I am afraid I have a serious accusation to make against you.'

* [Which aimed to bring about an improvement in Anglo-French relations, clouded by minor crises in Morocco and Tahiti.]

'Oh? And what is that?' I answered in some astonishment.

'You secretly added to your programme a piece of music calculated to arouse certain political passions which the government is endeavouring to suppress. I refer to the chorus from *Charles VI*, which did not figure in the original advertisement for the festival. The Minister of the Interior has reason to be gravely displeased at the demonstration it provoked, and I entirely share his feeling in the matter.'

'My dear Commissioner' (with all the calm I could muster), 'you are totally in error. The chorus from *Charles VI*, as you rightly say, was not part of the original programme. However, on discovering that M. Halévy had taken offence at being left out, when almost every important modern composer was represented, I agreed to include the piece at the instigation of his publisher. I chose it solely on the grounds of its being easy for a very large body of people to perform. The kind of nationalism which can get excited in 1844 over an incident from the reign of Charles VI leaves me cold; and so little did I contemplate secretly adding the piece to my programme that its name figured for more than a week on all the festival posters, including those put up on the walls of police headquarters. I should be obliged if you would rid your mind of any suspicion on that score and enlighten the Minister of the Interior accordingly.'

M. Delessert, looking a little shamefaced, declared himself satisfied with my explanation and actually apologized for having accused me unjustly.

Nevertheless, from that time forth a censorship of programmes was established, and today you cannot sing a romance by Bérat or Mlle Puget in a public place without a licence from the Minister of the Interior's office, countersigned by a police superintendent.

I had just completed this mad enterprise—which I should certainly not attempt today—when my old anatomy teacher and good friend Dr Amussat called on me. On seeing me, he took a pace backwards.

'Hello! What's the matter with you, Berlioz? You're as yellow as a piece of old parchment. You're obviously in a state of extreme exhaustion and nervous irritation.'

'Irritation? Why should I feel irritated? You came to the festival, you saw how it went off. I had the pleasure of paying four thousand francs to the poor-house tax-collectors, which has left me with eight hundred. What have I got to complain of? Everything's as it should be, isn't it?'

Amussat felt my pulse. 'My dear fellow, you're on the verge of typhoid fever. You must be bled.'

'Very well, let's not wait till tomorrow. Bleed me.'

I took off my coat. Amussat bled me liberally.

'Now,' he said, 'you will do me the kindness to leave Paris with all possible dispatch. Go to Hyères, to Cannes, to Nice, where you like—but go south, get some sea air, forget all about the things which overheat your blood and overstimulate your nervous system, which is highly strung enough as it is. Goodbye, and go—you really mustn't hesitate.'

I took his advice and went to Nice* where thanks to my eight hundred francs from the festival I spent a month, as far as possible undoing the harm it had done to my health.

It was a moving experience for me to see again all the places I had seen thirteen years before at the outset of my Italian travels, on the occasion of another convalescence. I swam a great deal in the sea and made many expeditions to places near Nice—Villefranche, Beaulieu, Cimiès, Phare. I resumed my exploration of the rocks, where I came across some ancient cannon, old friends of mine, still slumbering in the sun. I revisited the exquisite little bays and inlets where I had bathed in former times and where the rocks are a carpet of emerald seaweed. The room in which in 1831 I had written the *King Lear* overture was occupied by an English family, so I settled higher up, in a tower perched on a ledge of the Ponchettes rock, where I enjoyed with delight a splendid view over the Mediterranean and a calm whose worth I appreciated more than ever.† Then, cured of my jaundice after a fashion and relieved of my eight hundred francs, I quitted that enchanting

* [About 22 August 1844.]

† [A few weeks earlier his marriage had finally broken up. At Nice Berlioz wrote the first draft of the *Corsair* overture, performed the following January under the title of *The Tower at Nice*.]

Sardinian coastline which has such an abiding appeal for me and returned to Paris to resume my role of Sisyphus.

A few months later the director of the Théâtre Franconi,* impressed by the extraordinary receipts taken at the Festival of Industry, approached me with a proposal for putting on a series of large-scale performances in his arena in the Champs-Elysées.

I do not remember what terms we agreed on; I know only that it turned out badly for him. The takings of the four concerts, for which we had engaged five hundred performers, were inevitably insufficient to cover all the cost of such huge forces. Once again the place was quite unsuitable for music. This time the sound reverberated so slowly in that heart-breaking rotunda that compositions of any complexity gave rise to the most horrid confusions of harmony. Only one piece was really effective and that was the Dies irae from my Requiem. Its breadth of tempo and harmonic movement made it seem less incongruous than any of the others in those booming cathedral-like spaces. It scored such a success that we had to include it in the programme of every concert.†

The venture was not lucrative for me, and I was exhausted by it. But a fresh opportunity occurred to recuperate in the healing waters of the Mediterranean: I was engaged to give two concerts in Marseilles and Lyons, the proceeds of which would be bound at least to cover my travelling expenses.

It was the first time I performed my music in the French provinces. The letters that I addressed to my colleague Edouard Monnais in the *Gazette musicale* in 1848, though written in a rather light-hearted style, give an accurate account of my experiences on this expedition to the south and on another which I made shortly afterwards to Lille.‡ They are to be found in my book *Musical Grotesques*, under the heading of 'Academic Correspondence'.

* [Gallois.]

† [The four concerts were given on 19 January, 16 February, 16 March and 6 April 1845; the third included music from *A Life for the Tsar* and *Russlan and Ludmila* by Glinka. The Russian composer, then in Paris, was the subject of an appreciative article by Berlioz in the *Débats* on 16 April.]

‡ [He gave two concerts in the Marseilles theatre (19 and 25 June) and two in the Lyons (20 and 24 July). In August 1845 he went to Bonn to report the festival

A few months later I set out for the first time on a tour of Southern Germany, that is to say Austria, Hungary and Bohemia. What follows is the account of my travels which I addressed to my friend Humbert Ferrand in the *Journal des débats*.*

---

organized by Liszt for the inauguration of Beethoven's statue (*Débats*, 22 August and 3 September and *Evenings in the Orchestra*, second epilogue). The Lille concert took place on 14 June 1846 on the occasion of the opening of the Northern Railway, for which Berlioz wrote the cantata *Le chant des chemins de fer*, to a text by Jules Janin. The account of his French provincial experiences appeared in the *Revue et gazette musicale* on 10 September, 15 October and 19 November 1948.]

* [Berlioz's journey lasted from late October 1845 to early May 1846. He took Marie Recio with him, but this time she did not sing.]

TRAVELS IN GERMANY—II

AUSTRIA, BOHEMIA, HUNGARY

First Letter

Vienna

TO HUMBERT FERRAND

I have been to Germany again and, though only just back, feel the need to sit down at once and give you, my dear Humbert, an account of what I did there. You have often stood by me in the heat of the struggle and fortified me in times of despondency, and given me heart for future ordeals by recalling the victories of the past; to you with your keen and lofty feeling for beauty, your religious respect for truth and your belief in the power and greatness of art, the tale of my travels in Europe will not, I trust, prove without interest. No patronage it might win could be more sympathetic or discerning than yours. Despite the serious passions that absorb you and the labours you pursue (thanks to a royal bounty) in peace and seclusion in that delightful corner of the world,* I know that poetry and music are never far from your mind. Your love for them was too deep and pure ever to change, and I picture you among your island mountains, glancing northwards towards Paris and listening for echoes of great literary and musical deeds carried on the wind. But oh, how flat and dismal Paris seems—after this latest journey more than ever—and how I envy you, in these stifling dog-days, your reveries among the great scented orange-groves of Sardinia, the night-music of the Mediterranean, and even the simple songs of your Sardinian labourers, those Africans of Europe, ancient survivals into modern times. *Non nobis Deus haec otia fecit.*†

I come back to find our city steeped, as always, in material concerns, cynically indifferent to all that excites poets and artists, obsessed with scandal and the latest joke, shrill with the harsh, dry

* [Ferrand was spending some months in Sardinia, revising his earlier report on the island and on the agricultural and industrial schemes of Count della Marmora.]

† [An adaptation of Virgil's first Eclogue: *deus nobis haec otia fecit* ('a god has given us this peace').]

laughter that greets whatever feeds this strange appetite; back to the noisome stench of asphalt-burners tempered by the acrid fumes of cheap state cigars; to the bored expressions, the boring faces, the jaded intellects, the creative spirits in dejection, the fools swarming like ants, the theatres dying or defunct; back to hear the same barrel organ grinding the same barbarous tune beneath my window at the same hour, the same barbarous opinions churned out, the same barbarous men and works extolled.

In sum, a melancholy prospect and one that I am in no state of mind to see in a rosy light. Do you remember those fits of depression that used to afflict us in our adolescence the day after some ball or party? A kind of unease in the soul, a heart-ache, insidious, impalpable, a grief without cause, a nostalgia without object, a yearning towards the unknown, an indescribable restlessness in every nerve of one's being—do you remember? I am ashamed to admit it, but that is how I feel now. I feel as though it were the day after a party given by my foreign hosts in my honour. I miss those great orchestras and choirs, with their splendid warmth and responsiveness, whom I would gladly conduct every day of my life. I miss even the fatigue of the long rehearsals. I miss the brilliant audiences, so courteous, so attentive and enthusiastic. I miss the intense emotions of directing a great concert, the sensation of speaking to the multitude through the many-tongued medium of instruments and voices. I miss being able to study the varying impressions produced on an unprejudiced public by the latest experiments in modern art. In a word, the sudden stagnation after so much activity, the oppressive silence after all that musical confusion, fill me with such malaise that since my return I have had but one idea in my head, which I struggle against night and day—to embark on some ocean-going vessel and sail round the world. The day before yesterday, as if to undermine my good resolutions by a tempting example, fate cast in my way an old friend of ours, the great virtuoso Halma,* who had just arrived from Canton. You can imagine how avidly I questioned him about China and the other places he visited—the Malay Islands, Cape Horn, Brazil, Chile, Peru—and examined all the rare and

* [French violinist.]

curious things he had brought back with him. I was literally trembling with excitement, and would have parodied Richard III and cried, 'My kingdom for a ship', had I had one at my disposal. But having neither ship nor kingdom, I stay where I am, in this petty township which—to quote our charming poet Méry—stretches from the rue du Mont Blanc to the Faubourg Montmartre and is called Paris; and I walk about there each evening, repeating to myself in every conceivable key and rhythm that line from *Ruy Blas*:

God, but it's marvellous boring here!

Happily boredom is the midwife of invention, as the proverb might say, and it has suggested to me how I may forget Paris without quitting it. It is to see again and relive in spirit the far-off places that I saw, the artists that I met, the buildings I visited, the institutions I studied; in short, to write to you, choosing, however, only those times and days when the spleen forgets *me*, so that you too may not be bored more than is unavoidable. Will you ever read it, though? I see you from here, drowsing in the shade of the lemon trees, blessed, like the Roman poet's contented old man, by the hum of bees at work in the flowers around you,* a Virgil or Horace open in your hand, lulled by their immortal verse and in no need of my prose. But I know a way to rouse you without your reproaching me for it. Listen: I want to talk to you about Gluck—can you hear me?—Gluck, and about his country, where I have just been, and about Mozart and Haydn and Beethoven who like him lived a good deal of their lives in Vienna. Good, I knew those magic names would condone my untimely interruption. Now to begin.

Only two distinct impressions remain of the journey from Paris to Vienna. One was of a harrowing experience—a purely physical and thoroughly mundane one, with nothing romantic about it, I hasten to say—in the form of an acute pain in my side which forced me to stop off at Nancy, where I nearly died (but what of that, since we live with only that end in view?). The other was of a god whom I saw through the window of an inn in Augsburg. The worthy man, who had recently founded a species of

* A further reference to the first Ecologue.

neo-Christianity, was just getting into his carriage as the innkeeper, pale with emotion, pointed him out to me. I forget his name. I had a glimpse of a shrewd and lively face; he looked a decent sort of rogue. The journey, made partly by hackney carriage (like journeys in Italy), took even longer than it should have done. By the time I reached Ratisbon the last steamboat had left, and after being obliged to spend two days in that glorified market town I had the mortification, instead of steaming rapidly down the Danube, of being laboriously conveyed along its banks, reflecting on the centuries of progress which separate the two methods of travel: on leaving Ratisbon I could have imagined myself living in the time of Frederick Barbarossa; at Linz I slipped aboard a handsome, swift-looking steamer and was back in 1845. These two towns, by the way, reminded me of something that has often struck me: I mean the mania we have in Europe for altering or corrupting place-names when transferring them from one language to another. What possesses us, for example, to turn London into Londres? Why do the Italians find it necessary to say Parigi instead of Paris? I had with me on my journey a map of Germany which I often consulted. I found Linz, because we consent to speak and write it as the Germans do, but searched in vain for Ratisbon, for the simple reason that the name is our invention and has no relation to the correct one, Regensburg. We do certain names the honour of preserving them—including some of the most difficult to pronounce—and corrupt others, without any notion why we do it. We say Stuttgart, Karlsruhe, Darmstadt, the Kingdom of Württemberg, like the people who named them. The next moment, we are talking about Munich instead of München and the Danube instead of the Donau. At least there is some resemblance there between our translation and the original word. There is none at all between Ratisbon and Regensberg. Yet we should think the Germans singularly ridiculous if they had chosen to call Lyons Mittenbert and Paris Triffenstein.

On disembarking at Vienna,* I was at once given an impressive idea of the Austrians' passion for music. One of the customs-

* [3 November 1845.]

officers, examining the trunks and packages from the boat, caught sight of my name and cried out (in French, I may add):

'Where is he? Where is he?'

'Here—I'm here.'

'Thank heavens for that! M. Berlioz, what in the world can have happened to you? We've been waiting for you for the past week. All the papers said you had left Paris and were shortly to give concerts in Vienna. We were getting quite anxious about you.'

I thanked the excellent customs-officer as best I could, while reflecting that the Paris toll-house officials were never likely to be visited by such anxieties.

I had hardly established myself in this exhilarating city when I was invited to attend the first of the annual concerts in the Riding School. It is given for the benefit of the Conservatoire, and the immense body of performers, numbering over a thousand, is made up almost entirely of amateurs. As the government does little or nothing to support the Conservatoire, it is only sensible that the real friends of music should come to its assistance—though for the very reason that it struck me as sensible I was astonished that it should happen. Every year at this time the Emperor places the huge hall of the Riding School at the disposal of the Gesellschaft der Musikfreunde. Would-be performers put their names on a list at one or other of the music shops. There are so many competent amateur singers and instrumentalists in Vienna that it is quite difficult to choose the six-hundred-strong chorus and the four-hundred-strong orchestra, and each year more than five hundred people have to be turned down. The proceeds from these gigantic concerts (there are always two of them) are very large; the hall holds an audience of four thousand, even with the huge space taken up by the tiered platform on which the performers are accommodated. Normally, only the first concert is sold out; the second, which repeats the programme of the first, is not so well attended. Must one conclude that a great many Viennese would be bored if they had to listen to the same masterpieces twice in a week?

Audiences are the same everywhere in this respect. It is true that at these great Viennese functions the programme is nearly always made up of the best known works of the old masters. If there were a chance of hearing at the second concert some new work composed especially for the occasion and with those resources in mind, the public would very probably be just as eager to come to it as to the first concert. And it would, indeed, make a very interesting proposition. Works written with the breadth of style of the oratorios of Handel, Bach, Haydn and Beethoven no doubt have much to gain from being performed by large forces. But in such cases it is only a question of reinforcing the parts to a greater or lesser degree; whereas a composer writing specifically for an orchestra and chorus of this size and understanding the immense possibilities of such an agglomeration of forces could not fail to produce something as novel in detail as it would be imposing in general effect. This has not yet been done. In all so-called monumental works the form and texture remain unchanged. They are performed with pomp in huge halls but would not lose a great deal by being heard in more modest surroundings, with a small body of performers. They do not absolutely demand an exceptional concentration of voices and instruments; and when they get it, nothing extraordinary or unforeseen results, only a greater emphasis. Having said this I must admit I was profoundly moved by the concert,* above all by the effect of the chorus; I thought their ensemble excellent and the quality of the soprano voices incomparably beautiful. I had been alarmed to see the overture to Mozart's *Magic Flute* on the programme, supposing that this marvellous piece, with its rapid tempo and fine and closely woven texture, could not possibly be done well by such an enormous Mass of players. My fears were short-lived: the orchestra—an orchestra of amateurs—played it with a precision and verve not often found even among professional musicians.

A motet by Mozart, one by Haydn, an aria from *The Creation*, the aforementioned overture, and Beethoven's oratorio *The Mount of Olives* made up the programme. Staudigl and Madame Barthe-Hasselt sang the solo parts. Staudigl, a bass, has a voice as smooth and sumptuous as velvet, at once suave and powerful, with a range of two octaves and two notes (low E to high G). He never forces it, but sings with a calm, effortless flow of tone that can fill

* [11 November 1845.]

even a hall as huge as the Riding School with apparent ease. It is a voice which thrills and subjugates you by a quality of emotion inherent in its timbre and independent of the artist himself, who is normally rather phlegmatic. His singing has the simplicity and good taste that mark the virtuoso who has mastered the grand style. At the same time he can execute ornaments and fairly rapid divisions without difficulty. Finally, he is a thorough musician and reads at sight with complete assurance whatever is put in front of him. This extreme facility has its drawbacks. Staudigl takes a little too much pride in it; he never so much as looks at a piece of music which he is not required to sing by heart until he is actually standing before the orchestra. When the general rehearsal is about to begin he appears, takes out his copy—which he has not yet seen—and sings it through fluently, text and music, without getting a word or a note wrong. He reads it just as if it were a book put into his hands for the first time; but he does not read it any better than that, and it is precisely that better that is essential at a general rehearsal, where not only mechanical accuracy but also a lively and intelligent realization of the composer's intentions is involved. A performer who has not prepared any of it beforehand, to whom the general sense of the piece, the expression and even the tempos are unknown, naturally cannot hope to give it that warmth and feeling, that life, merely by reading through his part. I heard this mild criticism voiced while I was in Vienna—a criticism not of the artist's powers but of his use of them—by composers who on many important occasions had had cause to feel somewhat anxious about it. Louis XVIII used to say that one 'should not be more royalist than the King'; one might suggest to Staudigl that he should not seek to be more musical than the music. The aria in D major from *The Creation*, which he sang at the Riding School concert, roused the whole audience; and Staudigl, who had been on the point of leaving the hall, his presence being no longer necessary, had to come back and sing it again. Staudigl is both leading singer and stage manager at the Theater an der Wien (a company directed ably and with integrity by M. Pokorny). His magnificent voice, for all its exquisite beauty of timbre, is not one of those delicate organs which oblige their possessors to adopt a special régime and pay the strictest attention to their health. On the contrary, Staudigl will cheerfully go shooting in the coldest months of the year and spend all day in the snow, bare-necked as is his wont, and the same evening sing Bertram or Marcel or Caspar without the slightest vocal difficulty. The Theater an der Wien, so called because it is built by the little river of that name, was opened barely three years ago,* but is doing so well that it has already become a threat to its rival, the Kärntnerthortheater. Nearly all well-known artists who want to be heard in Vienna go to the Theater an der Wien. Pischek made his début there in the winter of 1846, and Jenny Lind shortly afterwards. Heaven knows what scenes of wild enthusiasm they provoked or what fabulous sums were taken.

The chorus there is not large but it is powerful, most of the men and women in it being young, with fine, fresh voices, though not all are good readers. The orchestra, which I heard strongly criticized from the moment I arrived in Vienna, is certainly not to be compared with the Kärntnerthor orchestra (of which I shall speak presently); but it is a serviceable body and the players are young and full of that enthusiasm and goodwill which can on occasion work miracles. The company includes a lady who impressed me as having a real gift for romantic and lyrical roles, and I regret that I cannot remember her name. She was particularly good as Agathe in *Freischütz*.

I should also mention Mlle Treffs, a very pleasing singer, and Mlle Marra, the prima donna, a performer remarkable both for her charm and for her panache, with a voice that is light and brilliant, if unsuited to certain kinds of florid singing; unfortunately she is a poor musician, with a feeble sense of time, capable of throwing the whole ensemble into confusion and confounding the most experienced and quick-witted conductor. Mlle Marra excels in Donizetti's *Lucia*. Last winter she sang with great success in North Germany and in one or two towns in Russia.

But the tenors! There is the weak point of the Theater an der Wien, as indeed of nearly every opera house in the world at the

* [Under Pokorny's management. The theatre had been in existence since 1801, when it was built as a successor to the nearby Theater auf der Wieden, where *The Magic Flute* was first performed.]

moment; and I fear it will be some time before M. Pokorny, with all his efforts, is able to strengthen it.

In this respect the Kärntnerthor is better off. It has Erl, a tenor with a high, 'white' voice—as an artist a little cold, more successful in placid than in passionate scenes and more a purely musical than a dramatic singer. The Kärntnerthortheater is directed by an Italian, Balochino. Everybody in Vienna—court, town, amateurs, professionals—is highly critical of his administration. I was not in a position to judge the reasons for this unpopularity, but its effect seems to have been to make the public stay away from the theatre, despite all the skill and energy of that distinguished artist Nicolai, who is in charge of the whole musical side—with which M. Balochino, as director of an opera house, is necessarily unacquainted. It says much for the latter that he has not recruited any tailors to play the cello,* and has thought of engaging violinists to play the violin. In France too they are usually forced to turn for their music to musicians; but they are working on a solution to the problem which will rid them once and for all of this disagreeable necessity.

Besides a very fine bass, deep and resonant, Balochino's company includes the singer whose name I mentioned earlier, Madame Barthe-Hasselt. Madame Hasselt is musically and dramatically an artist of the first rank. Her voice may be a little lacking in freshness but it is large in compass, unusually powerful, perfectly in tune, and with a timbre that moves one perhaps for the very reason that it is slightly veiled. I heard her sing, in magnificent style, the splendid but difficult soprano scena from *Oberon*. I doubt if there is one prima donna in a hundred capable of interpreting this inspired passage with such fidelity and fire, such grandeur and panache. In the last section of the final allegro, after Rezia's great outburst of joy, a battle royal was joined between singer and orchestra, from which Madame Hasselt emerged with flying colours, her voice defying the unleashed fury of the orchestra and ringing out triumphantly without a trace of forcing or a single dubious note. Few things that I heard left so vivid an impression on my memory as this concert performance of Weber's famous

* He used to be a tailor himself, I was told.

scene. Shortly afterwards I was able to recognize Madame Hasselt's abilities as a tragic actress when I saw her in Nicolai's opera *Il proscritto*, the last act of which is quite admirable and to my mind entitles Nicolai to a very high place among composers.

The heroine of this opera (which is based on a play by Frédéric Soulié) is a woman who, after marrying again in the belief that her husband, whom she respected but never loved, has died in exile, discovers that he is alive, and on his return is faced with the necessity of giving up her second husband, the man she has always loved; which grim ordeal proving too much for her to contemplate she poisons herself, having first reconciled the rivals, and dies with their hands clasped to her heart. Madame Hasselt sang and played the role like a consummate lyric tragédienne and recalled for me the wonderful bursts of eloquence, the blend of minutely studied effect and sudden unpremeditated genius, which made Madame Branchu so justly renowned in France forty years ago.

Alas, my dear Humbert, the great tragédiennes of opera are gradually dying out, like the tenors; yet without them the lyric drama is lost.* To judge from the ever-increasing rarity of singers capable of using our art as a medium for reproducing the noble passions of the heart, one would think such passions an invention of poets and composers, and nature's creating a few beings gifted with the power to understand and express them a kind of sport, a luxury which it did not propose to repeat, regarding such beings as beyond the scope of the human race.

Second Letter

Vienna (continued)

TO HUMBERT FERRAND

When I said that dramatic sopranos were becoming as rare as tenors and that nature seemed not to wish to produce any more, I was not referring to actual voices. Whereas true tenors are indeed pearls of great price, fine soprano voices, powerful, large in range,

* [A perennial cry! Cf. Wagner, writing about *Die Meistersinger* fifteen years later: 'It will not call for an outstanding tenor, which, as things are just now, is almost everything—nor for a great tragic soprano, which is a good deal.']

and even of exemplary method, are still to be found. But what is the use of such instruments without the feeling, intelligence and inspiration to give them life? It was genuine thorough-going dramatic talent that I was referring to. There are plenty of singers, popular with the public because they sing glittering nonsense glitteringly, and heartily disliked by great composers because they are incapable of interpreting their works with any reasonable degree of adequacy, possessing a voice, a knowledge of music and an agile larynx, but devoid of soul, heart or brains. These women are a species of monster, all the more dangerous to composers because they are often monsters of charm. This explains why many serious composers will weakly descend to writing roles which impose on the public by their superficial brilliance but in point of sentiment are fakes. Hence too the incidence of bastard works, the progressive debasement of style, stifling of sense of expression, neglect of dramatic proprieties and contempt for truth, grandeur and beauty, and the general state of cynicism and decrepitude into which the art has fallen in certain countries.

I have not yet told you anything of the Kärntnerthor chorus and orchestra. Both are of first-rate quality, especially the orchestra, which is selected, trained and directed by Nicolai. There are orchestras that are as good, but none that is better. In addition to its vivacity and poise and extreme technical efficiency, it has a most beautiful tone, due, I should say, as much to meticulously exact tuning between the instruments as to the accuracy and purity with which each individual part is played. People do not realize how uncommon this is, nor what a damaging effect poor intonation, supposedly so rare, can have on even the finest bands. The Kärntnerthor orchestra is adept at accompanying every style of vocal music and equally at taking the lead when it is required to dominate; but its forte is never noisy, except when it has to play one of those wretched concoctions which compel an orchestra to be as bad as the composer who perpetrated it. It is ideal in opera, superb in symphonic music and—to round off the catalogue of its virtues—wholly free from the type of vain, self-satisfied player who rejects just criticism as an insult, feels outraged at any hint of a comparison with foreign orchestras and considers he is doing Beethoven a favour by condescending to perform him. Nicolai has his enemies in Vienna. So much the worse for the Viennese. I regard him as one of the finest orchestral conductors I have ever encountered and one of those men whose presence in a town can give it a position of unchallengeable musical ascendancy when they enjoy conditions which provide full scope for their powers. Nicolai has to my mind the three indispensable qualities of a good conductor. He is a skilled, experienced and at times inspired composer; he has a thorough sense of rhythm and its complexities and an impeccably clear and precise technique; and he is a shrewd and tireless organizer who grudges neither time nor trouble spent on rehearsal and knows exactly what he is doing because he does only what he knows how to do. Hence the excellent moral and physical health of the Kärntnerthor orchestra, its confidence, discipline and stamina and its marvellous sureness and unanimity.

The *concerts spirituels* which Nicolai arranges and conducts every year in the Redoutensaal are worthy counterparts of our Conservatoire concerts in Paris. It was at one of them that I heard the scena from *Oberon* (referred to in my previous letter), together with the aria 'Unis dès la plus tendre enfance' from *Iphigénie en Tauride*, rather poorly sung by Erl, a fine symphony by Nicolai himself, and Beethoven's glorious symphony in B flat. The whole concert was performed with the passionate fidelity, disciplined force and refinement of detail which for me at least make such an orchestra, directed like this, the highest achievement of modern art and the most complete manifestation of what we mean by music today.

It was in this large and handsome hall, thirty years ago, that Beethoven performed his masterpieces, now worshipped throughout Europe but at the time received by the Viennese with lethal contempt. Count Michael Wielhorsky told me that he was one of an audience of fifty which in 1820 heard the symphony in A performed! The Viennese were busy going to Salieri's operas. Puny creatures! A giant had risen among them but they were happier with dwarfs.

You can imagine, my dear Humbert, how my legs trembled when I stepped onto the platform where that mighty foot not long ago had trod. Nothing has changed since Beethoven's time. The conductor's desk that I used had been his. There had stood the piano on which he used to improvise. Down that staircase he returned to the artists' room after the performance of his immortal works, when a few perceptive enthusiasts had the pleasure of calling him back and rapturously applauding him, to the astonishment of the rest who had come there out of idle curiosity and who could hear nothing in the sublime flights of his genius but the convulsions and brutal aberrations of a disordered brain. One or two of them privately agreed with the enthusiasts but did not dare join them, not liking to go against public opinion. Meanwhile Beethoven suffered. Under how many Pilates did this Christ endure crucifixion?

The huge Redoutensaal is excellent for music. It is a parallelogram, but the angles do not produce any echo. The hall consists simply of a level area and a gallery. At one of the concerts that I gave there the celebrated singer Pischek made his début in Vienna. I was delighted when he suggested it, having admired him in Frankfurt three years earlier. He chose 'Des Sängers Fluch', a ballad by Uhland set to music by Esser, which suited him admirably. As it is a piece with piano accompaniment, I asked Seymour-Schiff, a vigorous German pianist, if he would play it; which, like the artist he is, he agreed to do. We went off to Pischek's to rehearse the piece. I need hardly say that it has nothing whatever in common with the musical bric-à-brac that we know as ballads in Paris. Uhland's poem is of some length, and Esser has treated it spaciously in the manner of Schubert. The music is varied and powerfully dramatic in character and bears no resemblance to our meagre ditties with their patent Gothick veneer. I cannot describe the impression which Pischek's incomparable voice and thrilling vehemence made on me—so far has he advanced in the last three years. It was a kind of intoxication, not unlike the effect produced by Duprez on the Opéra audience the night of his début in *William Tell*. You can't imagine the beauty of this baritone voice, its intensity, the richness of its chest notes, the exquisite softness of its head notes, its power and flexibility. Its range too is considerable, extending over two octaves in pure chest register from low to high A flat. And what spirit infuses this rare instrument and gives it life! what passion—now skilfully contained, now leaping forth. The moment one hears Pischek one recognizes an artist, a true musician. He stirs or soothes the listener at will; one is held spellbound, one is swept away. From the very first bars of the ballad, his ardour possessed me. I felt myself flush to the eyes, my pulse beat violently and, beside myself with delight, I exclaimed, 'This man is Don Giovanni, Romeo and Cortez rolled into one!' Pischek has the further advantage of a striking appearance: a tall, well-proportioned figure, a glowing, expressive face. He is a fearless reader, a first-rate pianist and a sufficiently skilled contrapuntist to be able to improvise in fugal style on any given subject without difficulty. It is a tragedy for the Paris Opéra that he does not know a word of French. Born in Prague (in 1810, I think), his first language was Bohemian. Subsequently he acquired German, then Italian. He is at present learning English, in which language he will sing in London next winter.

His success in Esser's ballad at my concert was spontaneous and unqualified, and the encore it earned him—a romance sung, ravishingly, to his own accompaniment—captivated the audience and set the seal on his triumph. A few days later he appeared at the Theater an der Wien, first in Lortzing's *Zimmermann* and then in *Puritani*, in which the famous duet gave him the opportunity for a heroic encounter with Staudigl. He was about to play Don Giovanni when I left for Prague, and I keenly regretted that I could not hear him in the role of this embodiment of sexual fascination and effrontery, for he must surely be the ideal exponent of the part. Pischek had his critics in Vienna, among them highly intelligent people who found his singing mannered and artificial. I confess I never noticed anything that seemed to me to merit such a severe accusation, which has often, by the way, been made against Rubini too; and I repeat that if he would only learn to speak French really well (which, however, I fear is no longer possible) and if a brilliant and at the same time passionate role were written for him to sing, he would subjugate the Opéra audience at will and have all Paris at his feet.

The Redoutensaal takes its name from the great balls frequently held in the hall during the winter season. There the youth of Vienna gives rein to its passion for dancing, a genuine passion and a very agreeable one which has led the Austrians to elevate ballroom dancing into an art, as far above the conventional

Parisian variety as Strauss's waltzes and his orchestra are superior to the polkas and hack fiddlers of our suburban entertainment pits. I spent whole nights watching these incomparable waltzers whirling round in great clouds, and in admiring the choreographic precision of the quadrilles—two hundred people at a time, drawn up in two long lines—and the vivid character dances, which for originality and polished execution I have not seen surpassed anywhere except in Hungary. And there stands Strauss,* directing his splendid orchestra; and sometimes, when one of the new waltzes which he writes for every society ball makes a special hit, the dancers stop to applaud and the ladies go over to his rostrum and throw him their bouquets and they all shout 'bis' and make him come back at the end of the quadrille (since dancing feels no jealousy and allows music its share in the triumph and the fun). This is no more than justice; for Strauss is an artist. It is not sufficiently recognized what an influence he has already had on the musical taste of Europe as a whole by introducing cross-rhythms into the waltz. (Their effect on the dancers themselves has been so stimulating that they have devised the two-step waltz in an attempt to imitate it, although the music keeps the triple rhythm.) If the public outside Germany is ever brought to appreciate the extraordinary charm that can on occasion result from combined and contrasted rhythms, it will be owing to him. Beethoven's marvels in this line are too exalted to have affected more than a small minority of listeners. Strauss, on the other hand, deliberately appeals to a popular audience; and by copying him his numerous imitators are perforce helping to spread his influence.

The simultaneous use of different divisions of the bar and uneven accentuations of the melody—even where the shape remains constant and unvaried—is to simple rhythm as music written in independent and contrasting parts is to block harmony or, one could even say, as harmony is to the unison and the octave. However, this is not the place to go into the question. I ventured to do so, some twelve years ago, in an essay on rhythm,† and was violently abused for my pains by a large number of persons most of

* [Johann the elder, father of the composer of *Die Fledermaus*.]

† [*Journal des débats*, 10 November 1837.]

whom can have had no idea what I was talking about. I need not tell you that France, without being so reactionary as Italy on this point, is still the centre of resistance to progress in the emancipation of rhythm.

A small and scattered public in Paris, by dint of listening to Weber and Beethoven at the Conservatoire, is beginning to suspect that the constant use of a single rhythm may be a factor tending to monotony and even to gross platitude. But I no longer feel any desire to harry the dawdlers. Our French peasants sing only in unison. I am now satisfied that if the infatuated advocates of simple rhythm and eight-bar phrases with a thump of the bass drum on the strong beat ever acquire a feeling and a taste for rhythmic 'harmony', it will be on the day the peasants have learnt to sing in six parts and not a moment sooner. We should leave them to their primeval pleasures.

One evening at one of these midnight revels, while the stream of dancers flashed by me, I was brooding in melancholy fashion—for Strauss's waltzes with their yearning impassioned melodies have the knack of making me feel intensely sad—when a small man with a lively expression made his way through the throng towards me. It was the day after one of my concerts.

'Sir,' he exclaimed with warmth, 'you are French and I am Irish, so there is nothing chauvinistic about my admiration, and' (seizing my left hand) 'allow me to shake the hand that wrote the *Romeo* symphony. You understand Shakespeare!'*

'In that case,' I replied, 'you have the wrong hand. I always write with this one.'

The Irishman smilingly took the proffered hand, shook it very heartily, and went off saying:

'Oh the French, the French! They have to make fun of everything and everybody, even of their admirers.'

I never found out who this amiable islander was who mistook my symphonies for left-handed wenches.†

* [*Romeo* was performed, complete, at the Theater an der Wien on 2 January 1846, directed not by Berlioz (who was in the audience) but by the resident leader, Groidl.]

† [I.e. bastards.]

I have not told you anything of the good Ernst, who created a tremendous stir in Vienna at about this time: but I shall be speaking of him later when I come to give an account of my visit to Russia; for I met him when I was in St Petersburg, where he enjoyed an enormous and ever-growing success. At present he is relaxing by the shores of the Baltic, taking lessons in grandeur and sublimity from the sea. I hope to meet him again in some other corner of the world; for of all musicians, Liszt, Ernst and I are, I believe, the three biggest vagabonds that 'restlessness and the desire to see things' ever drove to leave their own countries and wander the earth.

It takes a talent as exceptional as Ernst's to attract attention at all in Vienna, where one hears so many eminent violinists, not counting the remarkable players who live there. Among the latter I would single out Mayseder, whose reputation is long-established and well-deserved; the young Joachim, a name that is beginning to count,* and Hellmesberger, son of the leader at the Kärntnerthor. Mayseder is a brilliant violinist, correct, poised, elegant, supremely assured. The other two, Joachim especially, are daring and impulsive players, as is natural at their age, striving after novel effects, gifted with abundant energy and not inhibited by a sense of the impossible. Mayseder is leader of Prince Czartorisky's admirable quartet; his second violin is Strebinger, his viola Durst and his cello Borzaga. All four are members of the Imperial Chapel. This quartet is one of the best things to be heard in Vienna and fully justifies the religious attention with which the Prince and a select audience listen to them once a week performing the masterpieces of Beethoven, Haydn and Mozart. Princess Czartorisky, a musician of wide knowledge and exemplary taste and a distinguished pianist, sometimes takes part in these private chamber concerts. After a performance of a Hummel quintet, which she had played in masterly style, someone remarked to me:

'There are simply no amateurs left.'

'Oh,' I answered, 'I think if you look carefully you may still find a few, even among professional musicians. But the Princess is certainly exceptional.'

* Joachim is now the leading violinist in Germany, if not in Europe, and a thorough artist.

The Imperial Chapel is naturally first-rate, being recruited from among the best players and singers in Vienna. The choir includes a number of boys with very attractive voices. Most of the solos are given to Staudigl. The orchestra is small but superb. The whole establishment reminded me of the Tuileries Chapel in the period of its greatest splendour, in 1828 and 1829. I heard them perform a Mass made up of pieces by various composers, including Asmayer, Joseph Haydn and his brother Michael. In Paris too they used sometimes to make a similar hotchpotch for liturgical use in the Chapel Royal, but only very occasionally. I imagine the same is so in Vienna, and I was simply out of luck (although the fragments that I heard were in themselves very beautiful). The Emperor, if I am not mistaken, had at that time three kapellmeisters: the learned contrapuntists Eybler and Asmayer, and Weigl, who died only a few days before I left Vienna.* In France we know Weigl by his opera *The Swiss Family*, performed in Paris in 1828. The piece had little success; musicians thought it feeble and colourless and the wags described it as a rustic idyll written in milk.

One thing that surprised and distressed me in Vienna was the general ignorance of Gluck. I was constantly asking musicians and music-lovers if they knew *Alceste* or *Armide* or *Iphigénie*. The answer was always the same: 'We don't know them, they're never done in Vienna.' But, you wretched creatures, you should know them by heart whether they are done or not! It is clear that entrepreneurs such as Messrs Pokorny and Balochino, more concerned with large receipts than with good music, are not going to waste their money putting on antiquated masterpieces after the example of the King of Prussia, when they have up-to-the-minute articles such as *Indra* and *Alessandro Stradella* to offer the public.†

People even mentioned as one of the events of the season the recent discovery of Gluck's tomb. Can you credit that, my dear Humbert? I visualize your astonishment. Its whereabouts had been completely unknown. My dear Viennese, you are worthy

* [Weigl, son of a cellist in the Esterházy orchestra and a godson of Haydn, died on 3 February 1846. Berlioz was proposed as his successor but could not bear the thought of being permanently exiled from Paris, so declined.]

† [Operas by Flotow. *Alessandro Stradella* was performed at both the Kärntnerthortheater and the Theater an der Wien during Berlioz's stay in Vienna.]

to inhabit Paris! Yet one should not find it so strange, considering that no one has the slightest idea where Mozart's remains are buried.

From the references in my first letter you will have formed no very brilliant impression of the Vienna Conservatoire. Despite all the ability of its director, Preyer, and the acknowledged talents of Joseph Fischoff, Boehm and one or two other admirable teachers on its staff, it does not correspond in size and importance with what one would expect to find in a great musical centre like Vienna. A few years ago it was apparently in such decay that without the ingenuity and Herculean exertions of Dr Bacher, who dedicated himself to saving it and putting it on its feet again, it would by now be defunct. Dr Bacher is not a musician at all but one of those friends of music, of whom there are two or three comparable in Europe, who out of pure love of art will take on and sometimes accomplish the most exacting tasks and who by the excellence of their judgment and taste acquire a real authority over men's minds, often achieving by their own efforts what sovereigns ought to do but don't. Energetic, persistent, determined, and generous beyond description, Dr Bacher is music's staunchest champion in Vienna and the good angel of musicians. The Conservatoire hall, which is small but excellent, is used for the Philharmonic concerts—ably conducted by Baron de Lannoy—and also for the meetings of the male-voice choral society, a valuable institution directed with enthusiasm and sagacity by M. Barthe. In this hall I heard the astonishing pianist Dreyschock on half a dozen different occasions, each time with renewed pleasure. He is a brilliant young man with a fresh and vigorous talent, a player of immense technical skill and a highly serious musician. His own pieces for piano are full of attractive and original inventions.

I must apologize to the many artists whom lack of space obliges me to treat so summarily. To do them full justice and list in detail all the musical riches of Vienna would require a book.

I have not yet said anything about some of its most distinguished spirits, those whose particular talent is expressed mainly in writing so-called chamber works such as quartets and lieder with piano accompaniment. One such is Becher, a taciturn, introspective spirit, a dreamer, a harmonist of unprecedented boldness, whose aim is to enlarge the form and scope of the quartet and give it a new character. Becher is also an eminent writer, and his criticisms are highly thought of by the leading lights of the Viennese Press.*

Another is Councillor Wesque de Puttlingen, who publishes his works under the pseudonym of Hoven. I spent some delightful hours listening to him singing his lieder. Their melodic style is deft and graceful and full of humour, and the accompaniments have many piquant touches of harmony. I was struck by similar qualities in the extracts which I heard (only on the piano, unfortunately) from two operas that he has written.

Josef Dessauer is better known to us, from the two years that he spent in Paris (1840 to 1842, if I remember rightly). While he was there he set to music innumerable pieces by our leading poets. He is still adding to his store of lieder, most of which are highly successful in all the salons of taste. Dessauer's predilection is exclusively for the elegiac. He feels at ease only with a melancholy soul; tears are his greatest happiness and the woes of the heart his chief joy. In Vienna, as in Paris, there was a state of gentlemanly war between us. His one idea is to convert me to some musical doctrine the nature of which I am still ignorant of, for he has never been able to bring himself to reveal it to me. Whenever the opportunity arose for having what he called a really good talk, and he was about to launch on his homily, I had only to look at him with my most serious expression and he would decide that I was going to laugh at him and put off my conversion until some more favourable moment. If all proselytizers had behaved like this, we would still be wallowing in the dark night of paganism.

I must not forget to mention the cordial welcome I received from my fellow-ploughmen who work the flinty soil of criticism, as I still do, for the thistles and nettles that are too often its only crop. They treated me as a colleague, for which I thank them. One of them, M. Saphir, holds an annual literary and musical forum at which he contrives, in defiance of the censorship, to castigate everything and everybody in the most brilliantly witty fashion,

* Unhappy Becher! I hear that during the recent uprising in Vienna he flung himself recklessly into the fray and was arrested, tried, convicted and shot.

to the delight of his audience who, like all the world, love nothing better than to see a reputation torn to shreds.

I shall refrain from telling you of the conductor's baton which my Viennese friends kindly presented to me at a supper-party given after my third concert,* the handsome gift I received from the Emperor, and many other matters with which you were regaled *ad nauseam* in the newspapers of the day. You know all about the nice things which happened to me during my visit, so it would be at best a waste of time to tell you again.

Third Letter

Pesth

TO HUMBERT FERRAND

There are at least three major cities that one positively must see when one visits Austria: Vienna, Pesth and Prague. Some perverse minds, it is true, insist that Pesth is in Hungary and Prague in Bohemia, but these two states are none the less integral parts of the Austrian Empire, attached and devoted to it body and soul and estate, much as Ireland is devoted to England or Poland to Russia or Algeria to France, as subject peoples have in all ages been attached to their conquerors. Accordingly let us set out for Pesth, a large Austrian town in Hungary. My relationship with the Danube was not a happy one. I have told you how at Ratisbon it spirited away the last steamboat when I wished to embark for Vienna. This time it hid itself behind a dense veil of fog so that I should not be able to travel down it to Pesth. As you will shortly see, the cantankerous old river's discourtesy did not end there. It

* The baton is of silver-gilt and bears the names of the numerous subscribers who gave it to me. It is wreathed in a sprig of laurel, with the titles of my works inscribed on the leaves. The Emperor sent me a hundred ducats (one thousand one hundred francs) after attending one of the concerts which I gave in the Redoutensaal. At the same time he instructed his servant to convey to me this curious compliment: 'Tell Berlioz it was great fun.'

[The supper-party was on 10 December 1845, the eve of his forty-second birthday. In Vienna Berlioz conducted or was associated with eight concerts; but it is clear that he, or his editor, had decided that the *Débats* readers wanted fewer musical details and more general chat than in his earlier series of letters from Germany and that Paris would be bored with what he called his 'dispatches from the Grand Army'.]

was clearly in a thorough ill humour at my arrival in its territories and was determined not merely to do nothing to assist my progress but to do everything possible to obstruct it. This was not for want of appreciative compliments on my part. I was forever expatiating on its majestic grandeur. But the more I rhapsodized, the more it took exception—like La Fontaine's 'lordly lion who was a kinsman of Caligula'.*

Before leaving Vienna I expressed the wish to be presented to Prince Metternich. But even those friends best placed to procure me the privilege seemed so genuinely nonplussed that my first reaction was to abandon the idea. I would have to see an officer who knew a councillor who would speak to a member of the court chancellery who was exalted enough to introduce me to a secretary at the embassy who would get the ambassador to have a word with a minister who would see what he could do to have me presented; which seemed an unduly roundabout route. Then I thought: why not simply dispense with officer, councillor, chancellery official, secretary, ambassador and minister, and present myself? My friends, when they saw me resolved to try, no doubt privately thought me an ass, or at least an incorrigible double-dyed Frenchman. Nevertheless, defying the rigours of Austrian etiquette, or the opinion of them held in Vienna, I set off for the Prince's palace. When I got there I went up to the reception room and handed my card to the officer on duty and explained why I had come. He went in to the Prince, and came back a moment later with the information that His Highness would be free in a few minutes and would be happy to see me. In due course and without further preamble I was admitted. The Prince was affability itself. He asked me a great many questions about music and especially about my own music, of which it seemed to me that His Highness, without having yet heard any of it, had formed a rather strange impression. I endeavoured to give him a different one. In a word, I withdrew at the end of the interview delighted with the way I had been received, astounded at how easy it had been to trample Austrian etiquette underfoot, and pleased with myself for having discharged the functions of officer, councillor, chancellery

* ['La cour du lion'.]

official etc., without fuss for a few moments. It only goes to show the truth of the parable which says, 'Knock and it shall be opened unto you' and the exquisite tact with which some princes know on occasion how to say *Sinite parvulos venire ad me**—always provided, of course, that the *parvuli* are foreigners with a modicum of intelligence who come from that useless class of people that the world is always so curious to see at close quarters, the class known today as poets, musicians, painters, collectively artists, and in the Middle Ages by the ruder designations of minstrel, troubadour, strolling player and gipsy.

You may wonder, my dear Humbert, that I made no use of my powerful influence to obtain leave to pay the imperial household my respects. The fact is there were reasons of policy behind my diffidence. I had been told quite early during my stay in Vienna that the Empress, who is an angel of sweetness and gentle piety, had an even stranger view of me than Prince Metternich had of my music. Some rather boorishly expressed passages in my *Travels in Italy*, which had also been cleverly criticized in Her Highness's presence by certain well-wishers (one has them everywhere, even at the Austrian court), had earned me in those exalted circles the reputation of an out-and-out brigand. To say that I felt flattered would be to put it mildly: I gloried in the bizarre reputation I had so unexpectedly acquired. I said to myself—as you would certainly have done in my place—that a delicate aureole of crime, since Byron made it fashionable, is too distinguished a thing not to be jealously preserved when one has the luck, however unworthily, to possess it. So I reasoned as follows: 'If I "present myself" at court, the Empress will probably vouchsafe me a word. I shall have to answer her, and in my best manner. Once the conversation is launched God knows where it may not lead me. Her Majesty risks losing in an instant the whole peculiar conception she has formed of my personality. She will simply see one more worshipper at the shrine of her grace and goodness, a man with nothing sinister or predatory in his look and nothing remotely tigerish in his tone of voice. There is always my aquiline nose; but in sum I shall not look the part. I shall pass for a thoroughly respectable citizen, incapable

* ['Suffer the little children to come unto me'.]

of "getting into trouble" or of so much as holding up a stage-coach, and my reputation will have gone. Damn it! Better remain a brigand and leave as quickly as possible; my aureole will be only enhanced by distance.'

That is why I steadfastly declined to do myself the honour of presenting myself at the Austrian Court, and one fine morning packed up and went to Hungary. Here I resume the account of my differences with the Danube. Each day the great river wrapped itself in cloud, like Homer's gods when dirty work is afoot. Result: suspension of all river traffic, necessity for travellers to Pesth to proceed by the land route. That is a polite way of putting it. The mud route would be a more accurate name. Do you know, over all that immense plain stretching from Vienna to Pesth even pebbles are as rare as emeralds, the surface being composed of dust so fine it might have been sifted; and when soaked by rain this dust forms quagmires which have to be struggled through with much heaving and floundering of horses and the ever-present possibility of sinking in so deep that one will never get out again? You may conceive the charms of such a progress. But it was nothing to what followed. The Danube in its wrath must needs overflow its banks, inundating the turbid trench, known locally as the Great Highroad, down which we had for the past fifteen hours been churning. At midnight I was roused from my patient dozing. The coach had stopped. There was a sound of water swirling about us. The driver, guessing at the road, had taken us into the river and dared not make another move.

The water rose steadily. A Hungarian officer in the coupé had spoken to me once or twice through a little opening cut in the partition which divided the ill-fated coach in two. It was now my turn to address him:

'Captain!'

'Sir?'

'It looks as if we are going to be drowned.'

'It looks as if we are, sir. May I offer you a cigar?'

His air of insolent unconcern made me want to punch him. I angrily accepted the cigar and began puffing furiously.

The water continued to rise. The driver now made a desperate effort and, risking a manœuvre that might have deposited us in the river, turned sharply round, succeeded in climbing the right bank (which fortunately we were still quite near), steered straight ahead—and drove into a lake. This time I was sure we were done for, and I appealed once more to the military gentleman:

'Captain, have you another cigar?'

'I have, sir.'

'Then give it me quick, for we really are going to be drowned.'

Luckily an obliging peasant who happened to be passing (where on earth can he have been going at such an hour of the night, with the road in that condition?) helped to extricate us and gave our hapless Jehu directions by which he was able to regain the route; and next day, by fits and starts, by ditch and fen, out of water and into mud and back again, we reached Pesth or rather the right bank of the Danube opposite Pesth; which in the absence of a bridge we were suffered to cross by boat. There is a tolerably large town on the right bank. I asked the captain what it was called.

'That's Buda,' he said.

'Buda? On my German map the town opposite Pesth has a quite different name. Yes, look—Ofen.'

'Yes, that is Buda. Ofen is a free German rendering of the Hungarian.'

'I see: German maps seem to be as ingeniously devised as French ones. All the same they should put "Ratisbon pronounced Regensburg" on the one and "Ofen pronounced Buda" on the other.'

On arriving* I treated myself to a little celebration which I had promised myself the night before if ever I came safely through the Danube and the mud. I took a bath, drank two glasses of Tokay and slept for twenty hours, not without dreams of drownings and lakes of mud; after which it was time to make the arrangements for my first concert, come to an agreement with the directors, see the kapellmeister, meet the singers, go in search of violins, etc., etc. Thanks to the good offices of Count Ráday, intendant of the National Theatre, where I had been strongly advised to give my concerts in preference to the German Theatre, the main difficulties were soon overcome. I had a moment's anxiety over the

* [7 February 1846.]

composition of my orchestra. The National's orchestra is tiny; I could not even consider putting on my symphonies with so small a force of violins. On the other hand there could be no question of bringing in players from the German Theatre, owing to a regulation which prohibits the employment at the National of any artist—singer, chorister or instrumentalist—from the German Theatre, no matter how urgently his assistance may be needed. This will give you an idea of the Hungarians' touching regard for all things German. What is more, any language ancient or modern may be sung at the Hungarian theatre with the single exception of German, which is expressly forbidden. This exception—an audacious one in a subject country of the Austrian Empire—is part of a general embargo directed by the Hungarian people, in imitation of Napoleon's Continental System, against Germany as a whole and Austria in particular. It is regarded as a moral duty in all classes of the population to use only goods manufactured in Hungary by Hungarians. Hence the sign *hony* which you see written up in large letters in most shop windows in Pesth, even the milliners', and which intrigued me the first day I was there; it means 'national'.

By great good fortune a Viennese music publisher, Heinrich Müller (the most helpful of men, and a devoted friend to me during my stay in Austria), had given me a letter to a colleague of his in Pesth, M. Treichlinger, one of the great German violinists of the old school. Treichlinger put me in touch with the leading members of the Pesth Philharmonic Society and promptly got me a reinforcement of a dozen excellent violins, beginning—as he insisted—with himself. All acquitted themselves admirably in the task they had so gallantly undertaken; the performance was, I believe, one of the best that had been heard in Pesth for a long time. Among the pieces in the programme was the march which now forms the finale of the first part of my *Faust* legend. I had written it during the night before my departure for Hungary. A few days earlier a Viennese amateur well up in the ways of the country I was about to visit had come to see me, bringing a volume of old airs. 'If you want the Hungarians to like you,' he said, 'write a piece on one of their national tunes. They will be delighted, and when you come back you can tell me what you thought of their *elyen* [bravos] and their applause. Just choose something from this collection.' I took his advice and chose the Rákóczy theme, on which I wrote the march that you know.

No sooner had the announcement of a new piece of *hony* music gone up all over Pesth than the national imagination began to seethe. People speculated as to how I had treated the famous, nay the sacred melody which for so long had set the hearts of Hungarians aflame with a holy passion for glory and liberty. There was even some anxiety about it, a fear of profanation—an attitude which, far from being offended by, I respected. It had, besides, only too much justification in the many pitiful medleys and arrangements in which the noblest strains were submitted to every kind of wanton outrage. Perhaps, too, there were Hungarian music-lovers who had been to Paris and had seen how we drag the immortal Marseillaise through the gutter on our national holidays.

At length one of them, a M. Horváth, editor of a Hungarian newspaper, unable to contain his curiosity, called on the publisher who was dealing with the arrangements for my concert, found out from him the address of the copyist responsible for making the orchestral parts, went straight there, asked to see the manuscript, and examined it attentively. He was not reassured by this inspection, and next day could not disguise his apprehensiveness.

'I have seen your score of the Rákóczy March,' he said uneasily.

'Well?'

'Well—I'm nervous.'

'Nonsense!'

'You state the theme piano; we, on the contrary, are accustomed to hearing it played fortissimo.'

'Yes, by the gipsies. In any case, is that all? Don't worry, you shall have such a forte as you never heard in your life. You haven't read it properly. One must always consider the *end*.'

All the same, on the day of the concert,* I felt a tightening of the throat when the moment came for this devil of a piece to be performed. After a trumpet fanfare based on the rhythm of its opening bars, the theme, you will recall, is announced piano by

* [15 February 1846.]

flutes and clarinets accompanied by pizzicato strings. During this unexpected exposition the audience remained calm and silent. But when a long crescendo ensued, with fragments of the theme reintroduced fugally, broken by the dull thud of the bass drum, like the thump of distant cannon, the whole place began to hum with excitement; and, as the orchestra unleashed its full fury and the long-delayed fortissimo burst forth, a tumult of shouting and stamping convulsed the theatre; the accumulated pressure of all that boiling Mass of emotion exploded with a violence that sent a thrill of fear through me; I felt as if my hair were standing on end. From that fatal bar I had to give up all thought of my peroration. The thunders of the orchestra were powerless against such a volcano in eruption; nothing could stop it. We had to repeat the piece, of course. The second time, the audience could scarcely restrain itself a few seconds longer to hear a bar or two of the coda. Horváth in his box was throwing himself about like a man possessed. I could not help laughing as I shot him a glance which said, 'Well—are you still nervous, or are you satisfied with your forte?' It was a good thing I had placed *Rákóczy-induló* (the Hungarian title of the piece) at the end of the programme: anything we had tried to play after that would have been lost.

These stirring events, it may readily be surmised, left me in a state of some excitement. They had a curious sequel. I was mopping my face in a little room behind the stage when a shabbily dressed man entered without warning, his face glistening and working strangely. On seeing me he fell on my neck and, embracing me passionately, his eyes filling with tears, barely managed to stammer out:

'Ah, monsieur—me Hungarian—sorry fellow—no speak French—*un poco l'italiano*—forgive—my ecstasy—ah! understand your cannon—yes—big battle—German dogs!—in heart of me' (striking his chest vehemently) 'I keep you—ah, Frenchman—republican—know to make music of revolution!' I cannot attempt to describe the man's alarming exaltation. He wept and gnashed his teeth. It was sublime.

You can imagine, my dear Humbert, that after this the *Rákóczy-induló* figured on every programme, and always with the same result. When I left I had to bequeath my manuscript to the town of Pesth. They had asked if they might keep it (I received a copy a month later in Breslau); and the piece is now performed on all important occasions in Hungary. But I must here inform the kapellmeister, Erkel, that I have made several changes in the instrumentation since then and have added a coda of about thirty bars which, I think, enhances the effect. I shall dispatch him the score, revised, corrected and enlarged, the moment my publisher allows me to.* Erkel is a most admirable and gifted person. I heard an opera of his during my stay in Pesth, ably conducted by himself and entitled *Hunyady*. The subject is drawn from Hungary's heroic past. It is a work full of originality and striking depth of feeling, as well as immaculately written and scored with great skill and refinement—which is not at all to say that the scoring lacks vigour. Madame Schodel, a true lyric tragédienne in the tradition of Madame Branchu (a lost tradition of which I had not thought to find a representative in Hungary), sang and acted the principal role

* 6 March 1861. I have just sent the score to Hungary. A few weeks ago an association of young Hungarians sent me a silver wreath of exquisite workmanship, bearing, on the coat of arms of the town of Györ (in German, Raab), the inscription: *Hector Berlioz, from the youth of Györ.* The gift was accompanied by a letter, to which I replied as follows:

14 February 1861.
Gentlemen,

I have received your handsome gift and the flattering letter which accompanied it. Coming as it does from a country which I recall with so much affection, this mark of friendship and solidarity has touched me deeply. I have no doubt that my work owes its effect to the feelings that your national air inspires in you. One day it will 'lead you to life', as your expressive phrase has it. Virgil might have been describing you when he wrote:

Furor iraque mentes
Praecipitant, pulchrumque mori succurrit in armis.

['Fury drives them on, and one thought is in their minds, that to die in battle is glorious.' *Aeneid*, II, 316–17; from Aeneas' description of the sack of Troy.]
But I regard myself as more than fortunate that you have discerned in my music even a spark of that fire which glows in the noble hearts of Hungarians, and count this success among the most precious an artist can achieve.

Please accept my grateful thanks and my warmest good wishes.

Yours sincerely,
Hector Berlioz

very finely. I must also mention a good tenor in the national company, called Füredi. He is a wonderful performer of the national songs and romances which the Hungarians love so much. Sung with this hauntingly individual inflection they would be bound to appeal everywhere. The leader of the orchestra, Kohne, is a highly talented violinist who was in Paris for a long time; I believe, in fact, that he is a product of our Conservatoire. The chorus at the National Theatre is very weak, both as to numbers and as to the natural quality and training of the voices. The Hungarian language is not at all unsuitable for music; indeed, to my mind it is a good deal less awkward than German. A splendid language, which no one understands—without learning it. Pointless to look for similarities between Hungarian and any other known tongue: there are none. Even certain musical terms, in every other European language preserved more or less unchanged in their original Italian form, are rendered by special Hungarian words, compound or simple, which are quite different. The word 'concert', for instance—which is virtually the same in Italian, French, German, English and Russian—appears on the posters as *hangverseny*. You may well look astonished. This curious word means, literally, 'combination of sounds'.

My musical affairs did not prevent me from attending two balls while I was in Pesth, as well as a large political banquet given by the Hungarian nobility. I have not seen anything to compare with these balls: on the one hand the incredible luxury of them, on the other the brilliantly exotic native costumes and the proud beauty of the Magyar race. The dances are quite unlike anything seen in the rest of Europe. Our chilly French quadrilles are almost unknown; the mazurka, the tarsalgo, the keringo and the csardas reign joyously supreme. The csardas in particular, a polished version of the rustic dance which Hungarian peasants perform with such wonderful abandon and energy, seemed in high aristocratic favour notwithstanding the fears expressed in a newspaper article by an ill-omened critic who claimed that the attitudes and movements of the csardas were a trifle indecorous, likening them—erroneously, in my opinion—to the irregularities of that unmentionable dance lately banned by the Paris police.* Imagine

* [The can-can?]

the reception he must have got when he showed his face at the ball after his article appeared! One can just picture the barrage of protests, the splendid eyes flashing in indignant scorn. *Hony soit.* (I spent two days thinking up this pun.) The political banquet which I was permitted to attend gave me the opportunity to see and hear the well-known orator Déak, the O'Connell of Hungary, a man whose name is a household word and whose picture is in every home. Déak's policy is—as the great Irish champion's was—to bring about the reforms his country needs gradually and by constitutional means, and he has great difficulty in restraining the impatient ardour of his party. I inferred the subject of his speech from the exclamation 'Fabius Cunctator!' uttered in a stage whisper and with an air of gloomy disapproval by one of my neighbours.

A young man with a very striking face was pointed out to me among the guests. 'He's an Atlas,' said Horváth.

'An Atlas? How so?'

'The fellow's a poet, and his name is Hugo.'

During dinner a small band of dark-skinned gipsies discoursed national airs in their own fashion, which is to say with a frantic, naïve energy; the effect of which, alternating with speeches and toasts and liberally seconded by the fiery wines of Hungary, was to rouse the company to a still higher pitch of revolutionary fervour.

Next day I had to say goodbye to my Hungarian hosts. I left still tingling with all the intense emotions I had experienced and full of sympathy for this warm-hearted, chivalrous and impetuous nation. During my stay in Pesth the Danube had subsided; not a trace of anger wrinkled its venerable face, and my progress upstream was smooth and untroubled all the way to Vienna. Hardly had I arrived when I received a visit from the music-lover through whose friendly advice I had been induced to write the Rákóczy March.

He was in a state of comical alarm.

'The repercussions of your Hungarian piece have been felt even in Vienna,' he said, 'and I have come to implore you not to breathe a word about my part in it. If it became known here that I had had anything to do with your composing the work, I should be severely compromised and could get into serious trouble.'

I promised secrecy. If I now reveal his name it is because this grave business has, I believe, had sufficient time to subside. He was called—but come, it really would be indiscreet to tell. I only wanted to frighten him.

Fourth Letter

Prague

TO HUMBERT FERRAND

I had already been all over Germany before the idea of visiting Bohemia occurred to me. When it did, in Vienna, I prudently rejected it on the advice of several apparently well-informed persons. 'Don't go to Prague,' I was told. 'It's a city of pedants. The only works they admire are works by dead composers. The Bohemians are admittedly first-rate musicians, but they come from a narrow, pedagogic mould. They can't bear anything new. The chances are you won't get on with them at all.'

So I had resolved to forgo the journey, when someone brought me the Prague *Musical Gazette*, with three long articles on my *King Lear* overture in it. I had them translated and was delighted to find that far from revealing the crustiness and pedantry I had heard ascribed to the Bohemians, they were the work of a critic conspicuously endowed with the very opposite qualities. The writer, Dr Ambros, seemed to me to combine thorough knowledge with balanced judgment and keen imagination. I wrote thanking him and sounding him about the attitude of his compatriots towards me. His reply dispelled all my misgivings and made me as eager to visit Prague as I had previously been afraid of showing my face there. When it was known that I had decided after all to go, there was much jesting at my expense: the people of Prague swore only by Mozart, they claimed they had discovered him, they had no desire to listen to symphonies written by anyone else. I would get a terrible reception, and so forth.

But Dr Ambros had given me confidence and it was not to be shaken. Despite the scoffers and their forebodings, I went.

When descending from the coach in a strange city more than a thousand miles from home it is gratifying, you will agree, to find an unknown friend waiting for you on the platform; who, promptly deducing from your lively and interesting physiognomy that you are his man, accosts you, shakes you by the hand, and informs you in your own language that everything is ready to receive you.

That was precisely my experience with Dr Ambros when I arrived in Prague, the only difference being that my lively and interesting physiognomy completely failed to make its effect, and it was on the contrary I who, perceiving a small man with a sharp yet benign expression and hearing him exclaim to his companion, 'How am I supposed to identify M. Berlioz in this crowd? I have never set eyes on him!'—it was I, I repeat, who had the sagacity to deduce that this was Dr Ambros and, going straight up to the two men, said:

'Here I am.'

'M. Berlioz?'

'In person.'

'Well, good day to you. We are very glad to see you at last. Come along, there's a set of nice warm rooms waiting for you and an orchestra the same. You will find them satisfactory. Have a rest this evening, then tomorrow we'll begin.'

And next day we set about preparing for my opening concert, having first made the acquaintance of the musical dignitaries of the town. Dr Ambros introduced me to the director of the Conservatoire, Kittl. Through him I met the brothers Skroup, kapellmeisters of the theatre and the cathedral, and the leader of the orchestra, Mildner. After that it was the turn of the singers, the Press, and the leading amateurs; and when all these visits were done, I suggested to Dr Ambros that he introduce me to the town; 'for,' I said, 'I see a hill over there literally covered with large and splendid-looking buildings, and contrary to my normal habit I feel the keenest curiosity to go and inspect them.'

'Come along, then,' said the genial doctor.

It is possibly the only occasion after such an ascent when I have not regretted my aching joints (I do not count Vesuvius, of course; Etna I have never visited). Jesting apart, the climb is a stiff one; but how wonderful it is, that great succession of temples and palaces, steeples, battlements, turrets, vast courtyards, soaring vaults! And the view from the summit of these marble-gleaming heights: on one side, a forest stretching down to a wide plain; on the other, a torrent of houses tumbling to the Moldau and, below, the river making its way majestically through the town to the sound of all the mills and factories that are worked by it, then streaming over the bar constructed across it to control the flow of water at that point, sweeping on past two small islands, and winding farther and farther into the distance until lost to view among a range of tawny-coloured hills which seem to escort it gently and solicitously to the horizon.

'That's Huntsmen's Island there,' said my guide, 'so called, no doubt, because there's no game on it. Behind, as you go upstream, you see Sophia Island. In the middle there is the Sophia Hall where you will give your concert; it's used almost entirely by the choral society, the Sophia Philharmonic.'

'And who is this Sophia, on whose island and in whose hall and by courtesy of whose philharmonic society I shall be giving my concert? A river-nymph of the Moldau, or the heroine of some rare romance enacted there, or merely a washerwoman with great coarse, chapped hands, who like a latter-day Calypso used to make the island ring with the roar of her singing and the crack of her wash-bat?'

'The latter is, I should imagine, the most likely conjecture. However, tradition says nothing about her having chapped hands.'

'Ah, Doctor, you look to me as if you had played Ulysses with this Sophia. Is there a Eucharis there? Come, I propose to be Telemachus and go in search of you on Calypso's isle.'*

A blush was the doctor's only reply; I saw that it would not do to harp too long on that string. Thus it was that I never found out the truth about Sophia, who was patroness of an island, a concert hall and a choral society.

Alas, this charming haunt set amid the purling waters of the Moldau, in summer shaded by luxuriant foliage and entwined with garlands of fair flowers, conceals, lurking within the very precincts of the Temple of Harmony, more than one of those

* [A reference to Fénelon's didactic romance *Les aventures de Télémaque* (1715). Eucharis was one of Calypso's nymphs, with whom Telemachus fell in love.]

deplorable establishments of which no abuse was ever adequate to express my execration, known—I shudder to pronounce it—as pleasure-gardens, where bad musicians make abominable music shamelessly in the open air and immodest young males and females indulge in blatant dancing, while idlers and wastrels, good-for-nothing fellows, lounge about smoking vile tobacco and drinking beer that is as bad, and the women sit and knit and wag their sinful gossips' tongues. What a desecration, thus to debauch this lovely bower, to pollute its sweet perfumes with rank odours, and crudely mingle its soft melodies with brute clamour! Is not Huntsmen's Isle at hand, with its taverns and the clatter of its mills and the tanneries near-by, and would it not lend itself in every respect more fittingly to these vulgar amusements? Between ourselves, I am very much afraid that Sophia did have chapped hands.

But to come back to music (on the understanding that I have the right to leave it and wander off again at the slightest provocation), I trust you are not expecting an elaborate disquisition, more soporific than scientific, of less utility than sterility (you see, I too can be a poet, my pen rhymes as readily as the next man's), on revolutionary developments in modern Bohemian music, whither the Slav mind, or the date on which the old masters of the country are thought to have first permitted the use of the unprepared dominant seventh. I must confess to a total and incorrigible ignorance where these important questions are concerned; and even were my apathy with regard to history or the superior chat which sometimes passes for it less profound than it is, I would rather inquire into the nature of the celebrated guitar ornamented with ivory that was used by the philosopher K'ung-Fu-tse, commonly known as Confucius, in order to improve the morals of the Chinese Empire—being, as I am, a guitar-player myself, yet never having so much as improved the morals of the population of a small bedroom (far from it). My guitar, admittedly, is rude and simple; the elephant's tusk plays no part in its workmanship. Never mind; the following passage, which I re-read yesterday for the hundredth time, may afford rich matter for meditation to philosophically-minded musicians (I do not say musically-minded philosophers; there haven't been any since Leibniz). Here it is; I believe I may have quoted it before.

It is related that K'ung-Fu-tse, having by chance heard the song of Li-Po—the antiquity of which was universally acknowledged to go back at least fourteen thousand years (thus confounding the vulgar delusion that music is a recent art)—was seized with such rapture that he remained seven whole days and nights without sleep, drink or food. He forthwith formulated his sublime doctrine and joyously preached it far and wide, chanting its precepts to the strains of Li-Po's music; and thus was able, by means of a five-stringed guitar inlaid with ivory, to improve the morals of all China.

Now consider my misfortune: my guitar is not merely five-stringed, like the one Confucius played, but is quite often furnished with as many as six; and, as I say, my reputation as a moralist is nil. Then again, had it only been ornamented with ivory, think of the benefits I might have brought, the heresies I might have rooted out, the truths instilled, the noble religion founded, and the happiness we might all be enjoying now. It seems hardly possible that such calamity should come simply for want of a strip of ivory. No doubt it contributed significantly, even greatly; but there must also be some other cause, one beyond my comprehension and I dare say worthier to have a series of human lives dedicated to its elucidation than questions appertaining to the Bohemians and the dominant seventh.

Be that as it may, it is time to return to the music of modern Europe; which, though it may not deprive anyone of drink, food or sleep, unlike the melody of ancient China, none the less has its value. That is to say, we must admit that it does not actually prevent one from eating and drinking; yet I have often heard it said by excellent musicians that trying to make a living out of their profession was like trying to get water out of a stone and that such and such a noted composer or performer was dying of starvation. As for depriving one of sleep, the most ancient works of our oldest masters have clearly never had the least pretension to that accomplishment. The question before us is my opinion of Prague as a musical establishment, and the taste and culture of its inhabitants. One would have to have stayed longer in that splendid city than I did to know it thoroughly in this respect; but I shall endeavour to collect my impressions and give the truth as I saw it. Accordingly I shall tell you about the theatre and the singers, orchestra and chorus that I heard there; the Conservatoire, the very capable composer who directs it, and the teachers and pupils I was able to meet; the choral society; the choir school and the liturgical music of the cathedral; the military bands; the composers and performers not connected with any of the aforesaid institutions; and finally, the public.

The theatre, when I saw it (in 1845), impressed me as being ill-lit, cramped, shabby and acoustically deplorable. I gather that since then it has been restored and its new director, Hoffmann, is making valiant efforts to rebuild its fortunes, which under the previous administration had apparently been going steadily downhill. His singers were on the whole superior to those of most German companies. The leading tenor, the baritone (Strakaty), Mlles Grosser and Kirchberger and Madame Podhorsky struck me as talented artists with fine voices in point of quality and keenness of intonation, and on top of that good musicians (Bohemians in fact). Unfortunately the size of the resident orchestra and chorus suggested excessive economies on the part of the management, being strictly related to the meagre dimensions of the theatre. It really is not permissible to attempt the masterpieces of the grand style with such a tiny force of performers; yet they sometimes did so. When they did, the destruction was terrible and every artist was a broken man. The decor on these occasions rivalled the performance in splendour and in punctiliousness; I remember that the ship which sails for Greece at the end of Gluck's *Iphigénie en Tauride* was equipped with cannon.

The regular repertoire was usually managed better from the point of view of the staging and had little to fear from the numerical weakness of voices and instruments, being composed of the feeblest and most undemanding type of rubbish translated from the French—works already sunk without trace in the great ocean of Parisian indifference and long since erased for ever from the bill-boards of the Opéra-Comique. Directors are all the same. Nothing is so impressive as their talent for nosing out the commonplace, unless it is their instinctive dislike of any work suspected of a leaning towards originality, grandeur, and distinction of style. In Germany, Italy, England and elsewhere, they are considerably below the man in the street in this respect. I exclude France, it being notorious that our opera houses have always been directed by men of superior capacity whose exquisite discrimination, when required to choose between two products, one crude and the other marked by some refinement, between a creative artist and an arrant imitator, between boldness and ingenuity on the one hand and feeble-mindedness and craven platitude on the other, can be depended on not to let them down. For these remarkable men the gratitude of all music-lovers is equalled only by their admiration. They have earned a place in history.

I have never been able to understand why the great majority of theatre directors in nearly every country have this invincible partiality for what to your true artist or man of taste, and even to a certain section of the public, is second-rate manufacture, inferior in workmanship and in the quality of the raw material, and guaranteed not to last. It is not as if the commonplace works were invariably more successful than the interesting ones; quite often the opposite happens. It is not as if the high-quality were necessarily more expensive than the shoddy; frequently it is the other way round. Perhaps the explanation is simply that whereas the one sort demands care, patience and application from everybody in the theatre from the director to the prompter, and intelligence, talent and inspiration from one or two specific individuals, the other, being devised expressly for mediocrities, drones, dabblers, ignoramuses and half-wits, is in no want of people to push its claims. What a director likes most of all is something that keeps his company happy and easily satisfied: something that everyone knows without having learnt it, that does not disturb accepted notions and settled habits of mind, that follows docilely the line of least resistance and wounds no one's self-esteem because it exposes no one's incompetence; something that above all does not require too much time to get up. His favourite compositions are the nice accommodating ones, the ones that do not struggle.

There are also the directors whose ambition is to control everything personally. This ambition is enough to prejudice them hopelessly against all works which cannot be put on without the help of the people who wrote them. The status the author acquires in such cases correspondingly diminishes the importance of the director, and he feels it keenly. A ship's captain demeaned before his crew does not forgive the pilot who consigned him to a role of onlooker and tactlessly reduced him to the rank of lieutenant; he heartily curses his foolhardiness in venturing into latitudes where the rocks and shoals were unknown to him, and vows in future to sail only in well-ploughed waters.

Then there are the infatuated directors, the directors obsessed with a particular kind of idea or object, a particular period of history, particular settings and costumes and stage effects, a particular singer or dancer, as the case may be. Whatever happens, a place must be found for their hobby-horse. The hobby-horse of M. Duponchel, director of the Opéra, was, is and ever shall be a cardinal in a red hat under a canopy. Operas without canopies, cardinals or red hats (and they exist in considerable numbers) have never appealed to him. If the good Lord himself had a part in a new work, as I once heard Méry remark, Duponchel would insist on his wearing the cherished headgear. It would be no use pointing out that, as the good Lord, it wouldn't look right if one were to come on like a cardinal. 'Excuse me, Almighty,' Duponchel would reply, 'it's essential that Your Eternity should kindly agree to put on this handsome costume and appear beneath the canopy, otherwise *my opera* will not be a success.' And the good Lord would have to give in. I pass over M. Duponchel's enthusiasm for horses, a serious passion too respectable to be mentioned in this context.

None of which, as I should perhaps have said earlier, has any application to the former director of the Prague Theatre. That worthy man was little versed in musical matters (like all his colleagues in the business), but he was exceptional in being liked and esteemed by his employees, who said goodbye to him with genuine regret when he was forced to yield the direction to other hands, his affairs being by then in a state of hopeless confusion. Pokorny, director of the Theater an der Wien, must also be included among these honourable exceptions. This type of director, the impresario who is in business on his own account and at his own risk, is fairly rare in Germany; I know of only five or six at the most—in Leipzig, Prague, Vienna, Pesth (the German Theatre) and Hamburg. The other houses are nearly all run by titled intendants who administer them on behalf of their princely masters. Although some of these men, who are barons or counts, treat their underlings with more than a touch of aristocratic aloofness, there is no denying that artists in general greatly prefer them to the commercial director who exploits their labours. Noble directors, besides often being persons of impeccable manners (a quality to which the other kind lay few claims), have the advantage of a literary education and sometimes even a musical one, which in the impresario class are even rarer accomplishments. Count Redern, who long controlled the destinies of the Berlin Opera, is a good example of the former. I dare say Germany has intendants as well as impresarios who are men of small intelligence or quite ignorant in matters of art, but I question whether it has ever known anything to compare with what France has produced in this line during the last thirty years. I would wager that every German director, aristocrat and commoner, has heard of Gluck or Mozart and could even name the titles of their chief compositions. In France, on the other hand, some scarcely credible enormities of the sort could be cited. There was the case of the director of the Opéra* who, on receiving a visit from Cherubini, languidly demanded of the great man (who had clearly stated his name) what he did, was he on the staff of the Opéra, one of the ballet people perhaps or on the stage management side? At about the same period Cherubini, having just had a new Mass performed with great acclaim, was paid this inscrutable compliment by the Secretary of Fine Arts† at a reception of his: 'My dear Cherubini, your Mass is splendid, yes, an undeniable success. But why have you always confined yourself to religious music? You really should write an opera!' One can dimly imagine the indignant consternation of the author of *Medea*, the *Deux journées*, *Lodoïska*, *Mont Saint-Bernard*, *Faniska*, the *Abencérages*, *Anacreon*, and other dramatic works, at this unexpected thrust.

A director of the Théâtre-Français‡ once asked the name of the man who wrote a comedy called *Le médecin malgré lui*, and was

* M. Duplantys [director 1824–7, and subsequently treasurer till 1831].

† Vicomte Sosthène de La Rochefoucauld.

‡ M. Buloz.

highly offended at the burst of laughter which accompanied the information that it was Molière.

Paris can also boast a director with an office more difficult of access than a cabinet minister's, a director who never answers when you write to him, and who carries his belief in his own ineffable superiority to the point of requesting those whom he 'needs' to be so kind as to come and see *him*:* the Director has a favour to ask them and considers it only natural that they should be the ones to put themselves out. It must be said, he does not always have cause to brag about the answers he gets.

It is only fair to add that there have been men in charge of our Paris theatres who combined genuine elegance and style with good sense, intelligence and literary cultivation (I do not say musical, such being quite unknown). One of the liveliest if not the most fortunate or the most idealistic was Harel, who died two years ago, after winning the Academy's prize for the best essay in praise of Voltaire. Harel was famous for his witticisms. None of them, however, was as good as the one he himself once prompted Frédérick Lemaître to make. Harel was at the time director of the Porte-Saint-Martin Theatre, where a very wealthy playwright, one of our patrician writers of the old school and a passionate devotee of poetry and art, had had a tragedy performed in return for handsome contributions to the running expenses of the theatre.† The playwright was in Harel's office one day when the famous actor happened to be there. Having just paid the bill for the scenery and the bill for the costumes, one for the properties and sundry other little accounts, he imagined that that finally settled the matter, when the insatiable director presented him with a bill of three or four thousand francs for the cost of the rope used to support the scenery. M. de C—— protested vigorously but in vain against what he called, with some justice, an act of robbery; he had to pay and went off fuming. When he had gone, Frédérick, who had been silently observing this instructive scene, clapped the director on the shoulder and said:

'You're getting slack! You let him keep his watch.'

* [Nestor Roqueplan.]

† M. de Custine. [The play was *Beatrix Cenci*.]

Fifth Letter

Prague (continued)

TO HUMBERT FERRAND

Today I feel in a sufficiently serious humour to tell you about the Prague Conservatoire and at the same time to say something of conservatoires in general—which institutions, with all their imperfections, I take to be the only ones concerned with the art of music that have been established under the aegis of reason and common sense. At the present moment every conservatoire in Europe is directed by a musician. It was not always so; and one can but offer thanks to providence for this surprising dispensation. At a time when there is a widely held belief that the more important and complex an artistic problem the more essential it is that the persons appointed by the government to deal with it be unacquainted with the art in question—a doctrine one would be tempted to ascribe to pure lunacy if the hand of envy were not so clearly recognizable—it is a matter for congratulation that the various branches of music should be entrusted to specialists reasonably competent in them. Of course many people, especially in Paris, would reply that this is a great mistake; much more sensible to get mathematicians to teach the violin, put men of letters in charge of the composition class, and choose singing teachers from the ranks of the medical profession. Others, the Academy of Fine Arts among them, maintain that as a general rule only painters, sculptors, architects and engravers really feel and understand music and are therefore in a position to judge it. The vast majority, however, subscribe to the good sound maxim that not merely are musicians not the right people to teach music and direct conservatoires and opera houses, but that mathematicians, men of letters, doctors, engravers, painters, sculptors and architects are also an unreliable lot, given to intelligence and a deplorable inclination to respect science and art, and that really the best musical directors and the best judges of music, those most likely to exert a healthy influence on its present and future state, are men without any distracting knowledge of science or art, any feeling for beauty, any dangerous hankering after perfection, any achievement to their name or any idea in their head, who have never done anything, do not know anything, do not believe in anything, do not care about anything, neither want nor are capable of anything, and in addition to the indispensable attributes of ignorance, apathy and incompetence are gifted with a kind of primordial inertia only just removed from imbecility. This splendid proposition has obvious attractions for an incalculable number of people, and it is not to be wondered at that it should make fresh converts every day. One is only surprised that their triumph should be less than complete and that they advance as slowly as they do towards the goal that lies before them. Hence the relevance of my observation that all conservatoires are at present in the hands of musicians.

The Prague Conservatoire, to boot, is directed by a talented composer, a man with a passion for his art, energetic, enthusiastic, untiring, capable of being severe on occasion but lavish with his praise when praise is due—and young. Such a man is Kittl. They could so easily have found some plodding mediocrity hallowed by time—Bohemia has them, like every other country—and appointed him to do what he could to paralyse the progress of music in Prague. Instead they chose Kittl, who is thirty-five, and music in Prague is flourishing. It would seem that the members of the committee who made the appointment must have been visited by some kind of mental spasm; alternatively, that the committee is composed exclusively of men of feeling and intelligence.

As I see it, a conservatoire of music should be an institution designed to *conserve* every aspect of the accumulated experience of music as a practical art, together with the theoretical knowledge that goes with it and the great masterpieces which the art has produced; and it should also stand in the vanguard of the progressive tendencies inherent in an art as young as European music, preserving the best that has come down to us from the past while moving forward soberly towards the conquests of the future. I do not think I am yielding to an access of nationalistic fervour when I say that of all the conservatoires I have seen, that of Paris comes nearest to answering this definition. After it, I would put the Prague Conservatoire.* This says a great deal for Prague, taking

* I know nothing as yet of the internal organization of the Brussels Conservatoire (ably directed by M. Fétis), except that it is one of the largest in existence.

into account the enormous difference in resources between a town of this sort and the capital of France. As you would expect, it is less lavishly set up in every respect than ours: it has fewer teachers and fewer pupils and receives nothing like the continuous and active support given to the Paris Conservatoire by the Department of Fine Arts; but the education is sound and the spirit of the school excellent. Among the teachers on M. Kittl's staff I must especially mention Messrs Mildner and Gordigiani. Mildner, a fine violinist who is also (as I have said) leader of the orchestra and solo violinist at the Prague Theatre, has produced a large number of good pupils. Gordigiani has long had the reputation of being one of the best Italian singing-teachers in Germany. He is also a talented composer: I know a Stabat Mater of his for double chorus, a beautifully written piece, and an opera, *Consuelo*, of which he wrote the words and the music, which is notable for the freshness of its melodies and the elegant restraint of its orchestration—a quality not often found nowadays. It is sometimes said—rightly, I believe—that it helps a composer to know how to sing. It is perhaps even more important for a teacher of singing to know how to compose; for the surest foundation of good teaching is an ability to perceive accurately the qualities that a composer may and must demand of his interpreters. The teacher who is himself a composer, unless he is an abject mediocrity, will have no sympathy with those perversions which today threaten the destruction of the art of singing in three-quarters of musical Europe. He will not teach his pupils to disdain rhythm and metre. He will never permit them the arrogant liberty of taking a melody which, as the musical expression of the passage, the character of the person represented and the composer's style all insist, must be sung exactly as written, and embellishing it according to personal whim. He will not let them grow accustomed to looking to their larynx as the sole guiding principle when they appear before the public. Consequently his pupils will not garble great works merely in order to avoid the uninteresting part of their voice or for the sake of prolonging, in the most absurd fashion, the more flattering notes that nature has endowed them with.

Such a teacher can be depended on to expound the art of singing to his pupils and to make them see that it has nothing to do with the degree of brilliance with which they can execute feats of vocal pyrotechnics devoid of dramatic meaning and musical interest, still less with the loudest, longest, highest, or lowest sounds that can be extorted from a human throat. He will require them to account for each expressive sound they produce and will show them that it is just as disagreeable to sing falsely from the point of view of expression as it is to sing falsely from the point of view of pitch; that a note sung flat or sharp may be an offence to the ear but a passage performed loudly when it should be soft, or feebly when it should be vigorous, or affectedly when it should be simple, is even more exasperating to an intelligent listener and more damaging to the work in question, and simply reveals the singer who perpetrated it—no matter how fine his voice or how exceptional his vocal skill—as an ass. The pupils of such a teacher will not, as happens everywhere nowadays, cynically impose on the forbearance of the conductor to the extent of forcing him to follow the wildest aberrations of rhythm, so that he must be ready at any moment to interpolate a beat, take the first half of a phrase or even of a single bar at a third of the tempo and gallop through the second half, wait with arm poised aloft while the singer sustains his favourite note until his breath gives out, and in general stand by, an indignant but helpless accomplice, while stupidity armed with a tyrannical pair of lungs insults art and common sense. Nor will such a teacher allow his pupils to begin learning a great work without having first grasped the content and background of the poem and without having duly reflected on the passions embodied in it and having tried to enter into them thoroughly. He will feel ashamed if a singer from his class fails to respect the language he is singing in and the fundamental rules of rhythm and euphony which govern correct diction. And he will make it abundantly clear to his students that if they are going to change the *fioriture* written by the composer, in cadenzas and elsewhere, they should at least make sure that their improvements harmonize with the accompaniment; the spectacle of the virtuoso singer swelling with conceit as he plays nonchalantly over the notes of a six-four chord while the orchestra holds the chord of the dominant, and vice versa, is one to be avoided.

From the conversations which I had with Signor Gordigiani, and from the style and method of those of his singers that I heard, it was clear he entirely shared these ideas.

It is not surprising that if there are many specialized studies in which the Paris Conservatoire does not offer classes the same should be so of Prague. Its syllabus, in fact, is far from complete. None the less it has produced a sufficient number of competent students to be able to give a satisfactory account of difficult works like the Choral Symphony of Beethoven with its own virtually unaided resources. This is one of the happiest effects of M. Kittl's régime.

If a conservatoire is an institution designed to conserve *every aspect* of music as a practical art and the theoretical knowledge that goes with it, it is odd that even in Paris they have not yet succeeded in establishing a really comprehensive curriculum. Our conservatoire was for long without classes in such essential instruments as double bass, trombone, trumpet and harp. These gaps have been filled in the last few years. Unfortunately many others remain, which I shall indicate. My remarks on the subject will provoke cries of protest from a number of people, who will declare them unwarranted and ridiculous (at least I trust they will). Here, then, is the reckoning:

(1) The study of the violin is incomplete. Pupils are not taught pizzicato. As a result a whole host of passages in arpeggios involving all four strings or in repeated notes with two or three fingers on the same string in rapid tempo—passages which are perfectly feasible, as any guitar-player will show you (on the violin)—are said to be impossible and consequently proscribed to composers. No doubt fifty years from now a director with a flair for innovation will take the plunge and lay it down that pizzicato is to be taught in violin classes; and then violinists, having mastered the novel and piquant effects that are possible with this technique, will laugh at our present-day players, just as ours now laugh at the fiddlers of the last century, with their cautionary 'Watch out for the C!'; and with reason. Another aspect of violin technique that is not formally and systematically studied is the use of harmonics. The little that our young violinists have learnt about it they have acquired for themselves since Paganini's appearance.

(2) It is lamentable that there should be no special class in the viola, an instrument which, although related to the violin, demands individual study and constant practice if it is to be played

properly. The ruinous old tradition by which the viola part is entrusted to second- or third-rate violinists—the usual reaction to a mediocre performer on the violin is: 'He'll make a good viola-player'—is obsolete where modern music is concerned. The leading composers at any rate do not write filling-in parts in orchestral music any more; they give every part an interest relative to the effect to be produced and refuse to regard some as inherently less important than others.*

(3) The omission of the basset horn from the syllabus of students of the clarinet was until recently a serious error, for it meant that a great deal of Mozart's music could not be performed properly in France—an absurd state of affairs. But now that Adolphe Sax has perfected the bass clarinet to the point where it can perform everything that lies within the range of the basset horn and more (it can play a minor third lower), and since its timbre is similar to the basset horn's but even more beautiful, it is the bass clarinet that should be studied in conservatoires alongside the soprano clarinet and the smaller clarinets in E flat, F and high A flat.

(4) The saxophone, the latest member of the clarinet family, an instrument which will prove extremely useful when players have learnt to exploit its qualities, should be given its own separate position in the curriculum, for before long every composer will want to use it.

(5) We have no class in the ophicleide, with the result that of the hundred or hundred and fifty persons in Paris at present blowing this exacting instrument hardly three are fit to be in a good orchestra and only one, M. Caussinus, is a really first-rate player.

(6) We have no class in the bass tuba, a powerful rotary-valve instrument differing from the ophicleide in timbre, mechanism

* [Cf. Ernest Reyer on the Théâtre-Lyrique orchestra in the 1850s: 'I was rehearsing a work of mine in which the viola part, without being unduly complicated, is of genuine importance. As I could hear nothing, I went over to the section of the orchestra normally occupied by the violas and found a solitary old man, his coat collar turned up to his ears (for it was very cold), timidly drawing a bow innocent of rosin across the silent strings of his instrument. I politely suggested that as he was the only one he might give a little more. He replied that there was no point in his doing so; and when I showed surprise, added: "I'm the rehearsal viola; there will be a different one at the performance: he will play with more tone than I."' (*Notes de musique*, 1875.)]

and range, its position in the trumpet family being exactly equivalent to that of the double bass in the violin family. Most modern scores include a part for either ophicleide or bass tuba, sometimes for both.

(7) The saxhorn* and the piston-valve cornet should be taught in our Conservatoire, both being now in general use, the cornet especially.

(8) There is no instruction at all in percussion playing. Yet is there any orchestra in Europe, large or small, which does not possess a timpanist? They all have a functionary of that name; but how many are true timpanists, thorough-going musicians, accustomed to every complexity of rhythm, masters of the technique of the instrument—which is less easy than is commonly believed—and gifted with a keen ear sufficiently trained to enable them to tune and change key accurately and to do so during a performance, with all the noise of the orchestra going on round them? I must positively state that, apart from the timpanist at the Opéra, M. Poussard, I know of only three in the whole of Europe—and I have had the opportunity of scrutinizing a few orchestras in the last nine or ten years. Most of the timpanists I met did not even know how to hold their sticks and were consequently helpless when it came to executing a true tremolo or roll. A timpanist who cannot manage a quick roll in every degree of loud and soft is a man of straw.

All conservatoires ought therefore to have a class in percussion, in which students can acquire a thorough proficiency in timpani, tambourine and side-drum at the hands of first-rate musicians. The old convention, now no longer tolerable and already abandoned by Beethoven and one or two others, whereby the percussion was neglected or treated in a crude and unimaginative way, undoubtedly helped to perpetuate its low status. Composers having till recently used it merely as a source of noise (more or less superfluous or actively disagreeable) or as a means of mechanically emphasizing the strong beats of the bar, it was assumed that this

* [A family of valved instruments of the bugle variety (developed by Sax), extending from high trumpet to tuba registers. The euphonium, the flügelhorn and the cornet are among the many related types.]

modest mission was all that it could or was meant to fulfil in the orchestra, and consequently that there was no need to go into the technique of the thing with any great care or to be a real musician in order to play it. In fact it takes a very capable musician to play even some of the cymbal and bass-drum parts in modern scores.

This brings me to another omission, perhaps the most serious of all in the curriculum of every conservatoire, Paris included:

(9) There is no class in rhythm, devoted to training every student without exception, singers and instrumentalists, in the hazards and complexities of divided time. Hence the depressing tendency of most French and Italian musicians to stress the strong beat, which reduces all phrasing to a monotonous dead level, so that most of them are quite unfit to perform syncopated music—for instance, the charming (our word for them is bizarre) popular airs of Spain—with any degree of finesse. French and Italian singers do not have the remotest conception of what is really meant by 'playing with rhythm'. Whenever they have occasion to try they go about it so clumsily that the result is an ugly musical effect instead of a pleasing one. So you hear them dismissing all music that is not what they call decent, straightforward music—i.e. (more often than not) commonplace—and airing the most childlike notions of what constitutes decency and straightforwardness, and expressing unashamed astonishment at any melody whose characteristic shape and accentuation differ from those generally in use in France and Italy. Hence, too, the flabbiness that is so common among performing musicians; it comes from being used to depending on strictly predictable stresses and divisions of time, as children who have not yet learnt to walk are supported by the handle of their push-carts. Beethoven's symphonies have rudely weaned many Parisian players from these infantile habits and given them a taste for fresh and unstereotyped rhythm. But as nothing similar has been done to rouse singers from their sleep and stir their blood and teach them a little vigilance and agility, their lethargy continues; it will require the discipline of a protracted course of special treatment to get them out of it. So it is they who would have most to gain from the establishing of a class in rhythm—though a large number of instrumentalists might also find that it benefited them.

(10) A comprehensive conservatoire, bent on conserving the significant facts and worthwhile achievements handed down from the past and the various revolutions through which the art has passed, would necessarily have a chair in the history of music, which would ensure that the works of our predecessors were studied and known, not only by means of oral and written instruction but also by the example of meticulous and authentic performances of the appropriate masterpieces. One would not then find students, even talented ones, who, so far as their awareness of the noblest works of great composers still living* is concerned, are as unenlightened as Hottentots. The general taste of musicians would be transformed, their whole conception of music would become larger and more serious, and in the ranks of the profession artists would at last outnumber artisans.

Sixth Letter

Prague (concluded)

TO HUMBERT FERRAND

Another subject yet to be included in the syllabus of any existing conservatoire—one which to my mind is becoming more necessary every day—is instrumentation. This branch of the composer's art has made great strides in the last few years and its achievements have attracted the attention of critics and public. It has also served with certain composers as a means of aping inspiration and concealing poverty of invention beneath a show of energy. Even with undeniably serious and gifted composers it has become a pretext for wanton outrages against good sense and moderation, so you can imagine what excesses their example has led to in the hands of imitators. These very excesses are a measure of the practice, or malpractice, of orchestration, which is for the most part mere whistling in the dark with blind routine to guide it, when it is not sheer accident. For it does not follow that because the modern composer habitually employs a far larger number of instruments than his predecessors he is any more knowledgeable about their character, their capacity and mechanism, and the

* [Berlioz is thinking of Spontini.]

various affinities and relationships that exist between them. Far from it: there are eminent composers who are ignorant of the most rudimentary part of the science, the range of many of the instruments. I know from my own experience of one who did not know the compass of the flute. Of the range of brass instruments and the trombone in particular they have only the most shadowy notion; you can see this from the way most modern scores, just as in the old days, cling to the middle register of these instruments and avoid taking them high or low, simply because the composer, not knowing their exact compass, is afraid of overstepping it; as he has no inkling of what can be done with the notes at either end of the scale, he leaves them strictly alone. Orchestration today is like a foreign language which has become fashionable. Many affect to speak it without having learnt to do so; consequently they speak it without understanding it properly and with a liberal admixture of barbarisms.

Such a class would be useful to aspiring conductors as well as to composition students. It will hardly be disputed that the conductor who does not have a thorough grasp of the technique of orchestration is not worth much, musically speaking. He should at least know the mechanism and exact range of each instrument as well as the player knows it, if not better. In this way he will be in a position to assert himself, especially when it is a question of some unusual combination or some daring or difficult passage which provokes the lazy or incompetent player to announce that 'It can't be done' or 'The note doesn't exist' or 'It's unplayable', or any of the other magic phrases invoked by ignorant mediocrity on these occasions. Instead of meekly accepting it the conductor will be able to reply, 'You're wrong, it can be done. Try it in such and such a way and you'll find you can manage it'; or, 'I don't say it isn't difficult, but if after working at it for a few days you still find it impossible we shall have to conclude that you don't know how to play your instrument properly, and engage a more capable player.' In the opposite instance—admittedly all too common—of the composer who through lack of technical knowledge makes cruel demands on the players and asks for things that are genuinely unattainable even by the most puissant virtuoso, the conductor who knows his business can take their part against the composer and point out to him his mistakes. While on the subject of conductors, let me also suggest that for composition students too some instruction in the difficult art of directing large vocal and instrumental forces (as far as that art can be taught) should have its place in a well-run conservatoire. This would ensure that, when required to, they could at least conduct their own works without making fools of themselves, and assist the performers instead of merely impeding them. The common assumption that every composer is a born conductor, i.e. knows how to direct an orchestra without having to learn, is a fallacy. Beethoven was a celebrated witness to the fact; and I could name many other composers held in general esteem who, the moment they take up the baton, become the most helpless greenhorns, not merely unable to indicate the time with any precision, let alone vary it, but actually capable of bringing the whole performance to a standstill but for the players' swift appreciation of their talents and consequent determination to pay no attention to the irregular convulsions of their arms. A conductor's work has two distinct aspects. The first, and easier, consists in directing the performance of a work which the players already know—a work in the repertory, as they say in the theatre. In the second instance he has the much more arduous task of rehearsing an unfamiliar score, which means discerning the author's intentions and transmitting them clearly and vividly to the band, working until he has achieved the accuracy, ensemble and expression without which there can be no music and, once these technical problems are mastered, identifying the orchestra with himself and animating and infusing it with his own enthusiasm and inspiration.

It follows that, quite apart from the working knowledge of his craft which a conductor acquires by study and practice, and the qualities of feeling and instinct which he has by nature or not at all—the presence or absence of which makes him the composer's most vital ally or his most dangerous enemy—there is a further skill that is essential to the conductor-trainer-organizer: the ability to read a score. The man who makes use of a simplified score or of a mere first violin part, as is often done, especially in France, cannot detect half the mistakes in the playing; and when he does point out an error, he is open to counter-attack by the player in question, who may riposte, 'What do you know about it? You haven't got my part there.' And that is the least disadvantage of this deplorable system.*

Whence I conclude that to become a real conductor a man must at all costs be thoroughly taught how to read a score. He may be expert in orchestration, a composer too, and proficient in the technique of rhythmical changes, and yet have mastered only half his art if this skill still eludes him.

Let me now tell you about the Prague choral society. It is like all such bodies in Germany in being composed almost entirely of amateurs from the middle classes. The choir, about ninety strong, is directed by the younger of the two Skroups. Most of its members are competent musicians, able to read music, and with fresh, resonant voices. Unlike some institutions of the sort it does not have as its sole aim in life the rehearsal and performance of ancient masterpieces, to the exclusion of contemporary works. Such institutions are, if I may so describe them, mere sects, musical consistories where under pretext of a real or pretended enthusiasm for the dead they complacently dismiss the living, of whom they know nothing, deplore the growing influence of Baal, and consign all supposed golden calves and their worshippers to perdition. These meeting-houses of musical puritanism are the repositories of the religion not of the beautiful, whatever its age, but of the old, whatever its quality: a narrow, rancorous religion with its own Bible and the works of two or three evangelists, over which the faithful pore tirelessly, producing ever more subtle interpretations of passages whose meaning is transparently clear, finding deep and mystical conceptions where the rest of the world sees only savagery and barbarism, and always ready with a Hosanna even when the God of Moses commands them to 'take the infants and dash them against the stones, and give the blood thereof for dogs to lick, and not suffer their eyes to pity them'.†

So beware of these bigots! They would almost drive a sane man into forgetting the respect and admiration due to the great achievements of the past.

* Habeneck used to direct the Conservatoire concerts from a violin part. His successors have, in this respect, faithfully followed him.

† [An allusion to the puritan Mucklewrath's tirades in Scott's *Old Mortality*.]

The Prague choral society, as I have said, has nothing in common with such people. Its director is an intelligent artist, not ashamed to admit modern composers, living ones at that, into the sacred precincts. Alongside a Bach or Handel oratorio the choir's repertory may contain the *Moses* of M. Marx, the gifted Berlin critic and theorist (still very much living), or some hymn or part of an opera which in point of age lacks all claim to academic consideration. The first time I went to hear the society they were singing a fantasy on Bohemian national airs by Skroup himself. The originality of this piece delighted me. I had never heard, and have not heard since then, such pungent vocal writing performed with such dash, precision, accuracy of intonation, command of vivid contrasts and splendidly sonorous tone. After the turgid compilations of chords that I had been subjected to on so many similar occasions my ear responded to this lively piece with the avidity of an escaped prisoner drinking in the keen air of the forest on a fine summer night after the stale atmosphere of his cell.

The Sophia Philharmonic (as I have already said it is called) gives a number of public concerts every year under the direction of the two Skroups, the elder brother's opera orchestra lending a hand to the younger's choristers. These are great occasions, prepared with exemplary care a long time in advance, and they always attract a large audience: an élite audience for whom music is neither a recreation nor a tiresome duty but a serious passion demanding, and receiving, all one's powers of intelligence, concentration, ardour and sensibility.

I promised to tell you about the choir school, or rather the liturgical music in the cathedral, and also about the military bands. I must confess to having included them in my list only for the sake of completeness. Religious Music, Military Music look well as headings to a report of this kind. I never meant to keep my promise, however, for the simple reason that I lack the requisite knowledge to say anything to the point about these two aspects of the richness of Bohemia's musical life. I have never been able to bring myself to dilate on matters of which I am quite ignorant. It may come, in time and by force of example. Meanwhile you must forgive me if I keep silent. Despite repeated invitations from Skroup I did not set foot in a church during my whole stay in

Prague. I am, as is known, a very devout sort of person, so there must have been some weighty consideration, since forgotten by me, which would explain this apparent apathy towards religious music. Or perhaps my phobia of organ gigues and fugues on the word 'Amen' got the better of me.

As for military music, I may plead this in justification: I listened to the band of the regiment at that time garrisoned in Prague playing, between noon and four o'clock on a public holiday, the hymn composed by Haydn for the Austrian Emperor. This tune, with all its touching dignity and majesty, is so simple that I was scarcely in a position to judge the quality of the performers. An orchestra, I think, would have to be made up of incompetent musicians indeed not to be able to give a tolerable account of such a piece (though this one, it must be said, played beautifully in tune, which is a rare thing, especially among military bands). Besides, having no idea whether the regiment in question was a native Bohemian force or hailed from some other part of the Austrian Empire, I would be naïve to construct a hypothesis on the basis of their playing which better informed persons might demolish with the simple observation that my 'Bohemian bandsmen' were actually Hungarians, Austrians or Milanese.

Among the performing artists and composers not connected with either the opera house, the Conservatoire or the Philharmonic Society, I would single out Dreyschock, Pischek and the veteran Tomaschek. The first two I have often had occasion to mention; they enjoy a European reputation. I have heard them many times, in Vienna, Pesth, Frankfurt and elsewhere, but not in Prague. It seems that each was badly handled by his compatriots on his first appearance there, and vowed never again to expose his talent to the disparagement of a Bohemian audience. No man is a prophet in his own country; the truth is valid for all times and all nations. However, the Praguers are now taking note of the admiring reports coming in from all points of the compass, to the effect that Dreyschock is an admirable pianist and Pischek one of the finest singers in Europe, and are beginning to suspect that they may have done them an injustice.

Tomaschek is a very well-known composer in Prague and even in Vienna, where his works are highly thought of. Not having the same reasons as Dreyschock and Pischek for bearing his fellow-citizens a grudge, he never denies them the opportunity to hear his compositions. I attended a concert at which, out of thirty-two pieces performed, thirty-one were by him. One of them, as I was informed in advance (but would have noticed in any case), was a new setting of the 'Erl-King', quite different in character from Schubert's. Someone—there are people who will find fault with everything—maintained that in comparison with Schubert's accompaniment, which catches so well the furious galloping of the horse described in the ballad, M. Tomaschek's suggested the ambling gait of a priest's nag; but a critic of superior wit and deeper penetration into the philosophy of art capped this taunt by observing very sensibly that 'it was just because Schubert had ridden the poor animal so hard that it had become lame and could only go at a walking pace'. Tomaschek has been composing for more than thirty years, and must by now have amassed a formidable list of works.

I must also mention a charming artist whose talent, all too unusual in Germany, was of great service to me personally: Mlle Claudius, excellent harpist, capital musician, and Parish-Alvars' best pupil. Mlle Claudius is also the possessor of a striking voice and often sings solos with brilliant success at the concerts of the Philharmonic Society, of which she is a member.

Of the public, what can I tell you? It is related of Louis XIV that, wishing to compliment Boileau on his lines on the crossing of the Rhine, he said, 'I would congratulate you if you had not congratulated me.' My difficulty is the same as the great king's: I would write panegyrics about the Prague audiences and their acumen, sensitivity and rapidity of understanding if they had not treated me so well. But I can say, since it is common knowledge, that the Bohemians are, generally speaking, the finest musicians in Europe and that a genuine love of music and a lively feeling for it are shared by all classes in society. Not only working men from Prague but also peasants came to the concert that I gave in the theatre, the low price of some of the seats having put it within their means; and I could tell from their fresh, uninhibited reaction to the more unexpected effects in the music how interested they were in what I was trying to do; they knew so much music that they had a standard of reference by which to compare the familiar with the unfamiliar, the old with the new, and the good with the bad. You will not expect me to enlarge here on what I think of the public as a general phenomenon. It would require a book and more to encompass a truly scientific study of the strange multitudinous creature, half just and half unjust, half rational and half freakish, ingenuous and cunning, enthusiastic and cynical, profoundly susceptible yet sometimes surprisingly independent, which goes by the name. Indeed, a book dedicated exclusively to the question would probably have come no nearer to solving it by the end. Even Voltaire's irony deserted him on the subject. He asked 'how many fools it took to make a public', but he ended his career suffering those same fools to crown him at the Théâtre-Français and finding their approval prodigiously to his liking. So let us say no more about it and leave the public to be what it is, a sea always in some degree of motion, but to the artist infinitely more dangerous in its dead calms than in its rages.

I gave six concerts in Prague, either in the theatre or in the Sophia Hall.* At the last of them, I remember, I had the great delight of introducing Liszt to my *Romeo and Juliet* symphony. Several pieces from it had already been heard in Prague, and the whole work was performed without arousing any violent controversy, perhaps because it had done so in Vienna; for the two cities are notoriously opposed to each other in matters of musical taste. The vocal side of the performance was exemplary and imposing, and marred only by a solitary mishap. The young person entrusted with the contralto solo had never sung in public before. Despite her extreme diffidence everything went well so long as she had other voices or instruments to support her; but when she came to the passage which begins:

Le jeune Roméo, plaignant sa destinée . . .

* [Berlioz made two visits to Prague, separated by two months during which he gave a further concert in Vienna and then went to Pesth and from there, via Vienna again, to Breslau (as described in the next chapter). The Prague concerts took place on 19, 25 and 27 January, 31 March, and 7 and 17 April. Although he does not go into great detail about it, his five weeks in Prague were among the most successful of his career.]

where the soloist is unaccompanied, her voice began to falter and lose pitch, to such an extent that by the end of the phrase, where the harp re-enters on a chord of E major, she had wandered into some unknown key a good tone and a quarter flat. Mlle Claudius, sitting alongside my desk, was afraid to go on. After a moment's hesitation, she addressed me in a low voice:

'Should I play E?'

'Certainly—we must get out of this.'

And the inexorable chord rang out, hissing and shuddering like a spoonful of molten lead in cold water. The poor little singer nearly fainted at this rude correction. I could not use my eloquence to reassure her, as she did not understand French. Happily she managed to recover her nerve in time for the stanzas 'Premiers transports', which she sang with great feeling and perfectly in tune. The role of Friar Laurence was superbly performed by Strakaty, with real fervour and nobility. The audience encored several numbers; but upon their demanding yet another, the orchestra begged me not to repeat it, as there was an opera performance that evening at seven. When the shouts continued, Mildner took out his watch and held it up in front of him to indicate that the orchestra would not be able to remain till the end if the movement were played again. This ingenious piece of pantomime saved the situation. At the end of the concert, as I was asking Liszt to interpret for me so that I could thank the admirable singers who for the last three weeks had rehearsed my choruses so punctiliously and had performed them with such prowess, a few of them came up to us and on behalf of all their comrades put the contrary proposal to him. There was a rapid exchange of German, then Liszt turned to me:

'My brief has changed,' he said. 'These gentlemen desire me to thank you for the pleasure you have given them in allowing them to sing your work, and to tell you how delighted they are to see you so happy.'

Altogether it was a great day in my life; there have not been many that I can look back on with such satisfaction.

Like the banquet in Vienna at which I was given the aforementioned silver-gilt baton, there followed a supper and the presentation of a silver cup from the musicians and amateurs of

Prague. Most of the performing artists, critics and music-lovers of the city were there; I was delighted to see, among the latter, a compatriot of mine, the witty and genial Prince de Rohan. Liszt was unanimously adopted as speaker in place of the President (whose French was not sufficiently fluent). When the first toast was called, he rose and in the name of the whole company addressed me for a full quarter of an hour with a warmth of feeling, a wealth of ideas and a turn of phrase that many orators would envy. I was deeply touched. Unhappily, if he spoke well, he drank likewise. That fatal cup set such tides of champagne flowing that all Liszt's eloquence was shipwrecked in it. Belloni* and I were still reasoning with him in the street at two in the morning, and urging on him the advisability of waiting until daylight before engaging in single combat with pistols at two yards' range with a Bohemian who had drunk even better than he. When daylight came we felt somewhat anxious for Liszt, who was giving a concert at noon. At half-past eleven he was still asleep. They finally woke him; he climbed into a carriage, arrived at the hall, entered to a triple-barrelled broadside of applause, sat down, and played as I do not believe he has ever played in his life.

Verily, there is a God . . . for pianists.

Goodbye, my dear Ferrand. I fear you won't complain that my letters were too laconic. Yet I have not said all that my fond memories of Prague and its inhabitants prompt me to say. However, you know my serious passion for music, and may guess from that whether I love the Bohemians. *O Praga! quando te aspiciam!*†

54

Concert in Breslau—my legend The Damnation of Faust—the libretto—patriotic German critics—The Damnation of Faust performed in Paris—I decide to go to Russia—my friends' kindness

IN THE PRECEDING letters to Humbert Ferrand I said nothing about having gone to Breslau. I do not know why I failed to

* Liszt's agent.

† [An adaptation of Horace (*Satires*, II, vi): *O rus, quando ego te aspiciam* ('O country home, when shall I see you again?').]

mention it, for my visit to the Silesian capital was both pleasant and profitable. Thanks to the enthusiastic efforts of a number of people who helped me—among others, M. Koettlitz, a young musician of great ability, Dr Naumann, a distinguished doctor and knowledgeable music-lover, and the well-known organist Hesse—the concert which I gave in the hall of the university, the Aula Leopoldina, was highly successful in every respect.* People came in from the townships and countryside all around to hear it. The receipts were a good deal higher than I usually took in Germany and the public gave my music a brilliant reception. I was all the more pleased because, the day after my arrival in Breslau, I had attended a concert at which the audience sat coldly unresponsive throughout the entire proceedings; to my astonishment, the performance of a work as sublime as the C minor Symphony of Beethoven was followed by total silence. I had never met anything like it; but when I expressed surprise and ventured to protest at Beethoven's being received in this manner, a lady, in her own way a devotee of the master, corrected me. 'You're mistaken,' she said. 'They admire this great work as much as anybody, and if they don't applaud, it's out of *respect.*' This word, which would have a profound significance in Paris and wherever the claque is traditionally active, gave me, I confess, the liveliest anxiety. I was terribly afraid of being respected. Happily nothing of the sort occurred. At my concert the audience (to whose respect I must have lacked sufficient claim) saw fit to treat me according to the vulgar convention in use for favoured artists throughout the rest of Europe, and I was applauded most irreverently.

It was during this journey through Austria, Hungary, Bohemia and Silesia that I began composing my *Faust* legend, which had long been taking shape in my mind. As soon as I had made up my mind to do it, I had also to resolve to write most of the libretto myself; for the fragments of Gérard de Nerval's translation of Goethe's *Faust* which I had set to music twenty years earlier and which I intended to rework and include in the score, plus two or three other scenes written to my instructions by M. Gandonnière

* [20 March 1846. Berlioz also made a return visit to Brunswick (not mentioned in the *Memoirs*) for a concert given on 21 April.]

before I left Paris, together amounted to less than one sixth of the work.

So, as I bowled along in my old German post-chaise, I attempted to write the verses that were to be set to my music. I began with Faust's invocation to Nature, seeking neither to translate nor yet to imitate Goethe's original but simply to take my inspiration from it and extract the musical substance it contained. The result, which I quote here, gave me the hope of being able to manage the rest:

Nature immense, impénétrable et fière!
Toi seule donnes trêve à mon ennui sans fin;
Sur ton sein tout-puissant je sens moins ma misère,
Je retrouve ma force et je crois vivre enfin.
Oui, soufflez, ouragans, criez, forêts profondes,
Croulez, rochers, torrents, précipitez vos ondes!
A vos bruits souverains ma voix aime à s'unir.
Forêts, rochers, torrents, je vous adore! Mondes
Qui scintillez, vers vous s'élance le désir
D'un coeur trop vaste et d'une âme altérée
*D'un bonheur qui la fuit.**

Once launched, I did the verses that I lacked as and when the musical ideas came to me; and I composed the score with an ease such as I have very rarely experienced with any of my other works. I wrote it when and where I could: in coaches, in trains, on steamboats, even in the towns that I visited (this despite all the various responsibilities that my concerts entailed). Thus I wrote the introduction, 'Le vieil hiver a fait place au printemps', in an inn

* ['Nature, immense, unfathomable, proud,
You alone give pause to my unending ennui,
On your omnipotent breast I feel my misery less keenly,
I regain my strength, and believe in life at last.
Yes, blow, you hurricanes! Roar, you mighty forests!
Crash down, you rocks, and torrents, hurl headlong your waters!
My voice delights to mingle with your majestic sounds.
Forests, rocks, torrents, I worship you.
Glittering worlds above, to you soars up the longing
Of a heart too vast and a soul thirsting
For a happiness it cannot seize.']

at Passau on the Bavarian frontier. The scene on the banks of the Elbe, Mephistopheles' aria 'Voici des roses' and the Dance of the Sylphs were written in Vienna. I have said how and on what occasion, in the course of a night—in Vienna again—I wrote the Hungarian march on the Rákóczy theme. The extraordinary impression it produced in Pesth induced me to incorporate it in my score; I took the liberty of locating my hero in Hungary when the action begins and of making him witness the passage of the Hungarian army across the plain where he wanders, wrapped in his thoughts. A German critic professed to find it most irregular that I should have done so, and said I had no business putting Faust there. I cannot see why. I should have had no hesitation in taking him anywhere in the world if the work would have benefited. I was under no compulsion to keep to Goethe's story. A person like Faust may after all have any journey ascribed to him, no matter how outlandish, without violence being done to plausibility. Later the same strange argument was taken up more vehemently by other German critics. They attacked me for the changes my libretto had made to the text and plot of Goethe's masterpiece—as if no other *Faust* but his existed,* and as if in any case it were possible to set such a poem to music complete and unchanged. I was stupid enough to answer them in the preface to the score. I have often wondered why those same critics have never lectured me about the libretto of my *Romeo and Juliet* symphony, which differs considerably from the immortal tragedy. No doubt it is because Shakespeare *was not a German.* Patriotism! fetishism! cretinism!

The choral refrain of the Peasants' Dance was written by the light of a shop's gas-jet in Pesth, one evening when I had lost my way in the town. In Prague I got up in the middle of the night to set down a tune that I was afraid of forgetting, the angelic chorus in the scene of Margaret's apotheosis: 'Remonte au ciel, âme naïve, que l'amour égara'. The students' song 'Jam nox stellata' was written, words and music, in Breslau. The big trio, 'Ange adoré dont la céleste image', I composed near Rouen at the country

* Marlowe's, for example, or Spohr's opera, neither of which resembles Goethe's *Faust*.

place of Baron de Montville, where I spent a few days on my return to France.*

The rest was written in Paris, but always in odd moments, unpremeditatedly—at home, at the café, in the Tuileries Gardens, even on a milestone in the Boulevard du Temple: I did not have to search for ideas; I let them come and they presented themselves in the most unpredictable order. Finally, when the whole score was sketched out, I set myself to work carefully over it again, to polish the various sections, to join and knit them together with all the tenacity and patience I am capable of, and to complete the orchestration, which had only been roughly indicated here and there. I regard the work as one of the best things I have done. The public naturally shares this opinion of it.

To have written it was nothing: it had to be performed. It was then that my frustrations and tribulations began. The copying of the orchestral and vocal parts cost me an enormous sum; the numerous rehearsals which I required of the performers, and the exorbitant fee of one thousand six hundred francs for the hire of the Opéra-Comique (the only place then available to me) further committed me to an enterprise that could not fail to be my ruin. But I went on. As anyone else would have done in my place, I fortified myself with plausible arguments. 'When I performed *Romeo and Juliet* for the first time', I reasoned, 'public interest ran so high that "corridor tickets" had to be issued to accommodate the people who could not get into the hall; and despite the enormous cost of putting on the work I made a small profit. Since then my stock has risen in the public estimation and the fame of my successes abroad has given it a prestige in France that it did not have before. As a subject *Faust* is at least as well known as *Romeo*, and generally considered to suit me; I am thought likely to have treated it well. All in all there is every reason to hope that people will be extremely curious to hear this new work, which is on a larger scale and more varied in colour than its predecessors. I should at least cover my expenses.' Delusion! Some years had gone by since the first performance of *Romeo and Juliet*, and in that time the apathy of the Paris public towards all that pertains to art and literature had made impressive strides. People

* [He returned to Paris from Germany at the beginning of May 1846.]

were now no longer sufficiently interested, least of all in music, to sit cooped up in the middle of the day (I could not give my concerts in the evening) and in the Opéra-Comique, a theatre which the smart world is not given to frequenting. It was the end of November (1846) and snowing; the weather was terrible. I had no star singer for the part of Marguerite. Roger, who sang Faust, and Herman Léon, the Mephistopheles, could be heard any day in the same theatre, and they were not smart either. The result was that *Faust* was given twice before a half-empty house. The fashionable Paris audience, the audience which goes to concerts and is supposed to take an interest in music, stayed comfortably at home, as little concerned with my new work as if I had been the obscurest Conservatoire student. For all the number of people that came to those two performances, it might have been the most footling opera in the company's repertory.

Nothing in my career as an artist wounded me more deeply than this unexpected indifference. The disillusionment was cruel but it was useful. I learnt my lesson, and since then have not staked twenty francs on the popularity of my music with the Parisian public. I hope I never will if I live to be a hundred.*

I was ruined. I owed a considerable sum of money which I had not got. After two days of unutterable depression, I thought I saw a way out of my entanglement: I would go to Russia. But to do so would again require money, the more so as I did not want to leave any of my outstanding debts unpaid. It was then that my friends came to the rescue, with a kindness that was a wonderful solace to me in my difficulties. As soon as it became known that I was driven to go to St Petersburg in an attempt to make good the loss in which my latest work had involved me in Paris, I had offers of help from all sides. M. Bertin got the cashier of the *Journal des débats* to advance me a thousand francs. Some of my friends lent me five hundred, others six or seven hundred. A young German named Friedland, whom I had got to know on my recent journey to

* I did not stick to my resolve. Having written *The Childhood of Christ*, I could not resist having it performed in Paris. Its success was immediate, and so great as to be positively insulting to my previous works. I gave several performances in the Salle Herz which, instead of ruining me as *Faust* had done, made a profit of a few thousand francs (1858).

Prague, produced twelve hundred. Sax, though himself in difficulties, did the same. Finally Hetzel, the publisher, who has since played a distinguished part in the Republican government, made me a loan, although he was only an acquaintance at the time. We met by chance in a café.

'I hear you're off to Russia,' he said.

'Yes, I——'

'It's a very expensive journey, particularly in winter. If a thousand-franc note would be any help, please take it.'

I accepted it as unreservedly as the excellent Hetzel had offered it. Thus I was able to face the world and fix the day of my departure.

I think I have said before, but do not mind repeating, that if I have come across a good many rogues and knaves in my life, I have been extraordinarily lucky in the opposite respect. Few artists have encountered such generosity of spirit and ungrudging loyalty as I.

Dear and excellent men! You have no doubt long forgotten the noble way you treated me. Let me here remind you and most warmly thank you for it and tell you how profoundly happy it makes me to think of all you did for me!*

* [Berlioz had been contemplating a Russian tour for over a year (the reason for his leave of absence from the Conservatoire library in October 1845 was given as 'to go to Austria and Russia'). He prepared the ground with the dedication of the Fantastic Symphony, published in the summer of 1845, to Czar Nicholas I.]

TRAVELS IN RUSSIA

55

The Prussian courier—M. Nernst—by sledge—snow—the silly crows—the Counts Wielhorsky—General Lvov—my first concert—the Empress—I make a fortune—journey to Moscow—a bizarre stumbling-block—the Grand Marshal—music-mania among the young—the Kremlin cannon

THE MOST CONVENIENT time in St Petersburg for giving concerts such as I wished to give is Lent, for the theatres are closed during this period, which covers the whole month of March. I set out from Paris on 14 February 1847. The snow was six inches deep on the ground when I left, and from then until my arrival in St Petersburg a fortnight later I never once lost sight of it. In Belgium there had been such a heavy fall that the train had to wait several hours at Tirlemont while workmen cleared the line. It may be imagined what bitter cold was in store for me the following week, when I had crossed the Niemen.

In Berlin I stopped only a few hours, to beg a letter of introduction to the Empress of Russia from her brother the King of Prussia; which the King, with his usual kindness, let me have at once.

From Berlin to Tilsit I had the misfortune to travel with a music-mad courier, who plagued me horribly from the moment I set foot in his post-chaise. The fellow had seen my name on his list and had at once decided to put me to good use. He composed piano polkas and waltzes as a hobby; and at each post-house along the route he would stop, sometimes for a considerable time, and while supposedly settling his accounts with the postmaster would rule some more staves and set down the dance tune that he had been whistling through his teeth for the last three hours; after which, getting back into the coach, he would condescend to give the order for our journey to continue, at the same time presenting me with the new waltz or polka and a pencil so that I could put in the bass and the harmonies. The bass being duly written, there would follow a stream of comments, whys and wherefores, exclamations of delight and astonishment, which at first I found very amusing but which, the second and third time, made me curse the good man's meagre acquaintance with music and the French language. One would never have such ill luck in France. On arriving in Tilsit I asked for the postmaster, Nernst (how I came to know his name and presume upon his good will I shall say presently). His office was pointed out to me, and I went in and found a large man in a cloth cap, severe of countenance yet with something both witty and benevolent about him. He was seated on a high stool, and remained there when I entered.

'M. Nernst?' I inquired, with a bow.

'Yes. May I ask who I have the honour of speaking to, sir?'

'Hector Berlioz.'

'You don't mean it!' he cried, bounding off the stool and landing in front of me, cap in hand.

Whereupon the worthy man overwhelmed me with every kind of polite attention, which grew even more civil when I revealed who had given me the introduction. 'On your way through Tilsit don't fail to look up the postmaster, Nernst,' a friend had said before I left Paris. 'He's an excellent man, and well-read and cultivated too, and you might find him useful.' The friend who gave me this advice, on the corner of the street where I met him at eleven one night on the eve of my departure, was Honoré de Balzac. He himself had been to Russia only a short time before. When I told him I was going to St Petersburg to give some concerts he assured me with great earnestness that I would come back with a hundred and fifty thousand francs. 'I know the place. You won't be able to bring back less.' It was a weakness of that great mind to see fortunes wherever he looked—fortunes already so sure that he would not have hesitated to ask a banker to advance him the money. He dreamed in millions; it was a mirage which the constant disappointments he suffered all his life were powerless to dispel. I smiled at his valuation of what the journey would be worth to me, without appearing to question its accuracy. It will be seen that if my concerts in St Petersburg and Moscow yielded more than I had hoped, I was able to bring back a good deal less than the hundred and fifty thousand francs prophesied by Balzac.

This extraordinary writer, the incomparable anatomist who has probed to the very heart of contemporary French society, naturally provided a fruitful topic of conversation between the postmaster and me. M. Nernst told me in fascinating detail of Balzac's affairs in Galicia and his hopes of marriage.* He is one of the small number of foreigners who are in a position to admire Balzac with true passion, knowing French well enough to be able to understand his prose.

I remember, on my return, describing to my family this episode in my travels, and my father bursting out laughing when I came to Nernst's exclamation 'You don't mean it!' He was by then very weak, in low spirits and constant pain. But the naïve pride which he took, in spite of all his philosophy, in this unusual evidence of his son's celebrity came out almost involuntarily.

'You don't mean it!' he would repeat, with renewed laughter. 'In Tilsit, did you say?'

'Yes, on the Niemen, on the eastern frontier of Prussia.'

'You don't mean it!'; and he would laugh again.

A few hours later, after this brief respite, furnished with instructions from Nernst and fortified by several glasses of an excellent curaçao which he had tirelessly pressed upon me, I set out on the most arduous part of my journey. A post-chaise took me as far as Taurogen on the Russian frontier. There I was encased in an iron sledge, not to leave it again until I reached St Petersburg after enduring, for four trying days and as many abominable nights, torments whose existence I had never suspected in my most lurid dreams.

Imagine a metal box, hermetically sealed yet subtly penetrable by the fine snow, which seeps in, powdering your face white. Imagine yourself shaken about in it, violently and almost without pause, rather as shot is shaken in a bottle to clean it. Imagine the resultant contusion to head and limbs from their being brought frequently into sharp contact with the casing of the sledge. Imagine, on top of all that, a general sensation of malaise plus a powerful desire to vomit, which can fairly be called snow-

* [A reference to Balzac's long courtship of the Polish countess Eveline Hanska. He married her three years later, a few months before his death.]

sickness, from its strong resemblance to the state known to travellers by sea.

The common assumption made in our temperate climes that Russian sledges, drawn by swift horses, skim smoothly over the snow as though crossing a frozen lake, has given us a rather agreeable idea of sledging as a method of travel. The truth is very different. Certainly, if you have the luck to encounter level ground where the snow is untouched or flattened into a regular, uniform surface, the sledge's progress is swift and impeccably horizontal. But you will not find one mile in fifty like that. The rest is all churned up, rutted across with trenches dug by the peasants' heavy carts (used, in this 'age of transport', for transporting wood in large quantities). The effect is of an angry sea frozen solid. The troughs between the snow-waves are veritable ditches; and the sledge, having laboriously climbed out of one trough onto the crest of the wave, plunges down into the next with a bump and a crash fit to crack your skull—especially at night when, nodding off for a moment, you can be caught unawares by the most horrible jolt. When the waves are smaller and less uneven, the sledge settles into a regular up-and-down motion like a canoe at sea, resulting in the aforesaid queasiness and even vomiting. And all this quite apart from the bitter, intense cold which, as the night wears on, becomes progressively more unbearable despite the protective layers of greatcoat, fur cloak and fur travelling bag and the straw with which the sledge is packed; until you have the sensation of being pricked all over your body by a million tiny needles, and whatever you may tell yourself you shiver almost as much from the fear of freezing to death as from the actual cold.

On days when the sun shone and I could see the great gleaming wilderness stretching forbiddingly about us, I kept imagining our poor shattered army on that murderous retreat and pictured the wretched men, coatless, no boots on their feet, without bread, without brandy to warm them, their morale and their physical strength reduced to nothing, wounded for the most part, by day dragging themselves along, a ghost army, by night stretched out in the open, corpselike, on that appalling snow in a cold more terrible still than I shivered in; and I wondered how even one soldier among them could have come through and lived to escape from this white hell. It must take an awful lot to make a man die.

Then I watched the famished crows with numbed wings following the sledge and alighting from time to time to feast on the horses' droppings, then squatting down on their bellies to get a little warmth into their half-frozen feet; and I laughed that they could be so stupid when, only a few hours' flight to the south, they might have found a mild climate, fertile land and lush pastures. Can its native country be so dear to the patriotic heart of a crow—if indeed, as our soldiers used to say, you can call it a country?

At length one Sunday evening,* a fortnight after leaving Paris, I arrived, wizened with cold, in the proud northern city of St Petersburg. From what I had heard in France of the strictness of the Imperial Police, I expected to have my bundles of music confiscated for a week at least; they had hardly been touched at the frontier. But nothing of the sort occurred. The police did not even ask me what they contained, and I was able to take them with me to my hotel. A pleasant surprise!

I had not been installed an hour, in a warm room, when M. de Lenz, a very agreeable man and a knowledgeable music-lover (see my analysis of his book on Beethoven in *Evenings in the Orchestra*), came to call on me and bid me welcome. We had met in Paris a few years before.

'I have come from Count Michael Wielhorsky's,' he said. 'We've just heard of your arrival. There's a big party at his house this evening, all the important musical people in St Petersburg are there, and the Count has sent me to say he would be delighted if you could come.'

'But how do people already know I'm here?'

'Well—never mind; they do. Come along.'

Pausing only to unfreeze my face, shave and dress, I accompanied my amiable mentor to the house of Count Wielhorsky.

I should say 'Counts', for there are two: they are brothers, each as intelligent and as devoted to music as the other, and they live together. The prestige of their justly famous taste, the influence of their great wealth and numerous connections, and their official

* [28 February 1847.]

position at court, close to the Emperor and the Empress, combine to make their house a little Ministry of Fine Arts in St Petersburg.

They received me with charming cordiality. In a few hours they had introduced me to all the leading personalities, musicians and men of letters, present in their salon. One of the first people I met was the admirable Henry Romberg, at the time conductor of the Italian Opera; with extraordinary kindness he at once constituted himself my guide to musical St Petersburg and promised to mobilize my performers for me. The date of my first concert was fixed on the spot by General Guedeonoff, intendant of the Imperial theatres, the assembly hall of the nobles chosen to hold it in, and the price of tickets settled, after discussion, at three silver roubles (twelve francs) each. So there I was, barely four hours after my arrival, already in the thick of it. Next day Romberg came to collect me and we went round the town together, visiting and engaging the principal artists whose participation I needed. My orchestra was soon complete. With the help of General Lvov, aide-de-camp and musical director to the Emperor and an exceptionally gifted composer and performer, in whom I at once discovered a kindred spirit, we contrived with equal speed to muster a sizeable and competent choir. That left only a bass and a tenor for the first two parts of *Faust*, which I had included in the programme. Versing, bass from the German Theatre, undertook the role of Mephistopheles, and Ricciardi, an Italian tenor whom I had known in Paris, agreed to sing Faust. He had to sing it in French, while Mephistopheles sang in German; but the Russian public, being equally at home in both languages, accepted this curious anomaly without demur. For the chorus, who were singing in German, the words had to be recopied in Russian characters, the only ones they were familiar with. Worse, at the end of the first rehearsal Romberg announced that the German translation which I had had made in Paris at great expense was very bad and so clumsy in point of prosody as to be virtually unsingable. So as not to delay the opening concert he quickly corrected the grosser blunders. But I made up my mind a few weeks later that I must look for another translator, and was lucky enough to find, in M. Münzlaff, a musician of wit and intelligence who acquitted himself perfectly and retrieved the situation. The evening of my first concert in the assembly hall of the nobles was a splendid occasion.* I had a large and well-rehearsed orchestra and chorus, and a military band to boot, chosen by General Lvov from among the musicians of the Imperial Guard. Even the two kapellmeisters of St Petersburg, Romberg and Maurer, had been recruited, to play the antique cymbals in Queen Mab. My artists were buzzing with excitement, which augured well for the performance, and I had just discovered a compatriot in their ranks—Tajan-Rogé, fine cellist and true artist, who was with me heart and soul. The programme, consisting of the *Roman Carnival* overture, the first two acts of *Faust*, Queen Mab, and the Apotheosis from my Funeral and Triumphal Symphony, was in fact very well performed. The enthusiasm of the great glittering audience which thronged the hall was beyond anything I could have conceived—not least for *Faust*. I was giddy with the number of recalls, the clapping and shouting, the encores. At the end of the first part of *Faust* the Empress, who was present, sent for me through Count Michael Wielhorsky and I had to appear before Her Majesty just as I was, flushed, perspiring, out of breath, with crumpled cravat, hot from battle. The Empress received me in the most flattering manner, introduced me to her sons, spoke of her brother the King of Prussia and the interest he took in me (as his letters showed), praised my music and expressed herself astonished at the exceptional performance I had obtained. After we had been talking for a quarter of an hour she said:

'Now I must return you to your audience. They are so excited, you mustn't keep them waiting any longer for the second part of the concert.'

I left the anteroom with a lively gratitude for all these marks of imperial favour.

The audience were beside themselves by the end of the Sylphs' Chorus. They were not prepared for music of such airy delicacy, so soft that one must listen hard in order to hear it. It was, I do not conceal it, an intoxicating moment for me.

Meanwhile I had been getting a little anxious about my military bandsmen. They were to play in the final piece, the Apotheosis;

* [15 March 1847.]

but there was no sign of them. I was afraid they might enter the orchestra in the middle of a movement and in doing so make a noise which would spoil the effect. I had reckoned without military discipline. On turning round after the scherzo—which, to be heard, requires the most profound silence—I beheld my sixty men drawn up in position, each man at his post, instruments at the ready. They had come in and taken their places without anyone noticing it. *Bravissimo!*

The concert concluded, the embraces weathered and a bottle of beer consumed, it occurred to me to inquire the financial outcome of the enterprise. 'Eighteen thousand francs.' The concert had cost six thousand. A clear profit of twelve thousand francs! I was saved. Unconsciously I turned south-west and, as I gazed in the general direction of France, found myself murmuring, 'My dear Parisians!'

I gave a second concert ten days later with the same results. I was rich. After that I set off for Moscow,* where third-rate musicians, incredible choristers and some bizarre obstacles awaited me, but a public every bit as enthusiastic and responsive as the St Petersburg public had been, and a profit of eight thousand francs. Once again I turned south-west and addressed my bored and blasé countrymen. Happily, not for the last time: in London, since then, I have often had occasion to turn south-east.

There are many people to whom a musician is a man who plays an instrument. It would never occur to them that there might be musician-composers, and composers who actually give concerts with the object of getting their works heard. Such people presumably think of music as a commodity which you get at the publisher's as you get cakes at the baker's, and which is simply turned out according to the standard recipes. Although this somewhat surprising theory is often in practice well founded, it does sometimes fall short of the truth. Yet the astonishment of certain persons when you speak to them of a composer is positively comical.

I was practically assaulted in Breslau by a respectable paterfamilias who was determined that I should give violin lessons to his son. In vain I protested that it would be nothing short of a miracle if I were able to play the instrument in question, never having

* [Beginning of April 1847. The journey took four days.]

handled a bow in my life. He refused to believe it and was quite sure that for some reason I was pulling his leg. I told him he must be mistaking me for the celebrated violinist Bériot; our names were rather alike. But he held his ground; had he not just read the poster which said I was giving a concert in the university hall in two days' time? What further evidence was required? 'Certainly,' I said, 'I am giving a concert, but I'm not playing the violin.'

'Then what are you doing?'

'Getting other people to play it. I'm conducting the orchestra. Come, and you'll see.'

But he continued to be very angry. Not until the concert was over, and he had thought the matter over, was he prepared to admit that it was possible for a musician to appear in public without actually performing anything himself.

In Moscow a similar misapprehension nearly proved my undoing. The assembly hall of the nobles was the only suitable place to give my concert in, so I sought to obtain the use of it and was taken off to see the Grand Marshal, a venerable old man of eighty, to whom I explained the purpose of my visit.

'What instrument do you play?' he promptly asked me.

'I do not play any instrument,' I said.

'Then how will you manage to give a concert?'

'I am having my works performed, I am conducting the orchestra.'

'Ah ha! a very ingenious idea. That is a new sort of concert to me. I am perfectly prepared to let you have our big hall, but as you are no doubt aware every artist to whom we grant permission to use it must in return, having done so, perform at one of the private gatherings of the nobility.'

'I see. Has the assembly an orchestra which it will place at my disposal to perform my works?'

'Certainly not.'

'In that case how are they to be performed? I presume I am not expected to spend three thousand francs on the necessary players so that one of my symphonies can be played at a private concert of the assembly's. That would be a rather high rent to pay.'

'Then I am very sorry, sir, but I must refuse you. I have no choice.'

And that was that; I had my answer. It looked as if I had come all that way only to see my purpose frustrated by this improbable stumbling-block. I described my discomfiture to M. Marcou, a French artist long resident in Moscow. He laughed very heartily but, as he knew the Grand Marshal personally, suggested that we both go to see him the following day and try a fresh attack. Second visit: second refusal; all explanations offered by my compatriot unavailing: the Grand Marshal shakes his snowy head and stands firm. However, fearing that his French is not fluent enough, and in case he has misunderstood some word or phrase in my request, he fetches his wife. Enter Madame la Maréchale, looking almost as venerable as her husband but rather less agreeable; she stares at me, listens to my story, then cuts the discussion short by saying in clear, precise and rapid French: 'We are neither able nor prepared to contravene the assembly's regulations. If we lend you the hall, you will play an instrumental solo at our next gathering. If you do not wish to play, we will not lend it to you.'

'Well, madam, I used to be quite a performer on the flageolet, the flute and the guitar. Choose which of these three instruments I am to play. But I must warn you that it is nearly twenty-five years since I touched any of them, so I shall play extremely badly. On second thoughts, I could probably manage a side-drum solo better, if you would consider that sufficient.'

Fortunately a senior official had come into the room during the foregoing scene. He was soon apprised of the difficulty and drew me aside:

'Don't insist, M. Berlioz, or the discussion may become a little unpleasant for our good Marshal. Be so kind as to let me have your request in writing tomorrow, and I shall see that everything is arranged.'

I took his advice; and thanks to the obliging colonel the regulations were waived for this one occasion. The concert could take place, and I was not obliged to entertain the aristocracy on the flute or the side-drum—which was a lucky escape for the aristocracy: I would have performed on the three-hole Provençal flute if necessary, rather than re-cross the Volga without giving my concert. Nevertheless the Muscovite nobles and their unusual club rule—of which I had unfortunately heard no mention in St

Petersburg—lost me quite a lot of money; for at the end of the concert,* which had been announced as the only one I was to give in Moscow, many music-lovers jumped onto the platform and shouted out: 'Encore! encore! You can't go away like this. You must give another one.' Had I done so, it might have brought me in more than the first. But I had no hall. The exception had been made only in consideration of my ignorance of the ruling and with the explicit understanding that I was not to treat it as a precedent. After all, a composer! A fellow incapable of playing anything! A trifler! Yet only think how many people there are in other sections of society, in the middle classes especially, people with little or no talent, for whom this arduous, almost impossibly difficult career is the summit of their dreams!

If the recurrence of an aptitude for music in certain artistic families can be explained quite simply by the influence of example and upbringing, by the fact that it is relatively easy for children to follow in their fathers' footsteps, and even by natural inclination transmitting itself, like physical appearance, from one generation to the next, how on the other hand is one to explain the extraordinary fantasies that visit so many young people quite out of the blue?

Leaving out of consideration the amateur who insists on taking useless lessons at exorbitant cost in defiance of a fundamentally inartistic nature against which the skill and patience of the cleverest teachers are of no avail, or the visionary who believes that music, like mathematics, can be mastered purely by the light of reason, and setting aside the worthy father who has a notion to make his son a colonel or a great composer, one comes across melancholy cases of music-mania among persons whom one would suppose perfectly safe from the disease.

I shall mention only two from the instances that have come my way—both, I fear, incurable: one a Russian, the other a Frenchman.

To take the Frenchman first. One day in Paris when I was alone, much preoccupied, there was a knock at my study door. 'Come in,' I called. The door opened and a young man of

* [10 April 1847.]

eighteen entered. He was panting for breath, because he had been running and because he was bursting with an idea.

'Do sit down,' I said.

'It's nothing—I'm a little—I have come—' then, like a pistol shot, 'I've inherited some money.'

'Have you? My congratulations.'

'Yes, I have, and I've come to ask you whether I should spend it on becoming a composer.' (I opened my eyes wider.)

'Please sit down. My dear sir, you credit me with unusual perception. Even prophecies based on fairly substantial works can be quite wrong. However, if you have brought some scores with you——'

'No, I haven't brought any scores. But you'll find I shall work very hard, I'm terribly fond of music!'

'You have already written something, I presume—part of a symphony, an overture, a cantata?'

'An overture? N-no. I haven't done a cantata either.'

'Well, perhaps you have had a shot at writing a quartet?'

'Oh, sir—a quartet?'

'Good heavens, you mustn't despise it. It's possibly the hardest of all forms of music to do well. Think how few composers have been successful at it. But, to aim a little less high, have you something simpler you can show me—a romance, for instance, or a waltz?'

'Oh!' (looking almost insulted)—'a romance? No, no—I don't go in for that sort of thing.'

'Haven't you done anything, then?'

'No—but I shall work very hard.'

'But you have at least studied harmony and counterpoint, you know the range of voices and instruments?'

'Well, not exactly, but . . . no, I don't know harmony or counterpoint or instrumentation. But you'll find that——'

'Forgive my interrupting you. You are eighteen or nineteen, which is late to begin studying these subjects to any purpose. I take it you have learnt to read music at sight and can write it at dictation?'

'You mean, do I know *solfège*? Oh, dear me! Well . . . no, I don't even know the notes at all, I don't know anything; but I'm really terribly fond of music, I would so like to be a composer! If you would give me lessons, I would come twice a day, I'd work at night.'

A silence ensued, during which I struggled against an impulse to laugh. Then I gave my young composer a detailed and suitably discouraging picture of the difficulties he would have to overcome simply to attain the most mediocre level of skill—in other words to be able to write bad music. I went on to describe the obstacles he would face even when he had become a composer of exalted rank. It was no use. He listened with an impatient, disgruntled air and went off with the obvious intention of looking for another teacher to whom he could offer his vocation and his inheritance. God grant that he has not found one!

There is nothing ridiculous about my second example of music-madness; quite the contrary. I had just given the aforementioned concert in Moscow when a letter was handed to me, written in excellent French. It was from a stranger, who asked for an interview. I replied at once, naming a particular date and hour when he could see me. This time my unknown friend had not inherited money—far from it. He was a tall young Russian, twenty-two or older, with a striking face and something a little strange about him. He spoke with fastidious care and with the intense, concentrated eagerness that denotes the enthusiast.

'Sir,' he said, 'I have a deep and unbounded passion for music. I have learnt it on my own, unaided—very imperfectly, as you may imagine. Moscow does not offer me much scope for pursuing my studies and I am not rich enough to travel. My parents have vainly attempted to deflect me from this course. Now one of the leading noblemen in Moscow is prepared to help me. He has informed my father that if some musician whose opinion is to be trusted were to find evidence in me of a genuine aptitude for music, he would undertake the entire expense of my education and send me to the best teachers in Germany and France to complete it. So I have come to ask if you will look at my efforts and then write and tell me candidly what you think of my abilities. If you will, I shall be eternally grateful to you whatever the outcome; but if the verdict is favourable, you will be restoring me to life—for I am dying; the enforced constraint of my existence is killing me. I feel I have wings but cannot spread them. You will realize what torture it is.'

'Indeed I do. I can imagine what you must be suffering, and I sympathize with you deeply. Pray make use of me, I am at your service.'

'Thank you a thousand times. I shall come back tomorrow and bring the works that I would like to submit to you.'

And off he went, his eyes shining, radiant with happiness.

Next day he came back. He was totally altered. The fire had gone out of him. Dejection was written all over his pale countenance.

'I have not brought anything,' he said. 'I spent the night going through my manuscripts. None of them seems to me worth showing to you, and honestly, none of them gives a true idea of what I'm capable of. I am going to set to work so that I have something better to offer you.'

'Alas, I have to return to St Petersburg the day after tomorrow.'

'Then I shall send it to you. Ah, if you knew how my soul is on fire—how inspired I sometimes feel. When that happens I cannot stay in the city. No matter how cold it is I go off into the woods and there, alone in the presence of nature, I hear a whole world of glorious, enchanted sound ringing and vibrating about me; my eyes fill with tears, I cry out, I fall to the ground in an ecstasy. It is a foretaste of heaven. They think me mad. Believe me, I am not mad, and I shall prove to you that I'm not.'

I again assured the young enthusiast how much he interested me and how anxious I was to be of service to him. Yes, I reflected when he had gone, these could be symptoms of an exceptional nature. The man might be a genius. It would be a crime not to help him. If need be I would devote myself body and soul to his cause; let him only give me some slight encouragement.

For several weeks I waited in vain. At last a letter came to St Petersburg. It contained no music. In it the young Russian apologized again for not sending me any. To his despair (he wrote), and in spite of all his efforts, inspiration had failed him utterly.

What is it, this coldly questioning, self-deprecating attitude to his own creations, this confessed impotence in a man who yet feels himself inspired and full of power? What is the ideal that draws him on, and has he travelled any distance in his search for it? In a word, what lies at the heart of that perturbed spirit? God knows. But in any case what is there remotely in common between this kind of passionate attraction towards music, whether well or ill founded (and that, time will reveal), and the dull spirit of petty, calculating ambition which impels so many young men to enter a conservatoire in order to take up the profession of music as one learns to be a tailor or a bootmaker? At least the music-maniac, near to madness though he be, hurts nobody, and his mania, when it is not ridiculous, is touching and poetic, whereas the artisan-musician is fundamentally hostile to art and artists, a cause of egregious and deep-rooted errors and capable, by sheer weight of numbers and the general depravity of his artistic impulses, of perverting the taste of an entire country. The most musical nation is not the nation which can boast the largest number of competently second-rate musicians but the nation which has produced the largest number of great composers and cultivated its taste for beauty to the most advanced point.

The semi-Asiatic city of Moscow is full of curiosities and items of interest from the architectural point of view, yet I spent little time looking at it during the three weeks that I was there: the preparations for my concert absorbed me completely. Besides, it would hardly have been possible to do so. The great spring thaw was in full spate and the streets were conduits of turbid water and half-melted snow through which a sledge could barely force its way. Even the Kremlin I saw only from the outside, and then only to tell the beads on the necklace of cannon that encircles it—grim trophies picked up in the wake of our shattered army. There are specimens of every variety and calibre, and from every country. Notices in French (horrid irony) give the name of the actual regiment—ours or one of our allies'—to which each item belonged. One of them bears on its lip the scar of a curious wound inflicted by a Russian ball, which struck it full on the mouth and then entered the barrel, ploughing up the interior. If the gun was loaded at the time, the cartridge must have had a shock at so rude a ramming, and imagined vaingloriously that the Emperor Napoleon himself had resumed his ancient trade of gunner.

In Moscow I heard a performance of Glinka's opera *A Life for the Czar.* The immense theatre was empty (I can hardly imagine it is ever full), and the stage represented an almost uninterrupted series of pine forests deep in snow, or snow-covered steppes with snow-white men moving about over them; I still shiver at the thought of it. The work contains some extremely graceful and original melodies, but I had virtually to divine them—the performance was so poor. One has the impression that, despite the zeal and musical knowledge of the director, Verstowsky, rehearsals are conducted in a very odd fashion at this theatre; or so it struck me when we came to prepare the chorus for the first two parts of *Faust*, which figured in my programme. On entering the room where the chorus rehearsals were normally held I found some sixty men and women standing silently in position, but no sign of a chorus-master or of an accompanist or even of a piano.

'Well, where is the piano?' I asked. 'And the pianist?'

'We don't have them here,' was the reply; 'we learn the choruses unaccompanied, on our own.'

'The devil you do! Some musicians! Your choristers must be the world's leading sight-readers.'

'Oh no, not at all. It's just the tradition. We get along as we can.'

'Come, you must be joking. Please be so kind as to fetch a piano—I need it. You will have to forgive my being so demanding. I'm a stranger here. We'll soon find an accompanist. I can even strike a few chords myself at a pinch—which will be better than nothing.' The piano arrived, to the amazement of the choristers; and with the help of M. Genista, a very able German professor who happened to be there and who agreed to play the accompaniment, we got through the choruses in *Faust*. By dint of a few more similar sessions it was learnt after a fashion. But one can only presume that the Russians are endowed with qualities undreamed of by other nations if they are really able to learn whole operas by a combination of trial and error, time, and a spirit of humility. Like their colleagues in St Petersburg they sang in German. But the roles of Faust and Mephistopheles, which Messrs Leonoff and Slavik, two Russian singers, kindly undertook, were both delivered in French (Baltic style). This was a step in the right direction; the two main characters at least were conversing in the same tongue. M. Grassi, a Piedmontese violinist living in Russia, helped me greatly with the organizing of the concert, as did M. Marcou, whom I mentioned earlier. The celebrated cellist Max Bohrer, who had come to Moscow at the same time as I had, generously offered to play in my orchestra—a most welcome suggestion which brought a powerful addition to the meagre ranks of my cellos, and an act of artistic unpretentiousness that virtuosos are not generally guilty of in such cases.

I had a brush with the censorship over some lines in the students' Latin song in *Faust*, printed in the programme of my concert:

Nobis subridente luna, per urbem quaerentes puellas eamus, ut cras fortunati Caesares dicamus: Veni, vidi, vici.

(While the moon winks down on us, let us search the town for girls, so that tomorrow, happy Caesars, we can say: 'I came, I saw, I conquered.')

The censor declared that he could not authorize the printing of so scandalous a song. In vain I pointed out that the entire libretto of *Faust* had been passed by the censor in St Petersburg, and showed him a copy which bore the seal of official approval. He replied testily that his colleague in St Petersburg was free to do as he thought fit but that he was in no way bound to follow his example; the passage in question was immoral and would have to be cut out. It was—in the libretto. As can be imagined, I was not going to mutilate my work to satisfy a little vulgar prudery. That would really have been immoral. The prohibited lines were sung at the concert, but in such a way that no one understood them. Which is why the inhabitants of Moscow are still the most moral on earth and why, in spite of all the moon's blandishments, the students never go searching the town for girls . . . in winter.*

* A Dresden critic, in 1854, solemnly protested against this song, claiming that German students were persons of high moral character, incapable of running about in the moonlight after grisettes. This same booby actually accused me, in the same article, of having 'maligned Mephistopheles' by making him deceive Faust. 'The German Mephistopheles' (I quote) 'is honourable and fulfils the terms of the agreement which he has made Faust sign; but in M. Berlioz's work he causes him to believe that he is taking him to Marguerite's cell, when in reality he is leading him to the abyss, which is monstrous.' Monstrous indeed—of me, to have slandered the father of all lies and wickedness! A fellow with whom no exclusively

Among the gifted teachers and distinguished amateurs living in Moscow, I must add to those already mentioned the name of M. Graziani, eldest son of one of the finest actors at the old Italian Opera in Paris.

There is a splendid establishment for young ladies, directly under the patronage of the Empress, where the girls' normal education is supplemented by a sound—if anything, an almost too serious—musical training. Three of the best pianists performed for me an ancient triple concerto in D minor for harpsichord by ——* which was very serious indeed. Yet I do not believe their teacher M. Reinhardt, an agreeable, lively man and a fine musician, actually meant me any harm when he chose it for his pupils to play to me.

From my stay in Moscow I also recall a charming little prodigy of ten, Princess Olga Dolgorouky's son, who quite alarmed me by the discerning passion with which he sang dramatic scenes from the great composers and some songs of his own composition.

Overwhelmed with civilities by several Muscovite households and by a French family which had settled there, I left Moscow as soon as my concert was over; for I was expected back in the imperial capital to direct the rehearsals of my *Romeo and Juliet* symphony, which General Guedeonoff had promised to have sumptuously performed at the Grand Theatre.

56

Return to St Petersburg—two performances of Romeo and Juliet at the Grand Theatre —Romeo in his gig—Ernst—the nature of his talent —music's retroactive power

ON REACHING THE Volga I saw for the first time a Russian river breaking up in the spring thaw. We had to wait five hours on the left bank until the ice had separated sufficiently to allow a passage;

disposed demon would care to associate! This delightful criticism was the hit of Dresden. I believe they still laugh about it.

* [Probably Bach, against whom Berlioz had a prejudice at that time.]

and when it was finally attempted, in a boat which was deliberately rocked from side to side to facilitate progress through the ice, I confess that the slow but inexorable drifting of the ice-floes, the small, sinister cracking sounds they emitted as they moved, the heavy load of baggage on board, and the shouts and general air of anxious vigilance of the crew, took a good deal of the pleasure out of the experience, and I was heartily relieved to set foot safely on the farther bank.

The sun was by now beginning to show itself, but still palely and without much strength; yet in several of the villages that the mail-coach went through I saw children naked save for their shirts, playing about in the snow and sliding down the icy hillocks as our children do on hayricks in summer. The Russians must have the fires of hell in their veins.

As soon as I arrived in St Petersburg I began rehearsing the chorus in the Grand Theatre. When General Guedeonoff had approved my plan to put on *Romeo and Juliet* I had asked him how many rehearsals I could have.

'How many?' he said. 'My dear fellow, as many as you want. They can practise every day; and when you come and tell me that you're satisfied, and not before, we'll announce your concert.'

'Capital! That is really doing it in the grand style. It's going to be good.' In point of fact, as I have said, this symphony cannot be even tolerably well done without prolonged and systematic rehearsal—as with an opera, in which the music is sung by heart. That is why it has rarely had a performance as confident and animated and grand as it received in St Petersburg.*

I had an enormous men's chorus and sixty young sopranos and contraltos with fresh, resonant voices, tolerably good musicians, drawn from the choruses of the Italian and German operas and from the theatre school (a kind of conservatoire where students learn music, French and the tricks of the stage). The Capulets practised in one place and the Montagues in another, while the Prologue was rehearsed in a third. When each chorister finally knew his or her part almost by heart, I brought the three groups together, and the precision with which their combined forces

* [23 April 1847.]

performed the finale was superb. My soloists were Versing for the role of Friar Laurence, Madame Walcker for the contralto stanzas in the Prologue, and Holland (a spirited actor, who 'spoke' the musical declamation with great subtlety) for the Queen Mab Scherzetto. The whole thing was imperially organized; the performance, as it could hardly fail to be, was marvellous. I remember it as one of the great pleasures of my life. And I was in such good form that I had the luck to conduct without a mistake, which at that time did not often happen to me. The Grand Theatre was full. On all sides uniforms, epaulettes, tiaras, diamonds, flashed and rippled. I was recalled I do not know how many times. But I confess I paid little heed to the public that day. I sang the divine Shakespearean poem to myself, for myself; and it had so great an effect on me that after the finale I fled trembling to a room at the back of the theatre, where Ernst found me a few moments later in floods of tears. 'Ah, nerves,' he said. 'I know all about it.' And he took my head on his shoulder and let me cry like a hysterical girl for fully a quarter of an hour. Try to imagine a bourgeois from the rue Saint-Denis or a director of the Opéra (Paris, of course) witnessing such an attack. What could they possibly understand of the storm raging in the composer's heart; of his vague but potent memories of childhood and early loves and the blue Italian sky, in imagination revived and flowering again in the glow of Shakespeare's genius; of the vision of a Juliet ever dreamed of, ever sought, never attained; of the revelation of unbounded love, infinite grief; and of his joy that his music had caught a few far-off echoes of that starry poetry of the spheres? One can only dimly picture them, mouths agape and eyes popping with astonishment. But the first bourgeois would be sure to say, 'The man's ill—send for a glass of sugar and water'; and the second, 'Pure affectation! I shall have him put in the *Charivari*.'

To tell the truth, for all the warmth of the reception, I think the public found the scale of the symphony and the sadness and solemnity of the final numbers a little wearying, and much preferred *Faust*. My belief was confirmed when we announced a further performance.* The box-office manager, though highly satisfied with the results of the first evening, admitted that he

* [30 April 1847.]

feared for the second unless I added at least two scenes from *Faust*, and I had to follow his advice.

I was told later of one very bored lady who was in the audience at the second performance. She was a frequenter of the Italian Opera but was not going to have it said that she couldn't enjoy this sort of music as well. She sat it out with exemplary fortitude, and as she emerged from her box, flushed with the achievement of having stayed to the end, exclaimed, 'Yes, I grant it's a very serious work, but, I assure you, perfectly intelligible. Oh, in that great business for the orchestra in the introduction, I saw at once it was Romeo driving up in his gig.'

I forgot to mention that at a benefit concert for Versing given in the Grand Theatre I directed a performance of my Fantastic Symphony, and that Damcke, the gifted composer, pianist, conductor and critic, had the extraordinary courtesy to offer himself as a humble percussionist and play, on the piano, the two low notes (C-G) which represent the tolling of the funeral knell in the last movement of the work.

The least successful of my scores in St Petersburg was the *Roman Carnival* overture. At my first concert it passed almost unnoticed, and Count Michael Wielhorsky (an excellent musician, I may say) admitted to me that he could make nothing of it, so I did not give it again. If you told that to a Viennese he would find it hard to believe; but scores, like plays and books, and roses and thistles, have each their own destiny.

In Austria the *Roman Carnival* overture was for long the most popular of all my compositions. It was played everywhere. I remember several incidents connected with it during my stay in Vienna. One evening Haslinger, the music publisher, gave a soirée at which the pieces to be performed included this overture, arranged for two pianos (eight hands) and physharmonica.* When its turn came, I was near the door which opened onto the room where the five performers were seated. They began the first allegro much too slowly. The andante was passable; but the moment the allegro was resumed, at an even more dragging pace than before, I turned scarlet, the blood rushed to my head

* [A kind of harmonium.]

and, unable to contain my impatience, I shouted out, 'This is the carnival, not Lent. You make it sound like Good Friday in Rome.' The hilarity of the audience at this outburst may be imagined. It was impossible to restore silence, and the rest of the overture was performed in a buzz of laughter and conversation, amid which my five interpreters pursued their placid course imperturbably to the end.

A few days later Dreyschock, who was giving a concert in the hall of the Conservatoire, invited me to conduct the performance of this same overture, which figured in the programme.

'I want to make you forget Good Friday at Haslinger's,' he said. He had engaged the entire Kärntnerthor orchestra. We had only one rehearsal. As it began, one of the first violins who spoke French whispered to me, 'You'll see the difference between us and those down-and-outs at the Theater an der Wien' (Pokorny's theatre, where I was giving my concerts). And, by God, he was right. The overture has never been played with greater fire, precision, vivacity and controlled vehemence; I cannot describe the sonority of the orchestra, the harmonious harmony of it (the tautology alone can suggest the effect it had). On the evening of the concert* it went off like a firework display. The audience encored it with the shouting and stamping of feet that you hear only in Vienna. Dreyschock, whose personal success was put out of joint by these ill-timed demonstrations, rent his gloves in his rage, naïvely exclaiming, 'If they ever catch me having overtures at my concerts again!', and glaring at me as though I were guilty of treachery towards him. I hasten to add that this comical ill-humour was short-lived; in Prague a few weeks later he treated me with the utmost cordiality.

I mentioned Ernst a moment ago. He had in fact arrived in St Petersburg on the same day as I did. We met there quite by accident, as we had done before in Brussels, Vienna and Paris, and as we have since then in other parts of Europe; it is as though the changes and chances of our artistic careers conspired to strengthen the links that an instinctive affinity had forged between us. I have the liveliest and most affectionate admiration for him,

* [17 December 1845.]

for his warmth of heart, his loyalty as a friend, his greatness as an artist.

People have compared Ernst to Chopin. There is some truth in this; but in the most important respects the comparison is a false one. Considered from a purely musical point of view, the two men are fundamentally different. Chopin chafed under the restraints of time and to my mind pushed rhythmic freedom much too far. Ernst can take liberties with the beat when artistic reasons, in particular the expression of passionate feelings, demand it, but he is essentially a rhythmical player; there is steadiness at the heart of his most daring fancies. Chopin simply could not play in strict time; Ernst is capable of abandoning strict time but only so that the underlying pulse may be felt the more strongly when he returns to it. One needs to hear him in Beethoven's quartets to appreciate this quality in his playing.

In Chopin's compositions all the interest is concentrated in the piano part; the orchestra's role in his concertos is confined to a frigid and practically superfluous accompaniment. Ernst's are the very opposite. The works he has written for his own instrument* and orchestra are conspicuous examples of qualities once thought mutually exclusive—brilliant technical display and sustained symphonic interest. Beethoven was the first to find a successful solution to the problem of how to give the solo instrument full scope without reducing the orchestra to a minor role. Beethoven himself, it can be argued, was inclined to let the orchestra overpower the soloist; whereas the plan adopted by Ernst, Vieuxtemps, Liszt and one or two others seems to me to strike the balance exactly.

Let me reiterate: Ernst, who is a great musician as well as a great violinist (as well as the most delightfully humorous man I know), is the complete, rounded artist, profoundly and predominantly expressive in everything he does, yet never neglectful of the craft, the disciplining art of music. He has that rare nature by which an artist combines a powerful imagination and the ability to realize his imaginative ideas unhesitatingly. He is a progressive musician and exploits all the modern resources of the art. He uses his violin to discourse poetry in the language of music, of which

* [The violin.]

language he is complete master. Chopin, again, was strictly the virtuoso of the elegant salon, the intimate gathering. For Ernst, vast halls, crowded theatres, the great pulsating public, hold no terrors. On the contrary, he loves them and, like Liszt, is never more potent than when there is an audience of two thousand to subjugate. If I had not already known it well, his concerts in St Petersburg would have convinced me of the fact. It was an unforgettable moment when he reappeared amid thunders of applause, after performing those glowing, grandly conceived works of his in his most imposing style, and as a farewell gesture to his audience played the variations on the *Carnival of Venice* (which he had the audacity to compose after Paganini's, and without imitating them)—a piece of sublime whimsy in which invention and technical wizardry are so skilfully blended that in the end one ceases to be astonished at anything and simply sits back, lulled by the constant rocking movement of the accompanying theme, as though the solo violin were not executing the most prodigious feats of agility and conjuring cascades of gleaming, iridescent melody the while. This fascinating display of virtuosity put to consistently tuneful ends, and performed with almost careless ease, never fails to dazzle and enthral the audience whenever Ernst plays it. He is like a juggler whose counters are diamonds. If old Councillor Krespel,* the curious eccentric who owned the Cremona violin, could have witnessed these fantastic feats of musical ingenuity, the poor man would speedily have lost what was left of his wits; he would not then have suffered so bitterly from the death of his Antonia.

Those variations affect me in a strange way now when I hear Ernst play them, as I have often since then (and only the other day in Baden). As soon as the Venetian air appears at the touch of that magic bow, it is midnight, I am in St Petersburg once more, in a great auditorium bright as day, experiencing again that curiously pleasurable sense of nervous fatigue one feels at the end of a splendid musical evening; there is a hum of excitement in the air and the glint of smiling faces; I fall into a romantic melancholy which I am powerless to resist, nay, which it would be painful to

* [The chief character in one of E. T. A. Hoffmann's most famous tales.]

struggle against . . . No other art has music's power to affect one retroactively. Not even the art of Shakespeare can evoke the past with this degree of poetic intensity. Only music appeals at one and the same time to the imagination, the intellect, the feelings *and* the senses; and from the reaction of senses on intellect and feelings, and vice versa, come the phenomena which people with the right physiological mechanism are susceptible to, but which to those not so endowed (otherwise known as philistines) will always remain a sealed book.

TRAVELS IN RUSSIA

SEQUEL

Return journey—Riga—Berlin—performance of Faust —dinner at Sans-Souci—the King of Prussia

LENT WAS OVER, there was nothing to keep me in St Petersburg; and I decided, with the keenest regret, to leave that brilliant city whose delightful hospitality had meant so much to me. My return journey took me through Riga, where I conceived the strange notion of giving a concert. The receipts barely covered the expenses; but it earned me the acquaintance of a number of notable artists and amateurs, among them the kapellmeister, Schrameck, M. Matinson, and the local postmaster. The latter had been unenthusiastic about my plan for a concert. 'Our little town is not St Petersburg,' he said. 'We're all good businessmen here. Everyone is busy just now selling corn. You will have an audience of a hundred at the most, all women; you'll see, there won't be a man among them.' He was wrong: there were a hundred and thirty-two women and seven men. I believe I actually made a profit of three silver roubles (twelve francs).* The postmaster also maintained that I 'did not look the part'. 'From your articles, which I read regularly,' he said, 'I had expected something quite different. You're not nearly ferocious enough. For, by God, you write with a dagger, not with a pen.' Perhaps; but the point is not envenomed; the 'precious villains' (to borrow Othello's expression for Iago) whose throats I am fondly supposed to have slit are all in excellent health.

In Riga I had a quite unexpected stroke of luck. The admirable German actor Baumeister happened to be there on a tour, and I saw him play—of all things—Hamlet.

Five weeks earlier, in Moscow, a letter had come from Count Redern informing me that the King of Prussia would like to hear my *Faust* legend, and urging me to stop in Berlin on my way home and put on a performance of it; His Majesty was placing the Opera and its entire resources at my disposal, with the promise of half the gross receipts. I could not but be impressed by this royal favour, so

* [29 May 1847.]

I stayed and spent about ten days in Berlin organizing the performance. It was first-rate from the point of view of orchestra and chorus but exceedingly feeble in certain other respects. The tenor charged with the role of Faust, and the soprano staggering under that of Marguerite, did me a great deal of damage.* The ballad of the King of Thule was hissed (since then it has been applauded everywhere else). Whether these expressions of disapproval were aimed at the composer or at the singer or at both, I could not tell. The last seems the most likely; the pit was full of malcontents, indignant, so I was told, that a Frenchman had had the insolence to set a garbled version of the national masterpiece to music. There were also the partisans of Prince Radzivill, who had himself set the songs from *Faust* with the aid of a number of genuine composers.

For sheer ludicrous ferocity I have not seen anything to compare with a fanatical German nationalist fully roused. This time, too, I had a section of the Opera orchestra against me, having forfeited their good will by my letters on Berlin, which had been translated by M. Gathy and published in Hamburg a few years before.† The letters contained nothing offensive to the Berlin players, as readers of these memoirs may see for themselves. On the contrary, I had praised them comprehensively, merely adding a few carefully qualified criticisms of minor points of detail. I called the orchestra magnificent and declared it exceptional in point of precision, unanimity, power and delicacy. But—and there lay my crime—I made a comparison between some of its principal players and those of Paris, and actually stated (perish the thought!) that where the flautists were concerned ours were better. These innocent words had planted a rancorous animosity against me in the breast of the Berlin first flute; and so far as I could make out he had persuaded many of his colleagues to believe that I had 'traduced the orchestra'. Fresh proof of the risks you run in writing about players, and of the advisability of not standing to leeward of their self-esteem when one has had the misfortune to wound it in the

* [19 June 1847. Faust was sung by Krause and Marguerite by Brexendorf. Berlioz spent about a month in Berlin, where Marie, who had not been in Russia, joined him.]

† [In the *Blätter für Musik und Literatur* during the autumn of 1843. Gathy was a Belgian littérateur with musical leanings who wrote fluent German.]

slightest degree. When you criticize a singer, you do not have his colleagues up in arms against you. Indeed, they generally feel that you have not been severe enough. But the virtuoso instrumentalist who belongs to a well-known musical organization always claims that in criticizing him you are 'insulting' the whole institution, and though the contention is absurd he sometimes succeeds in making the other players believe it. Once during the rehearsals of *Benvenuto Cellini* I had occasion to point out to the second horn a mistake in an important passage. I did so in the mildest and politest manner; but the player, Meifred, though an intelligent man, rose in wrath and, losing his head completely, shouted, 'I'm playing what is there. Why do you suspect the orchestra like this?' To which I replied, even more mildly, that it had nothing to do with the orchestra but only with him, and that secondly I suspected nothing, for suspicion implied doubt, and I was quite certain he had made a mistake.

To return to the Berlin orchestra, it did not take me long to notice a certain lack of geniality in its attitude to me during the rehearsals of *Faust*. The glacial reception I was given each day as I came in, the hostile silence which followed the best numbers in the score, and the irate glances, especially from the quarter of the flutes, made it only too obvious, and it was confirmed by what I learnt from the players who had remained friendly to me. They were too much intimidated by their comrades' antagonism to applaud me, and it was in a furtive aside that one of them who spoke French let slip discreetly, as he passed near me on the stage at the end of a rehearsal: 'Sir, ze music—it is vonderful!' Perhaps I may be permitted to suspect that some of those who hissed the ballad were not unconnected with the incomparable, not-to-be-criticized flutes of the Berlin orchestra. However that may be, I must repeat that orchestrally as well as chorally the performance could not be faulted.

Boeticher sang Mephistopheles like the admirable musician and true artist he is; the audience shouted 'da capo' after the Sylphs' scene, but I was in a bad mood and refused to repeat it. The Crown Princess of Prussia, who had twice come to the Opera at eight in the morning and sat in the cold, dark auditorium so as to attend my rehearsals, said all manner of agreeable things to me.

The King* sent me, via Meyerbeer, the Cross of the Red Eagle and invited me to dinner in the palace of Sans-Souci two days later. And the great critic Rellstab, the inveterate foe of Spontini and Meyerbeer, after expressing to me verbally his friendship and esteem, tore me to pieces in the most exemplary fashion in the *Vossische Zeitung*. Altogether, I felt I was being a success. The dinner at Sans-Souci was delightful. Humboldt, Count Mathew Wielhorsky and the Crown Princess were among the guests. After dessert, coffee was taken in the garden. The King strolled about, cup in hand. On catching sight of me standing on the steps of a pavilion some way off, he called across, 'Hey, Berlioz! Come and give me news of my sister and tell me about your Russian trip.'

I went over and talked I know not what nonsense to my august host, but it put him in a jovial humour.

'Tell me,' he asked, 'did you learn Russian?'

'Indeed, sire. I can say "*Na prava, na leva*" (to the right, to the left) when directing the driver of a sledge, and I can say "*Dourack*" when he takes the wrong turning.'

'And what does "*dourack*" mean?'

'"Idiot", sire.'

'Ha! ha! ha! "Idiot, sire"! That's very good. "Idiot, sire"!'

The King doubled up with laughter and waved his arms about with such abandon that he deposited most of the contents of his cup on the gravel. This scene of hilarity, in which I joined unceremoniously, turned me on the spot into an important personage. It was observed from the pavilion by a group of courtiers, chamberlains and gentlemen-in-waiting, who were all simultaneously visited by a desire to meet this man who made the King laugh so heartily and himself laughed with him in so familiar a manner. On returning to the pavilion a moment later I found myself surrounded by high-ranking noblemen, all perfect strangers to me, who bowed deeply and deferentially introduced themselves: 'Sir, I am Prince von ——, I am most happy to make your acquaintance.'

'Sir, Count von ——, permit me to congratulate you on the splendid success you have obtained.'

* [Frederick William IV.]

'Sir, Baron von ——, I had the honour to see you six years ago in Brunswick, and I am delighted,' etc., etc. I could not at first understand to what I owed this sudden status at the Prussian court. Then I remembered the scene in the first act of *The Huguenots*, where Raoul, having received the Queen's letter, finds himself the centre of a crowd of people singing in canon on every degree of the scale: 'Vous savez si je suis un ami sûr et tendre.' They had taken me for an influential favourite of the King's. A court is a very curious world.

Though neither a favourite nor influential, I am none the less profoundly grateful for the good will which the King of Prussia has so often shown to me; and there was no trace of flattery intended when I said to him, that day, during a few moments' serious conversation:

'You are the artists' king.'

'How so? What have I specially done for them?'

'To speak only of musicians, a great deal, sire. You have royally rewarded Spontini and Meyerbeer and loaded them with honours. You have had their works magnificently performed. You have had Gluck's masterpieces restored to the stage in the most imposing fashion; nowhere else but in Berlin can one hear them. You brought the ancient world to life again when you had Sophocles' *Antigone* produced and you commissioned Mendelssohn to write some choruses for the occasion. You got the same composer to write music for Shakespeare's exquisite fantasy *A Midsummer Night's Dream*. And so one could go on. What is more, the direct interest you take in all these high artistic enterprises is a stimulus to greater activity, a living encouragement to creative artists in their work; and this support that Your Majesty gives them is all the more valuable because it is the sole support of the kind they have in Europe.'

'Well—perhaps what you say is true. Only one shouldn't talk so much about it.'

It was certainly true. Today things are different. The King of Prussia is no longer the only European sovereign interested in music. There are two others: the young King of Hanover, and the Grand Duke of Weimar. Three in all.

57

Paris—I have Roqueplan and Duponchel nominated as directors of the Opéra—their gratitude—La nonne sanglante —I go to London—Jullien of Drury Lane—Scribe —he who serves at the altar

As soon as possible after my return to France, I went home for a few days to my family.* I had not been there for a long time and I wanted to show my father his grandson, whom he had never seen. Dear Louis! He enjoyed it so much: the loving welcome and tender cosseting by his grown-up relations and our old servants, the times spent exploring the countryside with me, a little gun under his arm. He spoke of it in a letter which came two days ago, posted in the Aland Islands, saying that those fourteen days at La Côte Saint-André were the happiest of his life. And now he is a sailor, on board a ship in the Anglo-French fleet blockading the Russian ports on the Baltic, at any moment liable to be engulfed in the hell on water that is a naval battle. The thought makes my head spin and turns my heart over. Happy those who do not love. . . . He chose this career himself. Could I have opposed it? It is a splendid career, after all. Besides, we did not foresee a war. Now I can only think of the ghastly apparatus of destruction, and hope and hope he comes out alive. The huge guns he has to 'look after', the crashing broadsides, the glare of the great Congreve flares, the hail of grapeshot, the ship on fire, the hold filling up, the boiler exploding—it will drive me mad. I must break off.

Two days later. I cannot stop thinking of it. Let us talk of something different. Ah, but a modern naval battle. . . . My story moves so slowly, is so wearisome to write, and no doubt to read, too. What purpose will it serve? Let me try to give the facts as briefly as possible, without comment or reflection. My poor boy!

After this visit to Dauphiné I returned to Paris.

(They are bombarding Bomarsund. Perhaps at this moment he is in the midst of the firing.)

Léon Pillet was on the point of giving up the directorship of the Opéra, and Nestor Roqueplan and the inevitable Duponchel had

* [Early September 1847.]

joined forces in an attempt to secure the succession. They came to see me.

'As you know, Pillet can't stay at the Opéra any longer,' they said, 'and we have a chance of getting it' (Duponchel could have said, of getting it again). 'However, the Minister of the Interior is not well disposed towards us, and you are the one person who could make him change his mind, by getting the proprietor of the *Journal des débats* to intervene for us. Would you ask Armand Bertin to approach the Minister? If we are appointed we will offer you an important position at the Opéra. We will make you general musical director, with the post of principal conductor thrown in.'

'Forgive my pointing it out, but that post is held by an old friend of mine, M. Girard, and I would not dream of being the means of his losing it.'

'All right; but two conductors are needed at the Opéra; we don't want to keep the second one, who is useless, so we will divide the position equally between you and M. Girard. Leave it to us; everything will be arranged to your satisfaction.'

Beguiled by these fair words, I went to see M. Bertin. After some hesitation, caused by his lack of confidence in the two gentlemen, he agreed to speak to the Minister on their behalf. Roqueplan and Duponchel were appointed.

The moment they were installed, I began to be snubbed in all manner of ways. Roqueplan would arrange to meet me at a certain time and then fail to turn up. Duponchel did the same. Or I would be kept waiting for two hours, and when one of them eventually arrived would be told that in the unavoidable absence of his fellow-director it was unfortunately impossible for him to talk business with me. I very soon realized what was in their minds. The indignation I felt at these manœuvres can be easily imagined, but I kept my temper; I wanted to see how far they would pursue their 'candour'. I was determined to get them in a corner, as the saying is. And I did, eventually. After countless comings and goings and appointments not kept, it had to end in our all three meeting; and then the recantation began. The trouble was, they said, they could not see how they were going to create a post for me at the Opéra. There was the chorus, of course, they might put me in charge of that, only I didn't play the piano, which I would be required to in order to take rehearsals. Girard was absolutely against dividing his authority as head of the orchestra with anyone else: 'You cannot share a throne,' he said (King of Yvetot though he was)* and so on and so forth. In short, it was all exceedingly difficult.

The climax was impressive. I had for some time been working on the score of a grand opera in five acts entitled *La nonne sanglante* which Léon Pillet had commissioned from me; the libretto had been sketched by Scribe and a contract signed between Pillet, Scribe and myself. In the midst of our discussion Roqueplan had the audacity to say to me straight out:

'You have a libretto of Scribe's, I believe.'

'Yes, I have.'

'Well, what do you intend to do with it?'

'What do you suppose? What one usually does with librettos.'

'But you realize there is a ministerial regulation prohibiting artists employed by this theatre from having their own works performed in it; and as you will have a position here you will not be able to write operas.'

'You needn't alarm yourself. I don't intend to write them by the dozen. I would consider myself extremely fortunate if I were able to produce two good ones in my life.'

'I'm afraid you won't even be able to have one performed. Your *Nun* will be wasted. You had better give it to us, and we will get someone else to set it.'

I controlled myself once more and in a choking voice replied: 'Take it!'

From that point onward the conversation became increasingly involved and unprofitable. It seemed my suspicions had not been altogether unfounded. I had divined my men correctly. They were bent on getting rid of me. Not only had they no intention of keeping any of their promises; they were determined they would never perform a work of mine at the Opéra, being convinced that as a composer I was a preposterous and dangerous figure who would inevitably imperil any theatre that attempted to

* [Berlioz means that the 'Kingship' Girard prides himself on is as laughable as that of the hero of Béranger's poem (and Adam's opera).]

put him on. For this reason they were going so far as to take back a work on which I had already begun and which had been offered to me by the previous director.

Duponchel said nothing; he found his colleague's cynicism a little embarrassing. Not that he had any greater faith than Roqueplan in my musical worth; but he seemed to feel that since they owed their position as directors to me they were bound, if not to make the sacrifice involved in putting on a work which in their eyes was doomed to failure, at least to dissemble what they thought and refrain from hurting my feelings.

I need hardly say it was not what those gentlemen thought of my compositions that angered me. I had heard them express their sovereign contempt for Beethoven, Mozart, Gluck and all the true gods of music too often not to have been heartily ashamed had it been otherwise. It was the colossal ingratitude of it, surpassing anything I had ever encountered in this line, that took my breath away. Consequently, on the day following this conversation—in which, although nothing had been settled, I had found out what I wanted to know, namely how far my two friends considered themselves committed by their obligations—I accepted an offer which happened to come at that time, to go to London to conduct the orchestra of the Grand English Opera. I wrote at once to Messrs Duponchel and Roqueplan, telling them of my decision, absolving them from all their promises, and wishing them every good fortune; whereupon, to exonerate themselves with those who knew what I had done to help them, they put it about that I had insisted on their making me principal conductor and dismissing Girard—which was doubly slanderous, as I had from the first made it clear that I would not accept anything to Girard's detriment. The upshot was that Girard believed the story, I took offence at his doing so, and since then we have been on bad terms—though for my part I cannot say I regard it as a calamity. However, I freely admit that I got what I deserved. I was well aware what values my two aspiring directors stood for. Musically speaking, they are heathen Chinese who believe themselves gifted with taste and discernment, thus embodying the fatal combination of unshakeable confidence in themselves with the most profound ignorance and barbarism. My duty lay not in smoothing their path to power but in stopping them by all possible means.

But their promise to make me musical director dazzled me. I immediately thought of the great things that might be achieved with such an instrument by someone who knew how to use it and who had as his sole object the grandeur and advancement of the art. I told myself that they would look after the finances and concern themselves with the ballet, the scenery, and so on, but of the Opéra properly so called I would be the real director. And I fell into their trap. *The undertaking made gratuitously by these gentlemen was no better kept than so many others had been, and that was the last that was ever heard of it.**

I had been in London a few weeks when I thought I would get my two directors in a corner again, on the subject of *La nonne sanglante*. I had admittedly replied 'Take it' when Roqueplan asked for it back, but rather in the spirit of Leonidas' reply when Xerxes demanded his arms: 'Come and get them!'

Besides, the issue had been the famous regulation which prohibits a composer employed by the Opéra from writing for it. The regulation had of course been overlooked in the case of Dietsch, chorus-master at the Opéra, who had had his *Flying Dutchman* performed there (this was a setting of Wagner's libretto which Dietsch, who inspired rather more confidence in the director than Wagner did, had bought for five hundred francs); in the case of Benoist, répétiteur at the Opéra, who had had his *Apparition* performed there; and of Halévy, whose *Juive*, *Drapier* and *Guido and Ginevra* had all been put on at the time when he was chief

* [The directors' reply, published in the *Revue et Gazette musicale* (1847), said: 'Your letter came as a surprise and a disappointment; but the friendly terms in which it was conceived encourage us to believe that you harbour no resentment at the unintended delay in the concluding of our arrangements. We like to think that you decided you would prefer not to stifle your musical genius by confining it in a position [that of chief coach] which is partly an administrative one, and that at your age, at the height of your powers, you would rather be free to pursue an unhampered career of noble artistic experiment. As for our regrets, they are sincere; it enhanced our prestige to have a name so closely associated with the advancement and restoration of music at the head of such an important department. We are losing one of our most glorious banners in the campaign we have undertaken. . . .']

coach at the Opéra. Nevertheless, Roqueplan had had the semblance of a pretext for ruling out any possibility of my *Nun* being produced. But now that I was established in London and the regulation no longer applied to me, I wrote to Scribe, begging him to get a definite decision from the directors. 'If they consent to abide by the agreement signed by us with Pillet,' I said, 'kindly ask them to allow me the time I need to finish my score. Directing the Drury Lane orchestra leaves me no leisure for composing. You on your side have still to finish your libretto. Even when the work is completed, I shall want plenty of time for pondering it and going over it again, and can't undertake to let it appear less than three years from now. If Roqueplan and Duponchel are not prepared to give us this latitude, or if, as is more probable, they refuse to be bound by our agreement, then, my dear Scribe, I will tax your patience no further but will ask you to be so kind as to take back your poem and dispose of it as you please.'

To which Scribe, having seen the directors, replied that they accepted the *Nun*—knowing very well that we were not nearly ready—on condition that it could be put into rehearsal immediately; and he ended:

'So I do not think our chances are exactly favourable; and since you have been so very decent as to allow me to dispose of our old libretto, which has been so long in hand, let me say frankly that I accept your offer and shall try to find a market for it either at the Théâtre National, which has just opened, or, failing that, somewhere else.' And that was that. Scribe took his poem back. He subsequently offered it in turn, so I was told, to Halévy, Verdi and Grisar, all of whom, knowing the facts and considering that Scribe had treated me rather shabbily, had the delicacy to turn it down. In the end M. Gounod took it, and his work is to be performed shortly.*

No more than two acts of my score had been written. Foremost among the numbers that I regard as good I would put the big duet containing the legend of the Nun and the finale which follows it.

* It had a very meagre success; and as for the poem, which had eventually been completed by Scribe and Germain Delavigne, it made such a dull and feeble impression that I am only too glad I did not hold onto it.

The duet and two arias are fully orchestrated; the finale is not. It is unlikely that this music will ever be heard.*

When I saw Scribe, on my return to Paris, he seemed a little embarrassed at having accepted my proposal and taken back his poem. 'But, you know,' he said, '"he who serves at the altar must live by the altar".' Poor man! With a bare two or three hundred thousand francs a year and only one town house and three country houses to his name, he could hardly have been expected to wait.

When I repeated Scribe's remark to Liszt, he replied, 'You mean, by the halter,' comparing Scribe to a hangman.

I will not go into great detail in recounting my first visit to England. If I were to I should never finish. Besides, it is the old familiar story. I had been engaged by Jullien, the celebrated director of promenade concerts, to conduct the orchestra of the Grand English Opera, a company he had set up at the Drury Lane Theatre in a moment of wild ambition. Jullien, in his capacity of indisputable and undisputed lunatic, had assembled a splendid orchestra, a first-rate chorus and a tolerably good collection of singers. All he lacked was a repertory. *The Maid of Honour*, a new opera by Balfe which Jullien had commissioned, was to be the great panacea. Meanwhile, while Balfe's opera was being rehearsed, the season would open with an English version of that sparkling novelty, Donizetti's *Lucia di Lammermoor*—which novelty would have to take ten thousand francs a night in order to cover expenses.

The outcome was inexorable. The nightly receipts of *Lucia* fell short of the required ten thousand; Balfe's opera had a very moderate success; and within a short time Jullien was ruined. I had received only one month's salary; and today, despite the ardent protestations of Jullien, who is after all an honest man—as honest as is compatible with such consummate recklessness—I look upon the money he still owes me as lost beyond recall.

It is Jullien and his improvident venture that are referred to in the passage on the Grand English Opera in my book *Evenings in the Orchestra*.† He is the hard-pressed impresario who seriously proposes to put on *Robert le diable* in six days despite the fact that he possesses neither music, English translation, costumes nor scenery

* It has since been destroyed, with the exception of the two arias.

† [Ninth Evening.]

and the singers in his company do not know a note of the work. That was pure lunacy, whereas the hilarious flight of fancy which I cannot resist retailing here is absolutely typical of the showman accustomed to appealing to the frivolous instincts of the mob and to achieving his successes by the most idiotic methods.

Jullien, at the end of his resources, seeing that Balfe's opera was not making money, and more or less persuaded of the impossibility of putting on *Robert le diable* in six days even if he rested on the seventh, summoned his committee of management to advise him what to do. The committee consisted of Sir Henry Bishop, Sir George Smart, Planché (the author of the libretto of Weber's *Oberon*), Gye (stage manager at Drury Lane), Maretzek (the chief coach) and me. Jullien explained his difficulties and mentioned the names of various operas—all without translation or music—that he would like to put on. You should have heard the ideas and opinions expressed by those gentlemen as each masterpiece came up for scrutiny! I was lost in admiration. At length we reached *Iphigénie en Tauride*, which the public had been promised by Jullien in his prospectus—as is the custom in London, where managers announce the opera every year but never give it. The other members of the committee, being quite ignorant of the work, were at a loss what to say. Jullien, impatient at my silence, turned abruptly to me and rapped out:

'Damn it all, say something. You must know it—you of all people.'

'Oh yes, I know it; but you haven't asked me anything. What do you want to know? Tell me, and I'll answer.'

'I want to know how many acts there are, what characters appear in the opera, what their voices are and, most important of all, what kind of scenery and costumes are wanted.'

'Very well, take a piece of paper and a pen, and write to my dictation: *Iphigénie en Tauride*, opera by Gluck (you know that, I presume) in four acts. There are three male roles: Orestes (baritone), Pylades (tenor) and Thoas (bass, going very high); one very important female role, Iphigénie (soprano), one small one, Diana (mezzo soprano) and several for members of the chorus. The costumes, unfortunately, are not what you would consider very glamorous. King Thoas and his Scythians are a tribe of down-at-heel savages on the shores of the Black Sea. Orestes and Pylades appear dressed in the somewhat limited garb of shipwrecked Greeks. Only Pylades has more than one costume. He reappears in the fourth act, wearing a helmet and——'

'A helmet!' interrupted Jullien, excitedly. 'We're saved! I'll write to Paris for a gold helmet with a coronet of pearls and a plume of ostrich feathers as long as my arm. We'll have forty performances.'

I forget how this remarkable discussion ended; but if I live to be a hundred I shall always remember the flashing eyes, the wild gestures and frantic enthusiasm of Jullien on his discovering that Pylades wears a helmet, his inspired plan to have it sent from Paris, no English craftsman apparently being capable of constructing a sufficiently dazzling one, and his hopes of achieving forty resplendent performances of Gluck's great work on the strength of the pearl coronet, the gilding and the interminable feathers on Pylades' helmet.

Prodigious, as the good Dominie Sampson* would say. Prodigious!

I need hardly add that *Iphigénie* was not even put into rehearsal. Jullien quitted London a few days after this learned conference, leaving his company to fall to pieces. In any case, the singers and the chief coach had declared against the 'antiquated piece'. The godlike tenor Reeves, when it was suggested he should sing Pylades, laughed like anything.†

* [The old tutor in Scott's *Guy Mannering*.]

† [On this first occasion Berlioz spent eight months in England, between November 1847 and July 1848, lodging first *chez* Jullien at 76 (now 27) Harley Street, then (after being turned out by the bailiffs as a result of Jullien's bankruptcy) at 26 Osnaburgh Street, where Marie joined him. He had been engaged for six years as conductor at Drury Lane at the splendid salary of four hundred pounds a quarter, with an additional four hundred pounds guaranteed profit on a month's concerts and eight hundred pounds for the composition of a three-act opera. The collapse of Jullien's enterprise soon put an end to all these prospects, and also to *Mephistopheles*, the stage adaptation of *The Damnation of Faust*, which was planned for the 1848–9 season (see *Correspondance générale*, III). Berlioz subsequently visited London four times: in 1851, as a member of the international jury on musical instruments at the Great Exhibition; in 1852, when he conducted the newly formed New Philharmonic Orchestra and gave two historic performances of

58

My father's death—La Côte Saint-André again —I visit Meylan—intense loneliness—the stella del monte once more—I write to her

IN ONE OF THE early chapters of these memoirs I describe the state in which I found Paris on my return from London, after the Revolution of 1848.

It was a depressing experience; but another grief, more personal, incomparably deeper, befell me soon afterwards. News came that my father was dead.

I had lost my mother ten years before, and that eternal separation had been a cruel blow. But my father and I were united by a friendship that was independent of, and perhaps stronger than, the natural ties of affection which exist between father and son. We thought so much alike on many questions, mere contact with which is enough to electrify some men's minds. His intelligence was so keen and lofty. He was so full of a profound natural goodness and humanity. He had been so happy to acknowledge that his prognostications about my career had been proved wrong.

On my return from Russia he told me that one of his greatest desires was to get to know my Requiem.

'Yes, I should like to hear that tremendous Dies irae which I have been told so much about. After that I would gladly say, like Simeon, "Nunc dimittis servum tuum, Domine."'

Alas, I was never able to gratify his wish, and my father died without having heard the least fragment of my works.

He was sincerely and deeply regretted, above all by our poor peasants, whom he helped in so many different ways. My sisters gave me some touching instances of this when they wrote to tell me of his end. But oh, his agony was long!

My sister Nanci wrote:

...We could not feel sorry to see our dear father go, his life had become such a burden to him. His one idea was to die as soon as

---

Beethoven's Ninth Symphony; in 1853 for *Benvenuto Cellini* at Covent Garden and one concert with the Old Philharmonic; and in 1855 for two concerts with the New Philharmonic. See Ganz, *Berlioz in London*, 1950, *passim*, and my *Berlioz*, vol. II.]

possible. It was obvious he no longer had any interest in the things of this world; he was eager to have done with it. A glorious procession of all the poor he had succoured and the sick he had relieved followed him weeping to his last resting-place. Two addresses were spoken over his grave, one by a young doctor who paid tribute to his skill, his learning and his virtues, the other by a man of the people, a natural spokesman of that class among whom he lived his unselfish and useful existence (the kind of existence that is becoming so rare nowadays!). I know how much you regret that you could not be here with us when he breathed his last; but if anything can comfort you, it will be the thought that he was far too weak to be clearly conscious of any deprivation. He slept almost continuously, and spoke to us very little. However, one day he did ask me if I had had any news of you and of Louis. . . .

I cannot refrain from quoting almost in full the letter which my sister Adèle wrote to me—a letter which brings out all her passionate tenderness and warmth of heart:

VIENNE, *Saturday 4 August 1848*

My dear brother,

I send you my deepest love and sympathy in this dreadful grief that we share. I knew only too well what a terrible blow it would be to you, and I felt so sorry for you being on your own, away from us; at such a time one needs so much the proximity of one's loved ones. You could not have got here soon enough for our beloved father to have recognized you. Let that console you for our silence, and forgive us for not letting you know. We had no idea whether you were in Paris or not, and for six days we expected every moment to be his last. It was agony. It went on like that from the Sunday till the Friday (28 July); he died at noon. He was delirious nearly all the time, and no longer recognized anybody, except at rare intervals. It was horrible to watch him during those final days. He was like a galvanized corpse. His head shook continuously from some nervous tic; so did his arms. His eyes were hollow and staring and his voice was cavernous. He kept asking us for impossible things. Sometimes our caresses succeeded in calming him. I would take him in my arms and clasp and hug him when one of his most violent crises was upon him (Nanci could not bear to stay in the room at those times). But he did not suffer pain—at least we hoped and believed this. The young doctor who attended him thought the same, he told us that the nervous convulsions were the result of opium, which he went on taking till the end. One day, my dear, our good Monique showed him your picture. He spoke your name and at once asked for pen and paper, which we gave him. 'Good,' he said, 'I shall write presently.' What did he want to say to you? No one knows; but this was the only time you came into his mind. I think he did not actually recognize us so much as sense us instinctively. One day, guessing from his restless look that there was something he wanted, I asked him what it was. 'Nothing, my child,' he answered, in a tone of unspeakable tenderness, 'I am looking for your eyes.' This remark, so full of fatherly affection, made us weep, and is something we will always remember. My husband was with him at the end. He had promised me to close his eyes, to perform that sad duty in your place. He kept his word; my heart will not forget. . . .

My father's death drew me back soon afterwards* to La Côte Saint-André again for a few days, to mourn with my sisters in the paternal home. The moment I arrived I went to his study, where he had spent so many long hours in pensive meditation, and where he had begun my literary education and given me my first music lessons, before the spectre of osteology arose to terrify me.

I sank down on his sofa, half-fainting; my sisters, in tears, embraced me. I touched with trembling hands everything of his that I could see: his Plutarch, his notebooks, his pens, his stick, his rifle (a harmless weapon which he never used), a letter of mine lying on his desk.

Nanci opened a drawer and took from it his watch. 'Here, keep it,' she said. 'Oh, so often during his last ordeal he used to consult it, as if to know how many hours he still had to suffer.'

I took the watch. It was going. It was alive—and he was alive no more.

* [Late August 1848.]

Before setting out again for Paris, I decided also to revisit Grenoble and the house of my maternal grandfather at Meylan.

A strange thirst for grief came over me: I must salute the scenes of my first intense emotions; I must embrace my past, steep myself in recollection, however harrowing the experience might be. My sisters remained at La Côte, knowing I would want to make my pilgrimage alone; for sensations such as I was exposing myself to are too personal to be witnessed even by one's nearest and dearest. Even now, at the thought of recounting it, I feel my pulse beat faster. Yet I will do so, if only to establish that certain feelings from the past, seemingly incompatible with new feelings, can go on co-existing with them, in a heart that forgets nothing.

So powerful is this inexorable operation of memory that I cannot look at a picture of my son at the age of ten without a pang. His appearance as he was then distresses me just as if I had had two sons and had now only the grown-up man, death having robbed me of the charming boy.

At eight in the morning I was in Grenoble. My uncle and cousins were away in the country, so I did not stop. Besides, I was impatient to reach Meylan. I went straight through the faubourg and set out on foot for the village. It was one of those ideally beautiful autumn days, serene, enchanted.

In Meylan, I stand before my grandfather's house, recently sold to one of his tenant farmers. I open the door and go in. There is no one there; the present owner has moved into a new house at the other end of the garden.

I look into the drawing-room, where the family used to gather in the old days when we came to stay for a few weeks with our grandfather. It is just as it always was, with the same grotesque pictures, the same fantastic multicoloured paper birds stuck on the wall. There is the chair where my grandfather slept in the afternoon, and his backgammon set, and on the old sideboard a little wicker cage that I made as a child. There I watched my uncle waltz with the beautiful Estelle. . . .

I went out again quickly. The orchard had been half ploughed up. I looked round for the bench where my father used to sit in the evening for hours on end, sunk in thought, his eyes fixed on the gigantic limestone rock of Saint-Eynard, offspring of the last great geological upheaval. The bench had fallen to pieces; nothing was left of it but the two worm-eaten feet.

There was the field of maize where I used to hide my sorrows, at the time when I first felt the pangs of love. At the foot of that tree I began reading Cervantes.

Now for the mountain.

Thirty-three years have come and gone since I went there for the last time. I am like a man who in the meantime has died and is returning to life. And in returning I recover all the feelings of my former existence, as fresh and intense as before.

I ascend the stony unfrequented paths in the direction of the white house that I had glimpsed in the distance sixteen years before, on my return from Italy—the house where the star shone.

On I went, climbing steadily. I could feel my heart beating faster all the time. I thought I recognized the avenue of trees that ran to the left of the path, and followed it for some way, but it was not the one I was looking for; it led to a farm which I had not seen before.

I turned back and continued along the path. It petered out among vineyards. I had obviously lost the way. In my mind's eye I could see the right path as clearly as if it were yesterday. There used to be a little fountain. I had not passed it. Where was I, then, and where was the fountain? My anxiety grew.

I decided to ask at the farm I had seen a moment before. I went into the barn. The threshers were at work. When they saw me they paused, with their flails in their hands. I stood trembling like a thief with the police on his track, and asked them if they could show me the way to the house formerly occupied by Madame Gautier.

One of the threshers scratched his head. 'Gautier?' he said. 'There's no one of that name in these parts.'

'Yes, an old woman—she had two young nieces* who used to come and stay with her every autumn.'

'I remember all right,' the thresher's wife broke in. 'Surely you recall them—Mam'zelle Estelle, so pretty she was—everybody would stop at the church door of a Sunday, to see her go by.'

* I am wrong: they were her granddaughters.

'Yes, of course, it's coming back to me. That's right—Madame Gautier. But it's a long time, you see. A tradesman from Grenoble has the house now. It's up yonder. You take the path to the fountain, behind our vineyard here, and then turn left.'

'The fountain? Then I know where I am. Many thanks. I'm sure I won't go wrong now.'

I crossed a field adjoining the farm and found the path I had been looking for.

Presently I hear the murmur of the little fountain; and there is the track, and the avenue of trees, like the one I mistook for it a moment ago. It is there that—I feel as if there I shall see . . . God! The air intoxicates me, my head is spinning. I stop for a second to control the beating of my heart. Now I am at the gate of the avenue. A man in a short coat, no doubt the prosaic owner of my sanctuary, is standing beside it, in the act of lighting a cigar.

He stares at me with an air of astonishment.

I pass without a word and continue to climb. My objective is an old tower that in my childhood stood at the top of the hill; from there I shall be able to embrace it all in a single glance.

I go on climbing, without turning round, without looking behind me; I must get to the top first. But the tower! There's no sign of it. Have they pulled it down? No—there it is. The upper half has been demolished, and the near-by trees have grown so high they hid it from sight. At last, I am at the tower.

Over there, where those young beech trees are shooting up, my father and I sat, and I played him 'Nina's Musette' on the flute.

Estelle must have come here. Perhaps I stand in the very same portion of air where her enchanting form once stood. Now—look! I turn and my gaze takes in the entire picture: the blessed house, its garden, its trees, below it the valley and the winding Isère and beyond, the Alps, the glaciers, the far-off gleaming snow—everything her eyes looked on. I breathe in the blue air that she breathed . . . Ah! A cry such as no human language can convey re-echoes from the Saint-Eynard. Yes, I see, I see again, I worship. The past is before me, I am a boy of twelve. Life, beauty, first love, poetry without end! I throw myself on my knees and shout, 'Estelle! Estelle! Estelle!' to the valley and the hills and the sky. I clasp the earth in a convulsive embrace and bury my teeth in the grass. And it begins: an access of loneliness, indescribable, terrible. Bleed, my heart! bleed! only, leave me the power to go on suffering. . . .

I get up and go on, noting avidly every landmark on the near hillside, sniffing to right and left like a lost dog in search of its master's scent. There, where the ground slopes down steeply, I was walking when she called out, 'Take care, don't go near the edge!'

Over this bramble bush she leaned to pick blackberries. And down there on that level ground must be the rock on which her lovely feet rested, where I saw her stand, tall and stately, gazing out across the valley.

That day I told myself, with a child's foolish sentimentalism, that when I was a famous composer I would write an opera on Florian's *Estelle* and dedicate it to her and bring it to this rock, and one morning when she came to see the sun rise she would find it there.

The rock! Where is it? Nowhere to be seen; it has disappeared. The vinegrowers must have uprooted it or the mountain wind covered it with sand.

This beautiful cherry tree—her hand rested on its trunk. But there was something else near-by—what was it?—something that should surely remind me of her more vividly than all the rest, something which was like her in charm and grace, but which eludes my clutching memory. Of course! a clump of pink vetch! She stopped to pick some. It was where the path bends. I quicken my pace. Eternal Nature! The pink flowers are still there, the clump richer and more luxuriant than of old; the light wind stirs its fragrant blossoms. Time, the inconstant reaper! The rock has gone, the plant remains. I bend down to take it all, to pluck it up by the roots. But no—dear plant, bloom on in your solitude. Be here the symbol of that part of my soul that I left here long ago, that will live here so long as I live! There—I take only two stems, with their delicate-coloured moth-like flowers, perennial butterflies. Farewell! Beloved tree, farewell! Valleys and hills, farewell! Farewell, old tower! Farewell, Saint-Eynard! Farewell, sky where my star shone! Farewell, my romantic childhood, last glimmers of an ideal, untarnished love! The stream of time bears me onward. Stella! Stella! Farewell!

And desolate as a ghost returning to its grave, I descended the mountain. I passed the drive that led to Estelle's house. The man with the cigar had gone; he no longer defiled the peristyle of my temple. Yet I could not bring myself to enter, eager though I was to. I walked on slowly, so slowly, stopping at every moment, tearing my gaze agonizingly from each cherished object.

I no longer needed to control my heart; it seemed to have stopped beating. I was becoming dead once more. And over all a stillness and solitariness, and the sun's soft glow.

Two hours later I crossed the Isère, and just before dusk reached the hamlet of Murianette. There I found my cousins and their mother. Next day we went back to Grenoble together. I had—it may be imagined—a strange, abstracted air. My cousin Victor,* when we were alone for a minute, could not resist asking me:

'What is the matter with you? I've never seen you like this.'

'The matter with me? Well—you'll jeer, but as you ask me I'll tell you. Anyway, it will be a relief to talk, I'm suffocating. I was at Meylan yesterday.'

'I know. What is there there?'

'Among other things, the house of Madame Gautier. Do you know her niece,† Madame F——?'

'Yes—the one they used to call the beautiful Estelle D——.'

'Well, when I was twelve I was madly in love with her—and I love her still.'

Victor burst out laughing. 'You idiot, she's fifty-one, her eldest son is twenty-two—we read law together.'

He laughed louder than ever, and I joined in; but mine was a bleak, nervous laugh, like the glint of an April sun through rain.

'Yes, I see that it's ridiculous, yet at the same time—it's ridiculous and it's true; it's childish and immense. Don't laugh—or rather, laugh if you like, it won't make any difference. Where is she now? You must know.'

'Since her husband died she's been living at Vif.'

'Vif? Is that far from here?'

* [Son of Dr Berlioz's younger brother Auguste, who was a doctor in Grenoble. Victor Berlioz was then thirty-one, and Berlioz forty-four.]

† Granddaughter.

'Seven or eight miles.'

'I shall go there. I want to see her.'

'Are you mad?'

'I shall find some excuse for calling on her.'

'Hector, I beg you not to. It would be extremely foolish.'

'I want to see her.'

'You'll never have the self-control to manage such an encounter properly.'

'I want to see her!'

'If you do, you'll merely make an ass of yourself and compromise her.'

'I want to see her!'

'But just consider——'

'I want to see her!'

'Fifty-one years old—more than half a century. What do you suppose you'll find? Much better preserve your youthful memories, keep your ideal unsullied.'

'Oh God! The whips and scorns of time! All right. At least let me write to her.'

'Write by all means. Ye gods, what a lunatic!'

He handed me a pen and subsided into an armchair, where he gave way to a fresh burst of hilarity, in which I joined in fits and starts; and between sunshine and shower, I wrote the letter which follows. It had to be copied out again because of the raindrops that blurred every line.

GRENOBLE, *6 September 1848*

Madam,

There are admirations so constant, so tenacious that they die only when we die. I was twelve years old when I saw Mlle Estelle for the first time, at Meylan. You must have been aware, then, how deeply you had affected that childish heart which was breaking under the stress of feelings too strong for it; I believe you were even at times so pardonably cruel as to laugh at it. Seventeen years later I passed through our valley again (I was on my way home from Italy) and my eyes filled with tears—the chill tears which come at the memory of the past—when I caught sight of that enchanted house high up under the Saint-Eynard where you had once lived. A few days after that, before I had yet learnt your new name, I was asked to wait for Madame F—— at the coach-station and deliver a letter to her. I handed over the letter—and my heart beat violently, and my hand trembled as it approached hers. You see, I had recognized her: my first passion, the *stella del monte* whose dazzling beauty illuminated the morning of my life. Yesterday, madam, after many years of effort and struggle, of travels all over Europe and exploits, some echo of which may perhaps have reached you, I made a pilgrimage which I had long been contemplating. I wanted to see it all again: the little house, the garden, the avenue of trees, the hill above, the old tower, the near-by wood, the eternal rock, and the sublime landscape, worthy of her whose gaze so often rested on it. And I have done so. Nothing has changed. Time has left my shrine as I remembered it. Only, strangers live there now; other hands cultivate your flowers. No one in the world could have guessed why a solitary man, with a sad, preoccupied air and the marks of toil and tribulation imprinted on his face, went there yesterday and walked about the secret haunts and by-ways of the place—no one, not even you. *O quante lagrime!* Goodbye. I am going back to my hectic existence. You will never see me, probably, nor know who I am, but you will, I trust, forgive the strange liberty I am taking in writing to you now. For my part, I forgive you in advance for laughing at the nostalgia of the man, as you once laughed at the adoration of the child.

'*Despis'd love*'*

And, regardless of my cousin's mockery, I sent the letter. What happened to it I do not know. Since then I have heard no more of Madame F——. In a few months I shall have to go to Grenoble. Oh, this time, I feel, I shall not be able to resist. I shall go to Vif.†

* A phrase of Shakespeare's in *Hamlet*.

† I never went. But five years ago I learnt that Madame F—— was living in Lyons. Is she still alive? I dare not find out (February 1864).

Yes, I have discovered: she is (August 1864).

59

My sister's death—my wife's death—her funeral —the Odéon—my position in the musical world—the theatre virtually closed to me owing to the hatreds I have aroused —cabal at Covent Garden—the Paris Conservatoire and its circle—a symphony dreamed and forgotten —the welcome I receive in Germany—the King of Hanover —the Duke of Weimar—the King of Saxony's intendant—my farewells

I AM EAGER TO have done with these memoirs, which are almost as wearisome to write as a feuilleton. Besides, when I have written the few remaining pages that I mean to write I think I shall have said enough to give a pretty well complete idea of the chief events of my life and of the orbit of emotions, aspirations, and frustrations within which I am fated to turn until I turn no more.

The road that lies before me, however long, cannot be very different from the one I have travelled. I shall find the same stony, uneven ways, the same ruts and deep pot-holes, with here and there a clear stream or the cool peace of a grove, or some sublime rock towering up, where I shall laboriously climb to dry myself in the evening sun from the chill rain endured all day in the plains.

Things change, it's true, and men with them, but so slowly that the alteration is imperceptible within the brief span of one human life. I would need to live two hundred years to taste the benefit of it.

I lost my elder sister, Nanci. She died of cancer of the breast* after six months of frightful suffering which day and night made her cry out in anguish. My beloved Adèle, my other sister, who went to Grenoble to nurse her and was with her constantly to the end, nearly died herself from exhaustion and the horror of watching that long agony.

Yet no doctor dared be so humane as to put an end to my sister's martyrdom by making her breathe a flask of chloroform. They do it to spare patients the pain of an operation that lasts a few seconds yet will not consider using it to save them six months of torment, when it is known for certain that no remedy, not even time, will

* [4 May 1850.]

cure the disease, and death is clearly their sole deliverance, their supreme happiness.

The law, however, forbids it, and the doctrines of religion are no less rigidly opposed. And my sister herself would have no doubt rejected that way of escape had it been offered her. 'God's will be done'—as if everything that happened did not happen because of God's will, and as if God's will would not have been as well manifested in the release of the patient by a swift and peaceful death as in the prolonging of her pointless and abominable torture. How senseless, how infinitely absurd are all these questions of fate, the existence of God, free will and the rest of it—an endless maze where human understanding wanders helplessly lost.

In any case, inexorable pain of that degree of intensity, with no possibility of remission, is of all things in this world the most hideous for us conscious, sentient beings; and it is sheer barbarity or stupidity, or both, not to make use of the sure and painless means available nowadays for ending it. Savages are more intelligent and more humane.

My wife too is dead. At least she did not suffer such great pain. Poor Harriet had been paralysed for the last four years, unable to move or to speak. I watched her dying. She expired on 3 March 1854 in Montmartre. Fortunately my son, who was at Cherbourg, obtained leave and was able to spend a few hours at her side only four days before the end. His coming sweetened the last moments of her life. It was a lucky chance, too, that I was not abroad at the time.

I had been out of the house for two hours when one of the women looking after her came to fetch me and hurried me home. It was all over: she had just breathed her last. A sheet already covered her. I drew it back and kissed her pale forehead for the last time. Her portrait, which I had given her a year before and which, painted in the days of her splendour, showed her as she had been in her radiant beauty and genius, hung beside the bed on which she lay inert, disfigured by disease.

I will not attempt to describe the grief that took possession of me. It was complicated by a feeling which, though it had never before been so intense, I had always found hardest of all to bear—a sense of pity. In the midst of all the regrets for our lost love, a wave of terrible, overmastering pity swept over me at the thought of everything she had suffered: her bankruptcy, before we were married; her accident; the deep disappointment of her last unsuccessful appearance on the Paris stage; her decision, which she made voluntarily but never ceased to lament, to give up her beloved art; the eclipse of her reputation; the spectacle of second-rate imitators, men and women, achieving fame and fortune; our bitter domestic strife; her ungovernable jealousy, which in the end had cause; our separation; the death of all her relatives; the enforced absence of her son; my long and frequent journeys; her distress, half injured pride, half genuine concern, at being to me a constant financial burden which she knew I could barely support; her delusion that she had forfeited the regard of the English public through her attachment to France; her broken heart; her vanished beauty; her ruined health; her growing physical suffering; the loss of speech and movement; the impossibility of making herself understood in any way; the long vista of death and oblivion stretching before her. Destruction, lightning and thunder, blood and tears—my brain shrivels in my skull at the horror, the pity of it!

Shakespeare! Where is he? Where art thou? I feel as if he alone of all men who ever lived can understand me, must have understood us both; he alone could have pitied us, poor unhappy artists, loving yet wounding each other. Shakespeare! You were a man. You, if you still exist, must be a refuge for the wretched. It is you that are our father, our father in heaven, if there is a heaven.

God standing aloof in his infinite unconcern is revolting and absurd. Thou alone for the souls of artists art the living and loving God. Receive us, father, into thy bosom, guard us, save us! *De profundis ad te clamo*. What are death and nothingness? Genius is immortal! What? 'O fool, fool, fool!'*

I had to attend to the last sad duties on my own. The Protestant pastor who was required for the ceremony, and whose parish covered the suburbs of Paris, lived on the far side of town in the rue de M. le Prince. At eight in the evening I went to notify him. One of the streets on our route had been taken up, and the cab had to make a detour which took us past the Odéon. The theatre was

* [*Othello*, Act V scene 2.]

brightly lit for a play then in vogue. There, twenty-six years before, I had seen *Hamlet* for the first time. It was there one night that the fame of my poor dead wife had blazed up like a meteor; there that I had seen a whole audience break down and weep at the sight of Ophelia in the ecstasy of her grief and heartrending madness; there that I had seen Miss Smithson, recalled after the final scene, reappear on the stage, dazed, almost appalled by the magnitude of her triumph, and tremblingly acknowledge the applause of the intellectual élite of France. There I saw Juliet for the first and last time. Beneath that arcade I paced on many winter nights in a fever of disquiet. Through that door I saw her enter for a rehearsal of *Othello*. At the time she was unaware of my existence; and had anyone pointed to the pale, dishevelled youth leaning against a pillar of the Odéon, staring after her with haunted eyes, and had prophesied that that unknown young man would one day become her husband, she would have considered him an impertinent fool.

And yet . . . he it is who now prepares your last journey, poor Ophelia, and who will say to the priest in Laertes' words, 'What ceremony else?'; he who was so cruel to you, who was made to suffer so much by you, having suffered so much for you; he who, with all the wrongs he did, can say, like Hamlet:

> *. . . Forty thousand brothers*
> *Could not with all their quantity of love*
> *Make up my sum.*

Shakespeare! Shakespeare! I feel the flood rising again, my grief sweeps over me, I drown! Let my cry come unto thee!

Father! father! where are you?

The following day, two or three writers—d'Ortigue, Brisieux, Léon de Wailly—and a number of artists brought by the good Baron Taylor, and a few other kind spirits, came out of friendship for me and attended Harriet to her last home. Twenty-five years before, all intellectual Paris would have been at her funeral, out of admiration, nay adoration, of *her*. Every poet, painter and sculptor, the entire acting profession, to whom she had given such noble object lessons in the art of movement and gesture and pose, every musician who, listening to her, had felt the music of her tenderness and the heartrending sincerity of her cries of pain, every lover, every dreamer, aye and more than one philosopher, would have walked in tears behind her coffin. . . .

Yet now she goes almost alone to the cemetery, while Paris swarms down there in the smoke, heedless, remembering nothing; and he who loved her but who lacks courage to follow her to the graveside weeps in a corner of an empty garden, and her young son is far off, battling with wind and weather, at the masthead of a ship above the heaving sea.

Hic jacet. She lies in the smaller Montmartre cemetery, on the side of the hill, facing north towards England, to which she never wanted to return. Her simple tomb bears the inscription:

HARRIET-CONSTANCE BERLIOZ-SMITHSON
BORN AT ENNIS IN IRELAND
DIED AT MONTMARTRE
3 MARCH 1854

The newspapers reported the event baldly, in humdrum terms. Only Jules Janin remembered, and wrote generously in the *Journal des débats*:

How sadly, how swiftly they pass, those legendary divinities, frail children of Shakespeare and Corneille. Alas, it was not so very long ago—we were young then, filled with the thoughtless pride of youth—that Juliet, one summer evening on her balcony above the Verona road, with Romeo at her side, trembling with rapture, listened—and heard the nightingale, and the lark, the herald of the morn. She listened with a pale, dreamy intensity, a bewitching fire in her half-averted eyes. And her voice! a golden voice, pure and vibrant, a voice through which the language and genius of Shakespeare in all their rich, perennial vitality and force found superb utterance. When she moved, when she spoke, her charm mastered us. A whole society stirred to the magic of this woman.

She was barely twenty, she was called Miss Smithson, and she conquered as of right the hearts and minds of that audience on whom the light of the new truth shone. All unknowingly she became a new passion, a poem unheard till then, an embodied revolution. She pointed the way for Madame Dorval, Frédérick

Lemaître, Malibran, Victor Hugo, Berlioz. She was called Juliet; she was called Ophelia, and was the inspiration for Delacroix himself when he drew his touching picture. Ophelia is shown in the act of falling, one hand slipping from the branch to which it still clings, while the other clutches to her fair bosom the last sad garland; the hem of her robe is about to meet the rising waters; around her a weeping landscape, and far off, hastening towards her, the wave that will engulf her in her sodden clothes, and 'pull the poor wretch from her melodious lay to muddy death'.

She was called, lastly—this admirable and touching Miss Smithson—by another name (Malibran bore it too): Desdemona; and the Moor, as he embraced her, called her his 'fair warrior'. I see her now just as she was then, white-faced as the Venetian woman in *Angelo, Tyrant of Padua*.* She is alone, listening to the rain and the moaning of the wind, the beautiful lass, enchanting and doomed, whom Shakespeare out of love and respect lapped round with his noblest poetry. She is alone, and afraid; an unutterable unease troubles the depths of her soul. Her arms are bare, a corner of her white shoulder is visible. The bareness had something pure and sanctified about it, the holiness of the sacrificial victim, the woman about to die. Miss Smithson was marvellous in this scene. She was more like a vision from on high than a creature of our clay. And now she is dead. She died a week ago, still dreaming of the glory that comes so swiftly and so swiftly fades. What images lie there, what worlds of poignant regret! In my youth they sang a chorus in homage to Juliet Capulet, a sad funeral march, with the same cry going through it, repeated again and again: 'Strew flowers! strew flowers!'† So they passed into the gloomy crypt where Juliet slept, and the dark melody ran its course, telling of the chill and terror of those mortuary vaults. 'Strew flowers! strew flowers! She is dead,' the dirge sang, like an Aeschylean hymn. 'Juliet is dead (strew flowers!). Death lies on her like an untimely frost (strew flowers!). Our instruments to melancholy bells are turned, our wedding cheer to a sad burial feast, our bridal flowers serve for a buried corpse!'

* [A play by Victor Hugo.]

† Janin is alluding to the Funeral Procession in my *Romeo and Juliet* symphony, in which the chorus chant these words continually.

Liszt wrote soon afterwards from Weimar, a warm, affectionate letter, such as he knows how to write. He said, 'She inspired you, you loved her, you sang of her, her task was done.'

I have nothing more to say of the two great loves that have had such deep and lasting influence on my heart and mind. One is a childhood memory. It was from the first associated for me with the delights of an incomparable landscape, by whose beauty I had already been stirred. Estelle was then truly the dryad of my Vale of Tempe; at the age of twelve Nature and Love awoke in me in the same moment and became conscious feelings.

The other came to me with Shakespeare in my manhood, a voice out of the burning bush, among the lightning flashes and thunderclaps of a poetry that was new to me. It struck me down; my heart and whole being were possessed by a fierce, desperate passion in which love of the artist and of the art were interfused, each intensifying the other.

The power of such an antithesis may be imagined—if indeed it is an antithesis. I never kept my Meylan idyll a secret from Harriet nor concealed how clear and fresh it remained in my memory. Who has not had some such early romance? Despite her jealous temper, she had too much sense to feel hurt. She would merely tease me gently about it from time to time.

Those to whom all this is incomprehensible will understand me still less when I mention another idiosyncrasy of my nature: the vague feeling of ideal romantic love that comes over me when I smell a beautiful rose. For a long time I used to have a similar sensation at the sight of a fine harp; when I saw one I wanted to go down on my knees and embrace it.

Estelle was the rose 'left blooming alone',* Harriet the harp whose strains were part of all my concerts, my joys and sorrows—of whose strings, alas, I broke many.

And now, if not at the end of my career, I am at any rate on the steep slope that leads with ever-increasing swiftness to the end; burnt up yet still on fire and filled with an energy that sometimes flares up with terrifying force. I begin to know French, to be able to write a decent page of music, of verse or prose. I can direct an

* ''Tis the last rose of summer' (Thomas Moore).

orchestra and give it life. I worship Art in all its forms. But I belong to a nation that has ceased to be interested in the higher manifestations of the mind; whose only god is the golden calf. The Parisians have become a barbarian people. In scarcely one rich house in ten will you find a library—I do not say a library of music. They no longer buy books. Execrable novels hired from the circulating library at a penny a volume are sufficient to satisfy the general appetite for literature in every section of the community. In the same way a subscription of a few francs a month paid to a music publisher ensures the right to select from among the infinite quantity of trash that stuffs the shops some particularly choice example of the genre for which Rabelais had a name.

We are witnessing the triumph of industrialism in Art, raised to power by the crude popular instincts to which it panders, and trampling with brutish contempt on the values it has dethroned. In short, Paris is a city where I can do nothing, and where I am considered lucky to fulfil the one task which is expected of me, that of feuilletonist—the only one, many would say, for which I was sent into the world.

I am conscious of what I could do in dramatic music, but to attempt it is as futile as it is dangerous. Most of our lyric theatres are houses of ill fame, musically speaking—the Opéra above all. Then, I could give full scope to my ideas only if I were sure of having absolute control of a great theatre, as I have of my orchestra when I conduct one of my symphonies. I would have to be able to count on the good will and obedience of everyone from prima donna, tenor, choristers, orchestral players, ballet-dancers and extras to producer, designer and scene-shifters. An opera house, as I see it, is first and foremost a vast musical instrument. I can play it; but if I am to play it well it must be entrusted to me unreservedly. That will never happen. Then again, I would be giving too easy an opening to the malice of my enemies. They may not have the face to boo me in the concert hall; but they do not waste such an opportunity in a theatre as large as the Opéra. That will always happen.

I would be exposing myself not only to the antagonism which my critical ideas have aroused but also to the equally violent opposition provoked by the style of my music—a style which is in itself the most scathing practical criticism of the works of certain composers who at the moment enjoy great popularity. These persons argue, quite reasonably, that if the public ever come to understand or even to like such music their own will cease to have any value. I had an example of this in London, where a gang of Italians virtually drove *Benvenuto Cellini* from the Covent Garden stage by hissing, booing and yelling from beginning to end.* They even tried to stop the performance of the *Roman Carnival* overture, which was used as an introduction to the second act, although it had been applauded on many occasions in London, among others at a Philharmonic Society concert at Hanover Square a fortnight before. Public opinion, if not mine, put Costa, the Covent Garden conductor, at the head of this lurid conspiracy. I had more than once attacked him in my articles for the liberties he took with the great masters, whose works he is given to shortening or lengthening, re-orchestrating, and generally mutilating. If it was Costa, as is very possible, then he is a master of dissembling; his eagerness to be of use to me and to assist during rehearsals allayed any suspicions I may have had.

The artists, indignant at the scurvy treatment I had received, expressed their sympathy by offering to give their services for a 'testimonial concert' in Exeter Hall. Two hundred and thirty put their names down, but it proved impossible to arrange. Beale, the publisher (now one of my best friends), brought me a present of two hundred pounds which had been raised by a body of amateurs headed by Messrs Broadwood, the famous piano manufacturers. Such a gift is too foreign to our French notions for me to feel that I could accept it. Not everyone is Paganini. But it had been inspired by genuine kindness and generosity.

I was far more deeply touched by these marks of friendly regard than I had been hurt by the derision of the cabal. No doubt, in a German opera house I should not have anything like that to fear. But I do not know German. I would have to compose to a French text, which would then be translated. That is a serious disadvantage. And to write a grand opera I should have to set aside eighteen months; during that time I would do nothing else and consequently earn nothing, and I would not be able to make up for it by

* [25 June 1853.]

drawing an advance on royalties: they are not paid to opera composers in Germany. And even in Germany (as I have described in my account of the first performance of *Faust* in Prussia) an inoffensive observation in the *Journal des débats* was enough to arouse ill-feeling against me among the players of the Berlin orchestra.

In Leipzig too, although my music is now listened to with other ears than in Mendelssohn's time (so far as I have been able to judge, and as Ferdinand David assures me is so), there are still a few petty fanatics, pupils of the Leipzig Conservatoire who, without knowing why, look on me as a scourge, a kind of musical Attila, and cultivate an insane hatred of me, writing me abusive letters and making faces at me in the corridors of the Gewandhaus when my back is turned. Then, there are one or two kapellmeisters, whose peace I have disturbed, who are capable of playing me rather low tricks on occasion. But such antagonism is inevitable, and even when added to the opposition I encounter from a small section of the German Press,* is nothing to the fury that would be unleashed against me in Paris if I were to lay myself open to attack in the theatre.

For the last three years I have been tormented by the idea for a huge opera, for which I would write the words and the music, as I have just done for my sacred trilogy, *The Childhood of Christ*. I am resisting the temptation to carry out this project, and shall, I trust, resist to the end.† To me the subject seems magnificent and deeply moving—a guarantee that Parisians would think it flat and tedious. Even if I were wrong in attributing to them a 'taste so different from my own' (to quote the great Corneille), where would I find a woman of the necessary intelligence and dedication, capable of interpreting the chief role—a role which demands beauty, a great voice, true dramatic ability, impeccable musicianship, and a heart

* Like the Paris Press, it has its cranks for whom the mere sight of my name on a placard or in a paper is like a red rag to a bull. These people ascribe to me a host of absurdities hatched in their own confused brains. They tilt with holy zeal at windmills, hear things in my music that are not there, do not hear what is, and if asked their opinion of a chord of D major, having been warned that I had written it, would exclaim indignantly, 'A vile chord!' But the poor devils are cranks, such as are to be found everywhere and in all times.

† Alas, I did not resist. I have just completed poem and score of *The Trojans*, an opera in five acts. What will become of this immense work? (1858).

and soul of fire? Still less could I be sure of all the other various resources which I would have to have absolutely at my disposal, without interference from anyone. My blood boils at the very thought of encountering, over the performance and production of such a work, the senseless obstacles that I have had to face in the past and which I see daily impeding other composers who write for our great Opéra. A clash of wills would be exceedingly dangerous, for I feel capable of anything where they are concerned; I would kill them like dogs. As to adding to the number of those pleasant and useful commodities which are daily manufactured in the manner of meat-pies, and which go by the name of opéras-comiques, I do not have the least desire to. In this respect, unlike the corporal whose 'ambition was to be a servant', I prefer to remain a private.* The influence of Meyerbeer, it must also be said, and the pressure he exerts on managers, artists and critics and consequently on the Paris public, at least as much by his immense wealth as by his genuine eclectic talent, make all serious success at the Opéra virtually impossible. This baneful influence may well continue to be felt ten years after his death: Heinrich Heine maintains that he has 'paid in advance'.† As for giving real concerts—musical as opposed to sporting events—I have already described the conditions which I had to contend with and the public's increasing indifference to all music that is not opera. I should add that the Conservatoire clique contrived to have me forbidden the use of its hall,‡ the Minister of the Interior publicly announcing at a prize-giving that this hall (the only suitable one in Paris) was the exclusive property of the Conservatoire Society and would henceforth not be lent to anyone for the purpose of giving concerts. 'Anyone' meant me; for, with two or three isolated

* A few years ago, however, I did agree to write a work of this type. Carvalho, the director of the Théâtre-Lyrique, now a good friend of mine, committed himself in writing to give me, at a specified time, a libretto which I was to set to music for his theatre, a penalty of ten thousand francs being stipulated in the contract. When the time came Carvalho had forgotten all about his commitment. Consequently, *this undertaking was no better kept than so many others had been, and that was the last, etc., etc.* [The 'corporal' alluded to here may possibly be Sterne's Corporal Trim.]

† I have said elsewhere, and here repeat, that Meyerbeer not only has the luck to be talented but, to a remarkable degree, the talent for being lucky.

‡ [In 1843.]

exceptions, I was the only person to have put on large-scale musical performances there in the last twenty years.

This celebrated society, most of whose performing members are my friends or my supporters, is controlled by a conductor and a small body of activists who are hostile to me. Nothing would induce them to give the smallest work of mine at one of their concerts. On one solitary occasion, six or seven years ago, the committee went so far as to ask me for two pieces from *Faust*. This was at least partly a concession to the views of my partisans in the orchestra, but they did their best to atone for their blunder by placing me between the finale of Spontini's *Vestale* and the C minor Symphony of Beethoven, in the hope that I would be crushed. Despite its formidable neighbours the Sylphs' scene aroused great enthusiasm and was encored; but Girard, who had conducted it clumsily and prosaically, pretended that he could not find the place in the score, and although the whole hall was demanding a repeat it was not granted. The success of the piece was none the less evident. Accordingly the committee has since that time avoided my music like the plague.*

Not one of the many millionaires in Paris thinks of doing anything for serious music. We do not possess a single good public concert hall, but it would never occur to any of our Midases to build one. Paganini's example was wasted. What that noble artist did for me will remain an act unique in our history.

No: the composer who would produce substantial works in Paris outside the theatre must rely entirely on himself. He must resign himself to sketchy and tentative and thus more or less misleading performances, for want of the rehearsals he cannot afford,† to halls which are inconvenient and uncomfortable from the point of view of both performers and audience; to the numerous difficulties raised, quite reasonably, by the opera houses,

* [The two excerpts from *Faust* (the Chorus and Dance of the Sylphs and the Hungarian March) were given at the Conservatoire concert of 15 April 1849. They and the overture *Rob Roy* (1833) were the only pieces by Berlioz performed by the Society in the thirty-two years during which Habeneck and, after him, Girard were in charge of it.]

† The most absurd piece of theatrical flummery is rehearsed almost daily for a month, whereas I had to produce my *Romeo and Juliet* symphony after only four rehearsals, and many works after only two.

whose players one is obliged to employ, and who naturally have the needs of their own repertory to think of; to the bare-faced appropriations of the poor-house tax-collectors, who take no account of what a concert costs and contribute to the deficit by walking off with one eighth of the gross receipts; and to the hasty and inevitably erroneous judgments pronounced on large and complex works which are heard under these conditions and rarely heard more than once or twice. He must, in the last analysis, have a great deal of time and money to spend—not to mention the exhausting expense of will-power and spiritual energy required to overcome such obstacles. The situation of the artist who possesses these qualities to the full is like that of a loaded projectile which goes straight for its objective, sweeping aside everything in its path; it undeniably makes a mark but is shattered to pieces in the attendant explosion. Normally, however, I would be willing to make every possible sacrifice. But there are circumstances in which sacrifices cease to be high-minded and become unforgivable.

Two years ago, at a time when my wife's state of health was involving me in a lot of expense, but there was still some hope of its improving, I dreamed one night that I was composing a symphony, and heard it in my dream. On waking next morning I could recall nearly the whole of the first movement, which was an allegro in A minor in two-four time (that is all I now remember about it). I was going to my desk to begin writing it down, when I suddenly thought: 'If I do, I shall be led on to compose the rest. My ideas always tend to expand nowadays, this symphony could well be on an enormous scale. I shall spend perhaps three or four months on the work (I took seven to write *Romeo and Juliet*), during which time I shall do no articles, or very few, and my income will diminish accordingly. When the symphony is written I shall be weak enough to let myself be persuaded by my copyist to have it copied, which will immediately put me a thousand or twelve hundred francs in debt. Once the parts exist, I shall be plagued by the temptation to have the work performed. I shall give a concert, the receipts of which will barely cover one half of the costs—that is inevitable these days. I shall lose what I haven't got and be short of money to provide for the poor invalid, and no longer able to meet my personal expenses or pay my son's board on the ship he will shortly be joining.' These thoughts made me shudder, and I threw down my pen, thinking: 'What of it? I shall have forgotten it by tomorrow!' That night the symphony again appeared and obstinately resounded in my head. I heard the allegro in A minor quite distinctly. More, I seemed to see it written. I woke in a state of feverish excitement. I sang the theme to myself; its form and character pleased me exceedingly. I was on the point of getting up. Then my previous thoughts recurred and held me fast. I lay still, steeling myself against temptation, clinging to the hope that I would forget. At last I fell asleep; and when I next awoke all recollection of it had vanished for ever.

'Coward!' some young fanatic will say (I forgive him in advance for his discourtesy). 'You should have taken the risk! You should have written it down! You should have ruined yourself! One has no right to suppress one's ideas like that. It's monstrous to deny life to a work of art, to force it back into the oblivion from which it is struggling to be born.' Ah, young man, who call me coward, you would judge me less harshly if you had seen what I had to see then. I never flinched in the days when it was still possible to gamble on a bold stroke. There was a small, select public in Paris in those days. There were the princes of the house of Orléans and the Queen herself who took an interest in music. And besides, my wife was full of life and the first to encourage me. 'You must compose this work, and have it really well performed,' she would say. 'Don't worry, we can survive any hardship it brings. Go on—you must!' And I did. But later, when she was lying there half dead, unable to do anything but moan, and needing three women to look after her and a visit from the doctor almost every day, and when it was certain—as certain as that Parisians are barbarians—that every musical venture of mine would have the disastrous consequence I have just described, was it cowardly to hold back then? Was it? I am conscious of having been human, that is all; and while I believe I am as dedicated to Art as you or any other man, I consider I honour it by not regarding it as a kind of Moloch hungry for human victims, and in proving that it has left me enough sense to distinguish between courage and fanaticism. If I have gradually yielded to the enticements of music in writing my sacred trilogy *The Childhood of Christ*, it is because my position is no longer the same; I do not have such pressing obligations. I can also count on getting this work easily performed in Germany, where several important towns have asked me to return. I go there frequently now; I have made four separate visits in the last eighteen months.* My welcome is warmer each time, and the artists ever more sympathetic and co-operative. In Leipzig, Dresden, Hanover, Brunswick, Weimar, Karlsruhe and Frankfurt they have treated me with a friendliness for which I cannot sufficiently thank them. For the public too and the intendants of the royal theatres and ducal establishments and most of the ruling princes I have nothing but gratitude. The charming young King of Hanover, and his Antigone, the Queen (the King is blind), are so interested in my music that they will come at eight in the morning to hear my rehearsals and sometimes stay till twelve, 'in order to understand the inner meaning more deeply', as the King said to me recently, 'and to get really accustomed to the novel methods and style'! He was immensely enthusiastic about my *King Lear* overture, and spoke about it in glowing terms.

'It's wonderful, M. Berlioz, wonderful! Your orchestra speaks, you don't need words. I followed it all: the king's entry into his council, the storm on the heath, the terrible scene in the prison, and Cordelia's lament. Oh, this Cordelia! How you have portrayed her—such tenderness and humility! It's heartrending, and so beautiful.'†

The Queen asked me, on my last visit to Hanover, to include two movements from *Romeo and Juliet* in my programme‡—one of them, the Love Scene, being a special favourite of hers. Afterwards the King formally requested me to go back next winter to

* Since this was written, M. Bénazet, manager of the casino at Baden, has several times invited me to organize the annual festival there, and has let me have everything I could possibly want for the performance of my own works. His munificence in this respect has far surpassed anything ever done for me even by those European sovereigns whom I have most reason to be grateful to. 'I give you carte blanche,' he said again this year. 'Get the artists you need from wherever you please and offer them whatever terms you think will satisfy them. I agree to everything in advance.'

† I never saw Harriet in this role, which was one of the sublimest examples of her art; but she would sometimes recite to me scenes from it (!!). Besides, I had already guessed what she must have been like.

‡ [1 April 1854.]

organize a performance of the whole work in the theatre at Hanover, where I have so far performed only fragments. 'If our resources are not big enough for you,' he added, 'we will get more performers to come from Brunswick and Hamburg, even from Dresden if necessary. You must have all you want.' The new Grand Duke of Weimar said to me on my last visit, as I was leaving, 'M. Berlioz, let me shake hands with you in sincerest admiration. And remember that the Weimar theatre is always open to you.' Baron von Lüttichau, intendant to the King of Saxony, has offered me the post of kapellmeister at Dresden, shortly to fall vacant. 'If only you would take it' (those were his very words), 'think what we could do here! With our artists, whom you find so excellent and who are so devoted to you, and you, who have few equals as a conductor, you would make Dresden the musical centre of Germany.' I do not know whether I shall decide on settling in Saxony when the time comes. It needs going into carefully. Liszt says I should accept. My friends in Paris are against it. I have not made up my mind, and in any case the post is still occupied.* They are talking in Dresden of putting on my *Cellini*, which has been resurrected at Weimar by the admirable Liszt.

If they do, I shall certainly go there to direct the early performances. But the future is not my concern here and I have perhaps dwelt too long on the past, though many curious incidents and sad particulars remain untold. I come to an end—with fervent thanks to holy Germany, where the worship of art burns still pure and strong; to generous England; to Russia, which saved me; to my good friends in France; to all the rare spirits and noble hearts, of whatever nation, that I have known. I have been blessed in knowing you; the memory is and always will be a precious possession. As for you, maniacs, morons, dogs, and bulls, and you, my Guildensterns and Rosencrantzes, my Iagos, my little Osrics, gadflies, crawling worms of every kind: farewell, my . . . friends. I scorn you, and hope not to die before I have forgotten you.

PARIS, *18 October 1854*

* [By Reissiger. This project was very much in the air in the spring of 1854 when Berlioz spent three weeks in Dresden, but it came to nothing. Reissiger, who had been thinking of retiring owing to poor health, remained in Dresden until his death five years later.]

POSTSCRIPT

*Letter to M. ——, accompanying the manuscript of my memoirs, in reply to his request for notes towards a biography**

PARIS, 25 *May 1858*

Sir,

You wish to know why I have encountered so much opposition as a composer in Paris during the last twenty-five years. The causes were many in number, but I am happy to say that they have to some extent disappeared.† This seems to be proved by the fact that, with the exception of the *Revue des deux mondes* (whose music criticism is in the hands of a monomaniac and whose editor cordially detests me), the entire Press was favourable to me on the occasion of my latest work, *The Childhood of Christ*.‡ Some people imagined they could detect in this work a complete change in my manner and style. Nothing could be more mistaken. The subject naturally prompted a naïve and gentle kind of music. That was why they found it more accessible—that and the development of their own taste and powers of understanding. I should have written *The Childhood of Christ* in the same way twenty years ago.

The chief reason for the prolonged war waged against me lies in the antagonism between my musical values and those of the Mass of the Paris public. It is only natural that many should regard me as a lunatic, since I regard them as children or half-wits. To such people all music that deviates from the narrow path where the makers of opéras-comiques toil and spin inevitably seems and has

* He studiously refrained from making use of them. The book is full of absurd tales and exaggerated appraisals. [Although Berlioz dates the letter 1858, it seems likely that the addressee is Eugène de Mirecourt, a hack biographer whose short life of him was published in 1856. Many of the anecdotes in the letter reappear in the book (often in garbled form); and we know, from a reference in a notebook preserved in the Musée Berlioz at La Côte Saint-André, that Berlioz supplied Mirecourt with notes.]

† They have since revived; the opposition is more violent than ever (1864).

‡ [Performed on 10 December 1854 in the Salle Herz, and repeated on 24 December and 28 January. The editor and critic of the *Revue des deux mondes* were respectively François Buloz and Paul Scudo.]

seemed for a quarter of a century the music of a lunatic. To them Beethoven's supreme masterpiece, the Ninth Symphony, and his colossal piano sonatas, are still the music of a lunatic.

Then, I have had the teachers at the Conservatoire against me—stimulated by Cherubini and Fétis, whose pride and principles were outraged by my heterodoxy in matters of harmony and rhythm. For myself, I am a free-thinker in music, or rather I am of the faith of Beethoven, Weber, Gluck and Spontini, who believe and preach, and prove by their works, that everything is 'right' or 'wrong' according to the effect produced, and that that is the sole criterion for condemning or exonerating any given arrangement of notes.

Nowadays even the teachers who were most rigidly bent on upholding the sanctity of the old rules are beginning to abandon them in their own works.

My opponents also include the partisans of the Italian sensualist school, whose doctrines I have often attacked and whose gods I have blasphemed.

Today I am more circumspect. I still abhor those operas which the mob acclaims as masterpieces of dramatic music but which to me are unspeakable parodies of feeling and passion; only I have the strength to keep silent.

Nevertheless my position as a critic continues to yield me a rich crop of enemies, the most rancorous being not so much those whom I have criticized as those whom I have failed to mention or have too feebly praised. Others have never forgiven some innocent jest of mine. I was rash enough, eighteen or twenty years ago, to make fun of a very dull little work of Rossini's, the three choral pieces entitled *Faith, Hope and Charity*. After hearing them, I wrote (I forget where) to the effect that the composer's 'Hope had disappointed ours, his Faith would never move mountains, and as for the Charity he had given us, it would not ruin him'.*

The Rossinians were of course furious—although I had previously written a long and admiring analysis of *William Tell* and repeated *ad nauseam* that the *Barber* is one of the great works of the century.

* [Rossini's work was performed on 20 November 1844 at Troupenas' music shop, conducted by Panseron. Berlioz referred to it in the *Débats* of 10 December.]

On another occasion, when M. Panseron sent me a fatuous prospectus announcing, in execrable French, the opening of a musical consulting-room where amateur composers of songs could have their effusions corrected for the modest sum of a hundred francs, I reproduced the whole thing in the *Journal des débats* under the heading: CONSULTING ROOM FOR SECRET MELODIES.*

Some years earlier an opera by M. Carafa called *La grande duchesse* was put on. It had only two performances. I was supposed to review the piece. My notice, written after the second, consisted simply of the famous phrase from Bossuet's funeral oration for Henrietta of England: 'Madame se meurt. Madame est morte.'†

M. Carafa has not forgiven me. I must confess that in conversation too I have sometimes inadvertently let slip remarks which could be taken as wounding by ill-natured persons. I remember an evening at my friend d'Ortigue's house. The company included M. de Lamennais and a departmental head from the Ministry of the Interior, M. P——. The talk turned on the dissatisfaction that everyone feels with his lot in life. M. P—— declared himself not at all dissatisfied with his. 'I would rather be what I am than anything,' said he. 'How odd,' I answered, without thinking. 'I am quite the opposite. I would rather be anything than what you are.'

He had the strength of mind not to make any reply, but I have no doubt our laughter, particularly M. de Lamennais', stuck in his throat.

In recent years the superiority which is generally ascribed to me as an orchestral conductor has made me fresh enemies. Nearly every conductor in Germany is hostile to me because the musicians play so much better under my direction than they usually do, and show and express their enthusiasm so openly.‡ A similar

* [*Débats*, 6 April 1853: a play on contemporary advertisements for cures of 'secret maladies'—i.e. veneral diseases.]

† [*Rénovateur*, 3 December 1835. 'Madame is dying. Madame is dead.' As Grande Duchesse d'Orléans, Henrietta (Charles I's daughter), was known as Madame.]

‡ [Cf. Hans von Bülow, writing to Liszt from Dresden (30 April 1854): 'Can you imagine it? Last week Krebs . . . actually rebuked the orchestra for having played so splendidly for a "foreigner"! What a public humiliation for the local conductors. . . . All the players and singers are plunged head over ears in enthusiasm,

situation prevailed in Paris for a long time. You will see from my memoirs what mortification I caused Habeneck and M. Girard, and the curious consequences which ensued. It is the same in London, where Costa secretly opposes me wherever he can.

You will grant that this is no mean force to have arrayed against one; and I have not mentioned the animosity of singers and instrumentalists whose tamperings with the great masters I am wont to rebuke without regard for their feelings, nor the general envy which anyone in the limelight automatically draws upon himself.

Yet I find this life of combat not without its charm, now that the opposition has shrunk to reasonable proportions. From time to time I enjoy breaking through a barrier instead of jumping over it. This pugnacity is a natural result of my passion for music, a passion always at white heat and never satisfied for more than a moment. Love of money plays not the slightest part in it. On the contrary, I have always been ready to make any sacrifice in my search for beauty and my determination to avoid the squalid commonplaces that win a cheap popularity. Offer me a hundred thousand francs to put my name to some of the most successful works of the day, and I would angrily refuse. That is how I am made. You may well imagine the effect of such a character and disposition, set down in the midst of the Paris musical world as it was twenty years ago.

If you were now to ask me, and I were to waive the normal conventions of modesty, I could give you the other side of the picture: the sympathy and understanding which I have met in France, England, Germany and Russia, and which have consoled me for many hardships. I could quote examples of the most extraordinary enthusiasm (I need not remind you of Paganini's royal gift and the marvellous letter, so generous in its artistic sentiments, which accompanied it). Let me quote you only a charming remark that Lipinski, leader of the Dresden opera orchestra, made to me when I was there three years ago. It was after a splendid concert at which my legend, *The Damnation of*

---

delighted that they have at last been made to show what they can do, thanks to this incomparable conductor. . . . They would all . . . like to keep Berlioz in Dresden as their musical director.']

Faust, had been performed.* When the concert was over, Lipinski introduced me to a player who, he said, was desirous of congratulating me but did not know a word of French. As I cannot speak German, Lipinski was offering to interpret for us, when the man, interrupting him, sprang forward, seized my hand, stammered out a few words, and burst into uncontrollable sobs; whereupon Lipinski, turning to me and indicating his friend's tears, said, 'You get the point.'

And one further remark, Roman in its simplicity. It was in Brunswick recently, when they were about to perform several movements from my choral symphony on *Romeo and Juliet* at a concert given in the theatre. On the morning of the concert a stranger sitting next to me at lunch informed me that he had travelled a long way to hear the work.†

'You should write an opera on this subject,' he said. 'From the way you have treated it as a symphony, and from the way you understand Shakespeare, you would do something quite new and wonderful.'

I replied that unhappily, even supposing I could find two artists capable of singing and acting the two main parts, which I doubted, the standards and values in our opera houses today were so low that were I to have such a work put into rehearsal I should certainly be dead before the first performance.

That evening my musical friend went to the concert; and during an interval, while talking to one of his neighbours, he repeated what I had said about an opera on *Romeo and Juliet*. His companion was silent for a moment; then, striking the rim of the box, he exclaimed, 'All right, let him die—but let him write the opera!'

And now may I say how grateful I am to you, sir, for the kindness you are showing me and for your wish to avenge (as you put it) all the injustice I have suffered from men and institutions. I believe, however, that where vengeance is concerned one must leave Time to do its work. He is the great avenger. For that

* [22 April 1854, 'the finest performance I have ever had of this difficult work', Berlioz wrote to Liszt the next day (*Correspondance générale*, IV, 521). It was repeated a few days later.]

† He was Baron von Donop, the Prince of Lippe-Detmold's chamberlain. [The concert was given on 22 October 1853.]

matter, the men and institutions that I had and still have cause to complain of are not worth getting angry about.

I realize I have said nothing from the technical point of view of my manner of writing, and you would perhaps like to hear something about it.

Generally speaking, my style is very bold, but there is no tendency in it whatsoever to destroy any of the fundamental elements of art. On the contrary, I try to add to their number. I have never dreamed of writing music 'without melody', as people in France have absurdly maintained. Such a school now exists in Germany and I abominate it. It should not be difficult to recognize that although I may not actually confine myself to taking a short subject for the theme of a movement, as the greatest masters often did, I am always careful to make my compositions abundantly melodic. The value of these melodies, their distinction, originality, and charm, may well be contested; it is not for me to assess it. But to deny their existence is, I submit, dishonest or simply silly. Only, as they are often on a very large scale, a shallow, undeveloped sensibility is slow to grasp their shape; they may also be combined with other subsidiary melodies which, for those same weak spirits, obscure their outline; or, lastly, they are so unlike the trivial little tunes which the riff-raff of the musical world understands by the term, that it cannot bring itself to admit that they are tunes at all.

The predominant features of my music are passionate expression, inward intensity, rhythmic impetus, and unexpectedness. When I say passionate expression I mean expression bent on reproducing the essence of its subject, even when that subject is the opposite of passion, and gentle, tender feelings are being expressed, or the most profound calm—the sort of expression that people have claimed to find in *The Childhood of Christ* and, even more, in the scene in heaven in *The Damnation of Faust* and the Sanctus in the Requiem.

In connection with the Requiem it is worth mentioning a field which I have been almost the only modern composer to cultivate, and of which the old masters did not even envisage the possibility. I refer to those enormous compositions which certain critics have designated by the name of architectural or monumental music, and which made the German poet Heine call me a 'colossal nightingale, a lark the size of an eagle, such as existed, we are told, in the primordial world'. Heine goes on: 'Indeed, for me there is something primitive if not prehistoric about Berlioz's music. It makes me see visions of mammoths and other beasts long extinct, fabulous empires of preternatural depravity, and many a cloud-capped, impossible wonder. Its magical strains conjure up Babylon, the hanging gardens of Semiramis, the marvels of Nineveh, the mighty constructions of Mizraim, as we see them in the pictures of the English painter Martin.'

In the same passage in his book *Lutetia*, Heine again compares me with the eccentric English painter and states that I have 'little melody' and 'no real simplicity whatever'. Three weeks after the book was published, the first performance of *The Childhood of Christ* took place. Next day I received a letter from Heine in which he apologized profusely for having misjudged me. 'I hear on all sides,' he wrote from his bed of sickness, 'that you have plucked a nosegay of the most exquisite blooms of melody, and that all in all your oratorio is a masterpiece of simplicity. I can never forgive myself for having been so unjust to a friend.' I went to see him. As he was starting on his self-recriminations again, I said, 'But in any case, why did you behave like a common critic and let yourself make a categorical statement about an artist when you know only part of his work? You are always thinking of the Witches' Sabbath and the March to the Scaffold from my Fantastic Symphony, and the Dies irae and Lacrymosa from my Requiem. Yet I think I have done and can do things that are quite different.'

The musical problems which I tried to solve, and which led Heine astray, are exceptional in that exceptional means are employed. In my Requiem, for example, there are four separate brass bands which answer each other from different points beyond the main orchestra and the chorus. In the Te Deum the organ at one end of the church communes with the orchestra and the two choirs at the other end, and also with a third, very large choir which sings in unison and represents the people adding their voice from time to time to the great ceremony of sacred music. But it is above all the scale of the movements, the breadth of style and the formidably slow and deliberate pace of certain progressions, whose final goal cannot be guessed, that give these works their 'gigantic' character and 'colossal' aspect. The consequence of such vastness of scale is that the listener either misses the point altogether or is overwhelmed by a tremendous emotion. Often at performances of my Requiem one man will be trembling, shaken to the depths of his soul, while the man next to him sits there listening intently and understanding nothing. The latter is in the position of the tourist who goes up inside the giant statue of San Carlo Borromeo at Como and is astonished when informed that the large 'room' in which he has just been sitting is the interior of the saint's *head*.

Those of my works which the critics have called architectural are: the Funeral and Triumphal Symphony for two orchestras and chorus; the Te Deum, the final movement of which, the Judex crederis, is unquestionably the most imposing thing I have produced; the cantata for double chorus, *L'Impériale*, which was performed at the concerts in the Palace of Industry in 1855; and, above all, the Requiem. As to those that are not conceived on any exceptional scale, and in which I use normal resources, it is precisely their expressiveness, their inner fire and rhythmic originality that have done them the greatest harm, on account of the qualities they demand from the performer. To perform them well, everybody concerned, the conductor most of all, must *feel* as I feel. They require a combination of irresistible verve and the utmost precision, a controlled vehemence, a dreamlike sensitivity, an almost morbid melancholy, without which the essential character of my phrases is falsified or even obliterated. For this reason I find it exceedingly painful to hear most of my works conducted by someone other than myself. I thought I would have apoplexy when I heard the *King Lear* overture in Prague directed by a kapellmeister of incontestable merit. It was approximately right; but in such a case approximately right is totally wrong. You will see in the chapter on *Benvenuto Cellini* how much I suffered from Habeneck's mistakes (unintentional though they may have been) during the long massacre of the work in rehearsal.

If you now ask me which of my pieces I prefer, my answer will be that I share the view of most artists: I prefer the adagio (the Love Scene) in *Romeo and Juliet*. Once, at the end of this adagio, when I was conducting it in Hanover, I felt something or somebody pulling me from behind. I turned round: it was the players nearest to my desk; they were kissing my coat-tails. However, before certain audiences (and in certain halls) I would take good care not to perform the piece.

With regard to French prejudice against me, I might also remind you of the saga of the shepherds' chorus in *The Childhood of Christ*, originally performed at two of my concerts* as a work by Pierre Ducré, an imaginary eighteenth-century choirmaster. How they praised that 'simple melody'! The number of people who said, 'Berlioz could never do anything like that!'

One evening, in a salon, a song bearing Schubert's name on the title page was sung in the presence of an amateur imbued with a pious horror of my music. 'Delightful!' he cried, 'now there's melody for you. What feeling, what lucidity and restraint! Berlioz would never have thought of that!' It was Cellini's song from the second act of my opera.

A dilettante once complained, at a party, of having been imposed on in a most ungentlemanly fashion. 'The other morning,' he said, 'I looked in at a rehearsal of the St Cecilia Orchestra, conducted by M. Seghers. They were playing a brilliant piece, a tremendously spirited thing, but quite different in style and orchestration from any symphonic music I knew. I went up to Seghers and asked him the name of the fascinating overture he had just played. He answered, "The *Roman Carnival* overture by Berlioz." Now you will agree that——'

'Yes,' a friend of mine broke in, 'we do agree that it's quite shocking to take advantage of an honest man's prejudices in this way.'

In France, as elsewhere, no one disputes my 'mastery of orchestration', especially since I published a treatise on the subject. I am, however, criticized for an excessive use of Sax's instruments, no doubt on the sound principle that I have often praised them, even if I do not happen to have employed them anywhere except in one scene of *The Capture of Troy*, an opera of which no one has yet seen a note. I am also criticized for being inordinately noisy and too fond of the bass drum—although I have included it in only a few works, where there is reason for it, and although I alone among

* [Late 1850.]

critics have been protesting for twenty years against the abuse of noise, the brainless introduction of bass drum, trombones and the rest into small theatres, small orchestras, operettas and comic patter songs, where even the side-drum is now pressed into service.

It was Rossini, in *The Siege of Corinth*, who first introduced noisy orchestration into France. Yet French critics never mention him in this connection, nor do they blame Auber, Halévy, Adam and a score of others for their hateful exaggeration of Rossini's system. Instead they blame me, nay they blame Weber (see his Life in Michaud's *Biographie universelle*)—Weber, who used the bass drum only once in his orchestra and handled every instrument with incomparable skill and restraint!

So far as it relates to me, I fancy this absurd delusion derives from the festivals in which I have often been seen to direct enormous orchestras. Prince Metternich asked me one day in Vienna whether it was I who 'composed music for five hundred players'? To which I replied, 'Not always, Your Highness. Sometimes I use four hundred and fifty.'

But what does it matter? My scores are now published, and anyone can verify the accuracy of these assertions. And if not, again what does it matter?

I am, sir, your obedient servant

Hector Berlioz

POSTFACE

I have finished—the Institute—concerts in the Palace of Industry—Jullien—the vibrations of eternity —The Trojans—performances in Paris—Beatrice and Benedict —performances in Baden and Weimar—visit to Loewenberg —the Conservatoire concerts—Festival at Strasbourg —death of my second wife—last cemetery tales —to hell with everything

NEARLY TEN YEARS have passed since I completed these memoirs. The events of my life during this time have been almost as momentous as those I have already related. I feel I must therefore describe a few of them briefly, before finishing with this long labour once and for all.

My career is over; 'Othello's occupation's gone'. I compose no more music, conduct no more concerts, no longer write prose or verse. I have resigned my post as critic. All the musical enterprises which I had begun have been terminated. I do not wish to do anything more; I do nothing except read, meditate, struggle against a deadly weariness of soul, and suffer from an incurable neuralgia which tortures me day and night.

To my great surprise I was elected a member of the Fine Arts Academy of the Institute;* and if, on the occasions when I speak, the criticisms that I make of our academic practices are to little purpose and produce no results, my relations with my colleagues are none the less friendly and in every respect pleasant.

There is much that I could say about the two Gluck operas, *Orphée* and *Alceste*, which I was invited to put on, the one at the Théâtre-Lyrique, the other at the Opéra.† I have, however, discussed them at some length in my book *A travers chants*, and although there are things that I could certainly add to that account, I shall not do so.

Prince Napoleon‡ had me put in charge of organizing a vast concert at the Exhibition in the Palace of Industrial Products on the day of the formal distribution of the prizes by the Emperor. I accepted this arduous task on condition that I had no financial

* [In 1856.]

† [In 1859 and 1861 respectively.]

‡ [Son of Napoleon's youngest brother Jérome, and first cousin of Napoleon III.]

responsibility. A shrewd and intrepid entrepreneur, M. Ber, came forward and offered his services. He treated me handsomely, and this time the concerts (there were several more, after the official ceremony) brought me in nearly eight thousand francs. I had twelve hundred performers, accommodated in a gallery behind the throne. In that position they made little effect; but in any case music was so unimportant on the day of the ceremony that in the middle of the opening piece (the cantata, *L'Impériale*, which I had written for the occasion) I was interrupted and obliged to stop the orchestra at the most interesting point, because the Prince had to make his speech and the music was going on too long. Next day the paying public were admitted and seventy-five thousand francs were taken. We had moved the orchestra down into the lower part of the hall and arranged it in proper fashion, and the effect was excellent. On this occasion the cantata was not interrupted, and I was able to ignite the crowning-piece of my firework display. I had called in an inventor of my acquaintance,* and he had come to Paris and set up an electric metronome with five separate arms. By simply moving one finger of my left hand, while holding the baton in my right, I could indicate the time to five different and widely spaced points in the huge area which the performers occupied; the electric wires transmitted my tempo to five sub-conductors who straightway gave it to the forces under their direction. The ensemble was marvellous. Since then, most opera houses have adopted the electric metronome for use with offstage choruses in cases where the chorus-master can neither see the beat nor hear the orchestra. The Opéra alone rejected it; but when I was directing the rehearsals of *Alceste* I managed to get this valuable device introduced there too. Some of the music at these concerts in the Palace of Industry sounded splendid, particularly the pieces in which the harmonies are broad and the tempo on the slow side; chief among them being, so far as I can remember, the chorus 'Jamais, dans ces beaux lieux' from *Armide*, the Tibi omnes from my Te Deum, and the Apotheosis from my Funeral and Triumphal Symphony.†

* [The Belgian inventor Verbrugghen.]

† [The ceremony was on 15 November 1855, the public concert on the 16th (repeated on the 24th). The previous April had seen the first performance of the Te Deum (composed six years earlier) in Saint-Eustache.]

Four or five years after this musical congress, Jullien, whom I mentioned earlier in connection with his management of the English Opera at Drury Lane, came to Paris to give a series of big concerts in the Champs-Elysées Circus. When his bankruptcy prevented him from entering into certain agreements, I was happily able to help him obtain his certificate and with it the power to make contracts. The poor man could hardly believe that I could so lightly waive my right to what he owed me; he broke down in the courtroom and embraced me in floods of tears. But from that time forth his mental condition steadily worsened. No one in London or in Paris seemed prepared to recognize how seriously his wits had already been impaired. For some years he had been laying claim to a remarkable discovery in the field of acoustics, which he eagerly imparted to everyone he met. He would place his fingers in his ears and listen to the dull roar produced by the blood passing through the carotid arteries, and firmly believe that what he heard was the cosmic A given out by the terrestrial globe in its revolutions through space. He would then whistle through his lips some shrill note—a D, an E flat, or an F—and exclaim with the utmost enthusiasm, 'Listen—it's the A, the genuine A of the spheres! The vibrations of eternity!'

One day he burst in on me with a strange air about him. He had 'seen God in a blue thunder-cloud', and God had commanded him to make my fortune; so he had come to buy my recently completed score of *The Trojans*, for which he offered me thirty-five thousand francs. He also wished, notwithstanding my waiver, to discharge his Drury Lane debt. 'I have money, money,' he said, pulling handfuls of gold and bank-notes from his pocket. 'Here, take it, pay yourself.' I had great difficulty in persuading him to keep his gold and his notes. 'My dear Jullien, we will deal with this matter some other time—and with the mission that God has entrusted to you. For that you must be calmer than you are now.' He had in fact already received substantial sums for his Champs-Elysées concerts from an entrepreneur whose confidence he had won.* A week later, after creating a public scandal by playing the piccolo in his gig in the Boulevard des Italiens and

* [Dejean.]

inviting passers-by to come to his concerts, he died of a haemorrhage of the brain.* How many musicians in Europe at the present time, who are as mad as he, are taken quite seriously!

I had now completely finished the dramatic work I mentioned a moment ago, and to which I referred in a footnote to one of the preceding chapters. Four years earlier, in Weimar, while talking with the Princess Wittgenstein—Liszt's devoted friend, a woman of great sympathy and intelligence who has often sustained me in my darkest hours—I was drawn on to speak of my admiration for Virgil and of the idea I had conceived of a grand opera on the Shakespearean plan, based on the second and fourth books of the *Aeneid*. I added that I knew too well the miseries such an undertaking must bring me ever to attempt it. 'But', replied the Princess, 'your passion for Shakespeare combined with this love of classical antiquity would be sure to produce something new and splendid. Come, you must write this opera, this lyric poem or whatever you like to call it. You must tackle it and you must complete it.' I continued to make objections. 'Listen,' she said, 'if you shrink from the difficulties this work can and must bring you, if you are so weak as to be afraid to face everything for Dido and Cassandra, then never come back here—I refuse to see you again.' Milder words than these would have been enough to decide me. On my return to Paris† I set to work to write the verses for my lyric poem. Then I started on the score; and at the end of three and a half years of corrections, alterations, additions and so forth, the whole thing was completed. While still polishing and repolishing the work, but having recited the poem on a number of occasions and done my best to profit by the various criticisms passed on it, I decided to approach the Emperor, and wrote the following letter:

PARIS, *28 March 1858*

Sire,

I have just completed a grand opera, of which I have written the words and the music.‡ Despite the boldness and variety of

* [14 March 1860.]

† [At the beginning of March 1856, after a 'Berlioz Week' organized by Liszt.]

‡ *The Trojans* was not then divided into two, but formed a single opera lasting five hours.

means employed, the resources available in Paris would be sufficient to perform it. Permit me, Sire, to read you the poem and then, if it should be so fortunate as to merit such a high honour, to crave your protection for the work. The Opéra is at present directed by an old friend of mine* who professes the strangest views about my musical style—a style which he has never understood and which he is incapable of appreciating. The two conductors on his staff are my enemies. Sire, defend me from my friend, and as for my enemies, as the Italian proverb has it, I will defend myself. If, having heard my poem, Your Majesty does not judge it worthy of being produced, I shall sincerely and respectfully accept your decision. But I cannot submit my work to the approval of people whose judgment is obscured by prejudice and preconception and whose opinions in consequence have no value for me. They would put forward the alleged inadequacy of the poem as a pretext for rejecting the music. I was tempted for a moment to request the favour of reading the libretto of the *The Trojans* to Your Majesty during some brief hour of leisure in Your Majesty's recent stay at Plombières; but the score was not then finished, and I feared lest, if the result of the reading proved unfavourable, I might be too discouraged to continue with it; and I wanted to write this great score, to write it wholly and completely, with the most constant and unremitting zeal, care and devotion. Now let discouragement and disappointment come if they will: nothing can take away the fact that the work exists. It is grand and powerful and, for all the apparent complexity of means, quite straightforward. Unhappily it is not vulgar, but that is a fault which Your Majesty will pardon; and the Paris public is beginning to realize that music has a higher purpose than the manufacture of agreeable sounds. Permit me therefore, Sire, to borrow the words of one of the characters in the epic poem from which I have drawn my subject, and to say: *Arma citi properate viro*,† and I believe I shall take Latium.

* Alphonse Royer.

† ['Quickly bring the man his weapons!' *Aeneid*, XII, 426: the call to rearm the wounded Aeneas during the battle against the armies of Latium.]

I remain, Sire, with profoundest respect and devotion, Your Majesty's most humble and obedient servant,

Hector Berlioz
Member of the Institute

Well: I did not take Latium. The Opéra people took good care not to *properare arma viro*, and the Emperor never read the letter; M. de Morny persuaded me not to send it. The Emperor, he said, would find it 'rather unsuitable'. When *The Trojans* was finally put on (after a fashion), His Majesty did not even deign to come.*

One evening at the Tuileries I managed to have a moment's conversation with the Emperor. He gave me leave to bring him the poem and assured me he would read it if he could get an hour's leisure. What leisure does one have when one is Emperor of France? I delivered my manuscript. He did not read it but passed it on to the office of the Controller of Theatres, where my efforts were regarded as absurd and nonsensical and slandered accordingly. The rumour was put about that the whole thing would last eight hours, that it required two companies the size of the Opéra's to perform it, that I was demanding three hundred additional choristers, etc., etc. A year later some faint signs of interest were discernible. One day Alphonse Royer took me on one side and

* [Berlioz had cherished a vain hope that Napoleon III would order the Opéra to put on the work, as Napoleon I had done fifty years earlier when Lesueur could not get *The Bards* accepted. He attended official receptions, at one of which the Emperor, wearing his '25 degrees below zero look', agreed to read the libretto 'if he could find a moment's leisure—since when I have heard nothing. The technique is as old as the hills. I'm sure King Priam did it in just the same way.' (Letter to Liszt, 28 September 1858.) The entry in the Goncourt brothers' journal for 15 November 1862 includes an anecdote from one of the Emperor's house-parties at Compiègne, told them by Berlioz himself: 'The Emperor was complaining that his sight was failing: "The queer thing is that I can't tell the difference between black and blue any more. Who is that over there?" "Sire, it is Monsieur Berlioz." He raised his voice.

'"Monsieur Berlioz, is your tail-coat blue or black?"

'"Sire," Berlioz hastened to reply, "I should never take the liberty of appearing before Your Majesty in a blue tail-coat; it is black."

'"Good," said the Emperor.

'And that is all the Emperor said to him in four days.' (Robert Baldick, *Pages from the Goncourt Journal*.)]

said that the Minister of State had authorized him to inform me that the Opéra was about to begin rehearsing my score, and that he wished to give me 'full satisfaction'.

This undertaking made gratuitously by His Excellency was no better kept than so many others had been, and that was the last that was, etc., etc. And that is why, after a long and fruitless period of waiting, tired of being treated with contempt, I gave way to M. Carvalho's friendly urgings and agreed to let him try producing *The Trojans at Carthage** at the Théâtre-Lyrique, despite the manifest impossibility of his doing it properly. He had just obtained an annual subsidy of a hundred thousand francs from the government. None the less the enterprise was beyond him. His theatre was not large enough, his singers were not good enough, his chorus and orchestra were small and weak. He made considerable sacrifices. So did I. I paid out of my own pocket for several players that his orchestra lacked, and I cut the orchestration about in many places to make it fit the resources available. Madame Charton-Demeur, the only woman capable of singing the role of Dido, treated me like a friend and generously accepted a fee far below what she had been offered by the manager of the Madrid Theatre. For all that, the performance was and could only be inadequate. Madame Charton had wonderful moments, and there were days when Montjauze, the Aeneas, showed some warmth and animation. But the staging, which Carvalho had insisted on seeing to himself, was quite different from what I had specified. In some places it was irrelevant and in others ridiculous. On the opening night the scene-shifter nearly brought disaster on the whole work by his incompetence during the Hunt and Storm. This scene would look thrillingly wild and beautiful at the Opéra; here it made a wretched impression; and when it was over there had to be an interval of fifty-five minutes while the scenery was changed. Next day, storm, hunt and scene were duly removed.

I have said before that if I am to be able to put on an adequate performance of a work of this scale and character I must be in absolute control of the theatre, as I am of the orchestra when I

* The second part of my lyric poem, to which I added an orchestral introduction (Lamento) and a prologue.

rehearse a symphony. I must have the co-operation and good will of everyone concerned and be obeyed without reserve. Otherwise, after a few days my energies are worn out in the continual clash of wills, the wasting struggle with crass ideas and crasser fears that is forced on me at every turn, and I end by resigning, sinking back exhausted and letting everything go to hell. I cannot describe how Carvalho, while protesting that he desired only to respect my intentions and do what I wanted, pestered me to obtain the cuts that he considered necessary. When he dared not ask me himself he would get some mutual friend to do it for him. One of them would write saying that such and such a passage was very risky; another would implore me—again in writing—to remove something else. And I was driven mad by niggling criticism of points of detail.

'This bard of yours with his four-stringed lyre: I realize, of course, that it accounts for the four notes played by the harp in the orchestra. No doubt it's archaeologically sound . . . but——'

'Well?'

'It's dangerous. People will laugh.'

'Yes, I see—it is awfully funny. Ha! ha! ha! a tetrachord, an antique lyre with only four notes! Ha! ha! ha!'

'There's a word in the prologue that worries me.'

'What is that?'

'*Triomphaux*.'

'Why should it worry you? It's the plural of *triomphal*, as *chevaux* is of *cheval*, *originaux* of *original*, *madrigaux* of *madrigal*, *municipaux* of *municipal*—isn't it?'

'Yes, but it's not a word one often hears.'

'Good heavens, if epic drama were limited to the vocabulary of vaudeville theatres and pleasure gardens, the list of prohibited expressions would be a somewhat lengthy one and the style of the work strangely restricted.'

'You will see, it will make people laugh.'

'Ha! ha! ha! *triomphaux!* It's killingly funny. *Triomphaux!* It's almost as good as Molière's *tarte à la crème*. Ha! ha! ha!'

'Aeneas mustn't come on in a helmet.'

'Why not?'

'Because Mangin, who sells pencils at the street corner, wears one—a mediaeval helmet, it's true, but a helmet none the less—

and the wags in the gallery will laugh and call out, "Hey, there's Mangin!"'

'Yes, of course, a Trojan hero shouldn't wear a helmet; it will make people laugh. Ha! ha! ha! a helmet! ha! ha! Mangin!'

'Look, will you do me a favour?'

'What is it now?'

'Leave out Mercury. The wings on his head and heels will make people laugh. No one has ever seen wings except on the shoulders.'

'Ah, so human figures have been seen with wings on their shoulders? But you are right, wings on the heels will make people laugh. Ha! ha! ha! and wings on the head even more so. Ha! ha! ha! Since one doesn't often run into Mercury in the streets of Paris, we'll leave him out.'

Can anyone conceive what I endured from such craven stupidity? Not to mention Carvalho's musical ideas: he wanted me to make the tempo of certain numbers slower or faster, to add sixteen bars, eight bars, four bars here and remove two or three bars or one bar there in order to suit some stage business of his own devising. In his eyes the production is not made for the music but the music for the production—as if, in any case, I had not carefully calculated my score in the light of the exigencies of the theatre as I had studied them for forty years at the Opéra. The actors, at least, refrained from plaguing me; and in justice to them I must say that they all sang their parts exactly as they were given them, without altering a note. This may seem incredible but it is true, and I thank them for it. The first performance took place on the date Carvalho had announced, 4 November 1863. The work still needed another three or four strenuous general rehearsals; nothing was running smoothly, least of all on the stage. But the director was desperate for something to keep his repertory going. The house had been empty for nights on end, and he was anxious to get out of this unsatisfactory position as soon as possible; and in such cases, as is well known, directors become very fierce. My friends and I imagined that the evening would be a stormy one and were expecting all kinds of hostile demonstrations, but there were none. My enemies were afraid to come out into the open. There was one solitary, rather subdued boo at the end, when I was called for, and that was all. The gentleman in question clearly regarded it as his duty to keep up the good work throughout the weeks that followed, for he came back with a colleague and booed at precisely the same point at the third, fifth, seventh and tenth performances. Others held forth in the corridors with comical vehemence, heaping abuse upon me, declaring that such music could not and should not be 'allowed'. Five papers were crudely insulting, in terms nicely calculated to wound my feelings as an artist. But more than fifty articles of appreciative criticism, written with genuine enthusiasm and uncommon perception, by men like Gasperini, Fiorentino, d'Ortigue, Léon Kreutzer, Damcke, Joannes Weber and many others, appeared during the following fortnight and filled me with a happiness such as I had not known for a long time. I also received a large number of letters, some eloquent, others naïve, all expressing emotion, which touched me profoundly. At several performances I saw people in tears. During the two months that followed the first performance of *The Trojans* I was often stopped in the street by strangers who wished to shake hands with me and thank me for having composed it. Was that not ample recompense for the sneers of my enemies?—enemies whom I owed less to my criticism than to the style and bent of my music and by whose hatred one can only feel honoured, for it is like the disdain of the whore for the honest woman. The muse of such people is called Lais, Phryne, occasionally but very rarely Aspasia* (she was too intelligent), whereas for noble minds and lovers of great art the goddess has names like Juliet, Desdemona, Cordelia, Ophelia, Imogen, Virgilia, Miranda, Dido, Cassandra, Alcestis—names that evoke images of poetic passion, dignity, restraint, self-sacrifice, where the former suggest only base sensuousness and prostitution.

I confess that I too was intensely moved by certain pieces in *The Trojans* that were well performed. Aeneas' aria 'Ah! quand viendra l'instant des suprêmes adieux', and above all Dido's monologue,

Je vais mourir
Dans ma douleur immense submergée

* [Aspasia was Pericles' mistress; Lais and Phryne were famous Greek courtesans of the fourth century B.C.]

overwhelmed me. Madame Charton declaimed with grandeur and dramatic force the phrase,

Enée, Enée!
Oh! mon âme te suit!

and, as she uttered the wordless despairing cries, struck her breast and tore at her hair, as Virgil describes it:

Terque quaterque manu pectus percussa decorum,
*Flaventesque abscissa comas.**

(Strange that none of my yapping critics should have blamed me for daring to produce such a vocal effect; I think it deserved their anger.) Of all the passionately sad music that I have ever written I know of none to compare with Dido's in this passage and the aria which follows, except for Cassandra's in parts of *The Capture of Troy*, which has not yet been performed anywhere. Oh my noble Cassandra, my heroic virgin, I must then resign myself: I shall never hear you—and I am like the young Coroebus,

Insano Cassandrae incensus amore.†

The following pieces in *The Trojans at Carthage* were cut at the Théâtre-Lyrique, as many of them during rehearsal as after the first performance:

1 The entry of the builders
2 The entry of the sailors
3 The entry of the farm-workers
4 The orchestral interlude (Royal Hunt and Storm)
5 The scene between Anna and Narbal
6 The second ballet
7 Iopas' air
8 The sentries' duet
9 Hylas' song
10 The big duet for Aeneas and Dido, 'Errante sur tes pas'.

Carvalho found the first three numbers dull; in any case the stage was not big enough for a procession of this size. The hunting

* [*Aeneid*, IV, 589–90.]
† ['On fire with wild love for Cassandra'; *Aeneid*, II, 343.]

interlude was lamentably staged. Instead of several real waterfalls, I was given a painted representation of a stream. The leaping satyrs were represented by a troupe of twelve-year-old girls, who brandished no flaming branches in their hands, the firemen having forbidden it for fear of a conflagration. There were no nymphs flying dishevelled through the forest with cries of 'Italy!' The female choristers were stationed in the wings; their cries were not strong enough to penetrate to the auditorium. Even the stage thunder could scarely be heard, despite the fact that the orchestra was thin and lacking in vigour. And when this miserable travesty came to an end, the scene-shifter always needed at least forty minutes to change his scenery. So I myself asked for the interlude to be removed.* Carvalho, against my furious resistance, remorselessly insisted on cutting out the scene between Narbal and Anna, the second ballet, and the sentries' duet (whose homely style he found out of place in an epic work). Iopas' stanzas disappeared with my approval, the singer charged with the part being incapable of singing them well. It was the same with the duet between Aeneas and Dido; I had realized that Madame Charton's voice was unequal to the vehemence of this scene, which took so much out of her that she would not have had the strength left to deliver the tremendous recitative 'Dieux immortels! il part', the final aria and the scene on the pyre. As for Hylas' song, which had been greatly liked at the early performances and was well sung by young Cabel, it vanished while I was in bed with bronchitis. Cabel was needed for the opera which was due to follow *The Trojans*, and since his contract required him to sing only fifteen times a month he had to be paid two hundred francs for each additional performance; so Carvalho, without telling me, removed the song on grounds of economy. I was so numbed and stupefied by this long torture that when the publisher of the vocal score, who shared Carvalho's view that it should conform as closely as possible

* [The *Journal amusant* commented on the fact in a cartoon by Grévin entitled 'Non-symphonic Interlude'; 'Well, what about this Royal Hunt? And the virgin forest? And the cave? The stream? The naiads? The satyrs? The nymphs? The storm? etc., etc.,' 'In the waste-paper basket'. 'Oh, M. Berlioz—but that was why I came! Didn't the public like it, then? What a dangerous admission! On that principle your waste-paper basket would very soon be full.' (28 November 1863.)]

to the performance, proposed to omit several of these pieces, I consented to it instead of opposing it with all my remaining strength. Happily the full score has not yet been published.* I spent a month putting it back into shape and carefully tending all its wounds. It will appear in its pristine integrity, exactly as I wrote it.

But oh, the agony of seeing a work of this kind laid out for sale with the scars of the publisher's surgery upon it! A score lying dismembered in the window of a music shop like the carcass of a calf on a butcher's stall, and pieces cut off and sold like lights for the concierge's cat!

Despite all the improvements which Carvalho lavished upon it, *The Trojans at Carthage* had only twenty-one performances. As the receipts were not coming up to expectations he agreed to cancel Madame Charton's contract. She left for Madrid, and the work, to my great relief, disappeared from the bills. Nevertheless, since I was author of both libretto and music, the royalties I received from those twenty-one performances were considerable. I had also sold the vocal score in Paris and London; and to my unutterable joy I perceived that the interest from these combined sums would just about equal my annual income from the *Journal des débats* and I at once resigned from my post as critic. At last, at long last, after thirty years of slavery I was free! Free—with no more feuilletons to write, no more platitudes to condone, no more mediocrities to praise, no more rage to repress, no more lies, no more make-believe, no more ignoble time-serving! I need not set foot in an opera house again, I need never speak of an opera house or listen to anyone speak of an opera house, nor even have to laugh at the messes they concoct in those great stew-pots. *Gloria in excelsis Deo, et in terra pax hominibus bonae voluntatis!*

To *The Trojans* at least, the unhappy feuilletonist owes his deliverance.†

*[It was not published till 1969, a hundred years after the composer's death. *The Trojans* is volume 2 of Bärenreiter's *New Berlioz Edition*.]

† [His last notice, a friendly review of Bizet's *Pearl Fishers*, appeared on 8 October 1863, but he did not formally give up the post until early 1864. He was succeeded by his friend Joseph d'Ortigue. On the latter's death in 1866, Ernest Reyer became music critic.]

After it had been written but before it had been performed, I composed *Beatrice and Benedict*, opéra-comique in two acts, at the request of M. Bénazet.* It was given with great success in the new theatre at Baden, under my direction, on 9 August 1862. A few months later, at the request of the Grand Duchess, it was produced at Weimar in a German translation by Richard Pohl and was equally successful. Their Highnesses had invited me to come and conduct the first two performances, and as always overwhelmed me with kindness.

The Prince of Hohenzollern-Hechingen was no less cordial. During my stay in Weimar he sent his kapellmeister with an invitation to me to come to Loewenberg, where he now lives, and direct one of his concerts.† He informed me that his orchestra knew my entire symphonic output, and asked for a programme made up exclusively of my works.

I replied that he had but to command, but as his orchestra was familiar with my symphonies and my overtures, let him choose the programme he would like me to conduct and I would conduct it. The Prince accordingly chose the *King Lear* overture, the Fête and Love Scene from *Romeo and Juliet*, the *Roman Carnival* overture, and *Harold in Italy* complete. As he had no harpist, he invited the Weimar player Madame Pohl at the same time as me, and she and her husband gladly undertook the journey. The Prince had greatly changed since my visit to Hechingen in 1842. He had become such a martyr to gout that he was confined to his bed, and to his keen regret could not even attend the concert I had come to give. He did not attempt to conceal his disappointment. 'You are not merely a conductor,' he said, 'you are the orchestra itself. It is a calamity that I cannot enjoy the benefit of your stay here.'

He has had a fine concert hall built in his castle at Loewenberg, excellent for sound. There, ten or twelve times a year, he assembles an audience of six hundred, selected from among the keenest and most knowledgeable music-lovers. The concerts are of course free. People come from all round Loewenberg and even from Bunzlau and Dresden and a score of castles equally distant. The orchestra has only forty-five players, but they are admirable

* Manager of the casino at Baden.

† [In early April 1863.]

players, experienced, alert and intelligent, and their director, Seifrids, is a conductor and trainer of rare skill and thoroughness. What is more, they have no lessons to give and, unlike the players in our symphony orchestras, are not exhausted by church or theatre work: they are entirely at the service of the Prince. He had me to stay with him. On the day of the first rehearsal a servant came to tell me that the orchestra was 'ready and waiting for me'. I walk down a corridor and enter the hall (which I have not yet seen), and find the forty-five musicians waiting in silence. No preliminaries, no noise or fuss of any kind: they have already tuned up. On the conductor's desk is the score of *King Lear.* I lift my baton and begin, and from the first everything goes with precision and accuracy and spirit. The most extreme irregularities of rhythm in the allegro are attacked and mastered without hesitation; and I inwardly exclaim as I conduct this overture, which I have not heard for ten years or more, 'This is tremendous! Did I write this?' It is the same with the rest of the programme, and I end by saying, 'Gentlemen, this is a joke. We are simply rehearsing for our own enjoyment. I have no criticism whatsoever to make.' The kapell-meister played the viola solo in *Harold* impeccably, with a beauty of tone and a rhythmic poise that absolutely delighted me (in the other pieces he resumed his violin). Richard Pohl played the cymbals. I may truthfully say that I have never heard *Harold* more irresistibly done. But the adagio from *Romeo and Juliet*—how gloriously they made it sing! Loewenberg was forgotten—we were in Verona. At the end of the movement, in which we had not had to stop for a single mistake, Seifrids rose, stood still for a moment, striving to master his emotion, then cried out in French, 'There is nothing finer in all music!' At which the whole orchestra burst into loud applause, the strings rattled their bows, the drums thundered . . . and I bit my lip. Emissaries went from time to time to the sickroom, bearing reports of the progress of the rehearsal to the poor disconsolate Prince. On the day of the concert a glittering audience filled the hall. It was obvious from their enormous enthusiasm that all the music had long been familiar to them. After the Pilgrims' March, one of the Prince's officers came up onto the platform and, amid great excitement, pinned on my coat the Cross of the Order of Hohenzollern. The secret had been so closely guarded that I had not had the slightest inkling I was to receive such an honour. This put me in high spirits, and just to please myself, without thought of the audience, I played the Orgy in my special *furious* style, with much gnashing and grinding of teeth.

Next day the players held a splendid dinner for me, followed by a ball. There were a number of toasts to reply to, which I did as best I could, Richard Pohl acting as interpreter and translating my words into German sentence by sentence.

There is a great deal more that I could say about that delightful expedition to Loewenberg, but I will mention only the charming courtesy with which I was received by the Prince's whole circle and especially by the family of Colonel Broderotti, one of his officers. I may add that the Broderotti ladies and the colonel himself speak impeccable French, which was a priceless boon for me, who hate to hear it spoken badly yet do not know a word of German. Two days after the artists' ball I had to depart. The Prince, who had not been able to leave his bed, embraced me and said, 'Goodbye, my dear Berlioz. You are going back to Paris, where you have friends who love you. Tell them I love them for it.'*

To return to *Beatrice*. For my libretto I had taken part of Shakespeare's play *Much Ado About Nothing*, merely adding the episode of the choirmaster and the text of the vocal numbers. The duet for the two girls, 'Vous soupirez, madame', the trio for Hero, Beatrice and Ursula, 'Je vais d'un coeur aimant', and Beatrice's big aria, 'Dieu! que viens-je d'entendre?' (sung at Baden with warmth, delicacy, great energy, and rare beauty of style by Madame Charton) made a prodigious effect. The critics who had come from Paris to hear the work praised the music enthusiastically, the aria and the duet in particular. One or two of them, however, decided that there was a good deal of scrub and dead wood in the rest of the score and that the spoken dialogue was dull. This dialogue is taken almost word for word from Shakespeare.

The work is difficult to perform well, the men's roles especially. To my mind it is one of the liveliest and most original things

* [Seven months later Wagner visited Loewenberg to conduct a concert, and was received with similar hospitality. In 1864 the Prince died and his orchestra was disbanded.]

I have done. Unlike *The Trojans*, it costs nothing to put on. All the same they will be sure not to ask me to give it in Paris; and they will be right: it is not Parisian music. Bénazet, with his usual generosity, paid me at the rate of two thousand francs for the words of each act and the same for the music—eight thousand francs in all—and a further thousand to go back and conduct it the following year. I have had the piano score engraved. The full score will appear later, along with the other three, *Benvenuto Cellini*, *The Capture of Troy* and *The Trojans at Carthage*, if I can find enough money to have them published. Choudens, when he bought *The Trojans*, committed himself in writing to publish the full score within a year of the piano score's appearing, but *this undertaking has been no better kept than so many others, and from the moment that the contract was signed, etc., etc.* The duet for the two girls from *Beatrice and Benedict* has become very well known in Germany and is often sung there. That reminds me of my last visit to Weimar and the small supper parties which the Grand Duke sometimes invited me to, and at which he would enjoy questioning me in minute detail about my life in Paris. He was astonished and sadly disillusioned when I told him what our musical world is really like. But I made him laugh one evening when he asked me in what circumstances I had written this duet.

'You must have composed it by moonlight, in some romantic spot,' he said.

'Your Grace, it sprang from one of those impressions of nature that an artist stores deep inside himself, to be released at some later time when it is needed, no matter where one happens to be. I sketched the music of that duet one day at the Institute, during a speech by one of my colleagues.'

'Indeed!' said the Grand Duke. 'That speaks well for his eloquence. He is clearly quite an orator!'

The duet was also performed at one of the concerts of our Conservatoire, where it aroused the most extraordinary enthusiasm and was encored with tumultuous applause by the entire hall. My faithful booers dared not utter a squeak. Mesdames Viardot and Vandenheuvel-Duprez, it must be said, sang it exquisitely and the marvellous orchestra played with surpassing grace and refinement. It was one of those performances one sometimes hears in dreams.* The Conservatoire Concert Society, again, chose to include the second part of my sacred trilogy, *The Childhood of Christ*, in one of its programmes this year.† It was admirably done and it too made a deep impression, though the audience for some reason did not encore the Repose of the Holy Family, as always happens elsewhere. My two booers condescended to announce their presence, to the general indignation. The society, which is now directed by a friend of mine, M. Georges Hainl, is no longer hostile to me. It proposes to perform excerpts from my works from time to time. I have made over to it, with full ownership, all the music in my possession, including separate orchestral and choral parts, engraved and manuscript, representing what is required for full-scale performance of all my works except the operas. This music library will have some value one day, and it could not be in better hands.

I must not forget to mention the Strasbourg Festival, to which I was invited eighteen months ago to conduct a performance of *The Childhood of Christ*.‡ An enormous hall had been built, seating six thousand, and there were five hundred performers. It did not seem possible that this oratorio, written almost throughout in a quiet and delicate vein, could carry in so vast an auditorium. To my great surprise, people were profoundly moved, and tears were shed at the mystic chorus, 'O mon âme', which is sung unaccompanied at the end of the work. How happy I feel when I see my audience weep! This chorus creates nothing like the same effect in Paris; it is, in any case, always badly done.

I hear that during the past year several of my works have been performed in America, Russia and Germany. Good! If I could only live to be a hundred and forty my musical life would end by becoming delightful.

I married again—it was my *duty*. After eight years of this second marriage I lost my wife. She died suddenly, struck down by a heart

* [22 March 1863, repeated on 5 April, and also given on 8 April at the Opéra-Comique at a benefit concert in aid of Rameau's descendants. Berlioz did not hear the latter two performances, as he was in Weimar, conducting the complete opera.]

† [10 April 1864.]

‡ [22 June 1863; the performance was part of the Lower Rhine Festival organized to celebrate the opening of the Kehl bridge.]

attack.* Some time after her burial in the larger Montmartre cemetery, my dear friend Edouard Alexandre (the famous organ-builder, whose kindness to me has been unfailing), thinking her tomb too modest, insisted on presenting me with a plot of ground which he had bought for me and my family 'in perpetuity'. A vault was built, and I had to witness my wife's exhumation and her re-interment in the new grave. It was a harrowing experience and I was deeply affected by it; but it was nothing to what fate had in store for me; it is as if I was destined to sup full with the worst horrors such rites can contain. Not long afterwards I was officially notified that the smaller Montmartre cemetery, where my first wife Harriet Smithson was buried, was about to be demolished and that consequently any remains that I valued should be moved elsewhere. I gave the necessary instructions at the two cemeteries, and one morning† in dull weather went alone to the burial ground. A municipal officer, who had orders to witness the exhumation, was waiting for me. The grave had already been opened. On my arrival the gravedigger jumped down into it. The coffin, though ten years in the ground, was still intact; only the lid had decayed from damp. Instead of lifting out the whole coffin, he wrenched at the rotting planks, which came away with a hideous crack, exposing the coffin's contents. The gravedigger bent down and with his two hands picked up the head, already parted from the body—the ungarlanded, withered, hairless head of 'poor Ophelia'—and placed it in a new coffin ready for it at the edge of the grave. Then, bending down again, with difficulty he gathered in his arms the headless trunk and limbs, a blackish Mass which the shroud still clung to, like a damp sack with a lump of pitch in it. It came away with a dull sound, and a smell. The municipal officer stood a few yards off, watching. Seeing me leaning back against a cypress tree, he called out, 'Don't stay there, M. Berlioz, come over here, come over here!' And as if the grotesque must also have its part in that grim scene, he added (mistaking the word), 'Ah, poor inhumanity!' A few moments later we followed the hearse and its sad contents down the hill to

* [13 June 1862, aged forty-eight. Berlioz married Marie Recio on 19 October 1854, seven months after the death of Harriet.]

† [3 February 1864.]

the larger cemetery where the new vault stood ready, gaping open. Harriet's remains were laid in it. The two dead women lie there now in peace, awaiting the time when I shall bring my own share of corruption to the same charnel-house.

I am in my sixty-first year; past hopes, past illusions, past high thoughts and lofty conceptions. My son is almost always far away. I am alone. My contempt for the folly and baseness of mankind, my hatred of its atrocious cruelty, have never been so intense. And I say hourly to Death, 'When you will.' What is he waiting for?

TRAVELS IN DAUPHINE

Second pilgrimage to Meylan—twenty-four hours in Lyons—I see Madame F—— again—a heart in turmoil

RARELY HAVE I KNOWN such mortal weariness as I suffered in the early days of this last September, 1864. Almost all my friends had left Paris, as is the custom at that time of year. Stephen Heller was the only one who remained—that delightful humorist, learned musician, author of many admirable piano works, whose melancholy spirit and passionate devotion to the true deities of art attract me profoundly. Happily my son arrived soon afterwards from Mexico and was able to give me a few days. He was not very cheerful either, and we three, Heller, Louis and I, often pooled our depression and had dinner together. One day we dined at Asnières.* Towards evening, I remember, walking by the Seine we talked of Shakespeare and Beethoven and reached a state of intense exaltation. My son could join in only where Shakespeare was concerned, Beethoven being still unknown to him. But we all three finally agreed that it is good to be alive to worship the beautiful and that, if one cannot confound and root out its opposite, one must be content with despising it and having as little contact with it as possible. The sun was setting. After having gone on some way we sat down on the grass by the river opposite the Ile de Neuilly. As we idly watched the swallows looping and skimming over the water, my mind abruptly swung round: I recognized where we were. I looked at my son and in my mind's eye saw his mother. I had sat here half asleep on the snow, on this very spot, thirty-six years before, during one of my mad fits of desperate wandering around Paris. I thought of Hamlet's cold exclamation in the graveyard, when he learns that the funeral procession is Ophelia's, whom he no longer loves: 'What! the fair Ophelia!'

'Long ago,' I said, 'I was nearly drowned just here, one winter's day, trying to cross the river on the ice. I had been walking aimlessly about the countryside since morning.' Louis gave a sigh.

* [A village (now a suburb) north-west of Paris.]

The following week my son had to go; his leave was up. A strong desire came over me to see Vienne, Grenoble, above all Meylan, and my nieces—and someone else, if I could discover her address—and I went, after first letting my brother-in-law, Suat, know that I was coming. He and his two daughters were on the station platform to meet me when I arrived. Shortly afterwards they took me off to Estressin, the place in the country just outside Vienne where they spend three or four months every summer. My charming nieces (one is nineteen and the other twenty-one) were delighted to see me, but it was a painful moment for them when, entering the drawing-room of the house in Vienne, I saw the portrait of their mother, my sister Adèle, who had died four years before.* The violence of my emotion took them aback. For them, the room, the furniture in it, the portrait itself, were part of the ordinary unthinking pattern of their everyday lives. Custom had blunted the keen edge of memory. Time, alas, had done its work. Poor Adèle! She was a person of such spirit and warmth of heart. She bore so tenderly with the asperities of my nature and was ready to indulge my most childish whims. I remember, one pouring wet morning after my return from Italy when we were all together at La Côte Saint-André, suggesting we should go for a walk. 'Yes, I'll come,' she said. 'Wait a second while I put on my galoshes.' My elder sister said we were a couple of lunatics, no one else could conceivably want to go squelching about the country in weather like this. I fetched a large umbrella and, regardless of the jeers of the rest of the family, Adèle and I descended to the plain and walked for nearly five miles, pressed together under the umbrella, without speaking a word. We loved each other.

I spent quite a peaceful fortnight with my nieces and their father in the seclusion of Estressin. But I had asked my brother-in-law if he would make inquiries in Vienne about Madame F—— and find out her address in Lyons, and the moment he did so I could not wait: I left for Grenoble and from there set out for Meylan, as I had done sixteen years before.

A wordless anxiety possessed me. I quickened my steps. There, already visible on the horizon, its treeless crown standing out

* [On 2 March 1860, aged forty-five.]

clearly above the other hills, rose the Saint-Eynard. Soon I would be seeing the little white house again and its surrounding landscape and then tomorrow—tomorrow, Lyons, Estelle herself! Was it possible?

This time there is no losing the way. I find the fountain at once. Above it stands the avenue of trees and beyond, the house. I know it all as if it were yesterday; sixteen years roll back. I walk past the avenue and continue climbing towards the tower, without looking behind me. The near-by slopes are thick with vines; the grapes hang ripe and full. I reach the tower, panting, and then, as before, turn round and take in the glorious valley in one sweeping glance. Till then I have kept my feelings fairly strictly under control, only pronouncing her name, softly: 'Estelle, Estelle!' Now an overwhelming oppression floods over me, I sink to the ground and remain a long time stretched out in an agony of spirit, while with each pulse-beat the hideous words hammer in my brain: 'The past! Time! The past! Never! never! never!'

I get up, I wrench a stone from the tower wall: it has seen her once, it may have been touched by her. I cut a branch from a nearby oak. On the way down I see with a shock of recognition, at the corner of a field where I had not been in 1848, the rock that I had searched for so eagerly, the rock on which I had watched her climb and stand. Yes, that is it, a block of granite: how could it possibly have disappeared?

I climb it. My feet rest where hers rested. This time I know that I am standing in the very same portion of air where her enchanting form once stood.

I chip a fragment from my granite altar and take it with me. Of the pink vetch I can see no sign. Either this is not its season for flowering or it has been destroyed. But the cherry tree is there. How it has grown! I pull a little strip from its bark and take the trunk in my arms and press it passionately to my breast. Dear tree: you surely remember her, and understand me!

I walk back down the hill as far as the avenue gate without meeting a soul. On the spur of the moment I decide to go in and see the garden and the house. The present owners are not likely to take me for a burglar. And what if they do! I go in. An old lady gives a start of alarm when I appear suddenly round a bend in an alley.

'Excuse me, madam,' I mumble in a barely intelligible voice. 'Would you be so very kind . . . to let me see your garden? It—it has associations for me.'

'Pray come in, walk about where you like.'

'Oh, I only want to go once round.'

A few yards on I come upon a young girl on a ladder picking pears. I nod to her and walk on, pushing my way through a tangle of bushes that almost block the way—for the little garden has been badly neglected. I pick a piece of syringa and hide it inside my coat, and come away. On my way past the wide-open front door of the house I pause on the doorstep and look in. The girl has got down from her pear tree and, no doubt warned by her mother of the curious visitor who has called, has followed me. She comes up and politely asks me in. I thank her and enter, and stand again in the small room with the window which looks out on the great wide landscape far below, and from which, when I was twelve, she showed me with a gesture of pride and delight the fabled valley lying beneath us. Everything is as it was, and the furniture quite unchanged in the drawing-room next door. I gnaw my handkerchief. The young person looks on with an expression almost of fear.

'Don't be astonished, Mademoiselle,' I say. 'Seeing all these things again like this—you see, I haven't—I haven't been back here for forty-nine years.' And I break down and flee, weeping. What can those women have thought of this strange scene whose meaning they will never know?

He repeats himself, the reader will say. It is only too true. The same endless rhythm: remembrance, regret, a soul clutching at the past, a pitiful blind urge to arrest the present and hold it as it flies, a hopeless struggle with time, a mad desire to realize the impossible, a desperate craving for limitless love. How should I not repeat myself? The sea repeats itself; its waves are all alike.

The same evening I was in Lyons. The night was like a dream. I did not sleep; I was thinking of the visit I planned to make the next day. I had decided that I would call at noon. It seemed as if noon would never come. While I waited I wrote her a letter, so that she should read it before the name of her visitor was announced; for I thought it quite possible that her first impulse would be not to receive me. The letter was as follows:

23 September 1864

Madam,

I come once again from Meylan—a second pilgrimage to the haunts of my childhood fancies, more painful still than the one I made sixteen years ago. On that occasion I ventured to write to you at Vif, where you were then living. This time I do more: I ask you to receive me. Oh, don't be afraid, I shall control myself, chafing though my heart is in the grip of an inexorable reality. Grant me a few moments, let me see you again, I beg you.

Hector Berlioz

I could not wait till noon. At half-past eleven I rang the bell. Madame F—— was in. I gave her maid the letter, and with it my card. I should only have handed over the letter; but I did not know what I was doing. Yet, on seeing my name, she did not hesitate but gave orders for me to be admitted and came forward herself to meet me. I knew her step, her bearing like a goddess. God! how her face had changed—her complexion darkened, her hair going grey. Yet my heart did not waver for an instant. My soul leapt out towards its idol the moment I saw her, as if she had still been in the splendour of her beauty. She took me into the drawing-room. My letter was in her hand. I could hardly breathe; I could not speak. Then she, with a gentle dignity:

'We are very old acquaintances, you and I, M. Berlioz . . .' Silence. 'We were children together . . .!' Silence.

The dying man, faintly: 'The letter, madam, if you would be so kind as to read it—it will explain my visit.'

She opened the letter and read it and then, putting it on the mantelpiece, said:

'So you have been in Meylan again? I suppose it was a chance visit—you did not make a special journey?'

'Oh madam, can you believe it needed chance to take me there? No, no, I have long wanted to go back.' Silence.

'You have had a very eventful life, M. Berlioz.'

'How do you know that, madam?'

'I have read your biography.'

'Which was that?'

'I think it is by Méry. I bought it a few years ago.'

'Oh no, if it is the one I think, please don't attribute such a tissue of inventions and absurdities to Méry, who is a friend of mine and an artist and an intelligent man. But I shall have a proper biography, one that I have written myself.'

'Oh, I am sure you must write so well.'

'Nay, madam, I do not mean the way it is written but the truthfulness and sincerity of what it contains. I have put in everything that I feel about you, without reserve, but without mentioning your name.' Silence.

'I also found out a lot about you,' continued Madame F——, 'from a friend of yours who married a niece of my husband's.'

'Yes, it was he whom I asked to discover the fate of the letter which I took the liberty of writing to you sixteen years ago. I wanted at least to know whether you had received it. But I did not see him again, he is dead now, and I never heard.' Silence.

Madame F——: 'As for my life, it has been a very ordinary one and a very sad one. I lost several of my children, and I brought the others up myself; my husband died when they were quite young. I have done my best to look after the family.' Silence. 'I am most touched by the feelings you have kept for me, and most grateful for them, M. Berlioz.'

At these kindly words I began to shake more violently. I looked at her, devouring her with my eyes, in imagination reconstructing the form and freshness of her vanished youth and beauty. At length I spoke:

'Madam, give me your hand.'

She held it out to me at once. I carried it to my lips and felt my heart turn to water and a thrill shoot through every bone in my body.

'May I hope,' I said, after another silence, 'that you will allow me to write to you sometimes, and very occasionally to visit you?'

'Oh yes, indeed. But I shall not be in Lyons much longer. One of my sons is getting married, and soon afterwards I am to go to live with him in Geneva.'

I rose, not daring to stay longer. She came with me to her door. There she again said:

'Goodbye, M. Berlioz: I am deeply grateful for the feelings that you still have for me.'

I bowed and took her hand again, held it for a moment to my forehead, and had the strength to go.

Wandering about in the neighbourhood of her house, blundering into the trees in the Broteaux,* or pausing on the Pont Morand to look down at the Rhône sweeping past below me, then resuming my fevered progress, I met M. Strakosch, brother-in-law of the celebrated singer Adelina Patti.

'You!' he exclaimed. 'What luck! Adelina will be so pleased to see you. She's here for some performances. They're doing *The Barber of Seville* tomorrow at the Grand Theatre. Would you like a box? You must come and hear it.'

'Thank you, but I am probably leaving this evening.'

'Well, do come and have dinner with us anyway. You know how much we always enjoy seeing you.'

'I daren't promise: it depends . . . I am not very well. Where are you staying?'

'At the Grand Hotel.'

'So am I. Well, if I'm not feeling too unsociable, I will dine with you. But don't expect me.'

I had an idea: I had been given an excuse for going back to Madame F——, for seeing her again. I hurried to her house. She had just gone out. I asked her maid to tell her that I had a box at the Grand Theatre for the following evening, and that if Madame F—— would kindly agree to come and hear Mlle Patti, I would stay in Lyons so that I might have the honour of escorting her to the performance; otherwise I would leave this evening, so I begged her to let me have an answer by six o'clock.

I returned to the hotel. Twenty minutes went by. I tried to read; I had a travel book which I had bought in Grenoble. But I could not understand a word of it. I walked about the room. I flung myself on the bed. I opened the window. I went downstairs and out into the street. Within a short while I stood before No. 56 avenue de Noailles where she lived; my legs had taken me there automatically. I could restrain myself no longer. I went up and rang at her door. There was no answer. A horrible thought struck me, and my heart sank: had she suspected that I would return and

* [One of the main avenues in Lyons.]

given orders that I was not to be admitted? The idea was absurd but I could not rid my mind of it. An hour later I was back. This time I sent the concierge's little boy up to ring Madame F——'s bell; but the door was not opened to him either. What was I to do? Stand guard outside the house? That would be boorish and ridiculous. Oh God! Go, then? Where to? The hotel? The Rhône? Perhaps she wasn't trying to avoid me. Suppose she had actually gone out? An hour later I was once more climbing her staircase. From above came the sound of her door shutting, and women's voices, speaking German. I continued up the stairs; I passed a lady, a stranger, coming down, then another, and then a third. It was she. She had a letter in her hand. 'Oh, M. Berlioz, you have come for your answer?'

'Yes, madam.'

'I have written you a note, I was just going to take it to the Grand Hotel with these ladies. Unfortunately I am unable to accept your kind invitation. I am expected in the country tomorrow, quite a long way from here, and I have to leave at twelve. I am so sorry not to have let you know sooner. I only came in and got your message a moment ago.'

She made as if to put the letter in her pocket. I almost shouted:

'Please let me have it.'

'There's no point, it's only——'

'Please—it was meant for me.'

'All right.' She gave me the letter; for the first time I saw her handwriting.

'So I shall not see you again?' I said, when we were in the street.

'You are leaving this evening?'

'Yes. Goodbye, madam.'

'Goodbye. I hope you have a pleasant journey.'

I pressed her hand and watched her walk off with the two German ladies. And then—will it be believed?—I felt almost happy. I had seen her a second time, had spoken to her again, held her hand once more; I had a letter that she had written to me, a letter which ended by giving me her 'kind regards'. It was an unlooked-for treasure, and I went off to the hotel in the expectation of being reasonably composed for my dinner with Mlle Patti. As I entered her room the exquisite creature gave a cry of pleasure and clapped her hands like a child.

'Oh, how lovely! Look, here he is, he's come!' And she ran over to me and, as is her wont, offered her chaste forehead for my kiss. I sat down at the table with her and her father, her brother-in-law and a few friends. During dinner she paid me endless pretty, coaxing attentions, and from time to time would say, 'There's something the matter with him. What is it you're thinking about? I won't have you unhappy.' When the moment came for me to leave, they decided they must see me off. The diva herself, one of her female friends and her brother-in-law drove with me to the station, where they were all allowed onto the platform. Adelina did not want to let go of me until the last minute. The whistle had blown, the train was on the point of going, when the gleeful girl flung her arms round my neck, hugging and kissing me and crying, 'Goodbye, goodbye—till next week. We shall be back in Paris on Tuesday. Come and see us on Thursday. Is that a promise? You must, you must!' The train moved off.

What would I not have given for such marks of warmth and affection from Madame F——, and from Mlle Patti the gestures of a mere conventional politeness! When this delicious Hebe pampered and petted me, it was as if some marvellous glittering bird with eyes like diamonds were humming round my head, alighting on my shoulder, pecking at my hair and, with a flutter of brilliant wings, whistling me its gayest, sweetest tunes. I was utterly charmed, but not stirred; because this girl, young, beautiful, enchanting, famous, who at twenty-two has conquered the musical public of Europe and America—I do not *love* her; whereas the aged, saddened, obscure woman, who knows nothing of art—my soul is hers, as it was once, as it will be to my dying day.

Balzac, Shakespeare himself, the great painter of human passion, never imagined that such a feeling could exist. One poet alone, an English poet, Thomas Moore, believed in the possibility of it and was able to describe it in lines that come back to me now as I write:

Believe me, if all those endearing young charms,
Which I gaze on so fondly today
Were to change by tomorrow and fleet in my arms,
Like fairy-gifts fading away,

Thou would'st still be ador'd, as this moment thou art,
Let thy loveliness fade as it will,
And around the dear ruin each wish of my heart
Would entwine itself verdantly still.

It is not while beauty and youth are thine own,
And thy cheeks unprofan'd by a tear,
That the fervour and faith of a soul can be known,
To which time will but make thee more dear;
No, the heart that has truly lov'd never forgets,
But as truly loves on to the close,
As the sun-flower turns on her god, when he sets,
The same look which she turn'd when he rose.

(*Irish Melodies*)

How many times during that grim night in the train did I say to myself, 'Fool! Why did you leave? You should have stayed. If you had, you would be seeing her again tomorrow morning. There was no necessity for you to go back to Paris.' Yes, but the fear of interfering, of being a nuisance. . . . And then, what would I have done during the long hours when I was so near yet not seeing her? It would have been torture.

After a few miserable days, I wrote her this letter. The pages which follow reveal the wretched state of my mind and the calm tranquillity of hers. It will be more obvious still what I must feel, now that I do not even have the consolation of writing to her. To have cultivated this barren love into a romantic friendship would have made too sweet a conclusion to my life. No. I must be torn and bruised to the end.

First Letter

PARIS, *27 September 1864*

Madam,

How can I thank you for receiving me as you did? Few women in such a situation would have been capable of your simple kindness and dignity. A thousand blessings on you! None the less, since leaving you I have been on the rack. In vain I tell myself that you could not have received me better, that anything different must have been either heartless or wrong; my unhappy heart bleeds as though it were literally wounded. I ask myself the reasons and I find these: it is *absence*, it is because I saw you so briefly, because I did not say to you a quarter of the things that I had to say, and because I parted from you almost as though it were for ever. And yet—you gave me your hand, I pressed it to my forehead, to my lips, holding back my tears as I had promised you I would. But now I feel an irresistible, overmastering need of another word from you, which you will not, I hope, refuse. Think! For forty-nine years I have loved you. I have gone on loving you ever since I was a child, through all the ravages of a tempestuous life. The proof is in the depth of my feelings today; they could never have revived now, in these circumstances, if they had ceased to exist even for a day. How many women have there been who ever inspired such a declaration? Do not take me for a mere eccentric, a man at the mercy of his imagination. Oh no: it is just that it is my nature to feel very intensely and at the same time, believe me, to be able to see very clearly and steadily; but my true affections are immeasurably strong, and constant even to the edge of doom. I loved you, I love you still, I shall always love you—and I am sixty-one and know the world and have no illusions. Grant me, then—not as a Sister of Mercy graciously ministering to a sick man, but as a generous-hearted woman who cures the ills she has unwittingly caused—these three things which alone can give me peace: permission to write to you sometimes; your undertaking to reply; and a promise that once a year, at least, you will invite me to come and see you. My visit might be untimely and consequently tiresome if I came without having obtained your permission. Therefore I shall not venture near you, in Geneva or anywhere else, until you send me word to come. Surely there is nothing strange or unseemly in this. What could be purer than such a relationship? Are we not both of us free? Who could be so unfeeling or unreasonable as to find it wrong? No one, not even your sons, well-bred, sensible young men as I know them to be. I must, however, say to you that it would be dreadful if I were allowed to see you only in company. If you are to bid me come, it must mean that we can talk as we did at our first meeting last Friday—a meeting which I dared not prolong and whose sad enchantments I could not savour by reason of the intense efforts I was making to restrain my emotions.

Oh, madam, madam! I have one aim left in the world—to gain your affection. Give me leave to try. I will be discreet and complying. Our correspondence shall be as infrequent as you wish it to be. You need never find it irksome; two or three lines from you will satisfy me. My visits can only be few and far between. But I shall know that your thoughts and mine are no longer sundered, and that after the long bleak years during which I was nothing to you I can at last hope that I may become your friend. And a loyal, devoted friend such as I shall be is rare. Oh, I will surround you with such deep and tender solicitude, such entire affection—half man's, half child's in its strength of feeling and simplicity of heart. And perhaps you will find an attraction in it and may one day come to say, 'I am your friend', and acknowledge that I have deserved your friendship.

Goodbye, madam. I have re-read your note of the 23rd, in which you end by giving me your 'kind regards'. That is not simply a formality, is it? is it?

Yours eternally *Hector Berlioz*

P.S. I am sending you three books. Perhaps you will be kind enough to glance at them in an idle moment. As you will realize, this is a pretext on the author's part for getting you to think of him a little.*

Madame F——'s First Answer

LYONS, *29 September 1864*

Sir,

I should think myself guilty of wronging us both, did I not reply at once to your letter and to the picture you have of the relations you would like to see established between us. I am going to speak to you frankly, from the heart.

I am an old, yes, old woman (for, sir, remember I am six years your senior), my heart blighted by times of great affliction, by

* [These were presumably his three collections of essays and reviews, *Les soirées de l'orchestre* (1852), *Les grotesques de la musique* (1859) and *A travers chants* (1862).]

physical and mental distress, such as have left me with no more illusions as to the delights and the sensations of this world. In the twenty years since I lost the best of friends I have sought no other and have kept only those to whom I was linked by long association or the natural ties of family. Since the grievous day when I became a widow, I have severed all my connections with society, I have said goodbye to worldly pleasures, in order to devote myself wholly to my children and my home. Such has been my life for the past twenty years. I have grown accustomed to it, it has become a habit whose spell nothing can now break, for this emotional seclusion alone can give me peace of mind for my remaining days on earth. Anything that disturbed their even course would be unpleasant and burdensome for me.

In your letter of the 27th you tell me that you have only one wish, that I may become your friend with the help of an exchange of letters. Do you seriously think that this is possible? I hardly know you—I saw you briefly last Friday for the first time for forty-nine years—so I cannot judge your tastes, your character, your qualities—those things which are the only foundation of friendship. When two people have the same way of feeling and of looking at things, then an affinity may spring up between them. But when they are not thus alike, correspondence cannot suffice to bring about the kind of thing you look for from me. For my part, I think it is impossible. Moreover, I must confess that I am exceedingly lazy about writing. My mind is as stiff and slow as my fingers; I find the greatest difficulty in fulfilling even the most inescapable obligations in this respect. So I cannot promise to embark on a regular correspondence with you; I would break my promise too often for me not in fairness to warn you about it in advance. If you like to write to me sometimes, I shall accept your letters. But do not expect my replies to be prompt or to the point.

You also wish me to say: come and see me. That is not possible, any more than it is possible to say: you will find me alone. I happened to be alone when you called last Friday; and if, when I am living in Geneva with my son and his wife, I am alone when you come to their house, I will receive you. But if they are with me at the time, you will have to endure their presence; for I would think it highly irregular that it should be otherwise.

I have tried to show you with all the candour and the sincerity that are fundamental to my nature what I think and what I feel. It seems I should also tell you that there are illusions, dreams which one must learn to give up when grey hairs come and, with them, the end of all desire for new emotions, even for the emotions of friendship, for they can possess attraction only when they are born of close and intimate acquaintance and in the happy days of one's youth. To my mind, the time to begin on a relationship is not when one already feels the weight of years and has lived long enough to have had one's fill of life's disappointments. I admit to you that I have reached that point. The time left to me is short, and grows shorter every day. What is the good of forming a relationship which today springs up and which tomorrow may be cut down? It would only be to store up fresh sorrows.

You must not think that in all that I have just said there is any intention on my part of hurting you by disparaging the memories you have of me. I respect them and am touched by their persistence. You are still quite young in heart. With me it is not so. I am really and truly old, no longer fit for anything but to keep—as, believe me, I shall—a large place for you in my memory. It will always give me pleasure to hear of the triumphs that you are destined to win.

Goodbye, and once again let me assure you of my kindest regards.

Estelle F——

The books you so kindly sent me arrived yesterday morning. A thousand thanks.

Second Letter

PARIS, *2 October 1864*

Madam,

Your letter is a masterpiece of grim reason. I waited until today to answer it, in the hope of being able to master the overpowering emotion it aroused in me. Yes, you are right: you ought not to embark on new friendships, you should avoid anything that might disturb your existence, and all the rest. But I would not have disturbed it—be assured of that—and the friendship for which I humbly begged, at some more or less distant time, would never have become 'burdensome' to you (you will admit that was bound to seem a cruel word to use!). I am content with what you vouchsafe me: a few kind regards, a place in your memories, and a little interest in the events of my career. Madam, I thank you; I am at your feet, I kiss your hand respectfully. You say that I may sometimes, occasionally, at irregular intervals, have an answer to my letters. Again, thank you for your promise. What I crave, what I entreat with tears, is the possibility of hearing from you. You speak of old age with such courage that I am emboldened to imitate you. I hope to die first. May I only be sure of sending you my last farewell! If it be you, let me be told that you have left this harsh world: let your son send me word of it. Forgive me. . . . My letters cannot be sent at random. Grant me what you would give to any chance acquaintance—your address in Geneva.

I shall not come to Lyons this month to see you. Clearly you would consider such a visit an intrusion.* Nor will I come to Geneva for at least a year; I would be afraid of being a nuisance to you. But your address! your address! Send it to me as soon as you know it, for pity's sake. If by your silence you would have me understand that you are resolutely, implacably set against any relationship even the most modest and unassuming between us, wishing thus to be rid of me as one does of disagreeable or dangerous people, you will have set the final seal on an unhappiness which you could so easily have alleviated. Then, madam, may God and your conscience forgive you; I shall remain in the cold outer darkness to which you will have thrust me, wretched, forlorn, and yours until death.

Hector Berlioz†

Madame F——'s Second Reply

LYONS, *14 October 1864*

Sir,

As I do not know when I shall be able to write, I hasten to send you these few lines, so that you may not think I mean to treat you

* [This refers to a proposal made by him in a letter of 30 September, not included in the *Memoirs*.]

† Oh, what a confused and contradictory letter!

like a 'disagreeable or dangerous person'. My son is coming here tomorrow evening; he is getting married on the 19th. I shall have the place full of people for several days and will have a thousand and one things to see to, as mother and as mistress of the house, so will not have a moment's freedom or leisure. Immediately after the wedding I shall be preoccupied with the preparations for the move to Geneva, which will be no light matter for me, as my health does not always permit me to be as active as I should like. I shall be leaving about the middle of November. When I am settled in my new home I will let you have my address. I cannot do so at the moment, I do not know it myself. I would have waited until my son arrived and could tell it to me, had I not feared that you would misinterpret my long silence.

With kind regards,

Yours *Estelle F——*

Third Letter

PARIS, *15 October 1864*

Madam,

Thank you! thank you! I will wait. My warmest wishes to the young couple, and to yourself. Dear madam, may this solemn event bring you unalloyed happiness. How good you are!

Don't be alarmed, I shall be discreet in my adoration.

Yours sincerely, *Hector Berlioz*

Twelve weary days later I received a formal notification of the marriage of M. Charles F——. The address was in his mother's hand, a fact which filled me with a joy such as few will understand. I was in my seventh heaven. I wrote at once.

Fourth Letter

PARIS, *28 October 1864*

Life is beautiful when certain feelings colour it! I have received the notification addressed by you, dear madam. I recognized your hand. You had a thought for the exile. An angel will reward you for the good you have done me!

Yes, life is beautiful, but death would be more so: to be at your feet, my head on your knees, your hands in mine—to end thus!

Hector Berlioz

But the days went by and I heard nothing. I made inquiries in Lyons and found that Madame F—— had left for Geneva nearly three weeks before. Could she be meaning to conceal from me her new address, which she had expressly promised me, but which I had no wish to discover against her will? Was I to have the grief of seeing her break her word?

At length, as I tensely waited, I came to believe what I said earlier, that I was not even to have the consolation of writing to her, and I grew utterly despondent. Then, one morning, while I sat in gloomy thought by the fire, a card was handed to me. To my surprise and delight it said, 'M. and Mme Charles F——'. It was her son and daughter-in-law: they had come to Paris, and on her instructions had called on me. She had sent them! I was quite overcome at finding the young man the living image of Mlle Estelle at eighteen. His wife looked taken aback by my emotion, but he seemed less surprised. Of course they knew all; Madame F—— had shown them my letters.

'Was she so very beautiful?' the young woman exclaimed suddenly.

'Oh! ——'

'Yes,' broke in her son. 'I remember one day when I was five, seeing my mother dressed for a ball and feeling a kind of shock; I was dazzled. I still remember it clearly.'

I managed to control my feelings and began to talk sensibly to my charming visitors. Madame Charles F—— is a Dutch creole from Java. She has lived in Sumatra and Borneo, can speak Malay, and has met Rajah Brooke of Sarawak. How I would have plied her with questions had I been in my normal state of mind!

I had the pleasure of seeing the two young people quite often during their stay in Paris, and of arranging some enjoyable treats for them. We talked constantly of *her*, and when we knew each other a little better Madame Charles went so far as to scold me for writing to her mother-in-law as I did.

'You frighten her,' she said. 'That is not the way to speak to her. Remember she hardly knows you, and you are both of the same generation. I can well understand her saying to me sometimes, in a sad tone of voice, as she shows me one of your letters, "What am I to answer to this?" You must learn to be calmer, then your visits to Geneva will be delightful and we will have a lovely time doing you the honours of the town—for you will come, won't you? We so look forward to it.'

'What do you suppose? Of course I will, if Madame F—— says I can.'

So I schooled myself in reticence and, when the young couple left, would not even give them a letter to take to their mother. But as there was a plan to do the second act of *The Trojans* at a Conservatoire concert,* I sent her a copy of the poem, with a request that she read it at the page marked with some dried leaves, on 18 December at 2.30 in the afternoon, the time when the piece was to be performed. Madame Charles F—— was due to return to Paris to see to some business affair which concerned her husband (who was unable to leave Geneva), and looked forward to attending the concert, the announcement of which had caused some stir in the musical world. A fortnight went by and she did not come, nor did I hear a word. The strain was becoming unbearable when at last, on the 17th, Madame Charles F—— came back and brought me the following letter:

GENEVA, *16 December 1864*

Sir,

I would have written sooner to thank you for the friendly welcome you kindly gave my son and his wife, but for having been continually unwell and in consequence very idle. But I do not want to let my daughter-in-law go without expressing my gratitude for all the amusements you arranged for them, which made their evenings pass so pleasantly. Suzanne has promised to tell you all about our life in Geneva. For my part, I should be as happy here as I was in Lyons, did I not deeply regret being separated from two of my sons and also from close friends who

* [I.e. the second act of *The Trojans at Carthage*, the fourth act of the complete opera.]

were fond of me and whom I dearly loved. I must thank you, too, for the libretto of *The Trojans* and for the charming thought you had in sending me some leaves from the trees at Meylan; they bring back to me the bright days of my youth and the happiness I had then.

On Sunday my son and I will read your work together and imagine your success and Suzanne's pleasure at hearing your music.

With kind regards *Estelle F——*

This time I did reply:

PARIS, *Monday 19 December 1864*

Last September, while I was at Grenoble, I visited one of my cousins at Saint-Georges, a little village tucked away in the bleak hill country on the left bank of the Drac, where the inhabitants live wretchedly poor lives. My cousin's sister-in-law spends her time trying to relieve their misery; she is the good angel of the district. On the day I arrived in Saint-Georges she heard of a cottage a long way off that had been without bread for three weeks. She set off at once. When she got there she said to the mother, 'Why, Jeanne, you're in trouble and you didn't let me know! You know we want to help you all we can.'

'Oh, miss, we're not in want. We've still got potatoes and a few cabbages. It's the children—they won't eat them. They cry so, they want bread. You know, children—they're so unreasonable.'

Well, madam, dear madam, you too did a good deed when you wrote to me. I had imposed a strict vow of silence on myself in case my letters should weary you, and I kept waiting for your daughter-in-law to return so that I could have news of you. She didn't come, and I was suffocating like a man who has his head under water but won't take it out. You know, people like me are so unreasonable.

And yet I am only too fully aware of the truth; believe me, I reason only too well. And I had no need of the cruel home-truths I have recently been subjected to. . . . No, but above all I do not want to upset you nor cause you the least annoyance. I will write as seldom as possible. You will answer or not answer, as you will. I shall come to see you once a year, but only as one pays a pleasant call. You know what I feel, and you will thank me for everything that I am able to conceal.

It strikes me that you are sad, and this makes me all the more——

But no, from now on I mean to give up this way of addressing you and to speak to you only of external things.

You may have heard that the act from *The Trojans* was not performed at the Conservatoire yesterday after all. The committee wanted me to cut first one thing and then another; they exasperated me (and the singers too, who were losing opportunities to shine) to such a point that I withdrew the whole thing.

Thank you, though, for so kindly being there in spirit at half past two in the concert hall, wishing luck to *The Trojans*.

While I was having all this fuss and bother in Paris, my birthday (11 December) was being celebrated in Vienna with a performance of part of my *Damnation of Faust*. The kapellmeister sent me a telegram two hours afterwards: 'Very many happy returns. Soldiers' and students' chorus performed at Männergesangverein concert. Immense applause. Encored.'

The warmth and consideration of those German musicians towards me moved me far more than my success. I am sure you understand. Kindness is a cardinal virtue!

Two days later I had a wonderful letter from an unknown Parisian about my *Trojans* score, which he described in terms that I could not possibly repeat to you.

My son has just arrived at Saint-Nazaire after an arduous voyage to Mexico, on which he had occasion to distinguish himself. He is now second in command of a big vessel, the *Louisiana*. He tells me he is off again very soon and cannot come to Paris, so I am going to Saint-Nazaire. He's a fine boy but much too much like his father for his own good; he cannot reconcile himself to the beastliness and banality of the world. We are as fond of each other as a couple of twin brothers.

That is all there is to say at present about the outward events of my life. My old mother-in-law, whom I have promised never to desert, waits on me hand and foot and never asks me the reason for my fits of depression. I read, or rather re-read, Shakespeare, Virgil, Homer, *Paul et Virginie*, and travel books. I get very depressed and am in great pain from a neuralgia which I have had for the last nine years and which baffles all the doctors. In the evening, when the pangs of mind and body and spirit get too much for me, I take three drops of laudanum and go to sleep after a fashion. If I am not so ill, but only in need of the company of a few friends, I go round the corner to see the Damckes. He is a German composer of great merit and a very able teacher, and his wife is an angel of goodness: they both have hearts of gold. According to what mood they find me in, there is music or talk, or they draw a big sofa up to the fire, and I lie stretched out on it all evening without saying a word, thinking my own black thoughts. There you have it all, madam. As I believe I have told you, I do not write anything now, and I have stopped composing. The state of the musical world in Paris and in many other places—what passes for cultivation of the arts, patronage of artists, respect for great works—enrages and sickens me. Which would seem to prove that I am not dead yet!

The day after tomorrow I hope to have the honour of escorting Madame Charles F—— (who is absolutely charming, in spite of her home-truths) and a friend of hers, a Roman lady, to the Théâtre-Lyrique. We are going to hear the second performance of Donizetti's *Poliuto*—to the end, if possible. Madame Charton, who is playing Paolina, is letting me have a box.

Goodbye, madam. May yours be only peaceful thoughts and a tranquil mind, and may you be happy in the knowledge of the love of your sons and of your friends. But spare a thought sometimes for poor children who are unreasonable.

Yours sincerely *Hector Berlioz*

P.S. It was very kind and thoughtful of you to get the young couple to come and see me. I was struck by the resemblance of M. Charles F—— to Mlle Estelle, and I am afraid I told him so, though one is not supposed to pay men such compliments.

Not long after receiving this letter, she wrote me one which included these words: 'You must not think I have no compassion for unreasonable children. I always found that the best way to quiet them and make them sensible was to distract their attention by giving them pictures to look at. I am taking the liberty of sending you one. It will serve to remind you of present realities and to destroy the illusions of the past.'

It was her portrait. Excellent, adorable woman!

Here I stop. I feel that I can now live more calmly. I shall write to her sometimes; she will write back. I shall go to see her. I know where she is, and I shall never be left in ignorance about her; her son has promised faithfully to keep me informed of any changes that may occur in her life. Perhaps, as time goes on, despite her dread of new friendships, little by little she may find her feelings growing warmer towards me. Already I am aware that my life has changed for the better. The past is not wholly and irrevocably past. My sky is blank no longer; through tears I look towards my star—distant but bright, soft, seeming to smile on me from afar. True, she does not love me. Why should she? But she might have remained for ever oblivious of me, and now she knows that I adore her.

I must be reconciled to her having known me too late, as I am reconciled to not having known Virgil, whom I should have loved, or Gluck or Beethoven—or Shakespeare, who might perhaps have loved me. (The truth is, I am not reconciled.)

Love or music—which power can uplift man to the sublimest heights? It is a large question; yet it seems to me that one should answer it in this way: love cannot give an idea of music; music can give an idea of love. But why separate them? They are the two wings of the soul.

When I see what certain people mean by love and what they look for in the creations of art, I am reminded involuntarily of pigs snuffling and rootling in the earth with their coarse snouts at the foot of mighty oaks and among the loveliest flowers, in search of their favourite truffles.

But let us try to think no more of art. Stella! Stella! I can die now without anger or bitterness.

1 January 1865

THE END

EDITOR'S EPILOGUE

He lived another four years. During that time he was often in acute pain; but at first life still held interest for him. The *Memoirs* went to the printer early in 1865, and he was kept busy that spring reading proofs and making corrections. The book was being printed at his expense. It was ready in July, and twelve hundred copies were stored in his room at the Conservatoire. A few were given privately to family and close friends; the rest would be published by his son when he was dead. Louis, now a captain in the merchant navy, came to Paris occasionally on leave, which was a growing pleasure. Sometimes—not very often—Berlioz went to a concert or to the opera: to hear Beethoven chamber music played by Joachim and friends; to see *Don Giovanni*; once to conduct, for the last time in Paris; and to hear the *Francs-juges* overture and the septet from *The Trojans* applauded by an audience of four thousand. Carvalho talked of reviving *The Trojans at Carthage*, but Berlioz was implacably opposed to a 'fresh butchery':

> The work is too big, the theatre is too small and badly equipped. I would rather not be performed at all than performed like that. Oh God! Why can't I be left in peace? I cannot and will not have anything to do with the world of directors, contractors, tradesmen, merchants—grocers of every kind, disguised under different names.

By contrast there were reports of performances of his music abroad to raise his spirits. In December 1866 he went to Vienna to conduct *The Damnation of Faust* in the Redoutensaal. Some newspaper accounts were hostile (partly, perhaps, because Herbeck, who prepared the orchestra and chorus, was involved in one of Vienna's periodic musical feuds), and it is clear that Berlioz, weakened by illness, found the rehearsals exhausting; but the concert was a triumphant success. Shortly before, he had helped to supervise a revival of Gluck's *Alceste* at the Opéra, an experience which made him, for the moment, almost happy.

Above all, the relationship with Estelle was the thread by which his life hung. Gradually she came to accept his friendship. He visited her in Geneva every summer. In between there were letters. He wrote once a month, sometimes more frequently. It was almost as great a pleasure as receiving her replies. 'It's perhaps wrong of me to write today,' one letter begins, 'it's too soon. Forgive me, I could resist no longer.' The letter ends: 'Oh what a happy evening spent here by the fire writing to you.' The postscript of another reads: 'I have broken open the envelope, I must speak to you again. But what is there to say? It's just that I feel that if I keep the letter a few hours more, my loneliness is held at bay that much longer.' It was a joy he had not foreseen: 'I might have died without ever seeing you again.'

But the sands were running out. His disease continued to gain ground. He took larger and larger doses of laudanum, which left him dazed and stupid without relieving the pain. In June 1867 came the crowning blow. Louis died of yellow fever in Havana, aged thirty-two. Berlioz's last surviving letter to him contained the prophetic phrase: 'Dearest Louis, what would I do if I hadn't got you?' Now he hastened to cut the remaining ties that bound him to life. A week after receiving the news he went to his office in the Conservatoire library, emptied a trunk full of letters, press cuttings, citations and other relics of his public and personal existence, and had them burnt. In the autumn he visited Estelle, who had recently lost a son. They met for the last time on 9 September.

The winter of 1867–8 saw the final flaring up of his once prodigious energies. He travelled to Russia and gave eight concerts in St Petersburg and Moscow to huge and tumultuous audiences. On the rostrum something of the old authority and fire revived. He conducted Gluck, Mozart, Weber, and four Beethoven symphonies (Nos. 3–6). His own music had not originally figured on any of the programmes except the last, but he was persuaded to add several works. It was with *Harold in Italy* and excerpts from *Romeo* and *Faust* that his career as conductor and musical proselytizer ended. After his return he visited his beloved Riviera, drawn by the need for sun and the call of the past. While clambering down to the sea at Monte Carlo he fell head first on the rocks and was picked up stunned and bleeding. A day or two later, at Nice, he had another, more serious fall, caused apparently by a stroke; he was in bed a week before he felt strong enough to make the journey back to Paris. Soon afterwards disaster struck his oldest friend, Humbert Ferrand. A young man called Blanc-Gonnet, whom Ferrand and his wife had adopted as a child, murdered Mme Ferrand and ran off with her jewels. He was arrested and guillotined. Ferrand died a few days later.

In the final months Berlioz was a walking shadow. The critic Blaze de Bury (son of his ancient adversary Castil-Blaze), meeting him one evening returning from the Institute, saw 'an apparition like a ghost, ashen, bent, shaking; even his eyes, those great, vital eyes, had extinguished their spark'. There were moments when he feared that he had been mistaken, that his vocation had been only an illusion. Henri Maréchal, looking back on his conversations with Berlioz at that time, was convinced that the possibility of a turn of the tide in Paris, a posthumous reaction in favour of his music, was something he no longer envisaged: the end, when it came, would be the end of everything, in France at least. It came early in 1869. He took to his bed in January and sank slowly into a coma. Friends visited him—the Damckes, Saint-Saëns, Ernest Reyer—and he would half rise to greet them; but he was silent and could only smile. His mother-in-law and Mme Charton-Demeur, his Dido, were with him when he died, at 12.30 p.m. on 8 March 1869. According to Reyer, his last words were: 'They are finally going to play my music.'

APPENDIX I

BERLIOZ DESCRIBED BY HIS CONTEMPORARIES

Age: 18 [actually 17]; height: one metre sixty-three centimetres [just over 5 ft. 4 in.]; hair: fair; nose: good; beard: incipient; face: oval; forehead: normal; eyes: grey; mouth: average; chin: round; complexion: high; special marks: none.

—Berlioz's passport, stamped 'La Côte Saint-André, le 26 octobre 1821'.

. . . a pale, tense young man, with regular features, slim figure and commanding air. One could hardly fail to notice such a strikingly forceful face, with its fine sardonic smile, eyes deep-set and alternately full of fire and veiled with melancholy (faithfully reflecting the play of his passionate, mercurial feelings), and broad forehead overshadowed by an abundance of hair.

—Léon Escudier, *Mes souvenirs*.

Hector is not at all talkative this evening. With him, everything is spontaneous, he is always quite transparent—never the slightest effort to regulate the vagaries of his humour.

—Nanci Berlioz's Diary, 22 June 1824.

M. Berlioz? Ah yes—my grandfather often spoke of him. They used to say in the town that the Doctor's son had gone to the bad, given himself up to music, playhouses, Paris, and the Lord knows what else. It was rumoured his mother never got over it. He'd come back once in a while. There was a lot of whispering when he passed by; no one dared speak to him any more—he looked so out of humour with the place. But he didn't do too badly after all, did he?

—An old inhabitant of La Côte Saint-André, quoted in the *Nouvelliste*, 2 September 1934.

His dense shock of light brown hair, swept back, overhung the collar of his suitably threadbare coat. The magnificent, marble, almost luminous forehead, a nose that Phidias' chisel might have carved, the thin finely arched lips, the chin curved lightly, not excessively, the lean look of a poet or an ascetic, made an ensemble that would have been a sculptor's delight or despair. It was like the profile on a medallion or cameo. But all these details were eclipsed at the sight of his eyes, of a pale, intense grey, and fixed on Juliet with the expression of ecstasy that pre-Renaissance painters gave their saints and angels. Body and soul were wholly absorbed in that gaze.

Pontmartin, *Nouveaux samedis*, 18th series.

Berlioz is of average height and well-proportioned; yet seeing him seated you would suppose him much taller because of the vigour of his face. He has fine, very individual features: aquiline nose, delicate thin-lipped mouth, prominent chin, deep-set, penetrating eyes, sometimes dulled and clouded over with an expression of melancholy. His forehead, already furrowed with wrinkles, is partly covered by a mane of fair, wavy hair . . .

—D'Ortigue, *Revue de Paris*, December 1832.

Suddenly, in the middle of the introduction to Caspar's song, one of my neighbours rose, leaned over towards the orchestra and shouted in a voice of thunder, 'Not two flutes, you fools—two piccolos! two piccolos!' He then sat down again indignantly. In the midst of the ensuing hubbub I looked round and saw a young man literally shaking with rage, his fists clenched, his eyes blazing, and a head of hair—how can I describe it? An immense umbrella or movable canopy over-hanging the beak of a bird of prey. It was at once comic and diabolical!

—Legouvé, *Soixante ans de souvenirs*.

Two incidents will illustrate the two sides of his nature. One evening I had invited some friends to my house—Liszt, Goubaux, Shoelcher, Sue, and five or six others. Berlioz was also there. 'What about a Beethoven sonata?' he said to Liszt. We went from my study into the drawing-room. . . . The lights were out and the fire had been banked up. Goubaux brought the lamp from my study, Liszt went to the piano, and we all found somewhere to sit. 'Turn up the wick,' I said, 'we can't see properly.' Instead Goubaux lowered it, and we were plunged in almost total blackness. The sudden change from light to dark, coinciding with the first notes of the music, made us hold our breath. It was like the scene in Rossini's *Moses*. Liszt, whether fortuitously or moved by some unconscious influence, embarked on the sad, heart-rending andante of the C sharp minor sonata. We all sat motionless where we were, rooted to the spot. Occasionally, the fire glowed for an instant through the cinders and threw our shadows in weird shapes against the walls of the room. I had dropped into an armchair; above my head I heard stifled sobs. It was Berlioz. When the piece came to an end there was a moment's silence. Then Goubaux lit a candle and we went back to my study; as we did so Liszt took hold of my arm and pointed to Berlioz, who had tears streaming down his cheeks. 'Look at him,' he whispered, 'the heir apparent.'

There you have Berlioz the enthusiast. Now the other side: we were at the Théâtre-Italien, at a performance of *Otello*. The finale of the second act contains a famous passage, in which Desdemona, at her father's feet, cries,

Se il padre m'abbandona
Che mai più mi resterà?

'If my father renounces me, what will I have left?' The first line, which is sung twice, expresses Desdemona's grief in a slow and very poignant phrase. Then, at the second line, to depict her despair, there is a sudden flurry of scales and roulades. I found them very stirring, but they infuriated Berlioz. At the end of the act he leant over and murmured in my ear, in a voice as expressive as the melody itself: 'If my father renounces me, if my father renounces me.' Then a burst of savage laughter and, faithfully reproducing all the coloratura of the score:

'I don't give a damn, I don't give a damn, I don't give a damn!' There you have the two Berliozes, the enthusiast and the mocker.

—Legouvé, *Soixante ans de souvenirs.*

Few were at ease in his company. The most eminent artists, his equals, experienced in his presence a kind of awkwardness. Gounod has often spoken to me of this. I once saw Adolphe Nourrit, one morning at my house, launch into a Schubert song with great gusto, then suddenly grow nervous at seeing Berlioz enter the room, so that having begun like a master he finished like a schoolboy.

—Legouvé, *Soixante ans de souvenirs.*

I saw beside me a lean, spare man, with tousled hair, piercing eyes, and a lively, rather noble face. Legouvé came up to him saying, 'My dear Berlioz', and we were introduced. He turned out to be a true enthusiast, not at all talkative until the moment when his enthusiasm seizes him; then, he becomes full of eloquence.

—Guizot, *Lettres à sa famille.*

Guizot, who was a good judge of men, once said to me, 'I have met many famous artists at your house, but the one that impressed me most was Berlioz. There is a truly original being!' Guizot was right. Everything in Berlioz was original. An extraordinary mixture of enthusiasm and mockery; a mind that you could never predict; conversation that had you constantly on the alert by its very changeability; long brooding silences, with lowered eyes and a glance that seemed to plumb unimaginable depths—then a sudden dazzling recovery of spirits, a stream of brilliant, amusing or touching remarks, bursts of Homeric laughter, and a delight like a child's.

—Legouvé, *Soixante ans de souvenirs.*

Even more evocative [than his analyses of Gluck] was Berlioz expounding the Choral Symphony. His articles, admirable though they are, give an imperfect idea, for they contain only his opinions; when he spoke, the whole of him was in it. The eloquence of his words was enhanced by his expression, his gestures, tone of voice, tears, exclamations of enthusiasm, and those sudden flashes of inspired imagery which spring from the stimulus of a listener hanging on every word. An hour spent in this way taught me more about instrumental music than a whole concert at the Conservatoire; or rather, when I went to the Conservatoire the following Sunday, my mind full of Berlioz's commentaries, Beethoven's work suddenly opened before me like a great cathedral flooded with light, the whole design of which I took in at a glance, and in which I walked as though it were familiar ground, and confidently explored every recess and corner. Berlioz had given me the key to the sanctuary.

—Legouvé, *Soixante ans de souvenirs.*

An admirable face, unique in combining in equal degree two contradictory qualities—greatness and subtlety.

—Pontmartin, *Nouveaux samedis*, 7th series.

. . . a splendid head, like an exasperated eagle. . . .

—Gautier, *La musique*.

At Baden [in 1860] . . . I attended a rehearsal, conducted by Berlioz, at which he went through a large part of *Orphée*. I was deeply interested and learnt many things that I had not known before. But poor Berlioz distressed me deeply. I have never seen a man so changed. . . . He knows it, and speaks of it with a sadness which pierces one to the heart. He was so pleased to see me and to be able to open his heart in talking about music; he told me he had not felt so well for a long time as in those two days.

Hallé, quoted in *Life and Letters of Sir Charles Hallé*.

With Berlioz, one always comes back to love. It was the alpha and omega of his existence.

—Legouvé, *Soixante ans de souvenirs*.

One morning I met him in the woods below the old castle [at Baden]. He seemed different, aged and sad. We sat down on a bench, for the climb tired him. He was holding a letter, which he clutched convulsively. 'Another letter?' I said with a laugh, trying to cheer him up.

'As always.' 'Oh—is she young?' 'Yes, alas.' 'And pretty?' 'Too pretty. And with a mind, and a soul.' 'And she loves you?' 'So she says and writes.' 'Well, if she gives you proof of it?' 'Oh yes, but what do such proofs prove?' . . . When I had read it, I could not help saying, 'Come on now, what on earth do you find to get so upset about? It's a letter written by a superior woman, and full of tenderness and warmth of feeling. What's the trouble?' 'That I'—interrupting me desperately—'I am sixty.' 'What does that matter, if she sees you as thirty?' 'Look at me. Look at my sunken cheeks and grey hair, look at these wrinkles.' 'Wrinkles don't count in a great man. Women are quite different from us. We can hardly separate love from beauty; but they fall for all kinds of things in a man.' . . . 'That's what she says when she sees me in my moments of despair. Sometimes, for no reason, I sit down suddenly and begin sobbing: the terrible thought strikes me. And she guesses! And then with an angelic tenderness she asks me what she can do to convince me. . . . "Have I not forgotten everything for you? Am I not running countless risks for your sake?" She takes my head in her hands, and I feel her tears fall on my neck. And yet, despite that, I hear the dread message deep in my heart: "I am sixty. She cannot love me—she does not love me." Oh my friend, what torture—to turn a heaven into a hell.' I left him without having been able to console him and, I own, deeply moved, not by his grief alone but by his humility. How far from the pathetic arrogance of Chateaubriand and Goethe, who fondly supposed that their genius endowed them with eternal youth, so that no amount of adoration surprised them. I prefer Berlioz—he is so much more human. How touching I find it that this allegedly arrogant man should so far forget that he is a great artist, and only remember that he is an old man!

—Legouvé, *Soixante ans de souvenirs*.

After the dress rehearsal [of *The Trojans at Carthage*] he called on Madame d'Ortigue . . . wife of one of his oldest friends. His appearance horrified her—he looked gaunt and white, like a ghost. 'What is it?' she cried. 'Did the rehearsals go badly?' 'Not at all,' he said, dropping into a chair. 'It's beautiful.' And he began weeping.

—Daniel Bernard in *Correspondance inédite.*

[He pretended] that he hated mankind—he, whom the least sign of sympathy moved to tears. He hated only the *profanum vulgus*, like Horace, like all artists and poets. In reality, he was not merely sincere, he was naïve in the best sense, like Haydn, whose naïvety he was fond of laughing at.

—Saint-Saëns, *Harmonie et mélodie.*

I met Berlioz in 1865. A boy of twelve, I had come to Paris to study the violin with M. Massart, the great virtuoso. At the end of one of my lessons, M. and Mme Massart asked me to stay to dinner—Hector Berlioz and M. Tadou were expected. As he entered the room he looked a striking figure. I can see him now, very aristocratic, like an old émigré. Of medium height, his body was very emaciated. Thin-lipped, with a Roman nose, his long hair was white. It had been a reddish blond colour and he had the white skin of that type. If he had had his hair short he would have resembled a Roman emperor. He wore a black satin tie well up the collar. His trousers were white and black check. They told him who I was. He was very kind and gentle in his manner. I remember as he sat there he made me sit on a foot-stool and began plaiting my hair (I wore it long) at the back of my head, and talking about Shakespeare. Of course I did not know what it was all about. When he left, he put on a light grey overcoat with a fawn collar. This much impressed me and later on when I had the money I had one made of the same colours.

—Benoit Hollander, quoted in Ganz, *Berlioz in London.*

The melancholy and silent figure of Berlioz stood out from among the other members of the examination committees or the Conservatoire juries on which he sat. While they, grouped round the green baize table obligatory on such occasions, took notes or consulted in low tones, Berlioz, alone in a corner of the room, listened detachedly, his elbow resting on the back of his chair, hand buried in his hair, in that attitude which was so characteristic, and which is immortalized in one of the best pictures of him. We divided our judges into two camps—those whose well-known strictness we feared and those of whose indulgence we had high hopes. But Berlioz we couldn't make out. He seemed determined to stay neutral in the face of those scholastic contortions which he himself had had to go through in 1830. . . . Mysterious, enigmatic, he seemed to us like the Sphynx awaiting Oedipus. His scores, when we read them, were so much at variance with what we were daily taught that even the most adventurous minds among us were nonplussed; and when we asked our teachers, they refused to discuss them and confined themselves to advising us not to study them.

—Maréchal, *Paris: Souvenirs d'un musicien.*

To the end he indulged his taste for bizarre fooling. M. Heller has told us of his passion for saying goodbye to his companions on a white paving stone near his front door, [and has described] an extraordinary occasion when Berlioz forced him to look for it on an evening of thick fog.

—Hippeau, *Berlioz intime.*

We went a long walk together. . . . 'My whole life', he said, 'has been one long, ardent pursuit of an ideal formed in my own imagination. As soon as it found a single quality, a single charm belonging to that ideal, my heart, eager for love, seized on it. Alas, disillusionment soon proved that I was mistaken.'

—Pauline Viardot, quoted in *The Music Quarterly*, Vol. II, no. I.

Gounod gave a dinner to celebrate [his election to the Institute in 1866]. The party broke up at midnight. Berlioz was tired and found walking difficult. I offered to see him home to the rue de Calais and gave him my arm, and we found ourselves once again in the deserted streets, as on so many nocturnal rambles in our youth. He did not say a word, but toiled along, stooping and occasionally giving one of those deep sighs that I knew so well. I asked the inevitable question: 'What is the trouble now?' 'I had a letter from her this morning. [Berlioz goes on to talk about Estelle.] What are her age or her appearance to me? My friend, the only reality in the world is what happens in that small corner of a human being which is called the heart. . . . At first she was astonished and rather alarmed—then, little by little, moved. I ask so little, my poor passion needs so little to sustain it. To sit near her, watch her at her spinning wheel—she spins—and pick up her spectacles—she wears spectacles—and listen to her voice, read her passages from Shakespeare, consult her about my concerns, listen when she scolds me. Oh, my dear friend—first love! Nothing can equal its power.' And choking with emotion, he sat down on a kerbstone at the corner of the rue Mansard. The light from a gaslamp fell on his pale face, giving him the appearance of a ghost; and tears such as had so moved me when he was a young man flowed down his cheeks. A profound and loving pity came over me at the sight of that great artist chained to the wheel of passion, and with a sudden intensification of emotion I had a glorious vision of the aged Michelangelo kneeling in tears by the body of the woman he loved. . . .

—Legouvé, *Soixante ans de souvenirs.*

I remember a description of Berlioz by Rimsky-Korsakov who had met the French master after one of the famous Berlioz concerts in St Petersburg in the late sixties. Rimsky-Korsakov, who was then twenty-three or twenty-four, had attended the concert with other young composers of the group. They saw Berlioz—in a tail-coat cut very short in the back, Rimsky said—conduct his own music and Beethoven's. Then they were shepherded backstage by Stassov, the patriarch of St Petersburg musical life. They found a small man, Rimsky's words were 'a little white bird with pince-nez', shivering in a fur coat and huddled under a hot pipe which crossed the room just over his head. He addressed Rimsky very kindly: 'And you compose music too?', but kept his hands in his coat sleeves as in a muffler.

—Stravinsky and Craft, *Conversations with Igor Stravinsky.*

APPENDIX II

GLOSSARY

ACADÉMIE ROYALE DE MUSIQUE, L'. The Paris Opéra—the most prestigious operatic centre in the world and the ultimate goal of a composer's ambitions during the greater part of the nineteenth century; a success there meant lucrative royalties (unusual at that time) and the virtual certainty of being widely performed in Germany; Berlioz's incessant concert-giving in the 1830s and early 1840s was partly aimed at creating a reputation which would gain him entry to it and, later, retrieve the position lost owing to the failure of *Benvenuto Cellini*. At the same time, a byword for splendour of spectacle combined with musical negligence and shoddiness. Cf. Verdi's remark that he had attended hundreds of performances there but not a single one that was satisfactory from the musical point of view. *The Trojans* was written, hoping against hope, with the Opéra in mind—the Opéra not as it was but as it might have been. Directors between 1821 and 1869 were:

1821–4	Habeneck	Chief Conductors were:	
1824–7	Duplantys	1817–24	R. Kreutzer
1827–31	Lubbert	1824–31	Habeneck and Valentino
1831–5	Véron	1831–46	Habeneck
1835–41	Duponchel	1846–60	Girard
1841–7	Pillet	1860–3	Dietsch
1847–9	Duponchel and Roqueplan	1863–72	Hainl
1849–54	Roqueplan		
1854–6	Crosnier		
1856–62	Royer		
1862–71	Perrin		

ACADEMY, The French. See under INSTITUTE, The French

ADAM, Adolphe Charles (1803–56). Successful composer of opéra-comique; professor of composition at Conservatoire from 1849. His attitude to Berlioz, epitomizing the view held in orthodox Paris circles, is summed up in the following: 'However barbarous Spontini's music is now acknowledged to be, it is like Cimarosa beside the music of this lunatic, who fancies himself a Beethoven because he combines in himself in exaggerated form all the defects of that celebrated composer and none of his qualities.' See Adam's *Lettres sur la musique française* (*Revue de Paris*, August–October 1903), for many similar expressions of contempt. Ironically it was Berlioz who, on Adam's death, succeeded to his chair at the Institute.

ALEXANDRE, Edouard (1824–88). French organist and musical inventor. One of Berlioz's executors (the other being Berthold Damcke).

ALIZARD, Louis (1814–50). Violinist, then singer. His artistry and splendid bass voice were much admired by Berlioz, who chose him to sing Friar Laurence in

Romeo and Juliet (1839). His reputation at the Opéra, however, was made in baritone roles. Died of tuberculosis at the height of his success.

AMBROS, August Wilhelm (1816–76). Bohemian civil servant, musicologist, critic, pianist and composer. Author of four-volume history of music up to the sixteenth century (*Geschichte der Musik*, 1862–81). Friend and admirer of Berlioz.

AMUSSAT, Jean-Zuléma (1796–1856). A leading surgeon of his time, renowned as a brilliant operator and also for his kindness and consideration to patients. Pioneering work on torsion of arteries and haemorrhages, etc., and on development of surgical instruments. At seventeen, Amussat served as an assistant surgeon in Napoleon's army during the French campaign of 1814 and was decorated for bravery. Berlioz and he became close friends.

AUBER, Daniel-François-Esprit (1782–1871). The most successful and prolific French opera composer of the epoch. In *Mes souvenirs* Léon Escudier compares his creative vigour in old age with that of Titian, Tintoretto and Michelangelo. Auber was director of the Paris Conservatoire from 1842 till his death. He instituted the ban on outside concerts which excluded Berlioz from the Conservatoire hall.

BACH, Johann Sebastian (1685–1750). Berlioz remained aloof from the mid-nineteenth-century revival of Bach, whom he considered an old fogey, until Saint-Saëns converted him in his last years. (See Saint-Saëns, *Portrait et souvenirs*, 9.)

BACHER, Joseph (?–?). Rich Viennese lawyer, man of letters and patron of music, admired by Berlioz, but dismissed by Wagner as 'an agent of Meyerbeer's and a pettifogging little lawyer'.

BALZAC, Honoré de (1799–1850). He was a friend of Berlioz, whose music he admired. Berlioz may be the source of the opinions on Beethoven and Rossini expressed in his short story *Gambara*. Another story of Balzac's, *Ferragus*, is dedicated to Berlioz. It is also possible that Balzac based some of the details in *Le médecin de campagne* on conversations with Berlioz (see Barzun, I, 26 n.). Berlioz's letter to Balzac accepting his offer of the loan of his fur coat to take to Russia is given in *Correspondance générale*, III, 405–6.

BARBIER, Henri-Auguste (1805–82). Poet, co-librettist (with Léon de Wailly) of *Benvenuto Cellini*; he may have first met Berlioz in Rome in the winter of 1831–2. His poems much admired by Berlioz and quoted several times in the *Memoirs*. Barbier outlived his reputation. His posthumous book of reminiscences (*Souvenirs personnels et silhouettes contemporaines*, Paris, 1883) is catty and superficial, though appreciative of Berlioz. His eloquent letter after the first night of *The Trojans at Carthage* (beginning, 'Well roared, lion!') is given in *Correspondance générale*, VI, 506. Not to be confused with the co-librettist of Gounod's *Faust*, Jules Barbier.

BECHER, Alfred Julius (1803–48). Viennese composer and critic; born in Manchester of German parents; studied law, then music, and for a short while taught at the Royal Academy of Music in London. He wrote a biography of Jenny Lind. In 1842 he settled in Vienna and contributed to the newly-founded *Allgemeine Wiener Musikzeitung*. Wagner described him as a 'passionate, highly cultivated man'. Politically active in 1848, editing the republican journal *Der Radikale* and taking part in the revolution in October; captured by Imperial troops, court martialled and shot. The Paris Conservatoire has a portrait of Becher, inscribed: 'Remember from time to time, my dear Berlioz, one of your warmest admirers. Vienna, 27th February 1846'; and below, in Berlioz's hand, 'Shot by Windisgraetz in December 1848. Poor Becher'.

BEETHOVEN, Ludwig van (1770–1827). A few isolated performances in the early and mid-1820s excepted, his music was introduced to Paris at the Conservatoire under Habeneck in a famous series of concerts beginning on 9 March 1828 (just under a year after his death). Habeneck's earlier attempt to rehearse the Eroica, some ten years before, had been a failure, the players greeting the work with laughter. He tried again in November 1826, with the nucleus of the Opéra orchestra; this session, held at his house, was the origin of the Société des Concerts (see Elwart, op. cit., 61). Rehearsals of the Eroica continued during the next fifteen months.

The discovery of his music, dating from the first Conservatoire concerts in 1828, was one of the formative influences of Berlioz's career. The influence was not directly stylistic; Beethovenian fingerprints are comparatively rare in his works: in the slow movement of the Fantastic, for example, one can point to a feeling of Beethoven in the general atmosphere of the music and in some of the cadences towards the end, and also to specific echoes of *Fidelio* (the end of Florestan's scena) and the Fifth and Sixth symphonies. The Tomb Scene in *Romeo and Juliet* shows the influence of the fragmentation of melody at the end of the Eroica Funeral March. But few other examples could be cited (the *Francs-juges* overture preceded Berlioz's discovery of Beethoven and owes the 'Beethovenian' flavour of its opening to the influence of Cherubini, Berton, etc.). Rather, it was the example that was decisive—the revelation of the immense new possibilities open to the symphony, through thematic generation, contrast, rhythm, and expressive use of the orchestra; these things and the triumphant demonstration of an art in which each work is a unique dramatic statement. Berlioz summed up what it meant to him in the phrase: 'In Beethoven there is a poetic idea constantly at work. Music is the be all and end all.' Once the Société des Concerts was launched, there was ample opportunity for studying him in performance; for example, the C minor Symphony (the most popular) was given seven times in the society's first three seasons. By the time he left for Italy at the end of 1830, Berlioz could have heard (and certainly did hear) all the symphonies except the Eighth and Ninth, most of them several times, as well as the Violin Concerto, the Emperor, and the *Egmont* and *Coriolan* overtures, the latter invariably 'concluded by the choral finale from the same composer's *Mount of Olives*'.

Fidelio, with Schröder-Devrient and Haitzinger, was in the repertoire of the German company which played at the Théâtre-Italien in 1830. In addition, Berlioz had read the Ninth Symphony and in a short study of Beethoven published serially in the *Correspondant* in 1829 defended the work against the charge of incoherence, claiming that modern music began with it. The same article describes a performance of the C sharp minor Quartet: 'After a short while people grew restless and began whispering. . . . Eventually most of them got up and left, protesting aloud that it was meaningless, absurd, intolerable—the work of a madman. . . . After a few bars of the first movement, I too had begun to be afraid that I would be bored. All the same I went on listening intently. Then the confusion seemed to resolve itself, and just when the patience of most of the audience gave out, mine revived, and I came under the spell of the composer's genius. . . .' The view that Beethoven's later works were the products of failing faculties, if not of a diseased mind, was common far into the nineteenth century, even among his admirers. Berlioz's unbounded admiration for Beethoven's music, which he shared with many other young musicians, did not help to commend him to the musical authorities of the time. Most of the older composers were antipathetic to it. Kreutzer fled from a rehearsal of the Second Symphony with his hands over his ears, and refused to play the sonata by which his name is now remembered. Cherubini confessed that he lost all sense of the tonic key in the overture *Leonore No. 3*, owing to the confusion of modulation.

Berlioz's collected writings on Beethoven are to be found in *A travers chants*. The last concerts he conducted, in Russia in 1867–8, included the Third, Fourth, Fifth and Sixth symphonies, the Violin Concerto and the Emperor.

BERLIOZ FAMILY, The. Established (and prosperous) in La Côte Saint-André as tanners from at least the early seventeenth century; the name appears in the region much further back. By the end of the eighteenth century it could boast substantial property in and around La Côte and at Le Jacques near Grenoble (thirty-five miles to the south-east), and several members in the professions. Berlioz's grandfather, Louis-Joseph (1747–1815), was a prominent barrister and, later, commissioner of audit in Grenoble. His son, Berlioz's father, also LOUIS-JOSEPH (1776–1848), was a doctor of considerable local renown who, in the opinion of many, could have made a name far beyond the region had he been more assertive in temperament and less sceptical in outlook. His publications included, in addition to the work on chronic diseases, cupping and acupuncture mentioned in the *Memoirs*, a monograph on the onset of menstruation; he was also a pioneer in hydrotherapy. All accounts of him agree as to his generosity and active philanthropy expressed not only in free medical care but also in building and agricultural projects in the interests of the poor. A picture emerges of a humane, rather melancholy man, with a wide-ranging but meticulous mind (in his last years he used to calculate the precise amount of food that he could take without aggravating his gastric condition, and weigh each day's ration of bread), a voracious reader, by temperament and also experience (as reluctant mayor of La Côte for a brief and troubled period in 1817) a confirmed disbeliever in 'Politics', an agnostic, a child of the

Enlightenment. His warnings of the grave moral dangers of 'enthusiasm' show him as an authentic product of the Age of Reason (see the letter in *Correspondance générale*, I, 83). If he acted truly according to his lights in opposing his son's vocation and, later, his marriage to an actress, Berlioz's filial devotion and the complete lack of rancour in the *Memoirs*' account of Dr Berlioz are none the less admirable; Berlioz suffered real privations in the mid-1820s, and there must have been many times during the first years of his marriage when he longed for a friendly gesture, if not financial support, from his father. Dr Berlioz took a long time to be reconciled to the idea of a composer in the family; not until May 1830 was the question finally resolved, and Berlioz could write, 'My beloved father, I can't tell you how much good your letter has done me. So you have begun to feel a little confidence in me! May I only justify it! It is the first time you have written to me like this, and I can't thank you enough. . . .' Yet, for all their differences and the periods of open hostility between them, the sense of affinity on both sides evidently went deep.

Berlioz's relations with his son—his only child—LOUIS (1834–67) were at least as close. How close, may be seen from the shattering effect of his death on Berlioz, and from one of Louis' letters (nearly a hundred have survived), written to his aunt Adèle after the death of his mother: 'I could not love my father more than I do already. . . . God alone can measure the depth of affection there is between us. I know I have sometimes been a trial to him, but I am very young, dear aunt, and young people go through terrible times. Since the loss of my mother I have felt a new strength, and I am going to use it to prevent myself causing any kind of distress to him who is dearest to me in all the world. God willing, he will be proud of his son. I cannot think of the day when he will have to leave this earth; since I became self-aware, I have felt that that day will be my last too. The thread of my life is but the extension of my father's. When it is cut, both lives will end.'

With his death in 1867 and Berlioz's less than two years later, the direct line apparently comes to an end (though there is evidence that Louis had had an illegitimate daughter). The family house in La Côte Saint-André had already been sold. Berlioz's share of his father's estate included the property at Le Jacques (which was partly sold and partly rented to a tenant farmer).

Of Dr Berlioz's six children, three survived into adult life; two died in childhood, and the gifted youngest child, Prosper, died at boarding school in Paris in 1839, aged eighteen.

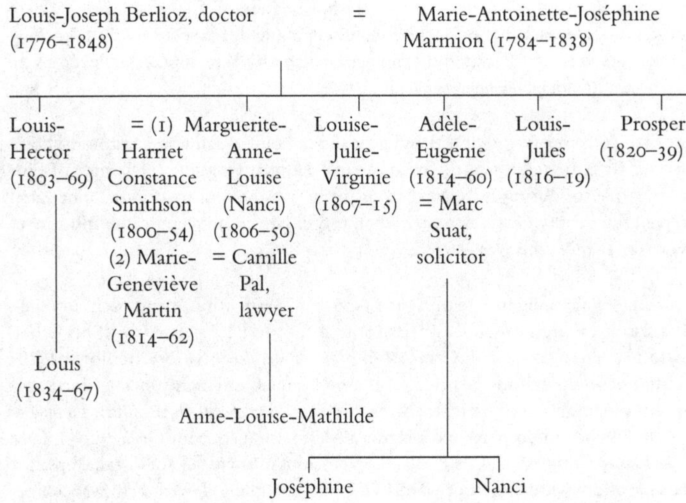

The senior living representatives of the descendants of Berlioz's sisters, Nanci and Adèle, are, respectively, M. Guy Reboul-Berlioz and M. l'Abbé Chapot.

BERTIN FAMILY, The. Patrons of Berlioz. The elder Bertin, Louis-François (1766–1841), founded the *Journal des débats* and edited it with his brother, Bertin de Vaux (1771–1842). After his death the paper was successively directed by the elder Bertin's sons Armand (1801–54) and Edouard (1797–1871). Edouard was an amateur landscape painter, and their crippled sister Louise (1805–77) an enthusiastic composer and poet; she published two collections of poems and had three operas performed: a one-act opéra-comique, *Le loup-garou* (1827); *Fausto*, a three-act Italian opera after Goethe (1831); and *Esmeralda*, the rehearsals for which were supervised by Berlioz. She also composed a *Guy Mannering* which according to Fétis was privately performed in the mid-1820s.

BERTON, Henri-Montan (1767–1844). French violinist, composer, conductor, theorist and teacher. His opéras-comiques were especially successful, but in the 1820s his fame was eclipsed by the vogue for Rossini, whom he attacked obliquely in a number of pamphlets; Berton originated the nickname Signor Crescendo. His *Virginie* (1823) was one of the works of the Gluckist school that Berlioz admired in his early days in Paris. Berton was one of Cherubini's few intimate friends; they were known as 'les inséparables'. Fouque (op. cit., 85–6) quotes a pleasant story of Berton during the French Revolution being stopped on his way to visit Grétry and arrested for not having his papers with him, whereupon his students vouched for his identity by improvising a round to the words: 'Citoyens, rendez-nous notre professeur—c'est un bon...' Berlioz's letter of 29 November 1827 to Ferrand singles him out among the members of the music section of the Institute as the one who first declared his cantata *La mort d'Orphée* unplayable 'even by an orchestra' (*Correspondance générale*, I, 161).

BLANC, Charles (1813–82). Brother of the famous socialist and historian, Louis Blanc; art critic, editor of the monumental *Histoire des peintres*, Director of Fine Arts 1848–50; during his period in office he was helpful to Berlioz. The latter repaid the debt twenty years later when, a dying man, he went to the Institute to vote for Blanc, who was elected.

BLAZE, François-Henri-Joseph (1784–1857). Music critic, composer, arranger, translator, calling himself Castil-Blaze (so as not to be confused with his father, who was also a musician). Critic of the *Journal des débats* before Berlioz; prolific author of books on musical history. His unprincipled and highly lucrative arrangements of famous composers' works included *Robin des bois* (*Freischütz*), *La forêt de Sénart* (Weber and others) and a Rossini Mass compiled from *Otello*, *Cenerentola*, *The Barber of Seville*, etc. Castil-Blaze's excursions into the field of original operatic composition were less successful. The one-act opera *Pigeon-Vole* was a flop; Berlioz savaged it in the *Débats* (15 August 1843, reprinted in *Les soirées de l'orchestre*, Eighteenth Evening, first edition only). Castil-Blaze was the leading exponent of an artistic morality widely prevalent at the time (and indeed for long afterwards). He was more enlightened than many, liking much of Beethoven's music (though characteristically arguing that it could sometimes be improved by shuffling the movements from one symphony to another). For Berlioz, however, he epitomized the Parisian musical creed against which he struggled all his life; one of his earliest published articles was an attack on Castil-Blaze for his disparagement of Gluck. Castil-Blaze's son Henry was also a critic, first under the pseudonym Hans Werner, later as Blaze de Bury.

BLOC, Nathan (?–?). Minor violinist and conductor. Befriended Berlioz and directed his first concert (26 May 1828). Leader of the first violins of the Odéon orchestra, 1824–5; in the following two years, assistant conductor there and in 1826 conductor, in which capacity he vigorously defended the musicians' interests against the management; a letter from Berlioz to his sister Nanci mentions a celebratory dinner at which the grateful orchestra presented Bloc with 'the complete works of Beethoven' (*Correspondance générale*, I, 211). In 1830 we find him in charge of the orchestra at the Nouveautés. From 1835 to 1849 he directed the newly founded Conservatoire of Music in Geneva.

BOÏELDIEU, François-Adrien (1775–1834). Composer of more than thirty operas, the most famous of which is *La dame blanche* (1825). In addition to finding the harmonies and rhythms in Berlioz's *Cléopâtre* incomprehensible, Boïeldieu played a minor part in his musical upbringing: a few of the romances transcribed for guitar in the museum at La Côte Saint-André are by him; and shortly after arriving in Paris, Berlioz saw his opéra-comique *Les voitures versées* at the Feydeau and was delighted by its gaiety.

BRANCHU, Alexandrine-Caroline (1780–1850). Leading soprano at the Opéra for most of the first quarter of the nineteenth century. Berlioz met her quite often during his student days. Her superb declamation in Gluck's operas made a profound impression on him and may well have been in his mind thirty years later when he wrote the roles of Cassandra and Dido. See my *Berlioz*, vol. I, 138–9.

BYRON, George Gordon, Lord (1788–1824). Cited by Berlioz in an autobiographical sketch of 1855 as one of the poets who have influenced him most (*Allgemeine Musikzeitung*, 11 December 1903, special supplement).

CARAFA, Michele Enrico (1787–1872). Italian-born opera composer active in France most of his career; disciple, close friend and collaborator of Rossini. In 1827 he finally settled in Paris. In 1838 he became director of Gymnase de musique militaire. Cf. Berlioz's letter to his sister Nanci after the failure of *The Damnation of Faust*: he is, he says, forced to leave France in order to live; the lucrative positions are 'gobbled up . . . by nonentities like Carafa, a musical odd-job man whose only recommendation is that he is not French'.

CARVALHO, Léon, *né* Carvaille (1825–97). Opera singer (baritone), then director (Théâtre-Lyrique, Opéra-Comique). His repertoire at the Lyrique included *Oberon*, *Orphée*, *Fidelio*, *The Pearl Fishers*, *Figaro*, and the last three acts of *The Trojans*. The most enlightened operatic impresario of his time (and renowned for a very untypical courtesy towards young composers). In 1857 Berlioz wrote enthusiastically about him after his revival of *Oberon*: 'chance has placed a man who feels and understands music at the head of a Paris opera house—a man of courage, intelligence, energy, and devotion to an idea once decided on'. However, Carvalho's enlightenment had its limits. To quote Mina Curtiss's *Bizet and His World*, 'His charm and amiability . . . were insufficient to sustain his composers and authors through the nervous strain he engendered by the perpetual changes he demanded during rehearsals . . . [and the] exasperation at his insistence on leaving the mark of his own frustrated creative urge on their creations.' He tried to get Berlioz to fill out *Orphée* with music from other Gluck operas. Carvalho can hardly be blamed for deciding not to produce the complete *Trojans*, and he took a risk in putting on as much of it as he did; but the *Memoirs*' complaints at his subsequent depredations are supported by the experience of other composers including Bizet, Saint-Saëns and Reyer. See also *Correspondance générale*, VI, 477, for Berlioz's (vain) request to Carvalho to be allowed to know best.

CASTIL-BLAZE. See BLAZE, F. H. J.

CELLINI, Benvenuto (1500–71). Florentine goldsmith and sculptor. His *Memoirs* contributed to the French romantics' neo-Renaissance cult of the artist as hero. Berlioz read the book in 1833 or 1834 in Farjasse's newly published translation and, no doubt seeing a parallel between his own struggles against convention, academic art and unhelpful authority, and those of this 'bandit of genius', based his opera on it. See also *Les soirées de l'orchestre* (First Evening): 'Le premier opéra'.

CHARBONNEL, Antoine (1803–76). Chemist, compatriot of Berlioz, from La Côte Saint-André. His adoptive great-grandson, Dr Aimé Suzet-Charbonnel, was proprietor of the *pharmacie* at La Côte in the 1960s.

CHARTON-DEMEUR, Anne-Arsène (1824–92). French lyric-dramatic mezzo-soprano, *neé* Charton; she married (in 1848) the flautist Jules-Antoine Demeur. Created the roles of Beatrice (1862) and Dido (1863) and, at the age of fifty-four, sang Cassandra in the first (concert) performance of Acts I and II of *The Trojans* (1879). In 1866 she prepared the role of Armide, under Berlioz's guidance, for a projected production at the Lyrique which was subsequently abandoned. An intimate friend during the last few years of his life, and present at his death-bed.

CHATEAUBRIAND, François-René, Vicomte de (1768–1848). Despite an unfashionably florid style and an ultra-monarchical outlook which alienated him from many of the young Romantics, his influence on them, and his intuitive understanding of the psychology of the Napoleonic generation, were profound. *Génie du christianisme* (with its discussion of epic poetry and the great tragic passions of antiquity) and *René*, the novel that originally formed part of it but was later published separately, were favourite books of Berlioz's youth and important influences on the growth of his poetic sensibility. The first version of the programme of the Fantastic Symphony postulates 'an artist, gifted with a vivid imagination, suffering from that state of soul which Chateaubriand has so admirably depicted in his *René* . . .'. In a later version this allusion was replaced by '. . . a young musician, afflicted with that psychological condition which a famous writer has called "intimations of passion" (*vague des passions*) . . .'. The symphony, a celebration of the pains and ardours of youth, might almost be a musical expression of Chateaubriand's analysis of adolescence in the *René* preface: love seeking an object, energy imprisoned in itself, 'living with a full heart in an empty world'. Berlioz not only wrote to Chateaubriand (the letter given in the *Memoirs*) but met him more than once, and at one time (1830) had hopes of being able to compose an *Atala* for the Opéra. Chateaubriand was a friend of Bertin's, and an important contributor to the *Débats* during its period of opposition to the government in the late 1820s. His autobiography, *Mémoirs d'outre-tombe*, serialized in the 1840s, may have helped to stimulate Berlioz to write his own memoirs.

CHÉLARD, Jean-Baptiste-Hippolyte (1789–1861). French composer and conductor; his father was a clarinettist in the Opéra orchestra. Winner of Prix de Rome, 1811. Violinist in Opéra orchestra. During the 1820s friendly with Berlioz, who names him as one of those who admired his *Huit scènes de Faust* (*Correspondance générale*, I, 255). Two of Berlioz's *Neuf mélodies* were performed at one of the concerts given by his Athénée Musical (18 February 1830). Chélard's

Macbeth (libretto by Rouget de Lisle, after Ducis and Shakespeare) was a failure at the Opéra (1827) but, rewritten, became a popular work in Germany, and also in London, where he conducted it at Drury Lane (1832). When the July Revolution ruined his music business, Chélard settled in Germany, becoming kapellmeister at Weimar (1836–52). He was one of the first to conduct with a baton.

CHENAVARD, Paul-Joseph (1808–95). French historical painter. In 1848 he began a vast series of frescoes for the Panthéon, depicting the progress of humanity from Genesis to the French Revolution, but the project was abandoned in 1852 when the Panthéon was restored to the Church.

CHERUBINI, Maria Luigi Carlo Zenobio Salvatore (1760–1842). Italian composer who in 1788 settled in Paris, where twelve of his twenty-four operas were composed, the most famous being *Médée* (1797) and *Les deux journées* (1800). From 1822 till his death, director of the Conservatoire. He was getting on for seventy by the time the young Berlioz came regularly into contact with him, set in his views and, by the standards of the day, conservatively minded: he admired Beethoven a good deal less than Beethoven admired him, and considered Bach's harmony dubious. He had a generous side (seen, for instance, in his treatment of Lesueur after the Bourbon restoration), but by this time he lived in a very narrow circle of friends (which included Ingres). His temper was notoriously short and he was known for a sharpness of tongue from which even his pupils suffered (e.g. his retort at the dress rehearsal of one of Halévy's operas when the latter, anxious at his continuing silence, asked him why he said nothing: 'I have been listening to you for two hours and you have said nothing to *me*!') In short, as Tiersot remarks, there were plenty of reasons why, despite their common enthusiasm for Gluck, the crusty old director and the determined young student should have clashed, and why manœvres which Cherubini would find impertinent, Berlioz would equally naturally see as mere common sense. It did not prevent Berlioz from sincerely admiring (and being influenced by) his music—an admiration which seems, however, not to have been reciprocated. Cherubini was one of the few members of the music section who voted for Berlioz in 1829 (the year of *Cléopâtre*); but, if the latter's letter to his father is correct, this was for 'considérations personelles'. Imitations of his strong Italian accent were not confined to Berlioz, as we can see from Gounod's, quoted in Fouque, op. cit., 134: Cherubini to Le Sueur—'Que zé n'y comprends rien—a la répétizzione z'ai toujours beaucoup de soussès, et à l'église c'est toi qui emporte tout.' If Cherubini is cast in something of the role of comic-strip villain in the *Memoirs*, this is no more than a burlesque presentation of the truth. Cherubini was symbolically and literally at the head of the musical establishment which was attempting to keep Berlioz out, and which in fact never accepted him.

CHOPIN, Frédéric-François (1810–49). Chopin was on friendly terms with Berlioz during the 1830s, visiting him at his house in Montmartre; he played at several of his concerts, attended a number of others (tickets and seating plans with his name survive) and helped him with the piano transcription (for four hands) of the *Francs-juges* overture published in 1836. But from various remarks it is clear that Chopin was not an admirer of Berlioz's music. For his pronounced rubato, on which the *Memoirs* comments adversely, cf. Hallé, op. cit., 34: 'A remarkable feature of his playing was the entire freedom with which he treated the rhythm'; but he adds, it 'appeared so natural that for years it never struck me. . . . I once ventured to observe to him that most of his many mazurkas . . . when played by himself, appeared to be written, not in 3–4, but in 4–4 time, the result of his dwelling so much longer on the first note of the bar. He denied it strenuously, until I made him play some of them and counted audibly four in the bar, which fitted perfectly. Then he laughed, and explained that it was the national character of the dance which created the oddity. The more remarkable fact was that you received the impression of a 3–4 rhythm whilst listening to common time.' To Berlioz's very precise, highly strung sense of rhythm, this (like the similar rhythmic freedom in Wagner's conducting) must have been disagreeable.

COOPER, James Fenimore (1789–1851). American novelist working in Paris in the 1820s, highly popular among intellectuals; his books were issued there in translation almost simultaneously with the English edition. The image of the noble savage in direct communion with unspoiled nature had profound appeal. Cf. Berlioz to J.-L. Duc (after the 1848 Revolution had apparently destroyed all remaining hope of his gaining an established position in France): 'Like a savage I hold on to my freedom, I keep moving so long as the earth bears me and there are deer and moose in the woods; and if I often suffer from cold and hunger, exhaustion, lack of sleep and the ravages of the pale-face, at least I can daydream in my own time beside the waterfalls and in the silent forests, and worship the grandeur of nature and thank God that I still have a feeling for its beauties' (*Correspondance générale*, III, 546–7). He read the novels avidly as they came out; see the following passage, from a letter to his sister Nanci: 'I am prepared to think well enough of you to assume that you know your Walter Scott inside out—that giant of English literature; but Cooper—do you know Cooper, the American Scott? Although he doesn't equal or indeed come anywhere near his model in dialogue and characterization, his pictures of untamed nature are marvellous, and his main characters are full of interest. Among others there is one who appears in three different books—the famous hunter Natty Bumppo, a unique figure, a European who from a taste for solitude has virtually become a savage. . . . As you read each book you get more and more attached to him, and his death, though bound to come in the end—he's 90—is indescribably affecting. *The Prairie* only came out a month ago. I devoured it straight off; I reached the end at 7 p.m., and was still there at 11, at the foot of one of the columns of the Panthéon, crying my heart out!' (4 June 1827, *Correspondance générale*, I, 155–6.) Berlioz's overture *Le corsair* was at one point called *Le corsair rouge*, which was the French title of Cooper's *The Red Rover*.

CORRESPONDANT, Le. Weekly journal of liberal Catholic and monarchical views, founded in 1829 under the patronage of St Peter and the Virgin Mary as a propagandist weapon, in a period of fierce—and fiercely resisted—clericalism in French public life. It aimed to reconcile the progressive forces in French society with the Church. Berlioz, who contributed to the paper off and on during 1829 and 1830, did not share its opinions, but was allowed a fair degree of freedom—though one article was rejected as 'a little too hard on the Italian school'. In 1831 the paper was replaced by the *Revue européenne*, which lasted till 1835.

COSTA, Sir Michael (1808–84). Italian-born conductor active in England for more than fifty years. A famous orchestral disciplinarian. Cf. Shaw: 'The [Bayreuth] orchestra, conducted by Felix Mottl, played with an absolute precision and a touch of austerity which reminded me of Costa, who, obsolete as his tastes were, and quickly as he has been forgotten, deserves this reminiscence for having kept his foot down so long on slovenly and vulgar orchestral work. So much so that I sometimes wish he were alive again; though there was a time when—musically speaking, you understand—I heartily wished him dead' (*London Music in 1888–89*, 184). Costa was given to 'trombonizing' Mozart's orchestration; Berlioz likened the process to 'slapping a trowelful of mortar on a Raphael painting'. On the other hand, Costa's puritanism was so offended by the brass chords accompanying the solo violin in the Benedictus of Beethoven's Mass in D that he is said to have struck them out of the score. Berlioz's suspicion of his intentions in 1853 no doubt sprang partly from Costa's having inadvertently forgotten to invite the critics to the dress rehearsal of *Benvenuto Cellini*, so that they heard the work only at the chaotic first night. True to his time, Costa composed several oratorios, on one of which Rossini commented: 'Ce bon Costa m'a envoyé une partition d'oratorio et un fromage de Stilton. Le fromage était très bon.'

CÔTE SAINT-ANDRÉ, La. Then, as now, a town of a few thousand inhabitants, lying a little to the east of the Rhône thirty miles from Grenoble, off the main route of commerce and armies. The natural setting is beautiful (*pace* Boschot—'ni de beauté ni de mystère'—and Tiersot—'cette vallée... triste et nue'), with a Berliozian mixture of grandeur and intimacy, a richness controlled by a classical spirit appropriate to a region that marked the furthest point of full Roman influence.

The first surviving sign of musical stirrings at La Côte is a letter written in 1805 by the Mayor to Bernard's music shop in Lyons, ordering instruments for a military band: clarinets, bassoons, horns, a serpent, a 'Chinese bonnet' and a 'fine pair of cymbals, from Constantinople or Smyrna—only, they must be Turkish—costing 15 louis'. Negotiations followed: 'You ask me the price of the serpent. You can have it for 16 bottles—i.e. half-litres—of Eau de Canel from the Durocher brothers' distillery at La Côte.' In 1807 Bernard supplied the town with a teacher, a M. Bouchmann, 'an upright and honourable man and a master of his trade; he plays clarinet, flute, bassoon and violin, and can teach the horn'. Bouchmann wrote to the Mayor a few weeks later: 'Je suis charmai de lai abithe Parmis vos amateur. Mais je ne peus parti que dans le couransd de la saimaine prochaine...' He was employed at a hundred francs a month, but for how long is not known. An 'inventory of the musical instruments of the National Guard at La Côte Saint-André, the property of the commune', dated 1 April 1821—seven months before Berlioz left for Paris—contains two clarinets in F, seven clarinets in

C, two piccolos, one bassoon, three horns, one old-style horn, an old-style trumpet and a valve trumpet, one trombone, bass drum, cymbals and triangle (see *Ménestrel*, 1904, 83–4). Local tradition, according to Edmond Hippeau, had it that Berlioz led the school outings with his drum: '*there* was a drummer' (*Berlioz intime*, 152). There seems to have been no piano at all in La Côte Saint-André during Berlioz's childhood; its great popularity as a domestic instrument came slightly later in France. But the folk-music of the region—litanies (one of which is used in *The Damnation of Faust*), hunting calls, *ranz des vaches*, etc.—must be accounted a vital influence.

DABADIE-LEROUX, Louise-Zuléma (1804–77). French soprano, *née* Leroux. She made her début at the Opéra as Antigone in Sacchini's *Oedipe* (1821). Madame Branchu's successor on the latter's retirement. Jemmy in the first *William Tell* (1829), in which performance her husband, the French baritone Henri-Bernard Dabadie, whom she had married in 1822, played Tell; he also created the roles of Cinna in *La Vestale* (1807) and Belcore in *L'elisir d'amore* (1832).

DALAYRAC, Nicolas (1753–1809). Composer of over fifty opéras-comiques, songs from which were part of the repertoire of music that Berlioz was brought up on. When he went to Paris he heard Dalayrac's *Azémia* (which he found 'enchanting') as well as the ballet created by Persuis (1813) out of the one-act *Nina, or the woman crazed by love* (1786). Opéra-comique of the late eighteenth and early nineteenth centuries was a not unimportant factor in the formation of Berlioz's musical style, and he remained fond of it in later life.

DAMCKE, Berthold (1812–75). German composer, violinist, pianist and critic who settled in Paris in 1859. He and his wife were near neighbours of Berlioz, who in his last years often spent the evening with them. They were among the few to whom Berlioz presented or lent a copy of his *Memoirs* when the book was printed in July 1865 (the others being his son, his uncle Félix Marmion, his nieces, his mother-in-law, Estelle, the Massarts, Reyer, and the Princess Sayn-Wittgenstein). He made Damcke one of his executors.

DANTAN, Antoine-Laurent (1798–1878). French sculptor, one of Berlioz's fellow-students at the French Academy in Rome; not to be confused with his brother, Jean-Pierre Dantan 'the Younger' (1800–69), who achieved great notoriety with his series of caricature-statuettes, including one of Berlioz.

DÉBATS, Journal des. One of the most successful and respected daily newspapers of the nineteenth century. Founded in 1791, it combined well-informed reporting of home and foreign affairs, detailed accounts of parliamentary debates, and serious political comment, with brilliant criticism of the arts, to which was added in 1837 the serialization of novels (*The Count of Monte Cristo*, Eugène Sue's *Les mystères de Paris*, etc.) Under Bertin the elder, his son Armand, and an editorial staff which included both academics and men with first-hand experience of politics and administration, the paper achieved exceptionally high intellectual and technical standards. Its period of greatest influence was the 1830s and 1840s; but its opposition to the ministries of Charles X after the fall of Chateaubriand (who wrote for it) was an important factor in the politics of the last years of the Bourbon Restoration. The *Débats* stood for constitutional monarchy, moderate Conservatism, and political liberties as interpreted by an 'enlightened' middle class.

DÉRIVIS, Henri-Etienne (1780–1856). The leading bass at the Opéra in the first quarter of the nineteenth century, noted for his powerful voice and energetic style. Rossini wrote the part of Mohammed in *The Siege of Corinth* for him; it was not generally thought to suit him, though he sang Italian roles as late as the mid-1840s; his greatest successes were in the works of Gluck and his school.

DESCHAMPS, Emile (1791–1871). French poet, an influential figure among the early Romantics; translator of Shakespeare's *Romeo and Juliet* and author of the text of Berlioz's symphony on the play. His brother Antony (1800–69) provided the text for the last movement of the Funeral and Triumphal Symphony in 1842.

DESSAUER, Josef (1798–1876). Viennese opera and lieder composer, born in Prague, where he was a pupil of Tomaschek. Berlioz first got to know him in Paris *c.* 1830. Wagner, who had met Dessauer in Prague, came across him again in Paris in 1841 and, at his request, drafted him a libretto on one of Hoffmann's tales for two hundred francs; but the project was turned down by the Opéra. Wagner corroborates Berlioz's picture of a very melancholy man.

DORANT, F.-X. (17?–18?). Dorant was employed by La Côte Saint-André from 24 July 1819 (the date of the only surviving contract), possibly earlier, and at least until 1 April 1821, on which date an inventory of instruments belonging to the town's National Guard names him as first clarinet in the band. Berlioz met his old music teacher again years later, when he went to Lyons to give a concert. Dorant, then living in Vienne, responded to the call for players to make up the ad hoc orchestra. Master and pupil met in the street. '"I'm playing for you!" exclaimed Dorant; "what shall it be—violin, cello, clarinet or ophicleide?" "Ah, my dear master, it's clear you don't know me. Violin—I can never have too many. No one ever has." "Very well—but I'm going to feel awfully awkward in the middle of your great orchestra, not knowing a soul!" "Don't worry—I'll introduce you." And next day at the beginning of the rehearsal I pointed him out to the assembled company: "Gentlemen, I have the honour to present to you a very remarkable teacher from Vienne, M. Dorant. There's a grateful pupil of his among us today. That pupil is I. In a moment you may decide that I don't do him any great credit; all the same, I want you to treat him as if you thought otherwise, and as he deserves." You can imagine the surprise and the applause. Dorant was more alarmed than ever. But once launched on the symphony, the demon of music took possession of him; before long I saw his bow bounding, his face flushed with excitement; I on my side felt a strange sensation at conducting the March to the Scaffold and Scene in the Fields, played by my old guitar teacher whom I hadn't seen for twenty years' (*Les grotesques de la musique*, 289–90).

DORVAL, Marie (1798–1849). The leading French romantic actress of her time; a great admirer of Harriet Smithson and much influenced by her.

DUBOEUF. See FORNIER, Estelle.

DUMAS, Adolphe (1806–61). Journalist, poet and dramatist; no relation of the great Alexandre.

DUPONCHEL, Charles-Edmond (1795–1863). Architect, designer, director of the Opéra 1835–40. Administrator under Pillet 1841–7 and director again 1847–9. 'A thin, yellow man, with a face . . . like an undertaker' (Heine).

DUPREZ, Gilbert-Louis (1806–96). French tenor who dominated the Paris Opéra in the decade 1837–47, displacing Adolphe Nourrit. Duprez was the thirteenth of twenty-two children of a Paris parfumier. Originally a rather light lyric tenor, he developed darker tones and considerable power in Italy, where he sang Arnold in the Italian première of *William Tell* (1831) and created the role of Edgardo in *Lucia di Lammermoor* (1835). He was reputedly the first tenor to sing top C as a chest note, with electrifying effect—though Rossini likened the sound to the 'squawk of a capon having its throat cut' and considered that the note in question (in Arnold's aria in Act IV) should be sung with head voice, as Nourrit, the first Arnold, had done. Berlioz admired Duprez's developed 'Italian' quality, preferring it to Nourrit's (*Correspondance générale*, I, 549), but he soon came to doubt his sensitivity and artistic humility. The parable of the great tenor's rise and fall in *Les soirées de l'orchestre* (the 'Astronomical Study' in the Sixth Evening) is partly based on Duprez. Duprez's *Souvenirs d'un chanteur* (Paris, 1880) gives an account of *Benvenuto Cellini* from the other side: 'In 1839 Auber's *Lac des fées* became my second major creation—for I cannot give that name to the role with which Berlioz charged me in *Benvenuto Cellini*, given in 1838 for only three performances. We know that Berlioz's talent, fine musician though he was, was not exactly a melodic one. *Cellini*, like his other works, was written in a style which to my Italian-trained ears sounded very strange. When this opera appeared, I was on the point of becoming a father for the third time. On the evening of the third performance I set out from home, leaving Mme Duprez in imminent expectation of the happy event—a fact which, as may be imagined, put me in some degree of agitation. Having had two daughters, I passionately wanted a son; and as I went out I begged Dr Gasnault . . . to come and inform me if my wife was brought to bed of a boy. While I was on stage for the last act, I perceived my faithful doctor in the wings, his face radiant. My delight caused me to forget myself. When one loses one's place in music as learned and complicated as Berlioz's, it is not easy to find it again. I got out of the business none too well. However, that had nothing to do with the very slight success of the opera, although the composer held me responsible and nourished a grudge against me because of it. The fact is that Duponchel soon wearied of a work which, novel as it was, made less money than the old-established operas, and *Benvenuto Cellini* returned to its drawer, never to emerge again.' Relations were not entirely severed, however, for Duprez appeared at Berlioz's concert of 19 November 1843, giving the first Paris performance of *Absence* and singing in the trio from *Cellini*. His voice, perhaps from ill-usage, seems to have declined rapidly in the late 1840s. In later life he was a successful teacher, running his own 'école spéciale du chant'. He composed a number of sacred works, songs, operas, etc. Duprez's daughter Caroline (1832–75) was also a professional singer, under the name Vandenheuvel-Duprez (referred to in *Memoirs*, 545); her husband was a répétiteur at the Opéra.

ERKEL, Ferencz (1810–93). Hungarian composer, conductor and theatre director, a sort of Hungarian Smetana. Still performed in his own country; and one at least of his many operas, *Bánk Bán*, is known outside Hungary.

ERNST, Heinrich Wilhelm (1814–65). German violinist and composer; a much travelled, brilliantly successful and versatile artist (he played the viola solo several times in Berlioz's *Harold*). In 1855 he settled in England and married. His health declined and he played little in the last few years of his life.

FERLOTTI-SANGIORGI, Santina (1805–53). Italian soprano; Mathilde in the Italian première of *William Tell* (Lucca, 17 September 1831). Sister of the well-known Donizetti and Verdi baritone Raffaele Ferlotti.

FERRAND, Humbert (1805–68). French poet and pamphleteer, close friend of Berlioz most of his adult life (Berlioz's correspondence with him, collected in *Lettres intimes*, runs with few interruptions from 1824 to 1867). Their characters were very different and they disagreed on religious issues (Ferrand being a devout Catholic). Boschot makes much of what he considers Ferrand's timid and lethargic nature; and despite all the plans for collaboration, Ferrand supplied texts for only two of Berlioz's works, *Les francs-juges* and *La révolution grecque*. Yet their temperaments seem to have complemented each other, and the letters Berlioz wrote to him are an invaluable biographical source; he was Berlioz's 'Horatio'. Ferrand spent a good deal of time in Sardinia, working on (and writing about) the Count of Marmora's schemes for agricultural reclamation, and was elected a member of the Turin Academy of Sciences. His poetry and fiction were published under the pseudonym of Georges Arandas. According to Berlioz's sister Nanci, whose interest in him had evidently been aroused by her brother's reports of his literary interests and high moral principles, the young Ferrand was small and unprepossessing, with a profile like a nutcracker and a voice that was alternately low-pitched and squeaky (see my *Berlioz*, vol. I, 135, 291–2). Ferrand's last years were clouded by poverty and ill health—he became partly paralysed—and his end was tragic, his wife being murdered by a young man whom they had adopted as a child. Ferrand died soon afterwards.

FÉTIS, François-Joseph (1784–1871). Belgian musicologist, critic, editor, teacher, administrator, composer; on the staff of the Paris Conservatoire, 1821–33; founder of the *Revue musicale* and editor 1827–33; director of Brussels Conservatoire from 1833. A man of astonishing energy; Fétis' eight-volume *Biographie universelle des musiciens* has been criticized for its many inaccuracies, but it was remarkable for its time, and represents a great feat of industry and persistence. His early relationship with Berlioz is somewhat obscure; the impression given by the *Memoirs*, though broadly correct, tends to overdramatize it and omits some relevant details. Berlioz is wrong, for instance, in implying that they were open enemies by the time he left for Rome. His exposure of Fétis for correcting Beethoven's harmony took place at the beginning of 1829; yet eighteen months later Fétis was treating him as a promising protégé, at the time of the rehearsals of the *Tempest* Fantasy. Berlioz, however, no doubt detected the element of gratified vanity in Fétis' approval (see Jullien, op. cit., 58 n.). He can have been under no illusions about the essential nature of his patron's musical taste; Fétis' reviews of Beethoven's symphonies at the Conservatoire concerts were full of observations such as this (on the Seventh Symphony): 'The first and last movements are protracted improvisations by a gifted composer on an off day. Occasionally the great man retrieves himself; more often he loses his way completely. I have no space to list all my criticisms of these two movements; I will cite only the second repeat of the first, which contains a series of dissonances that resolve upwards, in a manner excruciating to the ear. A grammatical error may be condoned if the effect is happy; when the effect is as outlandish as this, it is inexcusable.' The C sharp minor Quartet was 'the final spasm of a demented imagination'. In Berlioz's book, this sort of thing damned a man more than personal injury. The tone in which he speaks of Fétis in a letter written to Hiller from Rome (*Correspondance générale*, I, 515) is withering. But there may also be a personal motive at work here; it is not impossible that Berlioz believed, perhaps with reason, that Fétis, who was friendly with his fellow-Belgians the Mokes, had had a hand in breaking off the engagement. (Boschot even suggests that Fétis had been Camille's lover before Berlioz.)

Fétis' published criticisms of Berlioz's music after the *Lélio* episode are virulent. Later, there was something of a rapprochement. Fétis helped him during his visit to Brussels in 1842 (a fact acknowledged in *Voyage musical* but omitted from the *Memoirs*—which seems to show Berlioz putting a fictional gloss on the truth). The article on Berlioz written in 1855 for the revised *Biographie universelle* is quite moderate in tone, even expressing (in Barzun's phrase) 'a somewhat alarmed admiration'. Later still, Gluck and a common dislike of 'the music of the future' brought them further together. After the revival of *Alceste* at the Opéra in 1866, Fétis, now eighty-two, wrote to Berlioz: 'You have penetrated deeply into the great composer's mind. . . . Such an interpretation bespeaks not only a great musician but a poet and a philosopher as well. . . .' Berlioz answered: 'Your letter delighted me. . . . If anything could restore to me that courage which I no longer need, it would be approval such as yours. I defend our gods. But in the small band that fights—*nullam sperante salutem*—against the Myrmidons, you are still a spear, while I am now only a buckler.' On this note of faintly ironic respect, the relationship ended.

FORNIER, Estelle (1797–1876). Berlioz's 'Stella montis', *née* Estelle Duboeuf. It was her maternal grandmother, Madame Gautier, who owned the house in

Meylan. In 1828 Estelle married a man considerably older than herself, a lawyer called Casimir Fornier, who became president of the High Court in Grenoble. He died in 1845, three years before Berlioz first revisited Meylan. She had six children, of whom a son and daughter had long been dead by the time Berlioz met her again in 1864. In his will he left her a life annuity of one thousand six hundred francs which helped to make her last years more comfortable.

FRANCS-JUGES, Les. The source used by Berlioz and Ferrand for this opera was probably J.-H.-F. de Lamartelière's play *Les francs-juges ou les tems de Barbarie* (1807, revived 1823, published 1824). The opera, generally said to have been unfinished, was completed about October 1826; but the Odéon Theatre, for which it was intended, failed to get government permission to put on new French operas, and the work was not performed. It was the projected reworking of it for the Opéra that remained incomplete.

FREDERICK WILLIAM IV (1795–1861). King of Prussia 1840–61. A weak ruler, who failed to sustain his rather sentimental liberal impulses and finally died insane, but a king who took his responsibilities for the support of art seriously.

FUGUES. A bee in Berlioz's bonnet which had a rational origin but which was always liable to get out of control. He imbibed Lesueur's detestation of 'fugues which express nothing, and whose only object is to display the composer's vain erudition and the solution of some problem [and which] should be banished from our churches . . . resembling as they do the labour of that legendary pea-stringer who threw peas from a distance on to the point of a needle. It is true that he wrung a kind of admiration from the astonished Alexander the Great; but how did that judicious monarch reward his skill? He told his men to "prepare a bushel of the vegetable and make him a present of it"' (Fouque, op. cit., 178). On the whole, Berlioz's practice is consistent with his principle; the formal fugues in his works nearly always have a demonstrable dramatic motivation, though in general he is happier with free fugato, of which, as Wilfrid Mellers says, he is a master (e.g. the Convoi funèbre in *Romeo*, the Offertorium in the Requiem, etc.). His irrationality expresses itself, rather, in his refusal to recognize a similar validity in other composers' fugues, especially with regard to fugues on the single word 'Amen', a *bête noire* of his—although 'Amen' is a dramatic concept as sonorous and meaningful as 'pleni sunt coeli et terra gloria eius'. Berlioz's theoretical abhorrence of contrapuntists was partly a reaction against the unimaginative rigidity of Parisian musical academicism, partly a reflection of low standards of performance of sacred music, and partly a defence of his adored Gluck, but it did not prevent him from being, as Henry Barraud justly observes, an essentially linear and contrapuntal, because melodic, composer.

GANDONNIÉRE, Almire (?–?). An obscure journalist and man of letters, founder and editor of the short-lived political journal *Archives de la banlieue*, author of *Satires par Archiloque* (1844) and, in 1848, of the text of a 'republican cantata', *Le tour du monde*. He wrote some of the text of the first three parts of *The Damnation of Faust*.

GANZ, Leopold (1810–69). German violinist, leader of the Berlin Grand Opera during Berlioz's visits in 1843 and 1847. His brother Moritz (1806–68) was leader of the cellos in the same orchestra. The eldest of the three Ganzes, Adolph (1796–1870), was kapellmeister at Mainz and Nuremburg before he settled in England with his violinist son Wilhelm—later William—in 1848 (when Berlioz was at Drury Lane); both were naturalized. William (1833–1914) played in Berlioz's famous performances of the Ninth Symphony in 1852, and (as one of the antique-cymbal players) in *Romeo and Juliet* in the same year; later he became a successful conductor. He introduced the Fantastic Symphony to London in 1881. William Ganz was Patti's favourite conductor (see Shaw's account in *London Music in 1888–89*, 53–4). His barrister son Albert (1873–1947) kept up the family tradition with his pioneering monograph *Berlioz in London*.

GASPARIN, Comte Adrien de (1783–1862). Agriculturalist and 'Doctrinaire' (centre-left) politician, Minister of the Interior 1836–7 and again in 1839.

GAY-LUSSAC, Joseph-Louis (1778–1850). Leading French chemist and physicist of the day; discoverer of Gay-Lussac's law of the expansion of gases; made balloon ascents to verify theories about the earth's magnetic field. In 1841 he distinguished himself by opposing Guizot's measure banning the employment of children under eight in factories.

GAZETTE MUSICALE. Weekly, founded in 1834 by the music publisher Maurice Schlesinger; Berlioz contributed to it off and on (though with decreasing frequency) from its foundation until 1859, and occasionally edited it during Schlesinger's absences. In 1835 the journal absorbed its rival the *Revue musicale* and became the *Revue et Gazette musicale*. On Schlesinger's retirement in 1846, it was taken over by Brandus, the successor to Schlesinger's publishing house, and edited by Edouard Monnais. It lasted until 1880.

GERONO, Hyacinthe (1797–1868). One of Berlioz's select band of Gluckists at the Opéra. Gerono studied flute and cello at the Conservatoire. He published a few songs and cello pieces.

GIRARD, Narcisse (1797–1860). Violinist conductor of the old school; at first a friend of Berlioz's, then a rival on the latter's emergence as the finest conductor of the age. Succeeded Habeneck both at the Conservatoire concerts (where, except on one occasion, he maintained Habeneck's policy of excluding Berlioz's music from the society's programmes) and at the Opéra. He died while conducting a performance of *The Huguenots*.

GLUCK, Christoph Willibald (1714–87). With Beethoven, the great influence on Berlioz's music—which one could almost describe as a union between Gluck's melodic line and Beethoven's thematicism, Gluckian 'drama' and Beethovenian primacy of musical values. Berlioz was drawn to Gluck, instinctively, from the first. (For Rameau, with whom his music has certain affinities, he never had any conscious feeling. French classical opera, which was to be reborn in him, meant Gluck.) What he read in Michaud's *Biographie*, at the age of fourteen or fifteen, about Gluck's insistence on dramatic fidelity confirmed the interest already aroused by a few pieces from *Orphée*, and was to be a lifelong creed. His passion took firm root in the first four years in Paris, during which nearly all Gluck's major works were revived at the Opéra: *Iphigénie en Tauride* (1821), *Iphigénie en Aulide* (1822), *Orphée* (1824), *Alceste* (1825) and *Armide* (1825). Musically, Gluck's influence is both general, in its lofty temper and evocation of classical antiquity, and more specific, in its large melodic span, tragic declamation, and occasional harmonic asperity. It pervades Berlioz's career but is most prominent towards the end, above all in *The Trojans*, where it is part of a profound nostalgic return to the past and not the result of his revivals of *Orphée* and *Alceste* (which came later). His admiration was not uncritical: the overture to *Orphée*, for example, was an 'incroyable niaiserie', and he regarded Gluck's theoretical subordination of music to text, though in practice rarely observed by him, as 'impious'. To him, Gluck was not so much a god (as Shakespeare and Virgil were) as a spiritual father. His comment on the completed *Trojans* was, 'I believe that if Gluck were to return to earth and hear the work, he would say: "This is my son".' Berlioz's edition of *Orphée*, for female (contralto) voice (1859, with Pauline Viardot), is still the most commonly performed.

GOETHE, Johann Wolfgang (1749–1832). Gérard de Nerval's translation of *Faust* was published in the winter of 1827–8, but we do not know exactly when Berlioz came across it; the first reference in his correspondence is in a letter to Ferrand dated 16 September 1828, which speaks of 'Shakespeare and Goethe, mentors of my life, mute confidants of my grief!', and which goes on, 'The day before yesterday, while travelling, I wrote the ballad of the king of Thule.' Seven more pieces were composed during the next few months, and the whole published as *Huit scènes de Faust* in early April 1829. Berlioz addressed two scores to Goethe (not long before, Delacroix had sent Goethe copies of his *Faust* lithographs), and was delighted to hear from Ferdinand Hiller, who had written about it to Eckermann, that Goethe had been very pleased with his letter, was eager to hear the music, and would certainly reply. Meanwhile, however, Goethe had passed a copy to the composer and teacher Carl Zelter, his adviser on musical matters, asking him to satisfy his curiosity, aroused by the 'sight of these notes, which look so strange and marvellous'. Zelter replied dismissing the work as an 'excrescence, the aborted offspring of a hideous incest'. The long-awaited letter from Goethe never came.

There had been earlier French translations of *Faust*—one, for example, in 1822, by the historian and man of affairs, Guillaume de Saint-Aulaire (later French ambassador in Rome, and referred to in Berlioz's Italian chapters). But Nerval's came just at the right time. To quote Barzun, 'More than Werther and René, already a generation past, the figure of Faust seemed to embody the will of the moment, for Faust was more complete. Learned, passionate, curious, tender, courageous, bewitched and desperate, he stood for genius in all its greatness and misery. The "two souls within his breast" showed him at once a sufferer and a doer: "Unresting action proves the man". Yet Faust was a critic of himself no less than a critic of life, and his pilgrimage was a perpetual act of choice. To searchers like the young artists of the new era, it was wonderful to find a fable in which Experience and Wisdom were not shown as already bottled and labelled by the old for the use of the obedient young, but were purchasable solely with risk and effort.'

Not long after publication Berlioz withdrew his score, apparently because of certain technical faults that it contained. Sixteen years later the first intoxicated discovery of Goethe's poem reached fruition, and the *Huit scènes* became the nucleus of one of his greatest and most characteristic works, which closes the first, 'dynamic' part of his career as a composer. *The Damnation of Faust* is the great case-book of romantic defeat, of romantic man 'lost in a universe that cannot answer his desperate longings, "a speck of flesh upon an empty planet" . . .', the episodes of which are 'not a string of lurid or touching vignettes but a dramatization of the soul's condition, a nightmare progress from frustration at the failure of learning, of easy companionship, of God, of nature, of love, into an ever more terrible isolation, whipped by the devil who cannot be escaped because he is within, until journey's end is reached in the total dullness, the numbing of all sensation and the exclusion from any hope, that is Hell . . .' (John Warrack). After such a work, even without the material disaster in which its performance involved him, perhaps Berlioz could only have turned back, beyond Goethe, to the past, to childhood and Virgil.

GOUNOD, Charles-François (1818–93). One of Berlioz's friends and admirers among the younger French musicians (who were generally taught to distrust him as an artistic influence), but less intimate than Saint-Saëns. Almost the last pupil of Berlioz's master Lesueur, and winner of the Prix de Rome in 1839; he wrote successful operas on two subjects previously treated by Berlioz, *Faust* and *Romeo and Juliet*, and set Scribe's *La nonne sanglante*, which Berlioz had earlier abandoned. In the preface to *Lettres intimes* (viii–ix) he describes listening as a student to Berlioz rehearsing *Romeo and Juliet* and other works at the Conservatoire, where, hurrying out of Halévy's class, he would 'hide himself in a corner of the hall and listen intoxicated to this strange, violent, impassioned music which opened up before one such new and exotic horizons'.

GUHR, Carl Wilhelm Ferdinand (1787–1848). Frankfurt kapellmeister; renowned orchestral disciplinarian; Wagner was impressed by a performance of *The Magic Flute* which he heard him conduct in 1835. Guhr was apparently fond of extra-musical effects—on one occasion, during *The Creation*, he had all the gaslamps turned up at 'Let there be *Light*'.

GYMNASE DE MUSIQUE MILITAIRE. The conductorship was one of the posts on which Berlioz cast a hopeful eye; but Carafa was firmly entrenched there from 1838. Nothing to do with the Gymnase Musical, a short-lived orchestral society founded in 1834, which in 1835 gave two performances of *Harold in Italy* under the elder Tilmant.

HABENECK, François-Antoine (1781–1849). Violinist, conductor and composer. He conducted (with a violin bow) from a first violin part with cues written in, but by patience and thoroughness achieved results whose quality many musicians testified to; Wagner said he had never heard better prepared and more satisfying performances of Beethoven's symphonies than at Habeneck's Conservatoire concerts in 1840–1. As chief conductor of these and of the Opéra for the best part of two decades, Habeneck was entrenched in the most powerful executive position in the Paris musical world, and it was inevitable that his relations with Berlioz—a rival more than twenty years his junior and representing the new type of conductor, with which the future lay—should have been ambiguous and often stormy. He was the best official conductor there was and as such had sometimes to be used. The account of their relations given in the *Memoirs*, though heightened here and there for effect, will seem improbable only to those who have no experience of musical politics and no inkling of the peculiar venomousness of the French variety.

HALMA, Hilarion-Emile (1803–59). French violinist, pupil of Baillot. He appeared several times at Conservatoire concerts in 1829–31, but thereafter his career was largely spent in America.

HANDEL, George Frideric (1685–1759). It is hard to see Berlioz's failure to appreciate Handel's greatness, and indeed his frequently expressed antipathy for this 'gros tonneau de porc et de bière', as springing from anything more exalted than prejudice and ignorance, combined with an inability to forgive a man who could describe his cook as the equal of Gluck in contrapuntal skill. But at least Berlioz himself did not rate his own opinion much higher than that; see his letter written to Liszt from London, where Wagner had put his foot in it with the public by appearing to belittle Mendelssohn: 'Mendelssohn! who for many people is a sort of bigger and better Handel! In any case, if I weren't guilty of the same fault with regard to some other composers whom I abominate with the force of a hundred cannon, I would say that Wagner is wrong not to see in the puritanical Mendelssohn a fine and richly endowed artistic personality. When a master is a master, and when that master consistently honoured and respected his art, one ought to respect him, however much one may be taking a quite different direction oneself. But Wagner could turn the argument against me if he knew whom I so cordially dislike [Handel]. . . . No one is perfect' (*Correspondance générale*, V, 117–18).

HEINE, Heinrich (1799–1856). Settled in Paris in the early 1830s and lived there till his death. He sent regular news letters to the German Press, with idiosyncratic but penetrating comments on the Paris cultural and political scene. His knowledge of music (and regard for truth) may, however, be gauged from his account of the first performance of the combined Fantastic Symphony and *Lélio* in 1832, with Harriet in her box and Hector seated at the drums, his hair 'like a great primeval forest towering above a rocky precipice': 'every time he caught her eye he struck the drum with a kind of spasm of fury. . . . Miss Smithson, since then, has become Madame Berlioz, and her husband has had his hair cut. When I heard the symphony again last winter, he was there as before, at the back of the orchestra near the drums, and the large Englishwoman was in the stage box. Their glances met; but this time he did not strike the drums so furiously' (*Über die französische Bühne*: Zehnter Brief).

HELLER, Stephen (1815–1888). Hungarian composer and pianist who settled in Paris in 1838; an intimate friend of Berlioz; defended his music against Hanslick in the *Neue freie Presse*, January 1879 (and in *Revue et Gazette musicale*, 2 and 9 mars 1879). Heller's piano music later won a considerable vogue, especially in England, but he made very little out of it; he was saved from poverty by a testimonial organized by his old friend Hallé.

HILLER, Ferdinand (1811–85). German pianist, composer and conductor. Soloist at Berlioz's second concert, in the French première of Beethoven's Emperor Concerto. He lived in Paris 1828–34; close friend and confidant of Berlioz at this time. Kapellmeister in Düsseldorf 1847–50, then Cologne, where he helped to found the conservatoire. He became strongly anti-Wagnerian and openly hostile to Liszt and the Weimar school. Last meeting with Berlioz March 1867, in Cologne, where at Hiller's invitation Berlioz conducted what was to be his final concert in Germany.

HORN, The. The tremulous, watery French timbre so disagreeable to the ear of most other nations seems to have been adopted after Berlioz's day: see his description of contemporary French horn-tone in *Voyage musical*, I, 20–1 as 'slightly covered, but pure and noble'.

HOTTIN, ? (?–?). Conservatoire porter and music-binder. His name crops up in the accounts which survive for Berlioz's concerts in the Conservatoire hall. E.g. 20 November 1839, during rehearsals for *Romeo and Juliet*: 'to Hottin, for errands and supply of mulled wine, 26f.25'. The records also show him as having been responsible for blowing the organ of the Chapel Royal.

HUGO, Victor (1802–85). Berlioz set sèveral of his poems to music (including 'La captive' and 'Sara la baigneuse'), and may well have hoped at one time for his collaboration on an opera on his *Notre-Dame de Paris* (see *Correspondance générale*, I, 507–9, and the original of the same draft letter in Bib. Cons. Cat. 94); in the event the novel was set by Louise Bertin. Victor Hugo is one of the poets most often quoted in the *Memoirs*. The finale of the Fantastic was partly inspired by his Goethean ballad 'Ronde du Sabbat' and his novel *Le dernier jour d'un condamné*. The names of Berlioz and Hugo were often coupled as fellow-revolutionaries. But they were never close. Hugo did not have many connections with the musical world; and Berlioz found him rather pompous: 'Il trône trop'. He also—his earlier republicanism long forgotten—disapproved of the poet's self-imposed exile after

Napoleon III's coup d'état in 1851. Berlioz was at the famous first night of *Hernani* in 1830, on the author's side, though with some reservations about the play: see *Correspondance générale*, I, 321–2.

INSTITUTE, The French. Formally set up under the Revolution. It consists of five academies, of which Fine Arts is the fifth. Election, to a fixed number of 'seats' in each section of each academy, is by the members of the academy in question, and is for life. Berlioz campaigned for election four times, the last time successfully (1856). His interest in it was largely financial. 'It's worth only 1,500 francs [a year], but for me that is quite a lot. I don't speak of the honour, which is a myth, given the sort of people who belong and have always belonged to it. So far I have tried only twice. Hugo had to knock five times, de Vigny four. Eugène Delacroix has still not been vouchsafed entry, after six successive attempts. Balzac never got in. And the fools who are admitted! You simply have to resign yourself to treating it as a strict question of money, a kind of lottery, and wait patiently for your number to come up' (*Correspondance générale*, IV, 568).

JANIN, Jules (1804–74). Brilliant if rather frothy literary and dramatic critic, regarded in his day as the prince of feuilletonists, a maker and breaker of reputations.

JULLIEN (originally Julien), Louis-Antoine (1812–60). One of the originators of the idea of cheap popular concerts based on a shrewd blend of dance tunes and judicious extracts from the masters and on lavish spectacle. Conservatoire-trained, part charlatan, part serious musician, a mixture of practical horse sense and wild optimism, he believed in his mission to bring good music to the people. *Punch*'s description of him has often been quoted: 'The Mons., with coat thrown widely open, white waistcoat, elaborately embroidered shirt-front, wrist bands of extravagant length turned back over his cuffs, a wealth of black hair, and a black moustache—itself a startling novelty—wielded his baton, encouraged his forces, repressed the turbulence of his audience with indescribable gravity and magnificence, went through all the pantomime of the British Army or Navy Quadrille, seized a violin or piccolo at the moment of climax, and at last sank exhausted into his gorgeous velvet chair. All pieces of Beethoven's were conducted with a jewelled baton, and in a pair of clean kid gloves, handed him at the moment on a silver salver.' He toyed with the idea of setting the Lord's Prayer, fancying the look of the advertisement: 'words by Jesus Christ, music by Jullien'. The loss of many of his famous quadrilles in the Covent Garden fire of 1857 was a serious blow at a time when his wits were already deserting him.

KITTL, Johann Friedrich (1809–68). Bohemian composer, pupil of Tomaschek; director of Prague Conservatoire from 1843. Friend of Wagner, on whose libretto based on Heinrich König's novel *Die hohe Braut* he wrote the most successful of his three operas, *Bianca und Giuseppe, oder die Franzosen vor Nizza*, which aroused patriotic fervour at the time of the 1848 revolutions.

KREUTZER, Rodolphe (1766–1831). French composer, violinist and conductor. Assistant conductor, then conductor, at the Opéra 1815–24. Violinist in Napoleon's chapel orchestra and in the restored Chapel Royal under Louis XVIII and, briefly, Charles X. Author of famous '42 studies for the violin'. Prolific composer. His opera, *La mort d'Abel*, which Berlioz admired, was first performed in 1810, then revived in a shortened form on 17 March 1823, remaining in the Opéra's repertoire till 1826. *La mort d'Abel* was the occasion of a celebrated operatic rivalry between Kreutzer and Lesueur. Lesueur's *La mort d'Adam* had been waiting for ten years to be staged when Kreutzer wrote *Abel*, and the two works competed hotly for the honour of being put on first. Eventually, as Fouque remarks, 'Le premier fils des hommes céda le tour au père commun du genre humain.' See also under BEETHOVEN.

LACHNITH, Louis Wenceslas (1746–1820). German composer and horn-player, settled in Paris from 1773. His version of *The Magic Flute*, *Les mystères d'Isis* (1801), made his name. He followed up this success with *Saul* (1803), a macédoine of Haydn, Mozart, Cimarosa and Paisiello, then with *La prise de Jéricho* (1805), to which Mozart was again the principal donor. His own operas were less successful. Also composed symphonies, quartets, sonatas, etc., and wrote a 'Method of fingering on the fortepiano'.

LA FONTAINE, Jean de la (1621–95). An early and lasting love of Berlioz's, who quotes the *Fables* repeatedly in his writings and correspondence.

LEGOUVÉ, Ernest (1807–1903). French dramatist and poet, author of *Adrienne Lecouvreur*, etc. Close friend, for more than thirty years, of Berlioz, who consulted him on artistic as well as personal matters—e.g. on the libretto of *The Trojans*. *La mort d'Ophélie* is set to his paraphrase of Gertrude's speech. Full score of *Benvenuto Cellini* overture dedicated to him, in gratitude for the loan which enabled Berlioz to complete the opera. Legouvé's reminiscences, *Soixante ans de souvenirs* (Paris, 1886), contain a fascinating, if undependable, first-hand account of Berlioz.

LEIBROCK, Johann Adolph (1808–86). German composer, musicologist, cellist and harpist in the Brunswick orchestra. Translated Berlioz's articles on instrumentation (subsequently published by Berlioz as the *Grand traité d'instrumentation et d'orchestration modernes*), and made piano reduction of *King Lear* overture, published by Richault (Paris) in 1843.

LÉLIO. Berlioz's monodrama was not so entitled until the revival and publication of the work in 1855; in 1832 the principal character was simply 'the artist'. But the name occurs in connection with it as early as December 1832, the month of its first performance, in d'Ortigue's article on Berlioz published in the *Revue de Paris* (reprinted soon afterwards in *Le balcon de l'Opéra*); d'Ortigue refers to George Sand's story *La marquise*, comparing the strange passion of the Marquise de R—— for the actor Lélio, which it describes, with that of 'the artist' for his beloved. George Sand's novel *Lélia*, sometimes said to be the origin of the name, did not appear until the following year. Barzun suggests that the common source for the name Lélio in Berlioz and in George Sand was Hoffmann's tale 'The Empty House'. The spoken monologues were written and the work put together in Rome; but the idea for it was almost certainly formed in Berlioz's mind before he left for Italy; see the reference in a letter of 30 December 1830 to the 'great project [which] I shall try to realise during my exile' (*Correspondance générale*, I, 396). In other words, the 'return to life' which it celebrates, after the horrors of the Witches' Sabbath, was originally associated with his 'normal' love for Camille Moke, which had delivered him from his fatal obsession with the distant and unresponsive Harriet Smithson, and which inspired the life-asserting *Tempest* Fantasy that concludes the work. The pianissimo epilogue, with recall of the *idée fixe*, belongs to the 1855 revision.

LEMAÎTRE, Frédérick (1800–76). The leading French actor of his age, almost universally admired (though excluded by the rigid organization of the Paris theatre from appearing in the great classical and Shakespearean roles); see Gautier's tribute, quoted in Robert Baldick's *The Life and Times of Frédérick Lemaître*: '... Frédérick has the remarkable power of speaking to the highest intelligence as well as to the crudest instinct. Victor Hugo and the grocer's boy, Jules Janin and the duty fireman, George Sand and the attendant who peers through one of the windows in the boxes, are all equally impressed and applaud him with equal enthusiasm; Rachel, her face a pallid mask, leans out of her stage-box, panting with emotion....' Berlioz considered Lemaître's play *Robert Macaire* 'the drama of the century'.

LE SUEUR, Jean-François (1760–1837). A favourite composer of Napoleon's, whose *maître de chapelle* he became in succession to Paisiello in 1804. With Cherubini, director of the Chapel Royal under Louis XVIII and Charles X. Professor of composition at the Conservatoire from 1818 till his death. In his prime, celebrated in Germany as well as in France. Berlioz's first master in Paris, a counsellor and friend (he paid Berlioz's entrance fee for the Prix de Rome in 1828), and an important influence. There is abundant testimony not only to his personal kindness, consideration and old-world courtesy but also to his qualities as a teacher—quite apart from the fact that twelve of the seventeen winners of the Prix de Rome between 1822 and 1839 were or had been his pupils (including Gounod and Ambroise Thomas). The extent of Le Sueur's influence on Berlioz is exaggerated by Fouque (op. cit.), who sees Berlioz almost exclusively as a fulfilled Le Sueur. Berlioz did not echo Le Sueur's plea for a renewal of music through a detailed study of the modes and rhythms of the ancient Greeks, and he disagreed fundamentally with his Gluckian theory of music as the obedient servant of text and dramatic idea, believing instead in a Beethovenian symphonic ideal of a music 'wholly in command'. Nevertheless the list of 'Berliozian' characteristics foreshadowed in Le Sueur is an impressive one. They include a general insistence on the expressive integrity and dramatic uniqueness of each work of art, in sacred music as much as in secular; a belief that the 'rules' are there to be broken if the effect demands it; an interest in acoustics and the spatial element in musical performance (for his *Chant du Ier Vendémiaire* celebrating the anniversary of the Republic, in 1801, Le Sueur divided the orchestra into four groups and placed one at each corner of the Invalides); a special style of music for large, highly resonant buildings, marked by broad tempos and simple, deliberate harmonic movement; the use of huge forces to realize the Revolutionary concept of public ceremonial music, and to achieve particular effects of colour (e.g. ten harps in *The Bards*); a fondness, in his operas, for contrast and the combination of dissimilar dramatic, and therefore musical, ideas; timbre as a constituent of composition and of structure; the use of an explicit 'programme' supplied to the audience; the emancipation of rhythm; modal influences in melody and, hence, harmony; an unprecedented use of detailed dynamic and other markings in the score. It is a poetic injustice that he should have died a few months too soon to hear Berlioz's most Lesueurian work, the Requiem. Almost everyone, including his wife, wrote his name 'Lesueur', but he signed himself 'Le Sueur'.

LINDPAINTNER, Peter Joseph von (1791–1856). German composer and conductor, kapellmeister at Stuttgart, whom Mendelssohn at one time considered the finest conductor in Germany.

LIPINSKI, Karl (1790–1861). Polish-born violinist, leader of the Dresden opera orchestra 1839–60; a keen partisan of Berlioz, whom he tried (with Hans von Bülow) to have appointed kapellmeister at Dresden in 1854. He got on badly with Wagner during the latter's time there. Wagner thought him a dedicated and thorough musician but complained that he 'led' the orchestra too literally, always playing slightly ahead of the beat—a fault no doubt due to his having had formerly to take virtual responsibility for the performance under a series of weak conductors.

LISZT, Franz (1811–86). One of Berlioz's most intimate friends from the early 1830s to the late 1850s. He had already been living in Paris for several years (studying with Paër and Reicha) when they met. Liszt was one of the quite small company of non-relatives whom Berlioz addressed as 'tu'. Liszt wrote long analyses of Berlioz's music, as well as transcribing the Fantastic Symphony for piano and popularizing other works by performing fantasies on themes taken from them. He championed *Benvenuto Cellini*, which he put on during his régime at Weimar, and held a 'Berlioz week' there in 1852, 1855 and 1856. The long and close comradeship began to break up during the 1850s (at which time Liszt's voluminous correspondence with Berlioz is increasingly taken over by the Princess Sayn-Wittgenstein, his mistress) and ended almost in estrangement. Liszt in later life came to dislike what he felt to be the over-nervous intensity of much of Berlioz's music. Nevertheless, through its revelation of the orchestra as a medium of unprecedented subtlety and poetic sensitivity, Berlioz's music of the 1830s was a crucial influence on Liszt and, partly through him, on Wagner. Berlioz does not ever seem to have been particularly interested in Liszt as a composer (this and Liszt's increasingly fervent Catholicism, as well as his dedication to Wagner's cause, may have been factors in the decline of their friendship). Berlioz's passionate admiration for Liszt's playing never excluded disapproval of his occasional liberties with the written text. An autograph leaf of the *Memoirs* describing Berlioz's first meeting with Liszt includes the following, crossed out but still legible: '[our friendship has grown ever closer and stronger], despite differences of opinion on certain points of musical doctrine—differences which are solely concerned with his excessive rhythmic fluidity and the liberties he sometimes takes in interpreting the great masters' (Richard Macnutt Collection). On the former criticism, cf. Hallé (op. cit., 38–9): 'If, before his marvellous execution, one had only to bow in admiration, there were some peculiarities of style, or rather of musicianship, which could not be approved. I was very young and most impressionable, but still his tacking on the finale of the C sharp minor Sonata (Beethoven's) to the variations of the one in A flat, op. 26, gave me a shock, in spite of the perfection with which both movements were played. Another example: he was fond at that time of playing in public his arrangement for piano of the "Scherzo", "The Storm", and the finale from Beethoven's "Pastoral Symphony"; "The Storm" was simply magnificent, and no orchestra could produce a more telling or effective tempest. The peculiarity, the oddity, of the performance, consisted in his playing the first eight bars of the "Scherzo" rather quicker than they are usually taken, and the following eight bars, the B [D] major phrase, in a slow andante time; "ce sont les vieux", he said to me on one occasion.'

LOUIS-PHILIPPE (1773–1850). King of France (1830–48) under whom the greater part of Berlioz's music was written. His sons, the Duc de Montpensier and the Duc d'Orléans (to whom the Funeral and Triumphal symphony was dedicated, and whose death in an accident in 1842 was a grave blow to the hopes of the régime), were minor patrons, but the King himself took no interest in music. One of the few references to him in Berlioz's correspondence states: 'I wrote three times to Louis-Philippe when he was King, requesting an audience. I did not once receive an *acknowledgement*' (*Correspondance générale*, III, 546).

MARMION, Félix (1787–1869). Berlioz's uncle (his mother's younger brother). Lieutenant in Napoleon's army, serving in Prussia, Poland, Spain, Russia, at Waterloo; later rose to rank of colonel. Berlioz saw a good deal of him in the 1820s and 1830s, when he was stationed outside Paris, and remained in touch with him off and on throughout his life. Their last meeting seems to have been in September 1867 at the wedding of one of Berlioz's nieces in Vienne, shortly after the death of his son Louis: 'There were thirty-two of us, representing every side of the family, from Grenoble, Tournon, Saint-Geoire, etc.—we were all there, save one. It was the oldest of all that I was most pleased to see—my uncle the colonel, who is 84. We wept at meeting again. He looked ashamed to be still alive. I am much more so' (*Correspondance générale*, VII, 588).

MARTIN, Marie-Geneviève. See RECIO.

MENDELSSOHN(-BARTHOLDY), Felix Jakob Ludwig (1809–47). Mendelssohn's low opinion of Berlioz's music seems to have preceded their meeting in

Rome in 1831 (it is very likely that his teacher, Zelter, had shown him one of the two copies of *Huit scènes de Faust* which Berlioz sent to Goethe). As Ernest Newman remarks, the slightly priggish young genius 'could hardly be expected to grasp the paradoxical fact that [Berlioz] . . . had already written works . . . that would still be in the world-repertory a hundred years hence'. Although he came to regard Berlioz the man as something more than a poseur and an eccentric, he never really changed his attitude: in a letter to Moscheles written a dozen years later we find him agreeing that Berlioz's counterpoint is 'barbarous' and adding, 'His scoring is so messy and slapdash that you want to wash your hands after going through one of his works. . . . This saddens me, for his opinions are judicious and sensible; but he just cannot see how much nonsense there is in his music.' Berlioz's personal and professional admiration for Mendelssohn seems not to have been affected by knowing what Mendelssohn thought of him as a composer. His performances of Mendelssohn's music were considered masterly; Davison, for example, wrote that in the Italian Symphony every tempo was gauged perfectly for the first time in his experience (*The Times*, 29 May 1852). See also my *Berlioz*, vol. I, 487–92.

MÉRY, François-Joseph (1798–1865). French poet, satirist, novelist, short story writer and critic; friend of Rossini and Dumas.

MEYERBEER, Giacomo (originally Beer, Jakob Liebmann) (1791–1864). German-born composer, son of a Berlin banker, who by his genius for divining and satisfying the taste of the time, aided by his great wealth and the first modern publicity machine, dominated the Paris Opéra throughout the middle decades of the nineteenth century. His three great successes, *Robert le diable* (1831), *The Huguenots* (1836) and *Le prophète* (1849), had an enormous influence on the development of opera—an influence still seen in, for example, *Don Carlos* (1867) and *Die Meistersinger* (1867). The common disparagement of Meyerbeer as a mere calculating borrower of effects does not survive a comparison of dates (and is in any case based on a romanticized view of composition); it overlooks how much other composers, Berlioz included, learnt from him. Berlioz's attitude to Meyerbeer was ambivalent. *Les soirées de l'orchestre* admits *The Huguenots* to the pantheon of masterpieces which demand total silence and concentration from the orchestra; but we also hear of a conversation going on during a performance of *Robert*. Berlioz seems genuinely to have admired *The Huguenots* (even allowing for an element of diplomacy in his praise), but thirty years later found *L'Africaine* intolerably contrived. Meyerbeer's 'snakelike flexibility' both impressed and repelled him; and he recognized that the Meyerbeer/Scribe domination of the Opéra, and the public taste it expressed, effectively barred his entry. On his side Meyerbeer, as was his wont, studied Berlioz's music carefully, from 1829, when he sent for a score of *Huit scènes de Faust* from Schlesinger's, to 1863, when he attended several performances of *The Trojans at Carthage* 'for my pleasure and for my instruction'.

MOKE, Marie-Félicité-Denise, known as Camille (1811–75). 'The celestial pianofortist' (de Quincey); one of the most celebrated virtuosos of the nineteenth century, commonly considered the peer of Liszt (of whom she was a close friend); Berlioz's unfavourable judgment on her in 1845 (elegant but shallow and attempting to simulate feeling by affected changes of time) was exceptional. Brought up in Brussels and Paris; her father was Belgian and her mother German. Studied with Kalkbrenner and, later, Thalberg. Here she is, at the age of eighteen, as Berlioz saw her and described her in a letter to his sister Nanci: '. . . nothing is so absurd as a lover's pen-portrait. All the same, I would like you to have an idea of her. She is nearly as tall as me, figure slim and graceful, with magnificent black hair and large blue eyes which shine like stars but cloud over and become opaque like the eyes of a dying man when the demon of music takes possession of her. She is very lively, with a rather caustic mind but a fundamentally kindly nature. At times there's something a little childlike about her (she can be even more timid and nervous than you), yet she is strong when she has to be. In small things she is wayward and volatile. When her mother mentioned this fault to me, she stopped her and said, "Yes, I am changeable—as a silk dress is: the shade changes but the colour stays the same." At the piano she is a Corinne [the heroine of Mme de Staël's novel]. Nothing childlike or frivolous then. . . . It is almost too much to listen to her, and to *watch* her is positively so. Her talent has something miraculous about it, but she doesn't like hearing me praise it—she wants it to play no part in my love for her. In fact, deeply though I admire it, this is not what attracts me to her; nor has pride at being loved by such an angel anything to do with it, much though my vanity may be flattered. . . .' (30 June 1830, *Correspondance générale*, I, 339). There seems to have been a vein of archness in Camille's coquetry; when Berlioz finds Schröder-Devrient 'wonderful' in *Fidelio* she pouts and says: 'I forbid you to find any woman wonderful—other than a certain person that I know.' (From the same letter.) Nanci Berlioz confided to her journal that a letter she had received from Camille contained 'not one word written from the heart'. But that more than vanity was hurt when Camille jilted Berlioz is surely proved not only by the expedition to Nice but also by the tone of the two stories that he wrote about her, 'Suicide from enthusiasm' and 'Euphonia' (and perhaps too by the account, admittedly second-hand, of his conducting badly at a concert in which she played Weber's Conzertstück in London in 1852). 'Euphonia', though written thirteen years after the affair ended, is still full of the bitterness of a wound not yet healed. Camille is shown as a superficially fascinating but brittle, vulgar, self-seeking nymphomaniac. In fact she made a deep impression on many men, and not only her numerous lovers. But she was not to be tied down; no man ever completely possessed her. Berlioz spoke more truly than he knew when he called her his Ariel (it may have been because of this that Spontini tried to dissuade him from marrying her). Within five years of their marriage Pleyel had publicly repudiated her for disorderly behaviour and persistent infidelity. She really cared only for her art—'my one true friend', she told Janin—and she devoted herself to it with a single-mindedness which Berlioz might have applauded in different circumstances. The young Dutch pianist and composer Eduard Silas describes a visit to her in London in 1852, when she was just over forty: 'When I got there, she came in and said, "I must take off my bonnet, it interferes with my smoking". I thought I had misunderstood her; but when she presently brought out a box of big strong cigars, her meaning became clear. She offered me one, took one herself, lay down on the sofa and exclaimed, "now play me something". I soon saw that I had found more than my match in the consumption of big and strong cigars. Mme Pleyel is a fine woman, an excellent pianiste, has led rather a wild life and has all sorts of scandals attached to her name, but—I liked her, nevertheless.' See also Joan Hills, 'Ariel in Vienna', in the Bulletin of the Berlioz Society, XLIX, January 1965.

MONTFORT, Alexandre (1803–56). French composer, chiefly of opéra-comique and opéra-bouffe, in which he had great success during his lifetime; Berlioz's fellow-laureate in Rome 1831–2.

MOORE, Thomas (1779–1852). The collections of poems to which Berlioz refers, in the *Memoirs* and elsewhere, are *Irish Melodies*, *Sacred Songs*, *The Loves of the Angels* and *A Melologue upon National Airs* (which gave him the idea for *Lélio*). He read them, to begin with at least, in French prose translations by Louise Belloc, etc., which came out during the 1820s. It is not clear whether he knew any of the tunes to which Moore set his ballads.

MOZART, Wolfgang Amadeus (1756–91). Berlioz was not what modern opinion would regard as a complete Mozartian; by our standards, for example, he is distinctly cool about *Seraglio* (see *A travers chants*, 266–9); and there may be a grain of truth in Shaw's remark that 'Berlioz could never quite forgive him for possessing all the great qualities of his idol Gluck, and many others of which Gluck was destitute, besides surpassing him in technical skill'. But by nineteenth-century standards he was a fervent and perceptive admirer. *Idomeneo* delighted him. Near the end of his life we find him going to eight consecutive performances of *Don Giovanni* at the Théâtre-Lyrique. In so far as Mozart was a direct influence, it is to be seen in a general ideal of lucidity, lyrical grace, and wit combined with dramatic expressiveness, and not in any specific characteristics of style or form—though Wilfrid Mellers discerns a Mozartian quality in *Beatrice and Benedict*: 'Like Mozart ... the opera has a Mediterranean warmth in its acceptance of human frailty: and an implicit melancholy, because real life so seldom attains this union of creative understanding with critical wit' (*Man and His Music*, 768). *Idomeneo* in particular may be seen as an influence on Berlioz, not only because of its Gluckian affinities, but in its almost nineteenth-century use of colour.

NAPOLEON I (Bonaparte) (1769–1821). Like many of his generation—'the pale, nervous, fiery generation' of Alfred de Musset's *La confession d'un enfant du siècle*, 'reared in seminaries to the sound of drums'—Berlioz was attracted by the Napoleonic legend and way of life—'that mixture of recklessness, rapid motion, and obsession with glory ... which men as different as Balzac, Vigny and ... Stendhal ... found so gripping and so rich in artistic suggestion' (Barzun). His interest was fed by memories of the excitements of 1815 (when Napoleon passed up the near-by Rhône valley at the beginning of the Hundred Days) and by talking to people who had known or served under him—his uncle Félix Marmion, the surgeon Amussat, Horace Vernet, Lesueur (who refused to accept Charles X's award of officer of the Légion d'honneur, preferring to keep the chevalier's cross presented to him by Napoleon after *The Bards*). On returning from Italy in 1832 Berlioz noted down—'under the stimulus of the Napoleonic associations of the country which I had just travelled through'—an idea for a symphony in two parts on 'The return of the Army of Italy': '(1) Farewell from the crest of the Alps to the brave men fallen in Italian Fields. (2) Triumphal entry of the victorious army into Paris.' Nothing ever came directly of this, though he was still thinking of it in 1846 (see *Correspondance générale*, III, 368); but 'Napoleonic' influences and ideas are reflected in the Requiem, *The Fifth of May*, the Funeral and Triumphal Symphony and the Te Deum. At the same time, the anti-nationalistic, sceptical, humanistic side of Berlioz's mind increasingly deplored all that such a figure as Napoleon involved: 'Those pathetic little gangsters known as great men rouse me only to disgust—Caesar, Augustus, Antony, Alexander, Philip, Peter [the Great] and all the other glorified brigands' (*Correspondance générale*, VII, 438). But he could not quite bring himself to include Napoleon.

NOUVEAUTÉS, Théâtre des. Paris vaudeville theatre opened in 1827 (in the rue Vivienne, opposite the Bourse), where Berlioz performed as a chorister for a few months. In 1832 the company closed down and the theatre became for the next eight years the home of the Opéra-Comique.

O'CONNELL, Daniel (1775–1847). Irish Member of Parliament, patriot and radical frequently referred to in the writings and letters of Berlioz—who was himself described in the 1830s as a 'musical O'Connell'.

OPÉRA, The. See under ACADÉMIE ROYAL DE MUSIQUE.

OPÉRA-COMIQUE, The. The second of the three official opera companies (the other two being the Opéra and the Théâtre-Italien), housed successively, during Berlioz's Parisian years, at the Théâtre Feydeau, the Ventadour, the Nouveautés, and the Salle Favart. Berlioz's relations with the Opéra-Comique were sporadic and peripheral. *Benvenuto Cellini* was conceived for it, but turned down. His influence with the management helped to secure Marie Recio a brief engagement there in 1844, and *The Damnation of Faust* was first performed at two concerts given in the theatre in December 1846. In 1862–3 it considered putting on *Beatrice and Benedict*, but nothing came of the idea.

ORCHESTRATION. In the postscript to the *Memoirs*, Berlioz refers wryly to his acknowledged mastery of orchestration. As with all great composers since Mozart's time, but more than with almost any other, orchestration was with him an organic part of composition. In an age increasingly influenced by the piano and its pedal-suffused sonorities, Berlioz, who never played it, was unusual in thinking in directly orchestral terms. His use of instrumental timbres, singly and in groups, for expressive and formal purposes amounted, in the words of the French theorist Maurice Emmanuel, to 'a new conception of the orchestra, of which he was thoroughly conscious' (*Le correspondant*, 1920, 327–61).

ORTIGUE, Joseph-Louis d' (1802–66). French critic and musicologist from Provence, settled in Paris from 1829; disciple of Lamennais and contributor to many Catholic journals. One of Berlioz's most intimate friends, despite fundamental differences of opinion on religion and religious music (which d'Ortigue thought should be impersonal and 'inexpressive'). He was an assiduous publicist of Berlioz and his music, which he discussed and defended in many articles and in the book *De l'école musicale italienne et de l'Académie royale de musique à l'occasion de l'opéra de M. H. Berlioz* [*Benvenuto Cellini*] (1839). See also *Le balcon de l'Opéra* (1833) and *La musique à l'église* (1861); Berlioz's review of the latter is included in *A travers chants*. D'Ortigue's most substantial work is the *Dictionnaire liturgique, historique et théorique de plainchant et de musique religieuse* (1854 and 1860). He succeeded Berlioz as music critic of the *Débats*, but died of a stroke three years later.

PAËR, Ferdinando (1771–1839). Italian composer and pianist who spent the second half of his life in Paris, where Napoleon brought him in 1807 from Dresden to be his *maître de chapelle*. 1812–27 musical director of the Théâtre-Italien, except from 1824–6, when he had to make way for Rossini. Stendhal reports that for eight years Paër 'cleverly managed to conceal Rossini's existence from the Paris public'. Paër also tried to undermine Spontini's success in Paris. Auber parodied him as Signor Astucio in his opera *Le concert à la cour*. The name Paër does not require the diaeresis in Italian, but he himself adopted it when he settled in France.

PAGANINI, Nicolò (1782–1840). The diabolical, necromantic element in Paganini's public personality and appearance, which so impressed contemporaries (he was widely believed to have been taught his art by the devil in person), is largely absent in Berlioz's account of him in the *Memoirs* and in *Soirées* (Sixteenth Evening). He seemed simply to accept him, as man and fellow-artist. Except once in chamber music, he never heard the extraordinary violinist who played such an important part in his career. Paganini's appearances in Paris mainly took place in 1831, when Berlioz was in Italy. Thereafter he gave only one concert there (in 1833), which Berlioz missed because of illness. For a discussion of his famous gift to Berlioz, see Appendix III, 654–5.

PANSERON, Auguste-Mathieu (1795–1859). Professor of singing at the Conservatoire. Composer of operas and Masses, but chiefly known for his highly popular romances; author of several bulky works on the theory of music, and as a critic one of the first to pass judgment on Berlioz, making unfavourable comments on his concert of 26 May 1828. Panseron was a devoted friend of Rossini.

PILLET, Léon (1803–68). See under STOLTZ, Rosine and ACADÉMIE ROYALE DE MUSIQUE.

PISCHEK, Johann Baptist (1814–73). Bohemian baritone highly praised in the *Memoirs*, and in *Les soirées de l'orchestre*, where his voice is described as 'the finest in quality of any male singer that I know'. Pischek may well have had some influence on the characterization of Mephistopheles in *The Damnation of Faust*, part of which (including 'Voici des roses') was written during Berlioz's stay in Vienna, where Pischek was performing. Berlioz certainly had him in mind for the role in the stage adaptation which was planned for the 1848–9 season of Jullien's Grand English Opera at Drury Lane but frustrated by the collapse of the company. Pischek was a popular singer in England in the later 1840s and early 1850s. He remained with the Stuttgart kapelle until his retirement in 1863.

PONS, Augustin de (1803–48). Aristocratic friend and supporter of Berlioz in his early Parisian struggles, and a fellow-Gluckist. He sang, and later taught, under the maiden name of his wife, a student from the Conservatoire called Saint-Ange (possibly the Mlle Saint-Ange who sang in the 'Concert des Sylphes' at Berlioz's second concert). In 1839 de Pons started a school for singers. His bankruptcy and consequent suicide were among Berlioz's many personal reasons for detesting the 1848 Revolution.

PUGET, Loisa (1810–89). Composer of discreetly romantic and pious parlour songs which had an enormous vogue in Paris during the 1830s and early 1840s. After taking lessons from Adolphe Adam, she wrote a one-act opéra-comique, *Le mauvais œil*, to a libretto by Scribe and Gustave Lemoine (Opéra-Comique, 10 September 1836). In 1842, on her marriage to Lemoine (who wrote the words of most of her romances), she virtually retired from serious composition and 'broke silence only once again with an operetta called *La veilleuse, ou Les nuits de Milady*, to a libretto by her husband' (Grove).

PUTTLINGEN, Johann Wesque von (1803–83). Belgian-born civil servant of Polish extraction, councillor in the imperial chancellery in Vienna and amateur composer of opera, lieder, etc., who wrote under the pseudonym of Hoven (a place in Belgium where the family estates were located). Wagner in *Mein Leben* commends his prudence and taste in adopting only the last two syllables of Beethoven's name.

RECIO, Marie-Geneviève, *née* Martin (1814–62). Berlioz's second wife (he married her in 1854) and his mistress from about 1841; daughter of a French captain and a Spanish woman called Sotera Vilas. A mezzo-soprano with an attractive appearance but a weak voice, she was heard on the Paris stage between 1841 and 1844, and during Berlioz's German tour of 1842–3, when her insistence on appearing at his concerts was a considerable embarrassment to him (he tried, unsuccessfully, to escape from her at Frankfurt). To be allowed to go alone to

London without her in 1847 required 'a whole series of coups d'état'. Her hold on him must have been largely one of physical attraction. Berlioz seems never to have felt for her the romantic passion which was the mainspring of his existence, and such as he felt for several women in the course of his twenty-year relationship with her. Little that we know of her suggests a very agreeable person, even if Legouvé's story of her cruel behaviour to the ailing Harriet is not true (op. cit., I, 318–19). Life with her at home was not happy for Berlioz, and in public her gossipy tongue and quick sense of grievance were no help. One can say for her (as Beecham once remarked of an eminent English tenor) that she gave up singing; also, that she was an efficient and economical manager. When she died, at the age of forty-eight, this role was taken over by her mother, who remained devoted to Berlioz for the rest of his life, and of whom he was very fond, although his fastidious ear found her Spanish brand of French painful.

REICHA, Anton (1770–1836). Bohemian composer and flautist; friend of Beethoven and fellow-member of the Bonn Electoral orchestra. Particularly prolific composer of chamber music; his wind quintets are still played. Finally settled in Paris in 1808; taught at Conservatoire from 1818. His pupils included, as well as Berlioz, Liszt (privately), Gounod and Franck. Reicha was an experimentalist, writing whole movements in 5/4 time, and theorizing about quarter-tones.

RÉMUSAT, Charles de (1797–1875). French journalist, writer and politician. In 1830 a leading participator in the protest of the forty-four journalists which helped to touch off the July Revolution. Under Louis-Philippe one of the 'doctrinaires', the theorists of the left-centre. Minister of the Interior under Thiers from February to October 1840.

RÉNOVATEUR, Le. Legitimist daily founded in 1832. Berlioz contributed regular articles and reviews to it from 1833 to 1835.

REVUE ET GAZETTE MUSICALE. See under GAZETTE MUSICALE.

REVUE EUROPÉENNE. See under CORRESPONDANT.

REVUE MUSICALE. See under FÉTIS and GAZETTE MUSICALE.

ROCHEFOUCAULD, Sosthène, Vicomte de La (1785–1864). Director of Fine Arts under Louis XVIII and Charles X; largest landowner in France; a famous horse-breeder and a keen admirer of Rossini, whom he helped to engage for the Théâtre-Italien in 1824. Reputed, as the *Memoirs* states, to have asked Cherubini why he had never composed operas; but his most celebrated action as Director of Fine Arts was an attempt to purify the Paris stage by extending the length of the ballet-dancers' skirts. The young Berlioz described him as 'the most notable horse ever employed in the royal household'; but the dedication of the *Huit scènes de Faust* to the Vicomte four years later was a recognition of several useful services rendered in the interim. Rochefoucauld was responsible for having fig-leaves added to the statues in the Louvre. But he was also an effective and influential arts administrator, introducing changes which paved the way for Meyerbeerian grand opera.

ROGER, Gustave-Hippolyte (1815–79). French tenor highly successful at the Opéra-Comique 1838–49. Auber, Halévy, Thomas, etc., wrote parts for him. In 1849 he created John of Leyden in *Le prophète* at the Opéra, where he reigned for ten years, until a shooting accident deprived him of his right arm. He was Faust in the first performance of the *Damnation* in 1846, in which year he also sang the solo part in the Requiem. At his suggestion Berlioz orchestrated Schubert's *Erlkönig*, which he sang at the Baden festival concert in 1860. Fouque op. cit. describes him, as an old man at a performance of the *Damnation* in the 1870s, 'discovering' the music for the first time: 'It's a revelation to me. . . . Oh yes, I sang it, back in 1846, but I didn't *understand* it.' In his diary, published as *Le carnet d'un ténor*, Roger gives a lively account of musical life in France, Britain and Germany.

ROMBERG, Heinrich (1802–59). German violinist and conductor, son of the violinist Andreas Romberg of Hamburg and Gotha. In 1841 he directed the first performance of Berlioz's Requiem in Russia, where he was kapellmeister in St Petersburg.

ROQUEPLAN, Louis-Victor-Nestor (1804–70). French writer and operatic administrator. See under ACADÉMIE ROYALE DE MUSIQUE.

ROSSINI, Gioacchino Antonio (1792–1868). The prodigious vogue for his music in Paris, with intellectuals as well as with the general public, began in the early 1820s. Only if one is aware of its scope and the extravagant estimates of his greatness can one understand the force of Berlioz's reaction to it. Berlioz came to admire the *Barber* and *Comte Ory*, and parts of *William Tell*, and he relished his malicious wit; but they were never friends, hardly even acquaintances, though Rossini was a prominent figure in French musical society most of the rest of Berlioz's life: Hallé, for example, describes him at the dress rehearsal of Louise Bertin's *Esmeralda* (whose rehearsals Berlioz supervised), seated on the stage 'in an easy chair close to the scenery on the left side. . . . He gave no sign during the first act, but in the middle of the second, when a momentary pause had occurred, he rose and advanced slowly towards the conductor. Immediately a whisper ran through the whole house—"Rossini va parler"—everybody was all ears, and this was what he said: "Monsieur Habeneck, vous ne voyez donc pas? Il y a un quinquet qui fume? (one of the lamps is smoking)" . . .' In general he remained for Berlioz a genius, but one whose music was too often 'all artifice, knowledge of the world, sharp practice and manipulation of the public, and no true feeling'. Rossini's reported observations on Berlioz's music are rare and generally not encouraging. The failure of *The Damnation of Faust* elicited the comment that 'the Song of the Rat did not please because there was no cat in the house'. After perusing the score of the Fantastic Symphony he is said to have observed: 'What a good thing that young man doesn't know music – he would be very bad at it.'

ROUGET DE LISLE, Claude-Joseph (1760–1836). French poet and musician, author of words and music of the Marseillaise, written in 1792 when he was a lieutenant in the army. Berlioz made an arrangement for chorus and orchestra in 1830. The famous hymn, proscribed on various occasions before—and after—the July Revolution, was much in evidence at the time and was adopted by the new government. At the reopening of the Opéra on 4 August, the tenor Adolphe Nourrit, tricolour in hand, sang it at the conclusion of the performance of Auber's *La muette de Portici*; 'immediately afterwards, a note thrown onto the stage was read out to the audience, announcing that the author and composer of this sublime hymn, Rouget de Lisle, was living in extreme poverty, and proposing a collection for him. At that everyone streamed out into the foyer, where a considerable sum was raised for the modern Tyrtaeus' (Berlioz to his sister Nanci, *Correspondance générale*, I, 347). Rouget de Lisle, having just been granted a pension of fifteen hundred francs by Louis-Philippe, donated the collection to the wounded of the Three Days. Berlioz also made an arrangement of Rouget's *Chant du Neuf Thermidor*, a hymn celebrating the downfall of Robespierre.

SACCHINI, Antonio Mario Gasparo Gioacchino (1734–86). Prolific Italian composer of operas, of which the most famous, *Œdipe à Colone* (Paris, 1786), was a favourite work of Berlioz's in his early years as a student.

SAINT-SIMON, Claude-Henri, Comte de (1760–1825). French philosopher and social reformer. His doctrines—which included detailed practical schemes for industrial development in the interests of the working class—were widely subscribed to among the early Romantics. Berlioz was for a short time a convinced Saint-Simonian; see the letter to the journalist Charles Duveyrier in *Correspondance générale*, I, 476–7, and my *Berlioz*, vol. I, 504–7.

SALIERI, Antonio (1750–1825). Italian composer of operas and church music, etc. His one *tragédie-lyrique*, *Les Danaïdes*, was produced at the Paris Opéra in 1794; it was originally put about—with the connivance of Salieri's mentor Gluck—that the work was a collaboration between the two composers. *Les Danaïdes* remained in the repertoire off and on till 1828; it was revived shortly after Berlioz arrived in Paris.

SAX, Antoine-Joseph (known as Adolphe) (1814–94). Belgian musical inventor and manufacturer who in 1842 settled in Paris, where Berlioz was among the first to give him support (*Débats*, 12 June 1842), and the first to use his newly invented saxophone at a public concert (Salle Herz, 3 February 1844, in an arrangement of the Chant sacré for six wind instruments). Berlioz consistently advocated the adoption by military bands of Sax's improved woodwind and brass instruments. In two of his later scores, the Te Deum and *The Trojans*, he included parts for saxhorns, a brass family derived from the bugle.

SAYN-WITTGENSTEIN, Princess Carolyne of (1819–87). *Née* Ivanovski, daughter of a Polish landowner from whom she inherited large estates at Woronince and elsewhere. At the age of seventeen she married Prince Nicholas of Sayn-Wittgenstein, adjutant to the Czar. In 1847, in Kiev, she met Liszt, whose mistress she became; in the following year she went to live with him at the Villa Altenburg in Weimar. Her resolutely high-minded influence induced Liszt to give up his career as a world-famous virtuoso and devote himself to composition. A passionate bluestocking and a woman of immensely strong will, the Princess loved projects; after the completion of *The Trojans*, begun as a result of her encouragement, she nearly persuaded the now ailing and exhausted Berlioz to write an *Antony and Cleopatra.* (Her interest in Berlioz may have had, as an added motive, the desire to oppose Wagner, of whose influence on Liszt she was jealous.) In 1861 she and Liszt planned to get married; but at the last moment the hoped-for Papal annulment of her marriage to Prince Nicholas did not materialize. She lived in Rome from 1860 till her death (seven months after Liszt's), often seeing him, and maintaining in his absence a long and exalted correspondence with him. She was the author of *Causes intérieures de la faiblesse extérieure de l'Eglise*, a work in twenty-four volumes. Until Robert W. Gutman's recent study, books on Wagner tended to dismiss the Princess as a pretentious busy-body. The letters which Berlioz wrote to her in the period of *The Trojans* show him at his splendid best as a letter-writer, as well as providing the fullest documentation of the composition of any of his works.

SCHILLING, Gustav (1805–81). German musicologist, author of the seven-volume *Universal Lexikon der Tonkunst* (Leipzig, 1835–40). In 1857 he emigrated to New York, where he founded a music school. He died in Nebraska.

SCHLESINGER, Maurice Adolf (1798–1871). Son of the German music publisher Adolf Schlesinger. Maurice (originally Moritz) settled in Paris in 1819 and about two years later founded the publishing house which bore his name. Most of Berlioz's music published between 1829 and 1846 was issued by Schlesinger. In the latter year he retired and went to live in Baden, and the firm was taken over by Brandus. Berlioz was also closely associated with the weekly *Gazette musicale* (*q.v.*) which Schlesinger started in 1834. Other composers published by him included Chopin, Liszt and the young César Franck. His wife Elisa was the model for Mme Arnoux in Flaubert's *L'éducation sentimentale*, and aspects of Schlesinger himself appear in the character of Jacques Arnoux.

SCHLICK, Benjamin Gotthold (1796–1872). Danish architect, engineer and antiquarian whom Berlioz met in Paris and later in Italy. He designed theatres in various parts of Europe, and in the 1820s redecorated the Odéon and Variétés in Paris.

SCHLOESSER, Louis (1800–86). German violinist, conductor and composer. Fellow-student of Berlioz's under Lesueur in the early 1820s. Leader, then conductor at Darmstadt (where he composed an opera on *Benvenuto Cellini*). His younger brother Theodor, also a musician, was a close friend of Berlioz's in the late 1820s.

SCHRÖDER-DEVRIENT, Wilhelmina (1804–60). German soprano, daughter of the baritone Friedrich Schröder (Don Giovanni in the first German-language performance of the opera); married (briefly) to the Dresden actor Karl Devrient, the first of three husbands. While still in her teens she became famous in Vienna for the dramatic power of her performances as Pamina (1821), Agathe (1822, under Weber) and Leonore (1822, when she was highly praised by Beethoven). Also a prominent, if less generally admired, exponent of the roles of Donna Anna, Norma, Amina in *La Sonnambula*, Desdemona in Rossini's *Otello*, etc. She was Wagner's first Senta, Venus, and Adriano in *Rienzi*. Her art aroused widely differing feelings. Wagner said that her Leonore, which he saw as a young man, was the greatest single influence in his career as a composer; and he regarded her use of spoken inflections (which Berlioz disliked) as inspired. At the opposite extreme was the opinion of Chorley: '[Sontag and Jenny Lind] had learned to sing—Madame Schröder-Devrient *not*. Her tones were delivered without any care, save to give them due force. Her execution was bad and heavy.' But, like Berlioz in 1830, Chorley had once been under the spell of her Leonore. Similarly, as an interpreter of Schubert's and Schumann's songs she was adored by some, by others thought too dramatic.

SCHUMANN, Robert (1810–56). One of Berlioz's first admirers in Germany. His long analysis of the Fantastic Symphony (*Neue Zeitschrift für Musik*, August 1835), was written, by an extraordinary feat of understanding, from Liszt's piano transcription. When he met Berlioz in Leipzig in 1843, Schumann was half attracted by him and half disappointed, as the inconclusive entry in his diary shows: 'His face, otherwise so full of character, has a certain weakness about the corners of the mouth and the chin. Paris has corrupted him. Unfortunately, he speaks no German, so we couldn't have much conversation. I had pictured a more fiery personality. There is something very pleasant about his laugh.' Schumann's reaction to the works performed by Berlioz in Leipzig (which included what must have been the first performance of the Fantastic Symphony that Schumann had heard) was that they contained 'many deplorable things, but others that are extraordinarily distinguished, even inspired'.

SCOTT, Sir Walter (1771–1832). Like the rest of his generation, Berlioz came under the spell of the 'Waverley' novels, which he read avidly in the French translations available in the 1820s. In the *Memoirs* there are allusions to *Rob Roy*, *Old Mortality*, and *Guy Mannering*, and to the narrative poem *Marmion*.

SCRIBE, (Augustin) Eugène (1791–1861). Enormously industrious and successful French librettist and playwright, a master of his craft, and one of the principal architects of the Meyerbeer era. Twenty-six volumes of his complete works are devoted to opera librettos; he provided Auber alone with more than thirty texts. His collaboration with Berlioz on *La nonne sanglante*, which occupied them sporadically between 1841 and 1846, was almost inevitably abortive, owing to fundamental lack of confidence on both sides.

SHAKESPEARE, William (1564–1616). 'The English are quite right when they say that Shakespeare is the supreme creator, after the Good Lord. . . .' (Berlioz to Count Michael Wielhorsky, *Correspondance générale*, III, 433). To the young French artists of the 1820s he came like an unknown god. His example was the great catalyst of the Romantic sensibility, in a dramatic and poetic tradition in which his fantastic richness of imagery, power and depth of characterization, 'open' form, and deliberate mixing of genres were things hardly dreamed of. But whereas the example of Shakespeare's towering genius proved ultimately inhibiting to the Romantic dramatists, it was pure gain to an artist who worked in a different medium and who, like Berlioz and Verdi, could grasp its significance for his art. The directly Shakespearean works of Berlioz are: the fantasy on *The Tempest* (1830), the overture *King Lear* (1831), *Romeo and Juliet* (1839), *La mort d'Ophélie* (1842), *Hamlet* March (1848), *Beatrice and Benedict* (1862). Above all, *The Trojans* (1858) represents the supreme fruit of that seminal discovery of 1827; for, quite apart from its famous borrowing from *The Merchant of Venice*, the whole work shows at every turn an enrichment of classical *tragédie lyrique* by Shakespearean wealth of poetic (musical) language, unity-in-diversity, and irony of contrast.

SMITHSON, Harriet Constance (1800–54). Brought up in Ireland, where her Gloucestershire-born father, William Joseph Smithson, was the manager of touring theatre companies, and where she gained early experience of the stage. She made her London début in 1818. Harriet Smithson (whom Berlioz always called Henriette) was for about a year and a half the toast of Paris. In London she had been moderately successful and her looks were admired; an anonymous poet proclaimed, 'There still is purity on earth,/It sparkles on that beauteous brow . . . Can all be dark that life supplies/Whilst earth can boast of SMITHSON's eyes?' But her Irish accent was remarked on, and Drury Lane was reckoned too large for her. 'Her thrilling tones are lost; for the voice strained beyond nature, to insure distinctness, loses the beauty of its inflexions' (Oxberry's *Dramatic Biography and Histrionic Anecdotes*, Vol. 2, [195]–208. London, 1825). She created no great stir on her returns to England in 1829–30 and 1831–2; and the *Court Journal* of 12 October 1833, reporting her marriage, added, 'We trust this marriage will insure the happiness of an amiable young woman, as well as secure us against her reappearance on the English boards.' Berlioz may have been right when he described her—in a period of detachment—as an 'ordinary woman, with an instinctive gift for expressing agonies of the soul which she has never felt herself'. By 1830 her star, even in France, had begun to wane. But it was dazzling while it lasted. Some spark of genius in her responded to the mood of the moment. Her acting in the mad scene in *Hamlet*, which so moved the house that men wept and left the theatre convulsed by uncontrollable emotion, seems to have been almost an improvisation, owing nothing to traditional routines. Numerous accounts single out the power of her mime and a certain harrowing quality in her voice that spoke as if 'from soul to soul'. Macready said that in Rowe's *Jane Shore*, when she said she had not 'tasted food these three days', a frisson of horror ran through the audience. Even Stendhal, who was generally critical of the English players, had only praise for Miss Smithson: 'When she played the part of the widowed Queen of King Edward in *Richard III*, the scene in which she parts with her children, left not a single eye in the house which was dry' (*Selected Journalism from the English Reviews by Stendhal*, ed. Geoffrey Strickland, London 1959). At the height of her fame, when a benefit was given for her at the Opéra on 3 March 1828 (with Sontag in the second act of the *Barber*, Mlle Mars in Andrieux's *Le manteau* and herself in three acts of *Romeo*), a thousand people were turned away at the door, the Duchesse de Berry presented her with a magnificent Sèvres vase, and the King sent a purse full of gold. Her carriage bore the device *My kingdom for a horse*. Other roles which she played were Cordelia, Desdemona, Portia, Lady Teazle, Lydia Languish, Belvidera in Otway's *Venice Preserved* and Virginia in Knowles's *Virginius*.

The benefit performance of November 1833 described in the *Memoirs* was not her last appearance. She was seen briefly at the recently opened Théâtre Nautique in November–December 1834, in a ballet entitled *La dernière heure d'un condamné*; in the mad scene from *Hamlet* at a benefit for the actor Frédérick Lemaître (Variétés, 15 December 1836); and semi-privately in *Jane Shore*, Act V, May 1837. In French drama she was necessarily restricted to mute roles; and Berlioz's attempts to persuade various dramatists—Hugo, de Vigny, George Sand—to include a part for her in a new play came to nothing. This frustration was undoubtedly an important factor in the gradual worsening of relations which, after five or six years of happiness, led inexorably to the break-up of their marriage. The stress and hardships of domestic life during the late 1830s—the period of *Benvenuto Cellini*, the Requiem and *Romeo and Juliet*—must in any case have been considerable. She seems to have aged quickly and lost her looks and figure; and by the early 1840s had become a scold and taken to drink. But as Berlioz's passion for her waned and the reality eclipsed the dream, hers for him grew and became increasingly jealous and possessive. Despite the advent of Marie Recio in 1841 or 1842, they did not finally separate till the summer of 1844; thereafter Berlioz maintained two households. He continued to see and support her; and the vision of Ophelia never completely faded.

SOCIÉTÉ DES CONCERTS. Formally constituted in 1828. Its fortnightly concerts (held on Sunday afternoons every winter and spring) were famous throughout Europe for the quality of orchestral playing, most notably in Beethoven's symphonies. A vital formative influence on the early part of Berlioz's career, but later a stumbling block: the prohibition on his use of the Conservatoire hall for his own concerts from 1844 onwards had damaging consequences, helping to cause—among other things—the disastrous failure of *The Damnation of Faust* (1846). The society, founded partly to foster new music, performed works by composers as diverse as Rode, Schneitzhoeffer, Gomis, Rousselot, Masset, Schwenck and Turcas, but nothing by Berlioz between 1833 (*Rob Roy*) and 1849 (fragments from the *Damnation*) and nothing after that for another twelve years. The chief conductors were: 1828–48 Habeneck; 1849–60 Girard; 1860–3 Tilmant; 1864–72 Hainl. See also under BEETHOVEN, GIRARD and HABENECK. The hall, according to Elwart (op. cit.), seated just over a thousand people. It still survives, though alterations to its structure and furnishing have impaired the once-famous acoustics.

SPONTINI, Gaspare Luigi Pacifico (1774–1851). Italian composer who settled in Paris, writing for the Opéra his most famous works, *La Vestale* (1807), *Fernand Cortez* (1809), *Olympie* (1819). He was director of the Berlin Grand Opera 1820–41. Berlioz names Spontini, with Beethoven and Weber, as one of the three modern masters from whom he learnt the art of expressive orchestration, and he is emphatic in his belief—against the taste of the time or of posterity—in Spontini's genius and the grandeur and dramatic truth of his three masterpieces (above all of *La Vestale*). He got to know them thoroughly in the early and mid-1820s, when they were in the repertoire of the Opéra, and his faith in them never wavered—even when Spontini himself was at his most embittered and touchy. Berlioz conducted his music on many occasions, and withdrew from the Institute election in 1839 on learning that he was a candidate. 'I had grown to love him by dint of admiration', he wrote when the news came of Spontini's death in Italy.

STAUDIGL, Joseph (1807–61). German bass, very popular in London as well as in Vienna. Soloist in Berlioz's concerts in Vienna (where he sang Friar Laurence and the solo part in *The Fifth of May*) and in London (Ninth Symphony, fragments of *Damnation of Faust* and *La Vestale*, Handel's 'O ruddier than the cherry'.) His musical facility, on which the *Memoirs* comments, was demonstrated when he sang the part of Elijah at sight at the final rehearsal for the première of Mendelssohn's oratorio (Birmingham, 1846). Staudigl spent the last five years of his life in a lunatic asylum.

STOLTZ, Rosina (1815–1903). French mezzo-soprano, born Rose Niva Noël. An imperfect singer but by all accounts an original and compelling artist. As the mistress of Léon Pillet, director of the Opéra from 1841, she wielded great influence (Berlioz called her 'la directrice du directeur') until the collapse of the Pillet régime in 1847. Berlioz's relations with her fluctuated. She sang Ascanio in *Benvenuto Cellini* (1838–9) but throughout most of her reign at the Opéra was an enemy of his (Berlioz having insinuated in the *Débats* that she had become too stout to play the page in *Comte Ory* with conviction). In later years the hatchet was buried sufficiently for Stoltz to have been hurt at not being given the role of Dido in *The Trojans at Carthage*; but by that time her voice had largely gone.

STRAUSS, Isaac (1806–75). Jewish-Alsatian violinist, conductor and composer active in Paris from 1827. For many years leader of Théâtre-Italien orchestra, at the same time providing dance music at fashionable salons and, during the theatre's summer recess, in Aix-les-Bains and later Vichy. Directed the balls at Court under the Second Empire. Not related to the Vienna Strausses.

TAMBURINI, Antonio (1800–76). Italian bass with a voice of legendary beauty and suppleness, famous also in what we would now call baritone roles—e.g. Figaro in the *Barber*. Berlioz heard him in Naples in 1831 and wrote: 'What a man! An actor of wit and poise, voice admirable, method impeccable, unbelievable ease of delivery, power and sweetness combined—everything. It's superb!'

TAYLOR, Isidore-Justin-Sevérin, Baron (1798–1879). English-born traveller, playwright, administrator, engraver, patron of the arts; ennobled by Charles X for his part in Spanish campaign of 1823; director of Théâtre-Français during early Romantic movement, to which he was sympathetic; instrumental in bringing Luxor obelisk from Egypt to the Place de la Concorde; author of *Voyages pittoresques et romantiques dans l'ancienne France* (1828). 1838 Inspector of Fine Arts. One of the patrons of the short-lived Société Philharmonique founded by Berlioz in 1850. A pall-bearer at Berlioz's funeral.

THÉÂTRE-LYRIQUE. See under CARVALHO.

UNGER, Caroline (1803–77); in Italy her name was spelt Ungher. Hungarian contralto of unusual range who also achieved fame in soprano roles for a number of years; especially renowned as Donizetti's *Lucrezia Borgia*. She sang, with Sontag, in the first performance of the Ninth Symphony (Vienna, 1824); it was she who reputedly turned the deaf Beethoven towards the audience so that he could see the applause. Unger had a successful season in Paris at the Théâtre-Italien in 1833.

URHAN, Chrétien (1790–1845). German-born musician, a leading violinist in the Opéra and Conservatoire orchestras; also famous as one of the outstanding viola players of the age. Studied composition with Lesueur. Soloist in première of *Harold in Italy* (1834) and at many of Berlioz's concerts; played viola d'amore solo in first performances of *The Huguenots* (1836); violist in Anton Bohrer's quartet and, earlier, in Baillot's. Urhan was well-known for his musical purism and also for his prudery; his seat in the pit at the Opéra was turned away from the stage so that he would not have to see the dancers' legs.

VALENTINO, Henri (1787–1865). French violinist-conductor; conductor, with Habeneck, at the Opéra 1824–31 and, with Plantade, at the Chapel Royal 1824–30.

VANDENHEUVEL-DUPREZ. See under DUPREZ.

VERDI, Giuseppe (1813–1901). Berlioz admired Verdi's music more than he cared to admit, recognizing in him the reform-from-within of Italian music that he had implicitly stated to be impossible. He also warmed to Verdi for his integrity, his courage, and his uncompromising way with obstructive Opéra officials. On his side Verdi acknowledged Berlioz's genius but felt that it lacked the restraint necessary for the creation of truly great works of art. His expressions of friendly regard for the man were later qualified by what he called the 'sick hatred and bitterness' of Berlioz's last years. Berlioz lived long enough to have attended the première of one of Verdi's greatest works, *Don Carlos* (Opéra, 11 March 1867), but there is no record that he heard it. He wrote reviews of *Luisa Miller, Trovatore* and *Sicilian Vespers*.

VERNET, Émile-Jean-Horace (1789–1863). French painter and lithographer, renowned for his battle scenes and his studies of horses. His father (Carle) and his grandfather (Claude-Joseph) were distinguished painters. Napoleon admired his work and decorated him for personal bravery in 1814, and he was later to be a favourite artist of Louis-Philippe's. Sherlock Holmes claimed descent from him. Director of French Academy in Rome 1828–35; official artist of Algerian expedition and Crimean War. Berlioz described him in a letter to his sister Nanci as follows: 'A small, spare man, with an elegant figure; urbane but warm-hearted; an attentive son, loves his daughter like a brother and his wife like an uncle; earns twenty thousand francs a week; a swordsman and pistol-shot in the Saint-Georges class; a skilled performer on the drum, dances the tarantella with his daughter with a verve that brings the house down; austere, caustic, absolutely straightforward; fond of Gluck and Mozart, hates the Academy. A good man' (9 May 1831, *Correspondance générale*, I, 447). Some writers have detected an incipient *tendresse* between Berlioz and Horace Vernet's daughter, Louise, who later married the painter Delaroche.

VIARDOT, Pauline (1821–1910). *Née* Garcia, Michelle-Ferdinande-Pauline. Spanish-born mezzo-soprano, sister of Maria Malibran; in 1841 she married the French writer and impresario Louis Viardot. Her voice, like her appearance, had character rather than beauty, but she was an artist of exceptional intensity and perceptiveness. An intelligent and cultivated woman, a painter and a brilliant linguist as well as a gifted pianist, Viardot was on intimate terms with many of the leading artists and intellectuals in Paris (including, of course, Turgenev, with whom she lived for many years). Berlioz fell in love with her after working with her on the famous *Orphée* revival of 1859 (see her letters to Julius Rietz in *Musical Quarterly*, January 1916). She sang Cassandra in the only public performance of excerpts from the first act of *The Trojans* (Baden, 1859).

VIGNY, Alfred de (1797–1863). As poet, playwright and storyteller one of the most important figures in the Romantic movement; the preface to his *Chatterton* is a key document of the time. On very friendly terms with Berlioz; Barbier's and Wailly's text for *Benvenuto Cellini* worked over by him. (He is usually referred to as Vigny, on the grounds that 'de' is incorrect when not preceded by M. or Alfred. But Berlioz spelt his surname Devigny.)

VIRGIL (70–19 B.C.) The earliest and, after Shakespeare, the most important poetic influence in Berlioz's life; the tutelary genius of the 'classical' as opposed to the 'romantic', Shakespearean side of his art (though the dichotomy, beloved of some French commentators, is largely superficial). The *Aeneid* is quoted so often by him in the *Memoirs* and elsewhere that it seems to lead an independent life of its own in his imagination, and it is hardly fanciful to see the composition of *The Trojans* as inevitable, the culmination of a lifelong obsession. Cf. his letter of 20 June 1859 to the Princess Sayn-Wittgenstein, shortly after the completion of the opera: 'As for the principal object of the work, the musical rendering of the characters and the expression of their feelings and passions, that was from the beginning the easiest part of my task. I have spent my life with this race of demigods; I feel as though they must have known me, so well do I know them. And this recalls to me a childhood experience which will show you how deeply I was fascinated from the first by those splendid creatures of the ancient world. It was the period in my classical education when I was construing, under my father's direction, the marvellous twelfth book of the *Aeneid*; my imagination was possessed by the glory of its characters—Lavinia, Turnus, Aeneas, Mezentius, Lausus, Pallas, Evander, Amata, Latinus, Camilla, and the rest. I was like a sleepwalker, "lost in my starry meditation" (to borrow Victor Hugo's phrase). One Sunday I was taken to Vespers. The sad persistent chant of the psalm "In exitu Israel" had the magnetic effect on me that it still has today, and plunged me deep in the most real and vivid day-dreams of the past. I was with my Virgilian heroes again; I heard the clash of their arms, I saw Camilla the beautiful Amazon running, I watched the maiden Lavinia flushed with shame, weeping, and poor Turnus, his father Daunus, his sister Juturna, I heard the great palaces of Laurentium ring with lamentation—and was overwhelmed by an immense sadness. I left the church sobbing uncontrollably, and cried for the rest of the day, powerless to contain my epic grief. No one could ever get me to say the reason, my parents never knew nor had any inkling what sorrows had taken possession of my childish heart that day.' In his opera Berlioz, like that other Virgilian artist Claude in his last paintings, successfully translated into his own art the tragic power of *fatum*, as well as the heroic conception of the chief characters of the epic and the sense of the familiar, diurnal magic of nature.

VOGT, Gustave (1781–1870). Co-principal oboist at the Opéra 1812–24, and in the Conservatoire orchestra until 1844. His artistry was also admired in London—though English taste, used to a fuller, more robust tone, found Vogt's disconcertingly reedy.

WAGNER, Richard (1813–83). There were abundant reasons why Berlioz and Wagner should not have got on even as well as they did. Quite apart from external circumstances, tending to alienate them from each other—Marie Recio's unconcealed hostility to Wagner, Berlioz's resentment at the Opéra's accepting *Tannhäuser* but not *The Trojans*, the language barrier, Wagner's frequent disparagement of Berlioz's aims and achievements in his articles and books and the unfortunate coincidence of some local paper choosing to serialize the passage in question just when they happened to meet—there was their fundamental difference of outlook, which the ten years' gap in age only accentuated. In so many things they were antithetical: in their view of the roles of drama and music in opera, in their basic formal principles of composition (in Berlioz melody, in Wagner harmonic polyphony); as interpreters of the classics (Berlioz insisting on the sanctity of the composer's written intentions, Wagner prepared to re-create even to the extent of editing *Don Giovanni* or Beethoven's symphonies), as conductors (Berlioz being a Toscanini to Wagner's Furtwängler). As Wagner, under the influence of Liszt's harmonic innovations and the pressure of his own musical development and dramatic thinking, reached forward into the future, so Berlioz turned back to the past; at the moment of their closest rapport as men—in London in 1855—their respective paths were about to diverge furthest, towards *Tristan* and *The Trojans*. (At the same time Liszt, who had been the link between them and the champion of both, became increasingly preoccupied with Wagner's genius and thought.) The fact remains that the two artists were deeply intrigued by each other. Wagner could not ignore the composer who in *Romeo and Juliet* had revealed vast new possibilities for orchestral music; he had to try to get him on his side, and was irked when he failed to do so, yet still fascinated: behind his published statements that Berlioz's music lacked sense of beauty or coherent purpose lay a recognition of a creative force whose independent course was a constant puzzle and irritant to him. Berlioz, though much less of a proselytizer, could not altogether conceal his interest in Wagner under more or less dignified asides about the music of the future; rather like Lesueur with the C minor Symphony, he recognized Wagner's genius and power, while feeling in his heart that music like that of *Tristan* 'ought not to be written'.

WEBER, Carl Maria Friedrich Ernst von (1786–1826). The liberator of Berlioz's Romantic imagination, till then circumscribed within the limits of Gluck and his school. 'A new world opens before one,' he wrote a few years later, in a passage about Beethoven and Weber and their embodiment of poetic content in musical forms (*Correspondant*, 22 October 1830). As with Beethoven, it is not so much the specific parallels that strike us—though they are there: note, for instance, the use of flutes in thirds in the lower register in *Freischütz* (Agathe's scena) and in *Romeo and Juliet* (Love Scene), the very Berliozian rhythmic figure which depicts Max's anxiety, the triplet ostinato in the finale of *Romeo*, etc.—as the general influence of a vital example—of harmonic variation and of expressive orchestration in the interests of musical drama—studied and absorbed. In his *Carl Maria von Weber* John Warrack also points out a curious anticipation of Berlioz's *Les soirées de l'orchestre* in Weber's unfinished novel *Tonkünstlerleben*, in which the author dreams he overhears the instruments of an orchestra talking among themselves, and one of them opposing a threat of the Eroica with a plea for an Italian opera, so that they can 'at least drop off from time to time'.

WESTMORELAND, John Fane, eleventh Earl of (1784–1859). Previously Lord Burghersh, under which name he was widely known as an enthusiastic amateur composer. A contemporary account of an opera of his, quoted in J.W. Davison's *From Mendelssohn to Wagner* (79–80), suggests a musician of no great technical accomplishment. He is remembered chiefly as founder of the Royal Academy of Music. 1841–51, British Ambassador in Berlin. Berlioz may have met him first in Italy; Lord Burghersh was British Resident in Florence.

APPENDIX III

ERRORS, DISPUTED POINTS, AND OTHER MATTERS

In the following list I have set out the evidence as succinctly as I can and, where possible, my conclusions from it. In some cases I am not able to do more than draw attention to a conflict of evidence. I have also enlarged on matters touched on in the *Memoirs* and not dealt with in my footnotes. Here the dividing principle is that the appendix gives information that may be considered useful in a more general way whereas the footnotes take up points relevant to an immediate understanding of Berlioz's narrative. The designation CG refers to the seven-volume *Hector Berlioz, Correspondance générale*. The page-references to my *Berlioz* vol. I are to the revised edition of 1999.

Chapter 1

page
2, line 4: 'full of sound and fury . . .'
The first edition of the *Memoirs* has 'foul'—a reading not found in any of the modern variorum editions of *Macbeth*.

5, line 1: 'I was born on 11 December 1803 . . .'
At 5 p.m. (see birth certificate quoted in Tiersot, *Les années romantiques*, xli). He was baptized Louis-Hector on the 14th, the godfather being Nicolas Marmion, his maternal grandfather, and the godmother Sophie Brochier, his great-grandmother.

5, line 28: '. . . at the Ursuline convent . . .'
It was at the convent of the Visitation. The most probable year is 1815. See my *Berlioz*, vol. I, 572 (38).

6, lines 17: 'I recognized it when I heard it ten years later'.
Boschot (I, 62 n.) claimed to have seen it among the romances with guitar accompaniment in Berlioz's hand preserved in the museum at La Côte, but this seems to have been an error on his part.

Chapter 2

7, line 28: '. . . When I was ten years old'.
Boschot (I, 31 n.) believes 'dix ans' is a mistake—whether misprint or error of memory—for 'six ans'.

Hippeau (*Berlioz intime*, 152) also challenges Berlioz's statement that he went at the age of ten, and for a short time only, quoting the testimony of two of his former school fellows, Joseph Favre (with whom Berlioz played duets) and Charles Bert (a close friend of the family). But see the discussion in my *Berlioz*, vol. I, 46–7.

8, lines 22–3: '". . . he could not tell you how many departments there are in France"'. The young Berlioz's poor knowledge of French geography is corroborated by the certificate of his baccalauréat (1821), which gave him *médiocre* for 'Rivers of France, course of the Loire and the Rhone'.

Chapter 3

11, line 27: 'I was thirteen when I ceased to see her'.
I.e. in 1817. This would seem to conflict with the statement on p. 13 that he saw Estelle in the summer of the young Imbert's death, which can hardly have occurred before 1818; Imbert's contract was renewed on 20 May 1818.

Chapter 4

13, line 3: '. . . a copy of Devienne's *Method* . . .'
Méthode de flute théorique et pratique (1795).

13, lines 27–8: 'a copy of Rameau's *Treatise* . . . by d'Alembert'. *Eléments de musique théorique et pratique suivant les principes de M. Rameau, éclaircis, developpés et simplifiés par M. d'Alembert* (1752).

14, line 1: '. . . the quartets of Pleyel . . .'
In the Autobiographical Sketch of 1832 used by d'Ortigue in his biographical essay in the *Revue de Paris* in December that year (reprinted in *Le balcon de l'Opéra*) it was 'a quartet by Haydn'. This is however less sinister than Boschot and Malherbe would have us suppose. In the early nineteenth century, quartets by Pleyel were commonly ascribed to Haydn (his teacher). Berlioz corrected the mistake two years later in the *Gazette musicale* (9 November 1834), where he speaks of 'the quartets of Pleyel, with which the four amateurs who made up the philharmonic society of my native town used to regale me every Sunday after Mass'.

14, line 3: '. . .Catel's treatise . . .'
Traité d'harmonie (1805).

14, lines 5–6: 'I immediately wrote a kind of medley . . . on themes from a book of Italian airs . . .'
Possibly the same work that he tried to get published in the spring of 1819 (see CG, I, 20–2). The offer was turned down by both Pleyel and Janet et Cotelle; but he was more successful in his approach to another firm, le Duc, which published his romance 'Le dépit de la bergère' in about 1819 (see Cecil Hopkinson, op. cit., 6).

14, lines 15–16: '. . . who imagine that they can judge a string quartet from the first violin part'.
Curiously, in *The Life of Richard Wagner* (I, 130) Ernest Newman, led astray by a piece of false reasoning of Boschot's, imputes this very attitude to Berlioz.

14, lines 32–4: 'His place . . . was taken almost at once by . . . Dorant.'
For a discussion of the chronology of Imbert's and Dorant's residence at La Côte, see my *Berlioz*, vol. I, 70–2, 75–8, 87.

15, line 16: 'My father would not . . . the piano'.
Nevertheless Berlioz's early songs are nearly all written for accompaniment of piano and not guitar. For a discussion of this question see *New Berlioz Edition*, vol. 15, ed. Ian Kemp and Ian Rumbold.

16, line 10: 'I quote the first stanza'.
Berlioz actually quotes lines 1–4 of stanza 1 and lines 5–8 of stanza 2.

17, lines 12: '. . . the lives of Gluck and Haydn in the *Biographie* . . .'
Dr Berlioz was a subscriber to the *Biographie* (see an unpublished letter of 6 March 1846 in the Reboul-Berlioz Collection). Volume XVII (Ge–Go) came out in 1816 and volume XIX (Gu–He) in 1817.

17, lines 35–6: '. . . Monro's enormous treatise on osteology . . .'
Osteology, a Treatise on the Anatomy of the Human Bones, by the Edinburgh physician and anatomist Alexander Monro (1697–1767), originally published in 1726. The *Memoirs* spells him Munro.

19, lines 20: '. . . O'Connell's injunction . . .'
Berlioz, who quotes it in French, probably saw it in one of the *Débats*' frequent reports of O'Connell's speeches.

Chapter 5

20, line 27: 'On arriving in Paris in 1822 . . .'
It was 1821—late October or early November.

23, lines 23–4: 'The dissecting-room was abandoned for good'.
The *Memoirs* makes the breach more clearcut and dramatic than it was. The musical career and the medical overlapped. Berlioz remained sufficiently in touch with medicine to pass the examination for *bachelier ès sciences physiques* in January 1824, a whole year after becoming a pupil of Lesueur and about eighteen months after the discovery of Gluck's scores in the Conservatoire library. But the closure of the medical school in November 1822 for five months, owing to political unrest, was a providential event. See my *Berlioz*, vol. I, 115.

23, lines 30–1: '. . . when, after anxiously waiting, I was at last able to hear *Iphigénie en Tauride* . . .'
The event apparently took place much earlier than the *Memoirs* suggests; memory exaggerated the period of waiting. If the letter to Nanci in *Correspondance générale*, I, 34–7) is correctly dated, Berlioz had heard *Iphigénie en Tauride* by mid-December 1821—i.e. six weeks after his arrival in Paris. Six weeks may well have seemed a long time to a young man one of whose chief interests in coming to the capital was to see Gluck at the Opéra. But the impatience Berlioz refers to more probably concerns the three-month gap in the Opéra's performances of the work between

May and August 1822, by which time he was spending all his spare moments studying the score in the Conservatoire library. See my *Berlioz*, vol. I, 113. Cf. also *Gazette musicale*, 9 November 1834: 'After three months [*sic*] in the capital I had not yet seen the name of an opera by Gluck on the placards. [...] As you know, the Opéra always announces its performances twice; this gives the management the chance of changing on the day the work advertised the day before. One morning [...] I was glancing idly at the placards [...] expecting to see Rossini's name once more flaunted across the wall [...] when my teeth began to chatter and my legs to shake; barely able to stand up, I turned back to my lodgings in a sort of daze. "What is it?" said R[obert], seeing me wild and dishevelled, with a handkerchief to my nose. "Did you fall? You're bleeding—what happened? Tell me." "At the Opéra—tonight... they're doing... *Iphi–Iphigénie en Tauride*." "God!" And we both stood there, struck dumb at the thought that we were going to see Gluck's great masterpiece that very evening. R.'s nose, however, did not bleed.'

Chapter 6

24, line 16: '... The Arab Horse'.
Millevoye's poem, 'Le tombeau du Coursier, chant d'un Arabe', was first published in his collection of *Elégies* in 1812. In the *Œuvres Complètes* of 1822 it has the title 'L'Arabe au tombeau de son Coursier'.

25, line 10: '... what hours I wasted...'
Lesueur was, however, an important influence. See Appendix II, 605–6.

26, †n.: '... after the first performance...'
It was the second performance that Napoleon heard, not the first.

Chapter 7

28, lines 3–4: 'I was a great Piccini man—and a Gluckist too'.
Daniel Bernard, in his introduction to *Correspondance inédite de Hector Berlioz* (11–12), gives a fuller account of this incident, with Berlioz excitedly brandishing a saucepan of frying onions on hearing the old man confess that he liked Gluck, only to put it coldly down again when Andrieux added, in an undertone, 'I'm very fond of Piccini too.' Boschot sees a motive of self-interest behind the visit: Andrieux, on the point of publishing his complete works in five volumes, was anxious to court the younger generation, for whom Stendhal had recently spoken when he described Andrieux's witty, elegant poetry as too insipid 'for the strenuous and serious-minded age we live in'. Thirty years earlier Andrieux had written librettos. He is also remembered for his advice to Balzac not to become a writer.

28, line 14: '... *Beverley*...'
Laferrière, in his memoirs (see Bibliography), quotes several bars from Berlioz's scena, which is otherwise unknown.

28, lines 32–3: '. . . I . . . fled headlong'.
The date of this incident has been variously conjectured. Boschot identifies it with a benefit given not for Talma but for the singer Lays at the Opéra on 1 May 1823, at which Talma performed in *Athalie*. This would put the composition of *Beverley* before that of the opera on *Estelle et Némorin* and the approach to Andrieux, and not after as the *Memoirs* states; and the impulse to compose *Beverley* would have come directly from the announcement of the revival of Saurin's play (February 1823). Against this there are (*a*) the fact (apparently unknown to Boschot) that Berlioz was three hundred and fifty miles away in La Côte Saint-André at the time of Lays' benefit and (*b*) Berlioz's statement that the commission for the Mass—which definitely belongs to 1824—came 'shortly after' he had composed *Beverley*. Much of the confusion of chronology usually attributed to this part of the *Memoirs* is the creation of commentators. It springs from Boschot's misdating of the Innocents' Day rehearsal of the Mass (in which Newman and Barzun follow him). As is shown by a printed invitation in the Conservatoire library (CG, I, 72–3), and as Tiersot correctly guessed (see *Ménestrel*, 1906, 153), the rehearsal took place on 27 December 1824, not on 27 December 1823. This misdating was responsible for the ingenious but erroneous theory devised by Boschot, and adopted by Newman and Barzun, according to which the Mass and the oratorio *The Crossing of the Red Sea* were essentially the same work, the Innocents' Day rehearsal being not of the Mass (since it did not then exist) but of the oratorio, which was later reworked as a Mass. The theory involves a misreading of Berlioz's letter of June/July 1824 to Lesueur (CG, I, 60); for when he says that reading through the Credo and Kyrie has left him cold, he refers not to the music, which had not yet been composed, but to the text. In the light of the correct date of the rehearsal—December 1824—the confusion disappears; Berlioz's only mistake was to have placed the appeal to Chateaubriand three months after the rehearsal, instead of immediately afterwards and before the revision of the score and the recopying of the parts. The following chronology of this period may be hazarded:

1822	
Summer	visit to La Côte.
	Discovery of Gluck's scores in the Conservatoire library.
Autumn	Composition of *Le cheval arabe*.
	Gerono introduces Berlioz to Lesueur; Medical School closed for five months.
December	'Canon libre à la quinte' advertised—Berlioz's first publication to bear the inscription 'pupil of Lesueur'.
1823	
March–May	Visit to La Côte Saint-André.? Joséphine Berlioz curses her son.
June	Unsuccessful approach to Andrieux.
	Gerono agrees to write libretto.
August	First article in *Le corsaire*.

Late summer and autumn	Composition of *Estelle et Némorin.*
Winter	Composition of *The Crossing of the Red Sea.*
1824	
January	*Bachelier ès sciences physiques.*
Spring	Composition of *Beverley.*
	Project with Humbert Ferrand for opera on *Les francs-juges.*
	Mass commissioned for Saint-Roch.
June–July	Visit to La Côte Saint-André.
Autumn	Composition of Mass.
December	Abortive rehearsal of Mass.

29, lines 18–20: 'Valentino . . . was hoping to be appointed conductor of the Chapel Royal as well.'
He was in fact appointed shortly afterwards.

30, line 25: '. . . out of the question . . .'
Berlioz's letter of 12 December 1825 to Nanci (CG, I, 102), explaining why he was forced to borrow money, says the reason for his not being able to use the Chapel Royal forces as he had hoped was a visit by the King to Saint-Cloud planned for the day of the performance.

30, lines 25–8: 'At this point . . . approach Chateaubriand'.
As stated above, the letter to Chateaubriand preceded and did not follow Berlioz's revision of the score and copying of the parts.

31, line 2: 'You ask me, sir, for twelve hundred francs.'
In the original of Chateaubriand's letter (see *Lettres de musiciens écrites en français*, II, 155), the figure is fifteen hundred francs. Otherwise the two texts are the same.

31, n.: 'I must also have asked him to put in a word for me with the authorities . . .'
Chateaubriand had, however, been out of office since the previous June.

Chapter 8

31, line 31: '. . . in my articles in the *Journal des débats*'.
E.g. 26 April 1840.

33, *n.: 'I subsequently destroyed it as well.'
Berlioz is not 'mistaken' (Newman) but merely reticent. The Resurrexit survived only because of the copy he sent to the Institute from Rome (see Chapter 39). He destroyed the performing material of the Mass, and gave away the score (recently rediscovered and published in *New Berlioz Edition*, vol. 23), but he used some of its ideas in later works, most notably *Benvenuto Cellini* (Carnival scene), the Requiem (Tuba mirum and Offertorium), Te Deum (Te ergo quaesumus) and Fantastic Symphony, the main theme of whose third movement is prefigured in the Gratias agimus.

33, lines 10–11: '... an oratorio, recently completed, called *The Crossing of the Red Sea* ...'
The composition, however, belongs to 1823 (see CG, I, 60, and the draft of this letter quoted in Boschot, I, 140).

Chapter 9

34, line 21: '... the year before ...'
Probably 1822. His enrolment as a full-time student at the Conservatoire took place a good deal later, in 1826. It is this that he refers to when he says (Chapter 11): 'Cherubini ... knew that I had not been through the regular Conservatoire mill to get into Lesueur's class and had me enrolled in Reicha's ...'

34, lines 23–4: '... on the death of Perne ...'
1822 was the year of Perne's retirement, but he lived until 1832.

36, lines 7–8: '... twelve years later ...'
More like sixteen or seventeen: he was appointed assistant curator of the library in 1839.

Chapter 10

37, lines 9–10: '... I returned to La Côte.'
This visit is usually assigned to the summer of 1826. But Berlioz did not go to La Côte at all in 1826; this is clear from Dr Berlioz's *Livre de raison* and also from Berlioz's letter of 28 September 1826 to his sister Nanci (CG, I, 137–8). His last visit before 1828 was from August till November 1825; he left for Paris on 7 November. Was it on this visit that the events described in Chapter 10 took place? To my mind the incident should probably be assigned to spring 1823 (see my *Berlioz*, vol. I, 121 and 582). Berlioz's account in Chapter 10 conflates the visits of 1822, 1823, 1824 and 1825.

Chapter 11

41, lines 36–8: '... I had lately made friends with ... Humbert Ferrand ...'
The beginnings of their friendship go back earlier, as Berlioz himself suggests (see p. 30). This passage is concerned with events belonging to 1825 and early 1826.

42, lines 4–5: '... an oblivion from which it has never emerged.'
When the board of the Opéra turned down Ferrand's libretto (May 1829), Berlioz tried to have the work performed by a German company. As late as 1833 he was still hoping to get it put on (see CG, II, 109). However, nothing came of these various attempts.

42, lines 5–7: 'I have taken some of the best ideas ... and developed them in later works.'
Notably the March to the Scaffold and the second movement of the Symphonie funèbre.

42, lines 26–7: '... a positive panegyric a few months before'.
More likely two years before. Whereas the approach to Kreutzer belongs to late 1825 (see CG, I, 110), the letter (CG, I, 70–1) was probably written in the summer of 1823 (see my *Berlioz*, vol. I, 142–3 and 585). The letter began, 'Genius! I faint... I die... Tears choke me! God! *The Death of Abel!*...'

42, lines 35–6: '... where he was merely violinist...'
Kreutzer was leader of the orchestra.

Chapter 12

45, line 20: '... adapting Walter in *The Life of a Gambler*...'
Poetic licence: the Berlioz/Charbonnel ménage was set up in September 1826. Goubeaux's play did not appear until the following March.

46, lines 26–7: '... they only found out... seven or eight years after...'
Cf. Berlioz's letter to Nanci, 13 December 1839 (CG, II, 615): 'There's no point in my attempting to deny the facts: too many artists knew me then, and saw me at the Nouveautés, for it to be a secret. Besides, I was so desperate, so incensed at the opposition I was encountering, that rather than return home, as they were trying to force me to do, I made inquiries about going to East Africa or America. No opportunity came, and it was then that I went to the Nouveautés. I need not remind you that short of dying of starvation...' The rest of the sentence is lost.

Chapter 13

47, lines 1–3: 'It was during this period that I wrote... the overture to the *Francs-juges*. The *Waverley* overture followed soon afterwards'.
The chronology of the middle 1820s may perhaps be reconstructed as follows:

1825	
January	Family hears of Saint-Roch débâcle. Allowance cut off.
February	Berlioz asks his Uncle Victor to intercede for him.
Spring	He borrows from de Pons.
?June	*Les francs-juges* begun.
July	Success of Mass temporarily disarms opposition. Father orders him home.
August–November	Visit to La Côte Saint-André. Father agrees to further period of trial.
December	Composition of *La révolution grecque*. Unsuccessful attempt to get Kreutzer to perform it. Meanwhile, to economize, he has left his lodgings in the rue Saint-Jacques and moved to the rue de Harlay (c. June). Third article in *Corsaire*.
1826	
February	Weber in Paris.
March	Ferrand's text for *La révolution grecque* published.

Summer	Father hears of still outstanding debt to de Pons, pays it, but cuts allowance to fifty francs a month.
	Failure in preliminaries of Institute competition.
August	Berlioz enrols as full-time student at Conservatoire.
September	He goes to live in rue de la Harpe with Charbonnel. Ignores summons to return home. Engaged as chorister at Nouveautés.
Autumn	*Francs-juges* overture composed, opera completed.
1827	
March	Nouveautés opens after several postponements. Allowance increased.
July	Institute competition—*La mort d'Orphée*.
Late summer	Illness. Berlioz leaves Nouveautés.
September	English company at the Odéon: *Hamlet*, *Romeo and Juliet*.
November	Second performance of Mass.
1828	
Winter or early spring	Moves to 96 rue de Richelieu.

49, line 18: '. . . I do not think they were ever very close.'
Reicha and Beethoven were in fact quite close friends for a time. As Berlioz states, they were fellow-students, matriculating at Bonn University in 1789.

Chapter 14

50, line 24: '. . . and disqualified me.'
Berton later told Berlioz that there was nothing new to be done in music; 'the great masters abided by certain precise musical forms, but you are unwilling to. Why try to do better than the great masters?' (CG, I, 161).

51, line 4: 'Antoine was out chasing *grisettes* . . .'
The account-book for the household (see p. 46 n.) ends on 22 May 1827, when Charbonnel left for La Côte. But it was not till early in 1828 that Berlioz moved across the river to less modest quarters in the rue de Richelieu.

52, line 1: 'Weber had not yet produced his masterpieces . . .'
Der Freischütz had in fact reached Paris more than two years before Berlioz's period at the Nouveautés. His memory here and in the following chapter reverts to an earlier time, when Gluck and his school were his exclusive passion, and Rossini, the enemy, was conquering Paris. See also p. 80, lines 7–8, where he again implies that the revelation of Weber preceded that of Shakespeare by only a short time, instead of coming more than two and a half years earlier.

52, * n.: 'And without bass drum.'
The bass drum does appear briefly in six numbers of *The Barber of Seville*, but is not used in the ad lib. style typical of Italian operatic music of the period.

Chapter 15

60, n.: 'He was called le Tessier. I never saw him again.'
Berlioz wrote to le Tessier two days later (see CG, I, 80–2). In his letter, dated 21 January 1825, he apologizes for having asked him for his address. His excuse must be the state of ecstasy to which Dérivis and Sacchini had reduced them both. He will not abuse his confidence: '. . . you must be very busy, and are staying only a short time in Paris, so I shall not take the liberty of coming to see you,' but he cannot refrain from writing to him to express his delight at finding a kindred spirit, in these days when the public is so coldly unresponsive to true beauty. He ends by asking him—if he will still be in Paris on that date—to do him the honour of coming to a performance of a Mass of his which he hopes to give in the Panthéon on 19 March. The performance did not take place (the Mass was given, as we have seen, in Saint-Roch on 10 July). French etiquette and the shortness of le Tessier's stay in Paris no doubt explain why they did not meet again.

Chapter 16

63, line 12: '. . . the failure of *Oberon* killed him'.
Doubly untrue: *Oberon* was well received in London; and although the strain of rehearsing and conducting the opera must have hastened Weber's end, he was in any case a doomed man: the post-mortem found 'the lungs almost universally diseased' (Warrack, *Carl Maria von Weber*, 345).

64, line 9: 'The experience of 1828 . . .'
This should be 1830. The German company appeared in the early summer of 1829, and then returned the following spring; it was in the latter season that *Oberon* was seen.

64, line 11: 'The Mermaids' chorus . . .'
Presumably performed as a chorus at the time, but written for two solo voices.

67, lines 31–2: '. . . the miserable poetaster . . .'
Nahum Tate, librettist of Purcell's *Dido and Aeneas*, whose adaptation of *King Lear* (1681) was performed well into the nineteenth century.

Chapter 18

70, line 28: '. . . who five years later became my wife'.
It was six years. He first saw Harriet Smithson in September 1827 and married her in October 1833.

71, n.: 'Victor Hugo, *Chants du crépuscule*'.
The quotation is not from *Chants du crépuscule* but from *Les rayons et les ombres*: 'Regard jeté dans une mansarde'.

71, line 26: 'It was on my return from one of these wanderings...'
Newman (67 n., following Boschot) sees this as an error: Berlioz, he says, is here writing of the period 1827–8, whereas *Elégie* was composed much later. But the error is Newman's. The composition of the song was indeed later—probably January 1830—but Berlioz had not given up taking long solitary walks in the country by that time. The account of his unrequited passion for Harriet Smithson in Chapter 18 is not confined to the months immediately following her appearances at the Odéon but ranges over the whole period—i.e. September 1828 to early spring 1830.

73, lines 24–5: 'I was too overwhelmed ever to dream of such things [marrying Miss Smithson and composing a *Romeo and Juliet* symphony].'
Though Berlioz could conceivably have come out of the play with the wild idea of 'marrying Juliet', the thought of composing any kind of symphony would hardly have entered his head at that stage, with the inauguration of the Société des Concerts and the discovery of Beethoven still six months in the future. Once that had happened, the idea of a *Romeo and Juliet* symphony emerged very soon, if we are to believe Emile Deschamps, who wrote the text for the symphony, and who dates their first discussions to 1828. D'Ortigue's *Le balcon de l'Opéra* and Janin's review of the first performance of the symphony (*Débats*, 29 November 1839) both support Deschamps' contention.

74, line 2: '...keeping away from the English company.'
Berlioz's Autobiographical Sketch (1832), used by d'Ortigue (op. cit., 306), says that he attended the Odéon on nights when the English company was not playing.

74, line 5: '...several months in the kind of dull despair...'
This is not really contraverted by the fact that (as he himself states) he gave a performance of the Mass during the same period. Telling Ferrand about it shortly afterwards, he says, 'My friend, I write enthusiastically to you of all this, but you don't know how unimportant it seems to me. For three months I have been possessed by a sorrow so intense that nothing can take my mind off it. Life is hateful to me, I can't tell you how hateful; even the success I have just had only eased the burden for an instant, and now it weighs on me even more crushingly than before' (CG, I, 161–2).

74, lines 11–13: 'I would dare to attempt what no composer had attempted in France before...'
In a letter to the Press, published in the *Revue musicale*, *Corsaire*, *Figaro* and *Pandore*, he defended himself against the charge that this was an unwarranted thing to do, and at the same time publicized the concert.

76, lines 8–11: '... an exact account of our conversation... And I did send it, as it appears above.'
The account of their conversation in his letter of 12 May 1828 to Rochefoucauld is nothing like so colourful (though it contains the memorable reference to Cherubini as an 'agent subalterne' attempting to frustrate the Vicomte's

philanthropic intentions). It is possible that the conversation given in the *Memoirs* is a conflation of two separate encounters. It is also possible that the letter to which Berlioz refers was not filed in the public records. In general, the substance of what the *Memoirs* relates here appears to be true; but the details are not to be relied on. The documents preserved in the Archives nationales in Paris are given in CG, I, 175–84.

Chapter 19

77, line 11: 'The general rehearsal...'
His letters speak of two general rehearsals; see CG, I, 190 and 194.

78, lines 5–6: '... the final pages ought to have made me keep it.'
The autograph has indeed not survived and we know the work only because of a copyist's manuscript. From this we can see that the final pages, so far from being destroyed, became 'The Aeolian Harp' in *Lélio*.

78, lines 10–11: '... for the following day.'
According to Berlioz's letter to Ferrand (CG, I, 194) the second general rehearsal was on the Saturday, *two* days before the concert, which took place on Monday 26 May 1828.

78, line 15: '"... played on —— May 1828."'
Ferrand's copy of the score has the inscription: 'Work declared unplayable by the music section of the Institute, played on 22 July [*sic*] 1828'. The same date appears on his copy of *La révolution grecque*.

79, lines 6–7: 'It was never performed again, and I eventually destroyed it.'
Ferrand's copy of the work has survived. A second performance was planned, five years later, as part of a concert given in the Tuileries Gardens in commemoration of the July Revolution; but the candles ran out and the work was replaced by the Marseillaise and the 'ignoble Parisienne, which the orchestra could play in the dark' (CG, II, 110).

Chapter 20

82, line 34: '... you couldn't even if you wanted to.'
Boschot justly remarks that it is a little hard to expect an artist of seventy suddenly to respond to a totally different kind of music, virtually repudiating his own life's work in the process.

82, line 36: '... calling [Beethoven] a "great pianist" ...'
This is not an authenticated remark; but Berlioz may well have heard it from people who had known Haydn and Beethoven.

82, line 38–P.83, line 1: 'Handel claimed that his cook...'

What Handel apparently said was: 'Gluck knows no more counterpoint than my cook, Waltz'—who was, incidentally, a musician.

83, lines 1–2: 'Rossini's comment on Weber is that his music gives him colic.'
Berlioz cited Rossini's 'ridiculous gibes against Weber in the foyer of the German theatre' as a reason for refusing the offer of an introduction to him at about this time (CG, I, 257). However, they met soon afterwards.

Chapter 21

83, line 28: '. . . had recently founded the *Revue européenne* . . .'
This should be the *Correspondant*. (The *Revue européenne* did not appear till 1831, when it replaced the *Correspondant*.) It seems clear that the initiative in this particular instance came not from Ferrand but from Berlioz himself (see CG, I, 220–1). This does not of course preclude Ferrand's having previously suggested that Berlioz should try his hand at criticism. See also Berlioz's letter of 10 May 1829 (CG, I, 253).

85, line 3: '. . . I did nothing more about it.'
What this account does not tell us is that, presumably not long after the abortive attempt on the *Quotidienne*, he published an article on the same theme in the *Corsaire*, a daily arts and fashion newspaper. Two similar articles followed, on 11 January 1824 and 19 December 1825. After that he seems to have written nothing until 1829, when he began contributing to the *Correspondant* and to the *Berliner allgemeine musikalische Zeitung*.

Chapter 22

86, line 20: 'The government which instituted the Prix de Rome . . .'
I.e. for musicians. As a school for painters, sculptors and architects, the French Academy in Rome dates back to 1666, when it was founded by Colbert. Others before Berlioz had doubted the usefulness of sending young musicians there.

88, lines 25–6: '. . . to pronounce on an art that was not their own.'
The mixed voting procedure which he criticizes originated in a desire to lessen the risk of government interference. As it happened, Berlioz owed his second prize in 1828 to the painters, engravers and architects. The music section had awarded it to another pupil of Lesueur's, Julien Nargeot. The full jury reversed the vote, awarding it to Berlioz and Nargeot jointly. It has been suggested, by Newman (who really should have stopped to think!), that Berlioz is at fault in 'forgetting to mention' this fact. But to have done so would merely have drawn attention to his disinterestedness in attacking a system from which he personally benefited; it would not have weakened his argument, which is here concerned with general principles.

89, lines 18–19: 'The whole idea . . . is destroyed . . .'

For a musician of Berlioz's abnormal sensitivity to instrumental colour, the piano literally took the life out of an orchestral work by destroying one of the elements of composition, timbre.

Chapter 23

92, †n.: '... I doubt if [Méhul] was born at the time...'
Berlioz's chronology is equally suspect. Even supposing Pingard to have been in his late seventies when Berlioz knew him, he would not have begun his travels before the mid-1760s. Méhul was born in 1763. Levaillant (born 1753) did not go to the Cape till 1780.

93, line 16: '... if there was anything good in my score, it was that andante.'
Berlioz used this andante for the 'Chant sacré', the sixth of his *Neuf mélodies* published a year and a half later. The cantata contains something else which he does not mention, and which was certainly too good to waste—a substantial portion of what later became the main theme (the *idée fixe*) of the Fantastic Symphony, sung by the anguished Herminia to the words 'J'exhale en vain ma plainte fugitive, je l'implore, il ne m'entend pas'. It is none the less, as Tiersot remarks (*Ménestrel*, 1906, 270), the theme which enshrines the 'soul of the young Berlioz', expressing the pain of the lover separated from the object of his love.

Chapter 24

97, line 21: 'I wrote to her'.
For a few weeks in February 1829 he imagined that 'Ophelia' might after all be well disposed towards him. But his hopes proved illusory.

97, line 31: '... the French actor Huet...'
His memory apparently confused a benefit for Huet, held on 5 December 1827, which included the last two acts of *Romeo and Juliet* with Abbot and Harriet Smithson, and the performance given in aid of the poor on 25 February 1829, at which the same actors appeared in scenes from the play, and his overture *Waverley* was played. See CG, I, 236–9, where the details of the main part of the programme are in accord with *Almanach des Spectacles* and with *Figaro* of 25 February, which announced the overture.

99, lines 1–2: '... she left for Holland the next day.'
Actually six days later, on 3 March. See my *Berlioz*, vol. I, 302–3.

99, line 3: '... lodgings in the rue Richelieu...'
He moved there some time between January and April 1828.

99, lines 5–9: 'I had been lying since the previous evening... drove off on her way to Amsterdam.'

There is no need to follow the line of argument taken by Boschot who, with devastating literal-mindedness, doubts the sincerity of this account on the grounds that on the very day of Harriet's departure for Holland (3 March) Berlioz wrote a formal letter 'in a steady hand' to La Rochefoucauld, asking him to accept the dedication of the *Huit scènes de Faust.* In any case the incident referred to in the *Memoirs* clearly occurred on 26 February. Harriet had been expected to leave for Amsterdam that day, and when Berlioz saw her drive off he naturally assumed it was on the first stage of her journey.

Chapter 25

100, lines 36–7: '"You should not have done your best".'
Shortly afterwards Auber took Berlioz on one side at the Opéra and urged him to 'write conventionally, and when you have produced something that strikes you as horribly conventional, it will be just what is required' (CG, I, 270). Berlioz followed this advice a year later and won the prize.

101, line 23: 'Madame Dabadie is a very fine musician . . .'
Boïeldieu is referring to the performance given to the music section. According to Berlioz's letter to his father (CG, I, 265), when his cantata was heard at the full session it was sung not by the well-known soprano but by her sister, a 'totally inexperienced' student at the Conservatoire whom Madame Dabadie sent in her place because the session clashed with the postponed dress rehearsal of *William Tell*, in which she was taking the role of Tell's son Jemmy. A Mlle Leroux (the maiden name of Madame Dabadie) was one of the performers of the sextet from *Huit scènes de Faust* at Berlioz's concert of 1 November 1829.

Chapter 26

103, lines 2–4: 'One of them was seen by Marx . . . this unexpected encouragement . . .'
Berlioz contributed a review of Auber's *La fiancée* to Marx's Berlin journal not long before the *Huit scènes* was published; but the friendly tone of Marx's letter may still have been unexpected.

103, line 7: '. . . very differently developed . . .'
Most of the *Huit scènes* remained substantially unchanged.

103, lines 10–11: '. . . I rounded up all the copies I could get hold of and destroyed them.'
Fewer than twenty are known to have survived.

103, lines 13–14: '. . . my first concert.'
This should be 'my second concert'. The first was the concert of 26 May 1828, described in Chapter 19.

103, line 14: 'It was sung by six students at the Conservatoire...'
They were Mlles Leroux, Saint-Ange, Beck, and MM Cambou, Caneste, Devilliers.

104, lines 3–5: 'Immediately after the composition of the *Faust* pieces... I wrote my Fantastic Symphony'.
The gap between the completion of the *Huit scènes de Faust* and the composition of the symphony was about a year, but it is clear from his letters that the latter work had been germinating in his mind for a long time before he set it down on paper.

The March to the Scaffold was developed from *Les francs-juges* and the *idée fixe* had largely taken shape in the Prix de Rome cantata *Herminie*; but Newman's claim that the second, third and fifth movements came from the projected *Faust* ballet turned down by the Opéra in 1829 has no evidence to support it.

104, line 9: '... the March... was written in a night.'
Boschot (I, 230) argues that because the March comes from *Les francs-juges*, Berlioz's statement that it was written in one night is false. This is a good sample of his logic.

104 28–p. 105, line 14: '... when the day came for the rehearsal... and the enterprise was abandoned.'
Berlioz's letter of 28 May [1830] to his father says that two rehearsals ('très mauvaises') were held, and gives as the reason for the abandonment of the enterprise the fact that other concerts planned for the same day would have deprived him of singers, orchestra and audience.

Chapter 29

110, line 4: '... a battle hymn of my composition...'
The text of *Chant guerrier*, by his friend Thomas Gounet, does not correspond to any of Moore's *Irish Melodies*. It seems to be distantly derived from two of them, 'Forget not the field' and 'War Song' ('Forget not our wounded companions who stood' etc.).

112, line 19: 'The poor man died in the interval.'
Rouget de Lisle did not die till 1836, nearly four years after Berlioz's return from Italy.

Chapter 30

114, line 8: 'in the maternal eyrie...'
The quotation in the *Memoirs* reads 'maternelle' for the poem's 'paternelle'.

116, lines 7–8: '... and my mistress...'
Cf. his letter to his father (CG, I, 378–9): 'I was absolutely alone when I received my prize. M. Lesueur was ill in bed and unable to come; Mme Moke refused to

appear there. I had neither father, mother, master, nor mistress—nothing but a crowd of people who had come out of curiosity, attracted by the commotion caused by the final rehearsal of my cantata.' In the first published version of his account of the prizegiving (*Gazette musicale*, 5 February 1834) the identity of his 'mistress' underwent a subtle transformation, perhaps in deference to Harriet, whom he had lately married: 'Pour ma maîtresse; . . . oh! elle était loin . . . bien loin!'

117, lines 6, 9: '. . . Mme Malibran . . . the last time I saw her.'
Malibran, one of the two reigning stars of the Théâtre-Italien (the other was Sontag), went to Italy in 1832 and reappeared rarely in Paris in the remaining four years of her life.

117, lines 27–8: 'the much-heralded holocaust had turned into a damp squib . . .'
Madame Lesueur and her daughters apparently suspected sabotage by Berton: 'They have a mania for seeing plots everywhere' (Berlioz to his father, CG, I, 381). 'The players responsible—four in number—are good friends of mine', he goes on, 'and were genuinely in despair at their blunder.'

Chapter 31

118, chapter heading: 'I give my second concert'.
Once again he has forgotten the concert of 26 May 1828. This one was his third.

121, line 35: '. . . until the middle of January . . .'
This should be 'until the end of December'; he left Paris on the 30th.

Chapter 32

125, lines 14–18: '. . . a terrific gust caught the ship . . . the Venetian sprang forward . . .'
See the broadly similar accounts of the journey given in the letters of 2 March 1831 to his father and 6 May 1831 to his Paris friends (CG, I, 415–18 and 438–40).

Chapter 34

132, lines 12–13: '. . . I was allowed out for the first time and went to the post-office'.
Several days elapsed between his recovering from quinsy and his receiving the letter from Mme Moke; the reading of Shakespeare in the wood by the Arno and the episodes of Napoleon Louis' funeral and the *bella sposina*, which the *Memoirs* relegates to later visits to Florence, all took place in this interval.

137, n.: 'I think it was Ventimiglia.'
His letter to Horace Vernet is dated 'Diano Marina, 18th April 1831' (CG, I, 429). Diano Marina is about thirty miles farther east from Nice.

Chapter 35

140, lines 29–30: '... (despite the large hole ... in my funds) ...'
One thousand and fifty francs, according to the letter of 14 June 1831 to Thomas Gounet (CG, I, 457).

141, lines 1–2: 'Bellini's latest opera *I Montecchi* ... was being performed.'
It was on his first visit to Florence, in late February or early March, that he saw Bellini's opera.

143, lines 4–5: '... I went back a few days later to see Pacini's *La Vestale*.'
Like the performance of Bellini's *Montecchi*, this belongs to Berlioz's first visit to Florence.

143, line 20: 'His funeral service was being celebrated ...'
Napoleon-Louis' funeral had already taken place, not in Florence but in Forlì, where he died (17 March). This was the burial service in Santo Spirito, Florence, where his body was brought a few weeks later, in April.

143, lines 25–7: '... his mother fled to England ... and debarred from returning to France ...'
Hortense and Louis Napoleon did not reach England till May; they were allowed to stop briefly in Paris before resuming their journey.

144, line 3: '... the death of a hero ...'
Napoleon-Louis succumbed to pneumonia, caught while he was recovering from measles, but it was widely believed at the time and for many years afterwards that he had died of wounds received while fighting with Italian patriots against the Austrians—e.g. *Nouvelle biographie générale*, 1863, Vol. 37, 447.

Chapter 36

148, n.: '... her golden hair ...'
'The Countess Guiccioli remained a Titian blond until quite late in life' (Barzun, I, 212n). The 1878 edition of the *Memoirs*, used by Holmes and by Newman, erroneously reads 'blancs' for 'blonds'.

149, lines 24–5: 'I saw an English girl there ...'
Mendelssohn also saw her at a ball in Rome, in December 1830: 'Someone tapped me on the shoulder and said, "So you are admiring the English beauty? I am quite dazzled." It was Thorwaldsen [Danish sculptor and antiquarian], standing in the doorway, lost in admiration. He had hardly spoken when we heard a torrent of words behind us: "Mais où est-elle donc, cette petite anglaise? Ma femme m'a envoyé pour la regarder ... *Per Bacco!*" It was clear to me that the little thin Frenchman with the stiff grey hair and the Legion of Honour must be Horace Vernet. He and Thorwaldsen then set to work to discuss the young lady in the

most earnest and thorough manner, and it was delightful to see the two old masters admiring her, while she was dancing away quite unconcerned' (Mendelssohn, *Letters from Italy and Switzerland*).

150, line 30: 'My companions' . . .'
The following are referred to in his writings and letters: Cendrier, Dantan the elder, Debay, Delanoie, Duc, Constant Dufeu, Etex, Flacheron, Garrez, Gibert, Lefebvre, Montfort, Munier, and Signol.

Chapter 37

154, line 23–p.155, line 1: '. . . some passage from the *Aeneid* . . . The triple intoxication . . .'
The first published version of this passage, which appeared in *Italie pittoresque* (1834), also contained the sentence: 'I would deliberately get drunk on eau de vie'; and the beginning of the following paragraph read: 'Under the combined influence of drink, poetry (etc.) . . . The quadruple intoxication . . .' In *Voyage musical en Allemagne et en Italie* (1844) this was suppressed—whether from reticence, or because it was untrue (an example of what Berlioz calls 'the proneness of artists to write for effect'), it is impossible to say.

157, lines 8–9: '. . . the murmuring Anio . . .'
Anio is the Latin form. The modern name of this tributary of the Tiber is Aniene. In classical times its upper waters, which were exceptionally pure, were conveyed by a series of aqueducts to Rome.

158, line 25: '*The lovely Juliet* . . .'
A slight misquotation—'La belle Juliette' for Barbier's 'Divine Juliette'.

Chapter 38

163, lines 29–30: '. . . I had not been in the mountains since October . . .'
He was also at Subiaco in mid-November—see the letter of the 28th to Thomas Gounet (CG, I, 499).

Chapter 39

165, line 35: 'A very able German critic . . .'
His name, Joseph Mainzer, was given in the first published version of this passage (in *Italie pittoresque*, 1834) but subsequently removed. Mainzer changed from a supporter to an opponent of Berlioz's music in the mid-1830s. Berlioz here paraphrases his articles in the *Gaz. mus.* (1834).

172, lines 20–3: 'An overture, *Rob Roy* . . . I destroyed it immediately after the concert.'
It contained themes which Berlioz used shortly afterwards in *Harold in Italy*. The overture survives in the copy he sent back to the Institute from Italy.

172, lines 25–7: 'The Chant de bonheur . . . which came to me . . . in [the] Academy garden . . .'
The Chant de bonheur is based on the main theme of the Prix de Rome cantata of 1827, *Orphée*, but contains new material.

173, line 31: 'As to the Resurrexit . . .'
The Institute's approving report is in the archives of the Académie des Beaux-Arts, pièces annexes 1832 5 E 22.

Chapter 41

183, line 32: '. . . we sometimes omitted to consult the owners.'
In earlier versions of this passage Berlioz describes an unexpected encounter with one of them, who heard them throwing stones and knocking down pears in his orchard. 'I had got over to pick them up and was peacefully filling my hat when I saw him coming towards me shouting and gesticulating. Weighed down with plunder as I was, there was no time to get back over the fence. The only hope was to brazen it out. Just as the owner of the pears was about to seize hold of me, I addressed him with an air of furious indignation: "What the devil do you mean by keeping us hanging about like this? We've been calling you for the last half-hour to come and sell us your wretched fruit. Do you think we've nothing better to do? Here's six *grani*, take it, though your pears are not worth it, and another time try to behave a little more civilly to travellers or you'll find yourself in trouble." Thereupon one of my fellow-marauders, stifling his laughter, helped me over, and we left our man standing stockstill with amazement, mouth open, staring stupidly at the copper coin in his hand and wondering whether he oughtn't to apologise' (*Italie pittoresque*: 'Voyage musical', 12; *Voyage musical en Allemagne et en Italie*, II, 190–1).

185, line 21: 'M. Courrier is a Dauphinois . . .'
From Voiron, between La Côte Saint-André and Grenoble. See Berlioz's letter to his father, Monday 17 October [1831] (CG, I, 495–7).

188, line 17: 'On leaving Subiaco . . .'
The passage from here to the end of the chapter did not appear in *Italie pittoresque*; it was first published in *Voyage musical*. This difference of recension may explain the inconsistency in Berlioz's designating of the two Swedish officers, who, having been B—— and Kl——rn for most of the chapter, suddenly become Bennet and Klinksporn.

Anyone who has tried hopping on one leg for any distance may be forgiven for suspecting an element of exaggeration in Berlioz's account of his progress from Subiaco to Tivoli.

Chapter 42

190, line 15: '. . . the cartloads of dead . . .'
Cf. the painter Joseph Severn's account of a cholera epidemic in Rome in 1837: 'The sight after sunset at the Church of San Lorenzo was the most awful that could

be imagined. Carts were arriving continually, filled with naked dead bodies, which were at once on their arrival thrown into the fosse. These death-carts came in unbroken procession from sunset until two or three o'clock in the morning. There were innumerable torches to light up the dismal work. During a month, this rude interment was at the rate of three hundred corpses a day' (*The Life and Letters of Joseph Severn*, ed. Sharp, 180–2).

192, lines 3–5: '. . . a skull . . . I picked . . . up in the cemetery at Radicoffani . . .'
This skull was among a collection of personal belongings deposited in Berlioz's room in the Conservatoire library and destroyed on his instructions not long before he died. The library attendant later told Tiersot that it was 'the skull of his wife'.

Chapter 43

194, line 9: 'One evening, when I had gone to . . . the cathedral . . .'
Berlioz has transposed this episode by a year; it belongs to his second visit to Florence. See the letter of 6 May 1831, CG, I, 442–3. The same letter states that the *sposina* had died in child-birth, and contains medical details also omitted from the published account.

195, line 5: 'Give me *tre paoli*.'
In the letter of 6 May 1831 (see previous note) this is '*un paolo*'.

198, †n.: 'I do not yet know Verdi's works.'
This evasive sentence does not appear in *Voyage musical* (1844) and was presumably added some time after he began to compile the *Memoirs* in 1848. By the time the book was completed he had heard several operas of Verdi, whom he admired.

199, lines 14–16: *'Et maerebat/Et tremebat,/Cum videbat'*.
Misquoted for *'Quae maerebat/Et tremebat,/Dum videbat'*.

201, line 16: '. . . on 12 May 1832 . . .'
It was 31 May.

Chapter 44

202, line 3: '. . . before setting out for Germany . . .'
At that stage, he intended to proceed to Berlin early in the new year.

207, lines 12–13: '. . . with crescendo . . .'
There is no crescendo at this point in the slow movement of Beethoven's Fifth Symphony; but perhaps Habeneck was in the habit of making one.

208, lines 15–16: 'Thus on my departure for Italy I left . . . a dedicated opponent . . .'

This is not strictly true. Relations were still outwardly cordial. See Appendix II, under FÉTIS.

208, lines 29–30: '... that the world is bounded by the shores of their desert island...'
'Que le monde finit avec les rivages de leur île'. Perhaps an unconscious echo of *Paul et Virginie*, a favourite book of Berlioz's childhood: 'Ils croyaient que le monde finissait où finissait leur isle.'

209, lines 20–2: 'The strain... may be imagined...'
The stormy progress of the courtship may be followed in Berlioz's letters (CG, II, 42–114) to his friends and to his sister Adèle, the only member of his family with whom he remained on friendly terms during this period. Four letters written by Berlioz to his father in February 1833 survive, and are published for the first time in CG II.

210, line 30: '... in the summer of 1833'.
The autumn—3 October. Curiously enough, Berlioz's father made a similar mistake when recording the event in his *Livre de Raison*: '... marié malgré les Parens avec Henriette Smithson en juillet 1833'. The autumn in Paris that year was exceptionally warm and sunny.

210, line 32–p. 211, line 1: '... after having had to resort to legal action...'
By means of the *sommations respectueuses* a son could formally request his father not to disinherit him because of the action he was about to take.

Chapter 45

211, lines 16–18: '... my grant... which had another year and a half to run.'
It had just over two years—till the end of 1835.

211, line 18: 'The Minister of the Interior had exempted me...'
By this date the Department of Fine Arts had become (briefly) part of the Ministry of Commerce and Public Works and not, as formerly (and later again), of the Ministry of the Interior. The surviving documents suggest that the exemption of which Berlioz speaks was a less clear-cut process—more a matter of civil servants gradually accepting a *fait accompli*; for instance, as late as December 1834, an application made by Berlioz for a fresh instalment of his grant has, pencilled on it, the weary admonition: 'M. Berlioz devrait s'en aller en Allemagne' (Archives Nationales F^{21} 610, Dossier Berlioz, which contains all the relevant papers). It is of course quite possible that his statement in the application of 14 January 1834 that he was on the point of leaving for Germany was perfectly true, and that he then changed his plans on discovering that Harriet was pregnant; their son Louis was born the following August. His letter of 7 December 1833 to Spontini (CG, II, 136–7) had mentioned a plan to go to Berlin in the new year.

212, lines 8–9: 'The concert . . . would have gone on until one in the morning.'
According to the *Gazette musicale*, the show, announced for 7, did not begin until 8, 'devant un parterre irrité du retard à commencer *Antony*'.

212, lines 22–3: 'My wife and I were unfamiliar with the . . . manœuvrings which go on in the French theatre . . .'
This is a little hard to credit. Harriet had had several years' experience of acting in Paris, and Berlioz in his student days had worked for the claque.

213, line 36: '. . . on the stroke of midnight . . .'
In a letter to his sister Adèle written four days later (CG, II, 135), the time given is 12.30.

214, lines 10–11: 'The disappointed audience rose.'
According to the letter cited in the above note, there were cries of 'Next time—the Conservatoire!'

214, lines 17–18: '. . . about seven thousand francs.'
The same letter to Adèle gives the figure as 2,500 francs net, gross takings 5,000.

215, line 17: '. . . Paganini. The date was 22nd December 1833.'
This episode is obscure. The one surviving letter of Berlioz's which describes the concert (CG, II, 143–5) says nothing of Paganini. We know from another letter, however, that a few weeks after this concert Paganini did, as the *Memoirs* states, call on Berlioz to commission a work for viola. (See CG, II, 159.) But a meeting in the Conservatoire Hall, similar to the one described in the *Memoirs* (which is stated to have been the first encounter between the two men), was mentioned by d'Ortigue a year earlier in the *Revue de Paris* (reprinted in *Le balcon de l'Opéra*). It seems likely either that there were two separate incidents, which Berlioz's memory has run together, or that the meeting described in the *Memoirs* took place a year earlier, after the concert of 9 December 1832.

217, line 24: '. . . at the fourth performance . . .'
It was the fourth performance conducted by Girard; but there had also been two others under Théophile Tilmant at the Gymnase Musicale (4 and 25 June 1835).

217, lines 30–1: '. . . and not rely on anyone else . . .'
Two years earlier Girard, who was a violinist-conductor of the old school, had bungled a performance of the *Francs-juges* overture; and Berlioz entrusted his music to him only *faute de Habeneck*. His decision to conduct the next concert himself seems to have brought their friendship, temporarily at least, to an end. The concert, announced as including works by Girard, was put off a week and given without them. Yet the *Francs-juges* overture, published the following year, was dedicated to him.

218, line 31: '"It was pure chance . . .'
Contradicted by CG, II, 337. But there seems no doubt that bureaucratic delaying tactics were used to try to quash the commission.

220, lines 12–13: '. . . the annual service commemorating the dead of the 1830 Revolution.'
Berlioz has conflated two separate though closely linked events. The service planned for 28 July 1837 was also the anniversary commemoration of Fieschi's attempt to assassinate Louis-Philippe, in which the King escaped miraculously but fourteen people, including Marshal Mortier, were killed. 28 July was also the first of the Three Days of the July Revolution, and Fieschi's attempt had been made during the anniversary celebrations of 1835.

220, line 22: 'For five months I sought in vain for payment of these debts.'
Berlioz's application to the Director of Public Monuments (CG, II, 369–70) shows that the account was still unpaid on 21 October 1837. The bill for copying appears to have been settled by the end of October—(see CG, II, 372)—i.e. five months after the event, assuming the copying to have been done not later than June.

221, lines 21–4: 'His friends and pupils . . . tried to raise a storm . . . to oust the young man in favour of the old.'
This was evidently not the same as the manœuvre of which we catch a glimpse in Berlioz's diplomatic letter to Cherubini of 24 March 1837 (CG, II, 339–40).

223, lines 22–3: 'There are perhaps a thousand bars in my Requiem.'
There are some fifteen hundred.

224, lines 2–3: 'God forgive me if I do him an injustice!'
The arguments adduced by Boschot and others to disprove the whole incident largely depend on negative evidence. They may be summed up as follows: (1) Berlioz does not mention it in his letter to Ferrand of 17 December 1837 (CG, II, 391). He simply says: 'The Requiem was well performed.' (2) He took no steps to expose Habeneck's conduct; and a few days later he even inserted an editorial puff for a concerto of Habeneck's in the *Journal des débats*. Nor is there anything about the incident in contemporary newspaper accounts and gossip columns. (3) Stanford, in his *Pages from an Unwritten Diary*, reports an account by the composer George Osborne of a conversation with Berlioz in which the latter, asked why he had printed such a cock-and-bull tale, 'burst out laughing and replied that the story seemed to him far too good a one to be lost'. (4) The whole thing is too inherently improbable to be taken seriously.

Against this, the following points may be made: (1) The letter to Ferrand was written twelve days after the performance. Its tone is forward-looking; it is almost wholly concered with the great success of the occasion and the influence this is likely to have on the powers that be at the Opéra; it also refers to another letter written eight or ten days earlier to a mutual friend, from which Ferrand will have heard full details of the performance. In a letter written twenty years later, Berlioz took for granted Ferrand's knowledge of the incident: 'The latest numbers [of the *Monde illustré*, which was serializing chapters of the *Memoirs*] contain an account, very much watered down, of the crime attempted by Cavé and Habeneck at the first performance of the Requiem' (CG, V, 678). (2) It would have gone against his lifelong practice to attack Habeneck in print, and in this instance it would have been doubly fatal to his interests, which were concentrated on the Opéra, where Habeneck was chief conductor, and which needed an unqualified success. To draw public attention to a near-disaster caused by the wilful or inadvertent negligence of that conductor could only have harmed those interests. (3) The testimony of one Irishman reported by another is hardly to be weighed against the eyewitness account of Hallé (op. cit., 66–7), who corroborates the *Memoirs*, only differing over Habeneck's motivation, which he attributes to carelessness. Ernest Reyer's review of the *Memoirs* in the *Débats* (reprinted in *Notes de musique*) agrees with Hallé: the blunder occurred, though it was not deliberate. There is also the evidence of the critic Louis Engel (*Temple Bar*, October 1883), who describes Berlioz asking some of his friends whether he should include the story in his memoirs; here the question at issue was not the truth of the incident but only the advisability of publishing it. (4) The inherent improbability is less if we think ourselves back to a time when conducting was a rudimentary art, and mistakes which would damn a man now were all in a day's work. (Incidentally, Glinka in his memoirs, observing the Parisians at rehearsal, remarks on their penchant for taking snuff, especially in difficult passages.) The maestro was nothing like the sacrosanct figure of today. Berlioz was the first conductor as we would understand the term. In general, the concept had not evolved so very far beyond that of the late eighteenth century, when Mozart could write, from Paris: '[I was] determined that if my symphony went as badly as it did at the rehearsal, I would certainly make my way into the orchestra, snatch the fiddle out of the hands of Lahoussaye, the first violin, and conduct myself.' In a darkened church, Berlioz's action need not have excited comment. As to Habeneck's motive, this is pure conjecture. Hallé was sure it was thoughtlessness; yet, even allowing for the vast difference between modern and early-nineteenth-century notions, the opening of the Tuba mirum is of all places in the Requiem the most unlikely for snuff-taking if the conductor is merely negligent, the most likely if he is actuated by malice. There remains the possibility that the incident took place at the public dress rehearsal, not at the performance.

225, lines 1–2: '. . . the chorus rehearsals and the copying were paid for . . .'
The copying bill seems to have been settled by the end of October, but the rehearsals were not paid for till 15 December. This was five months late—not eight as the *Memoirs* states.

226, line 9: '. . . a bond for three thousand francs . . .'
The figure was 4,000—finally received on 1 February 1838, i.e. ten months after the official commissioning of the work (see CG, II, 408).

226, lines 14–17: 'Some time later . . . the Légion of Honour . . .'
10 May 1839.

226, line 23: 'Later still, when the Requiem was published . . .'
October 1838—i.e. shortly *before* the award of the Légion d'honneur. The Ricordi edition referred to by Berlioz was published in 1853.

Chapter 47

227, line 1: 'A few years after . . .'
A few months after: the performance took place on 25 June 1838.

229, lines 10–13: 'soon afterwards . . . I was at the Opéra . . . for the first performance of his *Ali Baba*'.
The first performance of *Ali Baba* took place five years earlier, on 22 July 1833. The work was not subsequently revived.

229, lines 34–6: '. . . the *Revue européenne* . . . the *Correspondant* . . .'
The *Correspondant* had been replaced, in 1831, by the *Revue européenne*. Berlioz's list omits the *Rénovateur*, for which he wrote regularly between December 1833 and December 1835.

231, lines 5–6: '. . . there are those who think me violent . . . in what I write.'
Berlioz's music criticism was too pungent for some tastes. Even Eugène de Mirecourt, author of the eulogistic short biography published in 1856, is shocked at the 'lack of restraint, unnecessary vehemence and acerbity, and humour in poor taste' displayed in his writings. 'One searches in vain for the literary delicacy, that niceness of discrimination which makes a writer reject the offensive ideas and retain only the wholesome ones.' Offenbach's marginal jottings in his copy of the *Memoirs* (formerly André Meyer Collection) are full of outraged whinnyings.

Chapter 48

233, line 12: '. . . 118 francs a month.'
The gross salary was 125 francs; 118 was what he received after the pension contribution had been deducted. According to a document in Mr Richard Macnutt's possession the Minister of the Interior decided in 1840 that the amount should be raised by 300 francs a year, but it is doubtful if the decision was ever implemented: see Berlioz's letter of 30 January 1866 to the Princess Wittgenstein, in which he says his salary has just been doubled and he is therefore getting 2,800 francs instead of 1,400.

233, line 24: '. . . I shall not forget'.
He did not. On 25 November 1868, not long before his death, he got out of bed to go to the Institute and vote for Charles Blanc.

233, [*]n.: (démarche of late 1838)
The question recurs five years later, in a letter from Berlioz to Montalivet's successor Duchâtel (CG, III, 165–7), in which he again solicits for a position on the staff of the Conservatoire. At present, he says, he lives almost entirely by journalism and as a result does not have time to compose; constantly interrupted and distracted, it sometimes takes him a year to produce a work which, if he were more fortunately and more normally placed, he would complete in two months. 'Dare I hope that you will see fit to carry through what M. de Montalivet began, so that my energies may be directed where they belong?' The request was not granted.

235, lines 1–2: '... I swear ... I did not write a note of it.'
Cf. his letter of 22 December 1836 to Adèle (CG, II, 319): 'The aria is a genuinely remarkable invention; it was encored at the first three performances. At the first, Alexandre Dumas, who is hostile to the Bertins, shouted out with the full force of his mulatto lungs: "It's by Berlioz, it's by Berlioz." There's justice for you. If I had anything to do with its success, it was in a very minor way. The music really is Mlle Bertin's; but (between ourselves) the very end was weak—it detracted from the effect of the good things in the aria. All I did was to suggest a more appropriate conclusion. That was all, and I have never told a soul.'

236, lines 33–4: '... this same saltarello that he could never get right ...'
Hallé's vaguer and less circumstantial account of the first performance of the *Roman Carnival* overture (wrongly transferred to one of Berlioz's concerts in the Champs-Elysées Circus) states that through an oversight it was entirely unrehearsed: 'Musicians who know the work, with its complicated rhythm and all its intricacies, will easily understand how bold the venture was, and will wonder that it could be successful. But to see Berlioz during that performance was a sight never to be forgotten. He watched over every single member of the huge band; his beat was so decisive, his indication of all the nuances so clear and so unmistakable, that the overture went smoothly, and no uninitiated person could guess at the absence of a rehearsal' (Hallé, op. cit., 68).

238, lines 10–11: '... not to reappear until much later—Alexis Dupont having taken five months to learn the part ...'
Three and a half months, not five. Berlioz originally hoped that the change of tenor would interrupt the run of his opera by no more than a week or ten days (see letter of 20 September 1838, CG, II, 459); but the fourth (and last) performance did not take place till 11 January. In addition Act I was given three times. Several other performances were announced and then cancelled because a singer was indisposed. In the spring of 1839 Berlioz wrote to Duponchel that he was withdrawing the work—'as I know you will be delighted to hear' (CG, II, 540).

238, line 28 and [†]n.: 'It is fourteen years ...' 'N.B. That was written in 1850.'
1850 was twelve years after *Benvenuto Cellini* was produced at the Opéra. In any case 1850 must be an error for 1851. It was in the latter year that Liszt asked him for the score (so that he could put the work on at Weimar) and Berlioz, before

sending it, went through it and revised it. His subsequent letter to Liszt is expressed in terms very similar to those used in the *Memoirs*: '... I swear I shall never again recapture this energy, this Cellinian dash and impetuosity, nor such a variety of ideas' (CG, IV, 84).

238, †n.: (Rosine Stoltz)
Stoltz's fall and the collapse of the Pillet regime go back to the opening night of *Robert Bruce*, a concoction from *La donna del lago* and other Rossini works. On being hissed, Stoltz tore her handkerchief with her teeth, shouted angrily at the audience and strode from the stage (30 December 1846).

239, line 32: '... the two thousand francs...'
Legouvé lent him two thousand in all, but in two instalments, not all at once.

Chapter 49

240, line 23: 'The first [concert]...'
He omits to say that it was conducted in his absence by Habeneck.

240, lines 28–31: '... the famous incident around which so much controversy and malicious gossip have collected.'
The sophisticated reasoned that Paganini was notoriously close-fisted and, anyway, such things do not happen in real life. One story, told many years later by the aged Liszt, maintained that the gift was purely an investment: Paganini made the gesture on Jules Janin's advice to placate the Parisian public who, angered by his refusal to play at a charity concert, had decided to boycott four recitals he was about to give; the gesture worked, and Paganini gave eight concerts to packed houses. The objection to this is that Paganini gave no concerts in Paris after this date. A less fanciful theory has it that Paganini merely acted as a cover for Armand Bertin. Hallé heard this story from Madame Bertin 'about seven years later' and reported it in his autobiography: '... in order to enhance the moral effect of this gift he [Bertin] persuaded Paganini to appear as the donor of the money. How well Bertin had judged was proved immediately; what would have been a simple *gracieuseté* from a rich and powerful editor to one of his staff became a significant tribute from one genius to another, and had a colossal *retentissement*. The secret was well kept and never divulged to Berlioz' (Hallé, op. cit., 69–70). The wording of the *Memoirs*, however, suggests that Berlioz was well aware of the various true versions circulating (of which that was one) and still thought his was right. In any case, that a man of Paganini's temperament should have been moved to a sudden act of generosity seems, however unexpected, far less out of character than that he should be prepared to act as a front for the philanthropy of others. His own account of the matter, given to Morel (*Journal de Paris*, 18 January 1839), is worth quoting: 'I did it for Berlioz and for myself. For Berlioz, because I saw a young man of genius whose courage and strength might in the end have broken under the strain of the struggle which he had daily to carry on against jealous mediocrity, ignorance and indifference, and I thought: I must help him. For myself because later [...] when my claims to musical glory are reckoned, it will not be the least

that I was the first to recognize a genius and bring him public acclaim.' See Geraldine de Courcy's *Paganini the Genoese.*

241, line 24: 'Two days later ...'
I follow the reading in Léon Escudier's *Mes souvenirs* (1863), which included this chapter of the *Memoirs* (its first appearance in print), and which has 'Le surlendemain'. The concert was on 16 December; Paganini's letter, and Berlioz's reply, are dated 18 December. The *Memoirs*' 'Le lendemain' is possibly a printer's error overlooked by Berlioz.

241, line 36: '*Mio caro amico* ...'
This transcription contains minor differences of punctuation and orthography from Paganini's letter, among which are:

Paganini: *degne di un genio*
Memoirs: *degne d'un genio*
Paganini: *dal sig. Baron*
Memoirs: *dal signor baron*
Paganini: *il vostro aff. amico*
Memoirs: il vostro affezionatissimo amico

(see the facsimile in Jullien, *Hector Berlioz: sa vie et ses œuvres*, 140).

243, line 6: 'I cannot bring myself to reproduce it here.'
The letter, given in CG, II, 489, said: 'Great, noble artist, How can I express to you my gratitude? I am not a rich man; but believe me, the approval of a man of genius like yourself moves me even more deeply than your regal gift. Words fail me. The moment I can get up (I am still in bed), I shall hurry round to embrace you.'

243, lines 29–30: '... whose words I could hear in the silence of the empty room ...'
His letter of 20 December 1838 to his sister Adèle states that he heard him clearly to begin with, but that later Paganini sent for his son to act as his interpreter (CG, II, 495–6).

244, line 29: '... no more newspaper articles, or very few.'
In fact he was reviewing almost as actively as ever during this period (though with one or two longish periods of remission). What he evidently remembers is the psychological relief of being no longer dependent on journalism.

246, lines 3–4: 'All the other modifications ...'
The work originally included, between the scherzo and the Convoi funèbre, a second prologue of seventy-five bars. A piano reduction of this prologue has survived. See *New Berlioz Edition*, vol. 18, 414–18. It was orchestrated in 1995 by Oliver Knussen, and included by John Eliot Gardiner in his recording of *Romeo and Juliet* (1997).

Chapter 50

247, line 2: '... the [Bastille] monument...'
The architect was Berlioz's former companion at the Villa Medici in Rome, Joseph-Louis Duc, at whose suggestion he wrote the piece which became the Shepherds' chorus in *The Childhood of Christ*, and whose name was used in the hoax attributing it to an unknown seventeenth-century composer, Pierre Ducré.

247, lines 8–9: 'In return I would receive ten thousand francs...'
The original agreement stipulated 7,360 francs, but the Minister increased it to 10,000 on being informed that Berlioz's expenses came to 6,901 francs 15 centimes.

247, lines 18–20: '... to conclude with a hymn of praise when, the tomb being sealed...'
According to the letter of 30 July 1840 to his father, the Apotheosis as well as the Funeral March was played (several times) during the procession through the streets of Paris (CG, II, 648–9). 'Hymn of praise' is of course figurative. The part for chorus was not added till 1842.

247, lines 37–8: 'The march and the funeral oration were completed...'
The funeral oration appears to have been largely a reworking of Arnold's scena in the third act of *Les francs-juges* (see *New Berlioz Edition*, Vol. 19, Foreword, ix).

249, line 1: '... engaged me for four evening concerts...'
The symphony was performed four times in the Salle Vivienne, but the third and fourth performances were separated from the first two by about eighteen months.

249, lines 24–5: '"I write ... under the impression of your shaking [*sic*] music."'
A facsimile of the letter is given in Charles Bouvet's *Spontini* (Paris, 1930, *Maîtres de la musique ancienne et moderne*).

249, lines 28–9: 'However, I am forgetting one other occasion...'
He has also forgotten Spontini's admiring remarks after the first performance of the Fantastic Symphony, on which occasion Spontini presented him with a score of *Olympie*, inscribed with a friendly dedication (see CG, I, 385, 388 and 390).

Chapter 51

250, line 15: '... towards the end of the same year (1840)...'
The visit to Brussels belongs to 1842 (September), not to 1840.

250, lines 24–5: 'An insane jealousy, for which I had long given absolutely no grounds...'

Legouvé maintained that Berlioz had a succession of love-affairs, of which Harriet was half aware (*Soixante ans de souvenirs*, I, 301). But there is no evidence to support this allegation.

252, lines 14–15: '. . . to bid Paris farewell with a gigantic concert . . .'
His memory seems to have confused two similar events: the 'festival' described here, which took place on 1 November 1840, and a performance of the Funeral Symphony, with 200 performers, on 7 November 1842 (also at the Opéra), which was his farewell to Paris before he left for Germany.

256, line 28: '. . . "the Marseillaise!" . . .'
Boschot (II, 319), following contemporary newspaper reports, places this incident after, not before, the encounter between Girardin and Bergeron, and states that it was the police commissioner, not Berlioz, who silenced the demand.

Travels in Germany—I

First Letter

259, chapter heading: '1841–2'
This should be 1842–3.

259, line 3: '. . . I gave fifteen concerts . . .'
This figure includes the charity concert in Leipzig (22 February 1843), at which Berlioz conducted several items.

262, line 8: '*Their eyes dissolved* . . .'.
I have not found the source of the French phrase.

262, line 16: '*Swore, somewhat late* . . .'
Both the *Memoirs and Voyage musical* have 'Jurait', a misquotation for 'Jura'.

262, lines 22–3: '. . . thanks to the good will of Messrs Henssens, Mertz and Wéry . . .'
In *Voyage musical*, I, 9 this read: '. . . thanks to the goodwill of Messrs. Henssens, Mertz and Wéry, and even of M. Fétis . . .'

264, lines 2–3: '. . . (that really would have been a Grande Harmonie) . . .'
He had hoped to use the military band there for a performance of the Symphonie funèbre (see letter of 29 October 1842 to Hiller, CG, III, 25).

268, line 12: '. . . the first Prisoners' Chorus . . .'
The *Memoirs* corrects the error of *Voyage musical* (I, 19), where the chorus is wrongly stated to be in C, instead of B flat.

Second Letter

272, lines 4–5: '. . . the unfortunate Guhr, who . . . seemed destined to find my music a source of embarrassment.'
According to Ferdinand Hiller (*Künstlerleben*, 91) Guhr had taken 'good care' there should be no evening free for Berlioz to give a concert. It is not impossible, from his jocular treatment of Guhr in the *Memoirs*, that Berlioz was aware of this.

275, line 25: '. . . Beethoven likewise.'
Not quite correct: there is a small part for harp in *Die Geschöpfe von Prometheus*, and also 'Easy Variations on a Swiss air, in F, for harpsichord or harp'.

275, lines 33–5: 'Molique . . . Paris Conservatoire . . .'
Molique played a violin concerto of his composition at the Conservatoire concert of 21 February 1836.

281, lines 7–8: '. . . Täglichsbeck (the Paris Conservatoire . . . performing his symphonies)'.
At the concerts of 24 January 1836 and 2 April 1837.

Third Letter

290, lines 10–11: '. . . he is about to perform his oratorio *The Fall of Jerusalem* . . .'
According to Hiller (*Künstlerleben*, 91 ff.), Berlioz left Frankfurt early, before the concert, in an attempt to shake off Marie Recio, who insisted on performing at his concerts ('she sings like a cat'). On the pretext of going to an official reception (to which she was necessarily not invited), he left her at the hotel and took the coach to Weimar, leaving behind a letter and enough money for her to return to Paris. Marie, however, found out where he had gone and followed him, and it was she who, shortly afterwards, indignantly answered Hiller's letter of inquiry. A few weeks later, writing to Morel, Berlioz was obliged to ask him not to mention Marie in his reply, 'because she caught me up at Weimar and we are reunited . . .' (CG, III, 71–2).

291, line 6: 'Schiller! you deserved a less human friend.'
Berlioz seems to have been completely misinformed about Schiller and Goethe.

Fourth Letter

293, line 21: 'That which we call a rose . . .'
I have corrected the quotation, which appears in the *Memoirs* as 'that we call a rose'. *Voyage musical* has 'that wich [*sic*] we call a rose'.

294, *n.: 'my Fantastic Symphony, which he had not seen . . .'
Mendelssohn had seen the symphony by this time. See letter of 15 March 1831 in *Briefe eine Reiser durch Deutschland*, etc. (1958).

295, lines 10–11: '. . . Gluck's Italian opera *Telemaco*'.
Rome, 1749. Gluck drew on it for some of his later scores.

295, line 32: '. . . the score of the *King Lear* overture . . .'
In a letter of 1 January 1832 to Hiller, he says he showed Mendelssohn the unfinished score of *Rob Roy* (see CG, I, 516). It is of course possible that he showed him *King Lear* as well.

299, line 15: '. . . an absurd dramatic incident'.
According to Mendelssohn's sister Fanny, Berlioz arranged to have a phrase from his letter ('Il est grossier, le tien est simple') inscribed on his baton, but the translator misunderstood it and rendered it as: 'I am coarse, you are simple' (Ernest David, *Les Mendelssohn—Bartholdy*, 177). Hippeau says that Mendelssohn's Lutheran piety was offended by Berlioz's invocation of the Great Spirit (*Berlioz intime*, 130).

300, line 3: '. . . having practically no tone.'
When editing this letter for the *Memoirs*, Berlioz removed a short technical passage about the Leipzig ophicleide which described, as an added practical disadvantage, the difficulties of transposition due to the instrument's being in B (*Voyage musical*, I, 81–2).

Fifth Letter

306, line 25: 'What about that!'
Here, in the *Débats* and in *Voyage musical* (I, 97), followed a reference to Marie Recio: 'Mlle Recio, who was in Dresden at the time, was good enough to sing two songs with orchestra; she was well received by the audience.'

306, line 31: 'Mlle Wüst . . .'
Berlioz spells her Wiest.

309, line 17: '. . . a young artist of rare talents.'
Originally (*Débats* and *Voyage musical*) this was followed by a sentence praising the 'uncommon energy and precision' of Wagner's conducting. Newman says that Berlioz 'seems to have deleted it after the Paris *Tannhäuser* episode of 1861', but there is no evidence that he did so then or for that reason. He had already decided, in London in 1855, that he did not admire Wagner's style of interpretation (an attitude reciprocated by Wagner). In general, the tributes paid—often for diplomatic reasons—in the *Débats* and *Voyage musical* tend to be toned down in the *Memoirs*.

309, lines 27–9: 'But the singer who impressed me . . . was Wächter . . .'

Wagner, on the contrary, thought Schröder-Devrient a superb Senta but considered Wächter psychologically inadequate.

309, lines 37–8: 'The composer . . . has gauged her powers to perfection.'
Offenbach, in a marginal note pencilled in his copy of the *Memoirs* (formerly André Meyer Collection), attributes this to Berlioz's pique at Wüst's refusal to sing the cavatina from *Benvenuto Cellini*. He sees the same motive behind the criticism of Schröder-Devrient in the Eighth Letter, although, according to Berlioz, Schröder-Devrient was not asked to sing the aria.

313, lines 1–2: '. . . the three weeks that I spent in this . . . city . . .'
He spent two weeks in Dresden, not three.

Sixth Letter

320, lines 1–2: '. . . the pizzicato passage in the Orgy . . .'
Presumably the bars for alternate pizzicato and arco (Eulenberg miniature score, pp. 144–6, repeated 169–71).

Eighth Letter

337, lines 25–6: 'I had no . . . predisposition for or against Madame Devrient.'
The criticism of her 'spoken inflexions' in the performance of *The Flying Dutchman* in Dresden (Fifth Letter) is already pretty vehement, however.

337, lines 30–2: '. . . all the more striking because the dramatic situations are more vivid and the music correspondingly grander and truer.'
Sc. than in *The Flying Dutchman*. Berlioz, though critical of Meyerbeer's eclecticism, and progressively more disenchanted with his later operas, rated *The Huguenots* very high among contemporary works.

340, line 36: '. . . "the heart knows no wrinkles".'
A slight misquotation: 'Le coeur n'a pas de rides' for 'Au coeur on n'a jamais de rides'.

Ninth Letter

349, lines 22–3: '. . . a battle symphony . . . by the Earl of Westmorland.'
When revising these letters for inclusion in the *Memoirs*, he cut out a sentence praising this 'most remarkable work' which 'reflects the greatest possible credit on the composer of *Torneo*, the Magnificat and many other dramatic and religious works that have made the Earl of Westmorland (better known to musicians as Lord Burghersh) one of the foremost amateur composers of Europe' (*Voyage musical*, I, 200).

350, lines 24–5: '. . . of the terrestrial globe, Alexander von Humboldt.'

Voyage musical, I, 202: '... who has revealed several different stages of its growth, and calculated the age of our planet by an examination of its mountain chains (those vertebrae of the earth), as Cuvier did with prehistoric animals'.

352, lines 6–7: '... G on the first beat ... B on the second ...'
Strictly speaking, on the third quaver of each subdivided (triplet) strong beat. A slight quickening of tempo indicated at this point may have helped to make the entries difficult for the players to get right.

356, lines 7–8: 'The King ... asked me for a copy of it.'
This manuscript (copyist, with autograph title and dedication) is in the museum at La Côte Saint-André.

Tenth Letter

360, lines 6–7: 'In the archives of one of London's theatres there is a letter to Queen Elizabeth ...'
Subsequently shown to be a forgery, and now no longer extant.

363, lines 20–1: '... superb valve-trumpet, with the same name as his Weimar rival, Sachse ...'
Carse (op. cit.) says they were brothers.

364, line 27: '... *The Fifth of May.*'
The Hanover programme (6 May 1843) also included *Harold*, *Waverley*, the Weber-Berlioz *Invitation to the Waltz*, and vocal items sung by Marie Recio.

366, line 15: 'the orchestra would have been only too happy ...'
Cf. Hallé, op. cit., 28–9, which gives an account of the Darmstadt orchestra a few years earlier, zealously rehearsing the Eroica under the same kapellmeister, Mangold: 'The rehearsals of this one symphony were continued a month ... far from being shunned by the members of the orchestra, as is so often the case, [they] were expected with impatience.'

Chapter 52

368, lines 25–7: 'I was on my way back from ... Germany when Léon Pillet ... decided ... to put on *Freischütz*.'
The production of *Der Freischütz* at the Opéra belongs to 1841. It therefore preceded Berlioz's tour of Germany. However, given his initial misdating of the tour as 1840–1, instead of 1842–3, the sequence is logical.

Chapter 53

373, lines 29–30: 'My life in the period which followed offers no musical event worth mentioning.'

It is not clear whether he is referring to the period which followed the production of *Freischütz* or the period which followed his return from Germany. The remark would apply equally well to both, however. He gave a number of concerts but composed little.

377, line 18: '. . . in Paris.'
They were also drawn from the provinces.

377, line 24: '. . . Madame Stoltz . . . declined.'
She was still, perhaps, annoyed with him for a notice in which, three years earlier, he had implied an unfavourable comparison between her physical appearance and that of Marie Recio in the role of Isolier in *Le comte Ory*.

377, lines 26–7: 'Almost all the members of the Conservatoire Concert Society . . .'
This would seem on the face of it to contradict the statement a few lines higher up, that he engaged 'virtually every orchestral player of any ability in Paris'. See also the letter of 25 June 1844 to Strauss: 'Habeneck (as was to be expected) is organizing his little opposition. His gang consists of seven people; we are already more than 900' (CG, III, 190). The explanation of this apparent contradiction may be that not all the musicians who regularly played in the Conservatoire Orchestra were members of the Society.

378, line 22: 'It consisted of the following . . .'
A copy of the programme in the Reboul–Berlioz Collection contains slight differences, viz.: the adagio [*sic*] and finale of Beethoven's C minor Symphony, not the scherzo and finale. However, as there is no mention of the chorus from *Charles VI*, which the *Memoirs* tells us was an afterthought, this programme may well represent an earlier and subsequently superseded order of events.

382, lines 1–2, line 1: 'I was in such a state . . . that there had to be a fairly lengthy interruption . . .'
In a letter written to his father soon after the concert, he places this incident at the end of the concert (CG, III, 197–8).

383, lines 8–9: '. . . thirty-two thousand francs, of which the tax-collectors took an eighth—four thousand francs.'
Thirty-seven thousand, in Berlioz's letter to his father (CG, III, 196), an eighth of which is 4,625 francs. The same letter gives the total tax on the festival as five thousand francs. However, Louis-Philippe's son, the Duc de Montpensier, who had been present at the concert, subsequently used his influence to get the tax reduced by a thousand francs (to four thousand), as well as sending Berlioz 'a magnificent porcelain vase' and a congratulatory letter (Boschot, III, 38).

383, line 13: '. . . a grand net profit of eight hundred francs . . .'
860, according to the letter from Berlioz to his father cited in the previous note.

383, line 24: '. . . one thousand two hundred and thirty-eight francs . . .'

One thousand two hundred and thirty-one, according to the letter cited in the two previous notes.

387, lines 3–4: 'the account . . . which I addressed to . . . Humbert Ferrand in the *Journal des débats*.'
Only the first three chapters were published in the *Débats* and addressed to Ferrand; the remaining five came out, addressed to Friedland, in the *Gazette musicale*, which had also printed the first three.

Travels in Germany—II

First Letter

389, line 2: '. . . though only just back . . .'
I.e. from Russia. The letters, which began appearing in August 1847, were originally designed to include the Russian journey.

390, lines 19–20: '. . . whom I would gladly conduct every day of my life.'
'. . . que je dirigerais . . .' The 1878 edition of the *Memoirs* misprints this as '. . . que je dirigeais . . .'

391, line 9: '. . . that line from *Ruy Blas* . . .'
The line is slightly misquoted: 'mais on s'ennuie' instead of 'mais je m'ennuie'. It occurs in Don César's soliloquy, Act IV scene 2.

395, lines 23–7: 'I heard this mild criticism voiced . . . by composers who . . . had had cause to feel somewhat anxious about it.'
He does not contradict the criticism, so it is possible he was able to confirm it from his own experience of Staudigl, who sang at several of his concerts in Vienna.

396, lines 28–30: 'capable of . . . confounding the most . . . quick-witted conductor.'
Again, perhaps he spoke from experience. Marra sang the cavatina from *Benvenuto Cellini* at his first concert in Vienna, on 16 November 1845.

Second Letter

400, lines 33–4: 'A giant had risen among them but they were happier with dwarfs.'
Cf. *Lélio* (1832 version) on Shakespeare: 'Colosse tombé dans un monde de nains!'

406, lines 16–17: '. . . performed in Paris in 1828.'
It was performed in Paris in 1827 at the Odéon (adapted by Crémont), and in 1830 in the German company's season.

409, n.: '. . . the names of the numerous subscribers . . .'

'The first forty subscribers', according to the *Gazette musicale* of 21 December 1845. These included Artaria, Asmayer, Bacher, Becher, Prince Czartorisky, Czerny, Diabelli, Ernst, Groidl, Haslinger, Nicolai and Staudigl.

Third Letter

414, lines 32–3: '... written it during the night before my departure for Hungary.'
Boschot, in his almost frantic determination to discredit this statement, comments (III, 57): 'Yes, it was written in one night, in Vienna, on the eve of his departure for Pesth; and in Pesth it took the audience by storm, all the orchestral parts being miraculously copied on the spot!' The parts, as the *Memoirs* states two paragraphs farther on, were copied in the normal way during the eight days which elapsed between Berlioz's arrival in Pesth and his first concert there. None the less, 'the Hungarian March', Boschot insists, 'was not written by Berlioz in Vienna "in one night" but in the course of the two months which preceded his departure for Austria', Liszt having suggested the idea to him in Bonn. However, Berlioz did not at that time intend visiting Hungary. (See Emile Haraszti, *Berlioz et la marche hongroise*, *Revue musicale*, special number, 1946, passim.) In any case, the composition in short score of a work of this length (some thirty bars shorter than in its present form) in eight or ten hours is an impressive but not impossible feat. It could have been scored in Pesth, and still have left time for the parts to be copied.

416, lines 24–5: '... a shabbily dressed man entered ...'
The Hungarian newspaper *Pesti Hirlap* of 19 February 1846 (four days after the concert) described an encounter—which has been taken to be the same as that described in the *Memoirs*—between Berlioz and a man in Hungarian national dress who came up to him at the artists' entrance, pumped his hand up and down and wept, but remained silent, not being able to speak any French. Haraszti (op. cit., 60–1) suggests that what the *Memoirs* gives is a touched-up version of this encounter. It is not impossible, however, that two Hungarians separately accosted Berlioz after the performance.

The phrase 'German dogs!' did not appear in the original version of this letter (*Journal des débats*, 19 October 1847), but was added when the passage dealing with the Rákóczy March was reprinted in the *Gazette musicale* fourteen years later (3 March 1861) on the occasion of the gift to Berlioz from the youth of Györ.

418, lines 1–2: '... a ... tenor ... called Füredi.'
Given in the *Memoirs* as Feredy.

419, line 24: '... goodbye to my Hungarian hosts.'
In the last week of February 1846.

420, lines 2–3: 'He was called— ...'
Haraszti (op. cit., 52) argues that he was probably Count Ráday, intendant of the National Theatre, disguised for safety under the misleading description of 'a

Viennese music-lover'. He was in Vienna at the time, and it was he who engaged Berlioz to come to Pesth.

Fourth Letter

425, line 8: 'The theatre, when I saw it (in 1845) ...'
It was in 1846.

Fifth Letter

435, lines 15–16: '... its timbre is similar to the basset horn's ...'
This may have been true of the bass clarinet in Berlioz's day, but reads oddly now.

Sixth Letter

445, lines 26–8: 'The young person entrusted with the contralto solo had never sung in public before.'
Her name was Rzepka; Berlioz had heard her sing one evening in January at a rehearsal of the choral society, and wrote from Vienna asking for her to be engaged (see the letter to Kittl, CG, III, 313). The Prague performance of *Romeo*, which took place on 17 April 1846, embodied several important changes made as a result of his hearing the work for the first time as a member of the audience, in Vienna. The changes included various modifications to the finale, the shortening of the first prologue, the omission of the second prologue altogether, the omission of the Tomb Scene, and a conciser version of the scherzo.

Chapter 54

448, line 33: '... twenty years earlier ...'
Actually seventeen.

452, line 4: 'It was the end of November ...'
Actually early December: the first performance had been announced for 29 November but was postponed a week.

452, lines 5–6: 'I had no star singer for the part of Marguerite.'
The singer was Mme Duflot-Maillard.

Chapter 55

459, lines 28–30: 'For the chorus ... the words had to be recopied in Russian characters, the only ones they were familiar with.'
This can have applied only to part of the chorus—the regimental singers and the court cantors—and not to the German choristers from the Grand Theatre, who took part. For the composition of Berlioz's chorus, see his letter of 31 March 1847 to Morel (CG, III, 413).

459, lines 36–8: '... was lucky enough to find, in M. Münzlaff, a musician ... who acquitted himself perfectly ...'
Münslaff's translation was included in the full score published in 1853, and is to be found in the current Eulenberg miniature score.

460, lines 17–20: 'The Empress ... sent for me ... and I had to appear before Her Majesty just as I was ... hot from battle.'
This recalls Lesueur's account of his summons before Napoleon after the third act of *The Bards* (see Fouque, op. cit., 120–2).

463, lines 20–1: '... it is nearly twenty-five years since I touched any of them ...'
A considerable exaggeration at least as far as concerns the guitar, which he had played in the early 1830s, if not later.

Chapter 56

474, lines 16–17: '... the two low notes ... which represent the tolling of the funeral knell ...'
This confirms that Berlioz had large bells in mind; the higher-pitched sounds we usually hear in the work are therefore incorrect. When William Ganz gave the first London performance, in 1881, 'he had large bells, of the essential deep notes C and G, specially cast' (Ganz, *Berlioz in London*, 214). They have apparently not survived, and were perhaps melted down in the First World War. Berlioz seems to have used a piano to represent bells at all performances that he conducted.

474, line 19: 'The least successful of my scores ...'
This paragraph precedes the previous paragraph, but I have taken the liberty of transposing them, assuming it to be a printer's error.

476, line 16: 'In Chopin's compositions ...'
I.e. compositions involving orchestra.

479, lines 11–25: 'Everyone is busy ... I saw ... Hamlet.'
Cf. CG, III, 432–3: 'The kapellmeister, Schrameck, collected me a little orchestra of about fifty, made up of local professionals and amateurs and a few players from Mitau. They were not at all bad, and actually played the finale of *Harold*, one of the most difficult pieces that exist, with commendable fire. [...] As you may guess, there was no harp: Schrameck stood in for it, on the piano. We did *Harold* complete (with an excellent solo viola), the *Roman Carnival* overture, two songs with orchestra tolerably well sung by a Mlle Bamberg from the opera, the Sylphs' Chorus (without chorus!!), and the Hungarian March. The audience was enthusiastic but thin; there are eleven hundred ships at the moment on the river at Riga, and everyone is busy buying and selling grain from eight in the morning till eleven at night. As a result, the concert was attended almost exclusively by women. All the same I don't regret either the fatigue it caused me or the loss of time; I think I have made firm friends of this new orchestra. What is more, I had the totally

unexpected good luck to see *Hamlet*. [. . .] As always, I was overwhelmed by this prodigious achievement of the greatest genius of mankind.'

480, lines 16–17: '. . . having forfeited their good will by my letters on Berlin . . .'
Shortly after his return to Paris from this second visit, he wrote to Leopold Ganz, sending a copy of his letters on Germany in an attempt to vindicate himself: 'you will be able to see and show your colleagues in the orchestra [. . .] in what terms I referred to them and whether the few detailed points of criticism that are included are of a kind calculated to offend or be taken in bad part' (CG, III, 440).

481, lines 31–2: '. . . orchestrally as well as chorally the performance could not be faulted.'
Cf. Berlioz to Morel: 'Part of the orchestra was hostile to me because of certain criticisms which they claim I passed on them in the letters on my first German tour. A few of them got into trouble over it, and all were given a severe ticking off by the intendant, who on this occasion at least did what was required of him. But none of this showed in the performance; on the contrary, the orchestra was superb. Don't say anything about the incident' (CG, III, 435).

481, lines 34–5: '. . . the audience shouted "da capo" . . . but I was in a bad mood and refused to repeat it.'
But see the letter to Morel above: 'As usual it [the Sylphs' Chorus] was encored; but I failed to catch the cries of "da capo"—the convention here in place of the normal "bis" (which one can hear through the bravos)—so I didn't repeat it. This offended the Berliners, so I was told' (CG, III, 435).

Chapter 57

484, line 2: 'I had not been there for a long time . . .'
It was only his third visit since 1832, the others being in September 1840 and July 1845. The former visit (not otherwise recorded) is referred to in a letter of 22 September 1840 to his father (CG, II, 659–60). For the latter, see CG, III, 259–60.

484, lines 29–30: '. . . the directorship of the Opéra . . .'
The negotiations over the Opéra came immediately after his return from Russia, before his visit to La Côte.

485, lines 13–14: '. . . an old friend of mine, M. Girard . . .'
This is not how Berlioz describes him on p. 257.

487, lines 22–3: 'I wrote at once to Messrs Duponchel and Roqueplan . . .'
See CG, III, 446.

488, line 22: '. . . a setting of Wagner's libretto . . .'
It was not Wagner's finished libretto of *The Flying Dutchman* that Dietsch set but a completion by Fourcher and Révoil of the sketch which Wagner had sold to Pillet.

490, *n.: 'It has since been destroyed...'
About 150 pages of score survive, however. They will form part of Vol. 4 of the *New Berlioz Edition*.

Chapter 58

494, line 21: 'Saturday 4 August 1848'.
The 4th was a Friday in 1848.

497, line 7: 'Thirty-three years have come and gone...'
This would mean that Berlioz was last on the Saint-Eynard in 1815, which must be wrong; Berlioz and his family continued to visit the Marmion house in Meylan and to go for walks on the hill above it long after 1815 (see for example the reference in CG, I, 474, to 'our expedition to the Saint-Eynard, with Adèle thirty yards ahead of us all the way'; in 1815 Adèle would have been one). But the date 1815 seems to have fixed itself in Berlioz's mind, and hence in Estelle's, as the year of his last childhood meeting with her; she makes the same calculation in her letter, given on p. 561: 'I saw you briefly last Friday [1864] for the first time for forty-nine years'.

501, line 26: '... September 1848'.
The *Memoirs* give the date of this letter as 6 December 1848. I have changed it to September, on the assumption that 'December' is a misprint or a slip of the pen. But it is not impossible that Berlioz did not post the letter till three months later, in Paris.

502, †n.: 'February 1864... August 1864'.
The *Memoirs* have 1854; but that is surely a misprint.

Chapter 59

504, line 19: 'At least she did not suffer such great pain.'
I.e. by comparison with Nanci. In a letter to Liszt written a week after her death, Berlioz speaks of her as 'delivered from... cruel sufferings which had tortured her for the last three years' (CG, IV, 473).

504, line 22: '... my son, who was at Cherbourg...'
Berlioz's letter of 6 March 1854 to Adèle implies that Louis was at Calais, not Cherbourg (CG, IV, 467).

505, lines 3–4: '... the deep disappointment of her last unsuccessful appearance on the Paris stage...'
In the context of the *Memoirs*' account this must refer to the benefit performance of 24 November 1833 described in Chapter 45. In fact Harriet made several

further appearances, in isolated scenes, and Berlioz campaigned energetically for several more years for her return to the professional stage. But she never again acted in a full-length play.

505, lines 12–14: '... her delusion that she had forfeited the regard of the English public through her attachment to France...'
A double delusion, for she never really won it.

507, line 4: '... she goes almost alone to the cemetery...'
This conflicts somewhat with the statement in the letter to Adèle cited above, in which he says that 'a large number of artists and men of letters... escorted her to the cemetery' (CG, IV, 467).

507, line 19: '... Janin... wrote...'
Débats, 20 March 1854.

514, lines 11–12: '... the C minor Symphony...'
According to the programme given in Elwart's *Histoire de la Société des Concerts* (241), the Seventh Symphony was played, not the Fifth.

517, * n.: '"I agree to everything in advance."'
In 1858, for example, there were eleven rehearsals for a programme which included the first four movements of *Romeo and Juliet*. Berlioz first conducted in Baden in 1853. He returned in 1856, and from then till 1861 gave a concert every August with a specially formed orchestra (the players being housed and fed at Bénazet's expense). In August 1862 *Beatrice and Benedict*, commissioned by Bénazet, inaugurated the new Baden theatre; it was revived the following year. In 1864 Berlioz was succeeded by Ernest Reyer.

518, line 1: '... organize a performance of the whole work...'
In the event it was his latest work, *The Childhood of Christ*, that he performed (3 February 1855).

Postscript

520, line 26: '... eighteen or twenty years ago...'
It was fourteen—in 1844.

526, lines 7–8: '... San Carlo Borromeo at Como...'
The statue is not at Como but at Arona, on Lake Maggiore.

527, lines 5–6 '... the shepherds' chorus... originally performed at two of my concerts...'
Only one performance is known about, on 12 November 1850, at a concert of the Société Philharmonique—though a letter of Berlioz's also speaks of there having been two (CG, IV, 139).

527, line 7: '. . . an imaginary eighteenth-century choirmaster.'
Les grotesques de la musique, and the first concert announcements, named him as choirmaster of the Sainte-Chapelle in 1679.

527, lines 7–9: "How they praised . . . could never do anything like that!"'
At least one such remark is attested, made by a friend of Joseph-Louis Duc: see *Grotesques*, ed. Guichard, 187–8, and CG, IV, 636, n. 4.

527, lines 32–3: '. . . except in one scene of *The Capture of Troy* . . .'
The scene where the wooden horse is brought into the city. A saxhorn is also used in the March at the end of the Te Deum. The score of *The Trojans* originally specified saxhorns for three of the Carthaginian scenes. This was before Berlioz divided the work into two evenings; the extra brass required for the scene of the Trojan horse being then no longer automatically available for the whole opera, the offstage saxhorn parts in the Royal Hunt were crossed out in the autograph score and either replaced by horns (in the orchestra) or suppressed altogether (see *New Berlioz Editions*, vols 2b and c). The reference to *The Capture of Troy* is presumably a later addition; the opera was not formally divided until the summer of 1863, five years after the date given to the Postscript.

Postface

529, lines 11–12: '. . . an incurable neuralgia . . .'
This seems to have developed in late 1855 or early 1856. The precise nature of the condition has still to be established, though Crohn's Disease is a plausible diagnosis. (Le marquis de Villemer's *Les portraits cosmopolites*, Paris, 1870, is so far as I know the only authority which speaks of a cancer.)

531, lines 20–1: '. . . The vibrations of eternity!'
The English music critic J.W. Davison had a similar experience at Jullien's country retreat at Abbaye d'Aywiers, in Belgium, Jullien 'darting to the trunk of a tree, listening intently and then silently beckoning his guest to approach and bear witness to the note'.

537, lines 1–2: '". . . there's Mangin!"'
A cartoon by Cham, during the run of *The Trojans at Carthage* at the Théâtre-Lyrique, showed 'M. Mangin lending his helmet to Aeneas in return for the latter's undertaking to sell some pencils for him at the court of Dido' (*Charivari*, 22 November 1863).

544, lines 24–5: '. . . the trio . . . "Je vais d'un coeur aimant" . . .'
The trio was not composed until the following month; it was first performed in April 1863 in Weimar.

Travels in Dauphiné

551, line 28: 'I chip a fragment from my granite altar . . .'
When Berlioz sent Estelle an advance copy of the *Memoirs*, the following summer, he enclosed this piece of granite, attached to a ribbon, for a book marker (CG, VII, 289–90).

559, lines 21–2: '. . . I am sixty-one . . .'
Actually sixty; his birthday was in December.

APPENDIX IV

SOURCES OF THE MEMOIRS

In compiling his autobiography, Berlioz drew freely on his published writings in book and newspaper form; his concern was, as he states, to 'complete and recast' what had come into existence haphazardly, to give coherent shape to an account of his life that in one form and another was already half written. The main source to hand was the *Voyage musical en Allemagne et en Italie* (itself based on newspaper articles), which had appeared in 1844 but had since gone out of print. Seventeen chapters of the *Memoirs* come largely from it: they are Chapters 15, 22, 23, 30 and 32–43 and the ten letters on Germany which follow Chapter 51. With the six letters on Austria, Hungary and Bohemia, and the two on Russia, they make up just over half the *Memoirs*. In addition, there was autobiographical material in his feuilletons which naturally lent itself to the purpose; in his articles Berlioz often described his experiences as a student to illustrate a point in the argument or as an escape from the antipathetic task of reviewing.

The following list gives the newspaper sources of the *Memoirs* by chapter (an asterisk indicates that the chapter also appeared in *Voyage musical*). It does not of course show the many changes of style and detail which the material underwent before taking its final form.

Chapter	
6 (in part)	Lesueur, the Chapel Royal: *Gazette musicale*, 10 June 1838.
12 (in part)	Audition for a job in the chorus: *Revue de Paris*, December 1832 (article signed by d'Ortigue but largely written by Berlioz; reprinted the following year in d'Ortigue's *Le balcon de l'Opéra*, 301–2).
13 (in part)	Lesueur's fugue 'Quis enarrabit': *Journal des débats*, 9 August 1835; also used in Berlioz's obituary of Lesueur in *Gazette musicale*, 15 October 1837.
	Reicha's interest in mathematics: *Journal des débats*, 3 July 1836; *Gazette musicale*, 15 July 1838.
*15 (complete)	*Journal des débats*, 13 September 1835.
	Also, the episode of the enthusiastic mathematician: *Gazette musicale*, 11 March 1841.
16 (in part)	Weber in Paris, *Freischütz*, *Oberon*: *Journal des débats*, 13 June 1841.
	Les mystères d'Isis: *Journal des débats*, 1 May 1836.
*22 (in part)	The composition prize, the regulations of the Academy: *L'Europe littéraire*, 12 June 1833; *Rénovateur*, 9 July 1833.
	Last paragraph: *Gazette musicale*, 2 February 1834.
	(See also *Gazette musicale*, 19 June 1836, which contains some of the same material as this chapter.)
*23 (complete)	The Institute usher: *L'Europe littéraire*, 19 July 1833.
29 (in part)	The Palais Royal concert, the Marseillaise in the Galerie Colbert: *Journal des débats*, 23 July 1836.

*30 (in part)	The Institute prize-giving: *Gazette musicale*, 2 February 1834.
31 (in part)	The French Academy in Rome: *Italie pittoresque* (1834), 'Académie de France à Rome'.
*32 (complete)	*Italie pittoresque* (1834), ibid.
*33 (complete)	*Italie pittoresque* (1834), ibid.
*35 (almost complete)	*Revue européenne*, March–May 1832; *Italie pittoresque* (1834), 'Voyage musical'.
*36 (in part)	Life at the Academy, etc. (less the passage on 'English concerts'): *Italie pittoresque*, 'Académie de France à Rome'. The Carnival: *Gazette musicale*, 21 February 1836.
*37 (in part)	Shooting in the mountains, the Campagna, Virgilian recollections: *Italie pittoresque* (1834), 'Voyage musical'.
*38 (in part)	Subiaco, St Benedict, a serenade, Civitella: *Italie pittoresque*, ibid. My gun, my friend Crispino: *Journal des débats*, 3 October 1841.
*39 (in part)	Church and theatre music, the *pifferari*: *Revue européenne*, March–May 1832; *Revue musicale*, 31 March, 9 April 1832. The Sistine Chapel: *Rénovateur*, 20 April 1834. The whole chapter up to and including the *pifferari*: *Italie pittoresque* (1834), ibid. The remainder: *L'Artiste*, 30 June 1844. (See also *Journal des débats*, 5 September 1835, where the description of the *pifferari* has certain similarities to the account in this chapter.)
*40 (complete)	*L'Artiste*, ibid.
*41 (in part)	The Teatro San Carlo: *Revue européenne*, March–May 1832. Vesuvius: *Gazette musicale*, 2 February 1834. The Teatro San Carlo, return to Rome on foot through the Abruzzi: *Italie pittoresque*, ibid. A crack of the whip: *L'Artiste*, ibid. The improviser of Capua: *Journal des débats*, 5 September 1835.
*42 (in part)	Last paragraph has similarities to *Italie pittoresque*, ibid.
*43 (in part)	Milan, the public, thoughts on the musical life of the Italians, etc.: *Italie pittoresque*, ibid. (Also, music and macaroni, the reference to the phrenologist Gall: cf. *Gazette musicale*, 11 January 1835.)
*51	Ten Letters on Germany: *Journal des débats*, 13, 20, 28 August, 3, 12, 23 September, 8, 21 October, 8 November 1843, 9 January 1844. First Letter, footnote on the two Strausses: *Journal des débats*, 30 January 1842. Eighth Letter, passage on Gluck's timelessness and on *Armide*: *Gazette musicale*, 26 February 1837.

53 Letters on Vienna and Pesth: *Journal des débats*, 24 August, 5 September, 19 October 1847; *Revue et gazette musicale*, 3, 19 October, 7 November 1847.
Letters on Prague: *Revue et gazette musicale*, 23, 30 July, 6, 20, 27 August 1848.

The *Memoirs* was not published until 1870, a year after Berlioz's death, but Chapters 1–14, 16–22, 25–7, 29, 31, 44–6, 48, 50–1 (beginning), 52, and 53 (beginning)—most of it material that had not appeared in *Voyage musical*—were serialized (with certain omissions) in the weekly *Monde illustré* in 1858–9. Chapter 49 was included in Escudier's *Mes souvenirs* (1863).

APPENDIX V

A SHORT BIBLIOGRAPHY

Berlioz's Writings

Italie pittoresque. Paris, 1834. A symposium which contains material by Berlioz later used in the Italian chapters of *Voyage musical* and the *Memoirs*.

Grand traité d'instrumentation et d'orchestration modernes. Paris, 1843. 2nd edn, Paris, 1856, including *Le chef d'orchestre: théorie de son art*.

L'Artiste. Paris, 30 June 1844: 'Italie, souvenirs d'un musicien' (containing parts of later Italian chapters not published in *Italie pittoresque*).

Voyage musical en Allemagne et en Italie. Etudes sur Beethoven, Gluck et Weber. Mélanges et nouvelles. 2 vols. Paris, 1844.

Les soirées de l'orchestre. Paris, 1852. Also Paris, 1968, ed. Léon Guichard, the first volume of the centenary edition of the complete literary works and letters issued under the aegis of the Association Nationale Hector Berlioz.

Les grotesques de la musique. Paris, 1859. Paris, 1969, ed. Guichard.

A travers chants: études musicales, adorations, boutades et critiques. Paris, 1862. Paris, 1971, ed. Guichard.

Mémoires de Hector Berlioz, Membre de l'Institut de France, comprenant ses voyages en Italie, en Allemagne, en Russie et en Angleterre; 1803–1865. Paris, 1870. Paris, 1991, ed. Pierre Citron.

Les musiciens et la musique. Paris, [1903]. Feuilletons from the *Journal des débats*.

Hector Berlioz: Cauchemars et Passions. Paris, 1981. Feuilletons, ed. Gérard Condé.

Hector Berlioz: La critique musicale, 1823–1863, ed. H. Robert Cohen and Yves Gérard. I, 1823–1834, II, 1835–1836, III 1837–1838. Paris, 1996, 1998, 2000: vols I–III of the projected complete feuilletons.

Le corsaire. 1823–5, passim.

Die Berliner allgemeine musikalische Zeitung. 1829, passim.

Le correspondant (later *La revue européenne*). 1829–30, 1832, passim.

L'Europe littéraire. 1833, passim.

Le rénovateur. 1833–5, passim.

La gazette (later *Revue et gazette*) *musicale*. 1834–59, passim.

Le journal des artistes. 1834, passim.

Le journal des débats. 1834–63, passim.

Le monde dramatique. 1835, passim.

Le chronique de Paris. 1837–8, passim.

L'Eclair (Brussels). 1842, passim.

Le monde illustré. 1858–9, passim (serialized chapters from the *Memoirs*).

Published Letters

Correspondance inédite de Hector Berlioz, 1819–68, ed. Daniel Bernard. Paris, 1879. (Contains errors and omissions, partly corrected in Tiersot's three volumes of letters.)

Lettres intimes, pref. Charles Gounod, Paris, 1882. 141 letters to Humbert Ferrand.

Briefe hervorrangender Zeitgenossen an Franz Liszt, ed. La Mara. 3 vols. Leipzig, 1895–1904. (First two volumes contain 61 letters from Berlioz.)

Une page d'amour romantique: Lettres à Mme. Estelle F. Paris, 1903.

Briefe von Hector Berlioz an die Fürstin Carolyne Sayn-Wittgenstein, ed. La Mara. Leipzig, 1903.

Revue musicale, Berlioz number. Paris, 15 August 1903.

Hector Berlioz: Les années romantiques, 1819–1842, ed. Julien Tiersot. Paris, 1904.

Hector Berlioz: Le musicien errant, 1842–1852, ed. Julien Tiersot. Paris, 1919.

Hector Berlioz: Au milieu du chemin, 1852–1855, ed. Julien Tiersot. Paris, 1930.

Revue de Paris, 1921, passim: contains letters on *Les Troyens*.

Lettres de musiciens écrites en français du XVe au XXe siècle, ed. Julien Tiersot. 2 vols. Turin, Milan and Paris, 1924–1936.

Revue des deux-mondes, March 1944: letters to Edouard Rocher.

Nouvelles lettres de Berlioz, ed. Jacques Barzun. New York, 1954.

Adam, 1969, nos 331–333: contains unpublished Berlioz letters.

Hector Berlioz: Correspondance générale, I, 1803–1832, ed. P. Citron, II, 1832–1842, ed. F. Robert, III, 1842–1850, ed. Citron, IV, 1851–1855, ed. Citron, Yves Gérard and Hugh Macdonald, V, 1855–1859, ed. Macdonald and François Lesure, 1859–1863, VI, 1859–1863, ed. Macdonald and Lesure, VII, 1866–1869, ed. Macdonald, Paris 1972–2001. Vols I–VII of the projected complete letters.

BOOKS AND ARTICLES

Arts Council of Great Britain, *Berlioz and the Romantic Imagination*: catalogue of the Berlioz Centenary Exhibition at the Victoria and Albert Museum. London, 1969.

Barraud, Henry, *Hector Berlioz*. Paris, 1955. Illustrated edition, Paris, 1966.

Barzun, Jacques, *Berlioz and the Romantic Century*. 2 vols. Boston, 1950, 3rd edn, New York, 1969.

Bloom, Peter, *The Life of Berlioz*. Cambridge, 1998.

Bloom, Peter, ed., *Music in Paris in the Eighteen-Thirties*. Stuyvesant, NY, 1987.

Bloom, Peter, ed., *Berlioz Studies*. Cambridge, 1992.

Bloom, Peter, ed., *The Cambridge Companion to Berlioz*. Cambridge, 2000.

Boschot, Adolphe, *Hector Berlioz*. I: *La jeunesse d'un romantique*. Paris, 1906. rev. 1946; II: *Un romantique sous Louis-Philippe*. Paris, 1908, rev. 1948; III: *Le crépuscule d'un romantique*. Paris, 1913, rev. 1950.

Cairns, David, *Berlioz*. I: *1803–1832: the Making of an Artist*. London, 1989, rev. 1999; II: *1832–1869: Servitude and Greatness*. London, 1999.

Carse, Adam, *The Orchestra from Beethoven to Berlioz*. Cambridge, 1948.

Cone, Edward T., *Music: a View from Delft*. Chicago, 1989: 'Inside the Saint's Head: the music of Berlioz', and 'Berlioz's Divine Comedy: the Grande Messe des morts'.

Fouque, Octave, *Les révolutionnaires de la musique: Lesueur, Berlioz, Beethoven, Richard Wagner, La musique Russe*. Paris, 1882.

Ganz, A. W., *Berlioz in London*. London, 1950.

Hippeau, Edmond, *Berlioz intime*. Paris, 1833.

Holoman, D. Kern, *The Creative Process in the Autograph Musical Documents of Hector Berlioz, c. 1818–1840*. Michigan, 1980.

Holoman, D. Kern, *Catalogue of the Works of Hector Berlioz* (*New Berlioz Edition* vol. 25). Kassel, 1987.

Holoman, D. Kern, *Berlioz*. Cambridge, Mass., 1989.

Hopkinson, Cecil, *A Bibliography of the Works of Hector Berlioz, 1803–1869*. 2nd edn rev. and ed. Richard Macnutt, Tunbridge Wells, 1980.

Jullien, Adolphe, *Hector Berlioz: sa vie et ses œuvres*. Paris, 1888.

Laferrière, Adolphe, *Mémoires* (*Ière série*). Paris, 1876.

Legouvé, Ernest, *Soixante ans de souvenirs*. 2 vols. Paris, 1886.

Macdonald, Hugh, gen. ed., *Hector Berlioz, New Edition of the Complete Works*. Kassel, 1967–.

Macdonald, Hugh, *Berlioz*. London, 1982.

Macdonald, Hugh, 'One Hundred Years Ago'. *Berlioz Society Bulletin*, April 1961–April 1969 (most numbers).

Macdonald, Hugh, ed., *Berlioz, Selected Letters*, trans. Roger Nichols. London, 1995.

Mellers, Wilfrid, *Man and His Music* (with Alec Harman). London, 1962. Chapter on Berlioz, pp. 759–81.

Mirecourt, Eugène de (pseud. of C. J. B. Jacquot), *Berlioz*. Paris, 1856.

Newman, Ernest, ed., *Memoirs of Hector Berlioz*. New York, 1932; reprinted 1965.

Ortigue, J. D', *Le balcon de l'Opéra*. Paris, 1833.

Primmer, Brian, *The Berlioz Style*. London, 1973.

Prod'homme, J. G., *Hector Berlioz: sa vie et ses œuvres*. Paris, 1904.

Prod'homme, J. G., *Les symphonies de Beethoven*. Paris, 1906.

Reyer, Ernest, *Notes de musique*. Paris, 1875.

Rose, Michael, *Berlioz Remembered*. London, 2001.

Rushton, Julian, *The Musical Language of Berlioz*. Cambridge, 1983.

Rushton, Julian, *The Music of Berlioz*. Oxford, 2001.

Tiersot, Julien, *Berlioz et la société de son temps*. Paris, 1904.

Tiersot, Julien, *Berlioziana*: a series in *Le ménestrel*, 1904–6, 1909–11.

Wotton, Tom S., *Hector Berlioz*. London, 1935.

Wright, Michael G. H., *A Berlioz Bibliography: Critical Writing on Hector Berlioz from 1825 to 1986*, Farnborough (St Michael's Abbey Press), 1988.

INDEX

IN THIS INDEX B = BERLIOZ

ABOUT THE TRANSLATOR

DAVID CAIRNS was chief music critic of the *Sunday Times* from 1983 to 1992, having been music critic and arts editor of the *Spectator* and a writer on the *Times Educational Supplement*, *Evening Standard*, *Financial Times* and *New Statesman*. From 1967 to 1972 he worked for the London branch of Philips Records. He has been Distinguished Visiting Professor at the University of California, Davis, a visiting scholar at the Getty Center in Santa Monica, and a visiting fellow of Merton College, Oxford. In 1991 he was made Officier de l'Ordre des Arts et des Lettres by the French government. The second volume of his life of Berlioz, published in 1999, won the Whitbread Biography Award and the Samuel Johnson Non-Fiction Prize. His other books include *Responses: Musical Essays and Reviews* and, as part-author, the ENO opera guides on *The Magic Flute* and *Falstaff*. He has been actively involved in music-making: he was co-founder of Chelsea Opera Group and is conductor of the Thorington Players.

19TH-CENTURY TITLES IN EVERYMAN'S LIBRARY

JANE AUSTEN
Emma
Mansfield Park
Northanger Abbey
Persuasion
Pride and Prejudice
Sanditon and Other Stories
Sense and Sensibility

HONORÉ DE BALZAC
Cousin Bette
Eugénie Grandet
Old Goriot

HECTOR BERLIOZ
The Memoirs of Hector Berlioz

CHARLOTTE BRONTË
Jane Eyre
Villette

EMILY BRONTË
Wuthering Heights

SAMUEL BUTLER
The Way of all Flesh

ANTON CHEKHOV
My Life and Other Stories
The Steppe and Other Stories

KATE CHOPIN
The Awakening

CARL VON CLAUSEWITZ
On War

S. T. COLERIDGE
Poems

WILKIE COLLINS
The Moonstone
The Woman in White

CHARLES DICKENS
Bleak House
David Copperfield
Dombey and Son
Great Expectations
Hard Times
Little Dorrit
Martin Chuzzlewit
Nicholas Nickleby
The Old Curiosity Shop
Oliver Twist
Our Mutual Friend
The Pickwick Papers
A Tale of Two Cities

FYODOR DOSTOEVSKY
The Brothers Karamazov
Crime and Punishment
Demons

GEORGE ELIOT
Adam Bede
Daniel Deronda
Middlemarch
The Mill on the Floss
Silas Marner

GUSTAVE FLAUBERT
Madame Bovary

ELIZABETH GASKELL
Mary Barton

J. W. VON GOETHE
Selected Works

IVAN GONCHAROV
Oblomov

THOMAS HARDY
Far From the Madding Crowd
Jude the Obscure
The Mayor of Casterbridge
The Return of the Native
Tess of the d'Urbervilles
The Woodlanders

NATHANIEL HAWTHORNE
The Scarlet Letter

JAMES HOGG
Confessions of a Justified Sinner

VICTOR HUGO
Les Misérables

HENRY JAMES
The Awkward Age
The Bostonians
The Golden Bowl
The Portrait of a Lady
The Princess Casamassima
The Wings of the Dove
Collected Stories (2 vols)

JOHN KEATS
The Poems

SØREN KIERKEGAARD
Fear and Trembling and
The Book on Adler

MIKHAIL LERMONTOV
A Hero of Our Time

HERMAN MELVILLE
The Complete Shorter Fiction
Moby-Dick

JOHN STUART MILL
On Liberty and Utilitarianism

EDGAR ALLAN POE
The Complete Stories

ALEXANDER PUSHKIN
The Collected Stories

WALTER SCOTT
Rob Roy

MARY SHELLEY
Frankenstein

STENDHAL
The Charterhouse of Parma
Scarlet and Black

ROBERT LOUIS STEVENSON
The Master of Ballantrae and
Weir of Hermiston
Dr Jekyll and Mr Hyde
and Other Stories

HARRIET BEECHER STOWE
Uncle Tom's Cabin

W. M. THACKERAY
Vanity Fair

HENRY DAVID THOREAU
Walden

ALEXIS DE TOCQUEVILLE
Democracy in America

LEO TOLSTOY
Collected Shorter Fiction
(2 vols)
Anna Karenina
Childhood, Boyhood and Youth
The Cossacks
War and Peace

ANTHONY TROLLOPE
Barchester Towers
Can You Forgive Her?
Doctor Thorne
The Eustace Diamonds
Framley Parsonage
The Last Chronicle of Barset
The Small House at Allington
The Warden

IVAN TURGENEV
Fathers and Children
First Love and Other Stories
A Sportsman's Notebook

MARK TWAIN
Tom Sawyer
and Huckleberry Finn

OSCAR WILDE
Plays, Prose Writings and Poems

WILLIAM WORDSWORTH
Selected Poems

ÉMILE ZOLA
Germinal

Everyman's Library, founded in 1906 and relaunched in 1991, aims to offer the most enduring library in the English language of the world's classics. This volume is set in the classic typeface *Bembo* and printed on acid-free, cream-wove paper with a sewn full cloth binding.